Savoring Power,
Consuming the Times

PINA PALMA

Savoring Power, Consuming the Times

THE METAPHORS OF FOOD IN MEDIEVAL
AND RENAISSANCE ITALIAN LITERATURE

University of Notre Dame Press
Notre Dame, Indiana

Copyright © 2013 by University of Notre Dame
Notre Dame, Indiana 46556
www.undpress.nd.edu
All Rights Reserved

Manufactured in the United States of America

Library of Congress Cataloging-in-Publication Data

Palma, Pina.
  Savoring power, consuming the times : the metaphors of food in medieval and Renaissance Italian literature / Pina Palma.
     pages   cm
  Includes bibliographical references and index.
  ISBN 978-0-268-03839-7 (pbk. : alk. paper) — ISBN 0-268-03839-2 (pbk. : alk. paper)
    1. Italian literature—To 1400—History and criticism   2. Italian literature—16th century—History and criticism.   3. Food in literature.   4. Gastronomy in literature.   I. Title.
  PQ4053.F58P36   2013
  850.9'3564—dc23
                                                            2012048959

∞ *The paper in this book meets the guidelines for permanence and durability of the Committee on Production Guidelines for Book Longevity of the Council on Library Resources.*

For Enzo,
In memoriam

CONTENTS

	Acknowledgments	ix
	Introduction: Taste and See the Power of Food	1
ONE	The Language of Food in Boccaccio's *Decameron*	33
TWO	Of Frogs, Giants, and the Court: Pulci's *Morgante*	89
THREE	Banquets of Power: Boiardo's *Innamorato* and the Politics of Gastronomy	153
FOUR	Meals, Transformations, and the Belly of History: Ariosto's *Furioso*	215
FIVE	Courtesans and Figs, Art and Nature in Aretino's *Ragionamento*	265
	Conclusion	317
	Notes	321
	Bibliography	383
	Index	411

ACKNOWLEDGMENTS

Many people have helped me during the years of work on this book. To them, I will always be indebted. I am especially grateful to my friend and colleague Jim Rhodes. With patience, wit, and wisdom he posed tough questions, pored through several drafts of the chapters, and commented on them. His criticism and suggestions improved the manuscript in more ways than I can say. Unflinching in his encouragement and unwavering in his confidence in the outcome, Jim provided generous and perceptive guidance, making me a sharper reader and writer. The privilege of teaching with him in the Honors College at Southern Connecticut State University led to lively discussions that drew me deeply into medieval texts and contexts. And when the complexities of the project became overwhelming, Jim remained a beacon of intellectual rigor, encouraging me to stay the course and to believe in myself. It is with pleasure that I acknowledge my debt to him.

Juliana D'Amato, OP, Dominican Sisters of Peace, read through the manuscript at various stages and offered advice and support despite the distance separating us. In many ways the seeds for this work were planted during the course of a conversation with her on the beach of Oyster Bay, Long Island. That conversation continued, perhaps unbeknown to her, throughout the years and from both sides of the Atlantic. With acute comments, piercing questions, and forbearance she guided me through discussions on Mary, the Gospels, Saint Dominic, Saint Thomas Aquinas, and everything else in between much as she did when I was her student at Albertus Magnus College. As my study on food took the medieval and Renaissance path, her suggestions were crucial at every stage. Above all, with humor and humility she helped me keep my feet on the ground.

I owe Giuseppe Mazzotta, my maestro at Yale, a special thank you. His courses on Dante and Ludovico Ariosto were fundamental in shaping my work and giving preliminary form to the ideas expressed in this book. Early on he embraced my project with intellectual enthusiasm. Over the years, he was an unmatched interlocutor, challenging me on many points and always suggesting the possibility of more riveting perspectives. This book is in part a tribute to his work and teaching, for without them it would not have been possible.

This list would not be complete if I did not mention Pete Wetherbee, who read the first draft of the chapter on Giovanni Boccaccio and made perspicacious comments. His criticism led to a complete revision of that chapter. Marcia Colish, during a break of the 8th Medieval Conference she was attending at SCSU, gave me an impromptu lesson on the days of Creation. Alaister Minnis, on several occasions, took the time to answer my questions about various aspects of medieval culture. During his stay in New Haven, and later from Pisa, Catania, and Milan, Silvano Nigro took a vivid interest in my project. Our long conversations about food, the Renaissance, Luigi Pulci, and Medici culture triggered my reflections in several chapters of this work. From the first time he heard me talk about food in literature in Cambridge, UK, Konrad Eisenbickler encouraged me to pursue the project and spurred me to bring it to completion. Rosa Morelli's remarkable ability to identify any passage from the sacred scriptures taught me to take a fresh look at familiar subjects. Zeynep Gürsel, former student and now colleague, was a constant source of wise counsel and encouragement.

I am also grateful to the three anonymous readers. Their significant suggestions transformed my manuscript into a book. Needless to say, the errors that remain are all mine.

Stephen Little, my patient editor, was equally supportive.

Finally, I owe a debt of gratitude to my children, Giancarlo and Flavia, patient allies throughout the whole journey, and to my husband, Jeff Stanton.

This book is dedicated to the memory of my brother Enzo with whom during our summers at Villa Beck I began to explore the complexities of foods and flavors. With him I discovered the happiness of brotherly wonderings and the sweetness of convivial gatherings. Without him I tasted the bitterness of death.

Shorter versions of some of these chapters were published in professional journals. I publish here the extended versions and gratefully acknowledge permission to reprint. Chapter 1 was published under the title of "Hermits, Husbands, and Lovers: Moderation and Excesses at the Table in the *Decameron*," in *Food and History* 4, no. 2 (2006): 151–162. Chapter 3 appeared as "Banquets and Power: Boiardo's *Innamorato* and the Politics of Gastronomy," *Quaderni d'italianistica* 27, no. 1 (2006): 21–29. Chapter 4 includes "Florinetta and the Food of Freedom: *Morgante XIX*," which appeared in *Table Talk: Perspectives on Food in Medieval Italian Literature*, ed. Christiana Purdy Moudarres (Newcastle upon Tyne, UK: Cambridge Scholars Publishing, 2010), 111–125.

Unless otherwise indicated, English translations are mine.

Introduction
Taste and See the Power of Food

"If you observe well, you will see that, from one age to another, there is a change not only in men's speech, vocabulary, dress, style of building, culture and such things, but, what is more, even in their sense of taste. A food that was highly prized in one age will often be found far less appetizing in another."[1] Thus Francesco Guicciardini in his *Ricordi* explains the fickleness, unpredictability, and inconsistency that characterize the human propensity for change. Arguably, the eagerness to accept and adapt to new systems, be they linguistic, artistic, or culinary, is the direct expression of the enduring human desire to discover, explore, and appropriate objects of wonder. The impulse driving this interest is to deepen human knowledge. This allows humanity to determine and assign meaning to the unintelligible. At the same time, it also engages the problematic and transforms the uncommon into the familiar. With refreshing directness in his aphorism, the Florentine historian seems to suggest that the penchant to replace the old with the new, the known with the unknown, or the tested with the untested mirrors, first of all, the appetite for innovative endeavors that sets the human mind afire.

By listing foodstuff among the elements that characterize a particular age and grouping it with widely recognized models that define the ever shifting landscape of cultural preferences, Guicciardini provides the clearest evidence yet for the Renaissance that food is a sign of its times. Indeed, through the particular ingredients and preparation techniques that any given epoch privileges, food bears witness to the many sociocultural facets and contradictions that shape an age. Of course, the sociocultural aspects that define any system are generally grounded in philosophical, political, and theological beliefs. As a result, food, as the historian describes it, turns into a nontraditional mode of assessing the currents that characterize the times in which it is consumed. In addition, it stands revealed as a highly reliable gauge of human endeavor. In the shifting trends that typify human progress, food exemplifies the departure from numbing ordinariness and, metaphorically, a change from resignation, denial, and quiescence. As a matter of fact, it also typifies risk-embracing creativity, unbending resoluteness, and inventiveness, all of which can pave the way to the moral truths after which humanity hungers.

Clearly, the sociohistorical traits Guicciardini assigns to food turn it into another cultural marker. As such, the historian reminds us that it can be used along with language, fashion, and architecture to assess the experiences that change, and at times mar, society as it pursues the knowledge that guides it to happiness, justice, and, ultimately, peace. The historian's assertion is especially momentous because it puts food on a par with language and architecture. By the time Guicciardini was confecting his aphorisms,[2] both these fields were highly established branches of study. In the middle of the fifteenth century, the Florentine Leon Battista Alberti had codified the rules governing modern architecture. Even before it was published, almost fourteen years after the author's death, Alberti's treatise *On the Art of Building in Ten Books* (*De re aedificatoria*) circulated among various groups of connoisseurs whose enthusiastic acclaim it won.[3] That the work focused entirely on architecture was one of the reasons for its immediate success. At the time of its publication, Pollio Vitruvius's *On architecture* (*De architectura*) was the only theoretical work specifically devoted to the art of building.[4] The wide range of interpretations and commentaries that throughout the centuries flourished around this treatise spawned a wide variety of works.[5] Nevertheless, this tradition produced mere variants of the original treatise the Roman architect and engineer had dedicated to Augustus.

The similarities between Vitruvius's and Alberti's treatises are few. The most obvious one is the ten chapters into which they both are subdivided. The differences, in contrast, are many and glaring. The most compelling one involves an innovative point of view. As Joseph Rykwert points out, Vitruvius's treatise looked at the past whereas Alberti's focused on the future.[6] Specifically, by making the designs of Hellenistic and early Greek architects the models for Roman buildings, Vitruvius did not strive for originality and inventiveness. He never endeavored to reach beyond the forms and designs that his investigations into the architectural past unearthed. Throughout his career Vitruvius remained a supporter of ancient construction rules and practices. Alberti's approach was exactly the opposite. He turned toward the imaginative new, a mode that enabled him to supersede the unimaginative, and no longer functional, old. For this reason, Alberti regarded the descriptions of ancient buildings he found in literary texts and the knowledge he gained from the ruins he studied as his points of departure.[7] In his view, the authority of the ancients could not function as a point of arrival because, among other reasons, ancient architecture provides neither answers to political demands nor spaces for social interactions and cultural sensibilities.[8] Because these concerns ranked high among the preoccupations of the modern age, Alberti looked for architectural solutions to those needs.[9] The new order of building he envisioned takes into account and attends to precisely the complexities and ambitions defining his age and society.[10] For him old models neither meet the expectations nor live up to the tensions, the curiosity, and especially the desire to exceed and improve on the past. Yet these are the tinders that kindle modernity. Not surprisingly, the far-reaching implications of Alberti's treatise on architecture not only influenced the political and social spheres, but also had impacts in the linguistic arena.[11] This latter field is of particular relevance for the purpose of this study because it elucidates the link that Guicciardini draws between architecture and language.

From Alberti's perspective, the idea of "inventing terms to explain matters,"[12] paired with his resoluteness about using "proper Latin, and in a comprehensible form,"[13] lays bare the necessity to rely on a language capable of expounding cutting-edge theories. As he emphasizes the need for a Latin suitable for his work's inventiveness Alberti, before Guicciardini, makes language and architecture part of the same discourse on creativity, innovation, and mastery. By insisting on a precise language that functions as an airtight system yielding the clearest meanings and measuring up to his new building criteria, Alberti establishes another fundamental difference between his work and Vitruvius's.[14] More than this, the necessity to adopt a language that is lucid and coherent intersects in a meaningful way with the Florentine's interest in language itself.[15] In various works he authored, Alberti reiterates his interest in the accurate use of language, whether Latin or *volgare*.[16] His specific concern with correct linguistic usage led him to write a *Grammatichetta*.[17] In essence, by opting for a language that conveys the precise meanings of his leading-edge building criteria Alberti foreshadows, and at the same time gives substance to, Guicciardini's assertion: together architecture and language are epoch-defining sociocultural markers.

There is yet another reason language and architecture are closely linked in Guicciardini's aphorism. In the sixteenth century the language debate, or the *questione della lingua*,[18] which spanned decades was reignited by Pietro Bembo's publication of the *Prose della volgar lingua* (1525).[19] To give uniformity to the linguistically fractured peninsula that comprised a variety of *volgari*, the Venetian humanist maintains that a canon must be set. As to the bases of this canon, he specifically pinpoints Petrarch's use of Tuscan for poetry and Giovanni Boccaccio's for prose. In contrast to Bembo's thesis, Giovan Giorgio Trissino theorizes about the use of a common language he defines as "Italian."[20] In the wake of his discovery of Dante's *De vulgari eloquentia* (1513),[21] Trissino argues that Tuscan is one of many variants that "Italian" must encompass. He puts forward his linguistic views in the *Epistola de le lettere aggiunte ne la lingua italiana* (1524) as well as in his dialogue *Il castellano* (1529). Writing within the same arc of time, Baldesar Castiglione, in *The Book of the Courtier* (1528), argues against Bembo's artificial use of Tuscan and moves closer to Trissino's position, advocating the use of *volgari*.

Niccolò Machiavelli does not shy away from this debate; rather, he lends his voice to it. In the *Discorso o dialogo intorno alla nostra lingua*,[22] he argues that the linguistic norms for Italy must be drawn from the Florentine. But he emphasizes that the rules ought to be based on the *volgare*—the spoken language. For him, the greater "constitutional and structural regularity" of this idiom gives it preeminence over other *vol-*

gari.²³ To lend credibility to his argument, the secretary argues that it was on the Florentine's linguistic foundations, not any other, that Dante, Boccaccio, and Petrarch found the means to express their ideas.²⁴ Accordingly, Machiavelli maintains that their use of the Florentine *volgare*, in turn, legitimizes its ascendency over other idioms. His reasoning undermines the artificiality of language that Bembo and Trissino advocate.²⁵ More importantly, although he never openly states it, it is evident that like his friend Guicciardini, Machiavelli does not lose sight of the geopolitical implications that the use and predominance of one language over others entail.²⁶

Against these theoretical disputations, Teofilo Folengo's *Baldus* (1517, 1521, 1539–1540, and posthumously 1552) adds fuel to the debate. Through a linguistic experiment, Folengo takes a bold anticlassical stand against Bembo's theory, openly questioning the validity of the rule imposed by the canon.²⁷ The macaronic Latin hexameters he uses in his *Baldus* provide a concrete example of the richness that idioms other than Tuscan possess. By parodying and ridiculing the excesses of "linguistic purity" in humanist literature, the Benedictine monk brings a fresh if rebellious perspective to the debate on language.²⁸ Through images of food and banquets that ground his discourse in popular culture and natural experiences Folengo with "verbal inventiveness and spontaneity"²⁹ pokes fun at the artificiality of pedantic linguistic rules.³⁰ And although these types of rules characterize the ongoing debate, Folengo demonstrates that a formalistic attitude toward language undermines its rich and fluid essence. Like food to be relished bite by bite, each mouthful appreciated for its own individual uniqueness and yet contributing to the whole meal's deliciousness, Folengo in his mock-epic poem posits northern Paduan dialects as constitutive parts of one idiom. In the end, by commingling Latin morphology and constructs with dialectal forms and uses, he shows another side of the complexities associated with selecting a specific *volgare* as the basis for an "Italian" language. Through the voices and works of these linguistic theorists and practitioners, among others, the *questione della lingua* occupies center stage in the literary landscape at the time of Guicciardini's writing. It is no surprise, therefore, that the historian speaks of language and architecture in the same breath with food.

There exists yet another strong nexus between language, architecture, and food. These elements lend themselves quite naturally to the consumption of users, readers, and viewers. Indeed, the way onlookers gaze at a particular building can be construed as a type of consuming. Visually appropriating an artistic, literary, or architectural object is comparable to taking in, to consuming it. Sight, the sense that occasions this phenomenon, functions like taste and smell. And just as these senses play an important role in tasting food, sight is central to partaking of the object observed. It could be argued that residing in and making a space one's own are comparable to absorbing into oneself what is outside of it (in this case, the surroundings). Like actual eating, both gazing at and inhabiting a space entail appropriating what is outside of the self and incorporating it. In anthropological terms, the absorption of the "other" into the self is a process that "synthesizes the other as part of the self."[31] While this notion accounts for different forms of cannibalism, it is obvious that living in a space or looking at an object is by no means the same as cannibalism. One is reminded, however, that internalizing ideas, forms, and spaces, in short, appropriating external objects through the senses, can be likened to the act of eating and ingesting. Isidore of Seville puts forward an intriguing common etymology for *aedes, aedificium* (room, building, edifice) and *edere* (to eat). The two words, he claims, share a common origin.[32] According to Ann W. Astell, Isidore's conjecture on this linguistic resemblance was seized on by medieval monastic orders.[33] The belief that the food (spiritual or physical) they privileged made it possible to build and reside in different types of houses (divine or worldly) originated in Isidore's pronouncement.

From a different perspective, the idea of building a beautiful edifice based on the spiritual, not the material, food consumed, was also derived from the notion of feeding on the sacred scriptures. For the medieval mind "eating" the scriptures was a commonly used metaphor. This idea traced its origins back to the Old Testament book of Ezekiel (3:3–4): "Son of man, eat what is before you: eat this scroll, then go, speak to the house of Israel. So I opened my mouth and he gave me the scroll to eat. Son of man, he then said to me, feed your belly and feed your stomach with this scroll I am giving you. I ate it, and it was sweet as honey in my mouth. He said: Son of man, go now to the house of Israel, and speak my words to them." Accordingly, it was believed that the spiritual nourishment provided by these texts strengthened, educated, and beautified the consumer.[34] The aesthetic value attached to the theological one lent force to the building theory the spiritual orders championed.[35] Guicciardini's terse statement indirectly calls attention to this tradition, underscoring once again that food, like architecture and language, heralds symbolic meanings that speak to the choices every society deliberately makes.

Understood in terms of a gastronomic taxonomy that assigns meaning to ingredients, preparations, dishes, and meals, the traditional role of food is upended. Its usefulness no longer limited by the nutritional values it delivers to an organism, food turns into something more than a mere means of sustenance. It becomes an element that possesses, among other attributes, aesthetic values. Eating thus stands for the internalization and appreciation of those values. In much the same way, the particular shapes and colors conferred to foodstuff for the purpose of stimulating and delighting the consumers' senses turn it into gastronomic works of art.[36] Like other creative works, gastronomic ones are influenced in part by the identity and personality of the artists shaping them. But the character, and in particular the social status, of those individuals for whom they are created also affect preparations. In fact, gastronomic creativity often aims at reflecting and affirming the latter's power, displaying their achievements, and conveying their sophistication.

Of course, there is another side to this. Admiring the attractive shapes into which expert hands turn food even before ascertaining its exquisiteness suggests a possible dichotomy between appearance and reality. Metaphorically, this is the equivalent of biting into an aesthetic layer without verifying the ethical one. The passage from the aesthetic to the ethical value of food is set in motion precisely by the pleasure of the senses that the former engenders.[37] By appealing to the senses of sight and taste, the attractiveness and tastiness of gastronomic creations bring out the whole problematic range of ethical implications.[38] This stems from the fact that the senses pave the way to bodily pleasures. And these, according to Aristotle and Saint Thomas Aquinas, among others, more often than not lead to immoderation, intemperance, and sin.[39] Yet the saint, in the wake of the philosopher's claim, maintains that "there is an art of making pleasure, namely, *the art of cookery and the art of making unguents*" (emphasis added).[40] Without ambiguity, this assertion posits cooking—the preparation of food and its final result, the dish and the meal—as a creative form of art that brings pleasure to the consumer. Yet, while substantiating the idea that gastronomic works of art engender pleasure, Saint Thomas's words straddle different types of pleasures. Thus, his pronouncement lays bare the shifting, thrilling, but also unsettling implications that gastronomy elicits. As one might expect, the degree of pleasure it engenders—immoderate or moderate— mirrors the individual's temperance. Like the art of making perfumed ointments intended to enhance the body's appeal, cookery does bring pleasure to the senses; but the temperate person steers clear of the excessive and unregulated behavior that sensual pleasures can elicit. For Saint Thomas, delighting in a sensible enjoyment of natural pleasures that are good for both body and spirit is not sinful. What he, and Aristotle, rejects altogether is the loss of self-control caused by sensual pleasures. In their respective views, yielding to them leads to the abrogation of moral and ethical principles. But Aquinas's assertion is fascinating for another reason also: it indirectly foregrounds the powerful role played by the artist charged with preparing the food. Cast against vulnerable consumers, who are more likely than not to give in entirely to the enticing delights, the cook—author and deviser of irresistible dishes—is unaffected by, and even unsusceptible to, their seductiveness. Because of this, the cook embodies control and authority; in short, he has power.

That food is a significant marker of culture, disclosing meanings that are fixed to culture and its milieu, just as Gucciardini claimed in the Renaissance, is a concept that modern anthropologists have long embraced. Although the anthropological analysis of food is beyond the literary aims of this study, it is important to remember that well before literary scholars, anthropologists probed the meanings of foodstuff and its relevance to the development of societies. More than forty years ago, for instance, Claude Lévi-Strauss argued convincingly that the universal transformation of nature into culture takes place through the cooking of food. In his seminal work, the anthropologist maintains that gastronomy "is a language in which each society codes messages which allow it to signify a part at least of what it is."[41] Lévi-Strauss's discourse makes it abundantly clear that food, including the ingredients used, the preparations chosen, and even the contexts in which it is presented and consumed, is an element that enables us to differentiate—either in its natural state or in its final preparation and apart from its nutritional value—among cultures and societies. To carry his assertion further, it would be accurate to say that food through its organizing and unifying properties becomes similar to a language. Its ingredients, spices, and cooking techniques replace the phonemes and morphemes that as a nonverbal language it lacks. And just like any language, it possesses a vast range of meanings. More often than not, these offer surprisingly arresting nuances. From these subtle differences one can analyze the context, culture, and society from which food is developed and within which it is consumed. To grasp the symbolic significance of food, accepting it as a sign of the culture of which it is part and which regulates it, requires understanding that it is itself a system governed by rules. These rules, not unlike social tenets, can either ensure or undermine the excellence of the final product that the cook, like a consumed leader and artist, aims to achieve. And as with any spoken language, food's rules are communicable and understandable only to those well versed in the code that defines them. Recognizing this system as one having the same force of a language gives rise to the same set of expectations the former provides. Food does meet them; and as an expression of social and cultural phenomena it discloses the sometimes riveting, sometimes repugnant principles every society champions as it seeks to advance itself over others—even if it entails subjugating them.

It is no wonder, then, that from the earliest times food has occupied a prominent place, first in the oral and later in the written literary tradition. Whether describing a shared meal or a solitary repast, storytellers and writers—from Homer and beyond—have used foodstuff as another means through which to plumb the depths of the human condition as it evolved under the extraordinary, and sometime intense, circumstances of the times in which the authors lived. An early example of this in the Latin tradition is Petronius Arbiter's *Cena Trimalchionis*. This work is an absorbing if occasionally unrefined model of food and dinner scene used to frame the social, political, and cultural practices shaping Petronius's society. Throughout the dinner the host's boasting is the common thread linking the various conversations taking place between him and his guests. In this work, Trimalchio's flamboyant pretentiousness is the supporting structure of Petronious's satire.[42] Indeed, the host's affectation is palpable in every aspect of the banquet, during which, what appears as spontaneous action, is the furthest thing from improvised.

From the beginning, it is obvious that Trimalchio's dinner is nothing other than a calculated maneuver staged to flaunt the wealth[43] he has amassed as a freedman of the empire.[44] Through it, he aims at garnering his guests' admiration. To add luster to his riches, and complement them, during the banquet Trimalchio seizes the opportunity to display his "erudition."[45] He does so by voicing his views on—and his interpretations of—philosophical, astrological, and mythological issues.[46] In his understanding, to be conversant in a wide variety of subjects lends a sophisticated sheen to the social status he has carved for himself; the intellectual curiosity he demonstrates adds legitimacy to it. Predictably, however, the very opposite ensues. Every time Trimalchio addresses subjects intended to show his literary taste and liberal education, fusing, in a sense, generosity of spirit with a light touch of pedagogy, he winds up revealing his utter ignorance. Mistakes, misstatements, and missed details sum it all up.[47] The coarseness and conceit Trimalchio embodies bear all the marks of the nouveau riche who closely track his fortune while feigning a lack of interest toward it. Despite his affectation, the host's vexatious obsession with his wealth is depicted in vibrant tones and hues especially as he boasts about the copious food and wine he offers to his guests.[48]

More than the speeches and dialogues intended to give substance to appearances and inspire awe in the guests, Trimalchio's raw ostentatiousness is manifest in the manner in which the dishes he offers are prepared and served. The culinary preparations disguise, and at times conceal, the basic ingredients used in their creation. For this reason, they turn almost into images of a textual banquet that Trimalchio authors throughout the evening. Arguably, this aspect of the meal hints at a link between the delicacies and the moral fiber of its provider. The privileged social position the host has reached is not the result of his moral character. On the contrary, insofar as he is concerned, moral values and forms of conduct do not traverse the road to riches. Trimalchio swanks about his cooks' culinary creativity, deeming it the gastronomic index of his own prosperity. As for his guests, whose sole objective is to "gaze and guzzle,"[49] they feign attention to the host's incoherent blather. In reality, it is the cooks' artistic renditions of food that turn into an evolving text that dazzles their eyes. In course after course, chapter after chapter as it were, this culinary text redirects their attention to the luxuries that affluence, and not moderation, self-control, or propriety, secures. To be sure, for the guests the lure of Trimalchio's wealth and all it promises, their steady increase—in short, the culmination of what they understand as freedom—vanquishes the mental numbness that overindulging at the table causes.

Undoubtedly, the cooks' culinary ingenuity and skillfulness reflect the host's own craftiness. The latter's extraordinary social trajectory, from slave to wealthy freedman, owner of an opulent villa equipped with a legion of slaves he governs with an iron hand in the privileged Puteoli milieu, is evidence of this. Yet Petronius's acerbic commentary on the depravity and dissoluteness that lie beneath the banquet's exotic fare summarizes the breakdown of social norms and civic bonds. Because he lacks the ability to make the subtle distinction between education and riches, reason and power, elegance and garishness, authority and tastelessness, Trimalchio's dinner highlights the very absence of self-restraint and, by extension, refinement. The presentation of a boar served with a cap of freedom—a *pilleus*—on its head graphically exemplifies this. The idea of serving exotic animals cooked whole and presented in spectacular manners is consistent with the host's intent of displaying his prodigious means. In Trimalchio's understanding, wealth turns the ordinary and formulaic into the exceptional and magnificent. But the effect the boar produces on the narrator Encolpio—and the readers through him—is quite different. At first, in fact, the significance of the cap eludes him completely. But as the mentor dining next to Encolpio points out, the peculiar garb with which the cooked boar is presented in Trimalchio's household signifies the freedom the animal gained on the previous night. Presented to other dining guests on that occasion, it was not eaten because of the copious food served. In the host's twisted logic, as a leftover, the boar gained an additional day of existence, and this earned it the freedom the cap signifies.

The parade of the freed boar is intended to crown Trimalchio's celebration of his wealth in the dining quarters of his villa. The dining hall is a context that controls his character and is simultaneously controlled by it because there he can sate his guests' physical hunger while they, in turn, can satisfy his hunger for social acceptance. The boar, however, illustrates the absurdity of Trimalchio's thinking. Rather than complementing the strident roar of celebration and the forced joviality the guests are expected to display, it highlights in a paradoxical way the host's misguided principles. An untamed and fierce animal known for the astuteness it deploys in concealing its own footprints to escape capture,[50] the boar is highly prized for its meat because hunting it down requires force and skill. Thus, reducing it to a prepared dish, taming, in a sense, the wild beast, turns into an image that invites the meal's partakers (and Petronius's readers) not simply to eat, but to take in the visual text of Trimalchio's entitlements. Served on his textual table, the boar exemplifies a chapter of the host's ascent to riches. That he can grant freedom to the animal is a further if ironic proof of it. On the table the boar becomes the image of the host's power, especially by way of contrast. In other words, while the first lost its freedom to satisfy human hunger for rare morsels, the latter gained it to gratify his desires for them.

While the spectacle of the cap is choreographed to emphasize the daily copiousness of Trimalchio's table, where the quantity and quality of food by far surpass the partakers' ability to consume it all, the *pilleus* does suggest that the boar is much more than just another course. The banquet of images and ideas that Trimalchio hosts lends itself to several interpretations. First of all, the cap brings the notion of freedom into play, suggesting, yet again by way of contrast, that it is never tied to mere appearance. For in spite of its symbolic cap the boar has been captured, killed, cooked, and served. A dead animal can hardly be thought of as free. Also, the paradox of the cooked/freed animal casts a penetrating light on the political implications of freedom. This idea, unsurprisingly, calls to mind the persistent tension between the social positions people hunger after and the moral and ethical values they willingly forsake to reach what they perceive as the pinnacle of prestige they covet. The cap becomes, then, a boldly imagined reflection on those who, like Trimalchio, perceive freedom as tied to affluence. The fact that the boar, like the pig, is associated with gluttony because of the tastefulness of its meat lends further meaning to the notion of human greed and the insatiable desires for material gratification it stimulates.

The display of the freed boar also points to the host's, and his guests', belief that even in death wealth provides a spectacle of power. With its stillness, passivity, and silence conquered by the distress and cries of survivors (who are after the deceased's fortune) death turns into another celebration of wealth. This, in Trimalchio's view, lends a degree of tolerability to the idea of leaving behind one's possessions. For this reason, the triumphantly free animal exemplifies the mark of distinction that, in the eyes of Trimalchio, only wealth imparts on death. Yet the *pilleus* forces a correspondence between animal and man. The ironic poignancy of this is made all the more pressing because Trimalchio fails to see the difference that exists between the two. For him, both man and boar are portrayed as having achieved a type of material freedom. But in both cases this is construed and defined by purely material terms: Trimalchio's freedom from slavery to riches and the boar's unconsumed flesh. The narrow perspective this type of freedom emphasizes and the false positive it sustains, as Petronius seems to suggest, result from a flawed understanding of the true meaning of freedom, the fullness of which gives life its genuine richness because it begins with the self.

According to Cicero, the secret path to true inner freedom is paved by moral and ethical principles that steer the mind. In contrast to this all-encompassing freedom, the boar's, like Trimalchio's, is a concoction of the unprincipled mind because it remains yoked to the universe of materiality. The freedman's beliefs, as Petronius describes them, turn on its head Cicero's notion of temperance and self-control. These are virtues the philosopher deems necessary in regulating human behavior, especially as it shapes political identities and these, in turn, inspire the collective project of society-building. Yet despite Cicero's teachings, Trimalchio remains enslaved by material preoccupations. This is the only reality with which he identifies because, in his view, through riches the abstract becomes concrete, the general particular, and the personal sacred. It is no wonder that the physical and financial freedom he has engineered—or cooked—for himself and which grants him the same rights from which Roman citizens benefit, neither gives evidence of his moral rectitude nor suggests a curiosity for what lies beyond the material. His gloating references to his wealth, his ferocious and barely hidden desire to increase it, along with the self-absorption he brazenly exhibits, are evidence of his warped understanding of freedom. More importantly, his idea of it does not turn into an experience for inquiring about truths and investigating claims of facts. Freedom for the freedman revolves around personal gains. And these bring no benefits to society, as would Cicero's model of the principled citizen who places moral dignity and goodness above all other qualities and possessions.

In the *De officiis,* the philosopher's advice to his son naturally intersects the social and public spheres. Within these, Cicero asserts, only temperance sets the boundaries conducive to carrying out the roles and responsibilities that free humanity from the bondage of corruption, fears, and violence yoking it. These failings, according to him, by undermining the moral principles on which righteous societies must be grounded cause social and political havoc. For Cicero, only truth and social justice lead to true freedom. For unlike the illusoriness of the material humanity too often pursues, truth and justice are the just ends society must strive to achieve. In his view, accomplishing this requires a steadfast adherence to a moral code of behavior that is rooted in the practice of self-restraint, propriety, and moderation.[51] As it struggles to balance patrician assumptions with plebeian realities the practice of these virtues enables humanity to overcome personal and political hurdles, as well as private and public challenges. Ultimately, Cicero's words make it plain that by abiding by virtues that lead to personal freedom, humanity reaches its fullest potential. This aim is neither determined nor improved by the glistening lucre of personal wealth.

Cicero's lesson of timeless and unchanging cardinal virtues that mold individuals' behavior and shape society as a whole is lost on Trimalchio, for he confuses freedom with worldly possessions. The freedom he advocates is of a material nature, and excludes the fundamental one of mind and spirit. His freed boar on the dinner table is a grim reminder of this. In fact, the animal's presence speaks to humanity's protean-nature. This leans toward what appears pleasurable even if flawed while loathing the flawless that requires discipline because it is perceived as unpleasant. Reading between the lines of Trimalchio's culinary text, it becomes evident that as copious and exquisite as the courses the guests eat their way through might be, they feed appearances not minds. Thus, consuming his food is more like tasting death than savoring life. The careful organization of appearances and the numbing seduction overtaking the guests as they passively observe in stupefied awe the succession of dishes in the peculiar forms they have been given illustrate this. As the foundation of Trimalchio's banquet, the overabundance, refinement, and presentation of food disclose the more pernicious and harrowing quality of the historical times in which Petronius's work was written. Marked by the influence of fears, political turbulences, mistrust, corruption, and profligacy, the universe Petronius depicts in the *Cena Trimalchionis* sums up the deep divide between the host's standards of value and those of its author.

Fittingly, to imbue his characters with vivid, complicated humanity that cuts deeply into their calculating manners, Petronius chooses satire as the literary device for his work. The etymology of the word, which retrieves the meaning of the abundance of food because it derives from *satura*, is telling. This was a dish of offering the Romans made to the gods on a yearly basis. It consisted of a medley of all fruits available at the given festival's time in a single dish. Aptly, the adjective *saturo*, "full," was the name by which the dish acquired its renown.[52] In later times, *satira* identified a type of drama popularized in Roman literature that integrated a mélange of music, words, and dancing, artistic forms that revolved around topics of ethical and historical themes. But the early tradition at times conflated the etymological origins of *satira* with Greek satyrs. These minor nature-deities were thought of as the brothers of nymphs. They were followers of Dionysus; Silenus, Dionysus's teacher, was considered their father. For this reason, satyrs were also called silens. Mythological creatures "primitive and semi-wild, the natural as opposed to the civilized man,"[53] satyrs were associated with libertine indulgence, uncontrollable lust, and unsophisticated behavior. Originally depicted with "bristly hair, broad noses, pointed ears, even tails,"[54] the part-animal part-man creatures embody the bestial instincts that

Dionysian rites celebrate.⁵⁵ As for Greek satyr plays, they are "viewed primarily as a contrast to, or relief from, the tragedies that preceded them."⁵⁶ Clearly, either one of the two traditions linked to *satira* contains elements that mirror the traits Trimalchio personifies. For this reason, the fact that Petronius opts for this particular literary style to illustrate his character's shameless escape into grandiose self-conception, tangled views, and shallow relations is especially revealing. Through this, with a master stroke he juxtaposes and parodies the human and divine, food and politics, literary style and lifestyle, meanings and values, men and animals. What ensues is an unvarnished picture of Roman society, engrossed with power and so prepared to forge its own brand of freedom.

The weakening bond between society and individual is caused by this egotistical attitude. It also results from the fact that for affluent Romans increasing personal fortunes comes at the cost of decreasing moral responsibilities toward society. Trimalchio's banquet, like a *satura* prepared for the gods, is full of mouthwatering delicacies. But unlike the gods' dish, the earthly bound *satura* is intended to satisfy human hunger. This appetite is as unconcerned with divine principles as it is with human ones. Petronius's fiery condemnation of the culture and times that privilege wealth over principled systems of beliefs points precisely to the devaluation of values Romans have conveniently accepted and foster. This attitude, he seems to suggest, occurs because their fantasies of power are more seductive than the certainty of powerlessness; and also because it is the former, not the latter, which allows people to identify with the affluent. The same excesses mark the dynamics at work in politics, where rootless figures control society. As an early example of the ways in which food intersects and defines, while simultaneously it is interconnected to and defined by historical times, cultural trends, and social mores, Petronius's *Cena Trimalchionis* sets an example for later Italian poets and writers. They will use food in their own works in an imaginative way as a means through which they identify, and critique, their own societies' flaws.

Trimalchio's banquet makes it clear that food evokes notions that go well beyond the idea of physical nourishment. Among them, there is the idea of emotional fulfillment. This, in turn, ushers in the idea of political triumph, spiritual gratification, and erotic pleasure. It can therefore be said that in literature as in the visual arts food by its very presence performs a complex, multilayered function. First, it adds a zest of authenticity to the actions narrated. Through this, it annuls the distance between fiction and reality. Second, through the process that transforms raw ingredients into prepared dishes, food becomes a sign encompassing more elaborate ideological, political, theological, and cultural concepts. As Louis Marin persuasively argues, it is through this metamorphosis that the comestible is transformed into the signified and the speakable is transformed into the edible.[57] According to Marin's analysis, food turns into a transignificant, and this, in turn, becomes a metaphor.[58] Through this conversion, food acquires new meanings that are completely disassociated from its original physical significance. Thus food—along with the setting in which it is consumed—serves to identify the motifs connecting individuals to their historically, socially, theologically, and philosophically determined environments.

It is interesting, however, that whether the writers' intent is to capture convivial occasions celebrating desire and power or to valorize the frugality that favors intellectual and spiritual growth, eating in the Middle Ages and Renaissance Italian literary landscape is directly linked to the humanistic concern with moralistic prescriptions. By tempering the impulsiveness that drives human desires, these play a dominant role in codifying the behaviors believed to dash the chances for earthly happiness and celestial joyfulness. It would seem logical, therefore, that individuals adhering to those principles were dissuaded from consuming scrumptious foods and indulging in copious meals.

Yet, the very opposite is true. While moralistic preoccupations ostensibly retain their theoretical relevance in people's lives, individuals—especially those occupying positions of power and authority—resist altogether the notions of restraint concerning physical pleasures. By appealing to the senses, food, with its tastefulness, complexities, and depths, becomes an ingredient that sates more than just the physical need. To please the palate, as well as the eyes and sense of smell of consumers, cooks enhance its taste, texture, shape, and color. In the kitchens the cooks' talent—the artists' creativity—turns cooking into a science, lending variety, subtlety, and luxuriousness to ingredients that social status, political dynamics, and cultural milieu desire and require. As it undergoes the changes necessary to impress, astonish, and entice—purposes far more worldly than the simple satisfaction of hunger—food acquires the precision of a language. In point of fact, it encodes and articulates with infallible accuracy sociocultural phenomena. Within the literary universe, it connects characters, as well as writers and poets, to the historical periods in which they live.

In the chapters that follow I analyze this concept first within the context of Boccaccio's *Decameron*. In this work the meals the characters consume produce an open system of meanings within the novellas; and the meanings stand in sharp contrast to the closed system that the historical background provides. The novellas are narrated according to the rules Pampinea sets down shortly after the *brigata*'s arrival at the country house. Her directives serve to maintain a constant, uncompromised order so that the young friends never stray from the objective they have set for themselves. Pampinea's organization can be interpreted as Boccaccio's dramatization of history: a succession of events from which spins a countless series of other occurrences. The events narrated result from, and at the same time also cause, society's adhesion to or rebellion against the rules that ostensibly ensure order. They also shape society and its culture in an impermanent manner because new occurrences bring on changes. History, by contrast, is permanent. The circumstances shaping it cannot undergo modifications. The only thing that can vary with regard to past occurrences is the meanings or interpretations people attach to them. The difference between the permanent and the impermanent is central to Boccaccio's understanding of the human condition. Just as significant is his awareness that history and laws—the permanent—can neither regulate nor assuage natural human desires. These, for him, account for the impermanent. To be sure, in Boccaccio's dramatization of history there is neither tension nor animosity among the ten friends. They take turns in leading the others as well as in narrating the stories on any given day. Their ludic diversion, carried out against the backdrop of the plague decimating their fellow-Florentines, does not bear out any form of conflict. Unlike historical events, among the ten friends emotions are neither unwieldy nor marked by jarring bursts of violence. In this serene setting Boccaccio uses foodstuffs to uncover and simultaneously test the limits of the political, theological, philosophical, and cultural tenets of his society. In so doing, he upends conventions, turning unbelievable fiction into believable lives. The novella of the marchioness of Monferrato (1.5), analyzed in chapter 1, is an example of this. In it the noblewoman counters the king of France's advances through a meal that she turns into her language of refusal. Although lacking phonemes and morphemes, this encoded form of communication conveys to the king her unambiguous rejection of his amorous advances. Through this simple but carefully conceived act, the marchioness, and Boccaccio through her, challenges and redefines the socially constructed model of masculine power. She forces the king to face up to the fact that a woman can choose according to her resolve rather than bow to conventions and socially prescribed roles. In so doing, she challenges not just political power, but also the theological and philosophical tenets ostensibly regulating human behavior. And this darkens the brew of the king's cup.

In a more striking manner, but still through food, *Decameron*, 3.10 focuses on the conflict between theological tenets and human desires. Alibech's journey of courage and discomfort to discover God, predictably enough, ends in a young man's cell. This particular detail exemplifies the tension between human intellect and appetites. The object of her wonder, curiosity, and also wanderings, in other words, the Christian God she hungers to know, drives the young woman's quest. The search for Him leads her to seek what is different and discover the unknown she wants to appropriate. In an ironic twist, however, she becomes the young hermit's object of wonder and discovery. As she travels through the desert, Alibech takes in and on the practices the hermits observe, eager to make them hers. Because of this, she compliantly adjusts, among other things, to their cuisine. Despite the austere diet Rustico observes to dampen enflamed erotic desires, the God about whom he teaches Alibech is Eros, not the divine one. In Rustico's desert, lack of copious and tasteful food neither extinguishes erotic desire nor does it eradicate the proclivity for self-indulgence. Against long-held beliefs, Boccaccio suggests that food in spite of its lack of succulence does not regulate human nature. This point leads to another reflection: the limits and flaws of rigid theological tenets governing the hermits' lives.

Through this the writer confronts the system of social inequalities that governs society. Looking at food as a sign of the unnatural bounds theology imposes on men and women in an attempt to still their inner desires forever leads Boccaccio to further question the political implications of desert life. This way of life, in his interpretation, is not just a rejection of the non-Christian culture. Indeed, viewed through the lens of political realism bending the will of weaker individuals to that of the powerful one results in abusive, oppressive, and, at times, brutal systems.

After Boccaccio the ideological and literary implications of food emerge in other Italian authors. Chapter 2 explores the ways in which Luigi Pulci uses food in his *Morgante* to critique the political and personal maneuverings shaping the Florentine court of Lorenzo de' Medici. In Pulci's epic poem food is also used to illustrate the corruption and greed that regulate the courtiers' lives. This, of course, occurs in spite of the humanist ideals set to guide the courtiers in mastering the beguiling ambiguities that hamper their goals. By embodying the ethical and moral ideals championed at the Florentine court, the knights populating Pulci's epic poem exemplify the more abstract expressions of humanist values. Over and against them, however, Morgante and Margutte, a giant and half-giant respectively, personify the radical opposite of courtly ideals. Their disproportionate bodies, ravenous appetites, unquenchable thirsts, and unrefined manners set them as models of the non-courtly. They are the "otherness" that courtly culture struggles against because in it, it perceives a threat to its privileged existence. Margutte's and Morgante's anomalous bodies match their unrestrained appetites. To satisfy the latter, they rely on any means and subterfuge available to them, and particularly on their physical might. By forcefully asserting their wills over others in order to secure what they hanker after, the two friends embody hunger for power. Yet to act as they do entails skirting the humanistic principles on which their society is theoretically founded. For this reason, they occupy a space outside the court. Paradoxically, however, Morgante's and Margutte's hunger is the same that pits courtiers, knights, ladies, leaders, poets, and philosophers against each other.

The savage wit with which Pulci uses food in his work ushers in more complex issues. By moving beyond political discourse, the poet focuses intently on the theological, philosophical, and linguistic spheres. The echoes of Bartolomeo Sacchi's (Platina) *On Right Pleasure and Good Health* (*De honesta voluptade et valetudine*) emerge from the initial analogy of frog meat that Orlando uses. The necessity to assign every animate or inanimate thing a proper Latin name gives Platina the opportunity to launch a scorching critique of the Roman curia. Filtered through Platina's argument, Pulci's own critique of and contempt for the Florentine court surface. For through the politics of gastronomy, which both Platina and Pulci describe in their respective works, the Roman as well as the Florentine courts' materialistic penchant is depicted in utter coarseness. Against Platina's treatise, however, there stands Marsilio Ficino's *The Three Books on Life* (*De vita libri tres*), a hybrid treatise of recipes and therapeutic advice geared for privileged people. For the most part, these individuals are unconcerned with ethical and moral questions. Unlike Pulci and Platina, in his work Ficino does not focus on the inconsistencies of political systems. For him, this is a logical choice. Because he is the personal adviser to the Magnifico, Ficino's ideas and beliefs influence Lorenzo. Through him, they shape the Florentine system. For this reason, Ficino does not question conventions; they serve his personal ends rather well.

In the *Morgante* personal gain is also the principle that guides Rinaldo's courtship of Antea. Even though as the adversary coming from the pagan camp she wishes to duel Rinaldo, the knight sets enmity aside. In a way, by shifting the field of play from the fighting camp to the banquet hall Rinaldo behaves like the king of France in Boccaccio's novella. And just like the latter uses a request to consume a meal at the marchioness's house as a ruse that barely hides his true intentions, the former exploits his invitation to a meal to win Antea over. Rinaldo's decision marks the precise moment when for Pulci food becomes a transformative force — erotic gastronomy — affecting human relations. But relying on a banquet as a means to conquer the desired woman is not the only way the poet uses food in his work. In a more fascinating manner the grotesque Margutte pokes holes through Ficino's theological beliefs through food. By making foodstuff, its procuring, preparation, and consumption, the underpinning of his religious doctrine the half-giant elaborates a detailed explanation of his philosophical axiom on faith.

His credo upends point by point Ficino's carefully constructed theological system. Control and authority, as displayed by the newly converted Morgante (much like Ficino, a translator-turned-priest) and not the nonbeliever Margutte (like Pulci), typifies the deceitful glutton whose deeds are concealed by mellifluous words. So the vivid scenes depicting the giants' truculent hunger disguise on the one hand the poet's defiant bitterness toward Ficino and the court that follows his teachings. On the other, they disclose the court's own ravenous desire for power.

Partiality toward rare morsels demands refined dishes. These are prepared with exotic ingredients, and are presented in eye-catching and imagination-stirring forms. The lavish meals these productions give life to characterize the Renaissance banquet scenes. Paradoxically, these sumptuous meals turn into a gastronomic definition, or even more precisely, an extension, of the self. This is the gastronomy of the self. According to it, the host, who is always a member of the powerful elite, identifies in the ostentatious food he consumes and offers. The staggering array of culinary delicacies his table presents ties in with his family's greatness. With searing effectiveness, Matteo Maria Boiardo in his *Orlando Innamorato* carefully seizes on this aspect of his culture. By integrating food and banquets with his hero's adventures, the poet depicts the materialistic universe the Este court and its courtiers inhabit. Chapter 3 probes the manner in which, through food and its symbolic meanings, the poet fuses together the span of his experience as an Este courtier and ambassador. Through this, he whittles away at the prestige and wealth his society ostentatiously flaunts in spite of the humanistic values rigorously instilled in young aristocrats at the school of Guarino da Verona in Ferrara and at that of his fellow-student Vittorino da Feltre in Mantua.[59] With leaders preoccupied with cultivating self-aggrandizement and seeking to gratify desires, the idea of keeping the senses in check through reason is spurned. This model turns the humanist upbringing into mere sophistry.

For Boiardo food becomes the conduit into the exploration of the tensions between ethics and aesthetics, form and substance, appearance and reality, permanence and impermanence. These strains hold a mirror up to the world of moral relativism the court espouses. The same contrasts, as the poet shows, threaten to split his already fragmented society asunder. Much like the historical men and women of the House of Este he served, Boiardo's characters do not acknowledge their flaws and faults. Yet, ironically, through the choices they make as they pursue their personal wants, they become humanized. For this same reason, they, like the Este leaders they emulate, often become ensnared in crises of their own making.

The historical context plays a large role in Boiardo's fictional work. Indeed, the intricate interplay of social, religious, philosophical, and economic forces surrounding figures like Ercole d'Este make up the nuanced background against which Boiardo's fictional characters play out their strengths and weaknesses. The many obstacles the knights and ladies face and overcome in the *Innamorato* are reminders of the self-contained and self-containing belief system that rational will affords. A rigorous moral and ethical compass, the rational will, can steer individuals to the right choices. The will also governs the spontaneous actions that knightly adventurous journeys frequently call for. By contrast, paying no heed to the rational will and the principles underpinning it inevitably leads to setbacks and losses. Boiardo's characters experience these too; and in powerfully moving scenes they are depicted in their agonizing reactions as they writhe in the physical (and emotional) discomforts caused by their unfulfilled desires. When this occurs, the urgency of their unhappiness and disappointments is distilled against the deceptively fulfilling sensual and material wants engrossing them. The gratification of desires thus turns into a force that hinders the knights' (and ladies') success. The poet describes these predicaments as wreaking havoc on the hero's self. Thus reduced, the heroes do not question their impulses, but they do act upon them. This recipe is not based on humanistic teachings; but neither are the ensuing destructive results that afflict the heroes, both from within and without.

As the knight who embodies the collective, modern struggle navigating through rigid principles and who tries to negotiate old values with new ones, Boiardo's Orlando allows the poet to delve into the manipulating power of language and poetry. Still, the moral universe he wrestles with evaporates in the face of his exacerbated desires. The imperfection of human thoughts, the inconstancy of human desires, and the shortcomings of human nature weigh down on his moral and ethical responsibilities and obligations. As a result, Orlando's perceptions misconstrue reality. From this perspective, food becomes the means through which Boiardo illustrates the tension between words and deeds, rational will and human passions, the ambiguous and the unambiguous.

The polarization existing between these extremes also subsists between illusion and reality, fiction and history. Ludovico Ariosto, in his *Orlando Furioso,* proposes different compelling ways of looking into the erosion of the boundaries that on the surface define and neatly divide each area. Against the inflexible idealism humanism champions, Ariosto conceives Ruggiero, the fictional Este forebear. This knight, much like his literary antecedents, tests the possibilities that the courtly universe offers. Through this, the poet discloses that the gratification of immediate physical needs and desires, rather than abstract idealized rules, drives human actions. What distinguishes Ruggiero from the heroes studied in the earlier chapters are his transformations into an acquiescent pawn in the hands of Atlante and Alcina. To be sure, both of these two magicians, albeit for different reasons, have an interest in keeping the knight yoked to their respective wills. In Ariosto's hands, the implications of Ruggiero's transformations are linked to the discourse on man's freedom. This notion is central to Renaissance philosophical thought. Chapter 4 delves into the study of this discourse through the hero's transformations. It also analyzes the manner in which Ariosto relies on food to underscore his character's moral and ethical fragility. In a masterful way, throughout his *Furioso* the poet shows that food exemplifies the flagging of the heroic will because it sums up the very process of transformations—negative or positive—that ingredients undergo as they are used in the preparations of different dishes. The power of transforming the transformed and of revealing new and unforeseeable culinary reconfigurations that food possesses, for Ariosto corresponds to the consumers'—as well as his heroes'—impermanent nature. There is no doubt that while this conflicts with the permanence of history, it does provide an accurate picture of the limits courtly ideals present. In light of this, the fleetingness of human nature the poet depicts also exposes the meaninglessness of the humanistic precepts it ostensibly champions. Over and against this belief system, Ariosto shows that in the universe of well-established theoretical abstractions aesthetics does not yield to ethics because the latter's seduction appeals not only to the corrupting nature of power, but especially to the exigencies the reality of a changed society requires.

In chapter 5 food and its political, philosophical, and historical meanings are explored from the perspective Pietro Aretino offers in his *Ragionamento*. Throughout this work Aretino, arguably the most controversial author of Renaissance Italy, uses food to launch a scathing condemnation of the self-indulgent lifestyles adopted by the princes of the Roman curia. By opening a window into the corrupt side of this court, Aretino, like Platina in his treatise, demonstrates that its members are neither immune to nor try to contain the flaws that are inherently human. On the contrary, they, like princes and courtiers from any dynastic court, seek to gratify every material want their prestige and power afford. Accordingly, they legitimize and disguise their appetite for pleasure that their extravagant way of life discloses through the vibrant palette of religion that offers a fluid interplay of the concrete and the abstract. But their crude behaviors, which conflict with the spiritual leadership their positions call for, reveal the full measure of the scandalous state of fraudulence that dominates the curia. And this erodes the spiritual foundations on which the Church was built. In other words, the curia's hedonistic lifestyle widens the gap between the secular and the spiritual, the powerful and the powerless, by erasing the line between the permissible and the deplorable, the ethical and the unethical, insiders and outsiders. This state of affairs has a ripple effect on society as a whole because in looking to emulate the model its spiritual leaders offer it finds no principled role model to follow.

This is the sociopolitical background against which Aretino's less-than-refined characters consume their simple meals while the urgency of their circumstances consumes them. Unlike the aristocratic prelates who make up the curia, the courtesan Nanna occupies the lower rung on Rome's social scale. Like them, however, she understands that affluence engenders power. But because she lacks their means she recognizes that to attain the material comforts they possess, and which she naturally aspires to achieve, requires a cunning recipe of astuteness and deceit. As the transgressive folds of life-experiences surface in Nanna's account to her friend and fellow-courtesan Antonia, the secrets of her professional career are revealed. In their concreteness they read exactly as a recipe for a dish. First, slowly entice the wealthy man to an adequate level of gullibility. Do this in the same manner one would slowly braise an ingredient in preparing a dish. Then, fleck him with occasional attentions and favors. Stir his imagination often by adding the zest of as yet unrealized sensual possibilities; slowly simmer his desires, mindful not to burn them to a crisp; add a small dose of flirtatiousness to his concrete demands while letting him stew in his carnal lust. Continue this process for as long as his wealth is made available to the courtesan. When it evaporates, and the man becomes no longer lucrative for her, in other words, when he no longer serves her interests, discard him. This procedure begins again with the next wealthy man who curries a courtesan's sexual favors. This play on recipes and food allows Aretino's Nanna to underscore the moral hollowness that the curia's greed has brought on Roman society.

Before turning to the chapters that follow, I wish to discuss the manner in which food links literature, philosophy, art, history, and theology. The question here is, how can the various meanings and implications of food start with the earthly and reach well beyond it? Food as a means to bring people and ideas together initially would seem to be self-evident; after all, everyone knows that the etymology of company is *cum panis*. Yet, perhaps, food is far more complex than one would think and its meaning is anything but self-evident. To my knowledge the words "gastronomy" and "astronomy" share no etymological root. In spite of their orthographic similarity in romance languages what sets them apart and gives each of the two words a different meaning is the addition of the letter "g" to one of them. This suggests that, at least in nomenclature, the divergence between the fields is simultaneously minuscule and vast: one of them concerns the earthly, the other the celestial. One entails the human, the other the heavenly. These two seemingly incompatible words and the areas of study they stand for bridge two worlds. To play with Lévi-Strauss's concept, one could say that they bring the raw closer to the cooked. The radical attitude this reading requires is the point of departure for lessening the distance between the human and divine. Among the other meanings that converge in the two words prevails the idea that the lowest earthly mind can soar to its highest potentialities through will and imagination. By rising above its fixed position through these means, the mind erases the distance between the tangible and the intangible, and even between the real and the imaginary. In this manner, it becomes, quite naturally, able to plot a course in, and thus becomes part of, both worlds. These meanings converge nowhere more clearly than in Dante's *Vita nuova*.

In chapter 2 Dante fuses cosmology and food in an unprecedented way. "Nine times already since my birth the heaven of light had circled back to almost the same point," he states. Then he continues: "She had been in this life long enough for the heaven of the fixed stars to be able to move a twelfth of a degree to the East in her time; that is, she appeared to me at about the beginning of her ninth year."[60] To accurately fix the time of his life-altering encounter with Beatrice through cosmological movements, Dante relies on his medieval grasp of astronomy. Through it, he establishes with mathematical precision his chancing upon a woman who, unbeknown to her (and, perhaps, precisely because of that), leads him to question every aspect of human existence and then to find answers to it in theological knowledge. In a self-reinforcing manner, Beatrice shows Dante the way to travel—intellectually, of course—from earth to heaven. As he tackles head on the pursuit of less materialistic objectives, which he now understands are the result of warped human aspirations, the poet brandishes a new type of weapon. Armed with his belief in the truths theology reveals, and with his faith in them, he faces up to the hardships confronting him. In his new understanding, theology and faith can turn any adversity—political, personal, and social—into a spiraling force for renewal and change.

Driven by this new understanding, Dante also establishes, without any possibility of error, an initial, circular connection between earth and heaven. He does so in the third chapter of *Vita nuova*. By way of a dream he illustrates the manner in which the earthly leads to the heavenly and from there, the latter in turn redirects, with newfound awareness and purpose, back to the earthly. In the dream immediately following the description of the poet's encounter with Beatrice, Dante traces in unmistakable terms and in a novel fashion the circular trajectory between astronomy and gastronomy. In it, the poet sees Beatrice held in the arms of Love.[61] He induces her to eat the poet's heart: "in one hand he seemed to be holding something that was all in flames, and it seemed to me that he said these words: *vide cor tuum*. And after some time had passed . . . he forced her cunningly to eat of that burning object in his hand; she ate of it timidly."[62] The symbolic implications this scene elicits point, first of all, to Beatrice's ingestion and taking in of that which, according to medieval understanding, is the "seat of vital forces" but also "of the moral conscience, of unwritten law, of encounter with God."[63] In short, it is the locus of human emotional and spiritual life.[64] But the eaten heart also suggests the assimilation of the values that the lovesick Dante embodies. As discussed above, to eat means to make one's own not just the nutritional values of the food ingested but especially to take in the qualities it exemplifies. Arguably, in their human limitations, these qualities are the counterparts to the divine values the Eucharistic sacrifice celebrates. The bold inversion Dante establishes in the scene of Beatrice eating his heart reveals that this, the receptacle of human values, when consumed by lady theology becomes part of her for whose love the poet is consumed.

The reciprocal act of eating suggested by this image—the idea of being eaten by her whose thought eats the poet—can be grasped first of all through John 14:6: "I am the way, and the truth, and the life." In the Middle Ages these words were construed as evidence of the open path the Eucharist provided between God and man. And, as Ann W. Astell states, for the medieval mind eating the Eucharist was to "be seen and eaten by Christ, drawn to Him, and incorporated into Him."[65] Augustine's *Confessions* lent further cogency to this notion: "I am the food of grown men. Grow and you shall feed upon me. And you will not, as with the food of the body, change me into yourself, but you will be changed into me."[66] In this passage the Bishop of Hippo underscores the power of the sacrament that mediates between God and humanity. Accordingly, by confirming the humanness of God revealed through His Son, the Eucharist discloses humanity's potential divinity. The dual roles Jesus embodies—food and consumer, eaten and eater[67]—encapsulate the process of restoration to spiritual life made possible by the Cross. To participate fully in the salvific journey toward redemption, humanity must willingly humble itself to be, like Jesus, food and consumer, eaten and eater. The reciprocity of this act, which erases the "I" and "you," sanctions the close relationship, shortening the distance as it were, between the human and divine, man and God.⁶⁸ In the following chapters the mutual effect of simultaneously being the eater and the eaten, subject and object (and the transformation this entails), is a recurrent theme among the authors studied. The spiritual redemption of their characters is not, however, their main objective. Indeed, the ways in which the heroes' moral and ethical probity is repeatedly questioned, undermined, and endangered is a far greater concern. The personal wants, corruption, and selfishness these characters privilege above principles, honor, valor, and duties emphasize the shift from the practice the Gospel proclaimed and Augustine championed. Thus, in the cases of the heroes considered in this study the roles of eater and eaten pertain specifically to the worldly circumstances in which they become ensnared out of sheer egotism. Because for them the "I" is the sole purposeful end of their actions, they imperil social stability. Through this, the authors considered launch a sustained social, cultural, philosophical, and political critique of their times. And the coherence with which these poets and writers sustain their respective assessments is a measure of their ability to depict their heroes as utterly consumed by the desires that, in turn, consume them.

The link between astronomy and gastronomy that Dante explicitly constructs in *Vita nuova* is emphasized in much stronger terms in *Inferno*, 6. Ciacco is among the gluttons the Pilgrim encounters there. The soul introduces itself through its sin, "per la dannosa colpa de la gola" (for the ruinous fault of gluttony) (6.53).⁶⁹ On the surface of it, this encounter could be interpreted as a representation of another type of human failing the Pilgrim must face on his way to purification. The lack of self-control gluttony presupposes results in moral failure; and this causes the soul to suffer eternal punishment. This reading of Ciacco's sin could be more or less on target if it were not for a crucial fact that sets this sinner, and his sin, apart from the others. Indeed, it is to the glutton Ciacco that the Pilgrim turns to ask about Florence's political future. That Ciacco complies with Dante's request, prophesying the defeat of the White faction through Pope Boniface's schemes, is beside the point. The important fact is that Dante, the poet who establishes in his earlier *Vita nuova* the link between heaven and earth, God and humanity, astronomy and gastronomy, with a bold stroke calls attention to it again in *Inferno*, 6. From Dante's perspective, putting faith in the political vision of Ciacco, a man whose life, by his own admission, was spent engrossed in the thrall of appetizing good food lays bare the intimate connection between gastronomy and astronomy.

Gastronomy, an art of this world, as Saint Thomas reminds us, etymologically derives from *gaster* (belly) and *nomos* (law). As the word indicates, it concerns the rules pertaining to good cuisine. This is the same as saying that it consists of the rules the cook follows to prepare food that the self internalizes. Metaphorically, then, gastronomy is tied to the self because it is not concerned with what is outside of it. But if it pertains to the inner self—as it does—it has vast consequences, for it can imply the notion of thinking, contemplating, reflecting, and meditating. And this, in turn, brings to mind the idea of foreseeing. These activities that begin "within the self" have bearings on the aptitude of "seeing" beyond the self. This fact can account for Ciacco's ability to "foretell" Florence's political demise. Astronomy, on the contrary, is the art of looking outside of this world. The word derives from *astron* (star), *nomos* (laws), and *nemein* (deal out). Originally, the field included astrology too. As the meaning of the word makes plain, astronomy is concerned with studying what is outside of the self (the celestial bodies) and giving order to it. One of the striking differences between the two disciplines is the direction to which they point. One aims at knowledge that leads inward, to the self. This indicates not just selfishness, but also self-knowledge, a quality that opens the doors to knowledge. The other discipline strives for the understanding of what is outside of the self, outside of the human world and beyond the grasp of human comprehension. Interestingly enough, humanity stands between the two opposite systems gastronomy and astronomy represent. Yet humanity is capable of reaching in both directions and participating in both systems. Indeed, it can master the two disciplines, making them means of its attempt to grasp and give meaning to the world surrounding it. Together, these fields erase the intellectual bounds of human limitations. Dante fully understands this original premise. The evidence of it is the manner in which he poetically links gastronomy and astronomy in his works. Through this, he unfurls the possibilities that the fusion of the human and divine, man and God, brings about. By the opportunities they lend to humanity, gastronomy and astronomy empower it to move beyond the ordinary.

At first glance, Guicciardini's aphorism cited above does not explicitly address a synthesis between the earthly and the heavenly. But the arts about which he speaks do liberate the mind from the fetters of conventional ordinariness. The changes (customs, mores, and systems) humanity is responsible for do suggest that a necessary fusion between the immanent and the transcendent occurs. This natural process allows humanity not only to envision, but also to bring to fruition, possibilities out of promising experiments. And these possibilities go beyond the limits of human experience and reach forward to new ways. Thus, through his assertion, Guicciardini intimates that the human determination to invent novel styles and forms derives from the desire to challenge the predictable. In his view, the systems that legitimize age-old norms rarely come to grips with the overwhelming sociocultural winds churning the waters of history. What results from the willpower to shift mores and customs, Guicciardini insinuates, are cultural changes. And although these are not always uplifting, they attest to the human trepidation over the diminished expectations that the known provides. By creating a new order out of the old one, mapping alternative paths that are wonderfully daring in their imaginative scope, and producing meaningful changes that yield greater returns in terms of the fulfillment they bring to humanity, the human mind soars to new heights. Guicciardini, like Alberti and Dante before him, understands this. The stretching out of and envisaging what is beyond the established, the scrambling of set notions of rules and regulations to supplant the pervasive pessimism and monotony that the tested—and tasted—expose, attests to the closeness between the human and the divine. Food through new and daring preparations, ingredients, and confections is an element that does away with the illusions of the certainties the past seems to offer. By keeping its ambitions alive, human inventiveness reinterprets the past and proceeds to conceive more visionary projects. In this manner, the human spirit shapes the future. In the end, savoring power does not mean indulging in narcissistic or hedonistic pleasures that give way to self-aggrandizement. Nor does it imply being disconnected from the divine and plunged into a world of sheer materiality. It means to plumb the soulful depths of the human spirit and understand the heights it is capable of reaching.

ONE

The Language of Food in Boccaccio's *Decameron*

The prominent place that food occupies in Giovanni Boccaccio's *Decameron* encapsulates the essence of two mutually exclusive worlds: the world of the powerful, who have access to it, and the world of the powerless, who do not. In the representation of the stronger and the weaker, of the empowered and the disempowered, created on the basis of those who have food and those who do not, there persists the systematic reinforcement of the mechanisms that accentuate social disparity. Subsumed and determined by both the quality and the quantity of food consumed, this social stratification constructs a system of political legitimacy.[1] Such a structure quite naturally dovetails with two intrinsically linked discourses. The first is the human appetite for material possessions; the second is the human desire for sexual gratification. In the *Republic* Plato explains social inequality and injustice as the desire of powerful people to subjugate and rule over weaker ones in order to extract personal benefits.[2] While on the one hand this failing of values leads to self-legitimization, on the other it results in self-indulgence. In book 9 the philosopher includes sexual pleasures among the impetuous desires that self-indulgence arbitrarily pursues.[3] It appears, then, that rooted in the notion of power and control that an individual can exert over others, both material possessions and sexual gratifications map out the terrain of a social structure. This configuration has as its trademark the ability of the stronger to satisfy material needs, as well as physical desires, at the expense of the weaker.

Beyond this, the images of food that spice the *Decameron* underscore Boccaccio's idea that sating hunger implies something more profound if less tangible than satisfying a physical need. For Boccaccio food exemplifies, among other things, knowledge. This belief is rooted in chapter 1 of the Old Testament book of Genesis. As a result, he sees the distinction between spiritual and sensual appetites as a blurred one. Yet he understands that society insists on demarcating those deceptive boundaries on which the conflict between moral absolutes and social ideals deepens. He also recognizes the dehumanizing, and at times tragic, compromises people make in the name of stultifying social codes. To demonstrate this point and chip away at old illusions that undermine the possibility of change, he incisively reconstitutes the elements that illustrate the error of that argument. By framing and supporting his discourse with wit and bold imagination, through food Boccaccio makes a passionate argument against social intolerance, religious fanaticism, and cultural prejudice. In his view, these issues make for a potent brew that destabilizes society from within because by force they narrow the road to social harmony. This situation unleashes the crises of values.

Boccaccio's discourse on the central role the senses play in human relations begins where the exegetical tradition left off. According to this tradition, the desire for physical fulfillment identifies man more closely with Adam who, in his inability to suppress his appetite, yields instead to the instinct of hunger and, consequently, of the flesh.[4] For patristic commentators and medieval exegetes alike, Adam's act exemplifies the transition from desire for food to carnal desire. In their view, this natural shift occurs because both desires are triggered by instinctive and uncontrollable forces. More specifically, in this tradition concupiscible appetites—the pursuit of external objects—are closely linked to the body and to the senses.[5] Yet Boccaccio considers them autonomous from the will. By emphasizing the instinctive nature of the senses, this interpretation privileges the role they play with respect to human biological development.⁶ Because of this, biblical commentators and theologians alike recognized the intrinsically powerful nature of appetites. In their views, appetites yoked humanity to the impulsiveness of desires. Predictably, this problematic truth uncovered a series of thornier questions. If humanity needs to satisfy its desires for self-preservation, how can they be restrained and kept in check? How can willpower rein in natural impulses? In dealing with these issues patristic and exegetical traditions concurred. By relying on the authority of the texts, they both demonstrated that appetites most frequently distort human judgment. And this fact, according to them, diminished humanity's potential capacity for self-control. For both traditions, Genesis 1 illustrated the powerlessness of human will when confronted by the senses. Indeed, in what happened to Adam they found the proof of the debasing changes that humanity suffers when sensual appetites rule the mind. Nonetheless, if exegetes and theologians alike concurred in the belief that the alluring pleasure of gratified desires caused Adam's fall from grace, they also agreed in blaming Eve as the true culprit of his error. For them, his savoring the fruit she offered him disclosed Eve's[7] ability to seduce the rational man.[8]

In patristic writings and beyond, this interpretation became the proof of Adam's surrender to the power of the senses. For although he had been empowered by God to rule over (and name) the creatures and objects surrounding him, by complying with Eve's proposition, Adam was irrevocably transformed into a pliant, submissive human being. Thus, his desire to *cognoscere* brought about a loss of innocence. This loss was caused in no small part by his *ignorantia*, that is, by his inability to grasp the way in which his action would shatter the predictable pattern of life, as he knew it. Like Eve's, Adam's desire "to know" entailed a new awareness of sexual desire. This correspondence is ingrained in the Hebrew word *yada*, which denotes "to know" as well as "to have sex."[9] It appears clear, then, that Adam's newly acquired knowledge and his newfound taste for carnal *sapere* attained through the fruit's *sapor* in Genesis 1 are played out on the ambivalent notes contrasting mind and body. The polarization this perception produces splits the world into absolute categories because it emphasizes humanity's disregard for the boundaries set by God. It is at this juncture, as Saint Augustine explains, that "the law of the mind" yields to carnal appetites. This for the Bishop of Hippo is "a law in their members,"[10] and discloses the full impact of Adam's loss of self-mastery.[11] Within this context, the intellectual ability that denoted Adam's prelapsarian experience, making him superior to Eve, is then tested and lost through desire.

In the interplay of the said and the unsaid, early commentators as well as theologians drew on Genesis 1 to underline not only the ruinous effects of a woman's persuasive voice on man, but especially her ability to shift the discourse from mind to body.[12] Through this process, they claimed, she engulfed man's rational mind in the tempest of libidinous temptations.[13] And these caused failures, dislocations, and horrors. The authority of these views made woman appear like a destructive force that turned man's normal life upside down. These interpretations also illustrated the devastating results that impulses engender when humanity gives in to them. Yet the various exegeses overlooked, it seems, the more fundamental idea that Genesis 1 unambiguously introduces. Palatable pleasure as a foretaste of bodily pleasure reveals a knowledge that is not the product of intellectual abstractions.[14] Rather, it is one of material concreteness.

Writing about Adam in the wake of the rich exegetical tradition that preceded him, Thomas Aquinas concurred, in part, with the earlier interpretations. He argued that Adam's sin was disobedience or pride, not gluttony,[15] a distinction that Dante too noted in his *Commedia*.[16] But even after differentiating between pride and gluttony, maintaining like Saint Augustine, that the former provoked Adam's act, Saint Thomas conjoined the two sins.[17] This strategy enabled him to assert that although they represented an inevitable aspect of human passions, and in a sense attested to the flaws that are inalienable from human nature, through imagination and cogitative power pride and gluttony could be controlled. More specifically, in exploring the connection between desire for food and sexual desire, Saint Thomas blurred the difference between the two appetites. By overlapping them, he held that humanity's erroneous pursuit of the pleasures these appetites engender is based on an unsound notion, namely, that they can be "medicine against manifold sorrow and sadness."[18] In the *Summa* Aquinas maintained that humanity is able to steer clear of this error by relying on both its particular reason, which deals with senses, and its universal reason, which deals with intellect and guides the former.[19] Through the rational web of his argument Aquinas made the case that reason can—and must—control passions so that they do not distort humanity's decision-making process.[20] In Aquinas's view, moral weakness in particular and sin in general, and in effect the whole gamut of human experiences, are products of concupiscence's powerful influence. This force, he claims, draws humanity to seek the gratification of bodily appetites. He further maintains that this choice eclipses humanity's judgment and, keeping it under its sway, renders it incapable of judging their inevitable repercussions. Drawing from and expanding on Aristotle's assertion that "the soul rules the body with a despotical rule, whereas the intellect rules the appetites with a constitutional and royal rule,"[21] Aquinas synthesized the manner in which intellect alone should guide human appetites with the deftness of a shrewd if sensible political leader. This strategy, Saint Thomas argued, can resolve the tension between reason and appetites, bringing humanity closer to this-worldly happiness.[22] The military analogy of the political ruler that the theologian avails himself of gives cogency to his argument. It suggests that in the realm of appetites, politics and power are not only intrinsically intertwined, but they are played out by the same rules. They are strands of the same knot; according to Saint Thomas, only a rational approach can disentangle them.

Boccaccio's familiarity with, and distrust of, the theological tradition surfaces in the *Decameron* as early as the proem. There the narrator asserts that *poco regolato appetito* (unregulated appetites) had governed his past amorous experiences.[23] With this ostensibly formulaic statement the author forges a provocative starting point for the discourse of desires in the *Decameron*. His statement in turn engenders a series of parallels with Adam's experience and Saint Thomas's elucidation of it. The elaborate strategy of reading the text that this approach puts into play is inscribed within a Christian teleology that draws from the prelapsarian era—by definition the time before the existence of sexual desire—and juxtaposes it to the postlapsarian era, a time shaped by the universality and ubiquitousness of desires regulating every facet of human experience. By linking his earlier condition of "unregulated appetites" with Adam's experience—and Eve's before him—Boccaccio essentially bridges the distance between the biblical archetype and the human experience. With this maneuver, he engages his audience in the discourse of the mind's inability to tame natural instincts or, more accurately, on the ineffectiveness of conventions to rule over and disempower the senses.

The radical subversiveness of Boccaccio's argument rests on the rhetorical strategy he deploys to prove his point. He first establishes a correspondence between Aquinas's beliefs and the dynamics that regulated the narrator's past amorous experiences. Accordingly, the theologian's claim that appetites are desires of the souls resulting from the senses,[24] not limited to craving for food, and encompassing the whole spectrum of sensual desires coincides with the narrator's experience as he describes it in the proem. The connection between the two, from which the unpredictable principle of desires that enliven, yoke, and liberate is forged, is then truncated by the revelation that desires, in the narrator's experience, cannot be repressed by way of a rational exercise. To illustrate this point Boccaccio equates appetite for food and sexual gratification to an interchangeable and self-contained symbolic and metaphoric system that serves to depict human limitations. Within this system, Boccaccio inscribes humanity's ineffectiveness in controlling its passions. Through the language of food that expresses the satiation of all appetites, including sexual fulfillment—because eating, as Genesis 1 demonstrates, is the act that at once negotiates and fuses oral pleasure with carnal gratification—Boccaccio articulates his understanding of the central role appetites play as a fundamental trait of human nature. That he accomplishes this while eschewing overtly erotic terms adds elegance and subtlety to his prose. But while in his *Decameron* the prominence of both appetites and food is readily identifiable, their metaphorical and rhetorical functions and values are not.

I

In the introduction to the first day of the *Decameron* Boccaccio emphasizes the fusion of the two meanings of appetite—for food and for sensual gratification. He does so by describing three very different codes of conduct the Florentines adopt in their efforts to survive the plague that is ravaging their city. Here the narrator depicts one group of people as adhering to a rigid diet of "dilicatissimi cibi e ottimi vini temperatissimamente usando e ogni lussuria fuggendo" (living moderately and avoiding any excess . . . eating the most delicate foods and drinking the finest of wines, doing so always in moderation).[25] To ward off the plague this group not only avoids indulging in culinary excesses, but also deliberately shuns all modes of lascivious behavior. This calculated choice marks the group's seemingly rational, but actually unnatural, control over human desires for pleasurable matters. The second group Boccaccio describes no longer forsakes any gratification. Instead, it seeks "il bere assai e il godere e . . . il soddisfare d'ogni altra cosa allo appetito che si potesse" (drinking excessively, enjoying life . . . satisfying in every way the appetites as best one could) (*Decameron*, 17). In striking contrast to the first group, but still endeavoring to shield itself from the disease, this group opts to satisfy its every desire.[26] The social (and political) crisis that is tearing Florentine society apart, and which the plague represents, is here powerfully portrayed in terms of the pleasurable excesses this group tenaciously pursues. Left to their own devices, these people strive to satisfy their every impulse. The third group adopts a strategy that falls between the extreme attitudes of the other two. Tellingly, the choice made by these people—"a sofficienza secondo gli appetiti le cose usavano" (they satisfied their appetites to a moderate degree) (*Decameron*, 18)—rests on a responsible satisfaction of human desires as they arise. By neither yielding to a descent into the senses, nor resisting their natural drawing power, the model of behavior this group adopts veers away from the affected conducts of the other two. This decision places desires in the sphere of constitutive traits characterizing human nature. For these people flesh and thought, material and spiritual, practical and theoretical, coexist and inform each other rather than mutually excluding one another.

As they struggle for survival the people Boccaccio describes in the proem anchor their hopes in the arbitrary choice of fully satisfying, fully renouncing, or just sensibly gratifying their appetites. Through this, they make their respective practices the illusory prescriptions with which to fend off the epidemic. In the resulting tripartite universe these modes of conduct engender, senses and reason function by virtue of one desire alone: survival. To this end, the people he describes steer clear of theological conventions. That two out of the three chosen courses of action transgress the limits of the rational serve Boccaccio to highlight the dialectic between the carnal and the spiritual. People are not concerned with the causes of the plague, but they are terrified by its symptoms and outcomes. By informing their decisions, this fear leads them to believe that the potential antidote to the disease is secured through the satisfaction of physical appetites in the measure that corresponds to a (group's) chosen behavior. For each group, the legitimacy of the preferred remedy hinges on this course of therapy. This understanding makes it clear that the degradation of human judgment brought about by the seductiveness of short-lived gratification is mediated by the fickleness of human nature. This idea retrieves—while simultaneously challenging—Saint Thomas's assertions. In the face of uncontrollable events fear, coupled with powerlessness, renders humanity incapable of acting rationally. Through the description of the Florentine people, Boccaccio parodies Aquinas's pronouncements on the ways in which the intellect guides and restrains human appetites. In Boccaccio's view, the illusoriness of resisting the epidemic through behavioral modes that privilege the physical rather than the spiritual redefines the constitutive essence of the human spirit.[27] This detail reveals it to be driven by a yearning for self-gratification rather than self-discipline. According to Boccaccio, against the backdrop of the social plague, humanity's enduring desire for survival is played out on the basis of its instinctive appetites.[28] Unbound from theological and philosophical bondage, these forge its coping mechanism. The awareness of having to fulfill its appetites according to its needs, Boccaccio suggests, enables humanity to remain fully integrated in, and be a dynamic part of, a society that progressively changes.

The ostensibly equalizing effects the satisfaction of varying degrees of appetites have on the three groups of Florentines function, it appears, to the exclusion of reason. Because of this, the groups' attitudes evoke the normative effects of courtly love. In other words, their commitment to—and credulity in—the medication they self-administer to keep healthy provides the people with an immediate sense of self-mastery. This goes hand in hand with a sense of fulfillment. Paradoxically, as they grapple with the turbulent emotions the plague unleashes in them, resolving to be their own saviors, these people turn their vulnerability into an instrument of power that depends on neither theology nor philosophy. Neither one of these spheres of knowledge, in fact, affords similar instantaneous gratification. The concern for survival, which rests on the satisfaction of bodily desires and appetites and is unconcerned with intellectual issues, illustrates Boccaccio's audacity in toying with Saint Thomas's pronouncements. By implicitly suggesting that the antidotes to human suffering must be found in one's own resolve to overcome the hurdles that impede the attainment of one's fulfillment Boccaccio—if only half-jokingly—points to humanity's innate ability to shape its own existence. And although this awareness does not provide a clear-cut solution to life's complexities and tragedies, because as Boccaccio intimates the plague and the market of shifting values it exemplifies changes people's lives in spite of the choices they make, it does ensure the gratification of the desires that are part and parcel of the human experience. Thus by way of a delicious play of metaphors and double entendres based on hunger, food, and appetites Boccaccio probes—and ultimately turns on its head—Aquinas's theory of the mind's ability to rule over the senses. And as he establishes a link between food and appetites, and the ambiguities that their meanings evoke with respect to the unraveling of human passions, the writer brings to light the most secret folds of human desires in a society eager to embrace more tolerant ideals. The society of merchants—of which he is a product as well as a sharp observer—has displaced and supplanted the courtly one.[29] Along the way, it has gradually replaced the abstract models the older system championed with more realistic ones. Still, even with a new belief system replacing the crumbling one, human desires persist unchanged, enduring as irreconcilable with anachronistic models. For this reason, in the *Decameron* appetites force the intensity and variety of human passions out in the open. And they are played out against a background of convivial gatherings that, at their core, center on the interplay of human appetites and social constraints.[30]

Love-struck Lisa (10.7) elegantly articulates the tension between these two extremes. "Niuno," she states, "secondo debita elezione ci s'innamora, ma secondo l'appetito e il piacere" ("no one on earth falls in love by deliberate choice but, rather, by impulse and desire") (*Decameron,* 1161). By explicitly equating appetite and instinct and in sharp contrast to Saint Thomas's assertions, her words underscore yet again Boccaccio's belief that the earthly love consuming men and women is based neither on rational choice nor on intellectual constructs. Instead, it is driven by natural impulses.[31] Through the prism of the exegetical elucidations, these urges can be defined as appetites that at once encompass and fuse both the desire for food and the desire for sexual gratification. For this reason, the meaning that Boccaccio confers on appetite continually shifts from the literal act of eating that reflects the convivial setting of the novellas narrated to amuse, to the more metaphorical allusions of the gratification of sexual desire. This point is further emphasized in the introduction. The scene is set in Santa Maria Novella. With the plague decimating the population, seven noble young ladies flock to the church for morning service. At the end of the service, Pampinea, one of the seven, with impassioned urgency suggests to her friends that they abandon the city by taking refuge in the countryside.[32] After initial hesitation, played on the notes of the inappropriateness of traveling without males accompanying them, the ladies agree to Pampinea's suggestion.[33] When three men with family ties to some of the women agree to join the group, her plan is put into action.

Pampinea's exhortation, "natural ragione è, di ciascuno che ci nasce, la sua vita, quanto può, aiutare e conservare e difendere . . . e se questo concedono le leggi . . . è a noi e a qualunque altro, onesto alla conservazione della nostra vita prendere quegli rimedi che noi possiamo" ("It is only natural for everyone born on this earth to sustain, preserve, and defend his own life to the best of his ability . . . and if the laws dealing with the welfare of every human being permit such a thing, how wrong or offensive could it be for us, or anyone else, to take all possible precautions to preserve our own lives?") (*Decameron*, 29), is intended to awaken the collective consciousness of the vulnerable group of friends. Yet it reveals a strikingly willful and audacious woman who, although fully aware of her social circumstances, refuses to become victimized by the same forces paralyzing Florence. Because of this, Pampinea is not afraid to defy the meaninglessness of conventional authority when the city's social fabric is tattered by human corruption. Her bold line of reasoning suggests that a woman's voice is not merely a conduit to seduction that corrupts man's rational nature, transforming him into a creature driven by carnal appetites. To the contrary, it is a voice of reason.[34] Her galvanizing argument reflects the urgency of the predicament in which she and the other women find themselves. And although her stance entails the displacement of male authority, it functions as a call to take charge of their lives. Only through this can the women alter the predictable outcome of their circumstances. To survive Pampinea must lay out the foundations of a viable strategy that protects the whole group from the anarchy that has overtaken their city.

By situating the women in a church gathered after the *divini uffici* (holy service), Boccaccio discloses more than just the spatial and temporal coordinates of the inception of his tale. Indeed, through this detail he swiftly establishes the metaphorical interplay of political discourse, spiritual food, and sexual desire. Pampinea's suggestion to abandon Florence with her friends calls attention, first of all, to the desire for self-empowerment that is an essential part of decision-making. As the assertive craftswoman stitching together the escape plan to lead the group to safety she defies "the patriarchal discourse in which women were defined primarily as sexual beings (virgin, wife, widow, prostitute)."[35] She embodies the power that is inherent to every human decision. The steeliness she displays amid all the uncertainties reveals that this power is not summoned out of pride but out of the desire to prevail over the social and historical upheavals the plague metaphorically represents. Because no other acceptable solution is available to them, and because exploring unexplored possibilities promises better returns than passively accepting what the system demands in terms of codes of conduct, Pampinea turns into a decision-maker. The courage she demonstrates through her decision allows her to assert herself and become an empowered leader.[36] In such a role she disempowers the social tenets ostensibly set to regulate her life.

The icy clarity of purpose with which she decides to move beyond the city limits openly defies the rules that govern her society.[37] In fact, even before it is acted upon, her plan not only conflicts with the socially acceptable feminine code of conduct, but also undermines the social and institutional practices her society embraces.[38] By transgressing the clearly defined boundaries in the gender hierarchy and breaching the unwritten rules that regulate the public and private spheres, her idea blurs the line between the proper and the improper.[39] As she engineers her plan of action Pampinea turns patriarchal hierarchy upside down because she breaks away from the domestic and circumscribed role she is expected to play. By placing herself in control of her personal, as well as her friends' welfare, she upends the fixed role that her society typically forces on upper-class women.[40] And even though in the city lawlessness and confusion prevail, her determination to move outside of it, albeit for personal safety, entails breaking away from the regulations her gender must observe. For the medieval mindset sexual gender determines the role the individual plays in society. While the inclusion of men will eventually lend a façade of propriety to the journey, Pampinea's resolve still suggests an arrogation of power. By defying the normative value system her conduct threatens the very order and stability of the patriarchal society itself.

This point becomes clearer by the fact that Pampinea gives voice to her design in a church. Because sacred scriptures focused on demonstrating the weakness of female gender, and because patristic thought posited male and female genders as opposites, as the world of intelligence and that of senses,[41] in the Middle Ages the woman embodied every evil. The cultural assimilation of female objectification was rooted in this perception and permeated every facet of society. As a result, women were mostly excluded from life in the public eye and confined to the safety of domestic walls. Against this backdrop, Pampinea's assertion in the church is momentous. Although the building epitomizes patriarchal culture, through Pampinea's plan it becomes the locus for the construction of female objectivity. Thus her plan of action foregrounds the precariousness of theological, political, and social systems. And as the soundness of these systems is challenged by her assertiveness and subjectivity, the stability of the economic order that depends on them is unsettled. To say that at this juncture Pampinea is cast as a new kind of Mary, like the church's name suggests, would be only partly accurate. In her leading role Pampinea is vested with the authority and privilege necessary to guide her close circle of friends to safety. Pampinea, unlike Mary, is an active doer. In this role, she persuades her listeners, subverts the norms, and provokes contradictions. In other words, her determination makes her a leader. She is not an acquiescent, forbearing, and yielding *ancilla Dei*, who follows orders imposed on her. For these same reasons, unlike Mary, Pampinea personifies resistance to the society and its rules, both of which she sees as lawless and corrupt. The little that is known about Mary comes from the New Testament, which is the earliest source for her.[42] In it, although she occupies a pivotal position, there are neither indications nor signs of social disenchantment on her part. Instead, she is portrayed throughout as the embodiment of compassion, thoughtfulness, and gentleness.[43] Lastly, the juxtaposition of Pampinea and Mary also calls attention to a more compelling difference. In the Gospel Mary through her son Jesus delivers hope for the spiritual life of believers, ultimately redeeming them from sin. Pampinea through her plan does show a concern with the group's wellbeing. But her solicitude pertains mostly to her friends' physical rather than spiritual welfare. Summed together, these differences fail to provide an adequate basis for likening Pampinea to a "new Mary." If anything, they emphasize the tension between the human and the divine.

The emotional and dramatic intensity with which the scene in the church is charged rather than pointing to Pampinea as one who fails her society by undermining its rules suggests just the opposite. It is she and her women friends who have been let down. They have been neglected, even ill treated, by the very systems set up to protect them.[44] Greedy strangers, as well as family members, eager to snatch any property the ladies' deaths may provide, have no interest in ensuring their safety. Left to fend for themselves, the women live in an anomalous system they no longer recognize as their own. Unable to function within it according to the old model, they decide to turn away from it. Breaking away from it, renouncing while simultaneously denouncing it, offers a viable solution for survival. For this reason, Pampinea never wrestles with the conflict between the role she is expected to uphold as a woman and the complications that the polarized sociopolitical environment presents. Instead, she remains a lucid leader, confidently in command of her plan.

To remind her friends that they are neither immune to the plague nor to the ruinous effects it has on society, Pampinea appeals to their sagacity: "noi erriamo, noi siamo ingannate, chè bestialità è la nostra se così crediamo" ("we are mistaken and deceived, and we are mad if we believe this") (*Decameron*, 32). These words draw attention to the necessity of facing reality with practical eyes. As the social order crumbles, their lives are falling apart. To survive they must forge their own path to safety. If they remain paralyzed by fear and the inability to simply act, or react, they will not change their predicament. The logic that undergirds Pampinea's reasoning is amplified by the inaction that thus far has marked their lives as women. At the same time, in a striking fashion Pampinea's words echo Ulysses's to his crew: "fatti non foste a viver come bruti" ("you were not born to live as brutes") (*Inferno*, 26).[45] The emphasis on the brutish, bestial lives that both Ulysses and Pampinea urge their respective groups to break free of has important implications. To begin with, Boccaccio vests his heroine with the same authority Dante confers on his Ulysses, in a sense, making her his counterpart. Like Ulysses, she simultaneously speaks within and against the rhetorical and social conventions of her times. In other words, she, like Dante's seasoned captain, is aware that her ability to persuade the rest of the women depends on the power of her words. Through this, she can first stir their emotions and anxieties about the plague and then arouse in them the aspiration for protection and wellbeing. But Boccaccio's audacious stroke is to cast her in a positive light regardless of her speech. He accomplishes this by showing that in spite of their rhetorical thrust, her words, unlike Ulysses's, emphasize the wisdom of Christian values.[46] Pampinea's objective is, after all, to get away from the pervasive human depravity and corruption surrounding her. She avoids Ulysses's error because of the principles underpinning her goal. Indeed, Boccaccio does not portray her as a selfish counselor whose advice to others serves solely to meet her ends. Unlike Ulysses's polarizing exhortation to his shipmates, her call to charge is not grounded in self-aggrandizement, but in securing a common good.[47] And this is the reconstruction of the social order.[48] Through this inversion, Boccaccio shows a woman who possesses the very qualities denied to her by both patristic and scholastic traditions.

If one follows Pampinea's perspective to its logical conclusion, according to which she acts out of reasoned need (*naturale ragione*) and within its limits ("senza trapassare in alcun atto il segno della ragione") (without trespassing in any action the mark of reason) (*Decameron*, 33), then Eve and Adam's sin in the "other" beginning can perhaps be seen under a less punishing light. Their transgression might be understood as something more than the result of concupiscence. Perhaps, they can be viewed differently than as two individuals driven by unrestrained pride.[49] In this reading, even the desire for the power of freedom that Eden irrevocably lacked can become part of the reason for their action. This idea is rooted in their determination to savor the unsavored, experience the unexperienced, and touch the untouched. The boldness of Eve's (and Adam's) act displays, therefore, a resoluteness that, like Pampinea's resolve, does away with intimidation and fear.

The Church of Santa Maria Novella also bolsters Boccaccio's argument on the complementary meanings of food that sates spiritual and physical hunger. As the group's point of departure and return, the church evidences the ostensible paradox between Christian morals and carnal pleasures. The metonymic value of the spiritual food consumed there stands out against the material one consumed outside of it. By abandoning the city, the group opts to forgo the former and consume the latter. This fact provides a richer subtext to Boccaccio's intricate discourse on food and appetites, reason and passions, power and powerlessness. Through it, he demonstrates the narrowness of old belief systems and the sterility of their discourses. Indeed, just as food and tasting metaphorically stirred Eve and Adam's craving for what they had never savored, Boccaccio's focus on food tests the soundness of rigid belief systems. The raw ambition of avid new learners his characters possess awakens in them a sense of resistance and resilience. And this stems from their desire to abandon the remoteness, abstraction, and ideological entrenchment that old models provide. Boccaccio's fascination with the changing political and cultural climate of his society that is enthralled with the riches the marketplace affords emerges throughout the *Decameron*. His novellas offer a tantalizing vision of a world driven by commerce and deceit. They also open a window into the seductive and subversive power of the senses regulating that world. By redefining humanity in opposition to the hegemony of past ideologies his novellas redefine the social, political, and cultural discourses of the period. They do so by unveiling a mode of thinking that is transparent, accountable, at times respectful of others, but always concrete. Through them, he weaves the strands laid out by the circumstances and events developing around him. Even so, the incessant oscillation between the literal and the metaphorical meaning of food remains constant. This technique draws attention to the pragmatism of human needs, contrasting it to the inadequacies of outmoded social ideals. It also lends new force to Boccaccio's discourse on the metaphorical significance of food in the stories narrated.[50] The banquet prepared by the marchioness of Monferrato (1.5) on the occasion of the unexpected visit by the king of France dramatically illustrates this point.

II

This novella centers on the interest the king of France has developed for the marchioness of Monferrato. While the marquis is away, the marchioness honors the king's request to dine at her house. Although she immediately understands the true purpose of his visit, her sense of duty compels her to comply with his request. Yet, to crush his plan and signal with exactness her refusal to accept his amorous advances, she devises a special meal. Based on the same type of meat dressed with different sauces, the banquet she serves honors the king's presence. At the same time, it conveys her rejection of him. When he fails to immediately understand on his own the implicit meaning of the unvarying fare, the marchioness provides him with an explanation. The meat, she tells him, like women, is the same in every dish. And while their attires change according to the country they live in, their substance remains the same. After this explanation, the king comes to grips with the marchioness's loyalty to her husband. Chastened, he praises her grace and virtues, thanks her for the banquet, and leaves her house. Clearly, in this novella Boccaccio redraws the contours of an amorous quest through food. He accomplishes this by making a meal the occasion for an encounter that from the male point of view stems solely from a desire to consummate a passion. As Boccaccio presents it, the banquet points to his mechanically exact but calculatedly subverted notion that eating cannot be automatically interpreted as the victory of the powerful over the powerless, or of a man's sexual conquest of the woman. By illustrating the manner in which the marchioness parries the king's appetite, Boccaccio describes her actions as those of a tactful if astute woman who successfully displaces and subdues a lover's intentions. Through her banquet, she effectively upsets the male hierarchy, in spite of the voiceless and acquiescent role society demands of her.

The marchioness is well aware that the king's visit during her husband's absence is a pretext he uses to meet her and satisfy the sexual fantasies he has been harboring for her: "e appresso entrò in pensiero che questo volesse dire, che un così fatto re, non essendovi il marito di lei, la venisse a visitare: né la'ngannò in questo l'avviso, cioè che la fama della sua bellezza il vi traesse" (she began to wonder what all this meant—that a king would come to visit her when her husband was away; nor was she deceived when she concluded that he was drawn there by the renown of her beauty) (*Decameron*, 87–88). Playing with the concept of courtly love, in which beauty and fame cast their spells over great distances, Boccaccio introduces the king as a man already consumed with passion for a woman he has yet to see. Interestingly, however, his desire to meet her, to know her, and to possess her is disguised as a simple request for a meal to be eaten at her table: "mandò a dire alla donna che la seguente mattina l'attendesse a desinare" (he sent ahead to the lady to tell her she should expect him to dine with her the next day) (*Decameron*, 87). The authority implicit in his demand is intrinsically connected to his rank. But it forges a solid link between food, desire, and power since ingesting food represents both the appropriation of a desired object and the fulfillment of an appetite.[51] Desire for food and desire for a woman are thus revealed as one and the same appetite—closely reflecting the common etymological derivation from *petere* that implies the desire to possess, as well as the desire to obtain. The power inherent in these acts, which the king of France embodies and exercises through his request, discloses Boccaccio's vision of a world in which appetites and power can never be separated because power saturates every action and appetite pervades every desire.

By juxtaposing the monarch's appetite for sexual fulfillment to his hunger, Boccaccio follows the Augustinian definition of carnal pleasure.[52] At the same time, he seeks to challenge its traditional meaning. For Augustine carnal pleasure is a craving similar to hunger and thirst.

Yet for Boccaccio, even against the filigree of the Augustinian interpretation and its Thomistic rendering, the elementary dynamism on which this analogy rests emphasizes the natural and instinctive aspect of the king's desire that is expressed as a wish for a meal.[53] Through this, Boccaccio introduces the notion of man's desire to transform the world by overpowering and ruling it. In the king's case this notion is conveniently couched in the parallel between the appetite for food and the desire for a woman. For if the act of eating suggests man's struggle and final victory in the hunt to procure the food from which he takes pleasure at the table, it also connotes man's ability to seize, subdue, and dominate.[54] Two crucial elements are embedded in this paradigm. The first is the physical force necessary to overpower and take advantage of another. The other is the freedom of hunting, a privilege reserved for the aristocratic elite.[55] Appropriately, the struggle that procuring the meat[56] evokes distinguishes and separates this elite socioeconomically from the legume-eating masses.[57] The sense of entitlement and haughtiness permeating the king's request is based on these principles. Indeed, while the solicitation for the meal is a legitimate request because of his rank, the timing of his demand discloses his true intentions. Still, as he defines himself through what he wants and in opposition to what he has, the king's desire to *cognoscere*—to know the unknown—and the correlation he establishes between eating, the physical, and sexual power recuperates the constitutive elements of Eve and Adam's experience. What drives the king in his quest is neither the safe awareness of his material possessions and privileged position nor the unambiguous certainty of what his act will beget. On the contrary, much like the biblical ancestors, it is the consuming knowledge of the unknown that appeals to him. He pines for what he does not yet possess and yearns to obtain it. But he is unaware of the fact—like them—that achieving the goal he has set for himself will force him to alter his understanding of his public and private personas. In other words, despite his social position he will have to face and accept the defeat that her denial to him encapsulates.

The banquet to be consumed at the marchioness's table will bring the king closer to the fulfillment of his sexual desire. One reason for this is the correlation between the meal to be consumed and the passion to be consummated. Another one is that the meat he anticipates finding there exemplifies the feast he hopes to make of her.[58] What the king envisions consuming at her house recalls Isidore of Seville's tantalizing notion of *conciliatio*, the joining together, rather than *convivium*, an activity that celebrates the essence of conviviality on a purely social level. Clearly, for Boccaccio the articulation of the king's desire rests neither on the harmonious Platonic dynamism championed by humanism nor on the more conventional topoi of courtly love. Instead, it shows the tension of dogmatic theological and philosophical models vis-à-vis human nature.[59] And this notion is subversive to the medieval mindset. For Boccaccio the human spirit reaches its highest potential when it is allowed to embrace the wholeness of its nature. Carnal pleasure is an inseparable part of it.[60] Eve and Adam first grasped the import of this lesson after eating from the tree of knowledge. The consciousness they acquired after tasting the fruit made them realize the incompleteness of life without desires. The king's desire "to get to know" the marchioness through a meal reenacts the biblical episode with a twist. He knows the reason he wants to consume a meal at her house. He also thinks he knows the outcome of it.

Ironically, although the king's request to dine at the marchioness's house is imbued with the power that is a constitutive element of his position and belongs exclusively to him,[61] it is also obliquely saturated with an explicit sense of self-abasement. While his position allows him to make an arbitrary request for a banquet, its fulfillment depends on her. As the hostess, she is charged with the responsibility to provide the meal. Yet as the provider she wields the power to organize it around her wishes. This peculiarity sets up a new paradigm. On it rests the development of the entire novella because it shatters the conventions of courtly orderliness and redistributes power not only from the hands of a monarch to those of a mere aristocrat, but especially from a man to a woman.[62] The shift of authority, with its unanticipated results, turns into a destabilizing factor that upends not just the social but also the political system the king incarnates. For this reason, the position into which the marchioness is thrust calls to mind Pampinea's and her resolve to abandon Florence with her friends. The striking poignancy of her argument reverberates in the marchioness's decision to take control of the predicament in which she unwittingly finds herself. Unlike the king, she envisions a different outcome for the meal he has requested. Accordingly, she prepares to thwart his plan by making a feast of him even within the confines of the power imbalance that exists between the two of them. While for him the banquet is a visual metaphorical representation of his intent to conquer, to possess, and to devour her, for the marchioness it is the mark of her ability to overpower him at his own scheme. In the interstices of her plan, however, are harbored the tensions and ambiguities that result from the contrast between mind and body, psychological strength and physical puissance, social haughtiness and personal dignity, self-reliance and dependence. All of these are rooted in the notion of power enshrouded in human willfulness. Like Pampinea, the marchioness must overcome the impasse with the only means available to her: by serving her guest the meal he asked for, but preparing it in a manner that delivers her implicit dismissal of his unspoken request. The dishes and the manner in which they are served must constitute the device through which she controls the potentially uncontrollable and flouts his authority, thwarting his appetite and refusing to become his edible feast.

The social difference between the guest and the hostess requires a precise ceremony of hospitality that follows rigid rules;[63] the king's presence must be celebrated with a lavish abundance of rich and exotic foods. These must turn the banquet into a spectacle that pays homage to the nobility he incarnates and simultaneously emphasizes the marchioness's subservient magnanimity.[64] Even within this context, her role as a deferential and submissive hostess transfers the symbolic significance of the table meat—the animal to be captured and eaten—to the marchioness. From the king's perspective, as a woman she must be seduced and consumed in an act of libidinous fulfillment.[65] But in spite of this, by engaging him in a palatable game, the marchioness uses the meal to displace his very desires. For the king the meal represents the symbolic and linguistic expression of his desires. In other words, by "concealing" his desire under the pretext of eating at her house he turns the meal into a mode of communicating his true intention. Still, as noted above, the marchioness immediately realizes what he is really asking of her. For this reason she turns it into her expression of defiance. The paradox of her decision is inscribed within the fact that the likelihood of her success revolves around, and is also limited by, the food she offers and its potential to signal her intentions to him.

The marchioness's carefully considered actions that dominate the novella map a new symbolic arrangement of feminine social conduct. If on the one hand this behavior is indicative of her determination, on the other it illustrates Boccaccio's awareness of a new social model that steadfastly challenges, and frequently uproots, the old one. This fact is evident in the marchioness's unwillingness to acquiesce to the king's advances. In fact, the way the story develops shows that there is more to her stance than just Andreas Cappellanus's codification of social behavior. In his *Art of Courtly Love*, he advises ladies courted by knights of greater nobility to turn down their advances.[66] The reason for this advice, he explains, is to avoid accusations of social-climbing. This charge can be leveled against those going beyond social boundaries imposed by birth. But in the marchioness's compliance to entertain the king with a banquet converge two important personas: the private one, enforcer of a self-chosen faithfulness toward her husband, and the public one. This latter persona behaves with calculated insouciance to fulfill her social responsibilities. By fusing public responsibility with personal accountability in one woman, Boccaccio does away with the biblical polarization of good and evil, originally typified by Eve. Indeed, in the novella opposites function not as a tearing apart of the sociopolitical fabric but as a rational and reliable mechanism of self-defense, much like Pampinea's decisiveness in the introduction. The fusion of conflicting forces enables the targeted prey to carry out her social obligations and to outwit the hunter who is prepared to seize and conquer. Viewed through historical and political lenses this model sets a fascinating paradigm for a potent foreign power seeking to overpower and rule a smaller, weaker one. As Boccaccio was all too aware, France's ambition to control Italy posed constant pressure on his side of the Alps.[67]

Serving an entire meal consisting solely of chickens, each one cooked in a different sauce,[68] is a striking contradiction to both the richness of the feast and to the culinary code that the marchioness should observe:[69] "quante galline nella contrada erano . . . , di quelle sole varie vivande divisò a' suoi cuochi per lo convito reale" (she collected as many chickens as there were in the countryside and ordered her cooks to use only these chickens in the various dishes for the royal banquet) (*Decameron*, 88). Ingrained in the cultural imaginary of medieval consciousness is the idea that the social identity of the eater is mirrored in the richness of the food consumed. One's power is reflected in the quality of the food consumed. Although the marchioness's meal is entrenched in "a courtly ideology of food,"[70] she purposely imposes a monotonous tone on it by repeatedly serving the same type of meat. Through this, she denies her guest the grandeur that a variety of more exotic meats would reflect upon his status.[71] Extant treatises on medieval diets detail alimentary regimens that individuals must observe according to their social rank.[72] These treatises mathematically equate quality with power. They highlight a similar correspondence between quality of the food and quality of the eater.[73] Thus, by serving only chicken, the marchioness defies a basic principle of courtly hospitality. This is based on the fact that although chicken flesh is deemed suitable for the aristocratic palate,[74] it does not quite project the sophistication of its consumer that more unusual meats would convey. Through this decision the marchioness implicitly refuses to become the king's intended meal even though she never openly articulates her refusal. The variety of sauces and quantity of (the same) meat she serves ensures that her banquet is entrenched in a gastronomic ideology of power. Yet the repetitious tone that she purposely imposes on it denies the sumptuousness with which her guest expects to be entertained.

As a perceptive strategist, the marchioness thus devises a system of repeated analogies and presents food as a scrutable text that obviates the necessity for language. Because her meal is a calculated plan to convey a specific message, it calls to mind Trimalchio's. It is clear, however, that the two banquets are intended to relay two very different messages to the commensals. By replacing her voice with food the marchioness can silently control the events unfolding in her household without ever confronting or openly turning down the king's advances. Most importantly, she can construe unconventional significance on the language that food produces. With her decision not to voice her denial to the king the marchioness retrieves—and simultaneously dispels—the notion of Eve's voice luring Adam into the discovery of his sexuality. By choosing not to speak her denial she is not just complying with a social convention. Rather, she is signifying her resolve to sexually distance herself from her suitor. Her sexual dismissal, carried out through a gastronomic text, juxtaposes the rationality of the mind to the irrationality of the flesh, just as biblical commentators had argued in the case with Adam and Eve. Boccaccio, however, reverses the roles in the novella. He does so by portraying the marchioness as the embodiment of the former while the king is the embodiment of the latter.[75] This significant shift marks Boccaccio's understanding of the politics of the self that is impervious to the pressures of power because of its deeply held beliefs. Through her tactful meal the marchioness reconciles the king's sexual fantasy with the reality of her lack of interest in him. In doing so, she breaches the bastion of his self-centered persona and never wavers on her principles. By shifting the linguistic power from the marchioness to the meat, Boccaccio replaces the logos with the meat.[76] This is a direct allusion to—and inversion of—the biblical Word that becomes flesh. Boccaccio's critical stance with regard to disingenuous and seemingly unchangeable social rules is exemplified here in the subversion of Christian dogma. The suggestion that this event, like the one in Genesis 1, can be challenged through acts triggered by sheer human willfulness shifts the power of control from divine intervention to human actions.

Not surprisingly, at first the king does not understand the visual text the food is set up to exemplify. Only the monotony of the same type of meat captivates his attention: "quantunque le vivande diverse fossero, non pertanto di niuna cosa essere altro che di galline" (he began to wonder, for at his table, no matter how many different dishes were served, all of them had been prepared with chickens) (*Decameron,* 89). Driven by the eros that does not require mediation with the logos, the king is unable to grasp the meaning of his host's culinary rhetoric. Ensnared by the senses, a state that both Augustine and Aquinas describe as one in which mental faculties are suspended[77] and that, in a similar vein, in the *Convivio*[78] Dante ascribes to those of "animal nature," the king's sole objective is to sate his sexual appetite. His ineptitude in reading and decoding the message delivered by the peculiar meal shows not only a man unaware of the fact that reading incites first of all a quest for knowledge that is inalienable from self-knowledge.[79] It also suggests that he is a man whose only desire is to study and decipher the body, the marchioness's body, to be specific, which is unfamiliar to him. The irrepressible appetite driving him at this point renders him incapable of seeing beyond the horizons of personal gratification and of grasping any correspondence between the representational force of the food and his desire. Thus he remains befuddled in a world of symbolic analogies that he cannot comprehend because they intimate an imposition of moderation and orderliness over physical impulses.

This is a pivotal departure from the abstract intellectualization of the Middle Ages with regard to love. By depicting a man incapable of reading the text before his eyes, Boccaccio discloses the radical shift in the cultural understanding of his period. He portrays a man whose sole objective is to seek and find the source of sheer physical gratification. The king is an earthly man (*homo terrenus*) who embodies earthly vanity and earthly transience as he stands at the crossroads of his historic reality. He has abandoned the rigid structures inspired by the monastic codex, and chooses instead the road toward humanism. Accordingly, his inability to read the message the marchioness presents to him crystallizes his powerlessness with regard to the old system. Emerging against an intransigent theological code that imposes strict frugality and self-restraint, because its opposite engenders sexual incontinence, the king is a man who is neither able nor willing to control his appetites. By portraying him as a failed *sapiens* incapable of making sense of the *sapor* presented to him, Boccaccio not only toys with the common etymology the two words share but also recalls Adam's experience, charging it with new energy. This draws from the marchioness's action and rewrites the text on female submissiveness.[80] Quite simply the difference between Adam and the king rests on two simple elements. The first one is the experience the food they consume yields. The other is the standpoint of the women providing it. By encouraging Adam to savor the fruit and its taste, Eve led him to the discovery of sexuality. Afterward, both participated in the revelations it brought to light. The marchioness offers the king a whole banquet. But instead of kindling his desire of sexually knowing her, the meal douses it. She is not interested in him. Her personal convictions, instead of philosophical or exegetical conventions, determine the choices she makes. This purposefulness bestows on her the authority of *sapiens* that the king lacks.

The climactic recognition of the king's inability to understand the meaning of her banquet is reflected in his need to rely on her for an explanation. Her terse reply, "le femine quantunque in vestimenti e in onori alquanto dall'altre variino, tutte perciò son fatte qui come altrove" ("though they may differ in dress and rank, the women here are the same as they are elsewhere") (*Decameron*, 89), intersects the tenuous boundaries that distinguish eating and sexual fulfillment, echoing the incongruous but clearly fabricated tension between reason and senses. By equating chicken meat to women the marchioness creates a direct analogy between morsels to be eaten and women to be possessed. Likewise, by intimating that the different sauces covering the chicken meats exemplify the fashions that women of different cultures adopt without altering their basic physical nature, the marchioness juxtaposes substance and appearance. Her words make her denial of his demand unmistakable. Yet the deeper meaning of her analogy lies in the emphasis she puts on the aesthetic aspect of the food served to make the king come to grips with her refusal to his advances. Accordingly, aesthetics turns into a means to gain knowledge,[81] for while it translates the harmony of the parts to the whole, it also forces the viewer to make a distinction between appearance and substance. Inevitably, this separation leads to ethical implications. According to the marchioness's argument, the attractiveness of apparel, the beauty—the outer layer—is subjective to cultures. As a result, it is an attribute relative to space and time. It has no bearing on the inner self, the human being. In fact, it neither defines it nor changes it. Her elucidation not only dashes the king's hopes but also especially reverses Aquinas's assertion on beauty. To be sure, while his *consonantia* (proportion and order) is part of her analysis, *integritas* (perfection of being) and *claritas* (radiance) are not. More specifically, while Aquinas maintains that these three qualities characterize and coincide with beauty and that inner splendor radiates through, making the form intelligible and beautifying it, the marchioness's words deftly erase every possible trace of this.

The measure of the marchioness's self-determination emerges, therefore, not just through her analogy, but is made more poignant by the manner in which she—and Boccaccio through her—tinkers with Aquinas's argument. The force of her rejection originally located in the chicken meat she has offered, and then reiterated with words, is made more cogent by the implications they carry. In the passage from the allegory to the symbol, there is again an insinuating inversion of the biblical *Verbum* that became flesh (*caro factum est*). Compelled out of the silence she has obediently accepted, the marchioness now embodies the teaching Logos. And in this role she informs the king of the meal's implications. In an unprecedented shift, the unity of the Logos that originally rested with a Man is now transposed onto a woman whose ability to maintain her composure and self-mastery exceeds the man's. Through this, she—and Boccaccio through her—also undermines the patristic belief in male intellectual superiority. Changing from the pleasure-giving object to the instruction-giving subject, the marchioness—much like Pampinea—redefines and asserts the parameters of her chosen position. In the process, she questions from within the system of values that the king is following and that takes for granted the libidinous nature of women.

The logos that the marchioness embodies defies the king. This becomes evidence of the fact that, for Boccaccio's heroes and heroines, the dialectical model of the Logos/flesh no longer suffices to pave the road to human redemption. To be sure, forces that arise from base instincts drive humanity. And these forces cannot be tamed through exempla or codes. They necessitate the mediation of language, a language that the marchioness first eschews, then attempts to substitute with food, and lastly must appropriate in order to fully succeed in her intent. Her unwillingness to yield to the king is the focus about which revolve the diverse, allusive, and enigmatic sauces that cover the chickens. This, from an anthropological point of view, could be interpreted as laden with symbolic possibilities. However, examining sauces against the filigree of a widely known medieval body of knowledge, they imply a bold departure from those very teachings because sauces[82]—as with any other delicacy—are considered corrupting condiments to be avoided.[83] Coupling oral and sexual pleasure as one and the same transgression because sauces make food pleasurable and awaken the senses, the marchioness's intentional recourse to chicken and sauces becomes problematic even as it encapsulates her strategy to repel the king's sexual advances.[84] By using food as a means to display her denial to him, she recasts herself as an empowered person within her domestic walls and responsible for her own choices.

Her determination, juxtaposed to his capitulation to her wishes, attests to his final cognizance of her lack of desire for him.

The way in which Boccaccio uses food in this novella shows that while the notion of courtly discourse rests on the assailable points of appetites and desire it no longer functions as the exclusive territory of man's unopposed pursuit. In his hands, food turns into the means to illustrate the cultural, philosophical, and theological failure to acknowledge the impulsiveness of human appetites. Through it, the writer also demonstrates the necessity to move beyond the paralyzing ideologies these systems enforce. For him, food, much like language, discloses humanity's failure to understand that letting affected beliefs shape moral behavior leads to unrealistic goals. The corruption these produce results in moral and ethical crises. And these set in motion irreversible rifts first among individuals and then between them and society. According to Boccaccio, if incessant appetites are to be fulfilled (because they are part and parcel of human nature) they must perforce coincide with corresponding desires in other individuals. This radical perspective is unimaginable for the medieval mind because it demands a reassessment and recalibration, and sometimes even upending, of the roles so heavily enforced. Only by adjusting to this practice, allowing, that is, for a harmony between the individuals' inner and outer state results in honest behavior. This, in turn, is reflected upon society. Thus, humanity's needs and desires can be met. The rich political overtones this scenario engenders make a compelling case for a reconfiguration of systems. At their foundations, these are more plastic and accepting. Although they cannot repair the errors of the past, they can prevent repeating them in the present. It is within this context that food serves Boccaccio to probe the nexus between humanity and the forces reshaping society. It is not by accident that Pampinea and her friends depart from a Dominican church. In other words, Aquinas's teachings colored by the Dominican vision of a universe governed by rigid rules and sustained by lives yoked to constrictive systems represent a mere point of departure. The new ethical prospect set in place by the *brigata*'s return to the city and to that same church, the marchioness's rejection of the king's advances, as well as Adam and Eve's act, suggests that savoring experiences outside of prescribed limits is a catalyst for asserting one's beliefs and not being cowed by silence.

Interestingly, Fiammetta narrates this tale. As one of the *Decameron*'s two central storytellers (Dioneo being the other),[85] she, according to Victoria Kirkham,[86] embodies temperance. The marchioness's story Fiammetta narrates exemplifies this quality. Yet in addition to self-restraint, as we have seen, the marchioness also illustrates Boccaccio's construction of a radically new female perspective. This idea reverberates in the manner in which she attempts to convey her message to the king via the banquet. By holding back from directly telling him where she stands, she avoids the use of language. Although her attempt is met unsuccessfully by him for the reasons discussed above, her conduct makes it clear that, having internalized the assumptions of her culture, she is mindful of the distrust it harbors for women and language.[87] Thus, she encodes her rejection in food. This is the secret language he chooses to set up his first (and last) encounter with her. Because she does not follow social expectations, but rejects and upends them, this woman is inscribed in a new cultural discourse. In much the same way, scholars agree that the Fiammetta of the *Decameron* is a persona vastly different from the various renditions of her Boccaccio gives in other works (*Comedia delle ninfe, Filocolo, Elegia di Madonna Fiammetta,* and *Amorosa visione,* among others).[88] In the *Decameron* she no longer incarnates Venus's traits as she did in the earlier works. Nor is she the seductive, carnal woman, origin of sin and perdition. Rather, she is the source of steadiness, strength, and self-restraint, of measured words and thoughtful actions, restorer of order, and re-shaper of ideals. It is no wonder, then, that among the cadre of narrators available to him, Boccaccio picks Fiammetta to recount the marchioness of Monferrato's tale.

III

In contrast to *Decameron,* 1.5, where a royal banquet is central to the development of the whole novella, scarcity of food characterizes *Decameron,* 3.10. Dioneo narrates this tale. Among the ten storytellers taking turns in telling the stories over the course of ten days, he is widely considered Fiammetta's counterpart. But unlike Fiammetta's, his tales are of a salacious genre, emphasizing carnal concupiscence.[89] In a sense, in them reason takes a back seat while passion drives human actions. For this reason, critics maintain that Fiammetta and Dioneo exemplify reason and desire respectively.[90] Yet reducing Dioneo to the champion of purely sensual pleasures strips the novellas he narrates of their deeper meanings and implications.[91] And this is tantamount to denying the importance of the issues and questions Boccaccio raises throughout his work and not with the exclusion of Dioneo's stories.[92] As it has been pointed out, Dioneo personifies Mars.[93] Accordingly, the bawdy narrator embodies the destructive force that desires to be unleashed. Naturally, this force is incompatible with self-control. As the god of war, Mars evokes the idea of devastation, chaos, disruption, and turmoil that every conflict engenders. Yet at the same time, there is another aspect to this god. The mythical father of the founder of Rome, he also symbolizes the possibility of fresh beginnings and new challenges brought about by the establishment of new systems. Because he is a warrior and protector while simultaneously a destroyer and creator, Mars's complex duality plays a large role in classical antiquity. Cato, for example, notes that Mars is the protector of fields, vegetation, and farm animals.[94] He is, in short, the god who turns the peace and unity of the past into political fuel for the future through his children's accomplishments. The complexities of Mars's mythological figure cast Dioneo, and especially the tales he narrates, under a more intriguing light. Given Mars's dual nature and the fact that the *Decameron* begins on a Tuesday (*martedì*), the day named after the god, it would seem that, at the very least, Boccaccio is setting the stage for the elaboration of a new discourse on society, human and divine laws, as well as traditions out of the chaos the metaphorical plague has unleashed.

In *Decameron,* 3.10, Dioneo narrates the story of Alibech, a young Muslim who becomes curious about the Christian God. After learning that hermits are the most knowledgeable people on spiritual matters, and that they can best answer her questions and instruct her, she travels to and through the desert outside of Thebes. Her objective is to find them in order to begin her Christian education. In the desert she meets Rustico. He is a young hermit who discovers that in spite of his chosen life of self-denial his hunger for physical pleasure equals Alibech's craving for spiritual guidance. In no time Rustico takes advantage of Alibech. He does so by claiming that the sexual acts he carries out with her are modes of serving God. Alibech believes his words. Only when Rustico becomes physically unable to sustain her insatiable desire to "serve God" does the narrator cut through the narrative. This move allows him to justify Rustico's waned interest in Alibech. For he attributes the hermit's weariness to the meager diet he consumes. Still, Rustico's toils end only when Alibech unexpectedly becomes the sole heir of her family's fortune. Her newly inherited wealth stirs the interest of Neerbale, a man from her native Capsa. He immediately begins to search for the new heiress. For this purpose he travels to the desert; when he finds Alibech, he brings her back with him, against her will, to their city of origin. There, to the laughter of town's women, Alibech explains how she "served God" in the desert: "rimettere il diavolo in inferno" ("to put the Devil back in Hell").[95] And in her explanation she appropriates Rustico's euphemism.

Played out against the ambiguous distinction of spiritual and sensual appetites, the story of Alibech dramatizes the conflict between moral absolutes and social ideals to which societies struggle to conform. To this end, for example, her simple desire to familiarize herself with the Christian God is described as a wish to "serve" Him. By borrowing the words from the Franciscan Rule and putting them into Alibech's mouth, Boccaccio establishes a correspondence between historical facts and narrative fiction.[96] This maneuver allows him to interpose historical events (Saint Francis did travel to the East to convert the pagans) to his fictional tales.[97] Through the fusion of reality and imagination he then explores the less appealing, but no less informative, aspects that make up the intricate consequences historical events have on humanity. With a deliberate irony that feeds on the pragmatism of passions, Boccaccio then demonstrates that by privileging only preconceived notions of sociohistorical occurrences, humanity turns them into fixed truths. And it is precisely through this conformity that he pokes holes. In so doing, he uncovers the deep ambivalence societies nurture toward those complex and restrictive absolutes that not only frustrate the possibility of sociocultural changes, but also foil religious tolerance.

Although at first Alibech's appetite is clearly a desire to acquire spiritual knowledge, the story soon changes it into one in which an intricate entanglement of carnal desires and misunderstood libido become forces possessing a transformative power. Against commonly held Christian beliefs based on long-held patristic and scholastic traditions, Boccaccio argues that natural impulses are not appeased by the scarcity or humbleness of food. On the contrary, they play a natural role in the dynamics of human relations. Thus they emerge unscathed against the systems humanity sets in place to resist them. This radical claim, aimed at subverting theological and social paradigms, is central to Boccaccio's understanding that the moral imperatives societies impose on individuals harbor hypocrisy and shortsightedness. In the same vein, he argues against models that reduce the full range of human expressions. For Boccaccio, codes lack personal validity because they belong to a social context focused on squashing human inquisitiveness for fear of the changes it may bring. Therefore, he sets out to demonstrate the manner in which the fundamental questions about selfhood, belonging, and conventional wisdom foisted on individuals turn into forces that warp political, philosophical, theological, and erotic expressions.[98] Food is among the elements he uses to prove this point.

Piqued by stories heard from Christians in her city and curious about a God about whom she knows nothing, Alibech is the embodiment of an idealized and innocent trust. She resolves to learn about Him and, more importantly, to serve Him: "un dì ne domandò alcuno in che maniera e con meno impedimento a Dio si potesse servire" (one day she asked one of these Christians how she could best and most quickly serve God) (*Decameron*, 433). Her quick decision to trade the comforts of her rich household and move toward an unmapped future provides more than just a counter-model to the conventional structure, dynamics, and codes that regulate women's conduct in her society. It suggests, among other things, that to leave behind the god of one's childhood in order to explore and gain knowledge of an unknown, unfamiliar, and culturally incompatible system of value requires an unwavering spirit of initiative. Although at this point there is no explicit textual link between Alibech and Ulysses, but rather an implicit echo, her quest to comprehend what she does not yet know calls to mind Dante's hero.[99] In the first place, both episodes emphasize the abandonment of private and public responsibilities in order to pursue personal interests. Also, Alibech's journey, like Ulysses's, involves leaving a father behind. In and of itself, this fact suggests dispensing with the experience and wisdom the paternal figure incarnates.[100]

Still, through her decision, Alibech becomes the embodiment of an authentic and irresistible force of change. This sets into motion, among other things, a new aesthetic understanding of the beauty of the unfamiliar. In other words, the power of the unexplored and the heightened expectations it produces superimpose themselves on the predictable and familiar. Envisaged as more than the commonplace and habitual, the attractiveness and wonder the unknown engenders cast an unflattering light on the familiar. The already-defined reality Alibech is accustomed to is perceived as unattractive because it offers little in terms of unanticipated possibilities. In this fashion, the unappealing known juxtaposes itself to the alluring unknown. Arguably, this same principle guides the king of France in his pursuit of the Italian marchioness. But there is more to Alibech's desire. For through her decision Boccaccio illustrates with sustained precision humanity's attraction to the "other" to which diverse cultures give life. This idea is based on the fact that beauty, the power of aesthetic—another form of forbidden fruit—transcends cultural divergences, social differences, political interests, and economic pressures. Its glitter, and the aesthetic accomplishments it brings to every culture, is gripping and thought-provoking. Moreover, it is never indifferent to moral and ethical integrity. As a result, beauty permeates and enhances the cultural consciousness of every system. It also suspends, if only momentarily, the divisiveness, contradictions, prejudices, and equivocations pervading societies.

Alibech's vivid and crisp desire to become skilled in the ways that will enable her to function in a radically different cultural milieu is manifested in her hunger to become knowledgeable about what is unknown to her—the "other" god. As she begins to act on her yearning, her quest for spiritual sustenance and knowledge of God bridges an apparently unbridgeable gap. In point of fact, she not only envisions the possibility of overcoming the vast cultural gulf separating her Muslim culture from the Christian one, but she effectively changes from a passive listener into an active doer. Her decision to entrust her spiritual education to learned tutors echoes an Augustinian belief. According to Augustine, those unable to directly perceive the divine must rely on the authority of others. He goes on to say that these individuals, through contemplation, can confirm the existence of the divine.[101] In light of the advice she receives, Alibech is confident that she can penetrate, and become part of, the universe that lures her and that, in her new awareness of the "other," supersedes the one she knows.

Alibech's is a liberating vision that endorses the logic of going against the norm and, because of it, of trading off one set of standards for another. But beneath its surface, her yearning discloses the dynamic and palpable opposition between appetites and reason. The crucial tension between the two, as Aquinas postulated, forever tests the limits of humanity's resolve to restrain its passions. For Aquinas yielding to human appetites and rejecting the moral and ethical guidance that reason affords inevitably spiral into the perversion of both value systems. By functioning either as a paralyzing force that deters one from pursuing unconventional goals or, on the contrary, as an inducement for undertaking audacious endeavors, the tension between desires and reason evolves almost naturally into a dialectical pattern. This system associates unbridled desires with defeat and reason with success. As noted above, the echo of Ulysses's journey in *Inferno,* 26 reverberates through Alibech's decision. In both instances, a single, pivotal decision illustrates the strain between reason and passion. In Ulysses's case, it also coincides with the notion of reason that yields to desires and results in a catastrophe.

Yet again, there appears to be a direct contextual, rather than textual, link between Dante's and Boccaccio's characters. The unequivocal resonance between the journeys Alibech and Ulysses respectively undertake is, however, played out on the notes of different objectives. Specifically, as he recounts his final voyage, Ulysses explains his desire to explore the unmapped world as the "ardor / ch'i'ebbi a divenir del mondo esperto, / e delli vizi umani e del valore" ("the passion I had to gain experience of the / world and of the vices and the worth of men") (26.97–99). These words are simultaneously imbued with the self-absorption of the yet unvanquished hero and the memory of his humiliating, unexpected defeat. Although the passion that drives him to experience the world conflicts with both moral and social duty, Ulysses remains resolute. In point of fact, his desire is based neither on a fixed moral code nor on unshakable ethical principles. Rather, it derives from the hero's misplaced self-centeredness. Looking back at his decision, Ulysses notes that his unmitigated desire to explore the unmapped world prevailed over his responsibilities, laws, and traditions. But he was determined to resist them in order to undertake the journey. The menace of the dangers it could bring on was quelled by the enticement that the beauty of the unexplored provides. Most importantly, buried under the appetite to learn about what he is ignorant of there transpires the arrogance of the fame and glory that the journey can deliver. Ulysses craves the renown that rising above rigidly fixed rules will bring him. Yet he disguises his personal ambition as an achievement that will also benefit his crewmen. In a single moment Ulysses decides for all. While Dante does provide a lucid account of the captain's stirring words, he does not note the shipmates' reaction to them. Ulysses's carefully constructed abuse of power, the partial truths and contradictions his speech evidences, is all that readers have to grapple with. Through his words, he manipulates the logical argument for self-serving reasons and seduces his crewmates into savoring the triumph and fame that crossing the columns of Hercules will bring.[102] By imposing his own value system on them, Ulysses displays his power and ambition. Yet through his decision, he not only flouts divine decrees, but he is especially heedless of the price his action will potentially exact on others. The desire to defy the established system for self-serving purposes turns, for this reason, into a form of despotism. From a political dimension, imposing one's own moral and ethical principles on others is synonymous with autocracy. As canto 26 of the *Inferno* draws to a close, the suggestion that human tragedy codifies the strident failure awaiting those whose pursuit of personal desires have made them lose sight of moral values is made evident. Still, Dante's silence throughout the whole episode is nothing if not highly ambiguous.[103] It suggests, among other things, the poet's uneasiness with the notion that to remain fixed in a moral position guarantees triumph whereas attempting to negotiate a compromise results in complete failure.

Although Ulysses's hunger for knowledge and glory and his ensuing defeat appear inscribed within these coordinates at the outset, the Pilgrim's deliberate silence is telling. It leads to the belief that the hero's failure must also function as a provocative invitation to probe the contradictory implications of his action. This in turn reveals the poet's mature vision of his personal and political experience, suggesting that it is not sustained by a sharply delineated notion of rights and wrongs. As a web of inferences is spun deliberately and obliquely, much in the same fashion as Ulysses incites his men without revealing his true ambition, the poet shares the powerful feeling of identification with Ulysses. The hero's literal and metaphorical decision to go beyond the geographical threshold finds its correspondent in the Pilgrim's journey through realms deemed unfathomable for the human mind. But precisely because of the silence he maintains throughout the canto, the Pilgrim seems to possess an acute awareness of the moral imperatives and implications dictated by moral codes and their troubling legacies. This fusion of rule-breaching and the result it produces raises some questions. Is it possible that for Dante faith and reason can bring about a defeat, as his personal experience attests and Ulysses's example confirms? Or is defeat merely a setback on the road to triumph and fame? Is it conceivable that political and personal freedom is more than just different from oppressive ideologies? Is it possible that, in fact, freedom is inherently more enlightened and therefore more accepting of half-won victories? That these eventually lead to a greater tolerance of human nature? Of course, Dante offers no clear answers to these questions. But in spite of this, in Ulysses's canto he has sown the seed for the syllogism between failure and desire, success and reason. Here the gratification of desires seems to carry inevitably the weight of failures, whereas the guidance reason provides appears to lead to success. This logic grows increasingly louder as the poet's silence pierces through the ethical and moral veil that envelops his hero's actions.

Perhaps, precisely because of Dante's undecipherable and deliberately ambiguous silence about Ulysses's maneuvers, Boccaccio describes Alibech's yearning for the unknown as a fusion of reason and desire. To make an implicit connection clearer, even though by way of contrasting motives, Boccaccio describes her decision as "non da ordinato disidero ma da un cotal fanciullesco appetito" (moved by childish impulse rather than deliberate decision) (*Decameron*, 433). In other words, although Alibech's desire is not tempered by reason, it is nevertheless caused by her young age.[104] This seemingly innocuous assertion carries important implications.[105] First, it suggests that a woman's place from a young age is under the control of a man (father, brother, husband). Because she is considered both physically and intellectually weak Alibech should rely on her father and brothers to make decisions for her. But Boccaccio is interested in questioning the tradition and finding new answers. Accordingly, he shows that she removes herself from living under their authority through her unconventional behavior. This enables her to re-inscribe herself in a new social model. The emphasis on Alibech's "childish impulse" casts her as an innocent player in the larger game of life. Her motivation is different from Ulysses's, yet it is based on both desire and reason. These for Boccaccio are synonymous with intellect and imagination. And as the first turns into the fulfillment of the latter this, in turn, becomes the rationalization of the first. Specifically, if, like Ulysses, Alibech has a firm grasp on her hunger for knowing, unlike him, she does not embody the contradictions and deceit that he personifies. Because she is not seeking self-aggrandizement Alibech is recast in the image of her hopes. She follows her inspiration "spirata da Dio" ("inspired by God") (*Decameron*, 433)—her appetite—to find meaningful answers for her intellectual inquisitiveness. Accordingly, the opacity that veils Ulysses's rationale stands out against the transparency of Alibech's impetus. Indeed, the fulfillment of her desire rests solely on the strength of the convictions guiding her actions. To pursue her objective she need not prod others' sense of pride by way of galvanizing their self-esteem. Nor does she have need of concocting relative truths. Personal ambition and desire for glory do not fuel her determination. On the contrary, a desire to understand and overcome a deep-felt cultural divide drives her.

A young woman struggling to figure out who she is and what she wants, of growing self-awareness and of as yet unrealized independence, Alibech is alone in her decision. And alone she remains through its implementation and realization. This idea is made clear in the description of her departure from her city: "senza altro farne ad alcuna persona sentire, la seguente mattina ad andare verso il diserto di Tebaida nascostamente tutta sola si mise" (she set out for the Egyptian desert all alone, without a word to anyone, the next morning) (*Decameron*, 433). The silence she maintains about her decision aside from revealing her resoluteness shows her desire to construct herself through her experiences. Most importantly, because it is neither fulfilled by, nor does it require, shared sacrifice, her hunger for knowing the God she does not yet know is neither a morally reprehensible choice nor one that exemplifies the erosion of her society's moral fiber. Through her desire Boccaccio toys with the possibility that seeking knowledge of God is a fundamental urge that is implicit in Adam and Eve's story too. Accordingly, he depicts Alibech as a person who sees Christianity's meaningfulness in a way that Christians (or the clergy) do not. For her, Christianity is more than a spiritual union with God: it is, as discussed above, the physical link, the corporal bond that ties her to Him and changes her into Him. This suggests that for Boccaccio Christian views of sexual appetite are completely out of harmony with human nature—as the story of Adam and Eve demonstrates.[106]

Clearly, in Boccaccio's hands Dante's syllogism that reason leads to success and desires to failure loses its strength; Alibech's desire represents neither a moral flaw nor a failure to embrace ethical restraint. Casting away passivity and inaction, a stance that her gender and privileged status require, she is driven by the awareness that cloistering herself in the security of the familiar shuts the door to the exhilarating possibilities that the knowledge of the unfamiliar promises. Organized around a lucid resolve to explore these possibilities, the appeal of the new eclipses old modalities that no longer—or perhaps only partially—fulfill her expectations. By reorienting herself along new cultural and ethical coordinates that cut across wealth and social class she not only challenges her society and culture but also explicitly rejects their customs and mores. This attitude becomes synonymous with constructing a historical perspective that emphasizes the centrality of desire and reason. As forces mediating the conflicts that simultaneously reflect and mold human existence, together desire and reason shape a new understanding of the world and of human nature. The same forces lead one to a self-awareness that turns into an ethical life of the present. This life is not crushed by contradictions. To the contrary, it prevails over them by deftly navigating the conflicts that humanity must negotiate on its way to achieving its desired objectives. Because of this, Alibech is more like the Pilgrim than

Ulysses. Unlike the latter, she is not motivated by the desire to burnish her reputation as one who proudly sets herself to overstep the boundaries of human knowledge. Like the former, however, she attempts to make sense of that which ostensibly has none. Through her actions she shows that the world of contingencies does not lend itself to unambiguous explanations. Similarly, she proves that intellect and imagination—reason and desire—are the tools through which the apparent contradictions between belief systems, cultures, and individuals can be reconciled. As a result, her whole experience, like the Pilgrim's, becomes proof of the fact that human experience must necessarily be a fusion of both reason and desire. As they converge together, reason and desire, intellect and imagination, like tributaries merging into the mighty river of the human spirit, reveal that all that pertains to human experience shuns codifications. They naturally go beyond the rules humanity sets, and often they question divine decrees. While Dante through his silence in *Inferno*, 26 clearly if obliquely acknowledges this, Boccaccio, on the contrary, boldly articulates it through Alibech's experience.[107]

Because of her life-altering decision, Alibech becomes the embodiment of an authentic and irresistible force of change. Yet to move beyond the sensitivities and values of an established system is, at the heart, a rebellion against the traditional order. But abandoning the system in which she has lived her entire life, forging ahead, seeking to change by way of learning about how to function within a different system is also a way of defying the conflicts and incongruities that are inherently part of the former. From a political standpoint, her decision brings to mind the struggle over contending belief systems that a society or culture imposes by grounding them firmly in the context of moral imperatives and social order. Ultimately, with her decision Alibech rejects the elements that are central to her culture and is won over by the colonizing politics of Christian fervor. This ardor exerts its power on the Muslim society and seeks to gradually conquer it from within. Alibech's rebellion against the present in order to be the architect and not just a bystander of her future suggests a firm awareness of her own potential to carry out with energy, zeal, and tenacity the task that gives her a renewed sense of selfhood.

If the eager appetite stirring Alibech's desire betrays something peculiarly childlike, such as self-absorption, lack of self-doubt, and lust for control over what is essentially uncontrollable, it also reveals an innocent trust in the range of possibilities the unfamiliar reserves for her inquisitive mind. The sophistication Alibech lacks about the modes of decoding the mysteries surrounding the Christian faith is mitigated by her single-mindedness. This trait is simultaneously a strength and a flaw. Yet it is precisely for this reason that she exemplifies the audacious if fledgling enthusiasm that energizes the infancy of every radical endeavor. Still, she sets out on her quest. As she embarks on her journey seeking answers that are neither shaped nor narrowed by conventional beliefs, more than just a discontented child Alibech personifies a transformative social force.

Alibech's single-mindedness functions as a countercultural strength to the prevailing ideological and political imperatives of her Muslim tradition. Her impetus to search for an alternative to the familiar sociocultural framework, paired with her desire to succeed within it, suggests her receptiveness to and flexibility regarding the vibrant waves of change and possibilities that invigorate the world. As Boccaccio is well aware, this is a universe incessantly crisscrossed and crosscut by the vitality of human impulses and wants that shape history. Alibech's simple but radical idea stirs those waves of changes because, despite the initial sense of dislocation that the crossing of cultural boundaries entails, it holds the promise of bold changes and unimagined possibilities. In an apparent contrast to Dante's Ulysses, these are obtainable only by those selflessly willing to explore beyond the complacent experiences a familiar cultural system affords. As a result, Alibech's appetite to find new answers unshackles her from a foreseeable social predicament and leads her literally into the unfamiliar terrain of Christianity. Figuratively, however, it takes her into a universe that negates and defies the secular world she knows.

The desert outside Thebes, where Alibech has been encouraged to find answers to her spiritual hunger, turns into the epicenter of her quest. Historically, this desert is regarded as the place in Egypt to which the first anchorites withdrew[108] in order to escape the material concerns of the secular world.[109] According to tradition, by leading a separate existence away from what they perceived to be the demeaning influences of the world,[110] and to which the Church was not immune, those early ascetics gave rise to desert monasticism.[111] In the isolation of that desert, in its desolation and harshness, the anchorites believed they could raise their minds above their human appetites. As Peter Brown has shown, for the desert fathers "food and the unending battle with the ache of fasting always counted more than did sexual drive."[112] In his view, human food, or better, the deprivation of it and the physical aches it caused kept their bodies shackled to, and their minds in constant battle with, their humanity. Yet at the same time, it was precisely the suffering caused by the lives of renunciation they led that, in their understanding, facilitated their closeness to God. The lifestyle of deprivation they chose purified them, making them feel closer to the state of grace Adam (and Eve) had lost forever because of their greed.

Along with food, sexual desire remained the other, reproachable link to humanity that the anchorites sought to erase. By retreating into the desert's unspoiled wilderness they sought to break this last chain to the world. For them the desert offered the possibility of living in a state of detachment from the world. Through assiduous self-denial and privations that the desert life made necessary because of its inhospitable environment, they fully believed in the possibility of freeing the body, as well as the mind, from defiling earthly concerns. Thus they considered the earthly existence they spent in the desert's inhuman environment a sort of decontamination process, the first stage toward the purification that led to a full spiritual existence. Once the transition was completed, the men and women living in the desert trusted that direct communion with God was again attainable. In their view, this state was modeled on Adam's experience before the Fall, when his "natural desires of the heart had been directed toward God."[113] Because they were of this world but essentially functioning outside of it, striving in this world to renew the sense of their Christian roots in order to secure the benefits of the one beyond it, the anchorites' demeanor had another side. It was, at its core, an act of rebelliousness against the permanence of historical occurrence.[114] Specifically, as they fought back the world and its enticements with asceticism the desert fathers in the third century refused to submit to the sociocultural pressures that did not meet with their moral and ethical standards. Theirs was also a way to reject the idea that Christianity was to be considered one of many religions practiced in Egypt. With unyielding conviction against widely observed customs, they refused to accept the notion of placing Jesus among other worshiped gods.[115] From a political perspective their detachment from society at large suggests a deep-rooted desire to sever ties from the Greco-Roman domination because, under the guise of Byzantine imperialism, this foreign power had begun to regulate Egyptian life by colonizing the minds. While the anchorites' defiance against societal mores brings to mind Alibech's rebelliousness, it also clarifies her determination to test the values of two allegedly conflicting systems. In a fascinating twist, while the anchorites' resolve led them away from a world they perceived as rife with sin, Alibech's decision propels her into their world. And this, as Boccaccio's readers soon realize, is not free of the "world's sinful ways."

The separation from the world that the anchorites sought essentially entailed a conversion of values. Accordingly, they traded riches and comforts for poverty and discomforts. They believed that in this manner impurity and corruption could be turned into purity and integrity. Moving away from the world to be part of the celestial one, for the anchorites the desert became a privileged place of suffering. In it, they denied the human self in order to come closer to the divine One; they wrestled evil in order to attain good. This experience made divine revelations possible, just as it had for Abraham, the patriarchs, John the Baptist, and Jesus before them. There, through sheer determination of will the spirit could test and refine its strength, triumph over matter, and thus be closer to God. Deprived of all forms of comfort and continually exposed to the appetites that persistent deprivations made more intense, the anchorites sought a union with God that was possible only in the measure in which they were able to transcend all forms of earthly pleasures. While representing an act of rebellion against history, their tormented existences also exemplified an act of tenacious submission toward divine hierarchy. This shifted the moral compass of early Christianity and turned the external struggle against the mores of the world into the inner struggle against the enticements the world continually posed on the body.

Incessant solitude, silence, nakedness, hunger and thirst, and lack of sleep and rest seasoned with constant prayers characterized life in the desert that away from mainstream culture and free of worldly concerns and desires the anchorites espoused. Subject to constant temptations just as in imitation of Jesus' battles with the demonic,[116] the anchorites interpreted the theophanies they experienced as the literal appearance of, the direct contact with, and the revelation of the divine that manifested itself on earth to the blessed few who steadfastly tested their will. They believed theophanies were the direct results of their determination to wage war against evil and their unyielding testing of the will against life's pleasure. Through deprivations they disciplined the body, emptying it of the impurities that it was capable of producing. In a sense, they made of their bodies deserts in the desert, in the belief that the Spirit could then overtake them and fill them with its grace. The inner desert, the desert of their physical and psychological loneliness, empty of worldly distractions, naturally permitted this spiritual transition just as the geographical desert allowed for the conversion from cultural aesthetic concerns to spiritual ones. While in the desert the beguilement of material appearances and worldly events had no meaning for those engaged in spiritual battles, the knowledge of, and the will to overcome, the temptations they imposed affected personal spiritual practice.[117] This space, fraught with extraordinary physical and emotional challenges, is the one that Boccaccio's God-seeking Alibech enters with a sense of self-reliance and fearlessness that belies both her innocence and her ingenuousness.

In pointed contrast, to the desert of Egypt where early Christians consumed their lives struggling to prevail over human weakness, the desert that Alibech traverses also calls to mind the mythological world of Statius's *Thebaid* in Boeotia. Only on the surface does the homonymy between the Greek Thebes and the Egyptian Thebes evoke this idea. In reality, Boccaccio's well-established familiarity with Statius's work in general and his epic poem in particular[118] suggests that the two Thebes, and especially what they stand for, are fused in the space that Alibech enters. This fact becomes more and more apparent as her story develops.

In the *Thebaid* Statius describes the events that led to the fall of the great House of Thebes. He does so by exploring the consequences of autocratic and selfish rule. Thus, he brings to life the pervasiveness of human wickedness, depicting it in its most insidious forms: as political and personal tyranny. Thirsting for power, because only through it they believe they can find self-realization, Statius's characters crave to appropriate it in any way they can in order to gratify their material desires. As Statius depicts it in the poem, tyranny like poison seeps through and corrodes all that it brushes past; not even family bonds are impervious to it. Unchecked and pushed to its extremes by self-serving intents, it forever tramples on the collective good, exposing humanity's utter contempt of human laws and divine will. Tyranny, Statius shows, is based on an unequal contest, where the stronger not only decides the rules but also changes them at will to serve his purposes. Its misplaced perspective of the vulnerability and fragility of human beings leads to precarious balances. These revolve around the manipulations of facts, not the pursuit of loftier ends. Ultimately, tyranny, as Statius describes it, seeks material dominance rather than legitimate authority. Because of this, it exposes humanity's utter contempt of the boundary between human desires and will of the gods because personal wants never reconcile with the latter. Tyranny's palpable paradox is precisely this: the betrayal of truth and its sacrifice on the altar of covetousness carried out at the hand of the powerful. Yet to spurn divine laws, to scorn them and diverge from them while simultaneously showing contempt for civil ones, while closing the eyes to human virtues, is tantamount to eradicating social and political stability. This naturally plunges society into utter chaos. As Statius narrates it, the rippling effects of betrayals created by misguided impulses and reckless decisions lead up to catastrophic events that cause the fall of the House of Thebes. Polynices's exile, his brother Eteocles's disloyalty toward both family and state orchestrated to assume absolute power as the king of Thebes, and the disastrous war that followed his actions are events suggesting that the capricious baseness of human nature is able, and willing, to mold its own brand of opportunistic morality to suit its ends. In the process, it willfully transcends every code that poses a threat to its aggrandizement. The horrific devastation that followed Eteocles's maneuvers meaninglessly claimed the lives of young and old alike. This fact makes the world of Statius's *Thebaid* one that is a fecund, fruitful, and fertile source of hatred, discord, and deceit.

The lawlessness and tragedy that saturate Statius's *Thebaid* stand in stark contrast to the order and calm that reign over the desert inhabited by early Christians. For this reason, the political and social tide flooding every corner of the former does not brush the latter. If the history of the mythological Thebes is the history of attempts to subvert social, political, and religious orders, the history of the spiritual Thebes traces the efforts to reestablish and maintain precisely those same orders. And just as almost every hero in Statius's work is ensnared in flawed situations of his own making,[119] the inhabitants of the "other" Thebes strive to prevail over the norms that society deems desirable. To those they prefer the spiritual rewards they believe eternal life will surely deliver. Statius's poem, therefore, seems to conjure up a universe in which the human perception of the gods' will jars with history. In his poetic account history leaves no space for divine musings. And this leads to the erosion of the spiritual bond between men, nature, and gods. In contrast, for the anchorites the spiritual link with God is strengthened precisely by the dissonance between history and the individuals' decision to put a distance between themselves and it. Outside of the culture, unchained from social constraints, and freed from the threats posed by its enticements through self-possession honed by harsh existences, the anchorites are a striking counterpoint to Statius's power-hungry tyrants. Yet for Boccaccio, who is redrawing the boundaries of the human condition in the desert's liminal space, pagan and Christian histories come to a head. Alibech straddles these two polarizing traditions, linking the two ostensibly disjoined universes—both of which are ironically regulated by the capricious fickleness of human nature. Thus her journey is simultaneously imbued with the rich symbolism of the mysteries and wonders that permeated early Christian spirituality and the tragic reality of human betrayals and perfidy that Statius's *Thebaid* unveils.

Alibech's journey ends in Rustico's cell. Rustico, who invites Alibech into his hovel for the express purpose of testing his continence, finds his resolve no match for his desire and her charm. By undertaking a journey of spiritual enlightenment, Alibech projects the resoluteness of a contemplative person. Contemplation and moral virtue,[120] which according to Saint Thomas are modes through which one attains the beatific vision that satisfies the desire for happiness,[121] require detachment from and disregard of worldly distractions. Accordingly, Alibech's quest for schooling among the hermits in the desert is the first step toward her spiritual edification. The rigor of their lives, which marks society as a conflict zone between materiality and spirituality, presupposes an alimentary code. In its plainness, it exemplifies the purity of the hermits' spirit. It also epitomizes their separation from society's ordered structure, as Claude Lévi-Strauss has argued.[122] Finally, the food consumed here is also a reminder of the simplicity of the Eucharist, with which, as discussed in the previous chapter, the medieval believer experiences God most profoundly. In view of this, the rawness of the first meal Alibech consumes evokes not only the coarseness of her knowledge but, more importantly, her integration into an order that entails an inversion of her societal values.

The frugal meals Alibech eats upon her arrival in the desert consist of grass roots, wild apples, water, and dates. This type of diet is suited to keep the body's cold humor in check.[123] It is a way to test—in an inversion of the biblical antecedent—the human will through taste. In contrast to the king's banquet in the marchioness's story, Alibech's new meals are based on a gastronomic ideology of powerlessness and humility. While her partaking of them turns into an act of allegiance with, and even conformity toward, the manners espoused by her hermit host, it also signals her integration into an order that has upended the social values she knows. Specifically, as she adapts to her host's gastronomic preferences, Alibech renounces the pleasures and self-indulgences the wealth of her former life afforded. According to Aristotle, *akolasia*—the vice of excesses or self-indulgence—occurs through touch or taste.[124] These senses, the philosopher argues, potentially lead to *akrasia*—the lack of self-control. Thus abstaining, as the hermits do, from consuming foods that excite lust is a way to stave off any sensual pleasure. Clearly, this implies the containment of human sexuality. For the medieval mindset appetizing foodstuffs stimulate hot humor and excite lust. Correspondingly, Aquinas argues, desire for sexual pleasures is the same as desire for pleasurable food.[125] As the antidote to gluttony and denial of bodily pleasures, fasting purifies both body and mind. As a device for self-control, it enhances one's aptness for contemplation.[126] But even through the lenses of the hermits' gastronomy of self-denial imposed by ascetic rules, the consumption of dates raises some perplexing issues because of the fruit's symbolic connotations. Named for their resemblance to a finger, *daktylos*, dates at once evoke the idea of the senses through touching and feeling. As the conduit to sexual arousal, touching and feeling are the gateway to a whole spectrum of sensual desires—tactile delights—that (potentially) lure mankind into the erotic transgression of every fixed rule.

By depicting Rustico and Alibech consuming dates Boccaccio cleverly undermines the rules about food and fasting long held by theologians and observed by the hermits. Through this fruit—dates—the author also sets the stage for the events that will unfold in the hermit's cell. The fact that the diet includes wild apples is also indicative of the type of knowledge that Alibech and Rustico will acquire together. As the two feed on this fruit, the direct allusion to Eve and Adam's experience and the metaphorical implications the fruit carries need hardly to be reiterated. At the same time, though, through these foods Boccaccio exposes not the weakness of human will, but its natural propensity for sensual pleasure. Navigating the countercurrents of his time, through the image of the dates and wild apples Boccaccio suggests that scarce food can neither curtail human appetites nor extinguish carnal desires. Indeed, these desires persist unabated in spite of the most stringent culinary restrictions. In short, neither dates nor wild apples are conducive to abstinence for human nature cannot be conditioned by a diet. Boccaccio illustrates the force of this belief by showing that what the two young people consume does not temper their sensual desires. On the contrary, by the rich traditions that subtend them, dates and apples retrieve the essence of human sensuality and want for material fulfillment.

The characteristics of date-producing palm trees make this correspondence more patent. While the biblical tradition of the apple is well known, the one pertaining to dates is less so. From antiquity botanical treatises emphasized the fact that in order to bear dates the female palm tree needs its male counterpart. The two genders necessary for fertilization is eerily suggestive of human reproduction. More than just this, the tree is known for not yielding to the weight of its top-heavy branches, but for sturdily striving upward. These characteristics make it a "noble" plant.[127] In Psalm 92:14 the tree is described as a symbol of unwavering justice, bearing fruit even in old age. For Saint Ambrose, the palm tree, like the laurel, is the emblem of victory.[128] By evoking notions of fecundity, genders, sexuality, strength, justice, nobility, and victory, date-producing palm trees exemplify the more provocative characteristics of the social system that the disciplined hermits seek to reject. Ironically, although they strive to erase the body's appetites and the pleasures unleashed by them, as they consume dates (and apples) the hermits paradoxically internalize and sustain their lives with fruits that exemplify the very desires and appetites that they steadfastly spurn. That in Rustico's cell Alibech's bed is made of palm leaves is especially important. For in Boccaccio's hand, it conjures up the very images of sexuality, physical strength, and victory that the palm tree exemplifies and the desert supposedly represses.

The clash between the life of self-denial that hermits champion in an environment chosen to stifle the senses and the notions of pleasure that dates evoke reintroduce the discourse of human desires on a new level. Through this circular image, Boccaccio synthesizes the illusoriness of the hermits' (and theologians') rejection of the physical world and shows that it is both an unattainable expectation and an inalienable component of human nature. With one stroke Boccaccio demonstrates that desires cannot be eradicated from human nature. Nor can their satisfaction be repressed because this entails the dehumanization of humanity. In pointed opposition to them, Boccaccio contends that appetites are not only part and parcel of the human condition, but that they possess redemptive values. These, in his view, exert a deep emotional pull capable of transforming and ameliorating human existence. Desires cannot be repressed. They can become the mechanism that leads to the knowledge and freedom (as Alibech will discover) that allows one to move beyond the rigid modalities frustrating the potential for change.

That Alibech's quest for God ends in Rustico's cell is not surprising. There, in a parody of the Gospel's event, his sexual awakening is described as "la risurrezione della carne" (the flesh was resurrected) (*Decameron,* 435). Although his awakened sexual appetite is a perversion of the biblical antecedent, it exemplifies the logical result of a self-imposed sexual deprivation. In striving for the nullification of libido, this forced regimen naturally explodes into a ferocious sexual appetite. This outcome is not the mere consequence of the persistent state of melancholy caused by the unappetizing diet the young man consumes.[129] On the contrary, it is Boccaccio's daring revision of farcical, shortsighted traditions imposed in the name of Christian values. In view of this, the writer suggests that the long-repressed desire brought to consummate gratification raises the sexual experience to new spiritual meaning. Paradoxically, Rustico's new awareness of his irrepressible desire emerges against the distorted ideals of self-denial that he has embraced in the desert. The deceptive language he relies on to keep Alibech with him illustrates the clarity with which he appraises his physical needs. Yet in a peculiar way, Rustico's misappropriation of language represents his own "grammar of sexuality."[130] Clearly, while living in denial of his physical needs Rustico has no necessity to lie or fabricate realities. He can hide in the illusory world of repressed desires that the hermits' lifestyle crystallizes. In this zone of silence, gastronomic restraint, and self-annihilation where the teachings of the past assured Rustico that the Word would suffice to displace the enticement of the present, Alibech's flesh disrupts the calm. With her presence she ruptures not only the silence but especially the coordinates of time and space. Because the desert is perceived as out of time and God's place, her presence forces Rustico to come to terms with the needs of his physical body. This, in turn, compels him to recognize his sexual appetite. The description of his "resurrection" becomes all the more potent because his experience is an incarnation, which, as the word suggests, entails to be made of flesh. It is also a release from the old mode of depriving the body of its needs. This, of course, brings about a reevaluation of the ascetic experience, whereby the flesh effectively and naturally rather than replacing the Word is made one with it. And because it is Rustico's senses that are stimulated by her presence Alibech gives new meaning to his understanding of a human-constructed spirituality.

"Putting the devil back in hell" (*Decameron*, 437) is the practice into which Rustico initiates Alibech. With words borrowed from Job 37:5–8, which set a precondition for what humanity needs to learn about God, Rustico euphemistically gives voice to, and disguises, his erotic desire. The immediacy of the language he deploys persuades Alibech of the legitimacy of her teacher's actions. Certain of the fact that as a hermit he already possesses the key that unlocks the door to the mysteries of God and has the spiritual wisdom she lacks, Alibech believes in Rustico. She also believes that his knowledge is implicitly paired with a cosmic understanding of avoiding the evil that the "devil" foments. By focusing on the "goodness and wisdom" that results from avoiding evil and by relegating the architect of wickedness—as she is led to believe—into the den from which he cannot impair her learning, Alibech has faith in the fact that she too can come to know the Christian God. The powerful imagery with which this scene is charged shows an Alibech defined by a dynamic and unquenchable yearning for God, but recklessly inexperienced. She is, therefore, naively unaware of the fact that more is going on beneath the surface of Rustico's words. To be sure, it is ironic that, unlike what she believes, Rustico's words serve as a vehicle for expressing an inversion of value not only with regard to what she believes in and what his intentions are, but also especially between his words and those used by Job.

In the biblical verses, Elihu admonishes Job to take heed of God's power and works and, at the same time, not to be preoccupied solely by his earthly suffering. To question God's judgment, Elihu argues, is a failure in understanding His power. This idea pivots on the notion that human suffering is a divine revelation and paves the way for knowledge. Through this, humanity is restored from the moral depravity to which it subjects itself as it wallows in material complacency. Once it is purified, as the anchorites believed, humanity is united with God.[131] Elihu elucidates this point by describing the meteorological cycles that instruct human and animal behaviors: "El thunders wonders with his voice, does great things we do not know ... On every human hand He puts a seal / so all man he has made may know. And the beast enters its lair, lie down in its den" (Job 37:5–8). This image emphasizes the power of divine will that directs and regulates the universe's movements. Humanity, however, remains unaware of how they work. The emphasis on humanity's ignorance effectively describes Alibech's unawareness with regard to what is truly unfolding in Rustico's cell. While the complexity of Job's couplet makes the precise meaning unclear, scholars agree that Elihu's words are a warning against sin because it leads humanity to self-destruction.[132] What can be inferred from the verses from Job is that while animals possess instinctive knowledge humanity does not. To learn, it needs divine teaching—and this is imparted through suffering. By shifting the frame of reference from Rustico's carnal desire to Job's words about the ways in which evil thoughts can enter the mind but through divine intervention they can be driven out,[133] Boccaccio upturns the biblical meaning of the expression Rustico adopts. Rustico has no intention of following the advice Elihu's words offer. Nor does he plan to tame the power of his desire by compensating it with other means. On the contrary, he is determined to sate his senses. Theology cannot regulate human appetites because the full realization of every human being rests on their satisfaction too. As a result, Rustico appropriates Job's language to sway Alibech, but for him, it does not resonate with any theological meaning.

The deceptiveness of his words eludes Alibech, for she believes in furthering her spiritual awareness through her actions. The aching simplicity that suffuses her understanding makes it clear that she misconstrues the events taking place in the cell and believes that they are part of her spiritual *paidea*. Arguably, the catalyst for Alibech's exploitation is not Rustico's sexual appetite but her ignorance. This renders her powerless and subjects her to his unbridled pursuit of erotic gratification. But as a strategy for survival in the desert, and as a tool for what she still perceives to be a Christian schooling, complying with Rustico's ways is her sole choice. In delineating Rustico's selfish behavior toward Alibech, Boccaccio implicitly describes the subtle tactics that a colonizing force uses to subjugate the "foreign other." Needless to say, the attractiveness of the colonized is measured in terms of the material gains it provides to the colonizer. It could be argued that the colonization of Alibech's mind occurs before she enters Rustico's cell, when the Christians in her city by stirring her curiosity for the "other" God effectively replace her religious and cultural beliefs with their own. Analyzed through the lens of expansionistic ideology that is subsumed to cultural imperialism and political domination, Rustico's appropriation of Alibech's body, achieved by employing a discourse of inversion of normative values, sums up the discourse of colonial expansion. The fact remains that by his deliberate lying to maintain his ascendancy over her, by his inversion of values skillfully carried out through his upending of Job's language, in short, by his lack of self-control to serve his own ends, Rustico overturns the fundamental bond of fellowship that sustains human existence. Also, by violating the trust she puts in him and encroaching on her intentions and desires, he takes charge of her life in ways she did not ask for or envision when she arrived at his cell. Because of this, he can influence and control her decisions and, through this, bar her way to attaining the goal she has set for herself. The ideological consistency between the Christians in Alibech's city and Rustico rests on the fact that while they lay claim to her mind, he takes possession of her body. In the end, both instances are fine examples of forces that surreptitiously seize what belongs to others.

What emerges from this situation is more than just the image of a defenseless individual subjugated by a powerful one; it is the image of an absolutist political force that does not accept compromises as it moves toward the goals it has set for itself. And in their pursuit, it crushes with visceral cunning the feeblest challenge it encounters. The astonishing display of Rustico's self-centeredness that precludes any consideration for Alibech's desire lies in his taking possession of, and penetrating, her body. This effectively reverses (and displaces) the terms of Alibech's quest. Although it was she who as an outsider planned to penetrate the desert of her ignorance with regard to Christian faith and to gain possession of it despite her pagan upbringing, it is Rustico who takes hold of and possesses her body. This inversion of roles, as well as of metaphoric values, signals the disruption of the kinship system. Rustico, neglectful of his obligations toward his belief system (his Christian religion) as well as toward her, abuses her trust. Because of this, she becomes the embodiment of a failed cultural and ideological conversion. With this brilliant but scorching shift Boccaccio questions the limits of absolutist ideals espoused in any ideological desert. And his criticism appears aimed at all coercive systems. More often than not corrupt and abusive systems produce results that drive humanity toward false objectives, transgressions, and impropriety. The vastness of this problem becomes even more conspicuous when those systems are foisted on individuals who are unable to gauge, much less to steer clear of, the results they produce. Alibech's experience is an example of this. The desert that for her represents the unknown exotic, for Rustico turns into the discovery of the unknown erotic. As he questions the repressive role that conventions play in suffocating human desires, Boccaccio yet again demonstrates that they inevitably lead to moral degeneracy and despotic behavior. And these, in turn, set in motion the crisis of political, social, and theological values.

In the provocative subversion of Job's imagery, Alibech's credulity in Rustico's actions—which marks the distance between an acknowledged human sexuality and a denied one—is not a false negative because it does respond to her desire, as she understands it, for spiritual growth. And she does find fulfillment in her spiritual apprenticeship with Rustico. Ironically, the search for physical gratification that both take pleasure from and that for her translates into spiritual fulfillment is attenuated neither by the simplicity of foods they eat nor by the austere environment in which their experience is consumed. But the language of deception that it necessitates to misconstrue the objective reality gives new meanings to old paradigms and undoes the truths the past held sacred. Alibech's impatient desire to grow spiritually factors as a driving force behind this fact. Conversely, Rustico's ability to capitalize on expressions that further his own end, making Alibech a vehicle of self-indulgence, mirrors his awareness of, but also his ability to rely on, the power language possesses. While Rustico is empowered by his shrewd exploitation of the biblical imagery, Alibech's inability to decipher his language is made persuasive by the fact that in his role as her teacher he has become her spiritual compass. So that even as divergent purposes drive their actions, Alibech's and Rustico's desires are shown as one because for both of them their respective experience sates a natural appetite. Specifically, although one individual seeks to gratify a physical appetite and the other longs to satisfy a spiritual one, together the two encompass the balance of powers through which the human spirit triumphs. In this manner the physical and the spiritual, the human and the divine, forces that forge the cosmological harmony and invest the universe with a seamless balance of higher value are no longer separated into a dialectical discourse. Most importantly, they no longer represent the limitations that cultural insularity imposes on both Rustico and Alibech. To the contrary, they allow for the fusion of the human with the divine and this leads to a more encompassing harmony of the human spirit. It is for this reason that Alibech and Rustico can both take refuge in and adopt a language that is based on inaccuracies. And as they pursue their respective aims, they succeed in communicating through the incommunicable and to remain connected and find fulfillment in spite of the divergent meanings they each assign to their words.

The pleasure Alibech and Rustico find in their respective discovery is not affected by the plainness of foodstuffs they have access to. In the same way, scarcity of food does not curb their appetites. Grass roots, wild apples, dates, and water do not diminish their sexual stamina because the revelatory pleasure of their libido becomes the quantification of what neither of them anticipated and both believed elusive. For this reason, Rustico thirsts to quench his desires while Alibech is a glutton for learning about God. Contrary to medical, theological, and culinary treatises of the time, through this inversion Boccaccio boldly contends that appetizing food neither affirms the identity of the individuals consuming it nor ensures their social standing. Food instills neither religious nor social conviction. In view of this, it neither validates the hermits' resolve to forgo earthly pleasures nor does it guarantee their future spiritual gains. According to Boccaccio, physical pleasure, the palpable result of desires, fulfills human yearnings in this world. But this newfound and unshakeable faith cannot be reduced to a rational exercise. It can, however, guide Alibech—and humanity as well—to navigate the inconsistencies the modern social paradigm presents. This is based on the notion that the new model is not stagnating in, nor is it a derivative of, anachronistic ones. But it is a society full of unruly passions and conflicting desires, shadowed by grief, disappointments, and deaths. This new paradigm requires a sense of adaptation to the new challenges that dynamic sociopolitical forces produce. As it is, these forces can enrich the human spirit and affect the mercantile morality society is forging. Boccaccio's prescient insightfulness into the philosophical paths that will define the Renaissance discourse on human nature and freedom emerges here.

When Alibech's unrelenting demand to serve God in the manner in which she has been trained outpaces his erotic desire, Rustico's inability to sustain the rhythms of her insatiability for spiritual wisdom is blamed on the meager diet they consume. This pretext the narrator introduces flies in the face of Rustico's initial behavior. Still, it does expose the shallowness of his commitment to search for a unity with the divine as well as with the human. For if Rustico is weakened by a diet that cannot sustain his physical demands Alibech is not enfeebled by the same one. Scarcity of food does not lessen her eagerness to succeed in her goal, as misplaced as it might be. On the contrary, her determination is only augmented by the physical pleasure she has found in "serving God" and this impels her to adopt Rustico's language. As he distances himself from her while she entreats him to continue to put the "devil back in hell" a role reversal occurs. Alibech's adoption of his language marks her metamorphosis into a liberated decision-maker and a *sapiens*. According to Isidore of Seville, the word *sapiens* derives from *sapor* and literally describes one capable of distinguishing among the various tastes of food.[134] Metaphorically, for him, the word depicts a wise person, that is to say, one capable of discerning between things and causes because he distinguishes each and every thing by his sense of truth. Applied to Alibech, this explanation suggests that she is not a failed *sapiens*. Even though her knowledge, seeped through Rustico's self-serving plan, is a perverted understanding of spiritual exercises, it still reflects her sense of truth. Through this, Boccaccio shows that what she has learned from Rustico blurs the lines between sexual gratification and spiritual growth. That for her the two coincide does not imply that she lacks moral values. On the contrary, it suggests that through her Boccaccio is describing a state of innocence in which the two appetites—sexual and spiritual—naturally converge. To be sure, for the medieval mindset the fusion of the human and spiritual, profane and sacred, is not perplexing. As James F. Rhodes has shown, this practice was widely used in the visual arts at the time.[135]

At this juncture Alibech is depicted as incapable of differentiating among things that she desires. But she enthusiastically pursues what gives her pleasure. Her appropriation of Rustico's language evidences this. And although her newfound voice is acquired through the appropriation of his misleading language, it, nonetheless, validates her self-assertion. Her words directly undermine his scheme, entrapping him in the very linguistic web that he has crafted. Here, with an exquisite twist Boccaccio portrays Alibech as the marchioness's specular image. For while the first adopts her lover's language to satisfy her desires, the latter turns the king's request into her way of declining and snubbing his sexual advances. Interestingly, in both Alibech's and the marchioness's resolve, there is a continuity that begins with Pampinea's. This is a bold counter-interpretative stance on Boccaccio's part, because it depicts Alibech (as well as the other two women) as free from sociocultural ideologies and unyoked from rigid models. For Alibech in particular, having harnessed the courage necessary to undertake her quest she now savors the joys of her newfound "spiritual knowledge." For this reason, her inability to decipher Rustico's language and behavior is made irrelevant by the fulfillment she finds in the belief of pursuing her goal. No less important is the fact that because her spiritual practice is unencumbered by the sense of guilt and degradation that assails those who like Rustico have bought into religious codes of behavior without questioning them, Alibech can live her faith free from the sense of shame and remorse. The fact that women laugh at her story when she returns to her city at the end of the novella is a further confirmation of this. Their laughter and pleasure over her experience (and naiveté) prove that the Muslim women, like Alibech, practice a sexuality that is in harmony with nature rather than the Christian ascetic ideal. For Rustico, gratifying his physical needs displaces—if only momentarily—his commitment to the desert life and to the past. For Alibech, on the contrary, it anchors her to the present. In her case, this fact makes it possible for the past to change her future. The quest that led her through spaces and meals of arguable beliefs and undeniable pleasures paves the way for her self-discovery. For her, the two blend seamlessly into a fulfilled existence. In the desert Rustico and Alibech, probing the finality of their respective searches, discover that they are neither of a contemplative nor of an intellectual nature but of a purely sensual one. The beauty of this image rests on the fusion of the spiritual and the erotic that ushers in the fulfilled moment, where time and eternity intersect. This becomes a communion that allows, first of all, for this-worldly freedom, openness, and understanding of the other; and these lead to the communion with the "other." To be sure, their lovemaking is not a relapse into a state of transgression. Instead, it is the discovery of two mutually fulfilling states: sexual gratification and spiritual comfort, each of which is the natural and direct extension of the other.

In direct opposition to Eve and Adam's experience, Alibech and Rustico's appears to be filtered through an inverted sieve of biblical analogies. She is not the temptress but the unwitting recipient not of the knowledge he promised but of the one he betrays. In an intriguing juxtaposition Rustico's role mirrors the function that hermits assign to the dates consumed in their desert. Just as the fruit gives the hermits a false sense of self-sacrifice, chastity, and security, Rustico purports to have one objective with regard to Alibech's tutoring. He veers, instead, to its opposite. Through the discovery and pursuit of sexual pleasure Rustico recasts himself in the image of his appetites; as her spiritual guardian he discovers that his own desires are stronger than the perils their satisfaction entails. In a symmetry of opposites, just as chicken meat and sauces could not incite the marchioness of Monferrato nor appease the king of France's desires, herbs, dates, and wild apples do not diminish Alibech's and Rustico's sexual appetites. Boccaccio's savage irony is here tempered by the many questions these novellas raise. Yet writing about appetite and desire, of food that purportedly bridles the senses and ostensibly restrains them, he maps the sociocultural anxieties and longings of his society. At the same time, through food he exposes the ineffectiveness of stultifying ideological models that can be neither substitutes nor replacements for human appetites. History and theology, in the end Boccaccio demonstrates, must be approached in a critical fashion, for fanaticism, obscurantism, and dogmatism do not provide for an extensive, objective view of society nor do they contribute to the formation of morally sound individuals. After Boccaccio, other Italian authors used food in their works as a defining element of their cultures. In the following chapters I explore the different ways in which Renaissance poets and writers made powerful statements about their times through food.

TWO

Of Frogs, Giants, and the Court
Pulci's Morgante

There is little doubt that in the *Decameron* Giovanni Boccaccio uses scarcity, abundance, quality, and variety of food to explore the hidden folds of the human condition. By turning his attention to the foods that the wealthy, privileged, and hermits consume, he draws attention to the disquieting effects that anachronistic codes have in regulating humanity's natural appetites. Indeed, throughout his novellas, he shows that imposing moral imperatives to uphold moral and ethical principles leads to double standards and dishonest practices. This awareness magnifies his unsparing critique of his society. The way Boccaccio used foodstuffs to illustrate his fundamental disagreement with the cultural assumptions his times upheld was not lost on later Italian poets and writers. Luigi Pulci stands out among them. In his *Morgante*, scenes revolving around banquets and meals are so ubiquitous that food appears to function on a par with, and not to the exclusion of, the knights' adventures. And the scenes that depict knights, ladies, and giants consuming copious amounts of foodstuff mark every important event of his epic poem. As Illidio Bussani noted long ago, in the *Morgante*, quite prominently, food and eating bridge the distance between poetic fiction and reality.[1]

In Pulci's epic poem food becomes a means to critique the political maneuverings and personal intrigues that are normative rules observed and practiced at the Medici court. With raw irony,[2] and through a web of subtle metaphoric meanings, the poet also uses food to expose the tumultuous philosophical, political, social, and cultural currents defining his times.[3] To be sure, the abundant meals his knights and giants consume reveal the tattered texture of the chivalric society that regulates court life.[4] At a time of social transition, Pulci makes a case against the old courtly system that remains ossified in outdated models. Through food and the body he offers a non-Platonic representation of Florentine life, imbued as it is, with the abstractions peddled by the Florentine Academy. Yet the powerful philosophical images this academy championed were espoused by a pragmatic Lorenzo de' Medici.[5] This fact proved disastrous for the poet. The cruelty, delusions, and losses he suffered for pointing out the absurd implications some of those beliefs led to ruined his career. And, as might be expected, this profoundly affected his personal life. Thus, by slicing through the literal level of the way in which the poet uses food, it becomes clear that through it he speaks of the struggle between politics and ethics and, by extension, between history and philosophy confronting his knights. In the shift from food to politics—and conversely from politics to food—Pulci reconstructs with explosive wit the events that marked his association with the Medici court, the intellectual circle that surrounded it, and his even more tempestuous rapport with Marsilio Ficino that led to Pulci's exclusion from the court.

The first illustration of the ways in which food richly evokes the excesses that courtly society enshrines as laws occurs in canto 2 of the *Morgante*. Here, as Orlando and Morgante travel at night to Caradoro's city, they stumble upon a magnificent palace.[6]

> E in questo, ragionando, hanno veduto
> Un bel palagio in mezzo del deserto;
> Orlando, poi ch'a questo fu venuto,
> Dismonta, perché l'uscio vide aperto:
> Quivi non è chi risponda al saluto.
> Vannone in sala, per esser più certo.[7]

(There in that desert a fair mansion stood / Towards it rode Orlando right away / and, seeing the door open, fast jumped down. No one was there to answer his Hello. Into a hall they walked just to make sure.)[8]

Lured by the open door and intrigued by the peculiarity of a palace in the middle of the desert, Orlando and his giant friend Morgante enter it without hesitation. The impulsiveness, laced with self-confidence, that marks their entry encapsulates the complex life lived by the ambitious hero Orlando personifies. Driven by a deep-rooted sense of moral and ethical duty that compels him to bring order and justice to the world surrounding him, the hero undertakes a journey that is continually hindered by a universe of beguiling ambiguities. Under different guises, these confront him at every stage of his journey. The difficulties, confusion, and ambivalences with which they present the hero expose the fragility of the human condition. Although they are meant to test his ability to master the circumstances he faces, by diverting his focus and energy to more seductive promises, the adversities the hero encounters lead him to question his understanding of self and identity. According to Renaissance humanism, the hero's *paidea* takes place as he grapples with the subtleties of the contradictions and ambiguities he faces, without yielding to impulses.[9] But resisting instincts and not to be made powerless by them to direct one's own actions also requires that the hero not remain trapped in fixed social, and political, positions.

For this purpose, an education that is rooted in sound moral and ethical principles must guide the hero. Acting as his compass, these values steer him in successfully restoring the world to its unified whole. The successful outcomes of his adventurous undertakings bring him fame. And the renown this lends him brings him closer to the object of his happiness (usually a lady's love). But the acquired knowledge and wisdom that the hero must rely on to reach his coveted goal are always anchored in self-knowledge. As the story of the king of France in the previous chapter illustrated, lacking self-knowledge makes it difficult, if not impossible, to decipher the circumstances in which one finds oneself. When this occurs, confusion arises and the hero becomes vulnerable.

Unable to untangle the situation he finds himself in, he becomes threatened by the very circumstances he should be resolving. As a result, the unresolved problems spawn into loss of harmony that thwarts his quest for fame. As a conduit for the hero's successful journey, through introspection self-knowledge turns into a powerful tool to resist the allure of distractions. In theory, the wisdom the hero gains through his experiences removes, or in part reduces, the potential for failure. When the readers meet Orlando in canto 2 of the *Morgante*, it is evident that the hero does not heed the lessons of his humanistic education.

Only when Orlando begins to wonder at and wander in the richly furnished but uninhabited palace does he become puzzled by it. For one thing, he cannot explain the absence of people. This fact alone makes it too removed from common human experience. Nor can Orlando find reasons for the exquisite décor and the lavish foodstuffs readied on the tables. Naturally, the palace's eeriness turns his initial curiosity into hesitancy. This realization troubles the knight as he begins to recognize that beyond the richness of the appearances may lie a trap or a murkier truth. He draws scant comfort from the fact that his initial enthusiasm goaded him to go inside, precluding him from envisioning dangerous surprises. Driven by the audaciousness and wild flight of his curiosity to learn about the mysterious place, which in the chivalrous universe is similar to testing challenging possibilities, Orlando plunges headlong into this adventure. That impulsive decision soon turns into the suspicion of seeing behind everything a shadow that presages his defeat and suffering. The apprehension this causes him betrays his sense of displacement. On the poet's part, though, the suspicion that replaces the knight's initial insouciance illustrates a deep understanding of the courtly system the hero inhabits. Orlando turns into a knight who does not trust the appearance of what he sees.

Orlando is aware of the fact that between appearance and reality there might be a radical difference. And although at first he does not voice his misgivings to his traveling companion, the knight does ponder the strangeness of the circumstances. As he reflects on the likelihood that the palace could be a hoax conceived to derail him from reaching his objective, Orlando's sense of helplessness emerges more clearly. His sudden awareness that ensnaring devices may lurk behind enticing deception and that nuanced realities might exist beyond the concreteness of what he sees illustrates the vigilance Orlando strives to maintain in keeping focused on his journey. This gradual change of perspective is a direct result of his humanistic education. Still, the self-possession and wariness the knight displays toward the luxuries the palace offers are surprising. Admittedly, he embodies a culture in which personal wealth and material gratification are powerful markers of social status. That he is uncertain about their legitimacy and not smitten by them at this point suggests that he is increasingly more cynical and diffident toward his own culture. And as he questions the nature of the rich surroundings and perceives their potentially misleading looks, rather than simply pursuing the sensual pleasures they afford, the knight distances himself from his culture. This radical departure from the Renaissance mindset gives pause. At the same time, Orlando's mistrust toward the social conventions that his rigidly hierarchical society upholds mirrors Pulci's own critique of them. It also reflects the poet's contempt for the sociopolitical system sustaining them. Pulci's attack on the elastic values the court has put into place to serve its own ends lays bare the fickleness of human nature that is quick to forgo moral and ethical principles in order to cater to its own desires.

Pulci's poetic invention at this juncture is genial in its simplicity, for it mirrors his personal experience. The poet's own pessimism and disillusionment with the allure of the court system and the culture of power it fosters surfaces as he depicts Orlando's pause when gazing at the palace's magnificence. By showing a knight who entertains doubts about the fact that his life depends on, and is made more fulfilling by, material gratifications, the poet reveals the compromised and complicated view of one who belongs to the court and, because of this, questions the values of its principles. As Pulci knows, the beliefs observed at court are subject to the prince's whims. Thus, Orlando's misgivings about the courtly lifestyle and the pressure of conventions that the palace encapsulates are not just the poignant measure of its diminishment. It is especially the evidence of the hero's disenchantment with the enmities, hostilities, resentments, anxieties, and grievances that the luxuries of the court deftly conceal but that are embraced by the political system it creates. At the Medici court Pulci experienced the viciousness of this system firsthand as it consumed his energy and his morale. There, his longstanding friendship with Lorenzo—friend and patron—was soured by the calumnies that Matteo Franco and Marsilio Ficino leveled against him. Despite a whole life spent attempting to disprove their increasingly more provocative allegations against him,[10] the poet never regained the closeness to Lorenzo he had enjoyed from his first arrival at the court. In much the same manner, the poet's best efforts to demonstrate his unyielding loyalty to Lorenzo proved ineffective.

Pulci's volcanic temperament and his impatience with the affected mannerisms Franco and Ficino espoused made the jovial camaraderie he shared with his young patron an easy target of their envious calumnies. That Lorenzo had at first fully embraced his friend's roguish cultural, social, and religious rebelliousness is demonstrated by the poetry he produced during the early years of his friendship with Pulci.[11] But the accusations cast against the poet by the two detractors pressured Lorenzo into alienating him from his circle. Political expediency, more than personal preference, forced Lorenzo to gradually distance himself from his older friend.[12] No longer a carefree member of the scandal-prone *brigata* but heir to the Medici power, Lorenzo marked the passage from youth to maturity by disavowing his earlier penchant for testing the limits of sociocultural norms.[13] By rejecting the impetuous and reckless behavior that marked his friendship with Pulci and moving closer to Ficino's sphere of influence,[14] Lorenzo sought to bolster his political ascent. Through this, he could strengthen the Florentine oligarchy. Politically, the magnificence of his court and the ideals it embraced no longer sufficed to fulfill Lorenzo's ambitions. And as his political ambition increased, the estrangement between him and Pulci became inevitable. Alienated from the court and bristling with resentment toward Ficino and Franco—though never openly against Lorenzo—the poet unleashed a critique of the ways in which the court fostered smiling deceitfulness, brutal treachery, and a voracious craving for power.

The poet's anguished outpouring of letters and conciliatory gestures toward his former patron did not achieve the results he had hoped for.[15] Instead, they provide solid evidence of his delusion with the court's unspoken and unfulfilled promises. They also demonstrate his awareness that the court remained deeply insensitive to the insidious perils engendered by ambitious aloofness. Pulci understood that because lofty ideals had not deterred Franco and Ficino from engineering his falling from Lorenzo's favor, the court retained a fluid and malleable sense of moral and ethical principles. The strong attraction and paralyzing fear this realization simultaneously stirred in the poet was in no small part the result of the lost friendship. But it was also due to the power Lorenzo personified and the loss of financial security that being estranged from him meant. Envy within the court failed Pulci both on a private and a public scale. Looking at that court through the prism of his personal experience not only allows the poet to document its flaws and deceptions, but also gives texture and nuance to Orlando's hesitancy with respect to the magnificence surrounding him in the palace he has entered.

While Pulci's bitterness is aimed at Franco and Ficino because he knows that they are stoking the fire of enmity against him, Orlando has no certainty about the person behind or the cause of his entrapment. To find an explanation for it, he strains to see a reality that fits his convictions. This leads him to hypothesize that the space he has entered is a hoax masterminded by the Saracens. In Orlando's view, they incarnate the antithesis of Christian and knightly values. This is why, he reasons, they would desire his demise. Orlando's conclusion, however, does not take into account the fact that his friend Morgante, who is also in the palace, is himself a pagan. Still, the knight's conjecture adds an intriguing layer to the scene because it shows the hero's (and his culture's) prejudicial attitude toward people he does not yet know. If Orlando's embroilment illustrates a whole range of trepidations and resentments with which Pulci identifies, there is yet another parallel the poet sets up between the knight and himself. The respective separations from familiar environments the two suffer at the hands of others create the effect of a specular but inverted image between the author and his character. More specifically, for Pulci the marginalization from Lorenzo's court marks a lifelong alienating odyssey. The expulsion from the Medici court, the center of Italian intellectual effervescence even if sustained by false dreams and hollow values, forces him into the world of financial destitution and artistic struggle. For Orlando, on the contrary, entering the palace and lingering within it brings about his estrangement from the vibrant world of contingencies, trapping him within the palpable isolation of courtly conventions. The humanist ideological divide that Orlando's and Pulci's respective states of alienation represent stretches in different directions. They function at the exclusion of each other because they both presuppose an insuperable distance between the universe of the court and the one outside of it. They also assume that there is no possible compromise between them because they do not share the same code of values. Lastly, they take for granted that the code that functions in one environment cannot operate in the other because this demands an increased cultural sensibility. Orlando still believes that he can impose his moral code on others, and thus overcome the predicament he is in. Pulci does not. He is aware that court principles hold a precarious value outside of it, and, more importantly, that they can be foisted on others by relying on an astonishing sense of self-centeredness.

Stealthy power ensures the downfall of the unsuspecting adversary. By the time the latter realizes the deception forced on him, it is usually too late to either contain or remedy it. This is precisely the quandary in which Orlando and Morgante find themselves. And as he chafes at his earlier decision, the knight finally voices his misgivings through an analogy that is inscribed within the imagery of frogs and food:

> —O qualche saracin molto malvagio
> Vorrà che qualche trappola ci scocchi,
> Per pigliarci al boccon come ranocchi;
> O veramente c'è sotto altro inganno:
> Questo non par che sia convenïente.
>   (2.21.6–8; 22.1–2)

> ("Either a very clever Saracen / has set a trap to catch some Christian thugs / and lure us here by food like stupid frogs / or there is a worse deceit beneath all this / it doesn't seem quite natural to me.")

The image of frogs lured by bait conjures up notions of helpless prey, predatory tactics, forceful captures, and powerful if cunning captors.

Through it the knight acknowledges, first of all, his lack of prudence and juxtaposes it to the adversary's watchfulness. By aimlessly meandering through the luxurious halls, Orlando (and to a certain degree Morgante) personifies moral and ethical ideals mired in the rigid and polarizing outlook of the courtly system. At this juncture he is certain that the aesthetic and gastronomic enticements are a ploy. But despite his best efforts, the knight fails to find his way out of the palace. His sense of bewilderment is matched only by the sumptuousness of the banquet readied on the tables.

For all that, Orlando's analogy of captured frogs suggests the notion of becoming unwittingly a prisoner of a system that forces one to comply with values and objectives one may not necessarily share. More than this, though, the analogy he uses calls to mind another literary figure whose writings had a profound influence on the intellectuals drawn to the Medici court. In 1457 Bartolomei Sacchi—Platina—arrived in Medici Florence from Mantua to study under John Argyropoulos. The Byzantine philosopher had been invited by Cosimo de' Medici to teach Aristotle at the university. Recommended by Ludovico Gonzaga, Platina became one of Argyropoulos's students.[16] Among his fellow-students were Lorenzo, Piero and Donato Acciaiuoli, as well as Pandolfo Pandolfini,[17] with whom Platina maintained a close epistolary friendship throughout his life.[18] At the time that Platina studied under Argyropoulos, Luigi Pulci was already part of Lucrezia Tornabuoni's circle. Through her, the poet had access to, and became a close friend of, Lucrezia's young son Lorenzo. More importantly, by 1461 Pulci had already been encouraged by Tornabuoni to work on the *Morgante*. Although Platina left Florence for Rome in 1462, he continued to correspond with Lorenzo. This suggests that Pulci not only knew Platina in person, but that he was most likely familiar with Platina's works, perhaps even before they were publicly circulating. In 1465 Platina began writing *On Right Pleasure and Good Health*, a treatise that was published in Rome in 1470.

Neither the medical advice that Platina provides nor the recipes he includes in the ten books make this treatise unique. But the documentary power of its narrative turns it into an exceptional document because it evidences the social and political mores of Platina's times.

By linking the well-established Renaissance tradition of the medical-therapeutic properties of food to the Galenic tradition of the body's humoral theory, Platina essentially creates a hybrid text. Only on the surface, however, does it aim to educate the wealthy on the ways in which they can be healthy. This approach differentiates *On Right Pleasure and Good Health* from Martino de' Rossi's *Libro di cucina*, a real recipe collection. Platina acknowledges de' Rossi's compilation as the primary source for the recipes he includes in his treatise.[19] Yet the similarity ends there. Unlike de'Rossi, Platina explains the qualities of specific foodstuffs and the therapeutic desirability associated with using them. De'Rossi's *Libro di cucina*, on the contrary, never digresses from the instructions on the ways to prepare particular foods. For this reason, underneath the veneer of the dietetic regimen the treatise purports to be and the medical advice it dispenses, *On Right Pleasure and Good Health* is more than a compendium of gastronomy and medicine or of the marriage of wealth and health. It is a social commentary that juxtaposes the society the author intimately knows with the unprincipled lifestyle its members lead.

Specifically, through the discussion on food the treatise focuses on the lack of ethical and moral values that the Roman curia fosters and displays. Because of his closeness to Cardinal Gonzaga and his circle, the mercurial Platina knows this court and its acolytes. Accordingly, his treatise turns into a scathing denunciation of the excesses sought and enjoyed by prelates who, as Platina tells it, are solely enchanted by and obsessed with the immediate gratifications that power and wealth provide. Platina doubles his dose of accusations as he intimates that material gains are the only currency of the Roman court. Its actions, he argues, are based on calculating principles that seek to find pleasure in material excesses and overindulgent lives. For this reason, in his view, they collide with the Christian principles the curia should uphold. According to him, self-absorption, not self-scrutiny, guides the members of the curia and this strips it of any credibility. Worse yet, the power wielded by the princes of Rome makes them highly influential in both the political and social arenas. Because of this, through their actions they shape the sociopolitical landscape not only of Rome and Italian principalities, but also of much of Europe. Through extraordinarily powerful prose Platina points out that the curial gastronomy is a compelling symbol of the corruption and greed reigning within the Roman court. And this understanding redefines the idea of power embodied by religious figures. More specifically, the narcissistic and supercilious stance that powerful prelates espouse illustrates the aloofness in which they live and the indifference they foster toward people who, like Platina (and Pulci), lack the means for self-support. To be sure, Platina's station within this court is not unlike Pulci's at the Medici court. Both writer and poet, in fact, find themselves ruthlessly marginalized because through their respective works they expose the provocative ambivalence and sheer hypocrisy the two courts thrive on. And in Platina's view (as well as in Pulci's), the court's callousness settles so deeply in its members' consciousness as to shape skewed political perspectives.

Throughout the treatise Platina illustrates the ways in which the curia's resolve to gratify its earthly appetites is made manifest at the table and shapes the political discourse it presses forward. By openly speaking about the gastronomic excesses that for the court translate into practicable ethics, Platina exposes the greed and unscrupulousness that the vice-infested Roman curia begets. The caustic words the humanist uses in his dedication of the treatise to Cardinal Roverella summarize his point:

> they upbraid me about food as if I were a gluttonous and greedy man and as if I were proffering instruments of lust and, as it were, spurs to intemperance and wicked people. Would that they, like Platina, would use more moderation and frugality either by nature or instruction; we would not see today so many so-called cooks in the city, so many gluttons, so many dandies, so many parasites, so many most diligent cultivators of hidden lusts and recruiting officers for gluttony and greed.[20]

At the heart of Platina's retort against his detractors are his own accusations of gourmandism and covetousness of which they accuse him. With *gula* and *avaritia*, Platina's critics, in his account, string sexual appetite.[21] While the three deadly sins are intended to demean Platina and cause his downfall within the curia, they also blur the lines between various types of appetites. Once again, as we saw in the previous chapter, appetite for food is entwined with sexual and worldly appetites. This triad, which according to Platina forms the basis for the accusations hurled against him, gives an idea of the ferocious atmosphere and even fiercer impulses engulfing the spiritual center of the world in the late fifteenth century. Yet in his cogent introductory remarks to Cardinal Roverella, Platina does not hold back from turning his own accusatory finger toward his critics.

At first glance, the explanations Platina gives with regard to his own cautious temperance—"by nature or instruction"—calls to mind the moderate behavior displayed by one of the Florentine groups in Boccaccio's introduction to the *Decameron*. But the combative response is just a precursor to Platina's more concrete shaming of his detractors. The strident tone of his reply makes plain an unyielding social consciousness; in it, there is no misplaced carelessness or feigned optimism, only the sour reflection about courtiers, whom he defines as "cooks, gluttons, dandies, and parasites." These titles sum up his view of the diluted morals prevailing among the prelates and their entourage. That he yet again ties together food and cooks with flatters and vacuous individuals in general demonstrates first of all that his text is, indeed, much more than just a recipe collection. It also suggests that Platina is not cowed by the criticism leveled against him. On the contrary, his retort shows that the transgressions his enemies accuse him of tarnish their own lives. And this has graver repercussions, for it casts a shadow on the Christian principles they ostensibly incarnate.

By placing the highest value in material pleasures, the curia, as Platina describes it, is not different from secular courts. On the contrary, with them it shares a self-serving elasticity about the malleability of ethical and moral principles. The humanist suggests that the peculiar subversion of values that changes and adjusts according to personal wants eventually leads to the collapse of the systems espousing it. Naturally, Platina's candid accusations against the rampant culture of greed the curia fosters do not go unnoticed. In fact, the reprisal soon follows. Powerless in a universe regulated by powerful men, he is charged of promoting perversion. To unleash a ferocious campaign against him intended to silence him while also erasing his presence from the Roman scene, his influential detractors need to look no further than the treatise's title.

According to them, *On Right Pleasure and Good Health* unlocks the door to the old debate of the *summum bonum*.[22] The title alone, his accusers claim, linking pleasure and good health, draws attention to immoral topics. In their view, these are not only mutually exclusive but lend themselves to potentially corrupting interpretations. Objectively, in the wake of the Stoic and Epicurean debates that inflamed the discussions of early humanists and the disputes between *virtus* and *voluptas* they engendered, Platina's treatise does seem to add fuel to the fire. In spite of this though, and aware that there is much more than the title in his treatise to unsettle his foes and draw their wrath, Platina works at dispelling those accusations. By arguing that moderation and even frugality—at the table as well as in every other aspect of life—are healthier courses for a gratifying and righteous existence, he voices his dissent against those who make unbridled excess a way of life.

The best-known fifteenth-century work on the discourse of virtue and pleasure is Lorenzo Valla's *On Pleasure* (*De voluptate*). Developed as a dialogue among Antonio da Rho, Cato Sacco, and Maffeo Vegio, who represent the Christian, Stoic, and Epicurean perspectives respectively for a cultured audience, the three books of the treatise delve into the exploration of the highest good engendering human happiness and how the two can be achieved. Through the figure of the Franciscan Antonio, Valla dissects the layers of perceptions created by the Stoic and Epicurean philosophical schools.[23] He does this by uncovering the limits and flaws that are inherent to both systems and showing the emptiness of their respective claims. Valla's argument, laid out with precise examples and rigorous language, first addresses the Stoic notions of *honestas* and *virtus* as they are embodied by the historical figures Cato uses in support of his argument. In the guise of the Epicurean Vegio, Valla first disproves Cato's assertion that humanity is both unable and unwilling to overcome vice because the latter proves to be more gratifying, and less repressive, than the practice of virtue. Against this argument, the humanist maintains that the Stoic notion of virtue is an end to itself because it does not take into account nature's providential attributes.[24] By this very fact, virtue, as the Stoics understand it, turns, according to Valla, into a deplorable, sterile quality that more often than not leads to vice. The Stoics' preoccupation with the evils that torment humanity and cause its perversion is offset by their notion of *honestas*. Yet this approach results in a skewed understanding of human nature. This is based on the fact that the rational and hostile relation with nature the Stoics espouse does not foster a kinder, totalizing rapport between the two.[25] As a result, the Stoics fail to benefit from the goods, the *voluptas*, which nature offers. Against the Stoic limiting point of view, Valla counters first with Vegio's Epicurean one. This too, however, he soon shows to be restrictive because it is limited to the world of the senses. In the end, it is Antonio's Christian understanding of virtue and his explanation of the ways in which faith, hope, and charity function that lay bare the most persuasive argument for the harmony of body and soul. By looking at nature and its manifestations with Franciscan kindness, the Christian Raudense defines virtue as "a step toward that perfect happiness which the spirit or soul, freed from its mortal portion will enjoy with the Father of all things."[26]

Thus, through Antonio, Valla turns his attention to the Epicurean notion of *voluptas*. Here, with studied elegance that is always seasoned with humility, the Franciscan refutes the principles that Vegio espouses. By demonstrating that the instinctive human desire for pleasure does not deviate from Christian moral principles, Antonio disproves his interlocutor's claims. At the same time, he reconciles the classical ethical system with the Christian one. Over and against his two interlocutors' materialistic stances, Antonio argues that the happiness humanity seeks, the *summum bonum*, is brought to fruition in the *caelestial voluptas* (heavenly pleasures), not in the fulfillment of earthly pleasures. For him, the benefits that faith, hope, and charity engender lead to the highest good. This is not earthly, but celestial, not transient, but eternal. In light of this, albeit in a less contemptuous tone, Antonio demonstrates that Vegio's understanding of *voluptas* is misleading because it steers toward a good that is entirely focused on and therefore yoked by the earthly materiality. By arguing that the word "pleasure" (*voluptas*) was originally used also to translate "delight" (*delectatio*),[27] Antonio concludes that pleasure is desired by "those who wish to experience joy" as did those who witnessed, and grasped, the mysteries of the Christian faith. For these individuals, Antonio reasons, hope—not the deceitful virtue of the philosophers—makes it possible to believe that the joys and pleasures that nature provides are precursors of otherworldly ones.[28]

Antonio further stresses this point by arguing that humanity's objective is to take pleasure in and benefit from nature's providential and generous physical essence. Nature, he emphasizes, was created so that humanity would take pleasure from it.[29] No longer split between body and spirit, and stripped of its Epicurean nuance,[30] the notion of pleasure, as Antonio describes it, is thus enriched with a strong Christian flavor. Antonio (and Valla) recognizes that among other necessities, humanity does have a concrete need for both pleasure and happiness. What he argues against, though, is that they are circumscribed by earthly experiences. These, in spite of their allure, are deceptive and fleeting. For him (and for Valla), faith and hope are the virtues that overcome the barrier the mind cannot rise above to envision otherworldly pleasures and joys. To emphasize this point, the Christian Raudense turns to Saint Paul's words.[31] In this manner, Valla shows that the Stoic idea of virtue and the Epicurean notion of pleasure come to full fruition only through the Christian theological virtues. From this Christian perspective, choosing to act with faith and hoping that joys will be savored in the future renew the essential contradiction between mind and body. Yet at the same time, Antonio makes it clear that the pleasure engendered by acts of faith and hope is the precursor of celestial ones and these represent the highest good humanity must aspire to achieve.[32] Pleasure, in his construction, derives from a Christian behavior and in it, it finds fulfillment.

Valla's *On Pleasure* in its study of human happiness, carried out with an even-tempered tone while the whole Stoic and Epicurean philosophical traditions are crushed, is not preoccupied with recipes. Charting a steady course to point out the flaws peculiar to the Stoic's logical argument in particular, the humanist leaves little room for food. When he does discuss it, it is part of Vegio's defense of the senses in the first book. Later, in the last book, Antonio picks up the subject. This time, it is to counter Vegio's view on the central role the senses play with respect to worldly pleasures. Predictably, Antonio's reply to Vegio shifts the focus from earthly to divine food. Yet the importance of the sense of taste, and the pleasures it produces, is not lost in the transition from human to heavenly food. On the contrary, the Franciscan emphasizes that taste is an exceptional mode of enjoying celestial fulfillment.[33] This fact is important for two reasons. First, it is a clear evidence of the manner in which Valla absorbs within the Christian tradition the Epicurean idea of pleasure elicited by the senses. Second, it places food, be it of a divine or earthly nature, yet again at the center of the philosophical and theological discourses that shape the Renaissance. On this last account, Valla's treatise is not different from Platina's *On Right Pleasure and Good Health*. In point of fact, both works argue for lives that do not stray from an ethical and moral code of conduct. More importantly, both treatises make a case for not lapsing into the narrowness of gratifying pleasures that power and occasions afford. Of the two works, however, Platina's, more than Valla's, traces a densely detailed portrait of the political and social landscape in which it was written. Thus with food as a thread that is a twist of several strands, Platina, unlike Valla, explores the complexity of human nature, extricating it from the ideals, delusions, illusions, corruptions, and hatreds that it creates for itself.

In book 10, titled "On Tidbits which We May Call Fritters," Platina discusses frog meat. From the outset he states that this is a delicious morsel. For this reason, he goes on to suggest that to ensure that the meat retains its flavorful taste, the animal must be "caught by a net." He also maintains that the frogs' skinned legs ought to be "soaked a night or a day." As he spells out the method for preserving that flesh's tastiness, Platina explains that frogs trapped by net are more flavorsome than those caught by trident. According to him, the manner in which the animal is captured affects the taste of its cooked meat. When it comes to food, sophisticated consumers prize quality, and this they measure according to the flavor it delivers. In subtle but substantial manners the analogy of frogs that Orlando voices in the palace, as a way to describe his own capture, brings to mind Platina's frogs for many reasons. First, like frogs caught to be consumed, the knight is entangled in a net set up specifically to get him. Second, like the type of capture Platina's frogs must undergo to provide tastier meat, the knight's does not entail physical pain. But it does inflict emotional anguish. The result of this ostensibly peculiar analogy is that just as the capture by net makes the taste of Platina's frog meat palatable and pleasing to the discriminating consumer, Orlando's captor can relish the hero's distress and humiliation caused by his entrapment. In point of fact, the emotional intensity of this scene increases as the knight pointlessly searches for and grapples with an as yet mysterious enemy, gradually watching himself succumb to it. For him, remaining in the enemy's net like a frog amplifies his inner turmoil.

The introduction to Platina's book 9 further enriches the complexity of Orlando's entrapment, filtered, as it is, through Pulci's own experience. As he discusses the dietetic value of tidbits to savor, Platina emphasizes the necessity of giving each one of them a name that possesses a proper Latin derivation. This detail is of the greatest importance because it shifts the discourse from the concern with food, cooking techniques, diets, and overindulgence and self-control at the table to philological accuracy. Philology, the discipline that underpins the humanistic belief in linguistic precision, aims at retracing and recovering the exact significance of words. Humanists believed that this retrieval would restore the authentic meanings with which early authors charged their writings. Accordingly, in making the case that the atypical and meaningless size of a tidbit is no reason for denying it a name from a Latin root, in an intriguing manner Platina retrieves the central argument of Lorenzo Valla's *Elegantie lingue latine*. This treatise focuses on the dignity of grammar. And just like Valla, Platina imbues his discourse with political and philosophical meanings. From a purely practical standpoint, Valla argues that by reading the best authors from classical antiquity, returning, as it were, to the original purity of the language, it is possible to extract the rules of good speaking. One striking implication this affirmation leads to is that for him grammar underpins rhetoric. Another equally important one is that the discourse on the relevance of grammar turns into one of aesthetic value.

Beyond this, the groundbreaking innovation of Valla's treatise (a work that is not a grammar manual as those known to the Middle Ages)[34] is that it calls for a reevaluation of medieval translations and commentaries. Valla's compelling point is twofold. Medieval Latin was corrupted by the linguistic interferences caused by barbaric invasions.[35] Because of it, unqualified translators and commentators, lacking rigorous linguistic accuracy, either obscured or altered the original meanings of documents.[36] The systematic adulteration of original sources led to the rise and perpetuation of irrational beliefs, illusions, failures, and shortfalls in subsequent generations of scholars. Worse yet, the loss of the true meanings, Valla claims, led to a tainted understanding of reality. For him, only the precise knowledge of Latin (and Greek) makes it possible to retrieve the original theological, philosophical, and juridical significances of old treatises. In shedding light on the past to illuminate the present, Valla's methodological approach is highly critical of those of his predecessors'. Nor is it sympathetic to his contemporaries'. Still, Latin stretched to all branches of knowledge. Indeed, applied to the political sphere, the power and prestige of Latin, according to Valla, turns into the weapon that brought territorial vastness and cultural renown to Rome. This theory would seem at odds with the military might that the Roman Empire achieved. And yet, as he sets out to account for his thesis, Valla steers clear of emotional ideas, tightly clinging, instead, to proving how the use of Latin and its legacy (and the culture from which it was spawned) came to dominate the world long after the empire had fallen.

In the introduction to book 1 of the *Elegantie*, the humanist affirms that the Roman Empire did not achieve its greatness through cruel and bloody wars. Instead, he claims, it resulted from the acts of kindness, love, and harmony its language provided.[37] The significance of this argument rests, among other things, on the fact that language is construed as a dynamic form of political maneuverings.[38] The departure from the safety of conventional wisdom, which dictates that the empire thrived because of its military puissance, alters the perceptions of how the Roman conquests and political triumphs were carried out. Tellingly, as he makes the case for harnessing history through language,[39] establishing the latter as a formidable manipulative tool of the political universe, Valla refers to Latin as the *Romane loqui* (Roman language).[40] This choice of words, together with the revisionist approach he takes, did not escape the criticism of his contemporaries.[41] But in spite of the polemics he raised, by designating Latin as the language of Rome and lending it the attributes of a powerful social and historical force, the humanist challenges the basic precepts of his times. In his understanding, Rome, cradle of Latin, is where through *usus* and *consuetudo* the language was honed.[42] From there, it trickled into foreign countries, where it was assimilated, becoming the parlance of choice that survived the empire's military demise. Latin, the point of convergence between politics and cultures, in Valla's view, affected and served the empire's ambitions. By cementing its philosophy, theology, and laws into the foundations of foreign cultures, it ensured that the Roman ethos survived even the loss of military power. Valla underscores this point anew by stating that the fame Latin acquired made it, in a sense, queen of idioms. As a proof of this he mentions that Latin was used not only throughout all of Italy, but throughout most of the Western world and large parts of Northern Africa.

The political analogy Valla uses—queen of languages—fuses two seemingly disparate discourses. In his parallelism, linguistic dominance becomes synonymous with, and in fact supersedes, political hegemony. Like a monarch establishing the laws and ruling over its subjects, grammar gives structure to language, setting its rules, giving order to, and establishing a place for, every component of a sentence. Beyond this, by linguistically binding different cultures into a coherent whole rather than causing deeper fractures among them, Latin turns into the currency of manipulation. It changes sociocultural attitudes because language connects the inner world with the outer one. By doing so, it also explores the connections between the two, placating the fraught relationship that may initially exist between them. Ultimately, as Valla describes it, the influence exerted by Latin turns into a collective renovation rather than oppression, and this leads to sharing sensibilities. As Alibech's novella evidenced in the previous chapter, the first step toward the thorough colonization of nations calls for swaying its peoples' minds. This strategy reduces the colonized into harmless, even willing subjects. Accordingly, they no longer feel locked in by obligation and duty. Instead, they are lured by the desire and commitment to understand the new model. Thus, they eagerly adopt the rules that the new language (and its speakers) enforces. As language and history converge, Valla's discourse reveals, the idea that philology can solve the riddles of long unacknowledged truths is a reminder that seeking answers to complex historical events requires careful study of the role that every element plays in the wider context of which it is part. This, as one would expect, implies that seemingly marginal factors must neither be excluded nor neglected because of their ostensible insignificance.

Clearly, Platina retraces Valla's discourse as he argues for the importance of assigning a proper Latin name to every morsel. His insistence on an exact nomenclature to establish philological accuracy for tidbits and frog meat is an artful arrangement of relationships that at first may seem peculiar. But hidden in plain sight of his search for linguistic precision lie the dark undercurrents and moral ambiguity of a political power play. Because his work and livelihood depend on the Roman curia, Platina is mostly concerned with the model this court sets and the power it exerts. In this respect, Platina's situation brings to mind Pietro Aretino's, an author whose work will be analyzed in chapter 5. Still, Platina grasps that the curia's central paradox stems from the presumption that its members can behave like those of secular courts. He also understands that persistently cultivating extravagant lifestyles leads to abrupt implosions. This fact is of particular cogency for the system designed to be the paradigm of ethical and moral conduct. For all these reasons, Platina's claim turns into a recipe for finding the right balance between theory and practice and between history and individuals, especially between those of means and those lacking them. In his view, substituting a model based on orderliness and implementing more sensible practices in the court's lifestyle would ensure that its princes not fall into ethical and moral lapses that turn them into secular predators.

The idea of naming, of course, implies taking possession of and retaining power over the objects named. In addition to establishing a hierarchical relationship, between object and name-giver, designating anything by name suggests orderliness between the newly named object and those surrounding it. Naturally, naming creates stability. As Adam's story illustrates, humanity is charged with the responsibility of naming and organizing, and through these activities, of mastering the world it inhabits. The resulting order is an ethical, legal, moral, social, and economic construct. In it relationships are fixed, and everything—foods, objects, and creatures, including those held in low esteem because of their small size—is part of the established and impartial system. Conversely, to be improperly named is the equivalent of being nameless. This, in turn, means to be excluded from any existing order, be it gastronomic, social, or political. In and of itself, this exclusion implies not only being dispossessed of any power, but also of selfhood. In short, namelessness means powerlessness, and powerlessness means not being part of the historical world. Plainly couched under Platina's discussion about frog meat fritters is the more striking discourse on the insidious ways in which power marginalizes powerlessness. This ingenious device becomes all the more compelling when we see that it draws from autobiographical elements.

Platina's personal experience in Rome, marked by his scathing critique of Pope Paul II that netted him two imprisonments and various forms of physical torture, made it clear to him that however gifted a scholar he might be, he remained a powerless man. Or, more accurately, he became a figure resigned and in need of the stability that only princely patronage ensured. The name he had coined for himself from the Latin derivation of his birthplace held no traction in a universe shaped and ruled by powerful personages. Thus, between frogs and fritters Platina suggests that the Roman court has no taste for erudition. Against the moral and ethical precepts of the Christian code of conduct, its courtiers crave the riches that wealth provides and corruption breeds. From the picture Platina draws of this court, the Rome of Paul II emerges as corrupt as the Florence of Lorenzo de' Medici. To deal with either one of these courts as a powerless individual requires audacity and cunning; these skills, however, do not necessarily guarantee success within them. Writing treatises on food and good health, or epic romances, turns then into an effective strategy to expose the courts' inner machinations. This tactic is all the more fitting when the individuals penning the critiques are small, "unnamed" tidbits like Platina and Pulci. Both of them, in fact, seem caught, like Orlando, in the net of greed their patrons cast.

Back in the palace, despite his suspicion with regard to "le mense riccamente son parate" (many a table richly set they viewed) (2.19), and stewing distrust of "tutte le vivande accomodate" (spread upon them, every kind of food) (2.19), Orlando and Morgante feast on a banquet that mirrors the intricate grandiosity of courtly gastronomic politics. As they savor the meal the apprehension troubling the knight is momentarily contained. Although he is portrayed as an ill at ease visitor in the exclusive space filled with expensive objects that enhance its wondrous beauty, Orlando takes pleasure in the dishes. Relishing them exemplifies the volatile relationship between the present and the past. The food he eats with Morgante in the palace-prison is a reminder of a courtly lifestyle and of its principles. But contrary to those meals, this one appears laced with inverted values. While court meals convey a (false) sense of freedom and power, this one is imbued with a deep sense of physical, as well as emotional, constraints and powerlessness. Also, the court is a system that pressures individuals into the convention of its well-displayed trappings. But in the palace, although the allure of the familiar is potent, Orlando is neither dreamy about nor enthralled by it. On the contrary, he is keenly aware that the embellishments are there to ensnare him.

In spite of this, the list of specific foodstuffs available to be consumed reads like a typical menu of a Renaissance banquet: "quivi vivande è di molte ragioni" (and there were countless appetizing plates) (2.24). The initial oversimplification suggests the beginning of a gastronomic seduction. Generally, within the court culture, elaborate banquets aim at reconciling conflicting interests and ambivalent values the courtiers embody with the powerful logic of the unremittingly idealistic responsibilities of knighthood. As events staged to excite and captivate the imagination of the partakers, sumptuous meals sustain the host's power. At the same time, because of the refined and exotic dishes they include, banquets are also intended to captivate the partakers' imagination. Through this, they turn into one of the more potent symbols of trumped justice, of hubris unleashed, and of upended values. "Pavoni e starne e leprette e fagiani, cervi e conigli e di grassi capponi" (Peacock and partridge, hare and pheasant, deer and rabbit and fat capon) (2.24.3–4) are some of the dishes Orlando and Morgante feast on that night. In terms of Renaissance gastronomic consciousness these are fixed delicacies. The richness of the foodstuffs prepared mirrors the knight's valor and reinforces his (and the court's) sense of social entitlement. Paradoxically, however, the ossified courtly society that at this juncture Orlando questions, by relying on these power-enhancing banquets is neither able to see its own flaws nor capable of providing reasons to believe in a future shaped and uncompromised by self-interests.

To mark the pervasiveness of the court's selfishness, Platina devotes the central chapter of his treatise, book 5, to the discussion of birds and their meats. But before he addresses the subject, in a brief introduction he explains that birds' flesh is foodstuff reserved for distinguished people. With palpable irony he explains that this elite consists of "those raised by look alone, from the depths, namely from cook shops, brothels, and cheap eateries, not only to riches, which would have to be tolerated, but even to the highest ranks of dignity."[43] The rawness of this sweeping attack makes it clear that for Platina discussing a foodstuff and dispensing information on how to prepare it, as he purports at the beginning of the treatise, is not to be taken at face value. Rather, it is part of a rhetorical and implacable denunciation of the curia's moral failing. Its courtiers hide behind the exquisiteness and beautiful presentations of gastronomic delicacies that wealth affords; but this stance pitches moral choices and ethical principles against the self-aggrandizing narcissism of its members. They have ascended to the highest ranks of their positions through political plots and intrigues. For Platina, who tests his ideas against the depth of his experience, the court is the locus of self-referential imitation and not of spiritual, ethical, civic, or moral accountability. Within it entertainment is politics and politics entertainment; love breeds hate and attraction repulsion. In short, the whole system is set up according to a game of power that cannot be reconciled with Christian values. Because of this, the court exemplifies the contradictions of the historical moment. Like a secular court, it clings to the belief that it can function in a self-sufficient manner; it is distrustful of outsiders and incapable of incorporating the perspectives of outsiders; thus, it is suspicious of their ideas. To draw a clearer link between the court's debauchery and its gastronomic preferences, Platina correlates the characteristics of specific bird meats to those who consume them. For him, peacock meat stands out among that of other fowls.

The rich animal lore that starting from Pliny reached the *Physiologus* tradition and worked its way well beyond the twelfth century sets forth an image of the peacock as a bird highly admired for the beauty of its feathers and elegant gait.[44] In medieval bestiaries, where animals' physical attributes are interpreted as manifestations of behavior, the peacock's aesthetic appeal is thought to coincide with ethical conduct. The most obvious lesson that is gleaned from the peacock's description is that it is a proud and ostentatious creature. As one would expect, commentators seized on the bird's traits, turning them into the image of spiritual and moral failing. In addition to this well-established tradition, another one gained a strong foothold. This tradition deemed the bird's flesh impervious to decay. In *The City of God*,[45] Saint Augustine draws an analogy between the peacock's incorruptible flesh and the spiritual soul. To counter those who do not believe that it can suffer the eternal torments of Hell without perishing, the philosopher offers, among those of other animals, the example of the peacock. Its flesh, according to him, does not putrefy. With this assertion Augustine lends a twist to the tradition, imbuing it with Christian principles.

Considering how attracted and attached to traditions and symbols Renaissance culture is, it comes as no surprise that the latter played a large role in turning peacock flesh into a favorite presence on distinguished tables. The qualities that the animal exemplified reflect the enduring self-absorption of those consuming its meat. Beauty, elegance, and haughtiness, along with magnificence, poise, and aplomb, are traits the elite not only identifies with, but also wants to be recognized for. Augustine's discussion on the peacock's imperishable flesh in part adds to the metaphorical significance of consuming it. Indeed, in a frivolous way the authority of his words shortens the distance between the spiritual and the material. It also impresses upon guests the host's power and prestige. More specifically, if banqueting is a closely choreographed performance, consuming meat held to be of an everlasting nature by a saint speaks to the host's enduring power. In a more radical sense, eating what does not perish dramatizes the host's invincible force. The political implications of this analogy could not be lost on Renaissance commensals. They translate the powerfulness exemplified at the table into the strength of the battlefield. Accordingly, it comes as no surprise that Orlando and Morgante dine on peacock meat.

Interestingly, Platina believes that this type of meat provides modest nutrition to those who eat it. This fact, he explains, is the result of the animal's traits. A "vainglorious" and "malevolent" bird, as he puts it, the peacock exemplifies the same values those consuming it embrace. The exotic vividness of the bird's plumage dazzles those feasting on its meat. Roasted whole and then covered with the entire plumage often coated in gold and silver leaves, the peacock thus reassembled is introduced to the banquet scene as a triumphant image of the host's sophistication.⁴⁶ The visual spectacle the prepared bird offers mirrors the exquisiteness of the partakers' magnificence. Yet the artifact that boosts the partakers' ego reveals the full extent of both their shallowness and their greed. Imitation becomes, for this reason, not a mockery of the imaginary but the cruel representation of the real. Starlings, the meat that Orlando and his friend also consume, for Platina also represent a poor meat choice. Like blackbirds and thrushes, he claims, they provide scarce nourishment. Worse yet, according to him, they increase black bile, which in turn, causes melancholy.

The concern with managing this ailment is of great importance for the Renaissance. Preventing its debilitating effects—especially on intellectuals—lies at the heart of Renaissance medical practice. In his *Three Books on Life* (*De vita libri tres*)⁴⁷ Marsilio Ficino considers black bile, or melancholy, as the madness that engenders genius: "the soul with an instrument or incitement of this kind (black bile), always seeks the center of all subjects and penetrates to their innermost core . . . (the soul), hereby called away from external movements and from its own body, is made in the highest degree both a neighbor to the divine and an instrument of the divine" (1.6). According to the philosopher, this form of melancholy is a "natural" one (1.5.28–29). In his view, black bile/melancholy "continually incites the soul both to collect itself together into one and to dwell on itself and to contemplate itself. And being analogous to the world's center, it forces the investigation to the center of individual subjects" (1.4). For Ficino melancholy is the means facilitating the investigation of the self in relation to the universe as well as to other objects with which it shares a place in it. Yet at the same time, Ficino also discusses black bile as a result of humors drying up. This, for him, is the "noxious form of melancholy" and the "most dangerous thing" that afflicts learned men because it renders them "stolid and stupid" (2.5.26). To illustrate the dangerous effects produced by this type of melancholy, the philosopher describes it as the monster that must be kept at bay because it dissipates one's energies in fruitless undertakings. His medical advice and medicinal recipes, based on Galen's theory of the four bodily humors (hot, cold, moist, and dry) aim at preventing melancholy, or, at least, at keeping it in check. Although he is as punctilious as, if not more than, Platina about choosing the suited types of meats in maintaining good health, Ficino's specific aim is to instruct the intellectual men of his city.[48]

The figure of Ficino looms very large in Medici Florence. By 1463 his works as philosopher, theologian, and translator of Greek at Cosimo de' Medici's court had earned him the financial security no other humanist of the time had enjoyed. Through his lectures, commentaries, letters, and treatises he introduced his Florentine audience to Plato's philosophy, which he infused with Christian theology. The discrepancy, however, existing between his earlier and later works gives pause. To be sure, on the one hand, Ficino takes a theologically minded position in his *Platonic Theology*. This earlier treatise comes through as a systematic reflection on light's gradation and qualities. As the metaphor for God, the sun and the light it produces provide the foundation for Ficino's claim that the soul in its desire to attain truth through the intellect is a movement toward God.[49] The soul's natural aspiration toward Him, according to Ficino, mirrors light's qualities. Interpreting the writings of Plato, as well as those of his commentator Plotinus, and fusing philosophy with theology, Ficino's *Platonic Theology* traces the stream of Christian doctrine to the Greek philosophers. His later *De vita libri tres*, on the other hand, is, among other things, a treatise on diets and astrology. These branches of knowledge, he claims, are ways of controlling human destiny and health. Ficino's fascination with, and exploration of, the notion that omens, astrology, and heavenly constellations influence intellectual men[50] is rooted in the complex discourse of astral determination that the Middle Ages transmitted to the Renaissance.[51] His interpretation, however, turns human history into a pawn of astral effects. His claim that a dietetic regimen can attenuate astral influence, that therapeutic diets counteract[52] the Saturnine influence at the root of melancholy, and that, by implication, they reconcile and solve the complexities of history, is not only startling, but irrational.

The ambivalence of Ficino's two treatises, characterized as they are by such divergent philosophical implications, lends a precarious credibility to his theological and philosophical soundness. Conversely, Pulci's controversial stance on religious matters, first voiced in his sonnets and then made more strident throughout his *Morgante*, may well explain the tension and antipathy between the two men. The poet, who had been Lorenzo's friend,[53] did not regard Ficino's professional ascent from translator of Greek philosophical treatises under Cosimo de' Medici's patronage[54] to the position of self-appointed new "Socrates"[55] and Lorenzo's moral adviser with much esteem. For this reason, throughout the *Morgante* Pulci ridicules Ficino's philosophical insights.

With regard to birds' flesh Ficino tends to be more general than Platina. True to his goals, he recommends only the types that keep black bile in check. He discourages the consumption of those meats that cause its development.[56] Peacock flesh, like that of capon and pheasant, he recommends because he considers it a "moderate sort" of meat that does not produce melancholy.[57] Deer meat he values only for the longevity it produces.[58] The similarity between Ficino's and Platina's gastronomic recommendations suggests a common source that can be easily traced to Pliny. The remarkable element that differentiates them, however, is the social portrait that emerges from these works. Unlike Platina, Ficino is never concerned about, nor does he ever draw a parallel between, his readers' predilection for culinary delicacies and the moral and ethical principles governing their lives. In other words, Ficino's study never turns into a reflection on the excesses of the court or on its guiding principles. When he does speak about the "quick corruption and putrefaction" (2.6) that certain foodstuffs cause to the human body, he keeps to the literal meaning of his assertions. The therapeutic value of his regimen is gauged by its success in cleansing the human body. The link between this and the corruption that afflicts the political body he never explores.

Ficino makes the case for the healthful values of peacock meat in the same chapter where he discusses the damaging effects of other foods (6.2). That he lists early gray hair, pallor, and wrinkles of old age, among them, suggests his concern with physical appearances. Because of this, he reveals himself as a true member of the court that discourages its members from questioning any aspect of its culture. This fact evidences Ficino's belief in the uncompromised truths and uncomplicated moral climate reigning over Lorenzo's Florence. Comparing his discussion on peacock meat to Platina's treatment of the same topic, it becomes evident that Ficino frames his argument within the safe confines of the privileged position he occupies. This is why he has no reason to critique the Medici court or to be concerned with its inconsistencies. Platina's discussion, on the contrary, sizzles with notions of greed and decadence festering within the Roman court. Indeed, it makes a point of poking holes through the worthiness of the principles on which that court stands. Buried deep inside Platina's accusations that are voiced through the curial gastronomy are the concerns of a complex man. Through them, he hopes to expose the inversion of normative values and the sullied narrowness of the court's culture in order to cause some changes. Although he is aware that this path is excessively overgrown with ambivalence and fossilized mindsets that can backfire on him, Platina perseveres in his charges because, in his capacity of mere literary scholar for the curia, he is financially teetering on its edge. He is driven by the need for fair rules to regulate the lives of those who, like him, have no assured security within the courts but whose livelihood depends on them.

Unlike Platina (or Pulci), Ficino has succeeded in reaching the highest pinnacle of fame. As an influential member of the Medici court, he reaps the benefits of power as well as of financial stability this position provides. For him the court's conspicuous and exotic gastronomic preferences can only be a legitimate identity definer. That the court aggressively promotes its self-interested standards of normalcy and justice does not trouble him because his philosophical theories have helped to lay the foundations for that court's way of operating. This perch informs his writings and his interest in dietetic regimens mirrors this position. The questions Platina, and Pulci, raise about the disjunction between individuals and systems, self-interest and selflessness, do not trouble Ficino. Where the elite comes into play, he has no personal reason to dissect their skewed layers of perceptions because he is part of it. These two divergent attitudes emerge in the image of Orlando trapped in the mysterious palace while yet feasting on exquisite fare. Like Pulci and Platina, not Ficino, the knight is suspended between two different worlds. The world of illusion and pleasures that he recognizes and that lures him in maps out a path that diverts him from his initial goal. The world of disturbing reality, plagued by self-doubt and frustrations that he begins to discern and that, by pulling him away from pleasures and self-enshrinement, redirects his attention to his duties. The pull and tug of attraction and repulsion and of his self-canceling wants are reflected in Orlando's attitude. Through the figure of the hero who begins to resist the beautiful veneer of material pleasures and shows the intent to break away from it, Pulci uncovers the tension that exists between these two worlds. In so doing, he emphasizes the practiced cunning of the court that behind a façade of respectability wallows in depravity. The delicacies Orlando consumes in that palace convey the anguish of the strong-willed knight lured by the desire to partake of them and yet disheartened by the morally ambiguous implications they entail. Thus frog fritters and peacock meat are Pulci's way of voicing his exquisitely refined rage against the cruel and arbitrary power Lorenzo's court and its courtiers have unleashed against him.

I

As events develop in the *Morgante* images of people and giants consuming food and feasting become a reference for desire and possibility. These elements play a large role in canto 16, where the encounter between the sultan's daughter Antea and the French knight Rinaldo takes place. In this canto Antea arrives at the French encampment with an ultimatum and a request. With regard to the ultimatum, she explains that the French must return to her family the city and lands they have seized and now occupy. Failure to comply will result in war. As for the request, she asks to duel Rinaldo. Her plan is to avenge the killing of Marcovaldo, the ambassador her father had sent to the French camp and who was killed by Rinaldo. As she voices both demands Antea displays a range of emotions. These are elicited by her encounter with Rinaldo who in this canto embodies the threatening realities of the visceral conflict between French and pagan factions. Her arrival at the French site dazzles the knight even though the objective of her visit is made crystal-clear by her forthright demand:

> Se voi volete lasciar la citade
> Sanza quistion, contento è il padre mio, . . .
> Se questo non farete, sia con Dio!

> Noi proverrén se taglian nostre spade,
> E così da parte sua vi dico io,
> E vengo a protestarvi nuova guerra,
> Se non ci date libera la terra.
> (16.10)

("My father will be pleased if you agree / to leave the city peacefully at once /. . . / If you do not comply, let God decide. / We'll prove to you how sharp our swords can be, / and so I tell you in my father's name, / to give this city to us once more, else I have come and have declared new war.").

Antea's request to have her father's territory returned to him offers her a vicarious hope for the reestablishment of the political stability the French have disrupted. More than this though, her unyielding demand blurs the line between occupier and occupied as it threatens to undo the injustice the French have inflicted on her family by waging a war. The attempt to solve a conflict with a conflict offers only slight comfort; it is a shallow refuge from the unavoidable fact that war is always a destructive process. It is also painfully ineffective at reestablishing the desired order because its outcomes are never ethically uncomplicated.

In contrast to the war threat she delivers, Antea's request to duel at once with Rinaldo reveals the moral beauty of her courage. It also shows her powerful appetite for what she considers just and honorable. Fearless and alone among the French enemy, she lacks neither the self-confidence nor the inclination to effect justice for the death of her father's representative. Her challenge to Rinaldo, that if she dies the French can keep her father's territory but if he dies they must withdraw immediately, underscores to a greater degree her bold self-assertiveness, a quality she does not mask with feminine mannerisms. Her reparative demands are not unreasonable. Yet, at the same time, they disclose her ingenuous belief that the world she inhabits is split along clearly defined cultural lines: the French occupy one side of it, she and her people the opposite one. The antagonism that flavors her language provides a distinct measure of her willingness to sacrifice all, including her life, rather than remaining subjugated by the French. Her political vision is shaped by her cultural values. These prevent her from seeing in a more expansive light the "other" and, quite naturally, also remove the possibility of finding a common ground with the enemy. By taking refuge in what she perceives to be the certainties her culture provides, Antea feels protected and, most importantly, is emboldened to pursue her ambitious vengeance.

In contrast to Antea's firm requests, Rinaldo's reply, although persuasive, hides an extraordinary tension. He speaks as an overpowered enemy and an already conquered lover. He submissively accepts the duel without flinching. But in so doing, he laces his words with a sexually suggestive ambivalence: "non ci è più giusta cosa che la spada / a solver nostra lite; e così vada" ("the sword alone is the best referee / to solve our problem—and it so shall be") (16.18.7–8). By acknowledging that the sword is the only just course to settle their enmity, Rinaldo ostensibly concurs with Antea. But his acquiescence conceals his true intentions, and this comes to light in his erotically charged language. Contrary to the literal meaning of his reply, the sword he anticipates using against her is one that will satiate his sexual desire. The conditions he puts to her request lay the foundations for his plan. Rinaldo entreats her to postpone the duel for three days:

> Ma una grazia prima ti domando,
> Che con la spada al campo ci troviamo;
> / . . . /
> E'l terzo dì, sopra il mio buon destriere
> Verrò in sul campo armato a tuo piacere.
> (16.19.1–2, 7–8)

("But there's one favor I would ask of you / before we, armed with swords, do to the field / . . . / astride my horse I'll come, on the third day, / just as you wish and say.")

Rinaldo clings to the idea that temporizing and delaying the actual conflict will give him time to resolve the lustful impasse he has reached. This thought, not the intractable political ultimatum Antea has made, preoccupies him. So, to exploit the unique possibility that Antea's presence in his camp offers him, he asks her to spend the day as his guest: "che insieme questo giorno dimoriamo" ("that we spend the day together")

(16.19.4). By asking her to share a meal prepared in her honor, Rinaldo gives voice to his irrepressible desire. In his understanding, the meal foreshadows his possessing her.

Rinaldo's emotional manipulation of Antea makes the banquet he organizes for her (which has more of the philosophical implications of Plato's *Symposium* and Dante's *Convivio*) titillating even before it begins.[59] Pulci depicts Antea and Rinaldo as physically attracted to each other:

> E cominciorno insieme a riguardarsi
> Ognun, più che l'usato, intento e fiso;
> Rinaldo non potea di lei saziarsi . . .
>   (16.21.1–3)

> (fixedly more than ever, so they kept / gazing and gazing at each other then. / Gazing upon her avidly, Rinaldo . . .)

Pulci characterizes the knight's attraction to the woman as an insatiable appetite. Through this, he connects with one stroke the pleasures of the table to the pleasures of the body, of the eater and of the eaten. Yet by framing the metaphor of food within the warfare context, yet again Pulci explicitly extends it to the realm of politics. Rinaldo's craving for taking possession of what does not belong to him draws attention to the audacity of human desire that emboldens individuals. At the same time, it also emphasizes the fact that no political boundaries can contain its gluttony. In more practical terms, Rinaldo's appetite for Antea's body calls to mind Lorenzo de' Medici's hunger to control and maneuver every aspect of the Florentine social and political body.[60] This element, along with Lorenzo's idealized pursuit of a contemplative life inspired by Ficino's works, is recognizable in Rinaldo's newborn desire—both the synthesis and the antithesis of his patron.

There is no mistaking Antea's reaction to Rinaldo's invitation. Although her graceful reply shows the self-possession that Rinaldo lacks, it appears evident that she feels increasingly besotted with him: "e la fanciulla cominciò a pensarsi / che così bel già mai fussi Narciso" (and the young lady suddenly was sure / even Narcissus's face was not so fair)

(16.21.5–6). The comparison she draws between Narcissus and the knight facing her is peculiar, for it lays stress, first of all, on her awareness of the latter's physical attractiveness. At the same time, however, it implicitly points to the knight's moral flaws. Indeed, by describing Rinaldo as a man more handsome than the mythical Narcissus, she suggests that he is more self-absorbed than the mythical youth. Through this, Antea unwittingly foregrounds Rinaldo's self-centered nature. This becomes more evident as the knight turns his back to his obligations and duties while simmering in his desire without regret or shame. Of course, Narcissus's death, resulting from the unappeasable attraction he felt toward his mere reflection, reveals his inaccurate understanding of reality. For his part, Rinaldo displays a similarly erroneous grasp of facts. His desire drives his action at the expense of responsibilities. But as he brushes aside the conflict dividing the two factions, closes his eyes to his responsibility toward his fellow-knights, and becomes prejudiced toward Antea's purpose and lacks concern for it, his sheer self-centeredness surfaces. By comparing him to Narcissus, Antea foreshadows Rinaldo's inability to distinguish objectively between reality and appearance. More specifically, Rinaldo is incapable of differentiating between the nature of the message—relinquishing to the rightful lord the lands that the French have taken—and the messenger—the beautiful woman. By ignoring the difference between these two parts, and in effect transgressing the limits that delineate personal gains and public responsibility, Rinaldo displays selfish haughtiness as well as a lack of moral temperance. These traits too evoke the figure of Lorenzo and of his mode of governing.

While the banquet becomes the immediate manifestation of Rinaldo's moral excess it also serves as his first—and ironically last—confrontation with Antea, as he will be emotionally unable to duel with her three days later. By inviting to his table Antea, who is a stranger and the daughter of a defeated enemy, Rinaldo counters her desire for a duel with his own culinary challenge. In so doing, he does not follow a codified form of chivalrous behavior. Substituting a banquet for a duel fundamentally moves the contest between the two—and its implicit antagonism—not only from the public to the private arena but also from the dispassionate to the erotic. Fusing food with conflict, Rinaldo effectively disempowers Antea because accepting a meal presupposes the reciprocity of giving. As the initiator of the invitation he becomes the dominant host, imposing his will on the obliging if hesitant guest.[61] By so doing, Rinaldo no longer needs to negotiate the hierarchical and cultural boundaries separating him and Antea. She recognizes this— "Ciò ch'a te piace a me conviene che piaccia" ("I much am pleased by what so pleases you") (16.20.2)—and reluctantly accepts his invitation. Indeed, the way in which she expresses her acceptance suggests that she will yield to his request because it is a necessary step toward achieving her goal. At the same time, she clearly understands that from Rinaldo's standpoint the banquet is an object of sheer pleasure: his, to be exact. By agreeing to be his guest, she condones his disregard for the other knights and resigns herself to the hierarchical dissymmetry imposed by the invitation. This last element especially provides Rinaldo with an opportunity to prove his ability to manipulate reality to his own advantage.

The knight's narcissistic opportunism and lack of judgment are reflected in the elaborate foods prepared for the guest:

> Furno al convito le vivande tutte
> Che si potevon dare in quel paese,
> Con prezïosi vin, confetti e frutte.
> (16.24.1–3)

(they served the best and most delicious food / that ever in that region could be found, with precious wines and sweets and varied fruit.)

The sophisticated culture of courtly banqueting, more than the knight's personal magnetism, is the crucial ingredient in this scene. Yet Pulci does not provide an accurate menu of the prepared dishes as he does in canto 2. In spite of this, here he does introduce *confetti* as part of the meal. Without a doubt, this new fare is a product of the particular time and culture. But brought to the table at this juncture, it becomes the gastronomic dramatization of Rinaldo's circumstances. The immediate subtext of the banquet is revealed by the presence of *confetti*. *Confetto* derives from the Latin verb *confingo*, which literally means "to prepare and to mix." Figuratively, however, its derivative, *confictio*, means "to fabricate, to cheat, to deceive, and to manipulate."[62] The art of making *confetti*, highly perfected in the Renaissance, involved coating any given food with sugar, often with the artistic aim of giving it a particular shape.[63] The more complex creations generally remained hollow inside, crystallizing the triumph of appearance over substance. Thus the culinary process of transforming raw food into a prepared *confetto* is an act requiring a metamorphosis from one "reality" (that of the original ingredients) to another and more esthetically pleasing one (the final dish). The new reality is a spectacular fabrication, always fanciful and often mythologically inspired. The beautiful and delicious final product the *confetto* sculpts marks the passage from the state of coarse food to that of refined representation, from the real to the metaphorical. In this fashion, the *confetto* itself acquires the power of transignificance. Although this process unavoidably leads to a visual falsification of the original nature of the ingredients used, the end results are visually enticing artistic elaborations that radiate a sense of energizing imaginativeness. From a historical perspective, a *confetto* re-creates an episode rather than giving an accurate rendition of events. It dramatizes rather than presenting unmixed and non-idealized facts.

Not unlike the transformative nature of the *confetti* served, the substitution of commensality for the duel alters the paradigm of battlefield courage. In return, it successfully constructs a strategic reality—the banquet—that is planned to sate Rinaldo's newborn passion for Antea. Yet his deliberate course of action turns a deaf ear to the political implications of her requests. Unlike a duel where the conclusion perforce results in a winner and a loser, the banquet, as Rinaldo correctly views it, not only celebrates, but also cements personal relationships. It also leads to equitable returns for the partakers, neither one of which needs to prevail over the other. Rinaldo reaches this conclusion based on the fact that through the ingestion of food and satiation, both he and Antea can partake of the same experience. Hoping to arouse in her the same craving that she stirs in him, the knight envisions the meal as a prelude to, and a metaphor for, the sexual fulfillment that he hungers for. But because the meal is the result of his manipulation of events, it undermines rather than invigorates reality. Reminiscent of the prepared *confetti*, his desire for her casts aside the more complex philosophy of love that Ficino expounds. Whereas the philosopher's theorization of love entails the sublimation of spirits that in seeking the highest Truth reach a loftier realm of fulfillment, Rinaldo's objective is to satisfy the simplest of his desires: the erotic.

In the hero's hasty impulse to possess Antea, Pulci couches his scorn for Ficino's theories. The philosopher's admonition that the desire for love is antithetical to the desire to physically possess flies in the face of Rinaldo's longing for the beautiful woman in front of him.[64] Accordingly, Rinaldo's banquet serves to gauge his acquired physical power over Antea. However, it measures neither his emotional attachment to her nor his adherence to the humanistic ideal of love. On the contrary, it spells out Pulci's criticism of Ficino's ideas that were embraced by the Florentine Academy. Apart from highlighting the hero's desire to prevail intimately over his adversary, the banquet offers yet another occasion to reveal Pulci's personal and longstanding antagonism toward the translator-philosopher, with whom he vied for—and in the end lost—Lorenzo's favor.[65]

When Antea returns to duel with Rinaldo three days later, Pulci brings into play a foodstuff very different from the dishes that marked the first encounter between the two. Throughout her absence, passion consumes Rinaldo. As he stews in ardor for her, he is on the verge of falling apart. His sense of courageousness abandons him; his compass begins spinning; he withdraws from camp activities and distances himself from his fellow-knights. When Orlando goes to awaken him on the morning of the duel, he hears Rinaldo calling Antea's name in his sleep and lamenting her absence from his side. The pang of loveless solitude that unconsummated love causes in him is not appeased by Orlando's comforting words. On the contrary, Rinaldo tries to keep secret the reason for his crying. But with a food-based analogy, Orlando admonishes him against hiding the truth from him:[66]

—Noi sarem que' frati
Che, mangiando il migliaccio, l'un si cosse;
L'altro gli vide gli occhi imbambolati
E domandò quel che la cagione fosse;
Colui rispose: "Noi siàn due restati

A mensa, e gli altri sono or per le fosse;
Che trentatré già fummo, e tu lo sai:
Quand'io vi penso, io piango sempre mai."
                                    (16.42)

("We are those two monks / who ate a pudding, and one burned his tongue: / one saw the other's eyes wide open, dazed, / and asked the reason for that sudden change. / The other answered, 'Just the two of us / are left to eat: the others are all dead. / Surely you know that we were thirty-three, / and so I'm mourning them, as you can see.'").

To persuade his cousin to reveal the true cause of his wretchedness, Orlando offers the example of two monks. One of them burned his mouth while eating *migliaccio*. Asked about his teary eyes he replied that he was crying, as he always did, when thinking about their other deceased brothers. Just as the scalded monk's lie is revealed by his expression of suffering following the consumption of a burning hot cake, Rinaldo's is revealed through Orlando's hearing Rinaldo calling Antea's name. Still, Pulci's recourse to an analogy based on *migliaccio*, a cake made with pig's blood and millet, marks an important change in Rinaldo's courtly standing.

Prepared with humbler ingredients and requiring less artful preparation than *confetti*, the *migliaccio* naturally evokes the food, and language, of uncouth and unrefined people. The shift to a lowly gastronomic model bears crucial implications for Rinaldo's character. To begin with, by introducing the *migliaccio* after the description of an earlier meal abounding with delicacies, Pulci emphasizes the difference between the elite and peasants. Rhetorically, he characterizes this difference in terms of those who have access to refined morsels and those who do not. In other words, while still a knight of the courtly scene, part, as it were, of the cultured universe it encompasses, Rinaldo had access to foods that kindled the imagination and indulged the palate. When he withdraws from that scene, abandoning his public duties to wrestle powerlessly with his amorous agony, the food the knight hears about neither feeds the imagination nor stimulates the palate. This exclusion from the courtly gastronomic zone of comfort is illustrative of the knight's demeaned chivalric status. And in fact, bemoaning Antea's absence while recollecting his first sight of her is the sole thought occupying Rinaldo. No moral or ethical responsibility preoccupies him at this point. The irresolvable struggle he faces does not project him as the victorious knight, but as a defeated one: he is inextricably connected to Antea, yet their separation appears unconquerable. As he takes stock of his predicament, Rinaldo understands that the duel in which they will face each other will not bring them together on a personal basis. Rather, by bringing about the death of either one of them, it will separate them forever. The loss of the object of his desire brings him discomfort and humiliation. Thus Pulci summarizes the erosion of Rinaldo's social standing resulting from his compromised moral and ethical standards in terms of food quality. In other words, if on the one hand it is ironic that Orlando uses the *migliaccio* as a food analogy to shake his cousin from the torments of passion, on the other hand it is through this device that the poet juxtaposes the elegance of the knightly world to the one lacking sophistication.

In the state to which he is reduced, the knight is governed solely by his desire for self-gratification, and pays no heed to civic-mindedness in so far as it pertains to his camp.[67] This makes him unfit to duel with Antea and marks his plunge into a world that is not regulated by the courtly values he is expected to personify. Clearly, vastly different foods capture two very distinct moments of Rinaldo's life. Of these, the practical one is shaped by unchecked impulses and transgressive desires. The other, ideal one is determined by theories and embellished with the luxuries wealth affords. Wrapped in a web of gastronomic leitmotifs, food signposts the hero's vicissitudes especially when he trades civic duty for personal interests. In this fashion, the artifice associated with the *confetti* corresponds to his scheme to entice Antea at the camp and make her the object of his erotic fulfillment; the humble *migliaccio*, on the contrary, corresponds to his fall from the position of paladin, which occurs when he sets aside both civic and moral duty to pursue Antea.

In the economy of the knight's amorous suffering, the fact that the duel is postponed for three days is significant. It suggests that the strategy Rinaldo adopts in trying to seduce Antea builds incrementally, varying the pattern while changing the dynamics of the objective she wished to achieve. Rinaldo's appeal to Cupid, along with the mythological love stories he evokes, dramatizes his misery. But it also draws a parallel with Jesus' Passion. Several vivid stanzas depict the knight paralyzed in the excruciating grip of love for three days. Rinaldo's, of course, is not a physical pain that reenacts Jesus' Passion. It is, instead, an inventive poetic imitation of His suffering that was caused by earthly greed. Through this, Pulci recasts the Passion in more immediate terms. With this twist, he depicts the conquered knight, at once the embodiment of Christian values that at times coalesce with and at other times collide with worldly ambitions, succumbing to carnal desires. The immeasurable contrast between the two passions played on the polarization of the earthly and divine, Christian and pagan, spiritual and carnal love, more than emphasizing the distances between the two experiences underlines their closeness. Carnal love, as Pulci suggests, is another facet of the polyhedric nature divine love takes on. This love is of and for men. It encompasses all aspects of human nature, including the carnal one. By focusing on the riddle of the unacknowledged hurts buried under the thick layers of conventions, Pulci highlights the palpable urgency about the erotic component that makes up human nature. Through this, he argues against the vision of divided selves that the court, swayed by Ficino's theories, maintains. Darting between private and public, love and politics, the poet thus thrusts his strongest blow to the Medici court's circle, underscoring its adherence to appearances and disregard of substance.

II

Much has been written about Morgante and Margutte with regard to their grotesquely voracious appetites. Indeed, their lives are etched with extraordinarily vivid details. For many, the ravenousness of the two who are, respectively, a giant and a half-giant, exemplifies their status, which ranges from the antisocial to the antiheroic.[68] Despite that, the first experience the reader has of the two friends and of their insatiable appetites is perhaps better grasped by first considering François Rabelais's Gargantua. According to Mikhail Bakhtin, Gargantua's renowned voracity and unrefined social demeanor posit him as a champion of folk culture, a fact that reflects Rabelais's biting criticism of the political and religious establishments of his times.[69] While the suppositions that led Bakhtin to these conclusions have vigorously been debated—and in some cases disproved[70]—he did formulate an accurate characterization of the metaphorical importance of food and eating within Rabelais's masterpiece.[71] Bakhtin's analysis of the meaning and function of food and banquets in *Gargantua and Pantagruel* can in part help shed light on the enigma and explain the importance of food in the *Morgante*, a literary work well-known to Rabelais.

From the onset, Pulci's giants with their disproportionate bodies and hyperbolic appetites appear to transgress the boundary between the human and the bestial, the proper and the improper. Because of this, their physiques clearly defy the humanist tenets pertaining to the human body. According to these, the human body exemplifies a proportional microcosm[72] of perfection and coincides with man's high moral purpose and achievements that Pico calls the "wonders" of man.[73] As the embodiment of "otherness" because of their anomalous shapes, Morgante and Margutte are outcasts from the privileged society that posits the harmonious proportionality of the body as the measure of moral excellence. Alienated from the court, the two appropriate a space outside of it. There they conform to their personal rules of conduct. Naturally, these abide neither by the courtly ethos nor by the Christian pathos. The significant social, moral, and cultural ramifications lurking behind the apparently simple change from the court to the space outside of it is evident in the empowerment of the outcast giants who, by constructing a new sociocultural model, undermine the mechanisms of social normality and give life to their own brand of it.

As outsiders, the two giants reject the abstract idealism of the court and turn its very opposite into the core of a new mode of thinking that shifts the operative power from the center to the margins. The Renaissance notion that symbolic imagery can be adapted to conflicting, and at times diametrically opposed, ideas is central to Pulci's discourse on power and desire. In fact, with his breaking away from the self-centeredness and the preoccupation with power and control that the court represents, unfamiliar, but no less effective, discourses develop. Accordingly, beneath the grotesque veneer of Morgante's and Margutte's bodies and appetites the potentially incomprehensible is made comprehensible and a non-Platonic representation of Florentine life emerges, saturated as it is with the abstractions and philosophical images promulgated by Ficino.[74] The resulting juxtaposition of the world of intellectual elitism personified by Lorenzo de' Medici and the inner circle of the *academia* to the world of ordinary people embodied by Margutte and Morgante encapsulates two distinct, and dissonant, voices that simultaneously capture the poetic and political pulses of Florentine culture. The self-absorption and withdrawal from the world of ordinary life implied by the former, paired with the despotic hand with which Lorenzo governed, helps to explain the events of April 1478.

Against this background, Pulci's giants emerge, symbolizing the transgressive, grotesque, and brutal force that confuses and deforms the foundations of civic-mindedness regulating Renaissance life.[75] Over and above that, they personify the transformative process that functions as a bridge between the past and the present. Yet more than this, through their transgressive conduct the giants mark the difference between the conventional and the unconventional, the center and the margins, the powerful and the powerless. In so doing, they (and Pulci through them) question the validity of the sociopolitical paradigms shaping Florentine society and expose the more hidden folds of the appetite for power espoused during the Renaissance.[76] Weaving the essence of defiant life into the tapestry of history with deliberate and audacious skills through his giants, Pulci brings to light his controversial stance toward Ficino throughout the *Morgante.* The fortuitous encounter between the two giants dramatizes the poet's loathing for the philosopher. In this scene, by lampooning point by point one of Ficino's more prominent theories, the poet's scorching criticism of the moralistic climate promoted by the philosopher at the Medici court surfaces. As a matter of fact, Ficino's unyielding belief in the moral life of the individual that emphasizes intellectual pursuits and leads to a system of political and cultural propriety shuns the simpler, but no less relevant, aspects of life.[77] In addition to that, it recoils from the jovial atmosphere that Pulci as Lorenzo's friend had cultivated. As Pulci sees it, the rigid intellectual climate of courtly life and its pursuits infiltrate the most private moments and most intimate relationships, poisoning them. The poet's brazen refusal to reduce the human experience to mere fragments of a vaster theologically minded and philosophically oriented mosaic surfaces, as a result, in his giants. Through them, he demonstrates that, as the poet cannot be constrained by theological beliefs, so his poetic genius cannot be controlled by the philosophical trends that saturate society and further divide the intellectual elite from the common man.[78]

Morgante and Margutte chance upon each other the first time at a crossroad:

> Giunto Morgante un dì in su'n crocicchio,
> Uscito d'una valle in un gran bosco,
> Vide venir di lungi, per ispicchio,
> Un uom che in volto parea tutto fosco.
> Détte del capo del battaglio un picchio
> In terra, e disse: "costui non conosco";
> E posesi a sedere in su'n sasso,
> Tanto che questo capitòe al passo.
> (18.112)

———

(One day, Morgante to a crossroad came / out of a valley into a thick wood. / Dimly he saw, still far away, a man / coming towards him, looking tough and grim. / He with his clapper knocked the ground and said, "Surely this thing I've never seen before." / So down he sat upon a stone to see, / when he got there, who that strange man could be.)

From the poet's perspective, the meeting place of the soon-to-become friends is not a random spot; on the contrary, it is one visually evocative of the convergence of two separate and contrasting forces that fluidly and purposefully come together. In fact, the limitations their difference may lead to turn into the advantages of new alternatives. But the crossroad Pulci introduces also evokes the mythological figure of Hercules.[79] As Prodicus tells it, the myth shows a young Hercules who, faced with a fork in the road, must choose which of the two paths that lay open before him to follow.[80] Naturally, the woman who entices him to take the left side of the road personifies pleasure. The one who sternly admonishes him about the right side represents virtue. The budding hero is hesitant at first. Because the divergent roads exemplify moral choices, he must decide on the type of life he wishes to live. To be sure, the left path will lead to unfruitful pleasures that yield no greater rewards while the right one will lead to hardship and suffering. By choosing the right path Hercules makes a self-defining choice that foregrounds his heroic character. The life of virtue he opts for entails struggles and deprivations, but his fame and glory, and ultimately his elevation to divinity, will result from them. The moral choice Hercules makes at the crossroad looms large in the encounter of Pulci's giants even though the poet redraws the mythical story with a twist.

That Morgante finds no personifications of virtue and vice to direct him where the road forks is a key point. Through it, Pulci suggests, first of all, that there is no clear difference between the paths that lay before the giants (and humanity). Unlike Hercules's onerous decision that Prodicus's myth emphasizes, when Morgante and Margutte begin their journey together, they do not dwell on which path to follow. Pulci's rendering of the myth is more ambiguous for it insinuates more than just the giants' antiheroic stance. Indeed, it reveals that fame and glory do not hinge on moral decisions taken a priori. This is based on the fact that neither one of the paths bears a clear mark of distinction. Through this, the poet intimates that neither one of them ensures with absolute certainty the type of (life) journey the travelers will face. This implies that both paths are equally fraught with vices and virtues, defeats and achievements. Accordingly, by entering either one of them the wayfarers do not violate any moral or ethical principle, as they will be exposed to hardship, travails, contentment, and pleasures, regardless of which road they travel. Pollio Vitruvius's *On architecture* (*De architectura*),[81] a study of Western architecture that discusses, among other things, urban planning, seems to reinforce this hypothesis. In it, the Roman architect and engineer claims that urban roads must run east to west. Most importantly, they must be built in areas not predisposed to winds because some of these, in his account, negatively affect the citizens' health. Written between 29 and 23 BC, the treatise became one of the fundamental texts on architecture, widely known to Renaissance humanists.[82] As discussed above, this treatise was the standard text on architecture before Leon Battista Alberti's. Petrarch possessed and annotated his own copy. Alberti, Lorenzo Ghiberti, Raphael, and Paolo Giovio also made use of the advice it dispensed.[83]

At first glance, Vitruvius's exhaustive explanations on the art of laying out urban centers with roads that are shielded from dangerous winds seem to deal strictly with the physical planning of cities and viable routes. But a closer look at his exposition reveals something different. The principles on which he bases the orientation of cities and streets emphasize not just the physical structures, but also the mental effects that natural elements have on citizens. According to him, "if the winds are cold, they injure; if hot, they corrupt; if moist, they are noxious."[84] By basing his thesis on Galen's theory of humors, Vitruvius concludes that in laying out the city "it seems best to avoid regions that can taint human bodies with hot vapors."[85] Although his primary concern is to set up a "scientific" model of the ideal urban setting, a medical understanding of the ways in which gales and latitudes affect bodies and minds informs his study.[86] Yet the painstaking explanations he offers entail a vast range of rhetorical implications. Among them stands out the parallel between the physical order and the political order of the city, both of which, according to him, can be undermined by the randomness of natural elements. This parallel is evidenced in the ways in which harmful gales impede the gatherings of city-dwellers.[87] More importantly, the corruption of health suffered by travelers journeying on roads exposed to particular gales calls to mind the unmarked road Pulci's giants decide to take. In other words, Vitruvius's subtle if unexpected introduction of a moral dimension in his architectural study suggests that every road is potentially exposed to harmful winds. Ultimately, it is up to wayfarers, and a city's leaders, to counteract the negative impact that they can inflict.

Given the renown this text enjoyed in the Renaissance, it is hard to believe that a metaphorical reading of Vitruvius's treatise escaped humanists, so skilled and attuned to seizing metaphors and interpreting meanings. That Pulci, at least in the beginning, moved with Lorenzo within the circle of Florence's humanists is undeniable. For this reason, it seems likely that in Pulci's treatment of the point of encounter between his giants, Vitruvius's study plays a role. In Pulci's narration neither the right road nor the left road is by definition morally correct or wrong. On the contrary, on either one of them Morgante and Margutte are susceptible and vulnerable to the political, philosophical, and theological winds blowing against them. With razor-sharp acuity that justifies the comparison between Vitruvius's "scientific" work and his epic poem, Pulci establishes a carefully nuanced link between historical reality and poetic imagination. Of the two, he suggests that it is the latter that powers social change because it rests on an inner compass, not on outside currents. What adds meaning to the Vitruvian echo in Pulci's work is the fact that for the poet the moral and ethical course of action the giants take as they journey together is not dictated by prevailing currents or ostentatiously flaunted principles. Rather, it is determined by a vigorous sense of necessity fused with a competitive desire for survival. This helps them to survive the circumstances they encounter. Yet the principles on which they base their actions are not the same as the ones upheld by the rarefied society of the court.

The latter point is made stronger by the image of Morgante sitting on the rock as Margutte approaches him. Toying with the Gospel's image, Pulci's version of Peter, and Paul, personified by a Morgante converted and baptized by Orlando to escape the labyrinthine palace of canto 2, gives originality to the scene.[88] At the same time, it draws attention to the truths it reveals. It would be reasonable to assume that as a new Christian convert, Morgante bases his actions on Christian principles. Yet the fact that he will soon model his conduct and adjust it to that of Margutte, the self-described atheist, is telling. It reveals that when Christian beliefs are embraced as a pretense, self-interest quickly prevails over public interest. It also suggests that achieving the latter, which advances the needs of the group rather than those of individuals, requires striking a credible and evenhanded balance between conflicting interests. This behavior, however, might be construed as self-defeating. Pushing aside one's own interests to put forward those of others, providing an all-encompassing sense of community, results in personal loss. The Christian principles guiding Morgante should provide an alternative value system to Margutte's. But, it does not. The underlying contradictory stance Pulci takes with regard to Prodicus's myth and the Gospel's episode anticipates the giants' trials of strength and wit that are imbued with impulsiveness, callousness, and selfishness. But it is also a pointed reminder of the poet's pain and ire interjected into his creativity. At the crossroad of personal suffering and political power Pulci understands that, like his giants, he possesses a beautiful sense of freedom. As a banished poet, he has learned the rules of the court; as an outsider, he can break them and deride their shortcomings. For this reason, the scene depicting the giants' first encounter expands from the initial mythological echo to chart the path toward a difficult and ambiguous reconciliation of conflicting, yet still coalescing, beliefs.

The conversation Morgante and Margutte strike focuses on the personal. Margutte describes himself to the inquisitive Morgante in terms of his wanton ways and debauched behavior.[89] By portraying himself as one who understands less through his head than his stomach, Margutte sums up his belief system with three words: "la gola e'l culo e'l dado" ("gluttony, ass, and dice") (18.132.2). According to him, these constitute the philosophical axiom on which his faith is based. More than just an outburst of moral dissonance in a universe ruled by the commonplace of theological beliefs, this flagrantly provocative answer points to a deeply anguished poet. Specifically, the uneasy mix of exuberance and rancor that transpires through Margutte's words dramatizes the poet's tension with court life. Separated from the prominence and expectations that culture demanded, indeed, no longer yearning to be part of it, through Margutte Pulci voices his stern refutation of the rules that regulated it. Soberly, bluntly, and constructively, with his "virtues" Margutte—and, through him, Pulci—deliberately sweeps aside Ficino's discourse on beauty and love that idealizes man's godlike figure and potential.[90] Margutte's belief system also ridicules the purifying effect that, according to the philosopher, moral virtues have in guiding man's ascent to God, putting the body instead of the intellect at the heart of man's pleasures. By substituting the Christian cardinal virtues with his personal version of them, namely, gluttony, sex, and gambling, Pulci mocks Ficino and rejects the idea that man's happiness is achieved through contemplation and philosophical knowledge.[91] Most importantly, through the half-giant's "virtues" Pulci exhaustively and relentlessly attacks point by point Ficino's description of the soul's ascent toward God.

In book 14 of the *Platonic Theology* Ficino explains that the process of the soul's purification, ascent, and union with God is achieved through moral philosophy, physics, mathematics, and metaphysics. Margutte challenges these beliefs one by one by creating a hierarchical ladder of earthly pleasures. Not by accident, he places gluttony on the first rung. On this ladder, man's yearning for this-worldly fulfillments has neither need for nor recourse to moral philosophy; he is self-motivated in his pursuit and self-sufficient in reaching his objective. In direct opposition to temperance and prudence, gluttony is revealed and satisfied through materiality. Because of this, it is divorced from philosophical inquisitiveness and unconcerned with the potentiality of human nature. Gluttony pursues bodily gratification and, like carnal desire, functions as pleasure in itself and outside of itself.[92] Most significantly, neither socioeconomic nor political circumstances hinder one from taking pleasure in it because it is neither enslaved by the rules of erudite sophistry nor bridled by financial circumstances. Margutte's interaction with the world is based on different types of hunger and this shapes the contours of his belief system.

As a middle step between gluttony and gambling, sexual desire for Margutte replaces hope. This virtue for Ficino bridges the distance between faith and love and connects the soul to God by distancing it from the material world. Margutte's second step on the ladder of earthly pleasures contrasts with the virtue of hope because sexual gratification is attained in earthly time, not deferred to future, however pleasurable but elusive, delights. The belief in man's attainment of earthly pleasures not only pulls the thread of Ficino's theological fabric but also upends Valla's Epicurean notion of *uti* and *frui* according to which the enjoyment of senses is a prelude to higher pleasures of the soul that arouse man's interest in civic responsibilities.[93] Neither one of these possibilities shapes Margutte's faith; in fact, his insistence on the pleasures of the body is a model of narcissism. In a striking contrast of opposites, this parodies Ficino's intellectual haughtiness, which is the result of the prominent status he has acquired within the Medici court.

The world of physicality transforms Margutte's faith into a theory of self-serving indulgence. Yet from it emerges a concrete sense of a modern, self-assured man in a way that is found in neither Valla's nor Ficino's writings nor, for that matter, in Lorenzo's own works. His interests—and gratifications—are not pinned to intellectual pursuits but are inscribed within the ever-fluctuating possibilities of the pragmatic universe in which he lives and by which his experiences are shaped. Ironically, both sexual desire and gluttony emphasize the reality of—or hunger for—power, an appetite with which both Ficino and Lorenzo, in their respective positions, are all too comfortably familiar. This suggests that for the giant, as for men and politicians alike, desire for power can be reduced to—and is synonymous with—yearning to possess the tangible, even though this entails neglecting a rather significant cardinal virtue: justice. While this implication contradicts Ficino's theological position, it reveals man's failure to govern not only himself but, especially, others. Margutte's apparently self-indulging creed, revolving around the enjoyment of the senses "that plague the mind" but "are a source of pleasure,"[94] becomes more complex as the political nuances of power arise from it.

Gambling, the last element of Margutte's faith, replaces Ficino's love and defies all of the Christian cardinal virtues.[95] Although placed on the highest rung of his hierarchical structure, the randomness that regulates this activity is neither based on intellectual pursuits nor capable of revealing the truths implied by Ficino's theological ladder. To the contrary, it hinges on the craftiness of the gambler who can alter, and elevate, a financial, not moral, standing. Clearly playing with Ficino's idea that through mathematics the soul reaches the celestial sphere and is closest to God, Margutte maintains that the highest level of earthly fulfillment is similarly achieved through the mathematical exactness that successful gambling requires.

Ingrained in a world of covetousness that neither inspires nor aspires to a hierarchical scale of moral and ethical values, Margutte's faith is a burlesque parody of Ficino's moral system. Unlike the philosopher's system, it emphasizes tact, taste, and smell, senses that supposedly anchor man to the universe of materiality.[96] Conversely, by rejecting sight and hearing, senses that according to Ficino set the soul free, Margutte sweeps away Ficino's belief that man's ultimate desire "consists in either the knowledge or possession of God"[97] and illustrates the suffocating intellectual isolation into which these ideas have plunged Lorenzo. This fact appears even more evident after Margutte finishes his presentation to Morgante. Margutte's lifestyle as a model of corruption and dishonesty does not trouble Morgante. On the contrary, he expresses an immediate liking for the rogue. Hearing the latter's adventures, or, more accurately, envisioning, and through it, tasting and smelling the foods that Margutte has brought to mind in his talk, Morgante is won over and becomes impervious to the implications that Margutte's behavior entails. In a similar fashion, leading Florence under the sway of the lofty, siren-like call of Ficino's teachings, Lorenzo misplaces—in fact loses sight of—the lucid sense of reality that his role demands and pays no attention to those senses that are the ingredients for, and denote, a less elitist and less despotic awareness of reality. The shift from poetry to politics, which the subtext suggests, reveals Pulci's wrenching concerns about himself as well as about social issues crippling Florentine life.

By making food, its procurement, preparation, and consumption, the underpinning of his doctrine Margutte shifts the fundamental core of the Christian profession of faith from divinity to animal—from the conventional to the unconventional.[98] Like Rabelais's giants,[99] Pulci's heroes launch a stinging criticism of the political and philosophical establishments of their time; this is fueled in no small part by the power of Pulci's personal experience at the Medici court. As Morgante and Margutte travel together they embark upon a series of adventures that fuse the culinary and chivalric worlds harmoniously into one. At times it appears as though the former devours the latter, eradicating, in the process, the ludicrous trust in a system of philosophical beliefs to govern life. On other occasions, it is the chivalric world that seems to consume the giants by confronting them with its rigid rules. The circular image of eating and being eaten that this fusion evokes draws attention to the fact that while power and authority rest in the material world, they are subject to the ebbing and flowing of personal circumstances.

This understanding transforms the world of humanistic precision into a universe of grotesque parody, of images reflecting "a phenomenon in transformation,"[100] and affirming that the grotesque is a dynamic state of "transformation or metamorphosis." Into it converge the ends of known ideas and the beginnings of those yet unknown. Accordingly, while the eaten and the eater on the surfaces function as equalizing elements, in reality they mark the boundaries of the Renaissance discourse on authority, power, and nobility. Indeed, the giants' culinary journey exposes their grotesque natures and, at the same time, reveals the incongruity of putting trust in the potential perfection of the human being. By highlighting the prominence of amorphousness, change, and ambivalence as coextensive and fundamental elements of the grotesque both Mikhail Bakhtin and Geoffrey G. Harphem disclose its radical subversiveness.[101] This property in literature, as well as in art, clashes against the rigidity of canonical models.[102] Also, this phenomenon engenders new ideas and forms that, despite their gross exaggerations, parody the very models they reject.[103] In the process, they construct new paradigms. This point is made evident in the giants' encounter with Florinetta, who has been held prisoner by two other giants, the siblings Beltramo and Sperante.

III

In canto 19 of Pulci's *Morgante* while traveling through a solitary and dark place Morgante and Margutte are struck by a plaintive voice that cuts through the air. Curious at first, then determined to identify its origin and put an end to it, the two giants follow the sound. Below a cliff they discover a disheveled maiden, chained and guarded by a fierce lion. To free the young woman Morgante kills the lion; afterward, he asks her to explain the cause of her captivity. More than just revealing the circumstances leading to the physical abuses suffered at the hands of her captors, Florinetta's harrowing account paints a lucid tableau of the disturbing reality at the heart of her society, and by extension, of Pulci's. Rather than a mere reflection on self-pity, the emotional description of the ordeal that shattered a privileged life draws the landscape of political and social self-advancement sustained by ruthless violence. In unambiguous terms, Florinetta's account of her captivity speaks of a society that is not only populated but also governed by individuals who hunger for material gains, even when acquiring them entails overpowering and subjugating vulnerable people. As she clings to the memories of her former lifestyle that make the present more agonizing, the young woman reflects on the changed reality of her existence. Feelings of betrayal, isolation, resentment, and yearning suffuse her words; at this juncture she incarnates human misery. The brutal system that has kept her shackled physically and emotionally for seven years exposes the collapse of the social order based on law and legitimacy. The acts of violence and abuses perpetrated in their name bring to light the moral and moralistic fiber of society, its power structure, and the way in which it willingly bends the first in order to legitimize the latter. For Florinetta, the difference between past and present is thus revealed at first in terms of ethical, as well as aesthetic, principles that resist corrupt and arriviste ideologies.

To lend force to her words, and to dramatize her displacement from the familiar, refined world of her home to the unfamiliar, uncouth one of her captivity, Florinetta makes use of, among other things, a gastronomic rhetoric. This rhetorical strategy compellingly juxtaposes the courtly universe she embodied as a free woman with the tribulations she has endured as a prisoner. By linking freedom and wealth with appetizing foodstuffs, and emphasizing her current lack of them, Florinetta shapes the story of her captivity into one of gastronomic ruin. As she understands it, her unexpected social downfall coincides with a squalid diet; and this, like other entitlements she was accustomed to and no longer benefits from, bears out the misery of her condition. The whole range of dismal emotions that season her account, including anger, fear, rage, and sadness, is summarized in the words that describe the foods she is forced to consume:

> E vipere e cerastre e strane carne
> Convien ch'io mangi, che reca di caccia,
> Che mi solieno a schifo esser le starne.
> (19.28)

("and snakes and vipers, I am forced to eat, / and the strange meats that from his hunt he brings / I, who the tastiest partridge once abhorred.")

The force and beauty churning beneath these verses, which are at once simple and complex, lie in the densely layered ideas that they simultaneously evoke. With verve, her words compellingly juxtapose the courtly universe she inhabited with the tribulations she has endured in captivity. They also disclose a strong-willed creature of unspoiled innocence, capable of using language with confidence to kindle her audience's interest. Despite the violence and exploitation she has suffered, through her words Florinetta projects a forceful presence and maintains an undiluted coherence with respect to the capacity for cruelty that individuals rely on to establish and sustain their reputation. Her discriminating palate reveals a socially privileged upbringing. Using this logic she correlates wealth with rare morsels and, presumes that the former, by entitlement, validates the latter. In Florinetta's understanding, the lack of exquisite foodstuffs bears out the misery of her condition.

Still, the wretchedness of her present circumstances, crystallized by the "vipere e cerastre e strane carne" she consumes, points to the clear-cut social divide she has unwillingly and unwittingly crossed. The authority of the real, exemplified by unsavory foodstuff, emboldens her to channel her suffering into a visceral condemnation of her abusers while unfurling her story to Morgante. Yet the strident tone in which she voices her accusations shifts her discourse from placid acceptance and self-negation, subjection and despair, toward denunciation and self-affirmation. The sociopolitical overtones that punctuate her argument impart new meanings to Florinetta's words—and Pulci's story. By underscoring the repressive practices governing her life, she implicitly suggests that her society has made envy, malice, and brutality fundamental, if unspoken, tenets of the system. Her sharp, albeit oblique, criticism of the resulting social and moral order is lent more incisiveness by the way in which she emphasizes her courtly sensibilities. For Florinetta the scrumptious foods she no longer savors shape the fixed, talismanic memory of life before her abduction. But in summing up the rudderless world she now inhabits their absence underscores yet again her role as a court outsider. The perils, humiliations, and powerlessness she endures because of that exclusion are made more piercing by the fact that they suggest living outside of history. Indeed, disenfranchised from the court, she is no longer an engaged participant in the expectations and aspirations it fosters. Instead, she is a submissive bystander to the norms and limits it enforces. Clearly, as a court outsider, Florinetta is like Pulci.

Still, in her understanding the foods she consumed there exemplify the food of freedom and justice. Both of these she is denied by her kidnappers, two giants who are empowered by ideas of what they want to achieve and gain by keeping her chained to their will.

The biblical resonance of Florinetta's food of freedom evokes an unbroken belief in regaining liberty because the events of the Old Testament book of Exodus foregrounds this concept. It also suggests a degree of acceptance on her part that is seasoned with a dose of defiance. In Exodus the Israelites agree to follow Moses but once they are in the desert they voice their protests when their hunger is not satisfied. Similarly, Florinetta endures the hardship put upon her without resigning herself to it. Pulci's audience, familiar with the historical moment, the life of material excesses the House of Medici favors, and the poet's personal experience at that court, could recognize the cultural subtext and the autobiographical resonances the poet weaves into Florinetta's story. In it, they could also perceive a critique of the system—and also of its prince— that has taken away the opportunities and freedom with which at first they provided him. Disconnected from the gastronomy of court and the privileges it entails, Florinetta now consumes any foodstuff her captors lay hands on. Her new reality also sums up the contradiction between what the nobility believes in and what the commoners practice. Because the meats she consumes in captivity are neither part of an aristocratic diet nor validated by recipes for people of her social standing, they become the symbol of a clear-cut social divide.[104]

The description of the meats Florinetta consumes is visually striking, politically charged, and poetically inventive. It allows Pulci to seize on the established tenet of the gastronomy of power and, through it, to probe the hypocrisy that lies at the heart of the system backing it. This is evident in the way in which Florinetta defines herself as much by the food she eats as by whom she has become. Through this, she unearths the contradictions between physiological hunger and hunger for self-advancement. Stirred by the desire for power and authority, the latter takes no account of the common good. As she conveys the entire arc of her experience through different types of appetites and foods, Florinetta exposes the humanization of violence. According to this, cruelty and wickedness are unavoidable ingredients in a universe shaped by selfishness and impelled by its cravings for power. To make sense of the grief, disillusionment, and failure that her unexpected reversal of fortune brings, she must resign herself to bear the sordid ruthlessness of her circumstances. Because of this, she bows down to treacherousness, degradation, and cold-bloodedness. These features are the new definers of her existence.

The image of the snakes she eats is telling for it evokes a narrowed vision of the world. The slithering, venomous animals that constitute her meals bring this image to mind because their field of vision is skewed and restricted to the horizontal plane. This earthly bound and partial range of vision is caused by the impossibility of an erect bodily posture that allows an upward gaze. Arguably, in metaphorical terms, these traits encapsulate the myopic, self-centered, and materialistic attitudes prevailing at court. Yet more than this, Florinetta's sharp description of her meals, which straddles between the confessional and the subversive, calls to mind the serpent of Genesis 3. However, the similarity ends there because in pointed opposition to the biblical text Pulci depicts Florinetta not as a woman induced to eating by the serpent but as an eater of serpent(s). Beyond the facile sexual connotations this image may bring to mind, the inverted image of Eve consuming rather than being consumed by snakes carries more intriguing metaphorical implications. It speaks of a woman neither swayed nor seduced by deceptively enthralling words. It portrays her as one unfazed by the allure of power. Most importantly, it presents her as a reshaper of human history because she plays a creative, active role in it. Liberated from the fixed stereotypes Genesis 3 sanctions with regard to women's shortcomings, Pulci's Florinetta breaks away from the perceptions within which centuries of exegetical analyses have entrapped the other Eve. In so doing, Florinetta blurs the line between the literal and the metaphorical, the reality and the fiction, peculiar to that text. The shift from entrenched biblical interpretation to poetic elaboration enables Pulci to redefine his personal experience while remaining firmly rooted in the political system affecting his life. Specifically, through his portrayal of Florinetta acting as an Eve in control of herself and of her circumstances, the poet shows that unregulated passions and conflicting desires, which according to Saint Augustine led to humankind's downfall, have a natural place in and are the spark that shapes human history.

In book 14 of *The City of God*, Augustine argues that freedom is attainable when the will is not ruled by vices and sins.[105] In times closer to Pulci, Valla's pronouncements on free will leave a mark on the poet's work. In a radical break from the Augustinian understanding of free will, Valla, as will be discussed below, in his *Dialogue on Free Will*, emphatically underscores the autonomy it retains from either theology or philosophy.[106] For the humanist neither of the two disciplines regulates the will because it is driven by mankind's enduring capacity—and desire—to choose what it deems more suitable or more gratifying to its existence. Valla claims that, as shaper of its life and of history, the choices mankind makes are driven by the returns they secure.

Into Valla's charged discourse that shifts the absolute into the ordinary, Pulci interjects Florinetta's—and his—respective ordeals. In both predicaments, the poet seems to suggest that breaking away from the chains of physical, emotional, and financial captivity requires altering the expectations cultivated under the spell of contrived courtly privileges. To accomplish this, he contends, requires not just an unprejudiced embrace of the untested, but also the firmness to believe in the meaningful potentialities that an existence outside of the court, shrouded in poverty and deprivations, offers. In his understanding, the painful extrication from the comforts of the past offers hope for redemptive possibilities. The prospect of this, Pulci claims, leads to the freedom one longs to achieve. To this end, Florinetta's emphatic *convien* with reference to the peculiar meats she consumes, which recalls Antea's use of the same expression in canto 16, denotes Pulci's sheer pragmatism: in the face of adversity, in order to triumph rather than succumb, the vulnerable and powerless must feign a compliant attitude toward powerful enforcers of rules. This approach is a coping mechanism that ensures Florinetta's survival. And this is the first step on the road to freedom.

Florinetta's metamorphosis into an indiscriminate, compliant eater, articulated with a verb that simultaneously conveys the ideas of need and expediency, functions as a referent of Pulci's own personal circumstances. Yet by also retrieving Antea's reply to Rinaldo's unanticipated invitation to a banquet (16.20), Florinetta's words redirect the attention yet again to a society weighed down by power seized through force and cunning. In both Antea's and Florinetta's respective cases, Pulci shows two heroines voicing their assent to those holding sway over them by way of agreeing to partake of the meals they offer. And although each woman is treated to very different foodstuffs, both of them are forced to bow to their respective hosts' wishes, consuming, that is, whatever they provide. The images of Antea and Florinetta compliantly eating at their respective tables the food that the enemy offers show a world swallowed up by seduction and violence.

Florinetta's former repugnance of partridge meat also becomes part of Pulci's critique of Lorenzo and his court. As discussed above, in the Renaissance the interest in food and its qualities brought about the standardization of courtly gastronomy. Michele Savonarola deems the meat that Florinetta used to find unsavory appropriate for "zentili e richi homini."[107] Yet, he also describes the bird as a deceitful animal renowned for stealing others' eggs.[108] According to Ficino, this act of violence is of no advantage to the partridges because the hatchlings return to their own mother, whose voice they recognize immediately. This would suggest that Florinetta's ordeal shares some common ground with Savonarola's explanation. Platina also considers partridge meat good for "distinguished people." But this assertion, as noted above, precedes the bolder one that exposes the corruption of the Roman court. With subtle irony, this is highlighted by the assertion that partridge meat stirs sexual desire.[109] This detail suggests that there are strong sexual connotations marking Florinetta's account to Morgante and Margutte. Yet more than this, both Savonarola's and Platina's explanations provide a cultural subtext to her dislike of partridge meat. On a literal level, the bird's deceitfulness portrays her captors' behavior, suggesting that their scheme will ultimately fail. On a metaphorical level, however, the bird meat inverts the equation of noble palate and delicious food and suggests that, in the Florence of the fifteenth century, noble palates describe men whose ascent to power and fame is based on the exploitation of authority rather than on personal accomplishments. Accordingly, in Florinetta's former revulsion of the fine bird meat are revealed Pulci's raw emotions against people driven by ego rather than principle and who seek personal benefits by manipulating the system and scheming against other individuals.

Derived from the Latin *convenire*, and evoking notions of agreements reached in spite of conflicting standpoints, Florinetta's *convien* uncovers Pulci's sense of the inevitability of acquiescing to the demands of threatening subjugators. At the same time, it also underlines his awareness of the ambiguous bond between captor and captive. With each side determined to resolve the conflict in ways that benefit its own interests, the tenuous accord between prisoner and captor is built on rivalry and hostility. The tension and false sense of security these create shape human interactions. Within the court setting—a system driven by desires and want rather than careful recognition of limits and capacities—the adversarial logic of personal interest regulating the captor/captive predicament is neither dissolved nor contained. Instead, it is replaced with the interplay of viciousness and deceitfulness. To thwart and undercut the boundaries of power set by (and within) social hierarchy, courtiers and princes alike exploit both of these. Although heavily suffused by pessimistic tones, Pulci's fundamental vision of subjugation and freedom that frames Florinetta's (and his) story is forged by this belief.

To this end, the poet's depiction of Florinetta suggests that despite— or more accurately because of—her physical confinement, she is focused on and clings to a youthful idealism that is balanced with emotional maturity. To be sure, she demonstrates a sensitivity and pathos that are not evinced from her own description of herself prior to the kidnapping. In the face of catastrophic events Florinetta no longer appears achingly vulnerable. As she tackles the challenges she faces, she appears emboldened by her misfortune, and this unchains her from the bonds of privilege. This, in turn, allows her to unwittingly explore the ambiguous moral folds of her former lifestyle, and results in a recalibrated ethical understanding of her world. Through a reversal of attitude and perspectives, it appears that while imprisoned Florinetta achieves a degree of freedom she never possessed as a member of the court. This seemingly contradictory idea is based on the fact that in captivity her decisions are driven by her desire to break away from the wicked mercilessness of her captors, not by material gains as life at court required and ensured. Her choices at this juncture are determined by her desire to find freedom from the yoke imposed on her. Yet the system her captors regulate with an iron hand is a microcosm of the court system. Accordingly, the freedom she longs to achieve is not reached by staving off worldly ambition for riches, fame, and power, as Saint Augustine claims. It is attained through a regained sense of ethical values that, more in line with Valla's claim about the randomness of human desires, ignores the precarious glitter of appearances. By refuting established assumptions, solid ethical foundations usher in achievable alternatives to the wretchedness that exploits the misery of the beaten to augment the oppressors' gains. Ethical principles probe, strive against, and challenge the layers of power, perceptions, perversions, and privileges the court counts on to plunder what others have and it craves. But to put trust in ethical standards and abide by them requires turning inward and grappling with the unsettling question of human desires and worldly goods. In contrast to the social dictum of the times, this struggle between coveting and disregard of material possessions leads to a sweeping search for authenticity. As a result, the journey toward freedom is an undefined and unsettling mode that involves, among other things, breaking away from conventions. It requires the courage to emerge from the court, be disenfranchised, and live outside of it in order to understand the demands it makes on the enfranchised, individuals enslaved by its codes. In Pulci's view, to act freely and innovatively calls for the unconventional. This mode of conduct, which calls to mind Cicero's notion of freedom discussed above, not only requires a poised detachment from materialism, but also clearly transcending rules the court enforces.

Pulci's understanding of freedom from the court's limits restores the human contours to Florinetta's ordeal. Still, on the poet's part there is a sense of calculated risk in exposing the failures of the system that she (and he) has long embraced and from which they are both irrevocably banned. The belief that Florinetta can retrieve and actualize her freedom through an ethical mode is illustrated by her adapting to unpalatable meats. This also suggests that the ethical principles on which she now bases her decision are impervious to the limiting aesthetic standards the court enforced. By portraying her as a woman cognizant of the threats confronting her, and aware that freedom comes at the cost of former beliefs, the poet shows that the human condition is neither a triumph of artifice nor a construct of philosophical theories, as Ficino—and Lorenzo—would have. To the contrary, it is an awareness of the concrete that is cemented in trusts, shaken by betrayals, rekindled in passion, and sustained by enthusiasm; that speaks with fervor and urgency against systems regulated by force and fear and motivated by the desire to control with twisted and closed logic. The subtle and far-reaching reverberations of Pulci's discourse make it plain that for the poet Florinetta embodies a fresh and unsettling force in the stale and ostensibly uncomplicated universe of her captivity. Like her, he, during the years of his friendship with Lorenzo, personified rebelliousness against and indifference to the controlled environment the House of Medici, in thrall to Ficino's philosophical pronouncements, favored.

With courageous poetic imagination and unflinching conviction, through Florinetta Pulci illustrates the disjunction between theory and practice at the Medici court and the political tensions it produces. Paradoxically, he accomplishes this by using Ficino's *De vita libri tres*. Here Lorenzo's philosopher explains that medicinal lozenges made from vipers cleanse the human body of its foul humors.[110] Undoubtedly, the healing qualities of viper preparations Ficino touts are a striking counterpoint to Florinetta's meals. She consumes them neither by choice nor to alleviate physical ailments. Indeed, rather than the advertised effects for Florinetta ingesting vipers opens the door to self-reflection that leads to a critical assessment of the political machinations the system encourages. The unexpected results of her diet enable her to make sense of the inexplicable abuses to which she is subjected. Arguably, the system she inhabits at this point is not the Medici court; but in a reversal of situation, the prism of her experience, shaped by repressive imperatives her despotic captors uphold, turns into a cautionary tale of Lorenzo's autocratic governance. For her, the realization that physical captivity cannot reduce one to emotional powerlessness turns into an impulse for renewal. This new awareness of the moral underpinning the court needs and lacks is a result of her predicament, which includes a diet of vipers. Thus upending Ficino's medical prescription, in Pulci's hand viper-based meals help clear the mind not the body and turn into the food of self-determination. These meals reverberate with political echoes, for they highlight not the physical freedom lost through the force of others, but the emotional freedom gained by leaving behind the false certitudes they cultivate. They also expose the enslaving illusoriness of the court's appearances. With a radical stroke, Pulci's use of Ficino's own theory amplifies the scope of his criticism of his nemesis's intellectual soundness and, more subtly, of Lorenzo's unquestioning acceptance of it.

In speaking to Morgante, Florinetta asserts that "non giudicate nulla innanzi al fine" ("until the end has come, you judge in vain") (19.26). The cogency of her words yet again redirects attention to Pulci's personal circumstances. But the lucidity of her language cuts across the grain of Renaissance commonplaces, suggesting that if anything can also be its opposite, possibilities and changes occur through human actions not through conventions. This also reveals that changes are subject to the insidiousness of human desires. Her remark evidences her determination to prevail over her captor-detractors by bringing about their downfall. The role reversal that Florinetta's words evoke essentially seeks to empower the powerless and to displace—or at least redefine—the authority of the powerful. The constructive transgressiveness—reverting to the original order—that this shift entails is rooted in the notion that social stability hinges on the evenhandedness of the powerful and must perforce be balanced with energies of divergent but harmonious forces. As a matter of fact, the opposite produces a destructive transgression that by destabilizing the social order ends up subverting it. Harmony— which for Alberti is the result of the "sonorous balance" from a variety of voices[111]—can be achieved and nurtured in political or intellectual circles through the balanced and complementary strengths produced by a plurality of modes of vision. Not unlike an architect or a musician, a perceptive leader must strive to integrate the dissonant voices into a work of parts that function together to benefit society at large.

Florinetta's awareness that she can change her circumstances through her actions becomes evident after Morgante and Margutte free her. As she journeys back home with them she turns into an indiscriminate eater. Indeed, the progress of her return is regularly interrupted by meals consisting of animals—a turtle, a dragon, a camel, and an elephant, among others—the giants hunt along the way. These meats provide another dimension to the grotesque nature of the giants whose uncanny[112] eating practices make them different from the norm[113] and thus upend the notion of unchangeable rules. Like vipers' meat, that of these exotic animals is neither part of the aristocratic diet nor does it appear in recipe collections of this period. Yet Florinetta consumes the meals she is offered without voicing any complaint. Her new eating practices suggest that, like the giants guiding her, she has become unconcerned with, as well as defiant of, courtly norms. More than this, the unusual meals she eagerly partakes of with her rescuers point to the fact that Florinetta, like Pulci, has put her hesitations, vulnerabilities, and aspirations behind her, thus acquiring a new perspective on the possibilities her changed circumstances usher in. This freedom, as a way of life, entails the awareness that new possibilities are feasible by resisting the constraints of perverted values. In the wake of the long tradition that from Aristotle to Petrarch places personal freedom at the heart of an ethical and civic-minded life, through Florinetta's story Pulci shows his final detachment from courtly rules aimed at keeping him and his bawdy creativity in check.

Buoyed by the independence she has gained once free from her captors, Florinetta savors her freedom through food that no power system foists on her. The transition from the food of captivity to that of freedom is based neither on quality nor on quantity of ingredients. On the contrary, it is rooted in the notion that as one freed from the shackles of conventions she can either accept it or seek alternatives to it. Although the newly found freedom outside of the court requires personal adjustments, it allows Pulci to persevere in his literary pursuits, unfettered by Ficino's limiting ideas. What surfaces in this depiction of Florinetta's experience, then, is the poet's lucid understanding of the tyranny of human passions, the cruelty of ambitious despots, and the subtlety human relations require. Florinetta's gastronomic education at the giants' tables—captors and rescuers alike—teaches her that the comforts of freedom are not found in lavish food, magnificent settings, and incongruous philosophical codes because they jar with the unpredictability of human nature. With an unerring feel for the nuances and subtext his own circumstances provide, Pulci thus signals his freedom from the Medici's yoke. Small hopes and expectations are now what drive him. But the awareness that his personal circumstances are only shadowed by courtly deceit, betrayals, resentments, and cowardice, not dictated by them, is a reenergizing—and much desired—consequence.

Curiously, the hunting expeditions the giants undertake to procure food while returning Florinetta to her family bring to light another important element: Morgante's selfishness. Yet again through food Pulci dramatizes the abuse of power-wielding demeanor. The ravenousness with which Morgante gulps down food paired with the deceptiveness he uses to trick Margutte out of his rightful share become, quite naturally, the source of the latter's increasing frustration and bitterness. The scenes depicting an angry and hungry Margutte also portray a self-absorbed and derisive Morgante. Unmoved by his companion's legitimate claims, Morgante remains entirely concerned with sating his own hunger because, he explains to Florinetta, "Il mio appetito / non può più sofferir, ch'è male avvezzo" ("My appetite," he to the maiden said, / "is not accustomed to more suffering") (19.82). While providing a truthful account of his need to eat, Morgante's words tread around the thorny question of sharing, in this case meals, in a fair manner. Actually, by veering toward the selfish his assertion underscores his indifference to fairness and friendship, ostensible bedrocks of courtly ideals. Beyond souring their friendship, eating of Margutte's share illustrates Pulci's awareness that the redemption offered by religion is offset by greed and hypocrisy. Specifically, while Margutte's earlier elucidation of his unethical and immoral faith cast him as the master of deceitfulness, Morgante's earlier conversion to Christianity should motivate him to share food and wine with his friend. Like fellowship and fairness, sharing—and partaking— of food is a fundamental tenet of the Christian doctrine.

But Morgante follows only nominally the teachings of his new religion. In this respect he is like Ficino, who converted from Platonic paganism to orthodox Christianity and was ordained as a priest in 1473. At the same time, he remained entwined in the knot of his philosophical/astral speculations and court intrigues while choreographing Lorenzo's personal and intellectual life. The image of a cunning Margutte helplessly plunged into famished isolation that is relieved only by the scraps of Morgante's dinners quantifies the distance between theory and practice, for Morgante as well as for Ficino. Paradoxically, by displaying a self-centered preoccupation with control and authority through food and eating Morgante, and not Margutte, embodies the deceitful glutton who conceals his true intentions with words but reveals them through his deeds. Through this inversion of roles the notion of human corruption emerges, giving prominence to the certainty of its unlimited potential. In the shift from words to deeds that shows Morgante taking pleasure in several gastronomic feasts at the expense of the ostensible true villain, the ambivalence between the professed and the real—or the eater and the eaten—reaffirms and reinforces Pulci's vision of a society perversely conforming to Ficino's (and Lorenzo's) shallow and unrealistic cultural models. If the thrust on human weakness that tears society apart and turns norms of courtesy on their heads drives a giant to betray his half-giant friend (and fellowman), moral principles are conveniently vaunted but seldom applied. In this fashion, the "outsiders" that on the surface confuse and deform the foundations of Renaissance ideals show that intellectual and civic-mindedness can be empty words if the ensuing deeds do not reflect the words. Alberti's Momus before Pulci had observed these traits in the human race and reported them to Jupiter:

> he realized that in all that pertains to war he had found nothing that smacked of fairness, nothing not utterly alien to justice. He saw that in all that crowd of soldier, there was nothing that showed respect for humanity or piety. He saw that everything turned on utility, on animal lust, on the disposition and condition of time and circumstance, as executed by violence and wickedness. The brave received no certain or deserved rewards; everything was weighed by the judgment and opinion of an ignorant rabble; plans and circumstances were judged by their outcome; and rewards were given not to virtue, but to reckless audacity.[114]

THREE

Banquets of Power
Boiardo's Innamorato *and the Politics of Gastronomy*

As we have seen in the previous chapters, power shapes people's social and political consciousness and, although it rarely reflects a consciousness of self, it is ever mindful of the privileged modes to which it is entitled. In Giovanni Boccaccio and Luigi Pulci, it is displayed through a variety of means, all of which are deliberate expressions and consolidations of grandeur and authority. This is the case for Matteo Maria Boiardo as well. In his *Orlando Innamorato*, food as a sociopolitical metaphor lends itself quite naturally to being a tool shaping social identity. In the *Politics* Aristotle characterizes the consumption of different foodstuffs in terms of the dissimilar "ways of life" that they produce.[1] The terms of the philosopher's argument appear inverted during the Renaissance. Still, to understand Boiardo's use of food we need to root him firmly in his historical context.[2] As discussed in the previous chapters, the culture of power clings to the notion that sustaining its sophisticated lifestyles requires the consumption of refined foodstuffs. Extant treatises available to modern scholarship attest to the fact that the culture and mentality of self-indulgent court life favored a diet based on rare delicacies elaborately prepared.[3] As a result, dietary conventions defined social identity. By emphasizing cultural divisions and social hierarchy, courtly society effectively conferred a status-building trait to gastronomy. The staging of stupendous and extravagant banquets in Renaissance Italy became another vehicle to express princely power. Through these lavish productions that ensured self-aggrandizement, the elite marked with food and banquets not only religious events and personal achievements, but also political alliances and exceptional loyalties.

For these occasions professional cooks transformed exotic ingredients into mouth-watering morsels and elaborate dishes that suited the sophisticated palates of those consuming them. Exquisite concoctions, prepared according to dietetic and culinary norms dispensed by highly regarded court doctors, philosophers, and humanists, translated the host's power into gastronomic spectacles.[4] Invariably, the theatricality associated with Renaissance banquets validated, and even magnified, his grandeur. As a coded but calculated language of persuasion, food ingratiated the host to the guests, and this enabled him to seize opportunities and capitalize on the advantages that the perception entailed. In view of this cultural reality, it is impossible to ignore the political and self-celebrating overlay superimposed to these convivial gatherings. Indeed, it is precisely because of the political implications (among others) that food transmits through its metaphorical or symbolic qualities that Renaissance banquets turn the host's private ambitions into public spectacles. The elaborately choreographed gastronomic maneuvers dazzled the guests while simultaneously securing the host's credibility through shrewdness. Of course, the sumptuousness of banquets was no evidence of either his competence or his integrity as a leader.

The banquet staged in 1473 by Sixtus IV's nephews Giuliano della Rovere and Pietro Riario to welcome Eleonora D'Aragona to Rome is a historical illustration of Renaissance gastronomic politics. Riario undertook intense efforts to ensure that before departing for Ferrara, where she was to become the wife of Ercole I, Eleonora and the duke's envoys, with Count Matteo Maria Boiardo among them, were entertained with unprecedented magnificence.[5] In the house he erected in her honor near the Church of the Holy Apostles, Cardinal Riario's wealth, power, and sophistication were meticulously displayed with clear objectives in mind. As to be expected, the splendid furnishings, new theatrical representations, and an opulent banquet left their mark on Riario's prestigious guests.[6]

Letters written by ambassadors, as well as by Eleonora herself, corroborate Riario's reputation as a powerful, worldly, and astute statesman. That Riario transformed the banquet into a formidable political maneuver is confirmed by the successful achievement of his immediate goal. By offering a public display of the pope's alliance with the Aragonese king whose daughter was marrying Duke Ercole d'Este, another papal ally, Riario simultaneously cast off the Orsini and the Medici, two powerful families that opposed Sixtus's territorial and political ambitions.[7] By astutely turning the political discourse into one of gastronomic seduction, and at the same time, by fusing the two into one ingenious triumph, Cardinal Riario gave new meaning to the Renaissance understanding of political strategizing. His deliberate substitution of a symbolically rich meal for a series of predictable political gestures demonstrated Riario's uncanny awareness of the possibilities offered by commensal diplomacy. He showed, among other things, that to influence people of power, diplomatic skillfulness must rely on, and permeate, every social activity in which those people took pleasure. At the same time, however, his strategy demonstrated that if eating at his table signaled the renewal of papal-Aragonese diplomatic relations, it also denoted the moral and ethical shortcomings of the parties partaking of the meal. The cardinal's banquet, devised as a carefully conceived scheme to promote papal interests, served as a stage for the porous and ambivalent relationship between the pope's power and the fickle nature of his political alliances. Yet, it left no space for Christian ethical values.[8]

Following the gastronomic conventions of the time, the three-course menu included stags roasted whole in their skins, goats, hares, calves, herons, peacocks with their feathers, and a bear—ostentatious dishes for a self-conscious group. Meats served covered in silver and innumerable sweets and confectionary shaped into artistic tableaux intended to stir and conquer the onlookers' imagination guaranteed the triumph of appearance. Every detail conjured up with a connoisseur's knowledge ensured that by adhering to the aristocratic culinary code, the far-reaching political implications of Riario's banquet served more as an attack on the pope's enemies than as praise of his new allies. An example of this is the bear meat that was served. The flesh of this animal was prized for its rarity more than its nutritional qualities. As

Platina explains in his *On Right Pleasure and Good Health*, and in accordance with the Galenic humoral theory, ingesting bear's meat "is not good for spleen or liver" because it "generates all kinds of indigestible residue."[9] Yet serving this meat implicitly evokes not only a man's hunt for, but also especially his overpowering of, a fiercely untamed force. The political message couched in the spectacle of a bear reduced to a meal obliquely calls to mind the powerful Orsini. This family was the pope's embittered rival and linked by marriage to the Medici. Playing on the homonym as well as on the meat's symbolic value, Riario's particular dish and the meal in general hinted at the Orsini's subjugation and ultimate downfall at the hands of the pope and his new allies. In this fashion, the pope's perceptive guests could foretaste, savor in fact, the political and economic benefits engendered by the newly formed alliance. Its powerful force, Riario intimates, would cause the decline and fall of his rivals.

Another passage in Platina's treatise emphasizes the weakness of the bear's head by contrasting it to the strength of the lion's. Accordingly, Riario's presentation of a "conquered" bear enhanced, by way of contrast, the mighty power that the Della Rovere, Aragonese, and Este families embodied. Above all, however, Riario's dish honored Ercole d'Este, whose name evoked the mythological figure of Hercules.[10] He, among his other labors, subdued the Nemean lion.[11] Thus, the presentation of the cooked bear when measured against the leonine strength Platina's treatise highlights directly calls to mind Hercules's power. And this, in turn, calls attention to Ercole d'Este's strength.[12] This audacious act of gastronomic politics on Riario's part is sustained by the notion that the diners' desire to crush the enemy is just as brutal. By suggesting that even feral nature could be reduced to submissiveness through resolute force, and in fact literally and metaphorically swallowed, Riario played on his (and the pope's) guests' eagerness to witness the Orsinis and their allies' demise. Through this, he intensified their urgency for action against them.

That Boiardo was present at this banquet as a member of the Este delegation infuses cogency to the meanings he assigns to food in his *Orlando Innamorato*.[13] In the shift from historical events to literary constructions, the interplay between power and banquets provides a riveting account of human behaviors, political discourse, social imperatives, and poetic imaginativeness. By marking moments of haughtiness, fear, happiness, and pleasure the presence of foodstuffs heightens the effects of the poet's purpose in subtle and stirring ways. The first canto of Boiardo's epic poem offers an elaborate example of this:

> Già sie appressava quel giorno nel quale
> Si dovea la gran giostra incominciare
> Quando il re Carlo in abito reale
> Alla sua mensa fece convitare
> Ciascun signore e baron naturale,
> Che vennero la sua festa ad onorare.[14]
>
> ———
>
> (The day drew near—that day on which / The titan tournament begins, / When, in his royal clothes, King Charles / Invited to his table each / Baron and knight of noble birth / Who came to grace his revelries.)

The octave places Charlemagne on the eve of the joust celebrating the feast of Pentecost presiding over a banquet surrounded by knights. The blend of power and self-awareness that inscribes the scene hinges on the fact that the meal is offered by the emperor to guests arrived to honor him in his city as he celebrates the Christian feast. This detail sets the political hierarchy clearly in focus. As the person who incarnates power, Charlemagne possesses the authority and means to declare a joust and invite all participants to his table. In point of fact, the Saracens asked to take part in the celebration amplify the magnitude of Charlemagne's political clout:

> Eranvi ancora molti Saracini,
> Perchè corte reale era bandita,
> Ed era a ciascaduno assigurato,
> che non sia traditore o rinegato.
>   (1.9)
>
> ———
>
> (And there were many Saracens, / Because court royal was proclaimed: / Anyone not an apostate / Or renegade was promised safety.)

These verses cast Charlemagne as an individual empowered to provisionally suspend the war and bring opposing factions together. Yet more than the joust, which recasts the idea of power in terms of adversarial forces confronting each other in a ludic context to affirm their supremacy, the image of enemies banqueting together suffuses the scene with an immediate, almost palpable sense of harmony. This idea shakes the foundations of hatred and antagonism on which wars are based. Coming together around a table gives a glimpse into peaceful possibilities that different cultural values make unconceivable. Unlike a joust, partaking of food (as we saw in the case of the freed Florinetta) does not entail forcing anyone to suffer a humiliating defeat. On the contrary, in a sense it binds people, friends as well as enemies, to a vision of a peaceful future. This future is built on the idea of shared goals and the ability—sometime flawed, but never unattainable—of achieving them.

The symbolism of Pentecost strengthens this idea. The feast recalls the Holy Spirit that empowered the apostles to speak in foreign tongues. Emboldened by this, they conversed in the different languages nonbelievers spoke, so as to deliver their message more effectively. In this manner they proclaimed the new covenant, converting a large part of the crowd that had gathered. This meaning of Pentecost is ostensibly retrieved through Charles's invitation to the Saracens. As the pagan adversary, they personify the foreignness that their language, practices, and conventions bring to the foreground. That the emperor, in an act of high-mindedness, reaches out to them through a meal on the religious holiday emphasizes the central role meals play within the Christian tradition. To be sure, the image of enemies sharing food infuses a symbolic value of sacredness into the scene, imbuing it with the notion of power that transcends—and unites—warring factions. This power, which has the capacity to suspend momentarily the reality of war and gather foes around the same table, effectively redraws the boundaries of Charles's authority. During the meal he watches not just over his knights, but also over his opponents and this, if only briefly, erases the dividing line that separates religion and politics. Conventions demand that, as guests, the Saracens must adjust to and follow the host's customs. Unsurprisingly, this norm relegates the Saracens to a position of passive power. In other words, although on the battlefield they personify the force that fights

Charles's, at the banquet, as his guests, they temporarily if unwittingly recast themselves in the role of his deferential subjects. At their enemy's banquet, they exhibit an impassive demeanor while he, paradoxically, takes on the role of their sovereign because of the food he provides. By temporarily turning into the nourishing emperor, fusing chivalric largesse with seeming Christian generosity, Charlemagne, like Cardinal Riario, forges a potent link between food and war that, in this specific case, is steeped in ambivalence. Through this, he conceals the chasm between the host's misleading generosity and the guests' indebtedness.

As the gastronomic translation of his power, Charles's banquet brings the stranger, the "other" that the adversarial Saracens embody, into the fold, transforming it into the familiar, friendly commensal. Yet in their temporary transformation—as invited guests—the Saracens are juxtaposed to the impermanence that food represents. The *finissime vivande* (food most succulent) served at the banquet requires turning ordinary ingredients into delicious bites. This is the same as creating new forms out of old ones. In gastronomy, this idea hinges on the process of transforming even decaying or fermenting ingredients into dishes appetizingly fresh and aesthetically pleasing. Blended together, seasoned, and cooked ingredients yield gastronomic dishes that retain the flavors, but not necessarily the shapes of original components. Through this process, culinary creations herald new and unforeseeable reconfigurations. But unlike other transformations, food transforms the transformed. Often, what appear to be spoiled ingredients, resulting from naturally occurring phenomena that entail organic decomposition, produce succulent edibles.[15] These, in their transient quality, mirror the consumer's impermanent nature, juxtaposing it with the permanence of history. Translated into historical terms, this culinary process can be compared to unexpected events rippling through separate actions that culminate in reshaping political realities and bearing social and cultural reconfigurations. Also like prepared food, historical developments set the permanence of outcomes against the impermanence of human nature.

At first glance, the constructive process of peace that Charles's food exemplifies suggests a correspondence with the role of dignified and obliging guests the Saracens play at his table. A rupture in this occurs, however, when the Saracens deride Rainaldo:

> Rainaldo avea di foco gli occhi accesi,
> Perché quei traditori, in atto altieri,
> L'avean tra lor ridendo assai beffato,
> Perché non era come essi adobato.
> Pur nascose nel petto i pensier caldi,
> Mostrando nella vista allegra fazza;
> Ma fra se stesso diceva: "Ribaldi,
> S'io vi ritrovo doman sulla piazza,
> Vedrò come stareti in sella saldi,
> Gente asinine, maledetta razza
> Che tutti quanti, se'l mio cor non erra,
> Spero gettarvi alla giostra per terra."
>
> (1.15–16)

(Rainaldo's eyes were lit with flames / Because those traitors, with proud airs, / Mocked him and laughed among themselves: / His clothes were not as rich as theirs. / He hid his thoughts inside / While showing them a face that smiled, / And he said to himself, "You rascals, / If you're found in the square tomorrow, / I'll see how solidly you're saddled! / Idiot family! Damned clan! / If my heart's true, I hope my lance / Will lay to earth each one of you.")

Set off by the mocking, the French knight bristles at being ridiculed for the modesty of his clothes; but with guarded emotions he conceals his resentment. In fact, his remarkable sense of self-control dominates the scene. By way of contrast, the Saracens' offensive remarks emphasize Rainaldo's courtly manners. Still, underneath the display of cordiality that the celebration calls for, his feelings toward them remain unchanged. Unconcerned with exercising any form of restraint, because he does not voice his thoughts, the knight considers the Saracens to rank somewhere between animals and humans, a combination, that is, of sinfulness, impurity, artificiality, and inauthenticity blended together with ambition. Although he reluctantly endures their taunting, he begins to grapple with the more vexing aspects of it. For him they suspend the peculiarity and wonder that result from enemies jointly partaking of a festivity. But by foretasting the sweetness of revenge he believes will be his the following day at the joust, Rainaldo's hatred toward the Saracens is unleashed, and this, paired with their insolent utterances, imbues their exchange with dark tension.

With a clear sense of wounded honor, the knight craves revenge while simultaneously concerned with keeping up appearances. The contrast between the inner and the outer states adds flavor to his nuanced ruminations over their mocking. It does not alter his perception of them. On the contrary, it reveals that despite superficial displays of kindliness, deep-seated hostility is not appeased through the celebration of religious feasts if a blind eye is turned to true meanings. That the celebration is a mere parody of Pentecost becomes evident as both factions carry on with the same fierce hostility that consumes them on the battlefield. They attack and deride each other's cultural mores with the buoyant certainty that comes from believing that they will respectively win the joust (and the war) they are fighting against each other and run the world, as they know it, according to their belief system. With each camp spurning the thought of accepting, assimilating, and celebrating the politics of identity that the different "other" produces and that the feast of Pentecost commemorates, the holiday turns into an empty spectacle of forms. By not paying heed to the basic norms of hospitality the meal requires from guests and hosts alike and using, instead, ferocious words to excoriate each other, both sides prove how dangerous and intransigent they remain. This type of conduct also attests to how insurmountable the cultural divide between them continues to be. Indeed, the banquet displays Charles's power and the influence he has over his guests, suggesting that for him and his knights, they, like *finissime vivande*, can be consumed, in fact devoured, by French power.

The fact that King Balugante, detecting Rainaldo's uneasiness, becomes embroiled in the searing exchange, adds combustibility to the fiery war of words that momentarily replaces that of the battlefield. Through a translator he pokes fun at Rainaldo by asking whether the court honors him for his virtues or his possessions: "Se nella corte di questo imperieri / Per robba, o per virtue se onorava" ("If honor in this emperor's court, / Was won by prowess or by wealth") (1.17). With this question, the king yet again draws attention to Rainaldo's simple outfit. Although the immediate goal is to humiliate him, the interesting point of Balugante's query is that it implicitly casts a serious doubt on the moral and ethical values of his Christian hosts. By raising the issue of appearances versus substance, hypocrisy versus sincerity, the pagan king strips the veneer of hospitality the banquet seeks to sustain. In so doing, he exposes it as a shallow ritual, organized for the superficial enjoyment of participants, guests as well as hosts, but lacking the true spirit of the event it seeks to reenact. Because it is a pagan who questions the authenticity and value of the occasion, Rainaldo's (and Charlemagne's) brazen misjudgment of the "other's" clear sense of the proper and improper is exposed. With extraordinary poignancy, through this suggestion Boiardo modifies the assessment Rainaldo formulates about the Saracens' character. They are not the only ones straying between the moral and immoral; the French too, and the emperor among them, are equally vulnerable to the paradoxical affectations that power can inspire. Constructed with a masterful circularity that aims at showing the cynical vision each side maintains in defaming the other without the pretense of being civic, Balugante's inquiry, while shaded with a deep sense of hubris, retrieves the symbolism of *vivande* in the way in which the appearance of a prepared dish disguises the nature of its ingredients.

The contempt in which the Christians hold the Saracens and their customs is emphasized by the manner in which the latter are described while partaking of the meal:

Saracini che non volsero usare banco né sponda,
Anzi sterno a giacer come mastini
Sopra a tapeti, come è loro usanza.
(1.13)

(Saracens / Who had no need of bench or couch; / Instead, they lay full length like hounds / On carpets, as they always do.)

The scene depicting them shifts the attention from the hosts' to the guests' culture. By displacing the focus from the meal itself and redirecting it to the social manners that the Saracens use, or more accurately lack when compared to the French counterpart, the scene dehumanizes them. As Boiardo knows, court protocol governing the practices and observances of Renaissance ceremonial banquets places the tables where aristocrats consumed their meals on raised platforms.[16] The spatial distance these structures enforce lays emphasis on the social rank of those gathered to eat. The ascending order, organized according to a scale of authority and power, distinguishes various degrees of nobility. This element visually reinforces the hierarchical ladder regulating the political structure governing the partakers' lives. Also, the arrangement implicitly suggests the moral, albeit self-ascribed loftiness, of those sitting on the dais. Most importantly, however, by enhancing the power and authority of those individuals, the raised tables construct a commensal hierarchy that furthers the separation of groups on the basis of their social standing.[17] In a marvelous illustration of the paradoxical power of commensality, the seating arrangements Boiardo brings into play result in two interlaced discourses. On the one hand, there is the strategic centrality—or marginality—of the participants based on the places they occupy. On the other hand, there is the actual duration—however long or brief—of the seating arrangements. Guests occupy more or less important places at the table for the span of the banquet. This is a reminder that high-ranking social positions are tied to time and subject to the capriciousness of the power-wielding leader. But because in this case time is determined by the length of the banquet, it is construed as a measure that transcends any other method or system of calculation, but it is tied to food. Thus, Boiardo links power and its duration to food.

Paintings of banquet scenes from this period and beyond attest to the presence of dogs at the feet of tables.[18] This presence ties in the convivial scene that rich meals tend to promote. It also underscores the host's wealth and power. Dogs positioned at the feet of tables where the elite consumes food and fed succulent leftovers tossed their way also enhance the sense of the owner-host's true worth.[19] Through a poetic image that retrieves the visual ones, Boiardo depicts the Saracens consuming their food not at the tables, but on rugs. By choosing to eat on the floor the guests occupy the space reserved for dogs. As perhaps to be expected, by following their customs rather than adjusting to those of their French hosts, the pagans separate themselves from their hosts and place themselves in the lowest space of the hall. Through this, they unwittingly relinquish the position of power that table seating affords. The implications of this eating arrangement feed the perception that the French harbor toward the guests' social awkwardness. And, in the illogical distortion at the root of intolerance, their seating choice is construed as moral depravity. In no time Rainaldo's loathing of the pagan guests becomes laced with sexual inferences. Specifically, by sitting below the tables and occupying the ambiguous space between the humans and nonhumans (men and dogs), the Saracens become the enablers if not direct architects of the sexual denigration to which their hosts subject them. Historically, Turkish—Saracen—customs were known to the Este court from as early as 1413, when Niccolò III, then marquis of Ferrara, went on a pilgrimage to the Holy Land.[20] Yet the contempt the aristocracy felt toward these people and their mores was never allayed. Infidels, pagans, barbarians, as well as homosexuals, sodomizers, and adulterer dogs, became part of the kaleidoscopic range of epithets Christians used to attack the Saracens because of their different customs and traditions.[21]

Rainaldo's view of Charles's guests reflects this awareness when with anger and unsentimental clarity he characterizes them as "gente asinina, maledetta razza" (1.16). By describing them as asinine people of a cursed race, he synthesizes his prejudices toward them: he explicitly labels them hybrid creatures. His opinion is based on a construction of "otherness" that excludes a priori the possibility of acceptance and inclusion because it would entail the acknowledgment and tolerance of cultural variables. Tolerance would also require the acceptance of ambiguities and tensions that are inherent to human interactions among individuals of different belief systems. From the position of moral superiority to which he feels entitled, the knight does not reason in this fashion. Because his certainties, however flawed they are, provide a sense of security and comfort that the uncertainty about the "other" removes, making him vulnerable, the knight doubles the dose of his vilification. He reviles the Saracens for lacking intelligence, a trait usually attributed to donkeys.[22] Curiously enough, his association of them sitting on floors with this particular animal recalls Isidore of Seville's explanation that the name *asinus* derives from *asedus*, "sitting."[23] Tapping into the deeper cultural currents of his times, Boiardo's poetic imagination floats unmoored, allowing him to skewer aristocratic beliefs in subtle ways. Accordingly, he depicts an insensitive Rainaldo who, oblivious to the moral implications his generalization entails, like a true Este courtier makes no attempt to understand the issues that shape the "other." In so doing, Rainaldo bases his belief solely on the platitude of constructs and learned hypocrisies rather than on personal experience. Needless to say, this attitude not only robs him of the possibility of extracting meanings from experience, but especially prevents him from differentiating between substance and appearance.

Predictably, Rainaldo does not take kindly to being publicly mortified by the Saracens. Still, he controls his simmering resentment against impetuousness and impulsiveness, maintaining an ostensibly unaffected behavior. But his retort to Balugante shows the increasingly more elusive possibility of finding a common ground between the two sides:

> ... Ch'e i giotti a mensa e le puttane in letto
> Sono tra noi più volte acarezate;
> Ma dove poi conviene usar valore,
> Dasse a ciascuno il suo debito onore.
> (1.18)

> ("Whores in bed and, at dinner gluttons / Most often get endearments from us, / But when our valor is on view, / Let each receive the honor due!")

Rainaldo's bitter words, steeped in the irrepressible confidence that comes from cultural beliefs and shapes a theory of self-serving indulgence, blur the line between civil and uncivil discourse, showing that humanity is incapable of understanding, or even sympathizing with, worlds and outlooks that are different from those that make it feel secure. By explaining that Christians indulge gluttons at the tables, pamper whores in beds, and confer honor only according to courage, Rainaldo defines his cultural understanding of appearance and substance.

According to Rainaldo's logic, gluttons who ravenously devour, and who are at the same time devoured by the rapacity of their desires, are appeased, and subjugated, by the French according to their want. Like gluttons, prostitutes are also enslaved by and succumb to the perversion of desires that makes them vulnerable prey in the hands of canny French pursuers. The sustained intensity of Rainaldo's argument, pairing gluttons and prostitutes, food and flesh, hinges on the deep-rooted Christian belief that, as discussed in the previous chapters, links the seductiveness of eating to sexual seduction. But as it seeks to shed light on and extol the French code of values while uplifting the knight's self-esteem, this argument only fuels tension between the two sides. To be sure, although driven by a fiercely defiant reaction to the grueling mocking he has been put through, Rainaldo's answer skirts the edges of ethical and moral principles, as well as of acceptability. For him, it represents a liberating act because it allows him to whip together religion and traditions, presenting them to his enemy as the proof of French high-principled character. Yet, when scrutinized more closely, his appealing answer turns appalling. Aside from the inherent spark of menace, it casts, first of all, the Saracens as people lacking a code of values and, therefore, willing to prostitute moral and ethical principles for material gains. As a result, it presents them as detractors, and destroyers, of traditions and conventions.

It goes without saying that the knight's tart indictment unveils the hypocrisy saturating his own (and the Christians') belief system. While he claims that honor at the French court is the measure of one's courage, his argument exposes deeper chords that resonate with his and his people's failure to understand that courage cannot be gauged by using flawed models. For the conscious, single-minded depravity necessary to preying on gluttons' and prostitutes' weaknesses discloses the perpetrators' cowardice. By depicting himself and his fellow-knights as men skilled at gratifying the wants of individuals incapable of self-control in return for personal gains, Rainaldo ascribes to his faction the same deceitfulness and immorality for which he faults the Saracens. Accordingly, his rationale for the validity of the honor system governing his camp fizzles out, leaving only the shell of his argument. The emptiness of his argument mirrors the ostentatious but meaningless celebration of Pentecost for which they have gathered. Reduced to a display of aesthetic, not ethical, importance, Charles's commemoration turns into a ritual of forms, hollow of spiritual meanings. The cornerstone of Christian beliefs, paraded into a spectacle of power to aggrandize the image of French superiority in the Saracens' eyes, only suggests the prostitution of moral and ethical values. This evisceration of principles on which Rainaldo's Christian camp bases its foundations logically rules out honor. Because of this, Rainaldo's scathing but flawed assertion with regard to honor shows both his unawareness of the subtle implications his own argument presents and his failure to recognize the facts as they present themselves.

Given his position as leader and role model, Charlemagne's opinion of the Saracens is more deceitful than Rainaldo's. He guardedly masks his disdain for the enemy-turned-guests with feigned cordiality. The scene depicting the emperor honoring every guest with a particular vessel and *vivanda*—"Chi de una cosa e chi d'altro onorava, / Mostrando che di lor si racordava" (honoring them for various / Deeds, showing no forgetfulness) (1.20)—makes this apparent. By acknowledging each prominent guest with special dishes and delicacies the emperor establishes a correspondence between the dishes' exquisiteness and the guests' individual worthiness. While this balancing act bolsters the self-image he painstakingly cultivates, it also ensures that he maintains his ascendancy over everyone present. On the surface, he remains the attentive, unprejudiced, and appreciative emperor for all of them. Yet this behavior too merely conceals the consuming hatred he feels toward the Saracens. In fact, his sense of superiority and self-righteousness, accentuated by the position he occupies on the higher table and stirred by the notion of the nourishing emperor he carefully cultivates, is underlined in the scene that juxtaposes his sense of greatness with the contempt he secretly feels for the Saracens:

> Re Carlo, che si vidde in tanta altezza,
> Tanti re, duci e cavallier valenti,
> Tutta la gente pagana disprezza.
>   (1.20)
>
> ———
>
> (King Charles, who basked amid his nobles, / Many kings, dukes, and valiant knights, / Scorns all the pagan populace.)

The social hierarchy that the eating arrangement emphasizes does not correspond to Charles's awareness of the degree of his bigotry. On the contrary, it clashes with the divisive thoughts occupying his mind. His hypocrisy calls to mind Boccaccio's king of France. In that case, the king disguised his true interest for the marchioness with the request of a meal. But once he was served it, he was unable to grasp its meaning because he assumed that she would yield to his advances. His inability to differentiate between appearance and substance that meat and sauces signified stemmed from the same root. But by drawing his attention to them the marchioness undermined the king's plan and remained faithful to her husband. Like the king of France, Charlemagne's attitude toward the Saracens is based on presumptions.

Reduced to a perfunctory act, his observance of Pentecost discloses on the one hand the underlying cultural divide separating the two groups and, on the other, the moral contradictions undermining the feast's true meaning. Boiardo makes it clear that the emperor considers the Saracens "come arena del mar denanti a i venti" ("as ocean sends before the winds") (1.20). This detail reveals the full measure of Charles's scorn toward people he perceives as inferior—in strength, character, and knowledge—to him. As he evokes the biblical image of sand blown by forceful wind, Charles misconstrues the meaning of the psalm.[24] There, man's vulnerability is counterbalanced by God's compassion, and discloses, instead, his misplaced sense of superiority. The emperor's misguided interpretation is reminiscent of the manner in which he fails to embrace the "others" in their diversities while pretending to welcome them at his table. By closing his eyes to the tolerance and to the human capacity for forgiveness that breaking bread with the enemy entails, Charles's hypocrisy is simultaneously opaque and yet obvious, even more so than his knight's. And the gastronomic utopia he devises and exploits to his own benefit mirrors his falsity.

In the wake of Charlemagne's barely concealed contempt, Balugante's insinuation juxtaposing wealth and courage indirectly exposes the moral inconsistencies cultivated by the sophisticated court culture with which Boiardo was familiar. From this perspective the banquet's refined *vivande*, transformed through the elaborate preparations of ingredients, is the symbolic correspondent to a mode of conduct that favors appearance over substance. The encoded meanings of the emperor's banquet disclose the layers of deceitfulness marking the French interactions with the Saracens. As the space where commensal politics take place to seduce the enemy, render it harmless, and even temporarily turn it into an obliging if not avowed ally, Charles's banquet is the literary counterpart to Riario's Roman feast. Like the historical one, rather than marking the hosts and partakers' moral and ethical integrity, this banquet highlights the way in which threats are turned into self-serving practices. Under the veneer of conventional Judeo-Christian symbolism both banquets offer a glimpse into the partakers' unscrupulous hunger for power: power of possessions, power of wealth, and power to enforce particular perspectives. For this reason, the banquets provide images of material and sensual desires that both hosts and guests yearn to gratify.

It is curious that Boiardo does not specify the particular dishes served at Charles's banquet. Rather, he vaguely refers to them as *finissime vivande*. This peculiar ambiguity contrasts with the precision the poet employs to describe the richness of the vessels used to serve the food. Boiardo's familiarity with the gastronomic practices the Este court favored unequivocally suggests that Charlemagne's Pentecost meal hinges on the gastronomy of power. The dietary rules the Este court follows were established under Borso d'Este. For him, Michele Savonarola wrote *Libreto de tutte le cosse che se magnano*.[25] Throughout its twenty-five chapters the treatise, a comprehensive work on foodstuffs and ingredients that provides explanations of their nutritional values, never loses sight of its audience. It is solely intended for "zentili e richi homini" (noble and wealthy men). This objective almost establishes a dialectic correspondence between food and consumers, whereby delicate, exotic, and delicious food is always associated with aristocratic palates. Coarser food, on the contrary, is deemed unappetizing for the elite and, as a result, only appropriate for plebeian stomachs. Given the specificity Savonarola's treatise offers and the prestige it sheds on a court that painstakingly cultivates its image of sophisticated wealth, it is surprising that Boiardo, the court's poet, would pass up the opportunity to showcase his patrons' culinary tastes. But the significance of this ostensible peculiarity lies in the wider context of the *Innamorato*'s crucial first canto. Here, more than just the action of the whole poem is set in motion. Indeed, the "ingredients for the whole meal," as it were, are organized. In other words, by not adopting the same accuracy he makes use of elsewhere in his poem, Boiardo deliberately speaks of *vivande* to broaden the possible meaning of food. The lack of precision the word suggests rather than being limiting, then, opens up to interpretative possibilities in a way that no one identifiable dish would. For Boiardo's courtly audience, *finissime vivande* evokes a large repertory of meltingly exquisite delicacies. It also conjures up seductive images of seizing, appropriating, and possessing that lead to nibbling, tasting, and devouring. Of course, these images are not restricted to foodstuffs per se. To the contrary, as it will be discussed below, relishing delicious *vivande* becomes one and the same with taking pleasure in another human being. Accordingly, in Boiardo's masterful use of *vivande*, food and physical pleasure overlap as irresistible physiological and subjective ingredients that humanity is willing to go to any length to obtain.

According to Louis Marin, through the process that transforms raw ingredients into prepared dishes, foodstuffs become a sign encompassing elaborate ideological, political, and cultural concepts. He argues that it is through this metamorphosis that the comestible is transformed into the signified and the speakable into the edible.[26] In his analysis, Marin defines food as a transignificant because it becomes a metaphor, acquiring new meanings completely disassociated from its original physical significance.[27] Marin's argument is especially relevant to Boiardo's lack of specificity with regard to the *vivande* served at Charles's banquet. It also helps us understand Boiardo's abrupt way of shifting attention from the banquet to Angelica.

I

At this point in the canto the meal is interrupted by Angelica's arrival. Followed by her brother and a retinue of knights, and surrounded by four giants, she explains to Charlemagne the reason for her coming. Her brother, she announces, wishes to duel the knights gathered for the joust, French and Saracens alike. She will be the winner's prize while the losers will be taken prisoners. What Angelica conceals from her attentive audience is the fact that her father, King Galifrone, intends to decimate the French force by capturing its knights. To accomplish this goal, he has provided both daughter and son with magical instruments. For this reason, Angelica's practical challenge is a mere ploy, a poisonous appetizer that appeals to, and stimulates, the bittersweet anxiety over the personal ambition and military prowess emboldening the French. The end foreshadowed in this beginning is camouflaged in her beauty. It ensnares every man, forcing him to abandon his duties:

> Però che in capo della sala bella
> Quattro giganti grandissimi e fieri
> Intrarno, e lor nel mezzo una donzella,
> . . . Essa sembrava matutina stella.
> (1.21)

(Because, far down the splendid hall, / Four fearsome and enormous giants / Entered, a maiden in their midst . . . / She seemed to be the morning star.)

By interjecting the strangers' arrival into the meal's convivial tableau, Boiardo infuses the scene with a sense of impending mayhem. While the presence of four giants surrounding a beautiful woman conveys the idea of protecting a weak person, a core tenet of knightly values, it also suggests a more nuanced understanding of the unsettling threat that she poses. As discussed in the previous chapter, humanistic theories associate anomalous bodies with transgression, lawlessness, gluttony, and, more generally, a villainess. For this reason, the fact that four giants safeguard the beautiful woman should raise the awareness of those gathered at Charles's celebration. By accompanying her as her bodyguards, the giants bear evidence that she belongs to the same system they inhabit and typify.

Yet, self-aggrandizing ideas are hardly compatible with perspicacity. As to be expected, Angelica's appearance disrupts the feast, wreaking havoc among the men, interrupting even the hostile verbal exchange between the opposing camps. Immediately, everyone's attention turns to her. Alluring and enigmatic, moving comfortably among the men, with her tale she captivates them all and with her dazzling beauty she distracts everyone. Unexpectedly, cultural and political divergences are forgotten; every man puts food and quarrels out of his mind and, in so doing, turns into a restless, jittery, impatient, and insistent person yearning for her. Both Christians and pagans are instantly inflamed by the desire to possess her. With a twist to Rainaldo's earlier assertion, Boiardo shows that the men's visceral reaction to her, the hunger they feel for Angelica, consumes and yokes them all. By seizing their attention, Angelica replaces the *vivande* they were consuming, effectively becoming the *vivanda* each man craves and believes he can feast on for his pleasure. In this ironic turn of events, just as the partaking of a meal turned powerful enemies into obliging if insincere guests, the new delicacy, the pagan Angelica, turns her foes, the Christian men (as well as the Saracens), into submissive subjects. The force of this shift is made particularly manifest by the way in which not only the knights, but the emperor too, are described as mesmerized by her beauty.

From the towering haughtiness of his dais Charles is not impervious to the power Angelica's attractiveness exerts. The irony that suffuses the scene rests on the image of a transfixed emperor whose life experiences have acquainted him with military triumphs and personal victories but whose composure crumbles as he confronts a beguiling woman. A greater challenge than the ones encountered on the battlefields because she appeals to the ungovernable passions of man, even though the man she addresses governs his subjects, Angelica pulls the thread to Charlemagne's fabric of self-possession:

> Re Carlo Magno con lungo parlare
> Fe' la risposta a quella damigella,
> Per poter seco molto dimorare.
> (1.35)

(In a long speech, King Charles the Great / Offered the damsel his response, / Keeping her long as possible.)

Charles's desire to indulge in Angelica's presence, to be the center of her undivided attention, is tactfully framed in his lengthy answer to her request. Charles's reply, as Boiardo puts it, registers not just his capitulation to her, but especially his craving to savor her company. This particular is underscored by Boiardo's use of *dimorare*, a verb that etymologically retrieves the meanings of both lingering and residing. Through his unanticipated behavior, the emperor upends the conventions of proper, wise, and vigilant conduct that he, more than the knights, is expected to exemplify. Also, by introjecting his power as a way of controlling events and keeping Angelica's attention, the emperor conveys the impression that while basking in the authority of conventions, he personifies the conflict between desire and norms, public duty and private desires. His sudden enthrallment with Angelica denotes his opportunistic sense of responsibility and this furthers the symbolic meaning of transignificance that Marin ascribes to food. For unlike the appetizing morsels he has magnanimously shared with both courtiers and enemy, the emperor greedily keeps Angelica—the woman who embodies everyone's new *vivanda*—to himself. The power play that is at work in this image is sustained by Charlemagne's desire to possess what no one else does. In other words, he wants what he perceives to be his entitlement. Perhaps, his fascination with Angelica is stirred by the desire to outshine the younger knights, showing them that his autumnal pulse is still receptive to the senses. Like the younger men, he has succumbed to the desire for her. Because of this, he agrees, without much consideration or a reflective moment to confront the possibility of error, almost as a transgressor silently reassuring himself, to the terms of her request.

Although Angelica's true intentions are hidden from him at this juncture, Charlemagne's lack of concern with the accuracy of her story suggests, like his banquet, his fascination with form rather than substance. His taste for aesthetic pleasures trumps the one for ethical conduct. This appears most conspicuously in the verse that describes him as a man who "mira parlando e mirando favella" (speaking he stares; staring he speaks) (1.35). The image of the aloof, vigilant, and focused leader is here countered with one that exposes a man bewitched by, and therefore vulnerable to, the attractiveness of his interlocutor. *Mirare*, which fuses both "to look" and "to admire," sums up Charles's susceptibility to Angelica's beauty. Yet it is his *parlare* ("to talk") that turns into *favellare* ("to tell tales"), suggesting a shift from self-controlled to unguarded and even fantastic conversation that more precisely discloses his capitulation to her. As he yields to her, the ethical and moral flaws of his character surface and this, in turn, makes his role as the French leader, closely attuned to maintaining a peaceful and controlled image, questionable. By turning into Angelica's pawn the power he imperiously embodied and displayed throughout his banquet teeters on the brink of powerlessness and subjection. The scrumptious but unspecified foodstuffs, in a sense the bait, with which he temporarily disempowered the Saracens, finds its correspondence in Angelica who thrusts him—Charlemagne—like all the men around him into a powerless position.

Charlemagne's inability to control his emotions at the sight of the charming Angelica stands in sharp contrast with another King Charles. In *Decameron,* 10.6, Fiammetta tells the tale of old King Charles who becomes intrigued by Messer Neri's garden. This Ghibelline knight, according to the narrator, left Florence and settled in Castel da mare di Stabia after Manfredi's defeat. While visiting the town, the king decides to see Neri's garden in person. He wants to verify for himself whether its beauty matches people's descriptions. Despite Messer Neri's political affiliation and lower rank, King Charles sends word of his wish to dine with him in the garden in the company of a few other courtiers. Messer Neri obliges. On the night of the visit, the king admires the host's garden and dines there on fine foods. But when Messer Neri's fifteen-year-old twin daughters suddenly appear to pay homage to the royal guest, the king, like all the men in his entourage, is immediately smitten—a scene that is repeated when Charlemagne is in Angelica's presence. That the two girls later get into the fishpond fully clothed further arouses King Charles: "ma sopra ad ogn'altro erano al re piaciute, il quale sì attentamente ogni parte del corpo loro aveva considerate, uscendo esse dall'acqua, che chi allora l'avesse punto non si sarebbe sentito" (he had been charmed more than anybody else, and so attentively had he been watching every part of their bodies as they emerged from the water that if someone were to have pinched him at that moment, he would not have felt it). He is mesmerized by the twins' beauty. While at first their courtly deportments charmed him, now it is their shapely bodies that bedazzle him. Even so, his awareness of the desire their sight has aroused in him conflicts with his inability to determine which of the two is the true cause of his newborn passion: "né sapeva egli stesso qual di lor due si fosse quella che più gli piacesse" (nor did he even know which of the two pleased him the most). King Charles's perplexity surprises him; he wrestles with the arduous choice and yet he finds no immediate answer to it. Thus, he questions their father Messer Neri about them. From him Charles finds out that Ginevra and Isotta are the girls' names. The king also learns that they cannot be given in marriage because the family lacks the means to marry them.

Caught in the throes of his newborn passion, King Charles does not make a connection between the girls' names and the literary heroines they evoke. He pays no attention to the fact that Ginevra and Isotta call to mind two queens of the Arthurian romances who were unfaithful to their husbands. Both queens, Guinevere and Isolde, incarnated unsurpassed beauty; at the same time, they loved young knights rather than their respective, much older husband-kings. Indeed, in Sir Lancelot and Tristan each queen found fulfillment for her passion. And although the two couples lived their respective loves according to the principles governing courtly love, their actions upended rules, caused mayhem, and defied both sociopolitical and religious codes. But Fiammetta's King Charles pays no heed to these antecedents. At the end of the supper, stirred by an emotion he cannot control, he returns to his palace. In the days that follow the thought of Ginevra in particular does not abandon him. In spite of the important affairs of state occupying his mind, his love for her grows stronger. Finally, when he can no longer keep it secret, he decides to take both girls for himself and reveals his plan to Count Guido of Monforte. The count, however, dissuades him from carrying it out. He accomplishes this by explaining to the king that this action would first of all break the bond of trust Messer Neri has put in him. Indeed, Neri opened his house for the Guelph king. Count Guido also reminds him that Manfredi's violence against women brought about his downfall.[28] By acting like his defeated enemy, Count Guido reasons, Charles would become himself a vulnerable target for retaliation. Lastly, the trusty counselor—a peak of strength, as his name Monforte suggests—reminds the king that conquering Manfredi was a small feat if he cannot restrain and control his passion. The truth of Count Guido's words persuades Charles to master his desire. As a result, he sets his personal interests aside. He even turns into a paternal figure for the two maidens by providing them with the needed dowries for appropriate marriages. True to the role she plays as a storyteller throughout the *Decameron*, Fiammetta ends her tale showing that by relying on reason social and political order is not disrupted.

But there are other elements in Fiammetta's tale that foreshadow the king's final change of mind. And these, obviously, have nothing to do with the girls' names. The first one is linked to their actions on the night they appear in their father's garden. There, after they pay homage to the king, Isotta and Ginevra return attired and equipped to catch fish for his table from the pond. For this purpose one of them has "in su le spalle un paio di vangaiole, le quali con la sinistra man tenea, e nella destra aveva un baston lungo" (two fishnets over her left shoulder and held a long pole in her right hand) while the other "aveva sopra la spalla sinistra una padella e sotto quel braccio medesimo un fascetto di legne e nella mano un treppiede, e nell'altra mano uno utel d'olio e una facellina accesa" (carried a frying pan over her left shoulder and a bundle of kindling wood under the same arm, with a tripod in one hand and a terracotta oil container and a small, lighted torch in the other).[29] As they are described in this scene the twins display an unseemly courtly demeanor. Not only do they carry working tools, they also look as though they are prepared to do the work themselves. And this strikes the king, as well as the readers, as out of character with the two elegant young ladies whom he first met. In and of itself, the spectacle of the twins wading into the water and later coming out of it with wet clothes adhering to their bodies is highly erotic: "le fanciulle . . . , essendosi tutto il bianco vestimento e sottile loro appiccato alle carni, né quasi cosa alcuna del dilicato lor corpo calando" (their white, thin garments clinging to their skin concealing hardly any part of their delicate bodies) (*Decameron*, 1145). That they prepare to catch fish by net is even more so because the notion of maidens taking on the role of fishermen entails codeswitching. In other words, their activity and conduct at this point conflicts with the social position they occupy; but it also coincides with an ambiguous inversion of gender. Typically, in fact, fish-catchers are represented as males. Yet Boccaccio upends this figural code. One possible explanation for this image is that he is toying with Matthew's account:

"come after me and I will make you fishers of men" (4:19). The words Jesus speaks to Simon and Peter, two fisherman-brothers, are reinterpreted, as it were, by Boccaccio through Messer Neri's daughters. It goes without saying that Boccaccio's rendering of Matthew's lines is empty of the spiritual meaning with which Jesus' words are suffused. For in this construal, the twins' fishing becomes metaphorically evocative of women ensnaring men. Also, if one follows this reading of Boccaccio's novella to its logical conclusion, it appears evident that just as fish trapped in nets die, men caught by women relinquish their power. This is in fact the case of King Charles, who finds himself quite spontaneously overpowered by Ginevra's and Isotta's attractiveness.

The second element suggesting that the king's course of action must change to avoid ruin becomes evident at the end of the dinner. At this point the sisters appear once again in his presence elegantly attired. This time they hold "due grandissimi piattelli d'argento in mano pieno di frutti vari" (two enormous silver trays filled with all kinds of fruits that were in season) (*Decameron*, 1146). As it will be discussed below, in medical-dietary treatises fruit is considered unhealthy, in fact, even harmful to the health of the individual consuming it. Depicting the girls offering it to the king could be construed, therefore, as Boccaccio's signal of Charles's impending ruin. Interestingly, the narrator does not specify whether the guests consume the fruit or not. But Ginevra and Isotta's proffering it to the already besotted king evokes the image of Eve's offer to Adam. The correspondence between the two images played on the notes of fruit that—like the beautiful girls—is simultaneously tempting and disastrous, amplifies Boccaccio's message, though still in a figurative mode, that the senses can play havoc with social order and political stability. For were King Charles to act on his impulse and feed his libido on the rhetoric of violence, he would be brought down by the shame it caused.

Of course, Boiardo's Charlemagne is not concerned with these issues. For this reason, at his banquet the scale of commensal hierarchy, diligently engineered to gauge the distance between social statuses and especially between pagan and Christian universes, is abruptly tipped by Angelica. As a Saracen and a woman who incarnates the unexpected and—no longer—unspecified morsel, with her presence she turns the tables on Charles's banquet. As the knights abandon the camp in her pursuit she destabilizes the order Charles has meticulously constructed.

We know that Cardinal Riario through his banquet succeeded in imposing his interests over his guests. The Pazzi conspiracy that exposed the Riario-Della Rovere plotting backfired in 1478, thus not immediately affecting papal maneuverings. Yet Boiardo, the ambassador-poet of the Este court,[30] who participated at the historical banquet and had firsthand experience of gastronomic politics at work, does not afford the same success to his characters. Time and again he questions and then undermines the legitimacy not just of their personal interests but the means by which they seek to achieve them. He probes into their obsession with rules and decorum by interrogating their inability to confront embarrassing truths. In canto 1 Rainaldo and Charlemagne, blind to what they perceive to be both irrelevant and extraneous to their moral superiority, do not question the principles on which they base their certainties. Nor do they show any propensity or ability to scrutinize themselves and their doings. As a conduit for exposing the duplicity, ambiguity, and limits of power devoid of self-analysis foodstuffs and banquets serve Boiardo formidably in this first canto of the *Innamorato*. They show that despite the sense of aloofness and control their cultivated images seek to convey, powerful individuals who lack a clear sense of introspectiveness, like elaborate *vivande*, conceal their true moral character under visual and ideological self-serving disguises.

This, of course, raises more intriguing questions. Does it represent Boiardo's oblique critique of the Este court? Does the prominent role he plays within it allow him a privileged perspective that is at once filled with wonderful incongruities and incongruous wonders? Is he too honest to accept them or, like his characters, too dishonest to denounce them? As part of the system and yet somehow apart from it, with tuned attentiveness the poet negotiates and understands the terms of the chivalric world the court embraces and that has gradually spent its promise of perfection. The immediacy of Charlemagne's capitulation to Angelica's charm evidences this. Still, could his unsuitable reaction to her just be a matter of a persuasive woman appearing at the wrong time and making an offer that no reasonable man could possibly resist?

II

Like all knights who instantly fall into a reverie of attraction for Angelica when they first see her, Orlando is smitten by her beauty. From the first moment he sees her, the urge to possess her drives all of his actions. Only for a moment is the sweetness of his new desire edged with a sour feeling of self-doubt. This occurs when the knight recognizes that by enfolding him in its grip, passion distracts him from his moral and ethical responsibilities. Yet, doing away with duty jars with humanist ideals that underscore reason's power to keep the senses under control.[31] This is why Orlando becomes acutely aware of the crippling ambivalence that Angelica's magnetism causes in him. He articulates his awareness in terms of a maddening, uncontrollable desire that by overpowering his reason diverts him from his obligations, leading him to err. Suddenly, his hunger for Angelica appears to him for what it truly is: a desire lacking a moral purpose. The resulting emotional struggle this realization entails by defying his anxiety also defies his reason:

> "Ahi paccio Orlando!"—nel suo cor dicia
> —"Come te lasci a voglia trasportare!
> —Non vedi tu lo error che te desvia,
> E tanto contra Dio te fa fallare."
> (1.30)

("Ah, mad Orlando!"—in his heart— / "How you let longing lead you off! / Don't you see sin entices you, / And makes you disobey your God?")

A note of sorrowful defeat reverberates in these words; and they vividly distill Orlando's preoccupation with the fact that Angelica's ascendancy threatens to transform, if not completely destroy, him. As he confronts his own fallibility, it is almost as though in trying to grapple with the fierce attraction simmering in his heart, Orlando pauses in pain, as if stung by the thought of her effect on his life. This idea is further emphasized by *desvia* (to lead astray), a verb that naturally calls to mind the opening canto of Dante's *Inferno*. There, where his "diritta via era smarrita" (the straight way was lost),[32] in order to resume his journey the Pilgrim must confront the threats that hinder his passage. The echo of the wayfarer's words reverberates within Orlando and fills him with a sense of impending failure. Like his literary antecedent, the knight painfully recognizes the impasse he has reached. Unlike the Pilgrim, however, and because of his humanistic education, Orlando believes that the power to prevail over, or more precisely, to achieve what he yearns for, rests solely with him.[33]

Orlando's analysis of his emotions and their implications points to Boiardo's fresh, subtle, and surprising depiction of a hero who is aware of the perilous path that lies ahead and yet cannot resist its biting allure (or is it power?):

"Io non mi posso dal cor dipartire
La dolce vista del viso sereno,
Perch'io mi sento senza lei morire . . .
Or non mi val forza, né lo ardire
Contra d'Amor, che m'ha già posto il freno."
(1.31)

("I cannot from my heart displace / The sight of her— her sweet, bright face— / Because I think I'll die without her . . . / Now neither strength nor courage helps / Against the bridling force of Love.")

The idea of the hero who cannot assuage his longing suffuses the scene with pain and beauty. Desire renders Orlando powerless and his words register his awareness of it. They also make it plain that at this juncture he harbors no illusions about his ability to wrestle with, much less overcome, the desire through courage and force—in spite of what he claims in canto 25. More importantly, though, Orlando's terse and lucid assertion discloses his understanding that sheer will cannot bridle the senses. The tension this admission conveys is due in no small part to the emphasis that humanists place on the will as the faculty guiding humanity through the labyrinthine maze of senses. Still, Orlando's words also serve Boiardo to invite a nuanced perspective on his hero.

In fact, they establish a correspondence between Orlando and the Petrarchan lover.

To begin with, both men are overwhelmed by the sense of anguish love causes to those individuals who willingly surrender to it. But the emotional awareness they both reveal also suggests that for Orlando, just as for Petrarch's lover, to be caught in the amorous web entails the suspension of rationality because love defies every reasonable thought. This makes Boiardo's lover incapable of harnessing his self-control. As a result, he becomes unable to either champion or defend the principles that define his courtly upbringing. More than this, however, for Petrarch the emotional instability that love engenders threatens the poetic voice.[34] For Boiardo, on the contrary, it especially imperils the political one. As Orlando yearns to conquer a human body, he turns his back on and forfeits his rights to the political one. With this unsurprising shift from the personal to the political Boiardo grounds the present of his knight in the lessons of the past. More precisely, given the scenario that the Petrarchan lover provides, Orlando should emerge as a man who has learned from the failed efforts of his literary predecessor whose enduring and unfulfilled desire drained him of every bit of energy, in the end crushing him. Availing oneself of examples the past offers in order to secure the present and ensure the future is a notion that Boiardo favors not just as a poet, but also especially as a political adviser and ambassador. This didactic model, he knows, can be particularly instructive for the Estes.[35] Emboldened by the power they wield, they are consumed by a ruthless desire to advance their personal ambitions.[36] Moreover, they close their eyes to people's needs. Thus, they neither strive for nor safeguard public interests. In political terms Boiardo's cautionary note aims primarily at Duke Ercole's unrestrained lifestyle:[37] his unconcealed political determination undermines the stability of the duchy. As a result, his corrupt and oppressive regime reinforces a culture of deeper political stagnation. The moral, ethical, and economic plundering this creates at every level of the system speaks of debauchery and decadence that cannot be reined in because leadership fails to set the example.

For Boiardo the effectiveness of the court's power is gauged through events that reveal a shift from the past. This is particularly true with regard to adverse or flawed conditions that negatively affect people's lives.

According to the poet, by improving people's circumstances the court can boast tangible proof of its power and success. This position informs his poetic writing. In gastronomic terms, this idea could be compared to improving an old recipe. As Francesco Guicciardini suggests, modern tastes and needs require adjustments and revisions of old models. In gastronomy, the adaptation to modern preferences takes place through unfamiliar and more appealing preparations. This practice may also benefit from the enhancement of flavors heightened by the use of spices.[38] This technique need not be forbiddingly extravagant; rather, it calls for more effective strategies that better satisfy modern palates. The resulting new spectrum of complex flavors and aromas the changes bring out gives way to unusual, improved twists on the familiar ones. Thus gastronomy turns old recipes into more appetizing dishes. By making a statement on their own the new culinary creations not only appeal to the senses, they especially attest to the cook's skillfulness in challenging the long-established norms. Through the improvement of results he ensures the consumers' satisfaction and they, in turn, become more receptive to his innovative creations. Applied to the sociopolitical arena, this model illustrates the way in which ineffectual systems can be improved on and changed to ensure that people outside of the court, and not just courtiers, benefit from better living conditions. The tax system levied on the citizens of Ferrara to finance the court's magnificence is an example of this. For the Estes, like Medici in Florence, Alfonso I in Naples (at whose court Ercole was raised), and the Sforza in Milan,[39] *magnificentia* was based on the Aristotelian principle that a great ruler spends lavishly to honor himself, his family, and his rule.[40] For this reason, for Ercole I d'Este the notion of ameliorating the living standards of his subjects is of little importance at first.[41] He makes it his concern much later, and only when the threat from Venice and the defeat that follows[42] jeopardize his political stability.[43] Before this time, he remains unaffected by, as well as indifferent to, life outside of his court.[44]

The ambivalence that briefly haunts Orlando, aside from turning him for a short moment into a tormented hero and creating a highly charged atmosphere in which his experience unfolds, makes him profoundly human. But even as he mulls over his pining for Angelica and frames his suffering within the context of madness, honor, courage, and fame, with a deliberate choice Orlando brushes moral imperatives, as well as humanistic teachings, aside. He cannot suppress his desire for Angelica, even though with grim certainty he understands the ill-fated consequences that his actions will invite. "Io vedo il meglio ed al peggior m'appiglio" ("I see what's best. I pick what's worst") (1.31), he states, summing up the mixed emotions of confidence, desperation, joy, and fear of error that entangle him, just like the Petrarchan lover.[45] As he oscillates between the two emotional poles, Orlando recognizes that his passion undermines his ambition for glory. For this reason, a heightened sense of poignancy marks his words. Yet despite the lingering uncertainty his emotional shifts hint at, the knight still displays a lucid sense of the repercussions that his impending transgression of and defiance to duty and conventions will cause. But in spite of all his misgivings, as the *vivanda* he desires, Angelica stirs his imagination. Like Charlemagne desired her before him, Orlando desires her too. For Orlando too she has become a delicacy he is unwilling to relinquish. Because of this, betraying duty and decorum in order to pursue her does not disturb him. Clearly, the sizzling turmoil Angelica stirs at Charlemagne's banquet not only brings the tempers of all those present to burn, it also boils over outside of the camp and, by charring Orlando's heart, it irrevocably changes him. From this point on, food, banquets, loves, and duties become inextricably intertwined with Boiardo's hero.

That Angelica is looked upon as a morsel that men crave to relish is made plain in canto 25 of the *Innamorato*. Here, Orlando's transformation from Charlemagne's paladin and savior of Christendom into a man enslaved by carnal appetite is crystallized. In the evening Orlando reaches the fortress of Albracà, where Angelica has found refuge. The place is surrounded by a raging war stirred and waged solely over lust for her. Orlando's disheveled appearance shows the signs of the most recent ordeals he has had to overcome to reach her:

L'arme ha spezzato ed è senza cimiero,
Arsa è la sopravveste e non ha lanza
E non ha scudo l'ardito guerrero.
                                    (25.36)

(His arms are split, his crest is gone, / His hauberk burned, he has no lance / And that bold fighter has no shield.)

Nonetheless, Orlando's countenance remains unshaken: "Ma pur mostrava ancor grande arroganza / Tanto superbo avea lo aspetto fiero" (But still he showed great arrogance / Such pride, such fierceness in his manner) (25.36). This scene draws its tension as well as its suspense from the contrast it creates between Orlando's appearance and his immediate objectives. To be sure, when he enters Albracà the knight is described as carrying himself with the pride and arrogance of a chosen knight whose power derives from his (misleading) sense of having achieved his final objective in spite of the obstacles encountered along the way. Without doubt, at this point Orlando's inflated sense of his own courage and strength mirrors Charlemagne's attitude at the Pentecost celebration. Still, such discrepancy between the knight's scruffy attire and his haughty demeanor, which is the impression he gives, suggests a counterpoint to Charlemagne's banquet in the first canto where refined appearances aim at concealing the loathing the French harbor toward the pagans.

In canto 25 Orlando's poorly clad superciliousness subverts the norm between the aesthetic and the ethical principles that emerge in canto 1 and that govern the courtly life Boiardo knew well. Specifically, moral urgency should be the force propelling Orlando's actions and this should render the aesthetic judgment irrelevant. Based on this, he should be driven exclusively by the desire to defend Angelica from the enemy surrounding her in Albracà. Instead, his only preoccupation is satisfying his sexual appetite. The portrait that emerges here is not of a hero of towering achievements who abides by the courtly ideals of courtesy, loyalty, and valor that lead to honor.[46] Rather, it is one of a pretentious and ambitious man so deep in the thrall of his desire for a body he longs to possess that he loses his sense of duty and place. Through this, Boiardo suggests that the badge of knightly pride Orlando carries in his bearing is transformed into the mark of his own downfall. Not unlike this knight, the Este's duke is seduced by the alluring power that political maneuverings provide. At the same time, however, the eagerness for self-aggrandizement underpinning his actions upends the humanistic ideals he should champion.

The scene depicting Angelica helping Orlando shed his armor immediately upon his entering Albracà lends validity to the idea of the hero who is completely consumed by his own desires. Although within courtly customs assisting the guest in removing his armor is a gesture that denotes the host's graciousness toward him,[47] for love-struck Orlando Angelica's kindness fuels his imagination. Indeed, he construes it as her eagerness to welcome him into her alluring universe of senses where undressing the knight is the prelude to possessing the man. Shedding the layers of his armor and gradually trusting his vulnerable body to her eager hands foreshadows for Orlando the realization of his dream. In his understanding, the sensual battle he believes she will keenly undertake with him will transform her body into his luscious *vivanda*. By shifting the action from the open field to the bedchamber, and turning the political battle into an erotic one the exquisiteness of which, paradoxically, he already savors, Orlando further chips away at the knightly conduct he should uphold. In point of fact, in the foretaste of the succulent pleasure that engaging Angelica in battle reveals Orlando revels. The unexpected and provocative kiss she bestows on him—"Di sua mano il disarmava / E nel trargli de l'elmo il bacia in bocca" (She doffed his arms in person, and, / Taking his casque off, kissed his mouth) (25.37)—magnifies his perception. As she insinuates herself with sensuous ease into his life, Angelica literally disarms him. Through this, she brings him down to earth where he trusts his desire can be quickly assuaged. By acting fluidly and moving with a looseness that is a counterpoint to the courtly norms in which she half-couches her hidden agenda, Angelica leads Orlando to believe that the attainment of his objective nears. Still, her kiss dazes the knight.

For Orlando, caught in the grip of his sensual desires, Angelica's kiss conjures up an intensely luscious world of physical delights he trusts will be his: "quando presso si sentì quel viso, / Credette esser di certo in paradiso" (when he could feel her face so close / He believed he had gone to heaven) (25.37). This inference mirrors the arrogant demeanor he vaunted upon his arrival. The range of emotions overtaking him is best illustrated by the analogy he draws with Paradise. In a glaring misconstrual of the Christian beliefs ostensibly shaping his political and moral sensibilities, Orlando replaces the spiritual Paradise with a sensual one. Also, in this personal understanding, the knight applies the prospect of his carnal gratification to the divine one. This inversion of values, according to which self-indulgence flouts self-discipline, yet again calls to mind Charlemagne's theatrical celebration of Pentecost. Like that feast, Orlando's doctrinal lapse turns the attention to the hero's selfish understanding of the world. In seeking the pleasure of the body, he turns a blind eye to the fact that the body he is pursuing betrays. The One that redeems does not give quick pleasure. For the bemused readers, who are aware of Angelica's love for Rainaldo, Orlando's words resonate with striking force. As for the kiss she delivers to Orlando, it suggests her singular if unsavory talent for stirring the dream of the gullible and smitten knight, making him the instrument of her immediate goals.

The extraordinary lucidity with which Angelica toys with, goads, and manipulates the knight hinges on the details of her hospitality and in those details lie her deceitfulness. As bait and bearer Angelica evinces the astuteness of a woman who with calculated perseverance engages the foe (Orlando, the suitor she does not love) in a battle of wills fought with physical intensity that is infused with unabashed erotic longing. She is aware of the dizzying effect her actions have on the knight. Because of this and to bend him to her will she deploys the skillfulness that her scheming demands. Through ruthless determination, she erases the image of herself as that of a helpless woman yoked to societal customs, preyed upon by several men, and intended as the exclusive prize to the bravest of them. As a result, she recasts herself as a person who is aware of what she wants and, most importantly, one especially able to orchestrate with raw tenacity its attainment. Angelica's single-minded fervor to wheedle Orlando suggests that for her, as for him, the satisfaction of personal desires requires brushing conventions aside and replacing them with one's own rules. The image of her literally (and figuratively) disarming the knight illustrates the essence of her resoluteness. By effectively "deconstructing" the knight, she "constructs" the man over whom she can claim her influence. Angelica's "new" man becomes an emasculated and vulnerable one blinded by the power of his desire. Because of it, like her, he is ready to turn his back to the norms that define his culture.

That Angelica does not hesitate to transgress those norms further emerges when she bathes, dries, and massages the knight. She adds zest to the procedure by kissing him again:

Avea la dama un bagno apparecchiato,
Troppo gentile e di suave odore,
E di sua mano il conte ebbe spogliato.
Baciandol spesse fiate con amore.
Poi l'ungiva d'un olio delicato.
(25.38)

(The maiden had a bath prepared, / Sweetly perfumed (perhaps too restful), / And she undressed the Count herself, / Kissing him ardently and often. / She oiled his body with a balm.)

With their erotic undertones Angelica's timely, nimble, and disciplined actions lend a disarming pathos to the scene. These gestures make her look as though for a fleeting moment she too is overcome with desire for Orlando. This further fans the flame of Orlando's passion because, yet again, he construes her conduct as the prologue to erotic possibilities. The divergence between what she should limit herself to doing in welcoming the knight and the thoroughness with which she carries out her sensual posturing once more underlines the disconnect between appearances and reality. But her gestures, like those Charlemagne uses toward his Saracen guests, are carried out solely for pretense. They bear no connection with the meaning that they intend to convey. Through such inconsistency between facts and gestures, Boiardo depicts a fragmented world that mirrors the materialist universe Ercole d'Este and his court inhabit.[48] Like other princely courts, this one measures its power and projects its prestige by displaying and flaunting its wealth. To this attitude corresponds, as the poet insinuates, the flawed moral aspect of the princely authority.[49] As a prominent member of Ercole's inner circle, Boiardo is aware that the duke's personal and political ambitions are conveniently tucked under the glamour of which his court boasts. The poet also knows that, following the Este's lead, the courtiers, whom Orlando and Angelica in point of fact personify, adopt the same self-centered stance in trumping with calculation and industriousness the normative ethical and moral system Guarino da Verona, and the humanists who followed him, championed in Ferrara.[50]

The sexual implications that with irony and wit season the scene of Orlando's bath are not the only ingredients lending it dynamism and depth. Indeed, what gives it poignancy is the manner in which it draws from earlier literary traditions. To make his characters' actions credible in the eyes—and to the ears—of the courtly audience Boiardo takes as his model not only the cycle of the Arthurian and Carolingian romances, but also Boccaccio's and Petrarch's works.[51] Yet the *Innamorato* is first and foremost an encomium for the Este dynasty within whose milieu Boiardo feels comfortable and moves about at ease.[52] Interestingly, in reconstructing the family's lineage the poet changes the time-honored Este's myth of origins. Instead of having the family descend from Gano di Maganza, Boiardo traces their ancestry to the Trojans, and, more specifically, directly to Hector.[53] In the third book of the *Innamorato* Ruggiero himself explains this lineage his own—as the Este's forebear to Bradamante (18.33). Boiardo's concern with ensuring that Ercole's dynasty originated with Hector adds rich nuances to the scene of Orlando's bath for it evokes, by way of contrast, a scene from Homer's *Iliad*.

In book 22 of the *Iliad*, looking forward to her husband's return from battle, Andromache readies a bath for him. "She called out through the house to her lovely-haired handmaidens / to set a great cauldron over the fire, so that there would be / hot water for Hektor's bath as he came back out of the fighting."[54] What she does not yet know, however, is that Hector is already dead. The scene's tragic exquisiteness fixes Andromache's preoccupation with preparing a soothing bath for her husband's fatigued body against the ignominious death to which he has already succumbed. Deceived and spurred by Athena, who disguises herself as his brother Deiphobos, Hector accepts Achilles's challenge to fight. Unsurprisingly, with Athena's help, Achilles kills Hector without much effort. Thus, he avenges the death of his friend Patroclus, who had been killed by Hector. At home his wife Andromache is unaware of this. And while she anticipates her husband's return, Achilles drags Hector's lifeless body behind his chariot around the walls of Troy. In one bold stroke, dirt, not cleansing, restoring water, enfolds the body of Homer's hero. This image, which becomes synonymous with reducing the hero as well as the glory and power he embodies to dust, superimposes itself with brutal irony on one of Andromache's preparations for his return. In Homer's poem the defeat of the hero is made all the more appalling by the way in which dirt shamefully desecrates the body that water should properly purify. Abandoned to the enemy's vengeful attack on its dignity, rather than released to the wife's care that would cleanse the corpse in preparation for the proper burial rites, Hector's lifeless body exemplifies the final crushing of the tested hero. Despite recognizing the goddess's deceitfulness he courageously faced death. Through this, Homer shows that man's irreducible ambitions and the impermanence of the fame he chases bear no relevance over his ephemeral nature. This, in turn, suggests that although empowered by the moral principles guiding it, humanity is rendered powerless when ruthless force becomes the magnet of its moral compass.

In contrast to Homer, Boiardo depicts a knight who turns his back on the battle to take pleasure in Angelica's inviting hospitality. Not surprisingly, this behavior shows remarkable similarities to the conduct the Este court embraces. Narcissism, ambition, brilliance, vengefulness, excesses, and selfishness define its members. Boiardo deftly synthesizes these traits in Orlando. The bath, the massages, the kisses with which Andromache was not able to coddle Hector Angelica brazenly lavishes on an acquiescent if weakened Orlando. Taken together the two scenes juxtapose Orlando's self-serving behavior to Hector's selfless courage. By vigorously defending his city and its citizens from the attacks waged by the Greek troops, Hector never forgets the moral responsibility his position demands. Even with his own life in danger he does not change his course of action; rather, with self-possession and a clear sense of reality, he faces death. Most interestingly, however, both scenes establish that the hero is dead before savoring the pleasure of the relaxing, albeit ceremonial, bath. Yet the striking difference between the two episodes remains that while for Hector death is solely a physical one, for Charlemagne's knight it is a graver one. His transcends the body and affects Orlando's moral and ethical understanding. In the service of social obligations and civic duty underpinning the humanistic ideals, those understandings require prudence and vigilance. Yet Orlando has closed his eyes to both of them. It is not surprising, then, that the nudity Angelica's bath requires exposes, in a sense, the knight's moral and ethical nakedness.

This is evidenced more forcefully in Orlando's lack of reaction to Angelica's unrestrained manners. This scene is more tragic than amusing in its depiction of the hero's inability to rule over the events unfolding around him. To be sure, as Angelica pampers him, Orlando does not respond to her fondling:

> Stavasi'l conte quieto e vergognoso
> Mentre la dama intorno il maneggiava;
> E benché fosse di questo gioioso,
> Crescere in alcun loco non mostrava.
>   (25.39)

(The Count was quiet, modest, while / Angelica massaged him, and / He felt tremendous joy, although / No part of him was seen to grow.)

Undeniably, Orlando's reserved and unresponsive behavior, coupled with his submissive acceptance of Angelica's uninhibited demonstrations of hospitality, is an incredible and shocking turn of events that contradicts his set objective. Yet to interpret his unresponsiveness to her advances solely as the mark of the awestruck hero's impotence strikes the reader as inadequate to the situation.[55] The irony that permeates the whole poem suggests that much more is at stake, even in the scene depicting an impotent hero full of libido.[56] For this reason, to write off this episode as a pure form of entertainment implies reading the text on a superficial level.[57] In addition, by accepting Orlando's impassiveness as a sign of mere impotence that traces its origin back to the Carolingian and Arthurian traditions, the audience, like the hero, becomes unreceptive to other possibilities that his reaction might suggest. This maneuver on Boiardo's part creates a comic tension that spills outside of the text as it, paradoxically, entraps readers as well as listeners in the poet's web.[58] Turning the audience into an unwitting accomplice by deflecting the possibility of its questioning the tradition is even more ironic. For all purposes, by clinging to the belief that Orlando's impotence is dictated by tradition and not questioning it, the audience is manipulated by the poet. With the hero and audience both turned into acquiescent personas, the poet, like the enchanting Angelica, plays with and diverts his public's attention. Through this, he compels it to believe that the knight's behavior is an unchangeable and unchallengeable condition because it is imposed by age-old tradition.

    Arguably at this juncture the diminished expectations one has of Orlando reduce the moral and emotional complexity that shape the hero.

Still, this is an ingenious move on Boiardo's part because it brings together and fuses different possibilities. The first one specifically calls to mind Borso's unexpected succession to his brother Leonello in 1450.[59] The two were both natural sons of Niccolò III. But Borso's accession to the marquisate was an achievement that took all by surprise for two reasons.[60] First, it bypassed Leonello's legitimate heir, his son Niccolò. Second, and more importantly, with Borso the line of succession also passed over Ercole and Sigismondo d'Este, Niccolò III's legitimate successors, born of his marriage to Ricciarda di Saluzzo.[61] Thus, an illegitimate heir took over, yet again, the lordship of Ferrara.[62] Borso himself engineered this feat through a series of clever maneuverings.[63] Once installed as Leonello's successor, he wasted no time in constructing a careful public image of himself.[64] This enabled him to further solidify his position and authority as the rightful heir to the House of Este.[65] He was acknowledged by some as the true embodiment of justice, prudence, temperance, strength, liberality, magnificence, magnanimity, humbleness, and beauty, among other qualities.[66] Others, on the contrary, saw right through his desire for power.[67] Nevertheless, his political climb defied expectations for it paradoxically trampled on the very humanist traits he was claimed to incarnate. By all accounts, Borso and his supporters with calculated cleverness suspended and dismantled the notion of legitimate succession. By putting himself forward as the new, uncontested marquis, he established himself as a peaceful—if cunning—ruler, able to govern in a manner that ensured tranquility for his people.[68] For this purpose, he did carry on "the pacific policies of his brother."[69]

According to Renaissance political theory, in the unpredictable and changing world of the time, peace and tranquility are the objectives that all rulers must seek.[70] As a result, Orlando's lack of reaction to Angelica's blandishments can be read, among other things, as the legitimate heirs' silent acceptance of Borso as the new (and their) marquis of Ferrara. In this way, just as through her enticing exploits the enchantress molds Orlando's outlook on his own quest and Boiardo sways his public, through his astute tactics Borso reshapes Ferrara's political landscape according to his own desire. But in addition to Borso's political manipulations, the scene of Orlando submissively accepting Angelica's fondling can also be read as a referent for Borso's personal life. He never married.[71]

Also, unlike his father and siblings whose sexual escapades were notorious and fully documented, nothing is known about Borso's private life.[72] Is it possible that in an unreceptive Orlando Boiardo is describing Borso's private life?

The scene depicting a submissive Orlando also underscores the tension between power and poetry. In other words, Angelica's power, which grows with her ability to disempower the hero, finds its correlative in the poet's artfulness that turns his audience into powerless listeners. Unwilling to question what it is told, this audience readily accepts it. As a result, Orlando's complaisant behavior becomes mirror and measure of a powerless audience. This suggests that the power of poetry—and of letters—far exceeds that of politics. In swaying people, it overtakes their minds, compelling them to believe in and consent to what the author affirms. This is precisely the principle Borso followed in creating an image that presented him as a benefactor of his society. Needless to say, unlike political power, poetry never overtly exposes its author's designs even though it often hits upon the truth while seeking to engage in a critique of values. Ironically, the tactic used by the poet to retain absolute control over his audience is one with which the Este were very experienced. In fact, they relied on it whenever they needed to further advance their interests.

These two ways of interpreting Orlando's docility in front of Angelica do not exclude a third one. Might it be that by depicting what appears to be an impotent hero Boiardo suggests that Orlando momentarily regains his self-control, his knightly composure, and projects it, by showing a man able to contain and control himself? Might it be that Orlando is *gioioso* in the presence of the woman fondling him and, for this reason, willing to postpone the erotic gratification he has been seeking? Is it possible that Boiardo is also hinting at a hero who is not overcome by his senses and who is willing to simply postpone gratification until he proves to the woman he desires that he is deserving of her? These possibilities are reinforced by the developments that take place in the subsequent scenes. At first glance the ridiculousness of the hero incapable of even reacting to Angelica's touches and kisses, let alone initiating them, suggests that the knight with uncontrolled desires, striking aristocratic background, and unrivaled accomplishments is not only a hero already dead for the chivalric society he willfully left behind but that he is also a man failing on a spectacular scale in his private pursuits. For the inconsistency between what Orlando has obstinately been seeking and what he finally does, or rather does not do, when at last he is in Angelica's presence can hardly be overstated. In a sense it is revelatory. It suggests first of all that for Count Boiardo, personal and political interests can neither be reconciled nor intermingled because the overt craftiness that the latter requires reduces the former to a thin pottage of hesitation, incapability, and powerlessness. Even worse, but clearly not inexplicably, this makes the individual thus reduced likely to be (figuratively) swallowed by those who cunningly hold on to power and who, with studied manipulations, often aimed at blurring the lines between the real and the desired imaginary to advance their interests. More specifically, by depicting the craftiness Angelica must rely on to gratify her lust for Rainaldo and the private and public failures that Orlando's own lust for Angelica produces, Boiardo draws attention to the chasm between idealism and pragmatism, aspirations and reality. This rift, which exposes the intellect as totally focused on personal gains rather than on defending the collective safety, dignity, and vulnerability, in turn leads to the collapse of the courtly system that the humanists envisioned and that Orlando embodies.

The failure, which Orlando exemplifies first by his stubborn urgency to sate his personal hunger and then by his inability to carry out his plan in Angelica's presence, also underscores Boiardo's growing impatience with the courtly model. This model, by legitimizing the implicit use of force, fraud, corruption, and abuses for its own gains, fails to revive and restore the values chivalric culture championed. It comes as no surprise, then, that the knight who has set himself on a perilous path, erroneously believing that he could feast on his long-sought *vivanda* by relying on his will, is curiously depleted of the very will necessary to consume what he craves. It is as though after his impulsive start Orlando seems to lose touch with his own desire. Humanistic ideals bent in the pursuit of non-humanistic goals fail to produce savoring results. The unexpected development of Angelica and Orlando's encounter challenges the foundation of an entire set of beliefs because he is a hero conceived within that tradition. Accordingly, he is aware that moral and ethical truths defy personal desires. In an ironic twist of occurrences, because of his inability to respond to Angelica's appetizing enticements, Orlando is depicted as devoured by their intensity. With his plan nibbled away by her captivating words and even more tempting gestures, Orlando's sexual unresponsiveness can mark, then, the mere postponement of the fulfillment of his desire.

With a skeptical eye directed to the political instability in which the Venetian war has thrown Ferrara and a grim vision of what the future holds for the Este duchy and its court, through Orlando and Angelica Boiardo illustrates the dangers lurking behind unbridled appetites.[73] As an aristocrat who is part of the court's inner circle, Count Boiardo knows that to sustain a desire without self-control is as catastrophic as its realization. As a historian he is also aware that the lessons history provides can help avert the upheavals that strike at the foundations of the princely, dynastic, and aristocratic state.[74] For him, the clashing of different ambitions and wills paired with attempts to assert oneself and prevail over others will cause every system to run amok. It is this idea that makes the scene portraying Orlando's passivity in Angelica's presence a pivotal one in the *Innamorato*. In it, the Este courtiers, as well as the duke himself, can see a correlative to their own libertine and opportunistic demeanors. According to the courtier-poet, the prince and his entourage must heed the lessons that history (and literature) provide to their advantage. To govern more effectively, to keep political corruption at bay, to put his abilities in the service of a vision of a stable, just principality, in short, to preserve and expand his power the prince must always question the soundness of his actions and weigh the repercussions they will have. Most importantly, by not succumbing to the deceptive allure that personal want holds over humanity, courtiers, as well as their duke, can eschew the failures that it unavoidably produces. With searing precision, through Orlando's reckless quest— a shifting brew of self-doubt and affirmation steeped in the confusion caused by a maddening yearning to gratify a personal desire—Boiardo offers the model the court must shun.

From a historical perspective Sixtus learned this lesson when Ferrara, by ceding the Polesine to Venice at the Treaty of Bagnolo, strengthened the Republic's power. As an ally of Venice his army had fought to erode the Este's power. But Venice's gains at the end of the war weakened the Papal States.[75] Unlike Sixtus, Ercole d'Este sought to put behind him the humiliation of the devastating attacks that Venice and the papal army had inflicted on his territories. The rebuilding and revitalization of Ferrara he undertook, along with his unequalled patronage of the arts, are a testimony to this attitude.[76] Still, the shadow that the Este's rapacious hunger for self-advancement cast on the courtly ideals that the dynasty had long vaunted left an indelible mark. Of this, Orlando's obstinate and irresponsible pursuit of Angelica, his subsequent hesitation to carry on with his initial objective because of what he perceives as the postponement of events, is an illustration.

III

The dinner Angelica offers to Orlando adds an additional layer of complexity to the knight's physical unresponsiveness to her. Predictably, it consists of "ogni vivanda delicata" served "Intro una ricca zambra ed apparata" (a richly furnished room) (25.40.2). Renaissance courtly ceremonial is reflected in this meal and its presentation, both of which aim at honoring the illustrious guest.[77] But that Boiardo yet again generalizes about the dishes, without specifying any one of them in particular, suggests first of all that his audience, entrenched as it is in the gastronomy of power, can envisage without difficulty the delicacies Angelica serves to her guest. The absence of details also renews the idea that the hostess is herself regarded as "the" delicacy that men, and Orlando in particular, aspire to devour. Convivial ceremonies aimed at celebrating significant events, important people, and remarkable accomplishments are an integral part of the Este court; Boiardo knows the value his culture and its members assign to them. Miguel de Cervantes too will draw attention to this issue when with mordant irony he recounts the episode of Sancho made governor of Barataria.[78] However, while Cervantes's Sancho after a brief tenure as a governor with surprising resoluteness abandons both island and governorship in order to return to the food he favors because for him its plainness typifies the gastronomic equivalent of the lifestyle he prefers, Orlando lacks the willpower necessary to decline Angelica's invitation. Because his still remains a journey of unrealized desires, for Orlando dining with his hostess becomes once again the foretaste and deferment of his goal. With visceral cunning, meanwhile, Angelica looks for a way to obtain what she wants. For this reason, she makes an art of the politics of food that Savonarola's treatise expounds and Riario's banquet put into practice. In short, through her dinner, she bends Orlando to her will.

The meal Angelica uses to further ensnare the knight has an overall effect of contrast. Put simply, though he is invited to consume artfully prepared *vivande*, it is she who devours him. While it could be argued that satisfying his physiological appetite rather than his sexual one is a maneuver consistent with her nature,[79] the significance of this episode lies in the complex interplay of food and power in the Renaissance. The intimacy Angelica and Orlando establish by eating together satisfies a need that can be as instinctive as a sexual one.[80] As they eat, Angelica and Orlando are symbolically united in sharing the *vivanda* that Orlando has unswervingly sought. Still, for Angelica the partaking of the meal becomes another subtle means to manipulate the knight who for her sake has lost both his sense of self-possession and his interpretative mastery. Indeed, while possessing her has been the propelling force of his quest, this desire has dispossessed him of his capacity to evaluate rationally both events and individuals. Having placed passion above reason, Orlando is unable to identify any event as a source of knowledge and experience and thus to differentiate between his sexual and physiological appetites. He, therefore, submissively assents to gratifying the latter in order to satisfy the former, never realizing that he has turned into a failed hero and a broken man. His willingness to accept the food she offers him as a substitute for satisfying the sexual appetite driving his actions mirrors his incapacity to fully discern the way in which Angelica now steers his actions. Amid the glint and glimmer of the dining chamber Orlando's knightly luster of honor and prowess shades into the evening dusk, its allure never materializing. The discrepancy between the inverted roles Angelica and Orlando now play is perhaps nowhere else in the poem made clearer. By leading him to a dinner that, as the audience and readers know, offers no spark of steaminess for his erotic expectations, but only the possibility of a libido set on a low flame,

Angelica shows the self-possession and cleverness that Orlando lacks. Indeed, he contentedly eats at her table and this crystallizes the contrast between the chivalrous knight that he once was and the boorish man that he has become.

Removed from the external world torn by the war, the boundaries of Angelica's and Orlando's selves are simultaneously fixed in their solitary sharing of the food and revealed in the abstraction from reality that typifies their respective selfishness. To be sure, Orlando's sole concern remains conquering her. She, on the contrary, is wholly engrossed in thwarting and subverting his plan for the advancement of her own conquest of Rainaldo. Still, the meal serves Angelica to establish a twofold correspondence between food as the ingredient of an intimate experience intended as a substitute for sexual gratification and as the means to exert power. As the provider of the meal, Angelica, like Charlemagne at his banquet, wields the unrestrained power that always rests with the one who feeds. This enables her to turn Orlando into her acquiescing dinner guest. Through this, she inverts the rules Charlemagne set for his own guests at Pentecost. Like the Saracens, Orlando is dispossessed of the power he valiantly embodied and is subdued by a Saracen's ostensible hospitality. More than this, and in contrast to Charlemagne's guests, by redirecting Orlando's sexual desires through and to food Angelica effectively emasculates her suitor, turning him into a pawn in her hands. By embracing Orlando again at the end of the meal—"Standosi al collo di quel conte abbracciata, / Lo prega e lo scongiura con bel dire" (Hugging the Count around his neck, / Conjured him and asked nicely) (25.40)—Angelica renews the hope of the disappointingly submissive Orlando who has put his erotic desire behind him. To him, her embrace suggests that the satisfaction of his craving is merely deferred; thus, her request that he prove his courage only heightens his future expectations.

The strategy with which Angelica sustains Orlando's belief of an amorous delay highlights anew the ferocious willpower that she keeps hidden underneath the courteous surface of a well-mannered lady. To ensure that his lingering desire does not evaporate, and that the (unfounded) belief of possessing her still simmers in Orlando, Angelica appropriates the language of commerce with its inferences on profit-making, marketable goods, and bartering:

—"D'una sol cosa, il mio conte,"—dicia
"Fammi promessa, e non me la negare,
Se voi che più sia tua ch'io non son mia,
Chè a tal servigio me puoi comparare;
... Ma sol cheggio da te che per mio amore
Mostri ad un giorno tutto il tuo valore."
(25.41)

("Only one thing, my Count," she said. / "Promise it. DO not say no, if / You want me to be yours, because / You'll win me if you do the service. / ... / I only ask that for my love, / For one day you show all your powers.")

The mercantile rhetoric that colors Angelica's words traces, first of all, the progression of roles Angelica has played until now for the unsuspecting Orlando. Specifically, she has turned from a hospitable maiden, into a purportedly doting lover, and finally into an expert businesswoman eager to negotiate a successful deal by trading a good—herself—in return for a proof of Orlando's courage. Although this new role too is part of her manipulative universe, it alone evokes a world devoid of empty ambitions and governed, instead, by exact calculations, unblinking, measured precision, and weighed thoroughness. To negotiate a successful deal and turn a profit from it, the practiced merchant controls the goods and takes advantage of these qualities. This rhetoric replaces the one of the caring lover. Now Angelica projects an authority that did not surface before because it draws from the business world of men.

By grounding her hopes in the certainty of achieving her goal through a business-like savviness, Angelica merges the world of economic affairs with that of politics. The plan she lays out for Orlando is one of an inveterate strategist who increases the reward in order to boost her returns. From a political dimension, this calls to mind yet again the Estes lords who are determined to reshape the universe they inhabit through the unrestrained power they wield within it.[81] Even the fact that Angelica simultaneously embodies merchant and merchandise mirrors the Estes' model. The duplicity with which the Estes conduct state affairs and the way in which they deal with forces that can be a threat to their hegemony (Sforza, Aragonese, Medici, and pope in particular) attests to this behavior.[82] For the Estes, expanding the radius of their influence and bolstering their power to its full potential in order to burnish their image entails currying the favors of adversarial forces, lying to them, and even cajoling them while promising to recompense any support they give. The many examples of this modus operandi that Pius II gives in his *Commentarii* are based on his personal interactions with Borso, a man he describes as "uomo vano e infido!" (a vain and treacherous man).[83] Although Borso's behavior in particular becomes the focus of Pius's acerbic criticism, the Estes' behavior in general does not escape the pope's condemnation. From this, Pius II draws with an insider's precision the picture of the Estes' exploitation of political situations to their advantage.[84]

Orlando's inability to tease out the complicated reality, and false premise, which through tears and caresses Angelica presents to him induces him to accept the seemingly generous terms of her offer. The intensity of his erotic desire prods him to accept her challenge. Because of this, the scene that is meant as a tableau of the hero's flawed understanding of truth also draws attention to the chivalric code still shaping his actions. Accordingly, for Orlando defeating Marfisa is not just the proof of prowess Angelica has demanded; it is a moral obligation. In Angelica's version of facts, Marfisa with French knights—now Orlando's enemy too—keep her prisoner in Albracà, which is under siege. Naturally, for the knight freeing her becomes synonymous with restoring the order and bringing justice to a woman who claims to be in danger. The beautiful contradiction this creates lends an exquisite complexity to the knight. The hero who earlier on abandoned his responsibility toward his fellow-knights now embraces it again. Except that this time he does so by turning against them because goaded by beauty that feeds desire:

> Dissegli il conte: —"Dama, a te servire
> Mi reputo dal cel a tanta graccia;
> E quella dama che me avesti a dire,
> Fia da me morta, o presa, o messa a caccia."
> (25.45)

(The Count said, "Lady, I consider / This mission heaven-sent, a grace, / And I will kill, or catch, or chase / The woman who makes you complain.")

At Angelica's bidding Orlando does not question her motives; nor does he take into account the moral and ethical implications of his assent. As a matter of fact, he does not see a conflict with battling his fellow-knights. Instead, he becomes again the knight driven by courage, proving his valor, and focused on undoing the villainies of others in order to achieve fame and glory. This return to chivalric principles, although transparently based on an inaccurate presumption, is sustained by Orlando's understanding that the pleasure of ultimately possessing Angelica is a fitting reward for defeating Marfisa.

Orlando's acceptance of Angelica's lying and his disregard for the real cause behind the events unfolding outside of the dining hall is reflected in the prolongation of their meal. That at this point Boiardo provides a more accurate account of the dishes brought to the chamber — "Frutti and confetti di molta ragione / Furno portati a quella zambra bella" (Sweetmeats of many sorts and fruits / Were carried to the splendid room) (25.46) — is telling. According to Renaissance dietetic treatises, consuming fruit is unhealthy. In the fourth chapter of his *Libreto* Savonarola discusses fruits and their effects on the human body. Like Galen and Avicenna, whose theories he closely follows, Savonarola does not deem fruits beneficial. Accordingly, his discussion tends to focus on the adverse effects of fruit because, in his view, it has meager nourishing value. Furthermore, he is very explicit about its harmful effects. Indeed, for each fruit he considers in his treatise Savonarola explains the harm it causes. For this reason, he cautions his patron Borso to consume fruit prudently. The assertion "Certo tua Signoria di lor non sia troppo vago" (Surely, your lordship should not be too fond of them) becomes Savonarola's overarching advice against fruit consumption for the ducal court.[85]

Like Savonarola, Platina considers fruit unhealthy for the body. According to him, by putrefying easily, fruits' juices harm the stomach. Marsilio Ficino also argues that fruit has detrimental effects on the human body. Its softness, the philosopher-doctor claims, "fill(s) up the veins with a perishable juice undigested and subject to putrefaction."[86] Clearly, the rapid decaying process to which fruit is predisposed determines the Renaissance's unfavorable view of its consumption. This understanding, which dates back to Galen, is also what informs Boccaccio's King Charles of his potential downfall. As we saw above, Isotta and Ginevra served him fruit on the night of his visit to their house. That Orlando is offered fruit by Angelica within a courtly setting, and presumably consumes it, suggests, first of all, that the hero is yet again defying conventions. Metaphorically, however, it insinuates the disintegration of the chivalric hero.

The *confetti* Angelica offers to Orlando carry similar implications. Made mostly out of sugar, because "(il zucaro) spesso viene in tavola cum altre vivande" (sugar often is brought to the table with other food),[87] *confetti* are ostentatious, aesthetically captivating edible arrangements.[88] The elite prizes them not because of their nutritional value, but because they are laborious culinary concoctions that in their concrete renditions turn into veritable works of art. The highly specialized preparations they require showcase the luxury, wealth, and social standing the elite cultivates. Also, the pronounced sweetness of the *confetti* appeals to the court's palates while the artistic arrangements of ingredients capture the consumers' imagination. Individually prepared and then combined to create the final *confetto*, these ingredients produce artistic tableaus that are, in a sense, another expression of the visual arts the Este court promoted and supported.[89] And just as through visual arts the Este built their iconography of power, gastronomy, and more specifically *confetti*, becomes another component of that iconography. In both cases, for the visual arts as well as for gastronomy, taste and sight turn into the guiding compass for people living within—and feeding on—the artificiality of entitlements. Both characteristics mirror the court's fondness for spectacles of power that rarely reflect the reality outside of it. The disconnect between the two worlds is discernible in Savonarola's discussion of sugar's qualities: "Questo è quello che farebbe li confecti a principi, ma se usa anche in le torte, che se ge dà una sola copertura per belleza" (This is the ingredient used to make *confetti* for the princes. It is also used for cakes, which are covered with it [frosted] so that they look beautiful).[90]

Sugar, as he explains, is used in the making of princely *confetti*. Through this simple statement Savonarola establishes, first of all, the social sphere to which *confetti*, and the sugar necessary to prepare them, belong. But, he adds, sugar is also used to give cakes "a coat of beauty." In culinary terms, the glaze Savonarola refers to is a technique widely used by cooks to this day. However, the metaphorical implications of his assertion, applied to his times, are striking. Like sugar-glaze that coats foodstuffs to embellish them, the manners and mores the court displays cover up the hollowness of its lifestyle. The assumptions and expectations the court harbors are buried under the façade of magnificence, a glaze that masks the unscrupulous conduct the duke and courtiers unabashedly embrace.

Like Savonarola, Ficino uses *confetti* to describe anything prepared with sugar. Unlike Savonarola, however, Ficino describes the use of these preparations as means by which to administer medicinal-curative treatments. Thus for him the sugary confections fill a strictly medicinal role. They are intended to alleviate, or even heal, afflictions of the body. As it turns out, the metaphorical implications of *confetti*, almost like those of fruits, lend themselves to controversial, if not altogether negative, interpretations. This suggests that beyond their scarce nutritive merit, the foods Boiardo introduces in the scene depicting Angelica and Orlando together are rich with symbolic meanings. And these, with metaphoric precision, capture Orlando's failings.

To begin with, rather than legitimizing his social standing, *frutti e confetti* denote Orlando's moral flaws. Lacking real substance even while bearing evidence of complex arrangements, compositions, and preparations, they exemplify the difference between appearance and reality. Their painstaking preparations, emphasizing the artistic beauty of the final products, obscure the role of individual ingredients. This fact also calls attention to the difference between acting out of free will and manipulation. For this reason, the *confetti* are the gastronomic equivalent of Angelica's concocted reality and Orlando's lacerated selfhood. For him in particular, the *confetti*'s aesthetic appeal mirrors the core of his unresolved shortcomings, pointing to his inability to stay true to chivalrous principles. His desire to impress Angelica leads him to commit to her request with stunning swiftness. Although this reaction is dictated by a residual sense of chivalrous duty, the fact that he is unable to sift through her lies reveals more than just his lapse of judgment. By sealing the agreement between two individuals who have selfishly "cooked" their own respective versions of reality, the *confetti* in the end only reveal the self-serving, personal as well as political, maneuverings of a society consumed by worldly possessions and bent on obtaining them at any cost.

By describing the *confetti* as "di molta ragione" Boiardo further enriches the symbolic meaning of the foods offered to Orlando. In the more literal sense this points to a variety of *confetti*. Metaphorically, however, the particular description intensifies the disjuncture between the scene in which the *confetti* appear and the one in which Orlando's lack of judgment is shown in his promise to Angelica. By toying with this ambiguity, Boiardo juxtaposes the lack of "reason" in a constructed reality—Angelica and Orlando's—with that of the hollow *confetti*. From this perspective, food as an edible as well as a visual medium takes on an explicit metaphorical role. This is highly evocative of Leon Battista Alberti's *De pictura*. In this treatise, which analyzes perspective and the creation of art, Alberti expounds on the artist's ability to make the absent present and the dead living.[91] Food, therefore, extends the modes of Boiardo's representation of Orlando's misplaced loyalties and flawed understanding. And the hero's unconditional capitulation to Angelica's manipulations mirrors this point.

Intrepid as he might be, the knight takes stock of his amorous pursuit, when he discovers that Rainaldo is among those fighting outside of the fortress to conquer Angelica. Stirred by jealousy, he writhes at the prospect that his cousin is a dividing force between him and her. For this, Orlando is overtaken by amorous despair. The wrought precision with which he articulates his anger against Rainaldo while keeping his own thoughts firmly anchored in the desire for Angelica charges the scene with intensity. As he broods on this conjecture and delves into the jealous agony that defines his yearning for her, Orlando accuses Rainaldo of lacking respect as well as love for him. Interestingly, to articulate his anger he uses an analogy that is based on eating:

"E sempre io volsi che la mia prudenza
La sua pacìa dovesse temperare;

> Or romper mi conviene la pacïenza
> Ché a tal taglier non puon duo giotti stare,
> Sì che a finirla io son deliberato,
> Ché compagnia non vôle amor né stato"
> (25.56)

("Thinking that my prudence / would moderate his craziness. / My patience now is wearing thin / Because one dish won't serve two gluttons, / And I am determined this will end: / Rulers, and lovers, need no friends!")

With these words the knight cuts through the rhetoric of courtly love and explicitly associates his and his cousin's desire for possessing Angelica with food. By using the analogy of two gluttons who cannot eat off the same plate, Orlando provides the most specific evidence yet that he, like the others pursuing her, considers Angelica a morsel to gobble. To lend more authority to his argument, he emphasizes that neither love nor political power can be shared. With increasing urgency his assertion fuses the notions of power, love, and food into one discourse. As he explores the past through the love and camaraderie that brought him and Rainaldo close together, Orlando fears the future and his preoccupation turns into open hostility. The tone of simmering regret arising from his words seems ambiguously complex: he regrets the past and yet grieves over the future: love has broken his and Rainaldo's familial bonds: time and experience have devoured their amity. The only thing left for Orlando is Angelica. Or so he believes.

Yet the peril in Orlando's formulation is that he assumes that like a political body waiting to be seized he, not Rainaldo, has a firm grasp on how to appropriate Angelica. Because of this, he dismisses his cousin's efforts, blames him for his impulsiveness, and swiftly if biliously speaks of his unwillingness to side with him. This fact underscores Orlando's sense of superiority. By speaking of power in terms of the force through which love and food are captured, attained, and controlled, Orlando, with unabashed arrogance, suggests that only he, as the most valiant knight, can and must have Angelica. For him love is synonymous with controlling power. But considering the fact that it is Angelica, not he, who wields power and that it is she who has yoked men of both camps to her will, Orlando's words resonate with ironic notes. Despite this, his remark highlights his unawareness of the flaws that veil the truths in his illusions. At the same time, through the explicit analogy of food that gluttons hunger after, Orlando effectively admits that he views Angelica like food that he craves to eat. As we saw, Boiardo establishes this perception in the first canto of the *Innamorato*. Thus, Orlando's admission is one that resonates with his culture.

Although the promise of the sexual postponement heightens Orlando's certainty of the outcome, it is not shared by Angelica. She is driven by different values and divergent purposes. Yet despite the gulf between Angelica's and Orlando's respective expectations, they are both motivated by their personal desires. The difference between the two is that, unlike Orlando, Angelica without ever losing focus adheres to the plot she has engineered. This allows her to fend off distractions and above all to maintain absolute control over Orlando, whom she considers the most effective means to pursuing and wooing Rainaldo. For this reason, the promise of a "proof of love" she coaxes out of Orlando is followed by another one. Like the first, this second one too is a ruse intended to pressure the knight into taking action on her behalf to reduce the time and space separating her from Rainaldo. In the aftermath of his first day on the battlefield, Angelica and her ladies pay a visit to Orlando. The meeting takes place in an atmosphere of polished luxury, where "Frutti, confetti e bon vino" (Food, fruit, good wine) (27.37) complete the setting that lends itself to conviviality. But the growing tension that charges this scene suggests just the opposite. An apprehensive, fretful Orlando who cringes with embarrassment about his disheveled appearance in the ladies' presence shows another side of the paradoxes defining him. This unconfident Orlando stands out against the self-assured knight who in canto 25 arrived at the fortress also in shattered armor but full of pride for the accomplishments that caused his dishevelment. The loss of the helmet and the breaking of the shield Angelica gave him in the morning cause his anguish: "Unde di doglia gli crepava il core" (Therefore his sorry heart beat fast) (27.37). The fear that she may ask him about the armor exacerbates Orlando's uneasiness:

> Ed avea tal doglia nel pensiero,
> Che non sa dir se egli è morto né vivo,
> Se quella dama chiedesse il cimiero,
> O domandasse come ne fo privo.
> (27.38)

(So wretched were his thoughts, he did / Not know if he were dead, or lived. / He thought she might demand her crest / Or ask him how it had been lost.)

The answer to Angelica's potential question would require acknowledging the blows Orlando suffered at Rainaldo's hands. With his mind engulfed in the confusion between form and substance, or aesthetics and ethics, like the *confetti* and wine prepared in the room, the knight sinks into a paralyzing despair. Still, the tension that grips him betrays the vainness guiding him. And this is reflected in the type of food made available in the chamber. The empty *confetti*, the easily perishable fruit, and the mind-altering quality wine possesses are all reminders of aesthetically attractive, pleasure-inducing foods that lack any nutritional value. According to Ficino, wine is harmful to the body because it "fills up the head with humors and very bad fumes."[92] Clearly, the fare intended to lend sophistication to the ambiance and enliven the courtly gathering despite its attractiveness is not only devoid of nutrients, it can cause more harm than benefit to the body. This fact mirrors Orlando's shallowness. He is concerned with his attire and feels shame because of his appearance; yet at the same time he fails to see the moral incongruousness of battling against the French and, more especially, his cousin. The rupture in the belief system that regulated his life before and after meeting Angelica is here underlined by way of his lost sense of which side he should be fighting against, as well as by his concern with his attire. The food provided in this handsome setting also points to Angelica's duplicitous strategy and her exploitation of truth and values. Through food that like Angelica's actions and Orlando's behavior feeds the perceptions and ravages reality, Boiardo continues to probe with subtle irony the moral challenges his heroes face.

Continually reassessing and recalibrating her strategy according to the situation, Angelica uses her persuasive manners and compelling talk to camouflage her interest in Rainaldo. Charming, scheming, and captivating, with gestures and words she confounds and confuses Orlando. She, meanwhile, remains fixed in her desire and hides the truth of her motivations behind her seduction of him. A turning point comes, however, when, after a restless night spent pining for Rainaldo, who occupies a nearby pavilion but whom she cannot visit, Angelica returns alone to Orlando's chamber. There, she briefly observes him also in a restless sleep that matches his state of mind: "Mirando il conte in quel sonno dissolto, / Tanto feroce e orribil è nel volto" ("To see that baron fast asleep: / He looks so terrible, so fierce") (27.47). As fleeting as it is, this image is enlightening first because it discloses Orlando's utter vulnerability. The word *dissolto* used to describe him retrieves the notion of "lost" as well as of "floundering." Both of these states aptly describe the knight who in the arms of Hypnos, just as if he were in those of his twin brother Thanatos, appears physically vulnerable, disempowered, disengaged, and removed from everything, including the misleading context Angelica has fabricated for him. This adds a layer of irony to Orlando's eagerness to meet the terms of Angelica's request. In his sleep, his "feroce e orribil" face gives away his unfailing earnestness to fulfill her request. But the fact that when awake he is incapable of peering beyond the illusion of stability and order she presents to him intensifies the paradox of his undertaking. For Orlando to remain true to the word given, complying with the promise is a moral imperative that consumes him even in his sleeping hours. Because of this, his sleep becomes the negation of a liberating dream. This suggests not only the fleetingness of life, but especially the inconstancy of human desires, the imperfection of human thought, and the shortcomings of human endeavors.

The scene of Angelica watching Orlando's restless sleep merits a deeper look, especially because it gives a unique insight into her arsenal of Machiavellian strategies. As she scrutinizes the knight, she embodies the seasoned strategist. Unseen, stealthily, relentlessly, and remorselessly, she studies the enemy in order to ascertain its vulnerabilities. These she will then target to bend the opponent to her will. While this strategy clearly enhances Angelica's power to keep Orlando yoked to her, it also underscores her willingness to test and overstep the boundary between the public and the private, the inside and the outside, the contained and the container. By making Orlando the object of her calculating gaze, the vigilant Angelica re-inscribes herself within the universe of deceit and artificiality she has crafted for Orlando. There, guided solely by ruthless self-centeredness she rules unchecked against his isolation and longing. More interestingly, in transgressing the limits between the private and the public and intruding in Orlando's space Angelica takes in and internalizes the sight of a powerless and innocuous knight. She consumes him, like food ingested, through her eyes in an act of voyeuristic appropriation. This magnifies her role as a controlling person who, again, prepares to cajole her adversary.

Immediately after this scene, with riveting verses Boiardo closes in on the growing erotic tension that motivates Angelica:

> Così la dama, che avea maggior fretta
> Che'l conte Orlando assai de cavalcare,
> Or col viso suave, or con la mano,
> Svegliò toccando, il cavalier soprano.
> (27.48)

(The damsel, in a hurry—more / Than Count Orlando was— to ride, / Now with her sweet face, now her hand, Touched him and woke the sovereign knight.)

Angelica's eagerness to be with Rainaldo becomes still more pressing than Orlando's own desire to possess her. Although this description singles out the basest type of human want, implicitly contrasting it to more edifying virtues, now there is no dissimulation on Angelica's part; at this point she is a compendium of desire. Her inner turmoil, the yearning consuming her, juxtaposed to her fudging of facts and manipulations, is a reminder of the beauty and hideousness defining humanity. This lends a delicious depth to her persona that is otherwise missed if one were to just focus on her scheming abilities. More importantly, it creates a bridge of empathy that connects her with the audience because her desire fits into a frame of reference with which the audience can identify. Here, there is no elliptical depiction of an Angelica simulating a response or misrepresenting her objective. On the contrary, her impatience to gratify her desires with the man she loves pulses through her conduct and this illustrates the interplay of ambition, craftiness, and love.

Orlando's reaction to Angelica's awakening is telling because it brings to an unexpected climax the assumption of the knight's impotence:

> Il conte al suo bel viso remirando
> Tutto se accese de amoroso foco
> E la dama abbracciò tutto tremando,
> Benché soletti fussero in quel loco.
> (25.50)

(Orlando saw her pretty face / And felt the flame of love ignite. / He trembled as Angelica / Embraced him, though they were alone.)

Despite his earlier failure to respond to Angelica's fondling, in this scene Orlando acts on his desire. By passionately embracing Angelica he dissipates any existing doubt about his maleness; he also momentarily regains control of the situation. By finding her near, in the act of awakening him, Orlando correctly surmises that she has walked into his chamber for him. What he ignores are the motives for which she is looking for him. Unlike what happened during their first encounter, his reaction to her is neither indifference nor capitulation; rather, it is one of strong erotic impulses. With a verse that echoes Dante's description of Paolo kissing Francesca "la bocca mi baciò tutto tremante" ([he] kissed my mouth all trembling),[93] Boiardo inscribes Orlando's reaction to Angelica within the sphere of tragic lovers. But there is a difference between the two couples. In Dante's scene, the lovers' yearning for each other adds dramatic tension to their awareness of defying social and moral rules in order to find fulfillment. As Francesca recounts it, their hope was pinned to the secrecy shrouding their mutual feelings. Paolo's quivering kiss suggests both the fear of being discovered and the exhilaration that their closeness arouses. In Boiardo's dramatization of the "lovers'" meeting, the knowledge that Angelica does not reciprocate Orlando's feelings makes his quivering embrace a diluted version of Paolo's kiss. Because he is sexually aroused and she is not, his embrace speaks to the intensity of his passion and also to her drive to manipulate him. She stokes the fire of his senses while remaining passive to his advances. Also, unlike Francesca who becomes caught up in the literary fiction of her readings, Angelica is firmly grounded in the concreteness of her wants. For this reason, although both Paolo and Orlando are doomed lovers, of the two Orlando is the foolish, innocent one because he is unable to reconcile the contradictions Angelica's nervous energy reveals. She is effusive and detached, deeply romantic and unresponsive. Her unsolicited arrival in his chamber feeds his imagination and he acts on the reality this creates without wrestling with it. Although his response to her presence restores his image from the unresponsiveness that immobilized him before, Orlando's new resolve is dampened by Angelica's determination to be with Rainaldo, not him. Because of this, she destabilizes Orlando's self-assertiveness by interjecting a new request to his passionate embrace:

> "Io ti prometto che a ogni tuo volere
> Soletta in questo loco, come io sono,
> Ti lascerò di me prender piacere,
> Se me prometti ed attendi un sol dono . . .
> E quel ch'io voglio e quel ch'io ti dimando,
> E' una battaglia sola al mio commando."
> (27.51).

("I promise I will let you have / Your way with me all that you want— / Right here, alone, as we are—if / You promise and provide one gift / . . . / What I desire, what I request, / Is just one exploit, when I ask.")

Angelica correctly surmises that Orlando will brave any risk to which she exposes him. She also understands that through this she can dispose of Orlando once Rainaldo is in close proximity. As a result, if the strategy she deployed until now aimed at keeping a distance between her body and Orlando's (implicitly separating the knight from the ordered body of politic of which he was part), Angelica's new request is designed to drive the unaware knight completely away from both.

Once again the agreement Angelica wants to extract from Orlando is based on deceitful terms underpinned by unscrupulous machination. She presents it, however, with finely honed sagacity. As the initiator of the promise, Angelica maps the road Orlando must follow and deflects the possibility of the knight turning down his end of the bargain. Through her request she not only gives voice to his desire, but also to the hopes that he continues to harbor. Angelica's emphasis on the "I" as the subject, active doer, and initiator of the promise that he must agree upon suggests to Orlando her own desire for him. Rhetorically, however, her words are another example of her willful manipulation. Analyzed through the prism of his unfounded hopefulness, the terms of her promise guarantee her commitment to him. That he neither suspects nor has any control over her scope and ambition, as well as her ability to disguise the truth, is a searing reminder of the knight's failure to discern the truth behind her maneuvers. Angelica's stipulation requires moral and ethical accountability, responsibility, and obligations—in short, the same traits that define knighthood. From Orlando's standpoint, the promise to which he is asked to keep faith is undergirded by the duties and expectations that he already embodies. What gives him even more verve to abide by her terms is that by eschewing ambiguity they clearly define, through personal details and specific location, her willingness to make herself the object of his pleasure. Although lacking authenticity, albeit brimming with emotional energy, her words reassure him that he will be allowed to take the physical enjoyment for which he longs. And the potential of the gratification distracts Orlando from the remote concreteness of its realization. He ignores the fact that the trust required in keeping faith to a promise rules Angelica out because he still does not see through her subterfuges. Were he to do so, he would recognize the contradiction between her words and her actions.

A promise stipulates the terms of an agreement between two individuals. The order a promise establishes is maintained by agreeing and adhering to the conditions and limits set to carry it out. By abiding by the rules, those sharing in the promise reap mutual benefits in its final implementation. Conversely, breaking the promise by not keeping faith to its terms undercuts the principles on which it is based. Violating the terms of a promise not only compromises, but also especially destabilizes, the normative system regulating it. In political terms, not keeping faith to a promise is tantamount to not observing the laws, a fact that Brunetto Latini emphasizes in his *Rettorica*.[94] The brutalities and destruction that the latter results in threaten not just the social order, but also individual lives. These are precisely the circumstances that define Orlando's existence ever since he abandoned the French camp in pursuit of Angelica. Dangerously linking his physical senses to his sense of duty in terms of private and public interests, being unaware of all the facts, and having failed to learn the lesson contained in Dragontina's offer of the cup of water (6.44) that led him to oblivion, Orlando agrees to help Angelica. With his pledge he blurs yet again the line between reality and appearance, reason and delusion. Most importantly, by accepting Angelica's words at face value he continues on his downward spiral. In so doing, he crushes the ideals of his humanist education. She is powerful, single-minded, and determined. He is powerless. She is in control. He has no control.

In sharp contrast to Orlando's acceptance of Angelica's food—and cooked reality—is Rainaldo's refusal to accept her advances. Upon entering the "palazzo zoioso" ("Pleasure Palace") (8.1), he is invited by her ladies into the garden and there he is served unspecified food and wine. This does not please him; rather, he is baffled by the rich surroundings and by the attractive maidens serving him. As soon as he learns that the opulence he is admiring is the result of Angelica's work, and that she is consumed by love for him, Rainaldo dashes away: "E cambiosse nel viso tutto quanto; La lieta casa ormai nulla non prezza" (His attitude completely changes. / Now he rejects that mansion) (8.12.4–5). Stylistically, what makes this scene especially suggestive is the compactness of the two verses within which Rainaldo's decisiveness is inscribed. With the sign of his disgust with her on his face, the clarity of his thoughts and the firmness of his will are figuratively measured against the allurement of the banquet prepared for him. Angelica's desire to draw him to her is made visible through the sophisticated meal she wants him to consume. Louis Marin's theory applied to this scene suggests that this meal functions precisely as a transignificant of Angelica's intentions. Accordingly, enticing Rainaldo to take pleasure in the intoxicating delights her table offers is a device to arouse his interest in her. It is also the conduit to her who, in the desolation of waiting for him, aspires to be the food of his passion.

In spite of Angelica's plan, and as if stung to fury by the contradiction between his ideals and her desire, Rainaldo rejects the maidens' invitation. His decision draws attention to the contrast between his and Orlando's course of actions. Rainaldo does not allow appearances to manipulate him. He is not enticed by the allurement of physical satisfaction. Most importantly, he is not controlled by his libido. By rejecting Angelica's advances and by not seeking self-gratification at her table he displays a sense of self-control that is unknown to Orlando. Rainaldo's impulsive flight from Angelica's table stands in stark contrast to the manner in which Orlando lingers at it in Albracà. Ironically, for Angelica the flight of the one she loves and the presence of the one she abhors illustrates the delusion of expectations that are not fed by deviousness. The two events are representative of the flight of the mind that affects one knight and the clear principles that guide the other. Ultimately, Rainaldo's resolve to abandon the pleasures evoked by Angelica's table reveals his understanding of and adherence to the normative code of chivalry. By leaving the enchantress's food behind he never relinquishes the qualities that a valiant knight must possess and thus, he never jeopardizes his sense of self.[95]

Through meals and banquets Cardinal Riario, Charlemagne, and Angelica whip their respective enemies into compliant allies. This strategy enables them to achieve their respective goals. For these individuals, much like the dukes of the House of Este, the politics of gastronomy turns into the enhancement of political strategies and linguistic persuasion because it negotiates meanings between actions and inaction, silence and words. With quiet force the politics of gastronomy says the unsayable. Most importantly, it gives voice to a range of meanings and possibilities, deeper insights and more nuanced stories. These go beyond rigid conventions, blur assumptions, and subvert impressions. The politics of gastronomy is an effective tool to rely on in a world in which powerful if narcissistic individuals (must) endeavor to coexist by artfully turning enemies into allies. In the following chapter we will see how in the *Orlando Furioso* Ludovico Ariosto relies on these same techniques to paint an accurate picture of his society.

FOUR

Meals, Transformations, and the Belly of History
Ariosto's Furioso

In the previous chapter I showed how Matteo Maria Boiardo relies on the politics of gastronomy to reveal the more hidden political, social, and cultural folds of his society. In this chapter I explore Ludovico Ariosto's use of food as a way to analyze in a more organic manner the sociocultural currents of his times. In canto 7 of the *Orlando Furioso* Ruggiero's quest for fame and glory is stymied by the enchantress Alcina.[1] Her illusory world, where the abnormal appears as the normal, transforms Ruggiero into a weak-willed character. This entails a transformative process that, by resisting and subverting the dominant courtly ideology that rests on power and authority, affects the hero's sense of both self and reality. Seduced by her intoxicating temptations, he becomes the embodiment of the complex dichotomy between reality and illusion — or reason and folly. Scholars have long probed the tricks, intrigues, deceptions, resentments, passions, and hatreds that change Ruggiero's course of action and result in his transformation from his chivalrous self into that of an unrequited lover. This painstaking canonical scrutiny has failed to appreciate the less obvious, but equally intriguing, presence of both food and banquets as a key to understanding the hero's experience.

In fact, these two elements have been subordinated to a third one: the idealized and impermeable notion of the hero's humanistic *paideia,* as if the three were dissonant chords in a musical measure.

To dismiss as mere reflections of Renaissance courtly practices the role that foodstuffs and banquets play in the *Furioso* is to diminish significantly the poem's complexity. It also detracts from the coded, multilayered range of metaphorical meanings that Ariosto injects, often inconspicuously, with potent doses of irony through food.[2] Like the authors considered in the previous chapters, this process allows him to question and often critique from within the sociopolitical atmosphere of his Ferrara and the Este court.[3] Against the filigree of the epic poem's main storylines, food and its presentations do more than spice up the hero's conventional chivalric-amorous undertakings. They are used by the poet as a means of playing off the porous and ambivalent relationship between the hero's moral fiber, the unpredictable force of his desires, and the limits of courtly ideals that perversely resist the reality of a changing society. Ruggiero's downfall, marked by the copious food he is offered and especially by the *confetti* he eats at Alcina's table, evidences this. His ensuing abandonment to the illusions that he "confects" from his newly erotic desire for the beguiling enchantress fuses the worlds of illusion and reality, fiction and history, impermanence and permanence. Food, as I have argued in the previous chapters, by its very nature exemplifies the process of change and transformation. The various preparations it undergoes before it is consumed connote impermanence.[4] Thus food lends itself as a formidable metaphor for the transformations Ariosto's hero experiences. Indeed, in Ariosto's poem one serves as a metaphor of the other.

More than just providing a conspicuous display of one's power and status,[5] foodstuffs in the *Furioso* function as a moral and aesthetic instrument through which the hero's education,[6] self-knowledge, and achievements can be gauged. More importantly, food serves as a means to maintain, as well as to negotiate, power, social hierarchy, and relationships between the powerful and the powerless. Offering and consuming it, taking part, that is, in commensal politics and sharing a meal with a host marks the potential progress, or regress, of the hero's journey.[7] In historical terms, Cardinal Riario's banquet offered to Eleonora d'Aragona's wedding party and Ercole d'Este's ambassadors is a good example of this type of political engagement. Yet, as we have seen, in the act of eating are also often embedded signs of the hero's moral and ethical fragility. Specifically, in Ruggiero's case food and banquets accompany the knight's progressive passage from a state of moral deterioration (and lack of self-control) to one of adhesion to the ideals of humanistic culture (and self-discipline). Unlike the earlier state of sensual subjugation to Atlante and to Alcina that diminished Ruggiero's character, the latter one, with its focus on restraint and willfulness, brings about his ethical awareness, psychological growth, and aesthetic insightfulness. Thus self-restraint and self-determination ennoble the hero by rendering him less vulnerable to intemperate yearnings. By depicting an inexperienced Ruggiero who abandons himself to the purely sensual pleasures that Alcina's culinary seductions metaphorically imply, Ariosto explores the permanent if tenuous balance between men and history through the context of foods and eating. The hero's lack of confidence and vulnerability that surface in the scenes portraying him at Alcina's table lend cogency to Ariosto's finely delineated critique of his culture and its leaders.

Vivande, mense, and *banchetti* ("food and drink," "festive boards," and "banquets") appear throughout the *Furioso.* Less frequently, only on two occasions, to be exact, does Ariosto specifically reveal that the food consumed at these events includes *confetti.* On the one level, the generalization about dishes and banquets suggests a powerful and deliberate authorial presence. This is one that eschews details ostensibly peripheral to the epic landscape. On another level, however, the broad assertion points to Ariosto's carefully devised poem that draws on a range of evidence to depict the experiences shaping his hero's character and juxtaposes them to those molding his contemporary audience. Ariosto accomplishes this even through broad statements because his distinctive poetic voice is often humorous, occasionally weary and defensive, but always intensively engaging. The poet is well aware that within the poem's fictionalization, no crumb of information is going to be overlooked by his audience's cultivated understanding. To this end, his words are very explicit: "A voi so ben che non parrà menzogna / Che'l lume del discorso chiaro" (I know that you, my sharp, / clear-headed listeners will see the shining truth of my tale) (7.2). These verses highlight Ariosto's awareness that his audience will recognize the cultural, social, and political references of its milieu.

To trace the symbolic meanings of food in canto 7 of the *Orlando Furioso* and to address the question of its connection to the critical events that transform the hero, it is necessary to begin with canto 4, where food first appears. Tellingly, in this canto, the presence of foodstuff coincides with the narration of Ruggiero's captivity in Atlante's castle. The magician keeps the hero as his prisoner in order to save him from death.[8] During his captivity the knight is entertained with "Suoni, canti, vestir, giuchi, vivande, / Quanto puo' cor pensar, puo' chieder bocca" (music and song, fine raiment, pastimes, food and drink, / whatever desire the heart can feel or lips can utter) (4.33). To keep Ruggiero enticed under his control, Atlante provides him with every form of leisure and satisfies his bodily desires. Clearly, these pleasures ensnare the body and the mind by appealing to the senses.[9] Because he is engrossed in music, songs, dressing, games, and food, Ruggiero's chivalrous resolve is undermined because, very simply, his desires are satisfied without any effort on his part.[10] To be sure, this process does not result in personal growth and maturity. On the contrary, it enfeebles the hero's will. For this reason, the experiences Atlante provides for Ruggiero typify the very subversion of humanistic ideals.

Interestingly, all the activities engaging Ruggiero's willpower involve a process of change. This system mirrors the transformation of self that the hero unwittingly undergoes. Specifically, just as music results from the sequence of distinctive sounds that individual notes produce and that in turn are transformed into the seamless texture of melodies, songs develop from the arrangement of verses and music that merge into one lyrical theme. Although products of the environment out of which they are created, both music and songs in the end give rise to their own, artificial and ephemeral, contexts.[11] As a result, they are unconnected to reality. They can even render it superfluous; yet, music and songs are never extraneous to the audience's cultural milieu. In point of fact, because in the courtly universe music and songs reflect the immediacy of the experiences out of which they are produced, they remain extraneous to social contexts removed from the courtly one. Ariosto's sophisticated audience could well relate to the types of diversion that music and songs provide for Ruggiero. In a similar manner, dressing is an outward makeover. It is composed of parts that alter one's appearance without ever modifying the substance.¹² Finally, games, in a less abstract way, require a change of both behavior and character from the individuals taking part and playing a role in them.¹³ By erasing the boundaries between reality and fiction, games, as well as music, songs, and dressing up, exceed the parameters of the conventionally possible and of life's ordinariness. In this manner, they usher the participants into the world of the extraordinary. In this world, time functions as a measure of the pleasures it affords while pleasures are visible gauges of the players' privileged existences. Yet again Ariosto's audience could find itself in a unique position to appreciate these forms of entertainment for they define the very identity of the Este court and its entourage. At the same time, however, the theatricality that these amusements require of the participants exposes the duplicity that is intrinsically part of the self-absorbed roles courtiers willingly play at court.¹⁴ In other words, by becoming part of the playful reality constructed to amuse them, players effectively capture and meld place, time, and yearnings in a way that speaks not only to the roles they play at court, but also to their sense of self.

By progressively marking the process of transformation as a phenomenon that takes place in sounds, words, clothing, and games, therefore both outside and inside of the self, Ariosto sets the stage for a further example of transformation. And this example encompasses all the others. By placing eating among the activities that entail a transformation of character and result in the flagging of the heroic will, the poet relies on food as the element that sums up the very process of transformation in both interior and exterior forms. As we have seen, food preparations change according to the cook's inventiveness and audacity. A combination of talent, inspiration, and skillfulness enables him to turn what may appear to be peculiar, decayed ingredients into gastronomic deliciousness. Perhaps these delicacies tickle the imagination even more than taste buds; and yet through them a rarefied culture defines itself. The process of generating appetizing and delicious dishes for a discerning audience foregrounds the cook's expertise. In a way, his interpretations of ingredients translate reflective moments about his sociocultural and historical context. His dishes are the gastronomic narrations of courtly conventions. This strategy is not different from the one adopted by Trimalchio's cook. Still, the gastronomic order to which a cook gives life overcomes and curbs the limits and variability that each ingredient possesses and offers. Even so, the resulting culinary achievements shape a gastronomic landscape that—like Francesco Guicciardini emphasizes—provides a cultural referent for a given time and mirrors a culture's sociocultural and political sensibilities. As for the writers and poets who in their works use food to convey a set of meanings, they often push against the conventions, logic, and chronology of particular dishes. Through this, they can better capture the anxieties, incongruities, and yearnings of their cultures.

Like the other transformations taking place in Atlante's *rocca*, a cook's creations herald new and unforeseeable culinary reconfigurations. From decay, maceration, and even fermentation different ingredients culminate in a product—the final dish. Thus, in its transient quality food mirrors the consumer's impermanent nature and wriggles it against the permanence of history. The combination of balanced flavors and unusual ingredients epitomizing the constructive process that prepared dishes exemplify is, for this reason, superior to all the other transformative instances that Atlante makes available for Ruggiero. The constructive transformation that food undergoes is a recognizable contradiction to Ruggiero's own transformation. At this point, his personal trajectory follows a moral and ethical sliding into the realm of excesses where the flagrant contradictions between courtly ideals and human selfishness are unearthed.

Atlante's actions, as he explains to Bradamante who arrives to free Ruggiero, are motivated by a selfless desire to protect the knight from death:[15]

> Nè per maligna intenzione, ahi lasso,
> (disse piangendo il vecchio incantatore)
> . . . .
> Nè per avidità son rubatore:
> Ma per ritrar sol dall'estremo passo
> Un cavalier gentil, mi mosse amore,
> Che come il ciel mi mostra, in tempo breve
> Morir cristiano a tradimento deve.
>
> (4.29)

("Alas, I had no wicked intention," explained the old enchanter, / weeping, . . . "And it is / Not avarice that has made me a robber: Love it was that moved me to / Rescue a gentle knight from extreme peril—for Heaven revealed to me, / That he is shortly to die a Christian, treacherously slain.")

Spoken with crystalline simplicity, Atlante's words reveal, first of all, his knowledge of Ruggiero's tragic end. Brimming with pathos, they echo Beatrice's "amor mi mosse" (*Inferno,* 2) ("love moved me"). Through the dynamic connection between thought and expression, that is, between words and feelings that retrieves Dante's verse, Ariosto lends power to the magician's desire to safeguard the knight. Like Dante's heroine, Atlante is driven by love. The magician's objective is to rescue his protégé from the impending peril and set him on a path toward a safer future than the one awaiting him. Yet Ariosto's parallel is striking not because of the poet he evokes or the gender contrast he sets forth, but because of the theological and profane discourses he pits against each other. Specifically, unlike Beatrice's love that is sustained by an unyielding commitment to the moral and ethical truths that theology imparts, Atlante's is unconcerned with them. For him saving Ruggiero entails bending the rules and doing away with the moral and ethical obligations the knight's position demands. By enveloping him in an uncomplicated universe where transient gratifications and pleasures need neither be gained nor desired, the magician shields Ruggiero from the world of losses and disappointments. Ironically, this experience enables Ruggiero, the forebear of the ruling Este family, to (erroneously) believe that his quest for personal fulfillment need neither be postponed nor earned through learned experiences and responsibilities. It is difficult to believe that this point would be lost on Ariosto's audience. The Este dukes, who ruled Ferrara with an iron hand, had their own notion of the privileges that life at court legitimated.[16]

Paradoxically, by contriving a world in which the hero can wallow in the bliss of unbridled delights, Atlante subjects the hero to the death of the will even while preventing his physical death.[17] By erasing Ruggiero's desire to pursue personal achievements and by suspending his yearning for heroic undertakings, the magician undercuts the knight's potential to learn through experience, test his will, and strengthen his awareness of his own shortcomings. In short, though the magician's actions preempt the knight's death, they also frustrate his chance to face the experiences through which self-knowledge is tested. In accordance with the humanistic tradition, only by gaining such knowledge can the hero apply it to his actions and, from them, secure the fame that results in the lasting gratification of desires. But the transformation to which Atlante subjects Ruggiero through controlling maneuvers does not strengthen the knight's moral and ethical perspective. It does not ground him in the rapidly shifting realities of the power-hungry world surrounding him. Nor, for that matter, does it hone the self-determination necessary for him to function in that system. Rather, it enhances the flights of the hero's imagination. And this widens the divide that separates it from reality. In a sense, through his machinations Atlante whittles away Ruggiero's identity, replacing it with a new, more vulnerable one. Not surprisingly, the knight's new identity casts a sharply revealing light on the ambivalence of sympathetic gestures and the dangers they inevitably usher in: reasoned capitulations, compromised ideals, and forsaken goals.

Quite naturally, in the face of tempting sensory delights Ruggiero undergoes a drastic change. Like food that no longer retains the tastes, the colors, or even the shapes of its original ingredients he is not assailed by guilt of who he was before entering Atlante's carefree world. Nor is he concerned with the man he has become. A subservient, if sensually fulfilled captive, the knight remains willfully blind by what he discovers in the magician's world. Here he is also unheeding of the fact that instant gratifications of desires reflect one's flaws rather than strength of character. Oblivious to the imbalance between the self-indulgent world of Atlante and the self-denying world of knighthood, Ruggiero becomes progressively more removed from reality. And as he loses sight of the contingencies it presents, his character cleverly typifies the princes of the Este court for whom Ariosto works: willful—and willing—captives of the "theater" of their court.[18]

While Atlante generalizes about the *vivande* available to Ruggiero in the *rocca*, well-known food treatises, recipe collections, and social manuals were widely circulated in the Renaissance.[19] As I argued in the previous chapter, these treatises focused not only on the preparation of exquisite dishes but also on the consumers' health. They did so by emphasizing the therapeutic qualities of specific foods and ingredients. With the *Erbolato* Ariosto adds his own voice to this fashionable trend.[20] Of course, there is more to it, for he addresses the issue with an inventive twist. The *Erbolato* is a humorous imitation of the pedantic treatises circulating at the time. It is above all, a concise but clearly outlined critique of the poet's culture. In this minor work, written around 1530, Antonio Faventino (the narrator) speaks of the medicinal qualities of herbs in general and of his *Elettuario vitae* in particular. He claims that this concoction—the *erbolato*—given to him by Master Niccolò da Lunigo not only cures every illness, but also ensures longevity. According to Antonio, "the Most Excellent Duke Ercole, Lord Sigismondo, Lord Rinaldo, and Lord Alberto, all brothers of the Most Illustrious House of Este," have benefited from the "therapeutic properties" of his *Elixir of Life*.[21] Thus, as an experienced impostor Antonio pitches the sale of his elixir. Clearly, throughout the work with wit and irony Ariosto criticizes his culture and especially its classicist leanings.[22] More than this, though, his work is a reminder of the self-absorption and conceit that rule at the Este court.

In the *Furioso* this critique is much more subtle; the treatise is, after all, an encomium to the ruling House of Este.[23] This notwithstanding, it is fair to assume that the intense interest in food and its properties experienced by Ariosto's culture suggests that an abundance of healthy and trendy culinary delicacies suitable for a knight of Ruggiero's prominence are available to him at Atlante's castle.[24] With regard to Renaissance recipe collections—compiled by doctors, philosophers, and cooks—they differentiate between the foods consumed by the elite and those eaten by the commoners.[25] This classification, like its medieval counterparts, and as Florinetta's words initially reminded us, highlights the correlation between the consumer's social status and food's scrumptiousness. In the passage from a system of nutritional theory to one mirroring the eaters' social standing, food becomes the edible symbol of social status. And, ironically, a creation resulting from ingredients transformed through cooking turns itself into an agent of social transformations. Equally interesting is the fact that, as food becomes a social symbol dividing the elite from the commoners a strong link is forged between the social consciousness[26] of the former and the *virtude* (virtue) and *sanitade* (health)[27] that only the former can derive from it.[28] Applied to Ruggiero, who at this juncture in the *Furioso* is the personification of unraveling courtly ideals, this idea begs a different, but not unrelated, question: is the *virtude* of the eater necessarily reflected in that of the exquisite food he consumes? Clearly, this question is nowhere explicitly articulated in the poem. Yet Ariosto's description of the hero's sojourn in the realm of illusoriness brings it to mind and the poet indirectly provides an answer to it.

Greedily engrossed in the meals and leisurely pursuits the magician provides, the knight shows neither desire nor need to dwell on his dereliction of public and personal duties. Both his lack of concern for these responsibilities and his new indifference to values that should define his heroic will reverberate in Atlante's vague reference to *vivande*. The ephemeral nature of food is an all-encompassing quality that reflects, and challenges, the notion of humanity's dispassionate sense of duty in the face of its fleeting desires. Longing and lusting only for personal gratifications, the hero is transformed, quite naturally, into a pawn of his own desires. Imprisoned by his yearnings and satisfying them without restraint, Ruggiero's new persona carries out Atlante's objective: stripped of self-control and made powerless by the magician, the knight's life becomes regulated by another's objectives. In such fashion, without relying on an inner compass he is ostensibly shielded from death.

I

Alcina's paradise is the other illusory world Ruggiero enters shortly after Bradamante frees him from Atlante's castle.[29] The place is tantalizingly rich, in both food and mirth. Here the knight is goaded to follow the trail of erotic fulfillment by Alcina's ladies who "con molte offerte e con buon viso / Ruggier fecero entrar nel paradiso" (All smiles and charm, they welcomed Ruggiero into / paradise) (6.72). For the still inexperienced, self-absorbed Ruggiero, the delights that Alcina provides are similar to those made available by Atlante. A true product of the court where the "real" is always an intimate part of the simulation,[30] Ruggiero— predictably—has learned nothing from his experience at Atlante's castle. As a result, he remains unable to distinguish between reality and bedazzling illusions; for this reason, he is easily seduced by the gastronomic and erotic pleasures the island and its hostess offer. To be sure, the fundamental difference between Atlante's and Alcina's enticements rests not on the captors' objectives but on their motives. Atlante holds Ruggiero in his castle out of selfless concern, by virtue of the affection that he feels toward the knight. Alcina, in contrast, imprisons him because of a capricious, selfish sexual desire. The different reasons that drive the two to hold Ruggiero captive is made more explicit by the symbolic value of the foods they respectively use to satisfy his hunger. To entice him the enchantress, who like Atlante is a master of transformations, changes her repugnant figure into an exquisite one. Through this, she becomes the object and subject of Ruggiero's erotic desire. Beguiled by her illusory beauty, he succumbs to her desire.[31] Consequently, he reverts to a state of moral idleness that, like his previous experience, is characterized by the wanton fulfillment of personal gratifications. Although the magicians' respective goal to trap Ruggiero is inherently problematic because, among other things, it speaks of the deceptiveness that pervades courtly life, the knight's thoughtless yielding to the pleasures they offer reveals his self-centered nature, as well as his gullibility. Ruggiero is contentedly unaware that what the captors provide is not only the product of their fabrications and transformations but also of his illusion. Clearly, here Ariosto depicts a knight whose desire for material pleasure is stronger than his chivalric idealism. The self-centeredness Ruggiero displays at this juncture overshadows the selflessness he should personify. It is this lack of moral and ethical judgment, his brazen disregard for the principles that should guide him on his journey, which splinters into shards the figure of the courtly hero. This fact is substantiated by the manner in which Ruggiero is portrayed as an effeminate man. Indeed, while the knight's desire for Alcina erases every trace of his former self, his new-fangled behavior is powerfully characterized as unmanly:

> Di ricche gemme un splendido monile
> Gli discendea dal collo in mezzo il petto;
> E ne l'uno ne l'altro gia` virile
> Braccio, girava un lucido cerchietto
> . . . .
> Umide avea l'inanellate chiome
> De più suavi odor che sieno in prezzo.
> (7.54, 55).

(A glittering, richly jeweled necklace / Fastened round his neck and hung to his chest, while his two arms, / Hitherto so virile, were each clasped by a lustrous bangle . . . / His curly locks were saturated / In perfumes, the most precious and aromatic that exist.)

The depiction of an effeminate Ruggiero, crystallized by the jewels and perfumes covering his body, suggests that he has turned his back on the core values of knightly ideals. The effects of his emasculation, made plain in the image of bracelets decorating his arms, stifle him physically and rationally. The hero's devastating enfeeblement is made visible by the way in which the strength that his arms once possessed is juxtaposed to their current weakness. Putting physical force in the same league with moral and ethical soundness, the poet draws an evolving picture of deception, desire, and assumptions. Through this, he zeroes in on the knight's moral decline. Indeed, Ruggiero's pursuit of pleasures at the expense of chivalric values leads to profound changes. Ariosto unfurls these to depict the tensions between the past and the present: "Non era in lui di sano altro che'l nome, / Corrotto tutto il resto, e più che mezzo" (All about him was sickly, all but his name; the rest / Was but corruption and decay) (7.55). That Ruggiero's name is the only trait that has not undergone any changes conveys the full measure of the strong-willed hero's undoing. What is left of his former self is the outer shell, his name. In spite of this, he is scrumptiously fed. "Stava in giuoco e in ballo / In cibo, e in ozio, molle e delicato" (He was passing his time now in amusements, in dancing and feasting, / In soft, pampered indolence) (7.40). Just as in Atlante's castle, on Alcina's island he wiles away his time in physical pleasures. These render him incapable of dismissing his experience as sheer illusion or of testing his endurance by reining in his desire. His sole concern is to savor the pleasures she provides for him. This suggests that Ariosto, with an unerring feel for nuances and subtext, is showing the baffling disjuncture between the food consumed and the worthiness of the consumer.

In stark contrast to the banquets Ruggiero partakes of while a prisoner of magicians are the ones he consumed as a child. This fact is stressed by Melissa when she arrives to liberate him from Alcina's yoke. One of the first things Melissa reminds him of is his childhood's meals: "Di medolle già d'orsi e di leoni / Ti porsi io dunque li primi alimenti" ("Early I fed you on the marrow of bears and lions") (7.57). Designed to strengthen his character and hone his moral fiber, the coarse meals of Ruggiero's childhood associate physical strength and high-mindedness. Not surprisingly, Melissa's claim suggests that she is well versed in the educational treatises of her times. To this end, Aenea Silvius Piccolomini's *The Education of Boys* (1450) takes Pier Paolo Vergerio's *Character and Studies Befitting a Free-Born Youth* a step further. In it, the future Pius II argues that a child's body must not be "nurtured too delicately."[32] More specifically, he states that "moderate and balanced food, as Jerome writes to Rusticus, is healthy for the body and soul . . . And although food that is difficult to digest should be refused, care must nevertheless be taken that you do not eventually come to refuse common food because you are used to delicate fare . . . sometimes you will be in camps, in forests, in desert places, where it will be necessary to take coarser food. The boy must be so nourished that when the occasion demands it, he does not shrink from red meat. Moreover, it is fitting to offer a future warrior such food as may produce a strong, not delicate body. Besides, if someone always eats thrushes, almonds, sugar confections, small birds, domestic kids, and lighter courses, with what dishes shall he then be relieved and cured if he should fall sick?"[33] Still, that Melissa's reproach to Ruggiero begins with the food he was fed reveals Ariosto's understanding of the lack of any connection between food's quality and man's character. The two types of food associated with the two different moments of Ruggiero's life unequivocally suggest that the excellence of the eater and of his virtues is hardly ever reflected in the deliciousness of the morsels he consumes.

To marshal Ruggiero back to the sphere of reason where Alcina has no place, Melissa continues her criticism of his capitulation to the senses, drawing attention to the weakness of his will. In doing so, she shifts between the threatening and the entreating, finally calling his attention to his progeny:

> La tua succession perchè defraudi
> Del ben che mille volte io t'ho predetto?
> . . . .
> Deh perchè il ventre eternamente claudi
> Dove il ciel vuol che sia per te concetto
> La gloriosa e soprumana prole
> Ch'esser de'al mondo più chiare che'l sole?
> (7.60)

("Why must you defraud / Your own posterity of all the good which I have a thousand times / Predicted to you? What of the womb in which—so Heaven has / Decreed—you're to conceive a glorious and god-like race, more radiant / Than the sun: why must you suffer it to remain eternally sealed?")

Although Melissa's reference to Ruggiero's Este descendants could be perceived as an appeal to his insecurity and arrogance more than a call to chivalric duties, it is especially an exhortation to gather momentum and correct the errors made. Coming shortly after her description of the unappetizing food Ruggiero was fed to forge his character, Melissa's words cast a shadow on the modern court. If the pleasures Ruggiero wallows in illustrate the fickleness of his will and his hasty forsaking of responsibility, they also reveal his heedless sense of aloofness and narcissism. This conduct mirrors yet again that of his Este descendants. They—Ariosto's patrons—are well accustomed to the privileges that their social status affords. Ensconced in the entitlements it provides, they brush aside the sociohistorical reality unfolding outside of the court. This is a provocative subtext in a poem written by a poet aware of the magnificent and extravagant excesses his patrons favor.[34] Ariosto also knows that they consider conspicuous food consumption one of the principal examples of their magnificence.

In contrast to Atlante's gastronomic generalization, the abundance of food welcoming Ruggiero's arrival on Alcina's island is conveyed at first through the image of a cornucopia: "Non entra quivi disagio, ne inopia, / Ma vi sta ognor col corno pien la copia" (There was no entrance here for Discomfort or Dearth, / But Plenty was ever in attendance with her copious horn) (6.73). More than simply revealing the copiousness of delicacies available to the new guest, the image of the cornucopia retrieves in one bold stroke the notion of the hero's transformations he undergoes when he is unable to keep his yearnings in check. By juxtaposing the idea of gathered food that the cornucopia calls to mind with the idea of transformation that its creation retrieves, Ariosto in canto 6 of the *Furioso* emphasizes the deep-rooted interconnection that underlies these two elements. In this manner, a new reading of Ruggiero's limitations is revealed through the prism of Ovid's poetry.

In book 9 of the *Metamorphoses*, Ovid describes Achelous's duel with Hercules for Deianira's hand. Like Atlante's ploys and Alcina's schemes, the contest that sets the two gods against each other is steeped in the notion of transformations, metamorphoses, submissions, sexual gratifications, and food. To describe his struggle with Hercules, Achelous recounts his transformations into animals that are physically stronger than humans:

> "Outmatched, out'man'ned, I used that art of mine:
> Changed to a long smooth snake I slid from him.
> In circling sinuous coils I wound myself
> And flickering my forked tongue hissed horribly . . .
> Vanquished again, my third shape still remained,
> A savage bull. A bull! And I fought back!
> . . . .
> (He) Kept pace and dragged me down and forced my horns
> Right into the hard ground and laid me low
> In the deep sand. Even that was not enough:
> He grasped my strong stiff horn in his fierce hand,
> Broke it, and wrenched it off—my brow was maimed!"[35]

By metamorphosing into other animal-figures, by "giving life" to, and at the same time, by "incarnating" creatures renowned for their force,

Achelous assumes that the impossible can be attainable. For him, this is the only way to overpower Hercules and possess Deianira. Achelous's perceived need to undergo physical changes in order to subjugate his adversary and achieve his goal calls to mind the transformations that both Atlante and Alcina undergo to capture Ruggiero. They, like Achelous with Hercules, believe that their respective success rests on their ability to disguise themselves and deceive the hero.

With his metamorphoses, first into a snake and then into a bull, animals that embody, respectively, slyness and strength, Achelous steels himself to confront the situation at hand. In his understanding this ploy will quickly restore what he believes is the legitimate order. Unaware that Hercules too is a god, Achelous believes that because of his own status as river-god he, and not Hercules, deserves Deianira. His beliefs as well as his plan rapidly prove incorrect on both of his morphing attempts. Hercules derides him for his first transformation by reminding him that "mastering snakes is a child's play, Achelous!" (66–67). Hercules punishes Achelous's second metamorphosis more violently, by tearing off one of the bull's horns. Unlike Ruggiero in his interactions with Atlante and Alcina, Hercules shrewdly recognizes and belittles Achelous's attempts to outwit him. It could be argued that Achelous is not clever enough to turn himself into an animal that Hercules has not already struggled against and overpowered. Still, by undermining his power Hercules forever crushes Achelous's hope to have Deianira.

Achelous's triple defeat, resulting from his three different efforts to succeed in his objective through physical mutations and deceptions—as a river-god turned man-suitor, as a suitor transformed into a snake, and as a snake changed into a bull—is most devastating in its third and last attempt at concealing his true nature. This is based on the fact that the tearing of the horn is strongly suggestive of castration. Dehorned as a bull, ridiculed as a snake, emasculated as a man, and powerless as a river-god, Achelous's trouncing is complete: he is not only physically wounded, but even more gravely culturally and morally scorned.

As he narrates his story in Ovid's work, Achelous transforms himself yet again, from a reactive god into an active and privileged narrator. The difference between these two roles evidences his skillfulness in retransforming his transformed self. This process requires at once a delicate albeit powerful shift from overpowered suitor to chronicler (and authorial) authority. In effect, through his narration of the events he has experienced Achelous reappropriates the power Hercules undercut from him and transmits it, through the details he provides, to his—and Ovid's—listening audience.

With his power temporarily reestablished and his authority regained in the persona of the omniscient narrator, Achelous foreshadows his impending catastrophe with a terse description: "At last, forced to my knees," he asserts, "I bit the sand" (61). By linking the experience of his downfall to chewing and, by extension, to the sense that detects and distinguishes flavors, Achelous relies on the image of eating to describe his defeat in terms of tasting that which he neither savored nor experienced before. Biting and tasting, which precede ingestion and reveal food's flavors, is used here as the device through which Achelous foretastes his loss and becomes aware of his own limitations.[36] Most importantly, through this experience the defeated god recognizes the uselessness of morphing into forms that—he wrongly believed—would enable him to overpower Hercules. From this vantage point Achelous's strategy bears a close resemblance to the process that a cook would adopt in tasting a dish to adjust the seasonings that diverse ingredients require in order to obtain the most palatable results.

The river-god, capable of metamorphosing into new and threatening forms, discovers the taste of unappetizing dirt. He gains knowledge of the unknown and untried: humiliation and dishonor. Nowhere is this new reality made more conspicuous for him than in the scene describing the Naiads getting hold of Achelous's broken horn. Seized by rivers' and springs' nymphs that personify earth's fecundity and abundance, his horn is filled with fruits and flowers provided by nature. This change epitomizes the disintegration of Achelous's former self: "My Naiads filled it full of fragrant flowers / And fruits, and hallowed it. From my horn now / Good Plenty finds her wealth and riches flow" (91–93). The juxtaposition of his newly dismembered and unproductive self with the fruitfulness the nymphs embody intensifies Achelous's sense of defeat and failure.

With the sign and symbol of his strength and masculinity severed, the reversal of his fortune is decided. His detached extremity, a phalluslike symbol, is not only appropriated by women who symbolize fertility, but is turned into a vessel for and container of products that signify the fertility and fortune of one other than Achelous. Foodstuffs and flowers, to be consumed and delighted in by others, make up the new inner parts of his former body. This suggests that his subjugation to the will of others (Hercules, Ceres, and the Naiads) is complete: he can claim neither credit nor pride for what his former horn now holds. By retrieving the image of the mythological horn, the cornucopia that welcomes Ruggiero's arrival in Alcina's world foregrounds the dissolution of the heroic will. In addition to this, it presages his impending subjugation to another's will. Thus the cornucopia's perceived abundance conceals a man's egotism turned into amorous defeat and public ignominy. But Ruggiero is unable to understand this. He remains, instead, awestruck by the appearances of his surroundings.

In Ovid's hands, as the gender hierarchy of power is upended and women become the undisputed holders and manipulators of man's willpower, the tentacles of his tale reach beyond the character of Achelous. In the rich tapestry of the myth, Hercules, Achelous's adversary, is renowned not only for his strength but also for his submission to, and emasculation by, Omphale. By succumbing to her sexual allurement, Hercules, much like Ruggiero with Alcina, embodies the undefeated hero who passively, if contentedly, is ensnared by his sexual appetite. Because of this, he undergoes a transformation that keeps him shackled to the desire for her; and this erases his awareness of social, as well as personal, responsibilities. Hercules's feminine attire,[37] like Ruggiero's "vestir delizioso e molle" (the delicious softness of his dress) (7.53), signals the hero's vulnerability and powerlessness in light of unchecked human desires. In the hero's new traits, which radically alter the established mythological and sociocultural patterns, is reflected the transitory nature of power. Although it can be either legitimately obtained or illegitimately seized, its impermanent nature defies any effort to preserve it at will. In the previous chapter we saw how Boiardo in his *Innamorato* linked power to the duration of Charlemagne's banquet.

Achelous's myth, etched, as it is, in the imagery of food and transformations, is itself framed within yet another myth that emphasizes in even stronger terms the interconnectedness of these two elements. In book 8 of the *Metamorphoses*, immediately preceding his account of the duel with Hercules, Achelous describes the punishment inflicted by

Ceres on Erysichthon as though to suggest the relative gravity of his own punishment. Erysichthon is a king who in an act of brazen effrontery hacks down an oak sacred to Ceres. His ferocity toward natural orderliness and, by extension, toward the established laws is exacerbated by his contempt for the oak's anthropomorphic qualities: "The holy tree / Shuddered and groaned, and every leaf and acorn / Grew pale and pallor spread on each long branch. / And when his impious stroke wounded the trunk, / Blood issued, . . . / Then deep from the tree's heart there came a voice: / "I, Ceres' nymph, Ceres' most favourite nymph, / dwell in this oak" (8.760–772). The voice from the oak evokes the scene of Astolfo's body imprisoned and transformed into a myrtle by Alcina shortly after her passion for him dwindled: "Il cor che m'avea dato si ritolse, / E ad altro nuovo amor tutta si volse" ("she took back from me the / gift of her heart, and threw herself body and soul into a fresh infatuation") (6.49). Ruggiero's doleful reaction to Astolfo's predicament coupled with his resolve to seek ways of freeing him, demonstrates that he has regained his sense of duty:

> Si dolse assai che in steril pianta e grama
> Mutato avesse la sembianza vera . . .
> Ma aiutarlo in altro
> In altro non potea, ch'in confortarlo.
> (6.54)

———

(He was deeply afflicted on seeing the change the knight had / Undergone from his true self into a scrawny, sterile shrub . . . He would gladly have been of service to him (if / only he had known how); but all he could do was to offer him / consolation.)

With refreshingly lucid understanding of the empirical evidence he faces, the knight readies himself to rectify the injustice. Ruggiero's awareness of his limits emerges as he recognizes that a force superior to his own—Logistilla's, to be precise—is necessary to undo Alcina's incantation. This detail too restores the hero to his former standing because it shows him wrestling with the hopelessness of changing newly imposed limits.

The strident difference between Erysichthon's and Ruggiero's reactions when facing the talking trees is illustrative of the ideals regulating their respective cultures and even more so molding their actions. Through them Ovid and Ariosto respectively mine the field of human interactions, showing that in a forsaken world humanity remains capable of rising above ostensibly irresolvable perspectives. But when it chooses not to, out of selfishness and self-enshrinement, humanity engineers its own moral downfall. Specifically, in the *Furioso*, Ruggiero, having recognized the voice of Bradamante's cousin Astolfo, feels pity for the forsaken lover; his comforting the imprisoned lover is imbued with a deep sense of regret over his own powerlessness in the face of Alcina's power. By contrast, when facing Ceres's nymph housed in the oak, Erysichthon displays utter contempt for both human and sacred laws. In point of fact, he remains unmoved by the nymph's plea not to hurt her and defiantly dismembers the tree. The callousness of his gesture reveals the arrogance of a man who misguidedly fails to differentiate between earthly and divine power and dismissively goes beyond the boundaries they set. Through his act, Erysychthon wreaks havoc on the tenuous harmony between man and nature. In so doing, he violates the defining principle of ordered societies that develop and flourish where nature generously offers her bounty (despite Achelous's experience).

In the economy of the hybrid myth, transgression is chastised by way of reciprocal transgression. And Famine, Ceres's nemesis and the personification of forever-unachievable personal satisfaction—because by her very nature Famine never finds satiety—is called upon to torment Erysichthon with her ravaging hunger. Her devastating effects on his body are soon apparent. Transformed into a shell of his former self, his emaciated body no longer projects the power he previously embodied. He turns, instead, into the personification of withered sociopolitical values. The incessant hunger that quickly dispossesses him of his sense of physical satiety epitomizes his former inability to recognize the limits of his power. At the same time, it also typifies the hopelessness of his new yearnings. Because of this, Erysichthon becomes the embodiment of wanton accomplishments, unbridled impulses, and depraved exploits. Having dilapidated his wealth in vain attempts to sate his appetite, he resorts to marketing his daughter for food. The depravity of this new ploy brings his selfishness to a new low, making even more real his defiance of moral and social values, the foundations of human society.

But unlike Ceres's oak-nymph, Erysichthon's daughter possesses the ability to metamorphose into other forms. She disguises herself as different animals in order to elude her father's plan. She returns home every time he sells her. Upon learning of her ability, Erysichthon persists in putting her up for sale. He is confident that she will come back and, through more sales, continue to be a source of revenue for his hunger. From an historical perspective, this mercantile mindset evokes Ercole d'Este's propensity for selling offices to the highest bidders for a two-year duration. This technique, as Ugo Caleffini argues, is fiscally if not ethically sound, for it ensures a continual source of revenue for the duke.[38] But returning to Ovid's Erysichthon, when nothing more can sufficiently satisfy his hunger, he gnaws his own flesh. The dehumanization of the self, articulated in terms of a man who "began / To gnaw himself, and dwindled bite by bite / As his own flesh supplied his appetite" (877–878), is complete. The destructive force that ravaged both natural and divine orders recoils onto the self in an unmitigated act of self-destruction.[39] This detail erases every last resemblance of humanity (in) nature. Stripped of his selfhood through his appetite and transformed by it into one (physically) other than himself, Erysichthon's undoing results from his gluttonous ambition to defy the laws that as a king he embodied and should have enforced.

Clearly, the intertextual references to and reversals of Ovid's myths, with their emphases on transformations and food, help to provide insight into Ariosto's characterization of Ruggiero's experience. This fact hinges on the incessant and all-encompassing changes that alter, redefine, and hone not just the hero's awareness of the events marking his journey, but especially on the manner in which, as he gains knowledge, he reacts to them. Not surprisingly, humanity's potential ability to transform itself from within and also of being transformed by nature is at the heart of Renaissance philosophical discourse on human freedom. To this end, Pico della Mirandola's core argument of the chameleon-like capacity of adapting to diverse circumstances and of maintaining in this fashion a central position in the order of the cosmos synthesizes the unparalleled power the human will possesses.[40] Although clearly Pico's theory does not involve physical changes, it is contingent on the will that leads humanity to self-realization. Human will, according to the philosopher, is mutable enough to either lead humanity to its highest potential or drive it to its lowest debasement. Accordingly, by relying on this inner compass, the philosopher argues, humanity can affect the environment and society in which it lives. In his *Oration on the Dignity of Man*, and even more compellingly in his exegesis of Genesis, Pico argues that by indulging in the senses, humanity's material and corrupted nature is revealed.[41] Its divine essence, on the contrary, is uncovered through its rational soul.[42] The dynamic role humanity occupies between animal and celestial worlds rests, therefore, not only on its freedom to choose between the two, but especially on its willingness to endure the changes each realm imposes. Pico's understanding of human freedom, with the consequences it entails, is gripping evidence of humanity's need to transform and advance itself in the pursuit of objectives that frequently change.[43]

Pico's argument is stretched to absurdity in the *Furioso* in the figure of Ruggiero. Here his transformation is triggered by the magic powers through which two magicians battle nature to enslave the hero. Self-knowledge, which underlies Pico's argument, neither guides nor defines the knight's decisions. Ruggiero is driven solely by the desires that the magicians can effortlessly gratify. In one bold stroke, Ariosto supplants the theological vision that frames Pico's claim on the freedom of man's will with magic and trickery. Like characters from Ovidian myths, both Atlante's and Alcina's raisons d'êtres are inscribed within their ability to mold reality according to their needs. And they accomplish this by taking on appearances that best suit their immediate interests. As a result, in Ariosto's hands Pico's view of man's ability to transform and be transformed from within drifts into a whirlpool of self-serving undertakings. These are transformative only in their outward manifestations and from them the courtly hero cannot be spared. Nor would he want to because his desires regulate his existence. Unlike Ruggiero, Atlante and Alcina act with a deep awareness of their objectives and with an even deeper determination to succeed in their schemes. They do so by regularly reassessing and modifying the tactics through which they can keep the knight yoked to their desires. And this, incidentally, is the same strategy Angelica uses in the *Innamorato* to manipulate Orlando. Still, because of the single-mindedness they exhibit throughout their maneuvers, the magicians' qualities are comparable to those of consummate leaders or skilled cooks.

The cook, by attentively evaluating and carefully selecting every ingredient to use in succulent *vivande* that will honor the prince's table, concocts meals that capture the eyes and stoke the imaginations of the persons whose palates will taste them. In the cook's experienced hands nature, through the ingredients he uses, is tamed, shaped, and rearranged. Indeed, some *vivande*, and especially the *confetti*, are transformed into mythological forms.[44] In Ariosto's Ferrara, the figure of the mythical Hercules is preferred to others in the shaping of *confetti* because it pays tribute to the duke's name. Of course, the *confetto* also suggestively links the accomplishments of the mythical hero to those of Ercole I. By evoking Hercules's mythological accomplishments through the *confetti*, the opulence of the meals and the power of the prince, not to mention the prestige of those eating them, merge into a fluid rendition of gastronomic politics. Cristoforo Messisbugo, renowned cook who—like Ariosto—worked for both Ercole and Ippolito d'Este, left ample testimony of his production of mythologically themed *confetti*, along with specific instructions about the organization of princely banquets.[45] In his compilation the celebrity status of his patrons is matched not only by the quantity and variety of food prepared for their banquets, but especially by the figures into which he shapes the *vivande* brought to the tables in-between courses.

The symbolic transformations and translations of Hercules's labors into sugary figures speak of the sophistication and bolster the prestige of the Este court.[46] At the same time, however, they also disclose its disdain for ethical and moral values. The hollowness of the figures the cook creates encapsulates the world of meaningless formalism that holds sway at court. In this universe of time-honored worldliness, fame and honor are inherited through heritage and lineage, not through personal deeds and achievements. The insistence on form rather than substance that the *confetti* emphasize foregrounds the court's recoiling into a world of constructed and empty appearances. Appetite for power and pleasures governs this cocoon-like universe in which time and space cease to have any real meaning.⁴⁷ This aspect of court life makes its members aloof, indifferent observers of reality outside the court and, therefore, disengaged from the struggles that commoners face. The tensions and contradictions between reality and illusion this system gives life to are exacerbated by the cult of the self it endorses. Restraint and curbing excesses are not the court's concerns just as solving and improving social ills is part of its poetic fiction not historical reality. Because of this, the court maintains its legitimacy through force and appearances. And the meaninglessness it typifies is captured in the hollowness of the *confetti* it so fondly produces and consumes. They serve no real function within either reality or history. Ironically enough, the court's appetite shows the same traits as Erysichthon's hunger.

By drawing this parallel, Ariosto's audience could be reminded of the foolishness of its own acts but still remain optimistic about the outcomes of its endeavors. The hedonistic life in which the Este princes indulge unmasks their distorted understanding of the sociocultural circumstances surrounding the duchy. Specifically, their normative excesses clash with the famine and plague raging outside the palace.⁴⁸ Nowhere does this contradiction become more evident than in the reconstruction of Hercules's achievements through edible confections that recall Achelous's empty horn.⁴⁹ These confections not only reduce the courage of Omphale's lover to ephemeral symbols, in both an outward and an inward sense, but also subject it to the destructive forces that human appetites generate. Molded and adorned by the artistic hand, marveled at, praised, and destroyed through eating by the prince and his guests, the cook's figures seek to recapture—if only visually—the power and determination that belonged to the mythical hero. Through this artifice, the court becomes engaged in its own mythologizing. With utter emptiness at its core, princely *confetti* allow gazers and commensals to fuse—or, more accurately, blur the difference between—Hercules's triumphs and Ercole's and his heirs' desire to increase the family's power.⁵⁰

In reality, the permanence and connection with the past that the edible figures promise is fleetingly admired and quickly crushed by the act of eating. In the same fashion, the heroic deeds they capture are neither embodied nor emulated by any of those privileged to admire and consume the *confetti*. On the contrary, the idleness into which the prince and his guests, as passive spectators and punctilious eaters are portrayed, stands as a vivid antithesis of Hercules's vigorous toils. As a result, the figures created in a vain and vainglorious attempt to equate Hercules's mythic triumphs with Ercole's accomplishments are mere depictions of strength, courageousness, and purpose. Individuals investing energy in the pursuit of creating self-images within the court do not incarnate these traits.[51] Hercules and his labors are, then, absent referents for qualities that can be ascribed to neither the prince nor his entourage. The cook, like the magicians and the poet, through his creations fabricates—and transforms—realities. In this manner, he smothers in artifice those, who by choice, not so much because of gullibility, prefer to misconstrue appearances. As for those able to discern between the intricate interplay of the real and imaginary, the cook's (as well as the magicians' and the poet's) labors illustrate the emptiness and vanity of pursuing elusive desires.

Yet, more than the cook's craftsmanship, the deceptiveness that Atlante and Alcina display adds another layer of complexity to their characters. In fact, just as the cook meticulously devises meals for his patron's aggrandizement, the talented prince-captain continually strategizes and implements plans of deception to bewilder the enemy and triumph over it. In his *Art of War* Niccolò Machiavelli suggests various techniques and strategies the captain should use to subdue his adversary. In book 4 of the treatise, Fabrizio Colonna, Machiavelli's main interlocutor, unambiguously asserts that the enemy deceived "by appearance . . . can easily be conquered."[52] The belief that deception is an effective mode of overpowering the opponent guides both Atlante and Alcina. Empowered by it, like accomplished captains, they rely on and cling to hoaxes, tricks, and illusions to keep Ruggiero under their respective yokes.

In the treatise, Machiavelli's piercing criticism of war tactics used despite their proven ineffectiveness is counterbalanced only by his biting disapproval of the conduct of Italian princes. A combination of their reckless debauchery and political ineptitude, the Florentine argues, caused the collapse of law and order.[53] These circumstances, he claims, ushered in the weakening of states, resulting in Italy's capitulation to foreign rule. The fact that Ercole d'Este is the only prince Machiavelli explicitly mentions as an example of a failed military leader is a striking blow to the magnified self-image the House of Este cultivated. As one may expect, it tears apart Ercole's efforts to project an inflated image not only of the Este's power and fame, but especially of his effectiveness as a ruler. This is an image he pursued as an irrefutable bit of logic. This idea—which was imprinted in the political consciousness of the Este court as the very truth that lent Ferrara its greatness—was only partly accurate. Famous Ercole d'Este was—but not because of his military skills. Machiavelli's assertion also chips away at Ercole's credibility to govern over the dynamic social and economic forces brewing outside his court.[54] Accordingly, Hercules's figures confected to contextualize Ercole's achievements and decorate his tables aimed at suggesting that more than just homonyms, the two were deserving of the same fame and honor. However, this attempt to present Ercole's actions as equal to those of the mythical hero functions only as a conceited exercise in self-worth.

Machiavelli argues that Italy's political decline was caused by Italian princes who "used to believe that it was enough for a prince to know how to think of a sharp response in his studies, to write a beautiful letter, . . . to be ornamented by gems and gold, to sleep and eat with greater splendor than others, to keep many lascivious ones around, to govern subjects avariciously and proudly, to rot in idleness."[55] As the Florentine sees it, complacency, fascination with and contentment in the glitters of appearances, materialistic abstractions from life's ordinariness, and personal agendas construct the princes' public image and steer their course of actions. It is no coincidence that his descriptions of the princes' failings seem to characterize Ferrara's princes. They also reveal an uncanny closeness to the enchantments that draw Ruggiero first to Atlante's and later to Alcina's realms. Ariosto's critique of the court and of its political and social shortsightedness is in this manner retrieved through his descriptions of the pleasures that in the enchanted realms captivate the hero and through Machiavelli's criticism of them. Remarkably, in fact, whereas Machiavelli's treatise ends with a disapproving assessment of Italian courts and Ercole d'Este, the works of Ariosto's magicians begin. By remaining entangled in a convenient denial of historical contingencies, the courts confect an alluring if meaningless reality that fascinates (and at the same time ensnares) its courtiers. This is the precise setting

Luigi Pulci's Orlando comes upon the night he and Morgante enter the enchanted palace while on their way to Caradoro's city. But the fantastic creations that offer Ariosto's Ruggiero the same lavishness of the court expose his delusive enticement. More generally, it also shows the narrow-mindedness—the narcissism, to be precise—in which princes and courtiers wallow. Ruggiero, who embodies the courtier, eagerly accepts the life of luxuriousness and idleness offered to him. His capricious nature, like that of Machiavelli's (and of the Este's) princes, is rooted not only in the incessant desire for personal gratification but especially in the sense of entitlement that his social standing (supposedly) legitimizes.

Translated into political terms—as well as ideological ones—Ariosto's depiction of the magicians' modus operandi, their ability to deceive, cajole, and control, evokes the tactics regularly used by the Este family to manipulate power in the advancement of its causes. The poet is familiar with their skillfulness at resorting to any stratagem deemed useful to enforce their rule over both people and territories of the duchy.[56] But while he does not condone them, personal circumstances and financial need force him to continue working for the ruling house, much like Boiardo before him.[57] The Estes' lack of interest in the problems outside of the court (a world with which Ariosto is well acquainted), coupled with their escapist attitude, produces a power imbalance affecting every layer of society.[58] The acute social malaise that ensues forces everyone, especially the powerless to adapt to the model the leaders offer. Like their leader, they adjust by espousing a relativist attitude toward the notion of fair play. And this heightens the tension between the two sides, engendering animosity against the ruling house. With poignant irony Ariosto's characters typify these social extremes. As a matter of fact, even the poet finds himself in this predicament.

The oldest of ten children, at his father's death Ariosto becomes the sole provider for his siblings. Struggling with this burden, the poet manages to pull through by working at the service of Cardinal Ippolito d'Este,[59] Ercole's son, even while the strong pull of literary studies makes itself felt.[60] Ariosto cuts his ties from Cardinal Ippolito and the Estes when he is asked to follow the prelate to his new bishopric in Hungary. Stuck between the constraints of laws and traditions, and between need and desire, the poet questions the very culture the court lives by.[61] Yet to the

Este service he must return; and so he does, this time at the service of Duke Alfonso, the cardinal's brother. While he recognizes that necessity requires that he serve it in various roles, the poet is acutely aware that for the court he embodies the world of the powerless. The condescending attitude it reserves for him stems from this. Needless to say, the Estes' opportunistic greed produces a ripple effect of lies and corruption. Ariosto describes the court's construction of self-serving discourses that makes it a universe of transgressions fueled by the deceptions in Atlante's and Alcina's respective abodes. And although he endeavors to find a balance between loyalty to his patrons, fidelity to history, and the fictive world of the *Furioso*, the Estes' haughty sense of authority paired with their self-ascribed brand of infallibility finds its counterpart in Alcina and Atlante. Like the magicians, the prince resorts to any stratagem deemed useful to enforce his rule over both people and territories of the duchy.[62] In the fiction of the *Furioso*, Alcina and Atlante are insulated from the rest of the world through the supernatural powers they wield. In a similar manner, albeit through a different type of power, the court in Ferrara insulates the prince and his entourage from the life in the raw of the outside world. This situation paradoxically distances him from the very people who empower him to govern and from whom he regularly draws the financial revenues necessary to sustain his ostentatious lifestyle.[63] Not surprisingly, the calculated enforcement of power intended to expand and preserve the Estes' interests and also project their power inevitably leads to a tense and more dangerous environment within Ferrara.

Ironically, if Alcina's fictional island—or, for that matter, Atlante's castle—provides the same luxuriousness that the court offers, the latter becomes their historical equivalent. Replete as they are with sumptuous banquets, splendid garments, precious jewelry, and lavish entertainments that stand for illusory and fleeting power, the magicians' worlds emulate the Este's own realm of illusoriness. This is an "island" in which reality is a more elaborate form of fiction. In it, transformations take place for and by its real inhabitants. Although the prince and his circle are allowed, in fact prefer,[64] to play out roles "assigned" to them in the artificial comforts of a palace that maintains its distances from the trite ordinariness of the life unraveling outside of its walls,[65] in the end, as in Ovid's myths and Machiavelli's treatise, they too personify a power that recoils onto itself and feeds on its own shortcomings only to finally consume itself.[66] Thus through Alcina's cornucopia that the inexperienced Ruggiero stumbles on in canto 7, through the Ovidian myths that it recalls and Machiavelli's military treatise that it evokes, Ariosto exposes, and most importantly critiques, the misuse of power that the Este court engenders and legitimizes. Through this, and because of it, the poet probes the limits of human willpower when confronted with the seemingly unproblematic gratification of desires. Far from being mere subjects of fables, these issues saturate the political and moral climate of the court the poet intimately knows. Here, carving out time from his official duties, Ariosto is creating and transforming his poetic masterpiece through three different editions.[67]

Alcina treats Ruggiero to a banquet the first night of his stay on her island: "E poi che di confetti, e di buon vini / Di nuovo fatti fur debiti inviti" (Once more he was pressed to partake of / Sweet delicacies and choice wines) (7.23). The ceremonial meal she has arranged for her latest guest leads to the ubiquitous *confetti*. But this banquet is more than just a spectacle of Renaissance culture, laced with music, songs, dances, poetry, and acting. The contextual convergence of biblical, historical, and mythological sources suggests that Ariosto envisions a more complex subtext to the meal. Throughout it, in fact, past human accomplishments are filtered through and measured against the events of his times reaffirming—with a new impulse—the timeless essence of human desire. The explicit reference to the *confetti* Ruggiero consumes is indicative, first of all, of the cultural framework within which Ariosto is writing. Indeed, besides reflecting the poet's familiarity with the practices of the Este court, it also mirrors the refinement of the poet's contemporary readers. These people could recognize in his text their social prestige and unmatched wealth and power. At the table this is translated into their own fondness for uncommon delicacies that the *confetti* represented.[68] Most importantly, though, the *confetti* epitomizes Ariosto's poetic boldness. Weaving in and out of his text, linking poetic creations with historical events, imaginary tales with actual food, Ariosto's poetry pivots inward to face the self and then outward into history. His strategy is similar to the one used in the preparation of *confetti*:

establishing the nexus between history and fiction. Like Messisbugo's mythological *confetti* that mesmerize the gazers, Ariosto's story tickles his audience's imagination. As a teaching device, it shows that those guided by self-knowledge and experience, and not misled by human desires, are capable of detecting at once the incongruity between appearance and substance.

Just as through the art of confecting[69] the accomplished cook fascinates his guests by transforming foods into breathtaking mythical scenes, so the skillful poet captivates his audience. He does so by continuously transforming vivid, but ephemeral images into other, but no less illusory, realities. By focusing on the hero who must continually modify his behavior according to relentlessly changing contingencies, the poet emulates the cook whose artistry enables him to give life to mythological tableaux out of edible ingredients. In a similar fashion, every reader can reinterpret the stories Ariosto interweaves in the *Furioso*. Like *confetti*, they are shaped according to the confectioner's creativity. Once they are shaped by the artist, the stories can be interpreted, or eaten, by the readers/diners. This phenomenon is similar to what happens in the visual arts. In that case, the gazers' interpretations of the work are also subjective. Interestingly, in the case of the cooks' creations, food becomes thoughts while thoughts are, simultaneously, shaped into food. Ultimately, for the cook as for the poet, the eaters and the readers identify themselves in the artists' works. And in both food and stories, it is as though the consumers and readers look into a mirror and recognize the salient characteristics of their own culture. Thus the literary text, just as the culinary work, confects and transforms both the world and the characters it reveals.

II

Ariosto describes the lavishness of Alcina's feast as exceeding that of the splendid banquets both Semiramis and Cleopatra prepared for their respective lovers:

Qual mensa trionfante, e sontuosa
Di qualsivoglia successor di Nino,

> O qual mai tanto celebre e famosa
> Di Cleopatra al vincitor latino,
> Potria a questa esser par, che l'amorosa
> Fata avea posta inanzi al paladino.
> (7.20)

(Which of the splendid and sumptuous banquets arranged by any of those who sat upon King Ninus's throne, which of the many celebrated feasts offered by Cleopatra to the victorious Roman, which of these can compare to the banquet that the loving sorceress prepared for the paladin?)

The poet's wry commentary on the gastronomy of power reaches here a kaleidoscopic historical span. In six lines he retrieves the figures of Semiramis and Cleopatra, etching their portraits and their stories against the meals they make use of to seduce their respective lovers. But the notion of power that is seized and retained through food lays bare, yet again, the manner in which commensality lends itself to political manipulation. Feeding a guest can be a courteous gesture and an act of undiluted generosity. It can also turn into the most palatable way of exerting control over others by foisting one's will on them. While some aspects of this strategy have been analyzed in the previous chapters, it is important to bear in mind another perspective. Hosting a meal involves making deliberate choices. Deciding on the foodstuffs to be served, even within a circumscribed universe of social norms, is among them. We saw an example of this practice with the choices made by Giovanni Boccaccio's marchioness of Monferrato. The power of selecting and choosing presupposes freedom because opting for what is preferred as opposed to what is imposed removes the possibility of being yoked to the will of others.[70] Grounded in self-assertiveness, freedom celebrates the domination—or influence—of one individual over another. For this reason it is linked to time and space. In terms of space, freedom reveals itself as the liberty to be and occupy a preferred place. But in terms of time, it is tied to history. The power it affords allows the strongest individual to withstand disappointments, overcome losses, and flourish within the timeless array of life's adversities. Through brash decisions, and sometimes subsequent regret, the strongest shapes human history.

The fact that a meal's choice rests with the host, while the guest remains a passive beneficiary, underscores the imbalance of power existing between the two. For Augustine of Hippo, freedom is achieved when the will is not ruled by vices and sins.[71] But in a shift from Augustine, Lorenzo Valla asserts that the will is autonomous from both theology and philosophy. In his *Dialogue on Free Will* he explains that the will is driven by humanity's enduring capacity—and desire—to choose what it deems more suitable or more gratifying to its existence.[72] Valla also claims that humanity bases its choices on the trust it puts on the returns they secure. The nature of the returns, whether material or spiritual, rests on individual aspirations. The options among which it can choose, the faith, trust, and hope in the returns that each choice yields become, in Valla's view, the needle of the compass that leads humanity to freedom. With regard to Ruggiero as a guest, he may choose among the dishes served what he will eat; but the decision of what choices to serve him lies with Alcina. As the hostess—like the marchioness of Monferrato—she is the person retaining power. In other words, because the decision of what food to taste follows, and is dependent on, the food served, the host is the empowered decision-maker.

By describing Alcina's meal as one more splendid than those of the mythical women, Ariosto sets a parallel of seductions at the banquet table. Through it, he invites a comparison between the past and the present. This comparison lays bare the hero's appetites, deeds, shames, and struggles. From Ariosto's vantage point, sexual allure camouflaged as lusciously ambivalent gastronomic enticement overpowers the hero despite his seriousness of purpose. In terms of appetite for power, disregard for those to whom it legitimately belongs, and contempt for the laws that regulate human societies, Semiramis and Cleopatra personify the same hunger that gnaws at Erysichthon. In fact, his resolve to sell his daughter mirrors Semiramis's and Cleopatra's determination to manipulate Nino and Antonio respectively. Both women's exploits are paradigms of *regni libidine*, wherein sexual enticements, transformations, and lingering wants are mechanisms through which their objectives can be pursued and achieved. In Boccaccio's *Famous Women* Semiramis's skillfulness and intelligence are emphasized.[73]

After her husband's death Semiramis reigned over the Assyrian peoples and territories he had conquered by disguising her identity and impersonating her son, and his heir, Ninyas.[74] The sham worked: by taking on Ninyas's role she misled the populations and attained the power she craved. But while on the political front she succeeded,[75] on the personal front her powermongering had tragic results. To shield the private persona from the public one in order not to imperil her illegitimate authority, Semiramis had every one of her lovers killed soon after their encounters. This practice calls to mind the transformations Alcina's lovers undergo when she tires of them. Both instances reveal that Alcina's— like Semiramis's—hunger for power, first introduced as hunger for political authority, flows into the erotic sphere. And the fusion of the two, political and erotic, results in the lover's death. The violation of laws her practice entails not only illustrates Semiramis's contempt toward them, but also her subversion of the basic principles on which any ordered society rests. Yet, her ferocious and misguided belief that power entitles her to take her lovers' lives culminates with her own death at the hands of her son. Once again, Ariosto reminds his culturally attuned audience that uncontrolled power, used for personal ends, ultimately brings on its own defeat. In political terms, this suggests that courts can do little to affect, let alone prevent, historical shifts when they fail to take into account the will—and needs—of people living outside of the privileged space, and whose toils and taxes sustain its splendors.

Although both Semiramis and Cleopatra achieve their objectives through their beauty, skills, lust, and audacity, the event that defines Ariosto's vision of their accomplishments in relation to Alcina's scheme is the feasts they offer to seduce the men whose power they crave. By casting the banquets as the conduit for the seductive deceitfulness that transforms the hero and flavors the events unfolding around him with the taste of sexual longing, Ariosto effectively recasts the discourse of food and power in terms of love and death. To draw attention to the eros that can simultaneously incite and subdue, engender and destroy, Ariosto's poetic imagination revives the stories of both Semiramis and Cleopatra, turning the two queens into classical predecessors for fleeting and fluid Alcina. Like Alcina, they appropriate authority by neutralizing the ones who rightfully wield it. They accomplish this through food and, of course, its implicit symbolic meanings.

If cleverness characterizes Semiramis, wickedness typifies Cleopatra. The full range of her antics emerges in Boccaccio's compilation where she is portrayed as a calculating political animal whose rapacity for wealth and power is unleashed at the table. There, in the poetic fiction, she uses her talents to carry on business and pleasure simultaneously. Under the sphere of her influence, her new husband Antonio wastes himself in the oblivion that she provides at her table, willfully blind to the harm it causes to his prestige and fame. Lazing there, "fattened" and engrossed "with sumptuous delicacies"[76] Antonio, with his flaccid resistance to her maneuvers, unearths the fully unresolved contradiction between the victorious hero and the overpowered man that results in the legitimization of the lover and the death of the hero.

Boccaccio inventively portrays this dichotomy in terms of enticing dinners that keep Antonio physically and sexually torpid while the dismal feast of his personal demise takes form. The image of Antonio's willpower vanquished by Cleopatra's banquets allows Boccaccio to use food as a sign and symbol of physical satiety that paralyzes the hero's resolve. At the same time, it also enables the poet to present a deliciously ambivalent but strategically effective method of portraying cunning Cleopatra who acquires power and authority through her banquets. These become her sexual campaigns and function as substitutes for Antonio's military ones. As he is ensnared and outwitted by the pragmatic woman who influences his decisions and takes his possessions[77] Antonio's sense of selfhood is progressively expunged by her maneuvers. The character of the new lover is carved out of the appetizing pleasures in which he blissfully flounders and not the military battles he should pursue. In stark opposition to his conduct, Cleopatra shows indifference to the opulence of the banquets. She remains focused on Antonio and persists in pressing, cajoling, and enticing him to surrender to her the gains of his military triumphs. And while he thoughtlessly savors her delicacies, fully absorbed by them, she relishes the power that his wealth accords her and, in a sense, devours him.

In this fashion, through gastronomic seduction that takes the place of the sexual one, the conqueror is conquered. Antonio is transformed into a weak (Boccaccio tellingly uses the adjective *effeminatus*)[78] man distracted from both personal and public duties. The hero's downfall, articulated in terms of luxurious morsels consumed at the lover's table, accentuates Boccaccio's fusion of erotic pleasure and gastronomic satisfaction. His bodily needs sated, Antonio is Ruggiero's forefather from classical antiquity. Like Antonio's, Ruggiero's selfhood is penetrated by a seductress's piercing lust for what he has and she wants. From this perspective, Cleopatra's banquets turn into the stage for the dramatization of power and weakness, courage and cowardice, life and death.

This becomes more evident when Antonio, fearing for his life, has his food tasted before eating it. To remove herself from his suspicions, Cleopatra first poisons his cup. Then, before he drinks from it, she stops him and explains that, had she so desired, she could have poisoned him. She believes that through this gesture she proves her fidelity to him. Contrary to her expectations, though, her gesture does not restore Antonio's trust in her (according to one version of the story, he has her killed for her action). Her bold act, though, is a measure of the power she maintains over him. But even her transformation into a "giver" and "taker" of Antonio's life falls back on her shrewd use of foods. The meals they consume together and through which she undercuts his productiveness to carry on his duties are, up until the moment of her death, the sign and symbol of her ability to control him.

These meals facilitate the transition between two different worlds: from the interior one that Antonio embodied, founded on the Roman ethos of honor and glory, to the external one that Cleopatra personifies, founded on deception and appearances. Yet by playing on the lack of confidence the inexperienced man shows at her table, Cleopatra undermines the structured social stability that a legitimate leader engenders and destabilizes the political hierarchy whereby heroic achievements are rewarded with deserved honors. As the drama of their relationship unfolds around gastronomic satisfactions that become one and the same with sexual fulfillments, Cleopatra, an expert "confectioner," creates and sustains a reality that, for Antonio, is visually, and sensually, appealing but substantially empty. This reality is not different from the one Messisbugo crafts for Ercole d'Este through his *confetti*. In fact, the misleading appearances Cleopatra and Messisbugo give life to stroke the narcissism of the men for whom they are fashioned. Accordingly, in her manipulation of Antonio every morsel of her appetizing dishes is, for the gullible man, a bite into her alluring beauty that transports him, as well as Boccaccio's and Ariosto's readers, into the world of deceptive fiction. Food, with its transient nature, is not unlike fiction. It must be consumed to nourish. Only when fully consumed does it achieve its ends and generate new energy. And from this comes a comforting sense of fullness that brings with it, for the cook as for the poet, unanticipated transformations.

Of the two versions of Cleopatra's death Boccaccio recounts in his treatise, the one in which Antonio orders her killed because he suspects her of unfaithfulness functions as his redemptive act. Awakened from his sexual stupor, he becomes again a man of action, capable of discriminating between the false lover and the real seductress. By ordering her death he reveals his new understanding that her actions entailed neither unfaltering love nor moral triumph. Instead, they incarnated the vengeful power of usurped authority illegitimately seized to satisfy wanton desires. Contrary to Antonio's self-regained awareness, Ruggiero requires the aid of Melissa's magic power to understand and escape Alcina's true nature. This suggests that the modalities of political and cultural understandings of Ruggiero's—and Ariosto's—world are different. Magic can only be conquered through magic or, better yet, transformations can only be crushed through other transformations. In other words, at the foundation of the individual's understanding of reality there must be a firm self-knowledge and a new awareness that craftiness, adaptations, and transformations are necessary means through which desired objectives can be achieved. Only through these, Ariosto suggests, can one escape, temporarily, from the world of history. But getting away from this world leads to one in which magic—the cornucopia—is a mark of one's defeat and self-deception, in short, a pure product of one's imagination. By recalling Cleopatra's and Semiramis's ploys in his description of Ruggiero's dinner with Alcina, Ariosto capitalizes on Boccaccio's compendium of cultural and political realities. This historical backdrop lends more depth to Ruggiero's failings and Alcina's plot. Like Antonio, Ruggiero is captured by a devious woman's beauty. More importantly, because of it, he willfully betrays both civic and personal commitments by enjoying the lustful enchantments her paradise provides.

In a sense, the meal Ruggiero consumes and his subsequent fall into the throes of sexual desire evoke the figure of Adam, whose sexual curiosity was also unleashed by eating. Yet Ruggiero's eating of *confetti* is more nuanced because the dish's metaphorical implications foreshadow his impending doom. This is based, first of all, on the etymological roots of *confetti*. It also stems from the visual deception that the creation of *confetti* provides and that Messisbugo's mythological renderings make plain. Still, the image of Ruggiero and Alcina consuming *confetti* exemplifies the fusion of gastronomy and eroticism.[79] As Alcina's unsuspecting prisoner eats the visually alluring *confetti*, he engages with her in "a vertical and horizontal communication."[80] In Ruggiero's case—like Cleopatra's and Semiramis's lovers—this suggests the connection between life and death, toil and idleness, faithfulness and betrayal, present and past. These are states that, in essence, constantly call to mind love and death.

With his mind inflamed by his desire for Alcina, Ruggiero cannot distinguish between responsibility and dereliction. Eating her *confetti* therefore is the precursor to his capitulation to Alcina's sexual ploys, while the *confetti* themselves become both object and sign of his intellectual subjugation. Specifically, *confetti* on the one hand refers to the food itself, while on the other it exemplifies the sensual appetites of the individuals who have "confected" them and are now sharing it. After eating the *confetti* Ruggiero is escorted to his chamber. There, tucked between linens that in their fancifulness recall Arachne's talent, he nervously and impatiently awaits for Alcina's arrival:

> Ruggiero entrò ne profumati lini
> Che parean di man d'Aracne usciti,
> Tenendo tuttavia le orecchie attente,
> S'ancor venir la bella donna sente.
> (7.23)

> (Ruggiero slipped between the perfumed sheets, which might well have been the handiwork of Arachne herself; he strained his ears now to listen for the approach of lovely Alcina.)

The state of suspense that Ruggiero experiences and the lines register lend psychological depth to the knight. In particular, while capturing the lover's yearning, it speaks of his sense of self. Although his thoughts are deeply imbued with a sense of power, Ruggiero clings to the expectation of Alcina's arrival. The juxtaposition of the pain her absence causes him and the elation that the thought of her arrival brings on conveys in vivid terms the anguish of the weak-willed hero tormented by the tribulation of a suffering lover. With delicate artistry Ariosto illustrates the breathtaking emotional force that seizes the man and keeps him engrossed in thoughts of lovemaking's plenitude while relying on his sense of hearing to detect her arrival. At this juncture Ruggiero shows no control over his emotions, no sign of introspection; this emotional state, which illustrates his vulnerability to readers, to him seems to lengthen the wait. Through this, the poet plays the ordinary against the highly charged for he peeks into a most intimate moment of the hero's life and darts between the public and the private, war and peace, adventures and sweet anxiety.

In doing this, Ariosto again draws from Ovid's *Metamorphoses*, reinscribing Ruggiero's experience onto the discourse of transformations and changes.[81] In the myth of Arachne the weaver loses the competition with Minerva. But the loss is not caused by her tapestry's quality for "In all that work of hers, Pallas could find, / Envy could find, no fault" (130–131). Rather, it results from the stories Arachne artfully weaves. They reveal the deceptions—and transformations—the gods used to take advantage of mortal women. The subject angers Pallas: "Incensed at such / success the warrior goddess, golden-haired, / Tore-up the tapestry, those crimes of heaven" (131–133). She is insulted by Arachne's audacity to divulge the truth about her peers' failings. By exposing the gods' flaws Arachne effectively undercuts their power and even challenges their claim of embodying divine justice. The weaver's work shows, in the first place, that gods, like mortals, are susceptible to desires. Beyond this, it demonstrates that the irresistible force of impulses drives gods' actions, and because of the power they wield, gods, like mortals, act upon their desires. As a result, the insidiousness of their want involves a radically more subversive force than humans'. Because of her bold assertion, Arachne is transformed into an animal. In and of itself the logic of Pallas's violent retaliation against Arachne reveals a form of impulsiveness that is comparable to the one the weaver has ascribed to other gods. According to this logic, if a mortal deliberately undermines the deities' perfection, then a goddess can demean a human being by turning it into an object or an animal. And Pallas does precisely this when she transforms Arachne into a spider.

Arachne's tale is suggestive of the crafter's lack of discretion as well as of her ingenuousness. These aspects of her story recall Ruggiero's own inexperience. Yet Arachne's metamorphosis, unlike any of the myths discussed earlier, unambiguously links physical possession to despotic power. In other words, her myth brings into focus the attainment of sexual consummations and the systems of power that surreptitiously validate and condone fraud. Pallas's punishment is primarily a mode of silencing, in this case by way of a metamorphosis, the individual who has the impertinence and courage to expose the divinities' world in its unvarnished reality. Through her tapestry Arachne unmasks the appearances that world strives to maintain. Still, her degradation from human to animal marks the vulnerability of human beings who, entangled in the web of social, financial, or political subservience, are susceptible to the capricious whim of those wielding power. By producing a work that divulges distasteful truths intended to be kept hidden, Arachne naively brings her demise upon herself. Ironically, in self-realization she finds self-destruction. The magnificence of her weaving is never challenged; Pallas actually acknowledges Arachne's unmatched talent. And in this acknowledgment the young weaver finds self-realization because it validates her initial statement that her weaving abilities surpass Pallas's. But her ability and talent are also imbued with a sense of hubris. As a result, her overconfidence drives her achievement. Yet, at the same time, it brings her down because it propels her beyond the boundaries set by the gods' presumptive and presumptuous claim of moral rectitude. Her attitude becomes for this reason a sign of the artist's reckless vanity. Accordingly, the intent to call attention to the vices and falseness cultivated by powerful entities turns into tragedy for the person exposing them. The truths Arachne reveals provoke the forceful retaliation of those whose exploits she exposes. Paradoxically, although in the end the artist's aim is to captivate and to please its audience, the crafty (and defenseless) weaver, like the poet, is trapped in a web of her own making.

The implications of this myth are not lost on Ariosto. His own disillusionment with the court as a model of life, which has cautiously but steadily simmered throughout the *Furioso*, is pushed to the limits of permissibility at this juncture. For the poet, the court, with its unrealistic partiality toward old cultural models, no longer suffices to contain and explain the complexity of human nature. The escapist attitude it maintains toward this new realization is revealed through the self-serving imaginary realities it constructs: the banquets, plays, music, and games hold Ruggiero in thrall, captured in illusory worlds. Simultaneously, however, the systematic disinterest in the problems outside of the island-like palace (the world Ariosto knows) makes the court a universe of transgressions and transformations fueled by the deceptions that self-interest engenders. The ceaseless lust for power and wealth that it craves and the belief that from them spawn honor and happiness makes him acutely conscious that the latter are courtly illusions.[82] History is not. For the poet who deliberately reinvents the world in the fiction of his poem, honor does not rest on the outward manifestations of wealth, privilege, and prestige.[83] Nor is it the product of calculated ambition. This belief pertains to a culture almost thoroughly collapsed. Titles, he contends, do not bestow honor unless their beneficiaries embody uncompromising high principles, that is, unless it is earned with extraordinary efforts through a continuous pattern of choices.[84] In veering from the personal to the moral, these remain grounded in a keen sense of socially concerned principles. Yet, the capacity to shed old illusions is impossible within the insularity of the court even though it is pivotal in adapting to both the limits and the potentials of realities that the modern individual faces at every turn. Only this ensures humanity's resilience in a world in which rituals are supplanted by necessities, and transgressions are commonplaces. Necessities and commonplaces require choices and with them comes the realization that one is inevitably on one's own. This demonstrates that idealized realities no longer exist. Clinging to the older model is, at best, pointless because it obscures the complexities that a reordering of priorities presents. It also precludes the possibility of looking with fresh eyes at traditional systems; and this makes it impossible to gain new perspectives on the ways to extricate humanity from moral recklessness. Ariosto's clear-eyed vision of a society splintered between the failed ideals of the court and the world of contingencies fizzing outside of it captures the vulnerability and inwardness of that society. It also suggests that greatness, honor, and privileges are not measured by fatuous standards, but by the individual's determination and steadfastness. This is the world of history.

Financial needs yoke Ariosto to his patrons.[85] His admission "pazzo chi al suo signor contradir vole, / se ben dicesse c'ha veduto il giorno / pieno di stelle e a mezzanotte il sole" (Mad is the man who would contradict his lord, / even if he were to say he had seen the day full of / stars and at midnight the sun) (*Satires*, 1.11–13) evidences his awareness that as he earnestly tackles a system of modern values in which human transgressions are just another side of history's unpredictable course, he cannot cut loose from, nor openly expose, his patrons' insensibilities and excesses. Like Ruggiero, the poet must perforce lie in a bed not of his own making but the one the Estes provide for him. And as Ruggiero lies down on the embroidered linens that evoke both the audacity and ruin of the mythological weaver, the focus shifts from the knight to the poet. The latter's bold questioning of his patrons' values is obliquely revealed by the image of the self-centered hero resting nervously on his hostess's bed. Not unaware like Ruggiero, but hampered by personal circumstances from openly criticizing the ruling family in order to avoid the likely outcome that criticism would cause, Ariosto reveals it through Arachne's myth. In this fashion the poet's (weaver's of tales) condemnation of his powerful patrons eludes their retaliation and, unlike Arachne, his personal (financial and social) standing is not affected.

Yet, after Arachne's myth Ariosto's criticism of the Estes is filtered again through the figure of Ruggiero. Only forty lines after eating the *confetti*, at Alcina's table, the knight turns into her sexual food:

> Come si vide il successor d'Astolfo
> Sopra apparir quelle ridenti stelle,
> Come abbia ne le vene acceso zolfo,
> Non par che capir possa ne la pelle.
> (7.27)

(When Astolfo's successor looked up to see those joyful-twinkling stars, he felt as though hot sulfur were coursing through his veins, which threatened to start out from his skin.)

Ruggiero's excitement about Alcina's arrival in his room is conveyed through the image of sulfur burning in his veins and through his body's incapacity to contain itself within the boundary of its form. The hero's lust for Alcina is self-devouring and consumes the reality of the moment. The blissful feast of senses he foretastes, the explosion of his desires, in concert with his hedonistic vision of life can neither be condensed into a fixed (physical) form nor be brought under reason's control. In a similar vein, the description of his embraces and kisses with Alcina points to the sexual gratification they seek while he wittingly ignores the moral implications of his actions:

> Non così strettamente edera preme
> Pianta ove intorno abbarbicata s'abbia,
> Come si stringon li due amanti insieme
> Cogliendo de lo spirto in su le labia
> . . . .
> Del gran piacer ch'avean, lor dicer tocca;
> Che spesso avian piú d'una lingua in bocca.
> (7.29)

(Ivy never clung so tightly to the stem round which it was entwined as did the two lovers cling to each other, drawing from each other's lips ... As for describing their pleasure, better to leave this to them—the more so as they frequently had a second tongue in their mouth.)

In Ovid's *Metamorphoses* (3.78), the image of ivy clutching and wrapping around plants denotes destructiveness. It is closely linked to the myth of Bacchus, the god known for destabilizing peace and established powers through the debauched and dissolute behavior he models. For this reason, in Ovid the image of ivy calls to mind the degradation of human nature that occurs when humanity becomes unwilling to function according to the rational knowledge it possesses. This discloses the pervasive effects of human wickedness as political and personal corruption, as the debasement of the body of politics, religion, and even language.[86]

Ariosto's description of the two lovers caught in an ivy-like embrace, blinded by lust and heedless to the reality unfolding outside of the chamber, brings to mind Ovid's myth. This is particularly true of Ruggiero. By giving in to his senses and impulses, the knight becomes the living symbol of the collapse of the courtly system. The interplay of object and sign, with its correlative in the artful preparation of *confetti* Alcina serves, is illustrative of her nature. The apparent beauty that conceals the repulsive sorceress signifies Ruggiero's physical subjugation, while her ability to physically metamorphose—like Achelous and Erysichthon's daughter—objectifies his rational degradation. In the actualization of these transformations and subversions, as the loyal and fearless knight is changed into a submissive lover and as the repugnant sorceress metamorphoses into an attractive woman, the real is transmuted into the imaginary and, in turn, the imaginary is transmuted into the real. Alcina—and Ariosto through her—is fabricating a reality that harmonizes with her desire for Ruggiero and, in fact, makes its fulfillment possible. At the Este court, in the same manner, the absent is made present (with a twist of the Albertian theory on painting)[87] by way of mythological representations that revive the memory of extraordinary achievements in which Ercole d'Este illusorily sees reflected the greatness of his own accomplishments.

Indeed, in an impermanent and unpredictable universe, relying on abstract and fixed codes to deliver honor and pleasures proves ineffective because humanity's natural desires can be neither bridled nor contained by the sheer exercise of the will. As a result, in the *Furioso* food in general and *confetti* in particular through their metaphorical meanings become a refraction of the glorious past. They actually supplant it, offering a mere glimpse of the ambiguous new. Alcina's *confetti* are therefore the bait necessary to draw Ruggiero into a world of self-indulgence he recognizes and willingly accepts by its appearances. He, unlike Pulci's Orlando in the palace he stumbles upon on his journey with Morgante, is never distrustful or skeptical about the rich tables he finds prepared for his enjoyment. This flawed understanding of reality makes Ruggiero, like Alcina's previous lovers as well as Ariosto's audience, vulnerable to the seductiveness of fiction.

Melissa's intervention, through her magic ring and especially her explanation of Alcina's true identity, has a sobering effect on Ruggiero:

> Perche` tu conosca chi sia Alcina,
> Levatone le fraudi e gli artifici,
> Tien questo anello in ditto, e torna ad ella,
> Ch'aveder ti potrai come sia bella.
> (7.64)

("Now that you may know who Alcina is, stripped of her artifices and deceits, put this ring on your finger and return to her, and you shall realize just how fair are her looks.")

The force of this argument runs swiftly through Melissa's commanding words. With directedness she instructs Ruggiero to become attentive, to understand the revelatory force of awareness, and to rely solely on the concrete. Through this, she indirectly informs him that trusting in appearances, however dazzling they might be, brings on disappointments and failures. From an historical perspective, Melissa's explanation reveals that reality—and history—must be confronted with clear eyes. And these must especially remain focused on the incongruities—social, cultural, and political—that surface because they consistently capture humanity's anguish and rebelliousness: in other words, its most concrete essence. For this purpose, courtly society, driven by material plentitude and dulled by traditions, must reevaluate its ideals. By reexamining events through a return to them from the vantage point of the still impermanent present, the "tornar ad ella" ("return to her") that Melissa instructs Ruggiero to do, fallacies are exposed. Understanding them means discovering the juxtapositions of contrasting elements that lead to truths. This knowledge gives the hero, and humanity, not only an organic and objective view of the past, but especially a full sense of the multifaceted events shaping the present. From their confluence history unfolds. Most importantly, the newness of this understanding guides the hero's awareness of the limited role he plays in defining history's meanings in view of his personal experiences.

III

Not incidentally, in the *Furioso confetti* reappear, for the second and last time, in canto 10. This is the second act, as it were, of Alcina's relentless ploy to keep Ruggiero yoked to her will. The event leading to the *confetti* is the knight's escape from the enchantress's island. Made aware of Alcina's real nature, he heeds Melissa's advice because through her guidance he recognizes every layer of his captor's repulsiveness. Displaying an extraordinary self-possession, Ruggiero prepares to flee the island. His regained sense of self guides him in his actions. Steered by it, he defies Alcina's cunning power with physical power, literally fighting his way out of her palace (10.80). Through this he turns from passive victim to merciless aggressor and gallops away. As he travels, though, he embodies the aching desolation of one aware of his errors, brought down by the seduction of senses, and enslaved by the pleasures they engender. For this reason, he pays no attention to the thirst and fatigue afflicting him:

> Mentre la sete, e de l'andar fatica
> Per l'alta sabbia, e la solinga via
> Gli facean, lungo quella spiaggia aprica,
> Noiosa e dispiacevol compagnia.
> (10.36)

> (Thirst, the exhaustion of plodding through the deep sand, and the solitude of his journey kept him tedious, unwelcome company as he rode along the sun-blinded beach.)

The physical exhaustion that overcomes Ruggiero making his getaway from Alcina stands in sharp contrast to the sense of relaxed plenitude that he took pleasure in throughout his stay on her island. Indeed, the self-centeredness that characterized that earlier behavior and translated into the gratification of physical desires is replaced by a freshly revived sense of purpose. This process is reflected and magnified through his ensuing actions.

Despite his thirst and fatigue, Ruggiero does not stop to assuage them. On the contrary, with an unblinking look he turns down the offer of three beautiful ladies who invite him to join them:

> Corcate su tappeti alessandrini
> Godeansi il fresco rezo in gran diletto
> Fra molti vasi di diversi vini
> E d'ogni buona sorte di confetto.
> (10.37)

(Reclining on Egyptian rugs, they were enjoying the fresh shade and a wide choice of wines in various jugs and all sort of delicacies to eat.)

Every aspect of the improbable oasis the ladies delight in echoes back to Ruggiero's experience on Alcina's island. The tranquil semblance of the place, the food, the beautiful women, and the drinks beckon the knight; at the same time, they are a reminder of the fictional universe lurking behind them. For Ruggiero, its memory is a reminder that the present can regress into the past and be consumed by it unless he controls his impulses by way of balancing his vulnerabilities with his strengths. Not giving in to the enjoyments the first promises insulates him from the moral and ethical chasm the second causes; and this lends legitimacy to the hero. By resisting their invitation, Ruggiero displays a self-restraint and prudence never shown while comfortably ensconced in his captors' palaces. Similarly, by rejecting the cup one of the ladies offers to him he gives proof of having overcome his weakness with absolute self-possession. For this reason, the fact that he turns down the wine is particularly significant not just because "sculta avea la sete in su le labbia" (thirst had left its imprint sculpted on his lips) (10.38) but because with it, Ruggiero rebuffs the corrupting pleasure it brings on.[88] This kind of pleasure no longer appeals to him because a new understanding informs his decisions. His resolute demeanor demonstrates that he is ready to set his own path, even if it leaves him alone and in discomfort. While this detail suggests that his awareness bears the marks of his experience with Atlante and Alcina, it also reveals that the self-knowledge he has gained from them carries the sting of solitude more than the song of pleasure. For as long as he was a captive of either one of them, Ruggiero slouched toward idleness, ceding to their predatory maneuvers that pandered to his every sensual whim. Yet the calculated intensity of their schemes disempowered him of the ability of decision-making. Deprived of the experiences and education that frustrations and failures, along with triumphs, provide, Ruggiero's potential for fame and success was thwarted. Finally free from the chains that both magicians forced on him, the knight is no longer a submissive man lolling in the illusions that knitted a whole universe smothered in artifice and deceptions. Outraged and bitter about the magicians' corrosive ways and the latter's paralyzing effects, perhaps even angry at his own gullibility, the knight becomes mindful of the deceptiveness they typify. As a result, he turns into a vigilant individual, especially distrustful of the pull that pleasure-giving illusions cause. This also raises his awareness of the suspicious nature of signs and sights. Motivated by a desire to shape events to his own purpose, with studied intent the knight, despite his thirst and fatigue, masters his body and passions. Through the hero's regained sense of the moral and ethical principles that must guide his actions if he is to triumph over adversities, marry Bradamante, and thus become the forebear of the Este dynasty, Ariosto cracks the mask of the debauched ways of the Estes of his times. And this reveals the corrupt face of their power.

Admittedly Ruggiero's experience, particularly on Alcina's island, is linked to the idea of the hero's moral education acquired through experience. For the humanists this education entailed the ability to decipher signs and, through philological education, to link them to their historical origins.[89] This type of decoding is precisely what Ruggiero does as he radically rejects both the *confetti* and the wine the ladies proffer:

L'altra con una coppa di cristallo
Di vin spumante, piú sete gli messe:

> Ma a quel suono Ruggier non entrò in ballo;
> Perché d'ogni tardar che fatto avesse,
> Tempo di giungere dato avria ad Alcina,
> Che venia dietro et era omai vicina.
> (10.39)

> (Another came with a crystal goblet of sparkling wine, which only excited his thirst. But Ruggiero was not going to dance to their tune; any delay would favor Alcina, giving her time to catch him up—she was now close behind him.)

Ruggiero's realization that the ladies are Alcina's agents marks the progress of his education. His ability to understand the hidden meaning of the signs presented to him results from a newly instilled awareness of her implacable ruthlessness and its outcomes. Accordingly, his rejection of their offer suggests that he has learned to recognize and mistrust, now like Pulci's Orlando, the emptiness of certain signs. As a result, the consummation that is achieved at this point is not carnal, but ethical.

A clearheaded evaluation of the threat the ladies pose, paired with a pristine sense of self-discipline, guides the new Ruggiero. The line in which Ariosto describes the knight's decision to keep on his way without stopping—"Ruggiero sicuro / Al suo dritto cammin la rena stampa" (Ruggiero calmly trudging on across the sand) (10.40)—bolsters this idea by obliquely calling to mind the beginning of Dante's *Inferno*. In both instances, moral and ethical irresponsibility is at the root of the characters' experiences. Yet, there, the Pilgrim who lost his "straight way" began his descent into Hell. Here, the knight is climbing his way out of the lowest depths of a sensual paradise that consumed him by corrupting his understanding of reality. His reintegration into a morally and ethically principled system begins with him following his *dritto cammin*. The poet, acute observer of the challenges facing the hero at every turn, past and current, historical and fictional, registers his ascent through the image of the straight line Ruggiero's footprints leave in the sand.[90] But the image of Ruggiero's unswerving footmarks impressed in the sand serves as a prism that simultaneously refracts and reflects the knight's attempt to making sense of the past while seeking to find his way across the perplexities and perversities of the present.

Ruggiero's new awareness of his surroundings is not etched against the backdrop of Ovidian myths. To the contrary, it is inscribed within the horizon of Dante's discourse on human salvation. This occurs because the hero who has learned to recognize the meanings of signs can deftly eschew their magnetism. For this reason, he is no longer vulnerable to the transformations their deceptiveness entails. Vacillation has turned into resoluteness. The self-control Ruggiero shows as he interacts with Alcina's lackeys earns him the passage to a new frontier: Logistilla's realm. As the knight navigates toward her place, his guide informs him that the happiness she provides, unlike the transient one Alcina personifies, is neither nourished nor satisfied by the senses. Rather, it is wisdom, acumen, and prudence, in other words, reason, that nurture and strengthen the happiness Logistilla exemplifies. These are the quintessential qualities that the hero has long brushed aside but must, at all cost, incarnate. For only through them will Ruggiero acquire lasting fame. In the hero's passage to a realm of knowledge, judiciousness, and principled happiness, the echo of the Pilgrim's ascent of Purgatory is unmistakable.

Still, while Ariosto's Ruggiero readies himself to take a new and sobering direction that redefines his place in the courtly universe after the disillusionment of his experience, Ferrara's ruling family, Ruggiero's descendants, continues to indulge in frivolous celebrations. Gastronomically, these continue to sustain and celebrate its beliefs with meaningless *confetti*—a discouraging fact for the poet-courtier, who is well aware that *confetti* are no matches for the true changes history inexorably brings. For historical changes are grounded in solid, courageous deeds. And these are not sustained by courtly confections. As we shall see in the following chapter, Pietro Aretino takes a similar approach with regard to courtly excesses. His attention will turn to one of the most opulent courts of the period: the Roman curia.

FIVE

Courtesans and Figs, Art and Nature in Aretino's *Ragionamento*

Food holds a special place in Pietro Aretino's *Ragionamento* because it amplifies the tension between power and morality, both of which are indispensible means to ensuring a stable, principled society. With radical aplomb and escalating intensity, through food the writer illustrates the imbalance of power that exists in Roman society. He also questions the morality of both pope and prelates practicing traditional power politics. As Aretino sees it, these circumstances result in a lopsided system. In this universe the stronger faces no restraint and the weak experiences no contentment—unless the latter resort to their own schemes. With a perspective that is less provincial and more rebellious than the ones embraced by the authors studied thus far, in the *Ragionamento* Aretino voices his discontent with the state of affairs this system has created. He does so with an attitude that mirrors his tempestuous life. Accordingly, foodstuff in his work conveys the rare decency of individuals kept outside the court's sphere of privilege. It also exposes the ordinary baseness of people intent on preserving and aggrandizing their positions of power. Through this, and also because of the specific characters involved, Aretino introduces the perspective of court outsiders. And their perspective is made more gripping by the food they consume. As he analyzes society through the prismatic, limpid light of a writer unafraid, in fact emboldened, to illustrate its debaucheries, Aretino turns into an unmatched chronicler of the paradoxes marking his times.

Pietro Aretino was one of the most controversial figures of Renaissance Italy.[1] Engaging and unpredictable, given to what for his times were contentious perspectives, his figure looms large in the Italian literary, and historical, landscapes. His vast production spanning across genres includes, among other works, the six volumes of "open" *Lettere* that he wrote and published as a marketing device to promote himself and his work.[2] Unconcerned about offending the sensibilities of the addressees, however high-powered they might be, the letters are for the most part biting indictments against them and their mannerisms. Ranging from dismissive casualness about the addressees' selfishness to vitriolic attacks on their avariciousness, corruption, and cowardice (depending on the specific case), the letters highlight the flaws of prominent figures, among them princes, popes, artists, high prelates, and many others in between.[3]

Aretino arrived in Rome prior to 1517.[4] In that city as a courtier/secretary of the powerful banker Agostino Chigi, the ambitious man of humble origins[5] had access not only to the Roman curia and its courtiers, but also to the most acclaimed artists who—like him—gravitated to that court's orbit.[6] Not surprisingly, Aretino's hands-on experience of Roman society and its powerful representatives found a central place in his works. Through a prose that is as sharp as his ideas, he exposes the crisis of values that the turn of events (historical and nonhistorical) has ushered in Rome.[7] At the same time, he also demonstrates that the new circumstances require fresh perspectives and responsibilities. These, he seems to suggest, force individuals to adapt to unscripted roles that are played within novel historical, social, and literary horizons. This adaptation paves the way for a cultural shift sustained more and more by the power of the few capable of manipulating the many. Aretino gauges the inequality between wealth and poverty in living standards, and in his Rome, nowhere is this made more palpable than at the papal court. Acquiring a position within the curia ensures material comforts the likes of which are unattainable outside of it.[8] Yet for this same reason, its courtiers' behavior exacerbates the social and religious tensions especially brewing outside of Italy.[9] The radical approach Aretino takes in questioning these men's concern with wealth and status provocatively challenges the idea of that court's unassailability. Never before had this type of openness and focused lens been used to lay bare the ills of a society. Never before had the finger directly been pointed to the unscrupulous and self-serving maneuvers of religious leaders whose ambitious interests lay in political power rather than spiritual matters. It goes without saying that this approach had a profound impact on the cultural, social, and political European landscape.

Early in Aretino's career, his abrasive style and self-promoting agenda earned him the title of "Flagello dei principi" (the Scourge of princes).[10] Even so, it is safe to say that no other author has been subjected to the same, unrelenting kind of moralistic prejudice as he.[11] Indeed, his literary achievements often have been glossed over because of the overtly erotic tone and uncensored language at the heart of his works. Among them the *Ragionamento* stands out.[12] As a dialogue with sexually explicit imagery and language, this work captures vividly society's dissatisfaction with the model set by the pope and his courtiers. It was often measured against Baldassarre Castiglione's *Libro del Cortegiano* and Pietro Bembo's *Prose de la volgar lingua*, both of which it brazenly parodies in style and subject matter.[13] This fact further contributed to the poor reputation the *Ragionamento* garnered over the centuries. Thus, except for sporadic instances, it received little attention from scholars.[14]

The last fifty years have witnessed a renewed interest in Aretino's works.[15] In spite of this, however, and much like the authors analyzed thus far, foodstuff, eating, and the range of possible meanings the two encompass in the *Ragionamento* have gone unexplained. And yet the rich symbolism of food Aretino's characters consume or describe adds a deeper and crisper flavor to his sustained criticism of the Roman curia and of the ways in which its weaknesses and iniquities are echoed in the lives of ordinary people. Indeed, it would be fair to say that in the *Ragionamento* foods turn into a device through which Aretino probes the pervasive sense of self-entitlement that permeates the papal court. The aloofness this sense of entitlement engenders has crippling effects on society. For one thing, the way in which spiritual leaders view ordinary people from a disdainful distance makes them incapable of understanding and resolving the pressing issues that concern society. The attitude curial princes keep, and in most cases the fraudulence of their positions, brings to mind the conduct of secular rulers. Among these stand out the familiar names of the Houses of Este, Medici, and Gonzaga. Not by chance, their representatives occupy preeminent positions within the curia. As a result, the Roman court's unwillingness to establish common ground with society at large increases the distance between insiders and outsiders. Inevitably, this disconnect forges a division that makes a sham of religious principles. By not fostering a universal sense of human fellowship the separation creates a divisive climate of self-centeredness. By resting on the authority of temporal power, the system the curia puts in place marginalizes the powerless. This practice, instead of solving social ills, creates new ones. As a matter of fact, the court's lax attitude toward moral and ethical principles encourages society to make a sport of them too.

Published in 1534 (and censured in 1554), the *Ragionamento* pushes the language of Renaissance dialogues beyond the limits of traditional discourses. By allowing the voices of courtesans, rather than those of aristocratic figures, to be heard without the filter of conventions, the work pokes fun at Castiglione's and Bembo's celebrated dialogues.[16] Specifically, while they sought to rationalize and even define both human activity and man's place in the courtly universe, the *Ragionamento* demonstrates that human nature defies rationalization. Indeed, it unequivocally shows that any attempt at rationalizing human nature remains incomplete because of the protean character it possesses. As Giovanni Pico della Mirandola argued well before Aretino's times, when this fickle nature is guided by the power the will can exert over it, humanity achieves its highest goals. But to accomplish this, the will must be grounded in sound moral and ethical principles. When it is not, humanity descends to the base sensuality of beasts. Yet, as the *Ragionamento* evidences, the ever-changing character of human nature, not norms, is a constant. For Aretino, what complicates this picture is the fact that a court represents a small stage of the vaster, dynamic social universe in which humanity plays out its experiences. Thus, it could be argued that for him, defining man's place and activity solely within such a finite sphere as the court's, however powerful it might be, is indicative of the pretentiousness, artificiality, and, above all shortsightedness that both Castiglione's and Bembo's dialogues promote.

With a bracingly fresh and disarmingly simple clarity, the *Ragionamento* lays out an ambitious two-pronged plan. On the one hand, it erodes from within the literary genres and moralistic interests that define Aretino's humanist predecessors and contemporaries. On the other, it unearths and exposes for public scrutiny the ravenous hunger for self-aggrandizement and material fulfillment that drives the Roman See and the members of its curia, despite the fact that it is the ostensible repository of Christian faith. This unusual act of defiance toward the system within which he himself hungers to work and be part of illustrates not just Aretino's ambition, but especially his impatience with the curia's hypocritical attitude.[17] A close reading of the *Ragionamento* strongly suggests that in Aretino's view, the courtiers' conduct kindles the fire of a moral and ethical breakdown, and the repercussions of their behaviors are visible in every layer of society. Subjecting both society and curia to internal lawlessness, greed and corruption not only enfeebles both of them, but also exposes them to external political and religious threats. Aretino's lucid if acerbic critique of the lives of coddled prelates reaping the benefits that their privileged positions command (in spite of their social disengagement) suggests that a corrupt system cannot be treated as if it were simply a "normal" part of society, with no outside perspective from which to criticize or condemn it.

Staged in Rome seven years after the troops of Charles V ravaged the city, making an example of the pope's vulnerability,[18] the *Ragionamento* brings to light a debased picture of the profligate curia. This court is a microcosm of privileges; unconcerned with the moral and ethical vacuum that greed has created within it, the papal curia sharply contradicts the apostolic mission it is charged to carry out. Instead of functioning as a compass of rectitude and integrity this court and its debauched courtiers trade these qualities for material comforts. Dominated by social-climbing in the service of which every type of appetite and interest is exploited, the curia openly flouts both divine and human laws.[19] This attitude calls to mind Erysichthon, whose own life was devoured and dissolved because of his wantonness. Indeed, as depicted in the *Ragionamento* the Roman curia turns into the most startling example of the venal, lecherous, and ruthless systems affecting Aretino's times. The originality of this work lies, therefore, in the way it sizzles with raw criticism of the self-serving maneuvers driving everyone associated with the curia. In the end, the work is a powerful reminder of the superficiality that it sanctions as it endorses an affectation of high culture and prestige, neither one of which says anything about the truths it conceals.

At the same time, the *Ragionamento* also underscores the flaws that are part and parcel of human nature. As his characters describe the ostentatious consumption and luxury the court craves and displays, Aretino convincingly demonstrates that that court sets the norms for people at every rung of the social ladder. Yet by striving to emulate the court's model, every individual, just like members of the curia, yields to base instincts. And because these remain an inalienable part of human nature, neither religious norms nor social restraints suppress them. Through this, and in bold contradiction to Castiglione's and Bembo's stances, Aretino demonstrates that dialogues and lewdness are not mutually exclusive. On the contrary, they are a genre that, by addressing themes outside of the province of virtue, nobility, and familial and civic duty, effectively exemplifies and responds to changed historical and sociocultural circumstances. To capture the spirit of the times without reducing the complexity of history into a simple account, Aretino seems to suggest, dialogues must look beyond the confines of moral and philosophical subjects. In so doing, they zero in on fickleness, capriciousness, and desires, traits that more straightforwardly reflect human nature. In this manner, while remaining within the realistic context of the historical, political, and cultural elements that shape society, dialogues also chart the trajectory of human experience. And this, Aretino's dialogues lead one to believe, is unbound from artificial conventions.[20]

From the outset the *Ragionamento* makes it clear that for the writer conventions cannot be counted on to guide human desires because they cross, rather than coincide with, human nature. Nor can desires be bridled by and through religious formulas. In a sense, Aretino's discourse on natural human desires (and especially on the ludicrousness of eradicating them through religious beliefs) evokes Giovanni Boccaccio's stance. Still, speaking through the wisdom of his experience, and perhaps from the indignation that his experience in Rome still causes him, Aretino suggests that the practice of using dialogues solely to probe into moral and ethical issues that every society strains to embrace is unsound. The narrowly focused dialogues reveal the senselessness of attempting to rationalize human impulses within the boundaries of conventional paradigms. It appears, then, that for Aretino the bankrupt culture the curia exemplifies paired with the deceitful machinations it relies on to mask its failures place it in the same league with any secular court. And because like any other Italian (or foreign) principality, it is driven by instincts and worldly concerns, the Roman court cannot serve as the model of integrity, nobility, familial, and civic duty it so carefully tailors for itself.

The lewdness with which Aretino foregrounds the *Ragionamento* reveals neither a predilection for crude erotic discourse nor a penchant for scandalous, shocking subjects.[21] Rather, it evidences the candid awareness—and depiction—of desires that regulate human nature. Trying to repress or cloak these desires under the decorum of religious vestments becomes, as Aretino shows in his work, an exercise in hypocrisy. This conduct not only discredits the reputation of the religious system, but it also makes it a target of choice for detractors. The awareness of the ever more determined German Reformers lurking not too quietly in the distance and eager to expose the curia's abuses of power tinges Aretino's assessment. Their resolve is made more tenacious as the curia construes a false model of human nature. But this model, kept up to maintain a high-minded image and purporting to be disengaged from, in fact even repulsed by, worldly seductions, barely disguises the curia's wants. The court's true features are renowned; and as these insinuate themselves in the social system, an ethical and moral breakdown ensues. Aretino's imaginative construction of courtesans discussing the social degradation they witness coincides with widespread discontent with the model set by the curia.[22] Thus, a papal court that professes to be the bedrock of moral and ethical principles, when in truth it is solely bent on satisfying its every material want and reversing, to this end, every moral and ethical principle, becomes the logical backdrop of the *Ragionamento*.

By openly discussing the lavish lifestyle curial dignitaries observe, Aretino offers a daring response to the acclaimed dialogues of his times. In point of fact, his choice of courtesans as main characters in the *Ragionamento* marks a crucial moment in the Italian literary landscape.[23] By abandoning the familiar territory—and platitude—of renowned interlocutors who speak from privileged perspectives, the *Ragionamento* engages ordinary individuals whose viewpoints are shaped by everyday experiences. For him, these, not the rarefied ones of the elites, provide meaningful perspectives that plumb the depths of human nature. The choice of unorthodox points of view, fused with the language that is consistent with and reflects the interlocutors' background, is simultaneously startling and thought-provoking. For one thing, by allowing the courtesans to speak freely of their society without interjecting his narratorial voice, Aretino paints a more accurate picture of that society. His artfulness in offering unpolished insights into society and its leaders through what courtesans say, and especially what they leave unsaid, is reminiscent of his friend Titian's art.[24] Renowned for his ability to translate the ideology of power onto the canvas, the painter was famous for "unmasking the ideal character of the sitter."[25] Titian's talent in exposing brutal truths and creating embarrassments through startling colors never turned away from verisimilitude. To the contrary, his artistry lent more accuracy to the veiled reality.

In much the same fashion, Aretino through his dialogues illustrates the meaninglessness of formality when truth is removed from it.[26] He believes that to reclaim the full sovereignty of truth is tantamount to restoring faith and dignity in a society corrupted at its core. This awareness points to the depth of his understanding of human nature. Therefore, he writes the *Ragionamento* in the form of dialogues, organizing them along the axes of sex and literature. On the face of it, the work's thematic concern is the explicit narration of all conceivable sexual experiences women might embark upon as either wives, nuns, or courtesans. In reality, throughout the work Aretino implicitly juxtaposes the beliefs dictated by his narrators' (and his own) concrete experiences to the Neo-Platonic conventions regulating Bembo's and Castiglione's works.[27] The radical notion of exploring society not just through the eyes of women, but especially those of high-end prostitutes, upends all theories of social decorum those treatises promote. Furthermore, by placing the courtesans within the orbit of the Roman curia, Aretino's denunciation of the inconsistency between theory and practice of that court escalates. To this end, he shows that Roman courtiers' behaviors conflict with the beliefs expounded in theological writings and embraced in literary treatises. The situation is made more appalling by the fact that the curia is a universe ostensibly striving to unyoke itself from the slavery of the senses.

Through this, Aretino challenges, among other things, the assumptions that philosophical theories lead to fulfilling lives. In particular, he questions the soundness of the idea that spiritual love facilitates the soul's ascent toward God. Throughout the *Ragionamento* one gets a strong impression that for Aretino this argument, which Castiglione, in the wake of Marsilio Ficino's Neo-Platonic theology champions, turns its back on historical truth, pays no heed to cultural referents, and closes its eyes to human needs. Taking the curia's paradigm into account, as well as his experience within it, Aretino appears to dismiss that notion altogether. At the same time, through this he implicitly attacks Bembo's linguistic theories.[28] He does this by allowing his uneducated characters to use their ordinary language, free of artificial tones, formulaic expressions, and conventional words.[29] For him, a contrived language, as will be discussed below, stifles more accurate linguistic modes that closely reflect the speakers' experience and background. In his view, by poorly reflecting the speakers' social status an affected language conceals the relation between reality and appearance. Ultimately, Aretino's dialogues, in their immanent transgressions of the norm, aside from striking a dissonant chord with Bembo's Neo-Platonic theory, turn into a lucid expression of his belief that historical experience dictates the means by which literature must encompass it.

I

The first day of the *Ragionamento* sets the tone for Aretino's entertainingly pugnacious criticism of the Roman curia. He accomplishes this by linking food and its symbolism to the whole discourse of the curia's hedonistic tastes. This strategy enables him to accurately depict the sociocultural reality of the court he intimately knows both as a dauntless writer and as a discerning courtier aspiring to a cardinal hat.[30]

Nanna and Antonia choose to discuss the former's concerns while consuming a meal. At first glance, it would appear that this detail instills a touch of homeliness to the scene and reflects the close friendship that exists between the two women. More than this, though, the food deliberately placed between them at the outset of the first dialogue functions as a strong link between them. Indeed, the image of two women connected by the food they share erases the divide between chewing as the actual action of eating and the idea of chewing over a course of action—or between doing and thinking. Thus, the food Aretino introduces in the first dialogue lends more than just a naturalistic touch to his tableau. It points to the central role the writer assigns to foodstuff. As will be discussed below, the specific foods the two friends consume translate into gastronomic terms Aretino's critique of conventions, people, and places that contain their own contradictions. He does this by depicting the lifestyles and experiences of people living outside of the privileged space of the papal court.

The dialogue opens with Nanna taking her friend and former colleague Antonia by surprise when she voices apprehension about her daughter Pippa. Nanna's unsentimentalized concern stems from her desire to ensure that the sixteen-year-old Pippa does not miss the material opportunities that a life of financial and personal autonomy secures. Nanna is a woman of instincts, earthbound, pragmatic, and ambitious. In this respect, she resembles members of the curia. At the same time, her lingering uncertainty about Pippa's future is a measure of her impatience with inflexible social conventions. These, in her view, are sanctioned by a flawed system that chains women to men's will. Her attempt to carefully confect Pippa's future shows Nanna's awareness of the consequences that each choice entails. It may look as if her own experience, first as a nun, then as a wife, and, lastly, as a famed Roman courtesan—the profession that still occupies her—would make her decision less daunting. But this is not the case. She is aware that each professional role demands a woman's art and artifice. She also especially recognizes that some of the roles, more than others, require total submission to men's desires and to the systems they have devised. Nanna's deep awareness of the lack of personal fulfillment and financial constraints these roles impose on women give way to her trepidation. As either a nun or a wife Pippa would be forced to lead an existence bound by conventions. And these are disadvantageous for her in financial, social, and personal terms. Still, by not immediately acknowledging that of the three possibilities only that of a courtesan would enable the young woman to achieve a life of independent prosperity, neither oppressed nor kept in check by men, Nanna shows an unprejudiced stance and open-mindedness with regard to her daughter's future.

As the most renowned and sought-after courtesan in Rome, Nanna incarnates freedom and affluence. She understands that her autonomous lifestyle hinges on the latter. She also realizes that unlike nuns and wives the financial freedom her profession ensures makes it possible for her to remain unshackled from men's authority. For this reason, she is set on exercising prudence and forswearing unwise decisions with regard to her Pippa's career path:

> "come non vuoi tu che io sospiri? Ritrovandomi Pippa mia figliuola di sedici anni e volendone pigliar partito, chi mi dice 'Fàlla suora, che, oltre che risparagnerai le tre parti della dote, aggiungerai una santa al calendario'; altri dice 'Dàlle marito, che ad ogni modo tu sei sì ricca, che non ti accorgerai che ti scemi nulla'; alcuno mi conforta a farla cortigiana di primo volo, con dire 'Il mondo è guasto; e quanto fosse bene acconcio, facendola cortigiana, di subito la fai una signora; e con quello che tu hai, e con ciò che ella si guadagnerà, tosto diventerà una reina."

("How can I help it? Now that my Pippa has turned sixteen and I must decide her future, they're really on my neck. One person tells me: 'Make her a nun. Just think, besides saving the three-fourths of her dowry, you'll be adding another saint to the calendar.' Another says: 'Marry her off. After all, you're so rich you won't even miss what she takes away with her.' And others urge me to set her up right off as a courtesan. 'This world is rotten anyway,' they say, 'and even if it becomes a proper one, by making her a courtesan you'll be making her a lady. And with what you own and she will soon be earning, she will become a veritable queen.'").[31]

As she sifts through the three options that are available to Pippa, nun, wife, or courtesan, filtering the flaws of Roman society through her own perspective, Nanna's hesitancy is indicative of her deep distrust for the world in which she lives. Still, her awareness that society is different from what it pretends to be—"Credilo a me, credilo a me, che questo è un mondaccio" ("take my word for it, this world is a filthy place") (7)—underscores the divide between the world of courtly assumptions and the world of frustrated possibilities. Her intransigent stance with regards to the hardship that people of limited means and especially women face is evidenced in her struggle to balance skewed assumptions with more radical beliefs. Naturally, through the latter she defies the former because, as she reasons, if moral principles play no role in the lives of courtiers, the same principle cannot thwart her daughter's career. According to Nanna, the fact that the curial elite has been pursuing her services, thus turning its back to the fundamental belief system it is expected to adhere to, proves her point.

Nanna's perplexity underscores her awareness that in such a world the power that affluence wields is the sole determinant of social order. To challenge this notion and cut across the grain of established norms only hinders one's possibility of success. As she sees it, this system creates insurmountable barriers for wives and nuns. Theirs is a solitary endeavor because the system gives them access neither to independent wealth nor to the influence that it commands. As a result, they are compelled to remain dependent, cloistered, invisible, and mute. To bear the abuses the system inflicts on them, nuns and wives become emboldened, Nanna argues, turning into the personification of deception. According to her logic, it is predictable that women trapped in intolerable living circumstances will manipulate those very circumstances, as well as men, for more liberating ends: "le moniche, le maritate e le puttane sono come una via croce, che tosto che giungi a essa, stai buona pezza pensando dove tu abbi a porre il piede; avviene spesso che'l demonio ti strascina nella più trista" ("becoming a nun, a wife, or a whore is like a crossroads—when you reach it, you stop for a long while and reflect on which road to take. But often the devil drags you down the worst") (9). Nanna's stern view of her society is laced with a sense of bitterness. Nonetheless, it describes a moral debasement that is particularly pernicious for it reveals that those who should counsel and guide vulnerable people are uninterested in, or have little capacity for, doing so. By perpetuating the latter's weakness the former bolster their power and this, in turn, strengthens the inequalities the system enforces. As for the crossroad to which Nanna refers, it, unlike the one Hercules reached, does not provide any warning as to the ordeals that women will encounter on their journey.

Courtesans, as Antonia asserts, are the only women who need not mask their deceitfulness: "La monica tradisce il suo consagramento, e la maritta asassina il santo matrimonio; ma la puttana non la attacca né al monistero né al marito: anzi fa come un soldato che è pagato per far male... perché la sua bottega vende quello che ella ha da vendere" ("The nun betrays her sacred vows and the married woman murders the holy bond of matrimony, but the whore violates neither her monastery nor her husband; indeed she acts like a soldier who is paid to do evil... for her shop sells what it has to sell) (139). Antonia's words attest to the fact that courtesans are the very embodiment of deceitfulness.[32] Through this, Antonia and Nanna—and Aretino through them—bluntly acknowledge the crisis of a system constructed on the premise that the stifling of human desires dissolves their force and turns into transgressions. The displacement of moral and ethical values occurs when the social system imposes stultifying normative constraints on natural desires. As Boccaccio showed through the figure of Rustico, every attempt at precluding the satisfaction of such desires is more often than not flouted and eluded through deceit. The corrosive effects this dialectic produces spawn into a moral relativism that engenders, among other things, the politics of possession. As a way of life, acquiring worldly goods, accumulating wealth, and flaunting possessions and their uncommonness is more stimulating than living in a temperate and disciplined manner. As the history of the curia during the Renaissance demonstrates, lifestyles of excesses only in part replace the necessity to gratify more basic human needs; yet those lifestyles turn into intoxicating gateways to overindulgent existences. Normative restrictions, ethical codes, or religious precepts have no leverage on these. Papal courtiers are especially attracted to them. Their gleaming court is a tangle of ambitions, rivalries, and achievements. And at its highest level—in the pope himself—the court acknowledges and condones every transgression that charts the progress from desire to the attainment of the pleasure sought.

Looking back at her own journey into adulthood with a pungent blending of disappointments and satisfactions, Nanna gives a provocative description of the curia's falseness. While projecting her knowledge into her daughter's life, she aspires to forge for Pippa a future in the shape of her dreams; she wants her Pippa's life to be fully satisfied and not ensnared by the false path of conventionalities. But in Antonia's view, to dwell on this is pointless. Despite the strained financial circumstances that a downturn in her career as a courtesan has caused—"Lascia star pensierosa a me che, dal mal francioso in fuora, non trovo cane che mi abbai" ("Leave the worries to me, who, save for the greetings of the French pox, can't even get a bark from a dog") (7)—Antonia is skeptical about Nanna's indecisiveness. Nevertheless, to help her friend see more lucidly into her own decision-making process, Antonia invites Nanna to discuss her experience as a nun, wife, and courtesan with her. The examination of Nanna's past intended to secure Pippa's future turns into a series of conversations. These are imbued with the sense of social dissolution that has left a deep imprint in Aretino's mind.

To enliven the conversation Antonia offers her provisions: "io ho pane e vino e carne salata," sufficient "per tre dì" ("I have enough bread, wine, and cured meat to last us for three days") (9). The plan is to consume the victuals in a setting outside the house and away from the city. Typically, scholars do not take these seemingly banal details into consideration. Yet even at first glance, the food and flavors Antonia supplies, coupled with the image of the vineyard in which they are consumed, confer a sense of immediacy to the material world the two friends—and Aretino—inhabit. For this reason, the provisions Antonia offers turn into a social commentary on her times; metaphorically, they capture a universe that is at odds with the gastronomic norms observed at court. But by indirectly emphasizing the dissonance between the gastronomy of power and that of powerlessness, Antonia's food redirects the audience's attention to the essence of the Renaissance political discourse.

The foodstuff Antonia offers adds more than just a realistic touch of conviviality to the scene depicting the two courtesans absorbed in conversation. As Francesco Guicciardini reminds us, food is the expression of a culture and of its time. Ingredients and flavors intersect the tenuous boundary between entrees and narrative themes, both of which are often evocative of political accomplishments, cultural trends, and historical events. Also, both preparation and consumption of food are always infused with and carry sociocultural meanings. These celebrate, among other things, kinships and relationships. In the political realm, food can be used to seal pacts and treaties just as often as it can be used to underscore the enmities that set rival factions against each other. Riario's historical banquet for the Este/Aragon families, as well as Charlemagne's fictional one offered to the Saracens in the *Innamorato*, are perfect examples of this. Thus, it would be appropriate to say that the metaphorical implications of food intersect time and space. In terms of time, by encapsulating the social codes of any given period, food becomes a poignant illustration of it. Through well-known ingredients and established preparation techniques, food recalls the past; through new ones, however, it emphasizes the concreteness of the present. In a way, this process brings the past (as a repository of methods and ingredients) into the present. To be fair, food also generates subtle clues about the uncertainties of the future. To a degree, these same characteristics confer a sense of space to foodstuffs. Depending on where it is prepared and especially consumed, food acquires metaphorical implications that hold different meanings. Yet in both cases, as a representation of space and time, food provides the means by which to convey the values that humanity clings to while struggling to break through the limitations that systems impose on it. Accordingly, food becomes the gastronomic translation of social norms that sanction sociopolitical beliefs.

By metaphorically fostering the shift from societal rules to political systems the discourse on food, as discussed in chapter 3, becomes one of gastronomic politics. As such, the copiousness or paucity that marks its consumption, the self-control or self-indulgence used at the table, can be construed as a moral and ethical gauge. As Matteo Maria Boiardo shows, at their finest, gastronomic politics function on a par with, or as a culinary version of, political discourse and maneuvers. As I have shown throughout the previous chapters, in some instances gastronomic politics replace the latter altogether. For this reason, in metaphorical terms it could be argued that the condensing and reducing of ingredients used in cooking to enhance flavors are the culinary equivalent of intensively planned political strategies. Devising these in terms of the highest returns they yield is one and the same with ensuring that a dish delivers the very essence of the flavors the cook wants to capture. Of course, to ensure that each ingredient asserts itself without overwhelming the others requires a delicate balance of proportions. This approach is what adds depth, complexity, and appeal to a dish. Yet, it is also true that to heighten a particular flavor the accomplished cook uses a contrasting flavor. For example, to intensify sweetness, a bit of salt is necessary, while to maximize tart, pungent, and peppery flavors the inclusion of a sweetener is essential.

Like the knowledgeable cook attentively producing new food combinations, the experienced leader achieves his highest and finest results by relying on the depth of his experience as well as on his audacity.[33] Thus, Aretino's choice of plain food for Nanna and Antonia is more than just a mere coincidence. His famed fondness for delicious fare and exquisite cuisine, as he asserts in his letters,[34] makes the choice for his heroines all the more intriguing because it conflicts with his own preferences,[35] not to mention the culinary rules the court follows. Yet, it is precisely through his selection of foodstuffs that Aretino highlights the gulf between the refined and the coarse, or hypocrisy and candidness, two antithetical worlds he knows well and purposely pits against each other. Strategically, this technique is similar to the one used by cooks to heighten the intensity of a flavor. In terms of Nanna and Antonia's choice, opting for unsophisticated food suggests the divergence between the ideal and the flawed, the latter of which both Nanna and Antonia, because of their professions, ostensibly incarnate. But more importantly, the simple food they prepare to consume calls to mind the difference between accidents and substance. The courtesans' unassuming ways and lack of conceit set them apart from the practices favored by courtiers. Lastly, there is no doubt that by choosing humble fare Aretino is emphasizing the divergence from the food of power the court prefers. By dispensing with the typical delicacies courtiers consume, the writer creates a direct counterpoint to the life of excess courtiers embody. Indeed, their lavish consumption of rich and exotic fare (even for outdoor meals) not only underscores their uncritical adulation and pursuit of wealth, but especially confirms their hunger for power and prestige. Paradoxically, the court barely conceals, and even justifies, these tastes through the misuse of religious authority.[36]

I

In striking contrast to the customs observed at the papal court, Nanna and Antonia's "court" convenes around a simple lunch of bread, wine, and salted meat. These provisions, as Antonia explains, are sufficient to last for three days. At once, the relevance Aretino assigns to food emerges from this detail. First, it reveals that food is inextricably woven into the fabric of his story. Second, it shows that food is tied to time. As quantifiable elements, each one of them becomes the measure of the other. Food and time are placed at the service of each other, functioning almost as an extension of each other: foodstuffs will last for a specific length of time while, simultaneously, there is a specified time necessary to finish the amount Antonia provides. Third, and perhaps most significantly, the importance Aretino assigns to food and time, as Antonia introduces them, evoke the symbolism of the sacrament of the Eucharist in which bread and wine are turned into the body and blood of Jesus. Aretino, however, plays out this idea with a masterful and revealing twist that parodies the whole spectrum of Christian dogmas. For example, the two who are in charge of breaking the bread and drinking the wine are women not men. Worse yet, they are prostitutes. Also, although they recognize Mary Magdalene as their patron saint—"Oggi è la Madalena nostra avvocata" ("this is the feast day of Magdalene, our patroness") (9)—unlike her, they have neither repented nor are they about to change their lifestyles. On the contrary, they are preoccupied with ensuring that one of their daughters maintains that same way of life. Finally, even though like Jesus, Nanna and Antonia choose to withdraw from the city, unlike Him, during their retreat they plan to test the soundness of their pragmatic views on human capriciousness, not the firmness of their high-principled wills. Accordingly, when contrasted to Jesus' withdrawal in the desert, Nanna and Antonia's turns into a calculated mockery of the Gospel's story.

Clearly, by drawing back from their familiar world in a *vigna* and, more precisely in a *ficaia* ("in the vineyard, beneath this fig tree") (49), the courtesans upend the story of Jesus withdrawing in the desert. This is also evidenced by the fact that He chose a barren place lacking food and comforts in order to test His determination against the temptations that the world stirred. The courtesans, on the contrary, choose a vineyard, which by its very nature provides both. In addition, they go to the vineyard to discuss the manner in which desires can continue to be gratified. Through this inversion of means and objectives Aretino deliberately mocks the clergy who, in his view, are emblematic of false values and in whose hands religion turns into a utilitarian pawn that thwarts and subverts Jesus' teachings. Like the prelates whom Aretino knows so well, Antonia uses wine and bread to advance her personal interest— in this case she wants to learn about Nanna's past. Also, Aretino shows that, as for the prelates, for Antonia and Nanna prosperity, contempt for moral values, and appetite for luxuries that enhance material comforts exemplify success and prestige, not moral degradation. As self-acceptance and moral degradation coexist in the same persons, with one attitude effortlessly displacing the other, Aretino highlights and scorns the practices that characterize the church. In his view, like these two women, it prostitutes itself to advance its interests.

Placed in the hands of a woman, Antonia's bread and wine is a distant reminder of the "other," spiritual one. But while the latter celebrates Jesus' life of total self-abnegation that is marked by a complete rejection of all forms of materialism, the former evokes its very opposite. By leading lives that are consumed by the thought of savoring every material fulfillment and through which they measure their successes, the courtesans trample on the examples set by Jesus. Yet again like prelates whose satisfaction of desires precedes and even eclipses religious vows and responsibilities, the two women believe that they can derive neither benefit nor profit by emulating Jesus' example. The world they know is one in which money begets power and this, in turn, authority. The way they see it, the combination of the two validates one's essence not the abstinence from pleasures or self-sacrifice.

The specific reference to the three days during which the bread and wine will last clearly evokes Jesus' Last Supper and His crucifixion, death, and resurrection. But Antonia and Nanna's actual "breaking of the bread" is not intended as a celebration of humanity's acknowledgment of its sins, repentance, and redemption. Their wine and bread memorialize no spiritual enlightenment; to the contrary, by consuming those victuals the courtesans epitomize the subversion of Christian beliefs. They also solemnize the human propensity to attain and preserve material wealth in a world that views them as the gauge of success. An inverted reflection of the Christian theology of the Eucharist, Antonia's wine and bread acquire the power of transubstantiation for the world of transgression and materiality to which the two women belong. At this juncture, the two not only incarnate the vices of society, but also, and especially, those of the papal court. There, despite the fact that Jesus' sacrifice is regularly memorialized, it is utterly devoid of its original meaningfulness because of the worldly interests driving its members. And so, rather than functioning as the model of humility and poverty that, according to His teachings, paves the way to greater, spiritual pleasures, the curia, like Nanna and Antonia, epitomizes the lack of those values. Aretino's ferocious criticism of it emerges as he describes two unschooled women whose material interests are in consonance with those nurtured in that court.

On the third day of their agreed-upon meetings, Nanna reaches a decision with regard to Pippa's future. After thoroughly analyzing the other options available to Pippa, the two friends conclude that only as a well indoctrinated courtesan will Pippa acquire independent wealth, preserve a self-mastery unknown to other women, and be able to act at will unencumbered by the presence of abusive men. For Nanna and Antonia a career as a prostitute is Pippa's only secure strategy against poverty and submissiveness. To this end, they also interject a moral element in their discussion. Cognizant of the fact that unlike other unscrupulous merchants, prostitutes merchandize only themselves, not what they do not possess, Nanna and Antonia determine that for this reason prostitutes are more virtuous than other women. The assertion "i vizi delle puttane son virtù" ("a whore's vices are really virtues") (139) juxtaposes acknowledged vices to hidden ones. This detail speaks of the greed that pervades court and society and that compels both of them to make every sort of compromise.[37] But the certainty that Pippa will derive material security from the career of courtesan also stems from Nanna and Antonia's conviction that Rome will always be "delle puttane" ("the whore's plaything") (140). With a fierce and fearless blow aimed yet again at the corrupt heart of the high clergy, the women—and Aretino through them—conclude that Roman leaders and representatives are people who sell themselves and, most importantly, what they represent for personal advantages. Nanna's conscious decision to engineer her daughter's career in order for her to maintain a luxurious lifestyle is not different from the aspirations of courtiers and princes of the church whose nepotism is intended to preserve riches within their families.

The salted meat Nanna and Antonia consume during their three days of conversations, confirms, first of all, the financial prosperity of its consumers. Beyond this, it is also suggestive of the independence that Nanna wants to preserve for her daughter. Salting meat is a process through which the animal's flesh is preserved. More specifically, curing ensures that meat does not spoil and can be consumed at a later time. But preserving something so as to make it available for future consumption is, metaphorically, one and the same with protracting the present into the future. Conversely, it is also a way of returning to—and tasting—the past in the present. In terms of Pippa's career, this is precisely what Nanna plans to do with her daughter. She wants her to continue experiencing in the future the comforts she has grown up with in her mother's household. Of course, the salted meat also points to the carnal aspect of Nanna's profession. Eating meat, swallowing it, digesting it, and ultimately expelling it after the body has absorbed all of its nutrients exemplifies the whores' conduct toward the men who crave their attention and lust for their bodies but remain entangled in the webs the crafty courtesans weave for them. Those men, who generously bestow money and possessions upon the women whose favors they seek, are predictably retained only for as long as their prodigality lasts. When largesse is no longer available, the skillful courtesans discard the impoverished suitors.

Curiously, on the third day of their conversation, the one reserved to the discussion of the lives of the courtesan—a discussion that ultimately leads Nanna to finalize her decision regarding Pippa's career—the first ingredient set on the table is plain salt. By itself this ingredient is never mentioned during the previous two days. *Sale e sole*—salt and sun, as Isidore of Seville pairs them—are essential to man's survival.[38] In the Judeo-Christian tradition, salt is a purifying agent. It prevents putrefaction and corruption. With its symbolic values diverging from the moral ones the two women espouse, the presence of salt, at this point, creates a piercing discrepancy with their ongoing conversation. After all, the two women advocate a life in which licentiousness is faithfully adhered to in order to preserve wealth and prestige. Similarly, as its redemptive symbolism in Baptism makes clear, salt ensures not only the attainment of purification and wisdom but also regeneration, or at least the potential for it. In spite of this, aside from the indication that Pippa will have a "new life" of financial independence after her apprenticeship as a courtesan, everything in Nanna and Antonia's conversation reverses the original symbolism of salt.

Yet at the same time, salt is also known as a corrosive agent. Through a chemical action it damages, and can destroy, any material subject to a prolonged exposure to it. Metaphorically, then, the salt on the courtesans' table also typifies destructiveness. By linking this characteristic of salt to the moral and ethical aspects of Nanna's and Antonia's chosen lifestyles, and by extension to those of papal courtiers, it would appear that the corrosiveness of salt evidences the ruinous consequences of the pursuits that these individuals have made their own. But Aretino is not a moralist. Instead, he is providing the opportunity for a candid assessment of this society. As a result, the transformative effects that the corrosiveness of salt produces brings to mind more complex political expansions, economic and military power, and identity-defining prestige.[39] For the courtesans' Rome, this corrosiveness is one and the same with the damaging influence those violent efforts for personal and political self-affirmation exert on society. In the end, through Aretino's patent inversion of the metaphorical meaning of salt, it appears as if the salt were put on the table to underscore yet again the dissoluteness ravaging Rome as the women and Aretino know it. As for the dangerous property salt possesses, it too becomes a symbol of greed's absorbing and caustic outcomes. All in all, these characteristics are incompatible with the high-mindedness, honor, and integrity humanists uphold.[40] In this manner, through the metaphorical value that can be assigned to food and his bristling wit, Aretino describes a world that no longer abides by rules that do not gratify natural human impulses.

That Nanna and Antonia's conversations take place outside the city in a vineyard rather than in a garden turns into another example of the originality of Aretino's argument. Renaissance authors preferred formal gardens as a frame for their disputations[41] on poetry, philosophy, and love.[42] Ficino's Platonic Academy developed in the paradisiac surroundings of Careggi—a gift to him from Cosimo de' Medici. There, the philosopher reestablished Plato's tradition of the academy at Colonus.[43] The area surrounding Careggi is perhaps the most celebrated example of a Renaissance garden constructed to create an intimate space, a closed system impenetrable to outsiders. Within it, decorative borders and margins were arranged and regulated according to specific architectural rules. The visual harmony these create makes the visitors feel protected, privileged, and contained. This setting provides a sense of intimacy with the natural world that daily activities hinder. Although this intimacy is laced with ambiguity, it lends itself to philosophical discussions. Ficino's *locus laetus* that makes the flight of the mind from daily *negotium* and the greed it breeds possible, draws, naturally, on Plato's model. Like Plato, within his garden Ficino and his followers believe that one could gradually progress from the physical to the spiritual world—or from *laetitia* (sensual joy) to *gaudium* (joy of the mind). According to him, by awakening the senses the exquisiteness of the surroundings negotiates the mind's passage from the concrete and utterly material to the realm of the spirit and of the otherworldly; and this, in turn, leads to God. Platonic philosophy, which Ficino translates into Christian theology, is brought back to life, and fully practiced, by shunning the materialism that *negotium* necessitates.[44] The *otium* that in the garden replaces it occupies the mind in its peregrinations toward higher principles. This exercise eradicates the craving for worldly possessions while instilling the desire to prize virtues. Thus, the mind "flee(s) excesses, flee(s) affairs, rejoicing in the present."[45] It would seem that for Ficino the cultivation of the mind is one and the same with the cultivation that beautifies Careggi. More accurately, in this construction one system gives

Courtesans and Figs, Art and Nature in Aretino's *Ragionamento* 287

order to chosen plants and flowers, allowing no intrusive vegetation to disrupt the botanical arrangements.[46] The other is one that plants the seeds for and cultivates high-minded thoughts that lead humanity to loftier ideals.

In his *Ragionamento*, with one stroke Aretino wipes away and simultaneously mocks the narrowly defined notion of Renaissance garden that Careggi exemplifies. After all, the perception this garden engenders is a powerful reminder of lives spent in the comforts conferred by donated wealth and bestowed privileges. Disengaged from the realities shaping the world outside of the garden, its patrons can reflect on, and pursue, stimulating philosophical subjects. They can also investigate theological issues, and ponder over the spiritual realm that, in their views, outshines the material one. But for the practical Nanna and Antonia these theoretical disquisitions hold no interest. In a similar fashion, for the Roman courtiers at whose services the two courtesans have worked, Ficino's philosophical and theological pursuits hold no relevance. Simply stated, the lives of Aretino's characters are all inscribed in the materiality of the world. Consequently, the space where Nanna and Antonia choose to meet highlights the paradox between garden and vineyard.[47]

Definitely, as the courtesans' place of choice, the vineyard is an audacious counterpoint to an elegant garden and the sumptuous banquets organized there.[48] The vegetation found in the vineyard makes this point evident. In Renaissance villas, the vineyard is often physically interconnected to the garden.[49] This fact suggests that both spaces are integral systems of Renaissance thoughts.[50] Even so, compared to the garden, the vineyard evokes more modest and unassuming connotations. Unlike the imposing, magnificent garden, in which the landscape is a perfectly manicured environment, graced by flower beds, decorative trees, and shrubs with luxuriant foliage,[51] the vineyard is associated with agricultural and farming activities. Instead of esthetic appeal, its organizing principle is the harvests it produces. Here the principles of beauty and harmony play no roles, but cede their place to needs. In other words, unlike the garden, the vineyard is not an esthetically controlled space. Generally, it calls to mind a more rustic style of living. Also, because a vineyard typically includes orchards, herb gardens, and farmland, and not decorative plantings, it is not devised as the visual expression of the owner's grandeur.[52] In contrast to this, Renaissance gardens are designed as another form of "monument" appropriate to princes mindful of the cultural and social demands for magnificence. Leon Battista Alberti's description in *On the Art of Building* makes this clear. He emphasizes that the planning of gardens requires the same principles regulating the visual arts: mathematical perspective, proportional relationship of parts, symmetry, and geometric forms. According to Alberti, man must artfully control the garden's physical landscape to create a space of aesthetic wonderment. In this manner, human craftiness transforms the garden into a fluid space defined by visual effects and illusions. By awakening the senses and swaying the mind, these transport it beyond the physical world it inhabits. As a place of selectiveness and sensory stimulations, the garden creates a sense of intimacy with the natural world. And this, in turn, becomes a conduit to introspection and ethical speculation that is imbued with the rhetoric of self-discovery. This is based on the notion that beneath the layers of plantings and labyrinthine paths that meander through and shape the garden are buried the ambiguities that the mind must untangle to grasp its innermost thoughts.

None of these attributes apply to the vineyard. Indeed, as the garden's aesthetic specter, the vineyard fails to make possible—and in point of fact is not conducive to—the elegant illusion that its harmonious beauty can gradually transport the mind to loftier thoughts. A vineyard does not induce a meditative state of mind because it is not a place for wandering guests; instead, it is one of work. Surely, for the people frequenting it, the vineyard is not a signifier of a set of symbolic associations. Accordingly, it does not make a visitor prey to delusions because its utilitarian plantings do not allow one to cross the border between the real space and the ideal space. The vineyard can only lay claim to the foods it produces. And this is not the product of human artfulness but of humanity's necessity to procure the food it needs.

By following the natural cycle of seasons the predictable harvests a vineyard yields may vary remarkably in quality and quantity. By the same token, a vineyard never tests, nor does it attempt to shape and modify, one's belief system. The natural bounty it provides is never the effect of human imagination. Nor is it the outcome of an intellectual journey to new spiritual insights. It is a place of exertion, not leisure. Through the food it supplies a vineyard serves mankind's basic needs rather than its wants. More importantly, its products suggest a relationship between fruitfulness and fecundity. The garden, on the contrary, does not readily bring this notion to mind. Its ornamental aims never fully hold on to the possibility of productivity over aesthetic unproductiveness. Applied to the *Ragionamento*, these distinctions are revelatory. First, they lead one to believe that as he deliberately and systematically upends conventions, Aretino makes a striking visual connection between his characters' qualities and the vineyard's characteristics. Second, as a space that privileges, among other things, the physical over the spiritual and, by extension, substance over appearance, the practical over the idealistic, and the earthbound over the otherworldly, the vineyard for Aretino foregrounds the pragmatism as well as the outward simplicity of his characters. Given the cultural predilection for sophisticated gardens as loci for philosophical (and theological) disquisitions among educated men, his choice for such an unconventional space—like his choice of subject matter—strikes at the heart of the Renaissance repertoire of places suitable for high-minded discussions.[53] And yet, the vineyard remains a place where natural events take place; for Aretino, this is one and the same with natural desires. For this reason, the courtesans' vineyard calls to mind the place Boccaccio's *brigata* reaches after leaving Florence. The country setting where the young Florentines choose to while away the time, like Nanna's vineyard, is a place where sociopolitical norms give way to conversations that emphasize the ludicrousness of codified systems intended to keep human nature in check. Finally, in the Gospel the vineyard, not the garden, is described as the place where one earns salvation. This fact is indicative of the toil, physical or spiritual, that the place requires.

By placing his two courtesans in a vineyard rather than a garden, Aretino underscores the correspondence between the elements that characterize the vineyard and the traits that distinguish the women.[54] Here they do not imagine anything but speak of the reality they know. By focusing on the humbler plenitude of the vineyard and contrasting it with the aesthetic triumph that the bareness of the garden legitimates,

Aretino implicitly privileges the physical over the philosophical/theoretical world. This is the realization of a vision that, as his whole body of work attests, Aretino has long harbored. The foods produced in the vineyard nourish the body not the mind; nature in its plainness can sustain humanity's physical needs. It can even lead it to a spiritual world that is disengaged from unnatural social norms. The consonance between the physical and the spiritual rests, Aretino claims, not in the sophisticated world of abstract ideals but in the unadulterated natural world. But when the natural is manipulated and its limits are pushed to the extremes, it becomes artificial. This manipulation makes art and nature no longer one fluid part of the natural but each an artificial extension of the other. Aretino's uncompromising stance against the glamour of appearances confected within gleaming princely courts and aimed at shrouding the corruption that pervades them surfaces as he lays the groundwork for the *Ragionamento*.

In the vineyard the two women sit and eat under a fig tree. The indelible image of two courtesans placed in the inelegant setting of a vineyard supposedly ties in with the moral coarseness of their lives. The unpretentious space with its unrefined nature also mirrors the crude topics of their licentious conversation. Similarly, the lack of the aesthetic beauty ingrained in the idea of the vineyard also calls to mind the moral degradation the two women personify. Through this, the writer retrieves the debate on ethics and aesthetics that absorbed humanists who believed that the two are always mutually connected. Drawing from Aristotle's moral philosophy, Italian humanists, albeit in different manners, saw in the political and ethical ideals of classical antiquity the models for their societies to emulate. For Lorenzo Valla a system of ethics can only be based on the Christian virtues of faith, hope, and charity.[55] According to him, it is these, not the Stoic ideal of virtue nor the Epicurean notion of pleasure, that lead humanity to the *verum bonum* and *verae virtutes* that make the *summum bonum* attainable. In a similar vein, for Ficino achieving the highest good requires that the mind, and thus humanity, "separates itself the more from corporeal things the more it is lifted upwards toward the contemplation of things spiritual, but the highest limit which understanding can attain is the substance itself of God, then it follows that the mind only ascends to the divine substance when it has become totally separated from the mortal senses."[56] Ficino claims that mankind aspires to become like God and that through sheer intellect and will it can come to know the beauty of truth and possess the good by turning away from corporal senses. His insistence on the necessity of distancing oneself from bodily appetites—"a body rarely needs to eat and even more rarely to have sex. But every single moment we wish for the true and the good"[57]—is removed from the world of immanence. Aretino's view is clearly incompatible with this idea.

From the safety of his ensconced Careggi where all of his needs are amply provided for by the Medici patronage, Ficino can claim that "the desire for sex can be mastered and the greed for eating lessened, the will for the true and good is never mastered or diminished; or rather, while the former wane with age, the latter increases . . . So to the extent the desire for the true and the good is more natural than that for food or sex, the guidance of nature has made even greater provision for its fully attaining its end."[58] The same principles are not true for society at large, just as it was not true for Luigi Pulci. For those like Aretino (and Pulci), living in the unremitting poverty outside of the guarded perimeter of the courtly garden, maintaining a comfortable lifestyle, and satisfying one's desires are all but unattainable. Because of this, Ficino's assertions are not so compelling for Aretino (just as they were not for Pulci). The philosophical abstractions that pervade Ficino's claims ignore, and even go against, the writer's experiences. His enduring desire for a rich and fulfilling lifestyle is not uncommon, but is shared by humanity. And for it, philosophical abstractions are no substitute for material comforts. According to Ficino, striving for the *summum bonum* of a spiritual nature is humanity's natural objective; and he claims that humanity constantly seeks it. Aretino's refusal to go along with this mode of thinking emerges in his presentation of the two courtesans. For them, as well as for him, the notion of highest good does not entail God; rather, it implies first and foremost the satisfaction of natural needs and appetites. And the Rome in which they—and he—live is a constant reminder of the fact that in a society especially corrupted by its spiritual leaders humanity does not naturally strive toward the good and the beautiful unless a monetary figure can be put on them.

Needless to say, Nanna's vineyard is no earthly paradise. In point of fact, it is neither a distinctive garden where the ploy of plantings creates a layering of images replete with ambiguities where, therefore, minds wander to higher ideals (Ficino) nor a place where the will is crushed (Ariosto and Pulci). To the contrary, because of its features Nanna's vineyard is a place that retains its connections with the fuller world outside of it. This is a world bustling with ordinary people who live behind the limits of the refined space. In the *Ragionamento*, the link between the vineyard and the outside world dissolves the ambiguity between outsiders and insiders. As a result, it erases the divide between alienation and integration that the formal garden accentuates. This idea is brought into sharper focus by the image of the two women seated under a fig tree. Here Aretino creates a geometric harmony through a triangular image that, more than providing a visual balance, retrieves, and simultaneously toys with, the Trinitarian dogma. Aretino's trinity is a human one, earthbound and ambitious. It is driven by a culture that has become narrowly money obsessed. Sex, riches, and luxuries characterize it. Unsurprisingly, this is the trinity the papal court also reveres for sustaining the prestige, independence, and authority it claims for itself.

Two women and a tree: this is the image of two individuals who have turned their backs on moral conventions because they have discovered the hypocrisy that social conventions lead to. Because of this, the two are more concerned with worldly matters than norms. For the first bolster and further their ambitions more than the latter or, for that matter, spiritual ones. The tree Aretino chooses for this image is of particular interest for it is steeped in political, sexual, and religious symbolism. Simultaneously suggesting male and female genitals, sperm, and copulation, the fig tree and its fruit imbue the entire scene with a sexually charged imagery. Indeed, the traits that characterize the tree evoke the sexual debaucheries (homoerotic as well as heterosexual) for which the papal court is notorious.

From a doctrinal perspective, together the women and the tree defy the Trinitarian dogma on several grounds. Among these prevails the maleness that defines God and Son. This earthly trinity, as Aretino portrays it, first and foremost foregrounds the lack of dignity the Church of Rome has come to exemplify because of the personal interests regulating it. And this, in turn, spawns into the lack of moral authority that it can hold over society. As it contrasts with the Christian dogma, Aretino's trinity becomes a vivid reminder of the clash between integrity and corruption, beauty and hideousness, virtue and vice. This human/vegetal triangulation makes the Protestant challenge looming in the distance all the more real for it literally and figuratively questions the assumptions that humanity is capable of changing its conduct and of acting in a way that privileges probity over personal desires.[59]

The figure of the two women mocks and subverts the Christian dogma by illustrating the moral decay to which society has succumbed. But through the fig tree Aretino endows Nanna and Antonia with an unexpected iconological stature that is enshrined within that plant and its foliage. Fraught with complex symbolic value, both tree and fruit shed another layer of symbolic ambiguities on both the courtesans and the society they represent. In the biblical tradition, this is the tree that provided the leaves with which Eve and Adam covered their naked bodies immediately after their eyes were opened to their sexuality. In sharp contrast to this, under the same type of tree Aretino's characters do not expose their bodies but the stark nakedness of their lives and their beliefs. These, ironically also encapsulate those of the papal court. As for their bodies, the courtesans prostitute them, thus exposing them to the carnal desires of the suitors to whom they sell their favors. The divergence between the biblical event and the Roman one re-inscribes Nanna's and Antonia's figures within the discourse of sexuality and desire. Yet in the Gospel of Mark (11:12–14, 20–21) the fig tree fills another role. Jesus curses it after His arrival in Jerusalem when He discovers that only leaves are on the branches. The figs are not in season and so He cannot sate His physical hunger.

Jesus' exclamation, "Never again shall anyone eat of your fruit," has received various interpretations, most of which show partiality toward the idea that Jesus is effectively talking about the Jews. Thus the assertion the "fruit that is out of season" is understood as a rhetorical articulation casting the Jews as spiritually unprepared for His arrival and His message. This interpretation appears corroborated by the fact that when He and His disciples reach the temple's precincts in Jerusalem they find its grounds packed with men conducting business transactions. He scatters them away, reminding them, "Does not the scripture have it, 'My house shall be called a house of prayer for all peoples'—but you have turned it into a den of thieves" (11:15–17) The two events, the cursing of the fig tree and the expulsion of merchants from the temple, evidence Jesus' disappointed expectations. With the fig tree, Jesus anticipated finding edible fruit; in the temple he expected to find people praying. In both cases, however, what He actually finds are just appearances: He discovers the bare façade of what He thought would be there: the tree has no fruit and the temple no true believers. This interpretation calls to mind the papal court Aretino knows. Like the temple in the Gospel, it has turned into a powerhouse of venality that vanity stirs. And like the fig tree of the same Gospel, the court is bearing no fruit but is solely engrossed in games of form. Egotism, self-importance, narcissism, and pride make up the unbridgeable distance that exists between Jesus' teachings and the curia's materialist dwellers. As the Gospel's episodes make plain, the examination of actions and introspection should result in changing the ways of those who ignore Jesus' example.

With its established sexual symbolism and as the background as well as the shelter under which the courtesans converse, the tree suggests more than the perversion of the Church. It also invests the scene with political implications, for it retrieves the notion of the foundation of Rome. In his *Lives of Noble Grecians and Romans* Plutarch recounts the story of Romulus's and Remus's births as told by Fabius Pictor. Here Plutarch details not only the circumstances of the legendary twins' births but also describes the place where the river's waters left the newborn brothers: "the river overflowing, the flood at last bore up the trough, and gently wafting it, landed them on a smooth piece of ground . . . near this place grew a wild-fig tree."[60] The fig tree, Plutarch goes on to say, "they called Ruminalis" because of "the suckling of these children there . . . and there is a tutelary goddess of the rearing of children whom they still call Rumilia in sacrificing to whom they use no wine, but make libations of milk." For Plutarch the tree represents the safe harbor under or near which the newborns suckle their way not just to life but especially back into the system that has rejected and alienated them. Because of this, rather than a symbol of weakness and powerlessness for Plutarch the tree is one of strength and power. These same traits characterize the actions that define the twins' adult lives. By prevailing over the adversities to which their uncle king Amulius, initially subjects them, Romulus and Remus's willfulness is tested and, with it, their moral fiber. But the fact that a she wolf nursed the twins adds fascinating nuances to Aretino's argument because of the ambiguous meaning of the name *lupae*.

As Plutarch explains "Latins not only called wolves *lupae*, but also women of loose life; and such was an (sic) one the wife of Faustulus, who nurtured these children."[61] The historian's elucidation that it was not an animal but a woman with an unsound moral character that nursed the forsaken twins lends powerful support to Aretino's argument. To reestablish the social order it is necessary to ruthlessly do away with appearances because they often only mask an unsavory reality. Facts and deeds, Aretino maintains, do not allow drifting away from reality. On the contrary, they are the powerful weapons in the war of ideas leading up to radical changes that restore law-abiding systems. And if individuals with less than sparkling moral traits are the ones carrying through the changes, the changes are just as meaningful. Reshaping and modifying an unjust system is more important than an individual's traits. As the events leading to their adulthood make clear, Romulus and Remus's survival marks not only the passage from excluded to included, from alienated to integrated, or from outsiders to insiders but especially restores the social and political order that Amulius's greed upended.

Dissatisfied with the mere inheritance he had initially assented to with his brother, Amulius craved Numitor's share. As a result, he decided to take the latter's kingdom by force. By seizing Numitor's kingdom Amulius violated the initial agreement that made him and his brother equal successors in the line of the kings of Alba. Worse yet, the fact that Amulius forced Numitor's daughter Rhea to become a Vestal, thus precluding the risk of legitimate heirs to his brother's kingdom, is another example of the lawful stability his greed undermined. Because of it, Amulius tore the fabric of a lawful society apart, overturning the rule of the law. Thus, Romulus and Remus's reinstatement into the folds of the system that tried to suppress them and squelch their legitimate rights illustrates the blend of drive, rivalry, vision, and courage—hunger, really—necessary to undo unjust systems.

The twins' new lives, which begin under a fig tree and from early on intersect the boundaries of religion and politics, set in motion the process that results in the foundation of Rome. Saint Augustine maintains that the establishment of this city stands from the failings and weaknesses afflicting humanity.[62] For him, the fratricide, or as he describes it, the "parricide,"[63] marks the moment in which in the history of Rome human impulses are given free rein and prevail over the laws of restraint that foster social order. Rome, he claims, from its inception had no moral compass guiding it. The self-assuredness it developed from military triumphs, though void of moral principles, made it oblivious to the obvious. It did not prepare it to battle the ruthlessness and greed that began to tear its citizenry apart. In Augustine's view, desire for riches,[64] refined foodstuffs, and the credulous belief in a gods-willed invincibility that ostensibly granted it absolute superiority over other cities and peoples turned Rome into a nest of materialism. With searing clarity the philosopher claims that the dissolute indolence that luxury provided resulted from a toxic mixture of misguided actions carried out by undisciplined men. Their lack of introspection and unwillingness to explore the deeper side of human fragility, Saint Augustine claims, did Rome in. Its stunning fall was a product of the people's own making. Internal, preventable forces, not external unavoidable ones, nibbled away the city's greatness.

Looking at Rome's foundation and at its collapse through the eyes of a courtesan who is witnessing a new "fall" of the same city gives a new pulse to Aretino's *Ragionamento*. Though at first glance the tenuous link between her Rome and Augustine's is a mere fig tree, the accounts given respectively by Saint Augustine and Nanna reveal similar causes for the city's undoing. The disintegration of Rome's social structure brought about by the fraying of its moral fiber is no less critical than the collapse of its physical structure. Obviously, Nanna harbors no illusion that as a courtesan her daughter will lay the foundation of a new civilization. Nor does she delude herself into believing that Pippa will follow the twins' path in establishing a new social/civil order. On the contrary, she is aware that Pippa will incarnate the dissolution of those long sought after and fought for ideals. She also knows, though, that as a courtesan Pippa will always be an insider of Roman society. Indeed, by virtue of the fame she will achieve, unlike the young twins, rather than an outcast Pippa will be the center around which the life of Roman society will revolve. Irrevocably prisoner of its impulses and desires, humanity will readily prefer the pleasures Pippa personifies to the chaste and virtuous ideals that conventions prescribe. Nanna is all too aware of this. But to illustrate further her awareness of human greed and loathing of hypocritical rules she describes to Antonia her experience as a nun.

II

Behind the walls of the convent she enters as a young novice Nanna discovers a world radically different from the one she envisioned. This is neither a place where lives are spent in silent prayer nor one in which worldly pleasures have been renounced in accordance with the literal interpretation of the Gospels. Instead, the women who inhabit it, and the clergymen who regularly visit, disregard the vows of chastity, poverty, and obedience they professed when they took their orders. Clearly, Nanna's startling discovery of a universe regulated by food, sex, and power is not unlike the one Aretino encountered when he moved to the Rome of Leo X. The glamour the curia achieved under this pope—its fame as the center of intellectual verve—was due in no small part to his refined taste for the arts. But the magnificence and brilliancy of the court that Leo cultivated around him had a less dazzling side. Rife with scandals, enmeshed in all sorts of political intrigues, and indulging in all kinds of excesses aimed at securing the immediate gratification of its members, this side trod upon the true meaning of the Church's mission. In fact, while reveling in the comforts of its power, the curia conveniently closed its eyes to the repercussions that its actions would have on both Christianity and Rome. In Leo's court, church and state affairs commingled because of the restless ambition of prelates who were driven by their rapacity for worldly possessions. The resulting system was one of unbalanced power and unbridled desires where greed and self-aggrandizement held sway. It is this world, unconcerned about the lack of moral values guiding its actions, that Aretino reveals and critiques through Nanna's experience. By describing a universe of women who, like their male counterparts, are driven by instincts, desires, and impulses Aretino deftly conjures up and brings to life a specular if feminized image, not just of Leo's court but also that of his successor and relative, Clement VII.[65] These two popes he served with unswerving loyalty.[66] Yet, through this depiction, and with no little irony, Aretino exposes the contradictions, failings, and wickedness in which the curia wallows. At the same time, he draws a detailed map of the politics, history, and religion shaping his times.

The lavishness that marked the first meal Nanna consumed in the convent is not stunted by the lapse of time that has occurred since she turned into a courtesan. For the attentive Antonia, to whom years later she recounts the event, Nanna recaptures that gastronomic magnificence of the meal: "e così vennero le vivande, e di sorte che il papa (mi farai dire) non ne mangiò mai tali" ("so then the food arrived, the sort of food that, I assure you, the pope in person has never tasted"). Her sense of wonder at the splendor of that banquet runs through her hyperbolized language. This detail dispels any doubt about the fact that the meal she consumed was based on a dietary regimen that, in the wake of Saint Benedict's Rule,[67] from the sixth century on all monastic orders adopted, albeit with some variances. Her recollection of the banquet does attest, though, to the widely recognized extravagant consumption that characterized the pope's table and translated in gastronomic terms the opulence he favored. Nanna's description foregrounds the curia's hedonism and its appetite for power and pleasure that sumptuous meals connote. Although pronounced by an uneducated woman, Nanna's candid comparison between the banquet devoured in the convent and those consumed by the pope strikes at the heart of the curia's lack of temperance.[68] But it also evidences the manner in which the pope's taste for lavishness is ingrained in the social consciousness. In this fashion, Aretino's acerbic critique against the self-indulgent and altogether worldly tendencies regulating life at the court surfaces through Nanna's seemingly innocuous comparison.

Nanna's reminiscence uncovers yet another aspect of convent life. As discussed in chapter 1, Aristotle speaks of *akolasia*—the vice of excess—produced, among other things, through the senses that can occur through touch. Accordingly, mouth, palate, throat, or tongue can arouse physical pleasure by heightening the senses. In this construct, taste, which results from the contact of tongue and palate savoring food's flavors, engenders a form of *akolasia*. But the arousal of physical pleasure, the philosopher maintains, leads to *akrasia*, which is lack of self-control. Applied to Nanna's experience Aristotle's analysis suggests, at the very least, that sensual pleasures are not extraneous to the convent. As a telling example he shows that the temperance plain meals exemplify is manifestly spurned there in favor of the self-indulgence that palatable meals typify. These, as discussed above, are emblematic of riches, sensuality, and power. Naturally, in the convent these attributes rule out poverty, chastity, and obedience on the part of those consuming them. Thus, Nanna's juxtaposition of convent and papal banquets reflects more than a simple inversion of codified monastic rules. In a compelling way, it clarifies and reinforces the conflict between an abstract if dehumanizing monastic culture and personal desires.

The silence that during the banquet envelops the refectory emphasizes the voracious greed the commensals display at the table. Nanna equates the sound of their chewing mouths disrupting that silence to that of silk worms devouring mulberry leaves. And yet, in her description to Antonia she does not mention the tree by its proper name; instead, she obliquely refers to it as the one standing at Pyramus and Thysbe's meeting place: "le bocche facevano il medesimo mormorio che fanno quelle dei vermi della seta finiti di crescere quando, indugiato il cibo, divorano le frondi di quelli arbori sotto l'ombra dei quali si solea trastullare quel poveretto di Priamo e quella poverina di Tisbe" ("their mouths were making the mumbling noise silkworms make when, fully grown and after a long fast, they devour the leaves of the tree in whose shade poor Pyramus and Thysbe played their little games") (12). With this deft stroke Nanna conflates persons and worms, humans and animals, mind and body. This word choice captures the multilayered complexity of human nature while also illustrating the long established disconnect between physical and spiritual pleasure. The uncanny juxtaposition Nanna voices turns her into a character who echoes, or at least unwittingly brings to mind, the values that Valla's Antonio da Rho champions in the third book of *De falso et vero bono*. There, arguing that worldly pleasures are an inadequate foretaste of celestial ones, the Franciscan voices a strong dissent against the materiality that humanity pursues and shows the error that is inherent to that belief system. To it, and to the short-lived earthly pleasures that it produces, Antonio counters the eternal, celestial ones: "we should not fear," he says, "to renounce the affairs of man. Rather we must take good hope . . . all things will be restored that we have entrusted to God here, and be restored a hundred for one, of the same kind or another, and yet always better and more sanctified, whatever its kind . . . So that whatever honor, praise, fame, delight, gaiety, or pleasure attract us, from which our spiritual health might in any way take harm, let us then promptly turn the eyes of our mind to the future reward, and let us always remember [that] every time that we are attracted by something delightful, we shall be all the more strongly drawn toward the hope of heavenly things."[69] This exhortation, as Valla's whole treatise evidences, refutes the values that the Stoic systems champions. But it does fuse some of the Epicurean values into a system of Christian practice.

In Antonio's view, only a life lived in a complete disinterest of material pursuits leads to the *delectatio* of eternal and more gratifying ones. Through his assertion "we must abstain from the pleasure here below if we want to enjoy the one above"[70] Valla shows the limits of earthly pleasures. Although Nanna — and through her Aretino — is obviously not modeling her line of reasoning on Valla's argument against the Stoics' and the Epicureans' seductive beliefs, her association of human and animal gratifications nonetheless discloses an oblique critique of the humanist's understanding of human pleasure. Her disenchantment with the social system is the result of her experiences. And these leave no doubt as to where her convictions lie. With the certainty of a woman who has tested the world and who has been both tested and tasted by it, Nanna paints a picture of moral sordidness that thrives in opportunism and shows no redemptive interest. Like the nuns, priests, and prelates she knows, attaining an afterlife more fulfilling than the life she is living is not what Nanna desires. For her, the future potentiality of pleasures, as Valla describes it, with its convergence of earthly and celestial fulfillments, only accounts for a vague promise. Thus, it can ill gratify individuals who are, quite naturally, tossed about by passions, betrayals, imperfections, and confusions and whose simmering impulses demand a more timely gratification.

As Nanna draws on the recollection of her novitiate days to reconstruct for Antonia the material pleasures adding zest to the lives of allegedly irreproachable people, she does not spare any tidbit of information. She describes the excitement experienced by nuns, priests, and prelates as they reveled in sexual excesses. She details the manners in which those individuals gratified their senses through luscious food, among other things. And in so doing, it is the descriptions of foodstuff in particular that illuminate the fraudulent culture promoted by religious hypocrisy. Through this, Aretino, with extraordinary realism, crushes Valla's claim that "pleasure must be desired for itself by those who wish to experience joy, both in this life and in the life to come."[71] By narrowly focusing on "pleasure that is love" of a celestial nature,[72] Valla calls to mind Ficino's understanding of Platonic love, which, as is known, is neither sustained nor underpinned by a material plenitude, but by a spiritual one. Neither Nanna nor Aretino can identify with Valla or Ficino's Christian understanding of pleasure. For the former, just as for the latter, the pressing urgency of human desires suggests that the vagueness of the future cannot sustain the needs of the present. Indeed, deferring natural pleasures to future gratification, or cloaking the same desires for pleasure under different disguises, creates a fragmentary reality that has only one outcome: it leads to opportunism and this, in turn, to the disintegration of moral, political, and ethical values. It is no surprise, then, that despite the finely creative unfolding of the humanists' theories Nanna's understanding of love is earthly bound, nourished by material comforts and driven by them.

Nanna's first six hours in the convent are marked initially by her passive behavior. She is puzzled by and tries to grasp what is taking place around her. In so doing, she faces the difficult choices and experiences of conflicting emotions that confront a still innocent young woman. She takes in the erotic drawings depicting Saint Nafissa's achievements and then spies, through a fissure in the wall of her cell, her fellow-nuns who industriously sate their sexual appetite: "e levatami in piedi, accosto l'orecchia ad una fessura; e perché nell'oscuro si vede meglio con un occhio che con dui, chiuso il mancino, e fisando il dritto nel foro che era fra mattone e mattone, veggio . . . in una cella quattro suore, il generale e tre fratrini di latte e di sangue, i quali spogliaro il reverendo padre . . . (che) parlando per 'ti' e per 'mi,' si diede a passeggiare sul passo grave di Bartolameo Coglioni" ("Rising to my feet, I put my eye to a crack in the wall, and since one sees better in the dark with one eye rather than two, I stood on tiptoe . . . In the cell I saw four sisters, the General, and three milky-white and ruby-red young friars, who were taking off the reverend father's cassock . . . then . . . the blissful General, to speak frankly, started strutting back and forth with the big-balled stride of a Bartolomeo Colleoni") (19). The sexual activities in which the other nuns revel with their male visitors in their cells seem at once peculiar and wicked to Nanna. But as she closes her left eye to better focus on the action unfolding in front of her, one could imagine Aretino's mischievous wink at his audience.

In her narration to Antonia, Nanna quickly explains that what she saw at that point is the norm for the monastery. Yet, the dislocation of expectations her initial discovery brings about underscores her original ingenuousness. Although still unsure of where she stands morally, Nanna understands that the idea of monastic life is irreconcilable with the behavior she witnesses. Nonetheless, the desire to become fully integrated in the closed system she has been forced to join, paired with the curiosity and desire to taste for herself what she is told is the dazzling sweetness of the pleasure of the flesh, becomes more irresistible than any prejudice she may hold against emulating her fellow-nuns. Gripped by the curiosity their actions unleash in her, Nanna is drawn to follow their example. Her eagerness to savor "i frutti paradisi" (the fruits of earthly paradise) (13) and relish for herself the sense of completeness that she witnesses in the other nuns, Nanna turns into a new Eve. By trying that which she has never tasted, she consciously oversteps the narrow limits set by the artificiality of the constructed system of which she has unwittingly been made part. Aretino's Eve—Nanna—like her biblical antecedent, negotiates for herself her desires and the terms in which they can be satisfied. But here too Aretino toys with the biblical precursor. The "fruit" or object that causes Nanna's sexual-awakening is not produced by a tree, but is an artificial phallic-shaped glass object. Yet again, the universe of artificiality that collides head on with that of nature resurfaces. And this gives Aretino another opportunity to criticize the hypocrisy that envelops every aspect of religious life.

Life in the convent does not lead Nanna to a spiritual awakening—at least not the type of spirituality that theologians and philosophers praise. That all the nuns received the phallus-like objects as gifts—and quickly put them to their intended use, describing them as "fruits of paradise" confirms this. The particular gift is a further proof of the sensual world the nuns inhabit, and it gives the full measure of the lewd and vulgar environment the unschooled Nanna is discovering. The monastery she has entered is no utopian paradise brought down by Eve's insatiable curiosity; instead, it is a space vibrant with human energy and sizzling with impulses and desires. In it, the new Eve-Nanna, more than just discovering her sexuality, learns about the shortsightedness of rules that repress human wants. Further, the food it provides is not spiritual, but physical. Because of this, the convent turns into a place where, paradoxically, the spiritual is reconciled with the physical. With this comes Nanna's full and precise understanding of the larger discrepancy, the knot of contradiction, between public façade and personal desires. Her realization that common perception incorrectly associates nuns' lives with sacrifices and abstinences is a catalyst for her repudiation of the spiritual purpose of the convent. Her fellow-nuns and their mates can neither repress nor deprive themselves of physical pleasures; instead, they balance the world of privations in which they are forced to live with the world of plenty they secretly construct for their gratifications. Both the lavish food they consume and the erotic games they engage in reveal their disinterest in and contempt for the rigorous lifestyle their roles demand. In Nanna's words, the hypocritical duplicity between reality and appearances results in her decision to pursue another vocation. As a matter of fact, her stay in the convent is followed by a short stretch in the role of wife. But ultimately, she opts to become a courtesan.

Eve's biblical model laden with obscure symbolism and metaphorical language is made clear through Aretino's straightforward and inventive rendition. His intention to provide a lively and precise picture of the contradiction between reality and theory emboldens him to articulate with meticulous precision the events taking place in a forced earthly paradise. Without distorting the truth or affecting it with elaborate words Aretino shows that, like Eve, Nanna discovers her sexual persona not through what she eats but through what she uncovers in her understanding of convent life. Her new awareness, brought about by the crudeness of the activities surrounding her, dictates that life demands much more than order, rules, and contentment. Because this awareness echoes the brutality and even the pain of human existence, it is startling, beautiful, and incredible, at odds with cultural circumstances and, at first, even distasteful. For the newly "educated" Nanna, it entails, first of all, the satisfaction of bodily wants that go hand in hand with spiritual needs. More importantly, both necessitate the free run of imagination and ideas.

This understanding informs the image of Pyramus and Thysbe that Nanna evokes. By fusing food and lust as a frame of reference for both the nuns' sexual trysts and the chaste if tragic love of the Ovidian characters, Nanna tramples upon the meaning regularly ascribed to the myth. This fact shapes an arresting, but not entirely surprising, new set of implications for the myth. In the classical love story tragedy befalls the lovers when one of them believes that the other has become a beast's meal. Because from its earliest beginnings Christian exegesis regarded gluttony and lust as sins sprouting from the same root, man's inability for self-control and desire to exceed the limits set for him, what lies beyond Pyramus's discovery is not just a false negative—Thysbe is not dead—but more precisely the frustrating sense of hopelessness, the unexpected loss of power and control that he has thus far experienced over events and, especially, over another individual. Although in the Ovidian myth food and desire are traditionally regarded as the ingredients exemplifying power, through Nanna Aretino suggests that there is yet another side to the myth—like the less dazzling side of the papal courts he knows. This side denotes, among other things, powerlessness, a profound isolation, the despair of one psychologically wounded, and the incapacity to reestablish a desired order. To Pyramus, as Nanna intimates through her juxtaposition, Thysbe's blood-stained veil suggests that she has been deflowered, physically possessed, by one whose desire to gratify the senses was greater than self-control and who—unlike Pyramus—could not restrain his appetite for her.[73] Accordingly, to explain Pyramus's self-inflicted death in Aretino's text solely as resulting from the grief caused by her death and by his inability to envision life without Thysbe's love is to foster the illusion that human nature can be compressed into one simple layer of rules and that its desires are always linear and not more complex. This awareness informs the new understanding of the stained veil's sexual implications. As a sign and symbol of her lost virginity the veil reveals to Pyramus the ambiguity and ambivalence of the world beyond its familiar limits. It also especially undercuts the moral certainty of his actions that he has—mistakenly—taken for granted.

Accordingly, Pyramus's inability to function in a universe of competing values, where what he thought was his, is taken by another, brings about his emotional undoing. If, then, on a literal level Pyramus's death is precipitated by his refusal to share his life with one whose virginity has been tasted and—in Pyramus's view—spoiled by another, in a figurative sense, through Nanna's rendition, the myth hints at more complex implications. It speaks of one's unwillingness to compromise his ambition even though it has been derailed by circumstances beyond his control. It also speaks of one's reluctance to be part of a new system in which another individual, through untamed and even brutal means, suddenly overtakes power and, by wielding it, subjugates those who previously possessed it. To be forcefully relegated to a powerless position after having occupied a powerful one, as at first Pyramus had in his ostensibly unrivaled love for Thysbe, illustrates the declining force of a dominating power. Naturally, this also entails the notion of wounded manhood, wrecked self-esteem, and loss of self-control, all of which potentially lead to self-destruction.

The political inferences that this reinterpretation of the myth present could not be lost on Aretino.[74] The Rome of the 1520s, so unrestrained in matters of consumption, so unabashed in its display of frenzied greed, and so certain of the unassailable nature of its own power, was soon to discover the unexpected but not unforeseeable effects of its pernicious actions. The full impact of its political collapse and the loss of its power made the reversal of its fortune all the more stinging. Pope Clement never fathomed the possibility of turning into a captive of Charles V. On the contrary, he firmly believed in the sacredness of power his position commanded.[75] Failing that, he trusted in his ability to barter for himself a secure spot in the chain of worldly power-wielding leaders.[76] Confident that Florence with the forces of the League gathered nearby[77] would engage the German and Spanish troops and disperse them, thus removing Rome from military danger, Clement failed to see the real danger in which he and his city were thrown. Wrongly convinced, like Pyramus, that his power could not be seized from him because it belonged solely to him, Clement was quickly overwhelmed when the events took a different turn. The historical implications that Nanna unveils as she retrieves the figures of Pyramus and Thysbe make it impossible to read the Ovidian myth as the dispersive and desperate nature of love that in its purest form, unencumbered by the allure of physical materialism, privileges a spiritual vitality. This form of self-control stands out against Aristotle's *akrasia* that the curia favors. In this construct, Pyramus's love, placing its fulfillment in death, is a bittersweet pleasure that in part echoes Valla's discourse of celestial pleasures to be savored after the earthly ones have been spurned. But this reading is not compatible with Aretino's intensely carnal universe. His "new" Pyramus calls to mind the dispossession of ownership—what one wrongly assumes to be one's own possession. The image of the innocent young woman defiled by a brute also serves to cast Nanna's personal experience in a new light. And as her hosts and their guests consume the copious banquet they become, albeit figuratively, the devouring beasts gnawing not only at the principles the Ovidian lovers personify, but especially at the innocence that accompanied young Nanna in the convent. She, on the contrary, as the young novice whose body the Baccelliere will try to sexually devour soon after the initial banquet in the convent, embodies Thysbe's innocence. Prior to this, Nanna has never experienced sexual relations. As she explains to Antonia during the course of their conversation, when the Baccelliere is called away to attend to other business, she deflowers herself with the phallic-shaped glass object that she was gifted at the banquet with the other nuns. Through the image of the innocent girl deflowering herself, Aretino captures two potent images. On the one hand, there is the sociocultural image of the physical materiality that the convent fosters. Through this image, the place in which the search for "spiritual" truths should eclipse material wants is revealed in its utter crudeness. This is a world galvanized by sheer self-centeredness. The second image that Aretino's description evokes is linked to the first, yet it is politically charged and, because of this, it directly mirrors the curia's self-inflicted undoing. Its attachment to the worldly comes at the cost of the spiritual values. This shift in perspectives and attitudes fanned the anti-curial sentiment that led to Protestant unrest.[78]

But Nanna's seemingly incongruous reference to Pyramus and Thysbe also calls to mind the religious tension brewing during Aretino's times. The German Reformers were stirring up animosity against the Church and its representatives[79] and in their attacks against the Church and the curial fondness for material wealth, they criticized artistic forms that, in their perception, brought pleasure to the senses. Visual arts and music became the immediate targets.[80] In his condemnation of the appropriateness of music in religious settings Andreas Karlstadt explained: "the lascivious notes of the organ awaken thoughts of the world. When we should be meditating on the suffering of Christ, we are reminded of Pyramus and Thysbe."[81] Clearly, in his theory, the two lovers only typify the sensual aspect of human nature. Yet by relying on the Ovidian myth to articulate his stern objection to the physical element of human experience, this German Reformer shows an unforgiving attitude with regard to human nature. More specifically, his critique seems to suggest that the universe of human experiences must be contained and regulated by strict behaviors. This, as Aretino demonstrates, is simply unrealistic. Karlstadt's life and works closely intertwined with those of Martin Luther. Also, he experienced firsthand the church's pervasive depravity in a visit to Rome in the early 1500s. In his *Disputation* Karlstadt condemned music in particular because it "puts a distance between the mind and God." Along with music, he also denounced visual arts in general. He claimed that these, as means to complement and enhance the spiritual experience of the believer, appealed to the senses. This fact, in his view, removed the spiritual element from the religious experience. That Aretino knew of Karlstadt and of the threat that the German theologian's views posed to the Church is unquestionable. That he was also aware of the Reformer's theory that "it would be better that oaths were discarded because through oaths no one becomes better; many, however, become worse," which he pronounced as early as 1521, is also beyond doubt.[82] Aretino's familiarity with the papal inner circle, and his own attempts to play an important role particularly within the court of Clement VII, lends strong support to the fact that he had intimate knowledge of the volatile situation existing in Germany and of the tension that the sale of papal indulgences caused with Reformers whose criticism of the pope was growing increasingly louder. In the wake of Karlstadt's remark, Nanna's analogy with

Pyramus and Thysbe becomes all the more poignant. By citing this myth, she unwittingly, perhaps, lends her voice to the objections raised by Reformers and presents a reality that tests the fragility of the misguided papal policies.

III

Returning to the banquet she describes for Antonia, we see that Nanna does not list the specific foodstuffs served. She does point out that once their hunger is satisfied the commensals amuse themselves: "scegliendo le punte delle ali di galline e alcune creste e qualche capo, e porgendo l'uno a l'altra e l'altra a l'uno ... e le risa e le voci che si udivano nel donare un culo di cappone, nè sarebbe possibile dire le dispute che sopra di ciò si faceano" ("they began picking and choosing the tender tops of chicken wings, combs, and heads and offering them to each other ... And I could not even begin to tell how they roared with laughter when they presented the capon's ass") (13). The playfulness that satiety leads to shifts the focus from food to body or, from gluttony to lust. Quite naturally, this shift also entails one from theology to politics. It appears that in the gastronomic index followed by the religious people Nanna has found, chickens' and capons' heads, combs, rumps, and wing tips are sought-after tidbits. The fact that proportionally they are just few morsels, not enough to please many people, makes them even more in demand. And supply always regulates demand. But the game's sexual innuendos foreshadow the sexual pleasures in which— to Nanna's incredulous eyes—the group of nuns, friars, monks, and prelates soon revels in and during which human bodies and their parts, like those of chickens and capons, are offered and enjoyed.

According to Ficino, chicken and capon meat is best suited to keep a learned person's health under check because it is of *mediae* moisture.[83] His whole theory to ensure the equilibrium of humors that prevents the black bile that brings on melancholy and results in a long life hinges on a strict dietetic regimen. In books 1 and 2 Ficino focuses on regimens and therapies that preserve his audience's health. For this purpose, he prescribes consuming the interiors and the extremities of chickens and capons because, in his view, they strengthen one's health, prolong one's life, and restore one's spirit.[84] But in book 3 of his *De vita*, he moves toward the more controversial part of his work. Here he discusses the effects of celestial influences on earthly products and claims that, when the products are consumed, those celestial influences they retain have an enduring effect on the consumers' bodies. Yet again, in this section of the treatise Ficino reiterates that chicken and capon meat brings a "solar" and "Jovial" temperament to both the human spirit and the human body. Both joviality and a solar attitude are necessary, he states, to preserve youth and health in the elderly.[85] It is for this same reason, however, that as early as book 1 he resolutely discourages sexual intercourse, for "it suddenly drains the spirits, especially the more subtle ones, it weakens the brain, and it ruins the stomach and the heart."[86] Not surprisingly, Aretino's Nanna reveals a deeply different perspective from Ficino's theories. She is an unlearned woman and thus the "other side," or the negative counterpart, of the learned men who are the focus of Ficino's study.

But besides the gendered, cultural, and social divide separating Nanna from Ficino's audience, the philosopher's advice conjures up images of a highly affected, laboriously coded lifestyle. This is achieved by living according to contrived rules that shun the natural world and, implicitly, the world of truth. By intentionally eschewing the world of sensual pleasure that is part and parcel of human nature, Ficino effectively devises an unnatural universe. The sensual restraint he upholds, his claim that in order to pursue loftier ideals lives must be sheltered not just from external events but especially from natural needs, engenders a sense of artificiality. This chips away at the reliability of the advice he purports to dispense; it also especially raises questions as to his credibility as doctor. His claim that the influence of celestial rays can improve human health, guard against all manner of illnesses, and safeguard the interest of the privileged few spurns life's most natural characteristics. Thus, his theory leaves the central aspects of human nature unexplored. Early on Pulci too had recognized and criticized this shortsightedness in Ficino's theories. Indeed, throughout the *Morgante*, in his portrayal of the philosopher's questionable values, ideas, truths, and religious beliefs Pulci bitterly derided him.

In his *Dialogo della Pittura*, written in 1557, Ludovico Dolce directly confutes Giorgio Vasari's assertion that Michelangelo was the greatest painter of the time.[87] Staged as a conversation between Aretino as the main interlocutor (and undoubtedly the one who inspired it) and Giovan Francesco Fabrini, Dolce's dialogue offers a new perspective on Italian painters through the analysis of "invention, design and coloring."[88] Through Aretino, Dolce maintains that these three elements are the constitutive parts of painting. In the dialogue, although Aretino concedes that Michelangelo is a great artist,[89] he concludes that Raphael's and Titian's mastery of invention, design, and coloring makes them, not Michelangelo, the most accomplished painters. While the critique of Vasari's (biased) preference for Michelangelo is Dolce's point of departure (Vasari had been a student of Michelangelo) the *Dialogo* forcefully speaks to, and about, the irreducible link between painting and literature.[90] Most importantly, however, throughout the dialogue Aretino argues with thematic coherence that "truth" and "natural" define excellence in both painting and literature. "Art is the hiding of art's presence,"[91] he asserts. Truth, he explains, "non si dee tacere" (truth should be spoken out)[92] even though it comes at a high, personal price.[93] With this pointed self-referential claim, in Dolce's dialogue Aretino insists that affectation does not denote excellence. On the contrary, by subscribing to it, he argues, both painters and poets[94] betray reality as nature presents it. For Dolce's Aretino, a painter (or a poet) who excels is one gifted to "rappresentare con l'arte qualunque cosa, talmente simile alle diverse opere della natura, ch'ella paia vera" (represent with his artistry objects of all sorts, and to render them so similar to nature in all its diversity that they appear real).[95] Aretino's assertions in the *Dialogo* make it clear that only a masterful writer or painter can recapture the effortless and varied beauty that nature produces.

This notion surfaces in more explicit terms in a letter Aretino addressed to his friend Dolce years before the publication of the *Dialogo*. In it, the writer maintains that the artist becomes a "secretary" to the beauty that nature effortlessly creates.[96] With typical caustic language, in the letter Aretino emphasizes the exquisite plainness of nature's creations. This, he stresses, is what must take place in both painting and poetry in order to seamlessly transpose on canvases or translate onto pages the truths by which every artist is surrounded. By claiming to be the secretary of nature's unadorned beauty, Aretino intimates not only that he is the keeper of its secrets, as the word "secretary" suggests, but especially that his talent lends him the authority to advise others about them. This position of privilege, as it were, of the artist who can guide others to truths that are known to him alone, casts a great artist as powerful beyond measure. Although it appears that with this sweeping claim he is specifically taking on artistic issues that establish the legitimacy of his unmatched finesse, in truth Aretino's words are casting a wider net. To begin with, on the linguistic level, his recommendation not to spoil language by using foreign expressions recasts anew the critique of affectation by recalling Castiglione's *Cortigiano*. The newness of Aretino's discourse is based on his explanation that to develop into a masterful carver and caster of human emotions, the writer must forgo elaborate but ineffectual words. Instead, through a linguistic system that is simultaneously poetic and unpretentious, the writer must humanize individuals by capturing the ostensibly unattainable: the complex ambiguity defining every human being in its elaborate simplicity. According to Aretino, the artist must then set what he gives life to into the fabric of history that is rife with unquenchable passions, wars, betrayals, losses, and political machinations. Through this, the vaster implications of Aretino's discourse that examines the relationship between individuals and their historical context become clear.

Aretino's insistence that poets and painters must not betray nature's example, but must instead faithfully portray reality in all of its cruelty, sufferance, and beauty, hinges on his understanding that art is a means through which human achievements and failures are illustrated as a way to educate. The role he assigns to Nanna is precisely one that recaptures images and events distilled from the experience of her convent days and his Roman stay. She recounts them as they occurred, using her ordinary and lowly language. The language the author chooses is neither sweetened nor embellished with pretentious jargon. But this style has a powerful effect because it is both hard and brutal and yet charged with human emotions. Naturally, this resonates with Aretino's idea that the artist is charged with conveying in an earnest manner, without altering the subtleties, the many levels of truth reality presents. His assertion about "art that hides the art" in Dolce's *Dialogo* further substantiates this belief.

Looking backward to recount her discovery of the nuns' world for Antonia, Nanna captures the coarse contradictions and inequalities that are an integral part of a lopsided and repressed society. This is one that cunningly tries to disguise its flaws. Yet, precisely because it tries to hide them, they become more conspicuous.[97] Indeed, by depicting the events taking place in the convent and describing them in their crude realism through Nanna, Aretino translates with precision onto the pages the reality that engulfs Roman society. More specifically, the facts she describes tap into the deep reserves of the author's personal experiences with the Roman curia. For while on the one hand the young novice's precise account paints a depraved picture of prelates', priests', and nuns' erotic trysts, on the other it pokes holes at the probity of religious life.

Tellingly, as Nanna engages Antonia with gusto in her description of religious life and squashes the confected perceptions the latter (and the readers) might have about it, Aretino documents the traits of a disenchanted world. And the disillusion about it, revealed in an unforeseen way by a novice turned courtesan and her friend, follows with cruel speed. Aretino registers this shift especially through Antonia. She has not experienced convent life directly; yet as Nanna's kindred spirit, and fellow-courtesan, she shares her friend's taste for finding meaning in the universe that surrounds her. In agreement with Nanna, because this is how they both have experienced it, for Antonia too, meaning comes from power. By contrast, women are synonymous with powerlessness; it is this awareness that has enabled them to imagine, and even realize, a life outside their prescribed roles. Accordingly, while Antonia's tart comments to the events Nanna recounts accentuate the gravity of the malaise that afflicts the Church hierarchy and spills out into society, they also suggest that to wrestle with a disenchanted world is fruitless.[98] Grappling with it neither eliminates nor solves issues that arise from basic needs. Instead, it dehumanizes people. With remarkable elasticity people turn into pawns of their wants because unmet needs result in wants. This the two courtesan-friends know from experience. As for the artist, whose talent is gauged in the measure in which he is able to capture the world of needs and convey its dispirited purposelessness to others, he must strive to create an authentic depiction of it. This accurate portrayal requires that he not do away with the natural human desires pervading it, however salacious they might be, because desires drive every human action. As he describes women and men whose wants have been forcibly bridled by financial calculations, Aretino unmasks the futility of oaths, as Karlstadt had voiced in his letter of 1521. Through this, he shows that by going against natural wants humanity turns its natural desires into depraved ones.

Despite the unpalatable taste Nanna's descriptions may leave, through her Aretino conveys the interplay of ambitions, jealousy, and slyness that exists in all rungs of the human ladder. In so doing he represents the wholeness of human nature thrust against the irrevocability of historical events. His acerbic critique of society in general and of the curia in particular is unequalled. His fiery words are pointed especially against the curia whose actions are impervious to Jesus' teachings. By straying from and trampling on the principles He embodied, it has made more than manifest its hollow purpose. The desire for power fueling its territorial expansions and personal aggrandizement are made at a cost that exceedingly surpasses any spiritual advancement. Its original mission is changed to the point that it no longer serves any ethical or moral purpose. Aretino conveys with persuasion the disillusionment that people feel in their spiritual leaders who have upended the very precepts on which their roles were founded. His awareness that human nature is not depraved, but that its complexity cannot be adumbrated or camouflaged by superimposing on it sets of convenient sociocultural norms surfaces in his depiction of Nanna's story. This, without exaggeration or artifice, mirrors the world he finds in Rome. The portrait of society Aretino paints is, in the end, one beset by deceitfulness and self-perpetuating greed: in it, obscene acts, abuses of power, and subversion of rules are the norm. Worse yet, this is a society riven at its core with personal animosities that spill out into political conflicts. By failing to acknowledge its corrupt and corrupting ways, it progressively moves toward its own undoing. In Nanna's personal recipe book food and sex, or better yet, their lack or abundance, and the dissatisfaction or pleasures they provide become ingredients that must be cautiously measured to lead fulfilling lives.

Clearly, Aretino provides these details to accentuate Nanna's deliberate transgression. Tweaking Pico's celebrated characterization of the dignity of man, as well as Alberti's fundamental idea of virtue,[99] in the same way in which he inverts Bembo's love triad, Nanna freely and with self-determination chooses for her daughter to become a courtesan. Through this choice she pursues the future by means of the past, defying yet again the values her society ostensibly holds as norms. In effect, her unconventional decision shows that she possesses a fluid sense of adaptation; thus she adjusts to, and even finds meaning in the cultural circumstances shaping her world. Through her decision she becomes a woman of her own making, one who is both genuine in her unpretentiousness and visceral in her awareness that the tentacles of power are swayed through power. Because she is capable of an incredibly precise analysis of the events she witnesses, eloquent, and above all unafraid of the complexities and contradictions her decision entails, Nanna's audacity mirrors her creator's. Like him, she dexterously navigates the treacherous financial and political waters of her times because the experience of poverty she has already absorbed drives her to action. Like him, she aspires to much more than she has. Like him, when honest means fail her, she resorts to other expedients to turn events in her favor. The fact that, like her author, she is not born into wealth and power is a reminder of how wrenching the freedom to shape one's future can be when one is shackled to a position of powerlessness.[100] In point of fact, through Nanna's choice, played on the tune of food and its symbolic imagery, Aretino shows that, generally, in a world lacking principled foundations, the views of truths, language, and self cannot be mirrors of reality. Instead, they are fictions through which the purposelessness of norms that look to regulate human behavior is explored. As his Nanna demonstrates, reality—however complicated or uncertain it might be—is shaped by people and events, and these can both be incessantly deceptive. To challenge them demands mustering the courage to operate within the constraints of social norms while exposing their sordid essence. In this manner, social codes are revealed for what they really are: masks employed to shroud flows and failures. This understanding invites a renewed appreciation for the way in which Nanna (and Aretino) grapples with the centripetal forces defining society. And although their respective impetus to call into question those forces may be interpreted solely as spurred by self-interest, and for that reason hypocritical, Nanna's (and Aretino's) predicaments and resulting transformations attest to a continuous struggle that involves adapting and adjusting to the sociocultural politics of her age. As times and mores shift, change, decline, and fade the figure of Aretino and of his heroine remain standing: the images of sureness, self-control, and resilience.

Conclusion
Is It Food for Fiction or Food for History?

Analyzing food within the context of the semiotic system, Roland Barthes asserts that what one eats is not just a series of ingredients and products. To the contrary, he argues that food is "a system of communication, a body of images," a defined—and, one could add, frequently a refined—"protocol of uses, situations, and behaviors."[1] Based on this, he maintains that food is an alimentary language. According to him, this language inherently possesses the same properties as a verbal one. As such, it includes, among other things, rules of exclusions as well as of associations. The rhetoric of this language, Barthes contends, surfaces in the rituals of food uses. To this end, he explains that buying, consuming, or offering specific foodstuffs summarizes and "transmits a situation."[2] Thus, he affirms that on the scale of values, the nourishment food provides occupies the bottom rung. For him, the more important value of food rests on the messages it conveys within the system of communication it establishes between and among consumers. One could argue that in this respect Barthes follows Giovanni Boccaccio's marchioness of Monferrato's deep and accurate understanding of food as conveyor of meaningful information.

Barthes's discourse, developed in the wake of Claude Lévi-Strauss's anthropological work, lends modern cogency to the notion that foodstuff stands for much more than nutritional usefulness. As the French philosopher emphasizes, food presents and signifies an entire world and social environment, while it also "*has a constant tendency to transform itself into situation.*"[3] Understood in terms of sign and system capable of capturing as well as of defining situations and events, food and its rhetorical functions within any historical context cannot be regarded as inferior to words. On the contrary, they illustrate the absorption of a whole system of sociocultural values. The marchioness of Monferrato's story exemplifies this point. The awareness that food is a code used to decipher meanings broadens the metaphorical implications that it holds in any given time. Juxtaposed to situations, events, cultures, and people preparing, consuming, or offering it, the ostensible ordinariness of foodstuff turns into the commentary on a complex if unspoken set of beliefs and way of life. There is a paradox, however, in the gastronomic system food engenders: while a culture always determines its gastronomic preferences, they, in turn, shape a culture. This phenomenon emerges in all the works analyzed in this book. Still, as a sign and symbol of the unstated, the gastronomic code manifests itself in life as well as literature. And in both instances it transcends the personal to embrace the universal.

Throughout this book I have argued that the medieval and Renaissance literary discourse on food is unequivocally circumscribed by social, cultural, political, and theological boundaries. Historically, it retrieves the convivial atmosphere of Boccaccio's *Decameron*. There the *vivande* served and consumed in the *novelle* analyzed are the immediate referent for the cast of characters that through food define themselves, their actions, and their cultures. Although with a more ironic tone, in these *novelle* food also retrieves Dante's stern judgment on gluttony in *Inferno*, 6 and *Purgatorio*, 24. Yet within these boundaries, the discourse on food operates unproblematically through the concepts of social ethics, metaphorical values, and literary traditions. But just as in Boccaccio's *novelle*, in Luigi Pulci's, Matteo Maria Boiardo's, Ludovico Ariosto's, and Pietro Aretino's respective works, food becomes an incisive commentary on the authors' cultures. At the same time, it is also a bittersweet assessment of the human condition. Through food, these authors voice the incongruities, limitations, and hollowness of rigid rules and philosophical abstractions their societies espouse. Indeed, although these authors are clearly distinct individuals with eclectic interests, tastes, and personalities, in their respective works food invariably brings out the intensely personal and reassuringly universal timelessness of human concerns: ambitions and frustrations, loves and losses, freedom and dependency, power and weakness. As these authors are acutely aware, these "ingredients"—these struggles—among others, shape the human condition and, by extension, human history. Through food, they add meanings and nuances to the events they narrate—sometimes with a bitingly wry and ironic tone, sometimes with a more tolerant one.

On one level, this occurs when these authors suggest that cooks' inventiveness turns common ingredients into refreshingly innovative dishes. The transformations the ingredients undergo enable the authors to demonstrate that through imagination, which often stokes the fire of social discontent that leads to changes, sociopolitical shifts occur. On another level, the authors also make it clear that basic food ingredients without undergoing elaborate preparations still convey precise messages. Like elaborately prepared dishes, plain ingredients too are manifestations of, and speak to the perception of values and the social, political, and philosophical currents of the times in which they are consumed. Therefore, in terms of metaphorical values food, in the works examined, establishes a symmetrical balance among the universes of the marchioness of Monferrato and the king of France, Alibech and Rustico, the courtesans Nanna and Antonia, the enchantress Alcina, and Orlando and Rinaldo. Mirrored and legitimized in this symmetry are the social positions and historical contexts of both the characters and their authors. More importantly, in this symmetry the language of food is the language of encoded messages, of palatable words, and of human desires. On their own, these defy and challenge political, theological, and philosophical discourses. Through them, ladies as well as prostitutes, paladins as well as enchantresses, hermits as well as lovers, and cooks as well as writers and poets make their culture manifest. Lévi-Strauss's assertion that "the cooking of a society is a language in which it unconsciously translates its structures, or else resigns itself, still unconsciously, to reveal its contradictions"[4] sums up this idea.

Clearly, both Lévi-Strauss's and Barthes's analyses suggest that food is a reliable register of meanings that transact social conventions. Francesco Guicciardini made this connection, articulating it in terms of language, architecture, and fashion at the dawn of modernity. Before his pronouncement, however, Boccaccio, Pulci, and Boiardo brilliantly made this understanding their own. After Guicciardini, Ariosto and Aretino, in the tradition of their predecessors, also used food as another powerful tool of their artistic arsenal. Like talented cooks taking delight in toying with and defying their readers and consumers' expectations, these authors relied on food as another means to explore the more hidden sides of human behavior in their respective works. In the end, whether they preceded or followed Guicciardini's assertion, these writers and poets in their respective works show that "eating the times" does mean taking in and on the specific sociocultural and historical currents of a given epoch. At the same time, they also demonstrate that for a small, self-conscious, and epoch-making elite, "savoring power" means—not so figuratively, after all—relishing the flavors that power affords. And this is food for history even if depicted in fiction.

NOTES

Introduction

1. Francesco Guicciardini, *Maxims and Reflections*, trans. Mario Domandi (Philadelphia: University of Pennsylvania Press, 1965), 69. "Se voi osservate bene, vedrete che di età in età, non solo si mutano e modi del parlare e i vocaboli, gli abiti del vestire, gli ordini dello edificare, della cultura e cose simili, ma quello che è più, e gusti ancora, in modo che uno cibo che è stato in prezzo in una età è spesso stimato manco nell'altro." Idem, *Ricordi*, intro. and comm. Emilio Pasquini (Milan: Garzanti, 1975), 91.

2. As Emanuella Scarano Lugnani points out, there were five redactions of Guicciardini's *Ricordi*. The first two date back to 1512; the third, from around 1525; the fourth, from 1528; and the fifth, from 1530. *Guicciardini e la crisi del Rinascimento* (Rome and Bari: Laterza, 1973), 61.

3. Leon Battista Alberti, *On the Art of Building in Ten Books*, trans. Joseph Rykwert, Neil Leach, and Robert Tavernor (Cambridge, MA, and London: MIT, 1990), 18.

4. For works on building and architecture that preceded Alberti's, see Caroline van Eck, "The Structure of 'De re aedificatoria' Reconsidered," *Journal of the Society of Architectural Historians* 57, no. 3 (1998): 280–297.

5. On the reception of Vitruvius's treatise among humanists in the Quattrocento, see Hubertus Günther, "Alberti, gli umanisti contemporanei e Vitruvio," *Leon Battista Alberti: Architettura e cultura. Atti del Convegno internazionale, Mantova 16–19 novembre 1994* (Florence: L. S. Olschki, 1999), 33–44.

6. Alberti, *On the Art of Building in Ten Books*, 10.

7. "No building of the ancients that had attracted praise, wherever it might be, but I immediately examined it carefully, to see what I could learn from it. Therefore, I never stopped exploring, considering, and measuring everything, and comparing the information through line drawings, until I had grasped and understood fully what each had to contribute in terms of ingenuity or skill." Ibid., 6.1.154–155.

8. On this topic Arnaldo Bruschi defines Alberti's architecture as "la costruzione di un nuovo 'codice dell'architettura' (generale; non solo linguistico, stilistico) fondato sulla Natura e sulla Ragione, rispetto al quale gli Antichi si

pongono, più che come modello da imitare, come esempio e come guida. Non dunque la restituzione di un'architettura veramente 'antica' ma la proposta di un'architettura almeno tendenzialmente 'moderna' che avesse tutta la dignità, la sapienza costruttiva ed espressiva, la logicità e la duttilità, la ricchezza e l' 'ornamento' di quella antica" (the construction of a new architectural code [general, not only linguistic, stylistic] based on Nature and Religion, against which the ancients stand more as example and guide than as a model to imitate. The new code is not the return to ancient architecture, rather, it is at least a proposal for what is potentially modern and possessing the dignity, wisdom, and expressivity of construction, the logic and adaptability, the richness and the "ornament" of the ancient). "Sull'Alberti architetto," *Leon Battista Alberti: Architettura e cultura. Atti del Convegno internazionale, Mantova 16–19 novembre 1994* (Florence: L. S. Olschki, 1999), 24.

9. Naturally, Alberti was also concerned with establishing his own reputation and fame as an architect in the Florence that hailed Filippo Brunelleschi as the "father" of Renaissance architecture. To this end, see Marvin Trachtenberg, "An Observation on Alberti's Choice of Antique Models: The Anxious Shadow of a Brunelleschian Anti-Canon," *Leon Battista Alberti: Architettura e cultura. Atti del Convegno internazionale, Mantova 16–19 novembre* 1994 (Florence: L. S. Olschki, 1999), 71–77.

10. "There is no reason why we should follow their (other famous architects') design in our work, as though legally obliged; but rather, inspired by their example, we should strive to produce our own inventions, to rival, or, if possible to surpass the glory of theirs." Alberti, *On the Art of Building in Ten Books*, 1.9.24.

11. See Alina A. Payne, *The Architectural Treatise in the Italian Renaissance: Architectural Invention, Ornament, and Literary Culture* (New York: Cambridge University Press, 1999), 73.

12. Alberti, *On the Art of Building in Ten Books*, 6.1.154.

13. Ibid.

14. Speaking of Vitruvius's work, he writes: "His speech (was) such that the Latins might think that he wanted to appear Greek, while the Greeks would think that he babbled Latin. However, his text is evidence that he wrote neither Latin or Greek." Ibid.

15. For an insightful analysis of Alberti's poetic language, see Mario Martelli, "La lingua poetica di Leon Battista Alberti," *Leon Battista Alberti: Architettura e cultura. Atti del Convegno internazionale, Mantova 16–19 novembre 1994* (Florence: L. S. Olschki, 1999), 79–105.

16. On this, see Bruno Migliorini, *Storia della lingua italiana* (Florence: Sansoni Editore, 1983), 262.

17. Migliorini quotes from Alberti's prologue to the third book of *Della famiglia*, "forse e prudenti mi loderanno s'io, scrivendo in modo che ciascuno m'intenda, prima cerco giovare a molti che piacere a pochi: ché sai quanto siano pochissimi a questi dì e litterati" (wise men will perhaps praise me for choosing to

be of use to many, but writing so that everyone understands me, rather than to please just a few, for you know how few erudite people there are today). *The Alberti of Florence: Leon B. Alberti's Della famiglia.* trans., intro., and notes Guido A. Guarino (Lewisburg: Bucknell University Press, 1974), 161; and also from the *Teogenio,* "e parsemi da scrivere in modo ch'io fussi inteso da' miei non litteratissimi cittadini" (I decided to write in a way that I would be understood by my not so well-educated fellow-citizens) to underscore the Florentine's interest in restoring the *volgare* as a language appropriate to his times. Ibid., 262, and n. 3.

18. Ibid., 339–360; see also Bartolo Tommaso Sozzi, *Aspetti e momenti della questione linguistica* (Padua: Liviana, 1955); Maurizio Vitale, *La questione della lingua,* enhanced ed. (Palermo: Palumbo, 1978); idem, *La veneranda favella* (Naples: Morano, 1988).

19. This has been defined as the "libro-simbolo del classicismo cinquecentesco." See Carlo Dionisotti, *Pietro Bembo: Prose e Rime* (Turin: UTET, 1966), 9–56; see also Paolo Bongrani, "Appunti sulle '*Prose della volgar lingua*': In margine a una recente edizione," *Giornale storico della letteratura italiana* 159, no. 506 (1982): 271–290; Mario Pozzi, *Lingua, cultura, società: Saggi sulla letteratura italiana del Cinquecento* (Alexandria: Dell'Orso, 1989); and Paolo Trovato, *Storia della lingua italiana: Il primo Cinquecento* (Bologna: Il Mulino, 1994), 111–121.

20. Trovato, *Storia della lingua italiana,* 109. See also Giovan Giorgio Trissino, *Scritti linguistici,* ed. Alberto Castelvecchi (Rome: Salerno Editrice, 1986). For a thorough discussion of Dante's *De vulgari eloquentia,* see Albert Russell Ascoli, "'*Neminem ante nos*': Historicity and Authority in the *De vulgari eloquentia,*" *Annali d'italianstica* 8 (1990): 186–231; for a more detailed and updated discussion, see idem, *Dante and the Making of a Modern Author* (New York: Cambridge University Press, 2008), 130–174.

21. Carlo Dionisotti, *Machiavellerie: Storie e fortuna di Machiavelli* (Turin: Einaudi, 1980), 289–90 and 320.

22. Dionisotti has convincingly argued that Machiavelli composed the *Discorso* around 1524 in response to Trissino's theory: "bisogna credere dunque che il *Dialogo* non è posteriore all'ottobre del 1524" (it is fair to believe that the *Dialogo* was written prior to October 1524). Yet the manuscript circulated unpublished until 1730 because of Trissino's powerful political supporters. *Machiavellerie,* 326 and 332.

23. Niccolò Machiavelli, *Discorso o dialogo intorno alla nostra lingua,* ed., intro., notes, and app. Bortolo Tommaso Sozzi (Turin: Piccola Biblioteca Einaudi, 1976), 49.

24. "E che l'importanza di / questa lingua nella quale e tu, Dante, / scrivesti, e gli altri che vennono / prima e poi di te hanno scritto, sia / derivata da Firenze, lo dimostra esser / voi stati fiorentini, e nati in una / patria che parlava in modo, che si / poteva meglio che alcuna altra / accommodare a scrivere in versi e in prosa. / A che non si potevano accommodare / gli altri parlari d'Italia" (That the

importance of this language in which you, Dante, and those who came before and after you wrote, derives from Florence is proven by the fact that you were born Florentines. You were born in a land whose language better than any other lent itself to writing in verses and in prose. The same could not be said of other tongues of Italy). Ibid., 777b, 46–778a, 6.

25. "Gli è impossibile che l'arte possa piú de la natura" (It is impossible for Art to be more powerful than Nature), states Machiavelli with regard to those who imitate the Florentine in their works. Ibid., 777a, 51–52.

26. See Dionisotti, *Machiavellerie*, in particular, the chapters "Machiavelli letterato" and "Machiavelli e la lingua fiorentina." The English translation of the first chapter can be found in *Machiavelli and the Discourse of Literature*, ed. Albert R. Ascoli and Victoria Kahn (Ithaca and London: Cornell University Press, 1993), 17–51.

27. On the "subversive significance" of Folengo's work vis-à-vis Bembo, see Ivano Paccagnella, "Plurilinguismo letterario: Lingue, dialetti, linguaggi," *Letteratura italiana: II, Produzione e consumo* (Turin: Einaudi, 1983), 103–167; see also Christian Bec, Stefano Carrai, and Ivano Paccagnella, eds., *Scarpe grosse: Contadini in letteratura* (Turin: Tirrenia Stampatori, 1999).

28. This is not to suggest that Folengo's criticism focuses solely on language. His denunciation of Church practices, of political corruption, and in general of human selfishness and greed are all integral parts of *Baldus*. On this topic, see Anthony Presti Russell, "Epic Agon and the Strategy of Reform in Folengo and Rabelais," *Comparative Literature Studies* 34 (1997): 119–148.

29. Marcel Tetel, "Rabelais and Folengo," *Comparative Literature* 15, no. 4 (1963): 357.

30. On this, see Michel Jeanneret, *A Feast of Words: Banquets and Table Talk in the Renaissance*, trans. Jeremy Whiteley and Emma Hughes (Chicago: University of Chicago Press, 1991).

31. See Peggy Reeves Sanday, *Divine Hunger: Cannibalism as a Cultural System* (Cambridge: Cambridge University Press, 1986), 51.

32. "The ancients called every edifice (*aedificium*) a building (*aedes*). Some think 'building' (*aedes*) took its name from 'eating' (*edere*) something, giving an example from Plautus . . . Hence also edifice (*aedificium*) because it was first 'made for eating' (*ad edendum factum*)." *The Etymologies of Isidore of Seville*, trans. Stephen A. Barney, W. J. Lewis, J. A. Beach, and Oliver Berghof (Cambridge and New York: Cambridge University Press, 2006), 15.3.308.

33. Ann W. Astell, *Eating Beauty: The Eucharist and the Spiritual Arts of the Middle Ages* (Ithaca and London: Cornell University Press, 2006), 66.

34. For an excellent study on the Christian concept of the spiritual dimension of beauty, see Richard Viladesau, *Theological Aesthetics: God in Imagination, Beauty, and Art* (New York and Oxford: Oxford University Press, 1999), 103–140.

35. Astell, *Eating Beauty*, especially "Taste and See: The Eating of Beauty," 1–26.

36. Cristina Mazzoni has an insightful study on sweets that resemble artwork. See "Sweet Traditions and the Martyrdom of Saint Agatha," *The Women in God's Kitchen: Cooking, Eating, and Spiritual Writing* (New York and London: Continuum, 2005), 74–86.

37. In the *Rhetoric,* Aristotle states: "everything, too, is pleasant for which we have the appetite within us, since appetite is desire for pleasure" (1.11.16–18); also, "pleasure is the consciousness through the senses of a certain kind of emotion" (1.11.26–27). Here, among the irrational appetites, the philosopher lists "those originating in the body, such as the appetite for nourishment [hunger and thirst] . . . and those connected with taste and sex and sensations of touch in general; and those of smell, hearing, and vision" (1.11.21–24). In the *Nicomachean Ethics* he asserts: "excellence and the good man are the measure of each thing" (10.5.16–17). *The Complete Works of Aristotle*, 2 vols., ed. Jonathan Barnes (Princeton: Princeton University Press, 1984). According to Thomas Aquinas, concupiscence—lust, desire—opens the gate to sin: "to crave for a thing under the aspect of something delightful to the senses, wherein concupiscence properly consists, belongs to the concupiscible power." Thomas Aquinas, *Summa Theologica, First Complete American Edition in Three Volumes*, ed. and trans. Fathers of the English Dominican Province (New York, Boston, Cincinnati, Chicago, and San Francisco: Benziger Brothers, 1947), I-II, q. 31, a. 1. For Saint Thomas, concupiscence is "disgraceful" because it does not "follow the judgment of reason." II-II, q. 156. a. 4. Aquinas also differentiates between the desire for good actions and that for evil actions much in the same way as he draws a distinction between the pleasures of good actions and those of evil ones. In the end, for him desires for sensual pleasures—bodily pleasures—"hinder the use of reason." I-II, q. 34, a. 1. Accordingly, for Aquinas lust, which "consists essentially in exceeding the order and mode of reason in the matter of venereal acts . . . (is) without any doubt a sin." II-II, q. 154, a. 4.

38. Plato, for example, in *Republic,* 10, criticizes paintings as deceptive; in his later *Sophist* he consigns visual arts in general to the realm of misleading appearances. See Jerome J. Pollitt, *The Ancient View of Greek Art: Criticism, History and Terminology* (New Haven and London: Yale University Press, 1974), 46–47.

39. Thomas Aquinas distances himself from Aristotle who, in the *Nicomachean Ethics*, 2.2.22–24, states "the man who indulges in every pleasure and abstains from none becomes self-indulgent, while the man who shuns every pleasure, as boors do, becomes in a way insensible." For Saint Thomas, evil pleasure is one "whereby the appetite rests in that which is discordant from reason and the law of God." *Summa Theologica*, I-II, q. 34, a. 2.

40. Aquinas, *Summa Theologica*, I-II, q. 34, a. 1, reply obj. 3; *Nicomachean Ethics,* 7.12.25–26.

41. Claude Lévi-Strauss, *The Raw and the Cooked*, trans. J. and D. Weightman (Chicago: University of Chicago Press, 1969), 142. "The raw/cooked axis is characteristic of culture; the fresh/decayed one of nature, since cooking brings

about the cultural transformation of the raw, just as putrefaction is its natural transformation." See also *From Honey to Ashes*, trans. J. and D. Weightman (New York: Harper and Row, 1966), 323.

42. Some scholars consider this satire as part of the Menippean tradition. They base this conclusion on general similarities found between Petronius's *Satyricon* (of which the *Cena* is a part) and Varro's *Saturae Menippeae*. Other scholars, however, maintain that in spite of some correspondences with the works of Varro and Seneca, the source of Petronius's *Satyricon* cannot be considered part of the Menippean tradition. On this subject, see Raymond Astbury, "Petronius, P. Oxy. 3010, and Menippean Satire," *Classical Philology* 72 (1977): 22–31.

43. On banquets in antiquity, see, for instance, Beryl Rawson, "Banquets in Ancient Rome: Participation, Presentation and Perception," *Dining on Turtles: Food Feasts and Drinking in History*, ed. Diane Kirby and Tanja Luckins (New York: Palgrave Macmillan, 2007).

44. On the language of the freedmen in the *Cena*, see Ilaria Marchesi, "Traces of a Freed Language: Horace, Petronius, and the Rhetoric of Fable," *Classical Antiquity* 24 (2005): 307–330.

45. Trimalchio's literary acumen is carefully analyzed by Nicholas Horsfall, "The Use of Literacy and the *Cena Trimalchionis*: I," *Greece & Rome* 36 (1989): 74–89; see also J. P. Bodel, "The Freedmen in the Satyricon of Petronius" (PhD diss., University of Michigan, 1984).

46. "Don't imagine I have despised studies, I have got two libraries, one of Greek books, the other of Latin," boasts Trimalchio. Petronius Arbiter, *Cena Trimalchionis*, trans. and ed. Michael J. Ryan (London and Felling-on-Tine: Walter Scott, 1905), 63.

47. Anthony Grafton shows that this is the sign of Petronius's "unclassical" style. In tracing the vicissitudes of the *Cena*'s literary reception, the critic concurs with Pierre Petit that the language used by Petronius is "the Latin of low society, of 'plebeian and ignorant men,' women, and provincials." See "Petronius and Neo-Latin Satire: The Reception of the *Cena Trimalchionis*," *Journal of the Warburg and Courtauld Institutes* 53 (1990): 237–249.

48. "Thanks to the gods I don't have to buy it," brags Trimalchio about the wine served during the meal. In the same breath he boasts that "everything here, good and all as it is, comes from one of my outlying estates, which I never heard of till now." Petronius, *Cena Trimalchionis*, 63.

49. Horsfall, "Use of Literacy and the *Cena Trimalchionis*," 74.

50. Pliny the Elder, *Natural History*, trans. H. Rackham (Cambridge, MA: Harvard University Press; London: William Heinemann, 1940), bk. 8, 72, 207–209. In the following chapter Pliny discusses the practice of serving boar meat at banquets. According to him, the custom began with Publius Servilius Rullus. This practice, the historian asserts, persists in excessive forms: "wild boar has been a popular

luxury ... So recent is the origin of what is now an everyday affair ... when it is the fashion for two or three boars to be devoured at one time not even as a whole dinner but as the first course." Bk. 8, 78, 210.

51. Marco Tullio Cicero, *On Duties (De officiis)*, trans. Harry G. Edinger (Indianapolis and New York: Bobbs-Merrill, 1974), bk. 1, 17–18.

52. J. W. Joliffe, "Satire: Satira: Σάτupos. A Study in Confusion," *Bibliothèque d'Humanisme et Renaissance* 18 (1956): 84–95; Peter E. Medine, "Isaac Casaubon's Prolegomena to the 'Satires' of Persius: An Introduction, Text, and Translation," *English Literary Renaissance* 6 (1976): 271–298.

53. Roger Lancelyn Green, trans., *Two Satyr Plays: Euripides' Cyclops and Sophocles' Ichneutai* (Harmondsworth, Middlesex, and Baltimore: Penguin, 1957), 10.

54. Ibid.

55. For a fascinating study on satyrs and their representation in art as well as in classical literature, see Guy Hedreen, "'I Let Go of My Force Just Touching Her Hair': Male Sexuality in Athenian Vase-Paintings of Silens and Iambic Poetry," *Classical Antiquity* 25 (2006): 277–325.

56. Mark Griffith, "Slaves of Dionysos: Satyrs, Audience, and the Ends of the *Oresteia*," *Classical Antiquity* 21 (2002): 196.

57. Louis Marin, *Food for Thought*, trans. Mette Hjort (Baltimore: Johns Hopkins University Press, 1989), 125.

58. Ibid., 122.

59. "At Ferrara he (Guarino) taught the young Prince Leonello, and an ever-growing number of others, drawn at first from Ferrara, but eventually (as the reputation of his school grew) from a catchment area that ran from England to Hungary," Anthony Grafton and Lisa Jardine, *From Humanism to the Humanities: Education and the Liberal Arts in Fifteenth- and Sixteenth-Century Europe* (London: Duckworth, 1986), 1. See also William Harrison Woodward, *Vittorino da Feltre and Other Humanist Educators*, foreword Eugene F. Rice Jr. (Toronto, Buffalo, and London: University of Toronto Press, 1996).

60. Dante Alighieri, *Vita nuova*, trans. Mark Musa (Bloomington and London: Indiana University Press, 1973), 3. All citations from *Vita nuova* are from this edition.

61. An important study on this subject is Robert P. Harrison's, *The Body of Beatrice* (Baltimore: Johns Hopkins University Press, 1988).

62. Dante, *Vita nuova*, 5.

63. Jacques Le Goff, "'Head or Heart': The Political Use of Body Metaphors in the 'Middle Ages,'" *Fragments for a History of the Human Body*, ed. Michael Feher (New York: Zone, 1986), vol. 3, 16.

64. See Heather Webb, *The Medieval Heart* (New Haven and London: Yale University Press, 2010).

65. Astell, *Eating Beauty*, 14.

66. Saint Augustine of Hippo, *The Confessions*, trans. Rex Warner (New York: Signet, 1963), bk. 7, 10.

67. For Karl F. Morrison to eat God and be simultaneously eaten by Him is essential for empathetic understanding. See *"I Am You": The Hermeneutics of Empathy in Western Literature, Theology and Art* (Princeton: Princeton University Press, 1988), 9–10.

68. Maggie Kilgour, in her *From Communion to Cannibalism: An Anatomy of Metaphors of Incorporation* (Princeton: Princeton University Press, 1990), 239, asserts that the act of eating blurs the distinction between "what is inside me or outside me," which is to say, between the self and the other. She also affirms that "communion sets up a more complicated system of relation in which it becomes difficult to say precisely who is eating whom." Ibid., 15. She highlights that "communion offers the beginnings of a model for relations that go beyond the binaries that lead to cannibalism." Ibid.

69. Dante Alighieri, *La commedia secondo l'antica vulgata*, ed. Giorgio Petrocchi (Turin: Einaudi, 1975), *Inferno*, 6.53. The English translation is from *Inferno*, trans. and comm. Charles S. Singleton (Princeton: Princeton University Press, 1975). All references to the *Commedia* are from these editions.

ONE The Language of Food in Boccaccio's *Decameron*

1. Massimo Montanari, *La fame e l'abbondanza: Storia dell'alimentazione in Europa* (Rome and Bari: Laterza, 1993), 91–98.

2. "So profoundly wise are you concerning the just and justice, and the unjust and injustice, that you are unaware that justice and the just is really the good of another, the advantage of the stronger who rules, but the self-inflicted injury of the subject who obeys; that injustice is the opposite, and rules those very simple just souls; that the governed serve the advantage of the stronger man, and by their obedience contribute to his happiness, but in no way to their own," states Thrasymachus in *The Republic of Plato*, trans. A. D. Lindsay, MA (London: J. M. Dent and Sons; New York: E. P. Dutton, 1945), 343b–344c.

3. Ibid., bk. 9.

4. "Adam had received from God the law of not tasting 'of the tree of recognition of good and evil,' with the doom of death to ensue upon tasting. However, even (Adam) himself at that time . . . yielded more readily to his belly than to God, heeded the meat rather than the mandate, and sold salvation for his gullet!" Tertullian, "On Fasting," *The Ante-Nicene Fathers, Translations of the Fathers down to A.D. 325*, ed. the Rev. Alexander Roberts and James Donaldson, bk. 8, ch. 3, vol. 4 (Grand Rapids, MI: Eerdmans, 1982), 103. "For it was by gluttony that he (Adam) took the food from the forbidden tree." *John Cassian: The Conferences*, 5.6.1, trans. Boniface Ramsey, OP (New York and Mahwah, NJ: Paulist, 1997), 185. "Finchè Adamo praticò l'astinenza, rimase nel paradiso: mangiò e fu cacciato" (for as long

as he practiced abstinence, Adam remained in Paradise: he ate and was driven out). Alcuin, *Liber de virtutibus et vitiis*, 16, ed. J. P. Migne, *Patrologiae cursus completus, sive bibliotheca universalis . . . omnium sanctorum patrum*, Series Latine. 221 vols. (Paris, 1844–1864), 101, c. 557. "El (sic) primo uomo più obbediente al ventre che a Dio, fu cacciato in questa valle di lacrime" (the first man, more obedient to the belly than to God, was chased out of Paradise and driven to this valley of tears). "Epistola di S. Girolamo ad Eustochio," *Scelta di curiosità letterarie inedite o rare dal secolo XIII al XVII*, ed. I. G. Isola (Bologna: Presso Gaetano Romagnoli, 1869), 72.

    5. Aristotle, *On the Soul*, 3.7.431a7–14.

    6. In the *Nicomachean Ethics*, 7.4.1147b 24–31, Aristotle states, "of the things that produce pleasure some are necessary, while others are worthy of choice in themselves but admit of excess, the bodily causes of pleasure being necessary (by such I mean both those concerned with food and those concerned with sexual intercourse . . .), while the others are not necessary but worthy of choices in themselves (e.g. victory, honor, wealth and good and pleasant things of this sort)"; see also Thomas Aquinas, *Summa Theologica*, I-II, q. 77, a. 5; I, q. 81, a. 2; and I-II, q. 66, a. 4.

    7. Augustine of Hippo sums up the tradition when he writes: "or is it precisely because he (Adam) could not possibly believe this that the woman was approached, as being of little intelligence and perhaps still living according to the sense perception of the flesh not according to the spirit of the mind?" And further, "perhaps he had not yet received what she was going to receive gradually as she came to recognize God under the guidance and management of the man." *The Literal Meaning of Genesis, On Genesis*, trans. Edmund Hill, OP, ed. John E. Rotelle (Hyde Park, NY: New City, 2002), 42, 58.

    8. Ibid., bk. 11, 4, 6. Here, Augustine examines the issue of why God allowed the first man "endowed with a spiritual mind" to be tempted and seduced by the serpent. He concludes that "God in this way would also demonstrate to the proud soul, for the instruction of saints of future generations, how fairly and squarely he himself makes use of even the bad wills of souls, when they make perverse and crooked use of natures that are good." On the spirit/body dichotomy, see E. Jane Burns, *Bodytalk* (Philadelphia: University of Pennsylvania Press, 1993), especially the chapter "A Taste of Knowledge."

    9. Clement of Alexandria states: "there is a proper time for the breeding of children and Scriptures calls it knowledge." *Stomateis*, trans. John Ferguson (Washington, DC: Catholic University of America Press, 1991), 3.81.5. Here, under note 351 the editor explains, "There is almost a triple meaning: knowledge, revealed knowledge (*gnosis*), and sexual intimacy." See also Elaine Pagels, *Adam, Eve, and the Serpent* (New York: Random House, 1988), 27; and Burns, *Bodytalk*, 103, n. 7. It is also important to remember that of the two accounts of creations the second one (Genesis 2:4f.), considered the older of the two, is narrated in the "language of folklore." Pagels, *Adam, Eve, and the Serpent*, xxii. The account now placed

first (Genesis 1:1–2:3) is newer. Called the "Priestly narrative," its language "is the result of intensive, theologically ordering thought." Thus, it is "succinct, ponderous, pedantic, lacking artistry." Gerhard von Rad, *Genesis: A Commentary* (Philadelphia: Westminster, 1973), 27.

10. Augustine, *The Literal Meaning of Genesis*, 11.3.

11. "And this lust not only takes possession of the whole body and outward members, but also makes itself felt within, and moves the whole man with a passion in which all mental emotion is mingled with bodily appetite, so that the pleasure which results is the greatest of all bodily pleasures. So possessing indeed is this pleasure, that at the moment of time in which it is consummated, all mental activity is suspended." Augustine, *The City of God*, 2 vols., trans. and ed. Marcus Dods, DD (New York: Hafner, 1948), bk. 14, 16.

12. "Woman must be silent. For Adam was created first, Eve afterward; moreover, it was not Adam who was deceived but the woman. It was she who was led astray and fell into sin" (1 Timothy 2:12–15). Also, "According to the rules observed in all the assemblies of believers, women should keep silent in such gatherings. They may not speak. Rather, as the law states, submissiveness is indicated for them. If they want to learn anything, they should ask their husbands at home. It is a disgrace when a woman speaks in the assembly" (1 Corinthians 14:34–35).

13. "And first he (the accuser) enticed the woman by fraud to take the forbidden fruit, and through her instrumentality he also persuaded the man himself to transgress the law of God." Lactantius, *The Divine Institutes*, bk. 2, ch. 8, vol. 7, *The Ante-Nicene Fathers, Translations of the Fathers down to A.D. 325*, ed. the Rev. Alexander Roberts and James Donaldson, bk. 8, ch. 3, vol. 4 (Grand Rapids, MI: Eerdmans, 1982), 62.

14. On this subject, see Burns, *Bodytalk*, particularly the chapter "A Taste of Knowledge: Genesis and Generation in the Old French *Jeu d'Adam*," 71–106.

15. "Hence the first sin of Adam was not gluttony but disobedience or pride." Saint Thomas Aquinas, *On Evil (De Malo)*, trans. Jean Oesterle (Notre Dame, IN: University of Notre Dame Press, 1995), 417. Saint Thomas's assertion echoes Augustine's "Pride is the beginning of sin" quoted from Ecclesiastes 10:13, *The City of God*, 14.13.

16. Dante, *Paradiso*, 26.115–117: "Or, figliul mio, non il gustar del legno / fu per sè la cagion di tanto essilio, / ma solamente il trapassar del segno" ("Now, my child, not the tasting of the tree, but the trespassing of the mark was the cause of such an exile").

17. "Lust is a vice opposed to temperance according as it moderates desires for the pleasures of touch in sexual intercourse, just as gluttony is opposed to temperance inasmuch as it moderates desires for the pleasures of touch in eating and drinking." Saint Thomas Aquinas, *On Evil*, 425–426.

18. "The reason why more seek bodily pleasures is because sensible goods are known better and more generally: and, again, because men need pleasures as remedy

for many kinds of sorrow and sadness: and since the majority cannot attain spiritual pleasures, which are proper to the virtuous, hence it is that they turn aside to seek those of the body." Thomas Aquinas, *Summa Theologica*, I-II, q. 31, a. 5, reply obj.1.

19. Ibid., I, a. 81, 3.

20. Ibid., I-II, q. 17, a. 7: "the apprehension of the imagination, being a particular apprehension, is regulated by the apprehension of reason, which is universal; just as a particular active power is regulated by a universal active power. Consequently in this respect the act of the sensitive appetite is subject to the command of reason . . . Hence the Philosopher says (*Polit.* i, 2) that reason governs the irascible and the concupiscible not by a *despotic supremacy*, which is that of a master over his slave; but by a politic and regal supremacy."

21. Aristotle, *Politics,* 1254b.2–5.

22. Denis J. M. Bradley uses this term to differentiate between the other, perfect happiness as Thomas Aquinas describes it. *Aquinas on the Twofold Human Good* (Washington, DC: Catholic University of America Press, 1997), in particular, "Imperfect and Perfect Happiness," 395.

23. Giovanni Boccaccio, *Decameron,* ed. Vittore Branca (Florence: LeMonnier, 1965). All citations are from this edition. English translations are from Giovanni Boccaccio, *The Decameron,* trans. M. Musa and P. Bondanella (New York: Penguin, 2002).

24. "The other is the sense of appetite following apprehension, in which (appetites) are the passions of the soul." Aquinas, *On Evil*, 412.

25. Boccaccio, *Decameron*, 17.

26. It goes without saying that this type of behavior directly contrasts the principles the church prized. For example: "Wine hath destroyed very many, and brought them into danger both of soule and bodie . . . Wheresoeuer fulnes doth abound, there luxurie doth domineere. A bellie that is strouted out with meate and wine, hath commonly luxurie for his companion." Bernard of Clairvaux, *A Rule of Good Life 1633,* trans. Antonie Batt (Menston and Yorkshire: Scholar Press, 1971), 193.

27. Aquinas, *Summa Theologica*, I-II, q. 31, a. 5, reply obj. 1: "spiritual pleasures, which are to the virtuous."

28. See Giuseppe Mazzotta, *The World at Play in Boccaccio's Decameron* (Princeton: Princeton University Press, 1986).

29. On the society of merchants, see Vittore Branca, *Boccaccio Medievale* (Florence: Sansoni, 1970), particularly the chapter "L'epopea dei mercanti," 134–164; Paolo Brezzi, *La civiltà del medievo europeo* (Rome: Eurodes, 1978), in particular, vol. 2, 557–567, and vol. 3, 444–449.

30. For a general study of conviviality in Boccaccio, see Laura Sanguineti White, *La scena conviavile nel "Decameron" e la sua funzione nel mondo del Boccaccio* (Florence: L. S. Olschki, 1983).

31. Aldo Scaglione, *Love and Nature in the Middle Ages* (Berkeley and Los Angeles: University of California Press, 1963).

32. Jessica Levenstein's article "Out of Bounds: Passion and the Plague in Boccaccio's *Decameron*," *Italica* 73 (1996): 313–330, addresses both the issue of the plague and Pampinea's role in the introduction of the *Decameron*. In particular, she focuses on women's fear of sexual transgression as their main reason for abandoning the city. For this reason, she links Pampinea's words "senza trapassare in alcuno atto il segno della ragione" ("without trespassing in any action the mark of reason") to Dante's account of Adam's Fall in *Paradiso,* 26.115–117, 319. For Mazzotta, however, reason is "to be understood as restraint, rather than as an abstract rationality which would conform either to the order of nature, which in reality is sheer chaos, or to the order of the garden, to which they move, for the garden is an artifice of nature." *World at Play in Boccaccio's Decameron*, 42.

33. For Victoria Kirkham Pampinea represents "the voice of reason." See "An Allegorically Tempered *Decameron*," *Italica* 62 (1985): 7.

34. On Pampinea and reason, see Janet Levarie Smarr, *Boccaccio and Fiammetta: The Narrator as Lover* (Urbana and Chicago: University of Illinois Press, 1986), 165–173, in particular, 167.

35. Alcuin Blamires, *The Case for Women in Medieval Culture* (Oxford: Clarendon, 1997), 137.

36. Albert Russell Ascoli appropriately describes Pampinea's role as "the Moses or *Numa* of the *lieta brigata*." He also emphasizes that "female empowerment is qualified, at least verbally, by explicit recognition of the Pauline notion that man is the head of woman." "Pyrrhus' Rules: Playing with Power from Boccaccio to Machiavelli," *Modern Language Notes* 114 (1999): 14.

37. For the role of women in medieval society, see Shulamith Shahar, *The Fourth Estate: A History of Women in the Middle Ages*, trans. Chaya Galai (New York: Routledge, 2003). Here the author quotes Frederick Pollock and William Maitland: "women must be kept out of all public office. They must devote themselves to their feminine and domestic occupations." *A History of English Law before the Time of Edward I* (Cambridge: Cambridge University Press, 1898), vol. 1, 485; ibid., 11, n. 2.

38. For a relevant discussion on the complete range of traditional medieval concepts about gender difference, see Alastair Minnis, "*De impedimento sexus*: Women's Bodies and Medieval Impediments to Female Ordination," *Medieval Theology and the Natural Body*, ed. Peter Biller and A. J. Minnis (York: York Medieval Texts, 1997), 109–139.

39. "In a dynamic, mobile, changing society, women offered a continuity of management over households, castles and estates essential to social progress. But no less remarkable is the prominence achieved by women in quite a different facet of medieval life—rebellious opposition to the social establishments of the medieval world, which similarly grows in strength from the eleventh century," asserts David Herlihy, *Women in Medieval Society* (The Annual B. K. Smith Lecture in History, 1971), 10.

40. "Implicitly, Boccaccio criticizes the urban bourgeois patriarchy which prevents women from exercising a range of options for release from love and its

melancholy," asserts Susan Noakes with regard to the proem. "The *Heptameron* Prologue," *Studi sul Boccaccio* 20 (1991–1992): 275.

41. "Man is associated with intelligence—*mens, ratio,* the rational soul—and woman, with *sensus,* the body, the animal faculties, appetite." R. Howard Bloch, *Medieval Misogyny and the Invention of Western Romantic Love* (Chicago and London: University of Chicago Press, 1991), 29, and "Early Christianity and the Estheticization of Gender," 37–63. See also Margaret R. Miles, *Carnal Knowing: Female Nakedness and Religious Meaning in the Christian West* (Boston: Beacon, 1989).

42. Marina Warner, *Alone of All her Sex: The Myth and the Cult of the Virgin Mary* (New York: Knopf, 1976), 3.

43. Ibid., 3–34; see also Miri Rubin, *Mother of God: A History of the Virgin Mary* (New Haven: Yale University Press, 2009).

44. "Many women in late medieval society, especially in the cities, were economically superfluous and regarded as a burden by their own families . . . the medieval world over the long course of its history improved the condition of life and lengthened the span of years allotted to women. But it never succeeded in (assuring) . . . personal and human fulfillment." David Herlihy, "Life Expectancies for Women," *The Role of Women in the Middle Ages,* ed. Rosmarie Thee Morewedge (Albany: State University of New York Press, 1975), 16.

45. According to Robert Hollander, "the importance of Dante for Boccaccio is overwhelming and significant." *Boccaccio's Dante and the Shaping Force of Satire* (Ann Arbor: University of Michigan Press, 1997), 12.

46. On the theological critique of rhetoric, see Giuseppe Mazzotta, *Dante's Vision and the Circle of Knowledge* (Princeton: Princeton University Press, 1993), 10.

47. Millicent J. Marcus is correct in maintaining that "though different from Dante's, his (Boccaccio's) is nonetheless a persuasive and coherent morality whose most effective vehicle is the *Decameron* itself." *An Allegory of Form: Literary Self-Consciousness in the Decameron* (Saratoga, CA: ANMA Libri, 1979), 110.

48. Levarie Smarr defines this as "the reestablishment of the rational government." *Boccaccio and Fiammetta,* 173.

49. Augustine, *The City of God,* 12.6; 14.13–14.

50. For a sociohistorical background on medieval food and society, see Antoni Riera-Melis, "Società feudale e alimentazione (secoli XII–XIII)," *Storia dell'alimentazione,* ed. Jean-Louis Flandrin and Massimo Montanari (Rome and Bari: Laterza, 1997), 307–324.

51. Yannick Carré, *Le baisir sour la bouche au Moyen Age: Rites, symbols, mentalités à travers les texts et les images, XIe–XVe siècles* (Paris: Editions Le Léopard d'Or, 1992), 19–31.

52. "But pleasure is preceded by a certain appetite, which is felt in the flesh like a craving, as hunger and thirst and that generative appetite which is most commonly identified with the name of 'lust,' though this is the generic word for all desires." Augustine, *The City of God,* 14.15.

53. On love and its natural aspects, see Scaglione, *Nature and Love in the Middle Ages*, particularly ch. 3.

54. Mikhail Bakhtin, *Rabelais and His World*, trans. H. Iswolsky (Cambridge and London: MIT, 1968), 281, asserts that "man's encounter with the world (that occurs in) the act of eating is joyful, triumphant; he triumphs over the world, without being devoured himself." As for banquet images he states: "(they) preserve their essential relation to life, death, struggle, triumph, and regeneration." Ibid., 282.

55. Massimo Montanari, "Strutture di produzione e sistemi alimentari nell'alto Medioevo," *Storia dell'alimentazione,* ed. Jean-Louis Flandrin and Massimo Montanari (Rome: Laterza, 1997), 220. Ibid., 226–228.

56. Massimo Montanari, "Verso un nuovo equilibrio alimentare," *Storia dell'alimentazione,* ed. Jean-Louis Flandrin and Massimo Montanari (Rome: Laterza, 1997), 305.

57. Giovanna Bonardi, "Manger à Rome: La mensa pontificale à la fin du Moyen Âge entre cérémoniale et alimentation," *Banquets et manières de table au Moyen Âge* (Aix-en-Provence: CUER MA, 1996), 37–51.

58. The idea that eating meat is inherently linked to lasciviousness is a common topos in the Middle Ages. The first outspoken critics of meat consumption were the church fathers. In Adam they saw the progenitor who yielded to gluttony and, after that, to the complete range of sensual pleasures. The words attributed to Nilus (d. 430) help explain this belief: "it was the desire of food that spawned disobedience; it was the pleasure of taste that drove us from Paradise. Luxury in food delights the gullet, but it breeds the worm of license that sleepeth not." Quoted in Caroline Walker Bynum, *Holy Feast and Holy Fast: The Religious Significance of Food to Medieval Women* (Berkeley, Los Angeles, and London: University of California Press, 1987), 36. Isidore of Seville provides a full-scale, "scientific" explanation of the lustful effects meats have on man. He explains that "meats (*carnes*) are so called because they are (*caro*) flesh ... Boiled (*elixus*), because it is cooked in water only, for water is called *lixa* because it is a solution (*solutus*)—wherefore also 'giving rein' (*solutio*) to desire (that) is called debauchery (*luxus*, noun)." Saint Isidore, of Seville, *The Etymologies of Isidore of Seville*, trans. Stephen A. Barney, W. J. Lewis, J. A. Beach, and Oliver Berghof (Cambridge and New York: Cambridge University Press, 2006), 20.2.20, 396.

59. See Timothy Kircher, "The Modality of Moral Communication in the Decameron's First Day, in Contrast to the *Mirror of the Exemplum*," *Renaissance Quarterly* 54 (2001): 1035–1073.

60. "Carnal knowing is both embodied and social; it includes the most private and intimate experiences as well as the most public and social experiences. Carnal knowing is not a kind of 'pure' subjectivity, untouched by social location and by all the particularities of experience that create one's perspective," Miles, *Carnal Knowing*, 9.

61. Massimo Montanari speaks of the binomial difference of potens and pauper, for they both must eat in quantities that reflect the quality of their persons. "Contadini, guerrieri, sacerdoti: Immagine della società e stili di alimentazione," *Storia dell'alimentazione*, ed. Jean-Louis Flandrin and Massimo Montanari (Rome: Laterza, 1997), 229–232.

62. For an analysis of love and economics in the *Decameron*, see Mazzotta, *World at Play in Boccaccio's Decameron*, particularly the chapters "The Riddle of Values" and "The Heart of Love."

63. See Bridget Ann Henisch, *Fast and Feast: Food in Medieval Society* (University Park and London: Pennsylvania State University Press, 1976).

64. Gerd Althoff, "Obbligatorio mangiare: Pranzi, banchetti e feste nella vita sociale del Medioevo," *Storia dell'alimentazione*, ed. Jean-Louis Flandrin and Massimo Montanari (Rome: Laterza, 1997), 234–242.

65. Gluttony and lewdness are here implicitly paired. For the theoretical explanations of them as sins, see Gregory, *Moralia*, ed. J. P. Migne, *Patrologiae cursus completus, sive bibliotheca universalis . . . omnium sanctorum patrum*, Series Latine. 221 vols. (Paris, 1844–1864), 76, 621B. In discussing lust, Aquinas cites Gregory. "Uncleanness," he states, "is assigned as a daughter of gluttony, according to Gregory." *On Evil*, 438.

66. "The woman says: Even though you might, by these arguments, compel me to love you, there is another reason which necessarily keeps me from doing so. Suppose everything did turn out prosperously for our embraces, if the affair came to the ears of the common people they would ruin my good name by blaming me openly on the ground that I had gone far outside my natural limits." Andreas Cappellanus, *The Art of Courtly Love*, trans. John Jay Parry (New York: Columbia University Press, 1960), 86.

67. For a discussion of the political scene in Italy and Europe during the Middle Ages, see Brezzi, *La civiltà del medioevo europeo*, vol. 3, 101–157. See also Michael Jones, "The Last Capetians and Early Valois Kings, 1314–1364," 388–421; Françoise Autrand, "France under Charles V and Charles VI," 422–441; John Law, "The Italian North," 442–468; Louis Green, "Florence and the Republican Tradition," 469–487; and David Abulafia, "The Italian South," 488–514, all in *The New Cambridge Medieval History*, ed. Michael Jones (Cambridge and New York: Cambridge University Press, 2000), vol. 6.

68. According to Terence Scully, for the medieval cook sauces were "a means by which to guarantee the salubriousness of what would go to the dining table." This was based on the "medical theory" that humoral balance could be controlled by diets based on different sauces. Maiano de' Maineri's *Opusculum de saporibus* deals specifically with "sauces required by particular foodstuff." "Tempering Medieval Food," *Food in the Middle Ages*, ed. M. Weiss Adamson (New York and London: Garland, 1995), 3–21. See also idem, *The Art of Cookery in the Middle Ages* (Rochester: Boydell, 2005), in particular, chs. 3, 4, and 5.

69. See Henisch, *Fast and Feast*, 190–205. She notes that at the noble's table "every effort was made to get as far away as possible from peasant life and peasant taste" (102).

70. Montanari, *La fame e l'abbondanza*, 108.

71. Ibid., 60.

72. Ibid., 62.

73. Ibid., 110.

74. Allen Grieco, "Les plantes, les régimes végétariens et la mé à la fin du Moyen Age et au début de la Reniassance italienne," *Le Monde vegetal (XIIe–XVIIe siècles): Savoirs et usages sociaux* (Saint-Denis: Presses Universitaires de Vincennes, 1993), 12. Also, "Alimentazione e classe sociali nel tardo Medioevo e nel Rinascimento in Italia," *Storia dell'alimentazione*, ed. Jean-Louis Flandrin and Massimo Montanari (Rome: Laterza, 1997), 370–380.

75. This inversion of roles that upends the *caput/corpus* paradigm strongly upheld in patristic writings finds some support in the Middle Ages. See Alcuin Blamires, "Paradox in the Medieval Gender Doctrine of Head and Body," *Medieval Theology and the Natural Body*, ed. Peter Biller and A. J. Minnis (New York: Medieval Texts, 1997), 3–29.

76. In the Gospels the Logos's function is to teach: Jesus teaches His disciples about everyday experiences. See Diana Culbertson, *The Poetics of Revelation: Recognition and the Narrative Tradition*, Studies in American Biblical Hermeneutics 4 (Macon, GA: Mercer University Press, 1989), 23.

77. Augustine, *The City of God*, vol. 2, bk. 14, 16: "at the time it (lust) is consummated, all mental activity is suspended"; Aquinas, *Summa Theologica*, I, q. 98, a. 2: "Beasts are without reason. In this way man becomes, as it were, like them in coition, because he cannot moderate concupiscence."

78. Dante Alighieri, *Il convivio*, trans. R. Lansing (New York: Garland, 1990), 95.

79. "Of all things to be sought, the first is that Wisdom in which the form of the Perfect God stands fixed. Wisdom illuminates man so that he may recognize himself; for man was like all other animals when he did not understand that he had been created of a higher order than they. It is written on the tripod of Apollo, . . . 'Know thyself,' for surely, if man had not forgotten his origin, he would recognize that everything subject to change is nothing." *Didascalicon of Hugh of St. Victor*, trans. and ed. Jerome Taylor (New York: Columbia University Press, 1961), bk. 1, ch. 1, 46.

80. Quite appropriately Noakes writes: "Boccaccio looks at the conventional view of women, promulgated by the Church, with considerable irony." "*Heptameron* Prologue," 274.

81. Mazzotta, *Dante's Vision*, 229. See in particular the chapter "Theologia Ludens."

82. Henisch, *Fast and Feast*, 74–75.

83. Saint Bernard of Clairvaux, "Meditationes piissime ad humane conditionis cognitionem," *Opera* (Lyons: Societas Biblipolarum, 1679), 5.93.

84. Piero Camporesi, *The Anatomy of the Senses*, trans. Allen Cameron (Cambridge: Polity, 1994), 69.

85. See Smarr, "Fiammetta and Dioneo," *Boccaccio and Fiammetta*, 174–192.

86. Victoria Kirkham, *The Signs of Reason in Boccaccio's Decameron* (Florence: L. S. Olschki, 1993), 153.

87. See Eugene Vance, *Mervelous Signals: Poetics and Sign Theory in the Middle Ages* (Lincoln: University of Nebraska Press, 1986), 529.

88. Smarr, *Boccaccio and Fiammetta*; Kirkham, *Signs of Reason in Boccaccio's Decameron*; Robert Hollander, *Boccaccio's Two Venuses* (New York: Columbia University Press, 1977), 94–97.

89. "Dioneo's joyful sensuality," states Kirkham, "literally puts 'carnal concupiscence' into the *Decameron*." *Signs of Reason in Boccaccio's Decameron*, 139.

90. Smarr, *Boccaccio and Fiammetta*, 174–192.

91. Kirkham accurately speaks of "the moralistic content of Boccaccio's minor works, which reappear in the general plan of his major work." *Signs of Reason in Boccaccio's Decameron*, 213.

92. Smarr, *Boccaccio and Fiammetta*, 201.

93. Ibid., 184.

94. Catone il Censore, *L'agricoltura (De re agraria)*, trans. Luca Canali and Emanuele Lelli (Milan: Mondadori, 2000), 83, 105.

95. *Decameron*, 3.10.

96. "As strangers and pilgrims in this world, who serve God in poverty and humility, they should beg alms trustingly," are the words that guide the Franciscan brothers in the Rule of 1223. See Saint Bonaventure, *St. Francis of Assisi, Writings and Early Biographies: English Omnibus of the Sources for the Life of St. Francis*, ed. Marion A. Habig (Chicago: Franciscan Herald, 1983), ch. 6, 61.

97. Bonaventure, in his *Major Life of St. Francis,* recounts Saint Francis's travels to Morocco and Syria "to preach the Gospel of Christ among the pagans." Ibid., 702–703.

98. According to Robert Hollander, the *Decameron* is characterized as embodying one of three central positions, but no one of them by itself is adequate in understanding the overarching purpose of Boccaccio's work. He offers a fourth possibility that expands and improves on the previous approaches. "The *Decameron* Proem," *The Decameron First Day in Perspective* (Toronto, Buffalo, and London: University of Toronto Press), 14–15.

99. The ways in which Boccaccio's and Dante's works are linked have long been established by Robert Hollander. See "Boccaccio's Dante," *Italica* 63 (1986): 278–289.

100. For a discussion on the meaning of old age and Ulysses, see Giuseppe Mazzotta, *Dante Poet of the Desert: History and Allegory in the Divine Comedy* (Princeton: Princeton University Press, 1979), 101.

101. Augustine, *The City of God*, 11.3.

102. On Ulysses's language, see Mazzotta, *Dante Poet of the Desert*, 96.

103. According to Mazzotta, Dante's aim in this canto is "to disrupt the complicity with Ulysses and to place his own voice in a condition of interpretative distance from both prophetic claims and rhetorical self-deception." Ibid., 105.

104. An important study on childhood in medieval times is David Herlihy's "Medieval Children," *Women, Family and Society in Medieval Europe*, ed. and intro. A. Molho (Providence, RI: Berghahn, 1995), 215–243.

105. It should be noted that the description of Alibech's appetite echoes the narrator's pronouncement in the proem. There, with regard to his own early amorous adventures, he states that *poco regolato appetito* (unrestrained desire) caused his suffering. The fascinating but contrasting parallel this statement sets up between the narrator and Alibech rests on the seemingly divergent objectives that author and character have as they set on the path of their life-changing experiences.

106. For an excellent discussion on sexuality and canon laws, see James A. Brundage, "Carnal Delight: Canonistic Theories of Sexuality," *Proceedings of the Fifth International Congress of Medieval Canon Law, Salamanca, 21–25 September 1976*, ed. Stephan Kuttner and Kenneth Pennington (Vatican City: Biblioteca Apostolica Vaticana, 1980), 361–385.

107. See James F. Rhodes, *Poetry Does Theology: Chaucer, Grosseteste, and the Pearl-Poet* (Notre Dame, IN: University of Notre Dame Press, 2001), especially ch. 1, "Poetry and Theology."

108. See, for instance, Saint Athanasius of Alexandria, *The Life of Anthony*, trans. T. Vivian and N. Athanassakis (Kalamazoo, MI: Cistercian Publications, 2003); Palladius, *The Lausiac History of Palladius*, trans. W. K. Lowther Clarke (New York: Macmillan, 1918); Dom Cuthbert Butler, *The Lausiac History of Palladius: A Critical Discussion Together with Notes on Early Egyptian Monachism* (London: Cambridge University Press, 1898); San Girolamo, *Vite degli eremiti Paolo, Ilarione, e Malco*, trans. and ed. Bazyli Degórski (Rome: Città Nuova Editrice, 1996); Giovanni Cassiano, *Conferenze ai monaci I–X*, trans. and ed. Lorenzo Dattrino (Rome: Città Nuova Editrice, 2000); P. G. Maxwell-Stuart, *Satan: A Biography* (Stroud and Gloucestershire: Amberley, 2008), particularly ch. 2, "Demons in the Desert: The Early Christian Centuries," 26–39.

109. Jacques Lacarrière, *Men Possessed by God: The Story of the Desert Monks of Ancient Christendom* (Garden City, NY: Doubleday, 1964).

110. "On the whole monks regarded wilderness as having value only for escaping corrupt society," states Roderick Nash, *Wilderness and the American Mind*, 3rd ed. (New Haven: Yale University Press, 1982), 18.

111. Susan P. Bratton, *Christianity, Wilderness, and Wildlife: The Original Desert Solitaire* (Scranton: University of Scranton Press; London and Toronto: Associated University Presses, 1993), 179, speaks of "the early monastic model of wilderness experience that has obvious similarities to the ascetic and contemplative models of the New Testament."

112. Peter Brown, *The Body and Society: Men, Women and Sexual Renunciation in Early Christianity* (New York: Columbia University Press, 1988), 218, and more generally, the whole chapter "The Desert Fathers," 213–240.

113. Ibid., 225.

114. See Pagels, *Adam, Eve, and the Serpent*, 32–56.

115. Lacarrière, *Men Possessed by God*, 40.

116. "Monks imitated Christ in his battle with the demoniac." Bratton, *Christianity, Wilderness, and Wildlife*, 178.

117. "They considered not only sexual desire, but also food and sleep to be sources of temptation. Self-denial was the ultimate virtue . . . They proceeded with unquenchable enthusiasm, to battle demons . . . they were convinced that . . . they were engaging in a spiritual warfare which would help to free the universe of the powers of evil." Ibid., 162.

118. On Boccaccio's familiarity with Statius's work, see Alberto Limentani, "Boccaccio traduttore di Stazio," *La rassegna* 8 (1960): 231–42; Giuseppe Velli, "Cultura e imitazione nel primo Boccaccio," *Annali della Scuola Normale Superiore di Pisa* 2, no. 37 (1968): 65–93; and more recently, Winthrop Wetherbee, "History and Romance in Boccaccio's *Teseida*," *Studi sul Boccaccio* 20 (1991–1992): 173–184; Dominique Battles, *The Medieval Tradition of Thebes: History and Narrative in the OF Roman de Thèbes, Boccaccio, Chaucer, and Lydgate* (New York and London: Routledge, 2004), especially 61–83.

119. Winthrop Wetherbee, "Dante and the *Thebaid* of Statius," *Lectura Dantis Newberryana*, ed. Paolo Cherchi and Antonio Mastrobuoni (Evanston, IL: Northwestern University Press, 1988), 73–92.

120. "Beatitude consists in intellectual contemplation," and "Beatitude consists more in the speculative than in the practical intellect" states Saint Thomas Aquinas. *On Love and Charity, Readings from the Commentary on the Sentences of Peter Lombard*, trans. Peter A. Kwasniewski, Thomas Bolin, OSB, and Joseph Bolin (Washington, DC: Catholic University of America Press, 2008), 341 and 345.

121. "The highest good is to be found in spiritual realities." Aquinas, *On Love and Charity*, 338. "The speculative intellect is nobler, simply speaking, than the practical, since it is on account of itself, whereas the practical is on account of its work; . . . and by this very fact, the practical intellect is shown to be at the assistance of the speculative." Ibid., 347.

122. Lévi-Strauss, *Raw and the Cooked*.

123. Grieco, "Les plantes, les régimes végétariens et la mé à la fin du Moyen Age et au début de la Renaissance italienne," 17.

124. To describe the vice of excess—*akolasia*—Aristotle includes the senses of touch and taste: "temperance and self-indulgence, however, are concerned with the kind of pleasures that the other animals share in, which therefore appear slavish and brutish; these are touch and taste." *Nicomachean Ethics*, 3.10.1118a.24–26. "Thus the sense with which self-indulgence is connected is the most widely shared

of the senses; and self-indulgence would seem to be justly a matter of reproach, because it attaches to us not as men but as animals. To delight in such things, then, and to love them above all others, is brutish." Ibid., 1118b.1–5.

125. "But from gluttony certain vices arise which are called its daughters as being those that can issue from immoderate pleasure in eating and drinking. Which can be considered either as regards the body, whose defilement readily follows from excessive consumption of food, and thus 'uncleanness' is designated as a daughter (species) of gluttony." Aquinas, *On Evil*, 422.

126. Bynum, *Holy Feast and Holy Fast*, in particular, ch. 5.

127. Pliny the Elder, *Natural History, with an English Translation in Ten Volumes*, trans. H. Rackham, MA (Cambridge, MA: Harvard University Press; London: William Heinemann, 1945), 13.26–35.

128. Saint Ambrose, *Hexameron, Paradise, and Cain and Abel*, trans. John J. Savage (Washington, DC: Catholic University of America Press, 1961), 108.

129. Grieco, "Les plantes, les régimes végétariens et la mé à la fin du Moyen Age et au début de la Reniassance italienne," 19.

130. On Alan of Lille's sexual metaphors see, Jan Ziolkowski, *Alan of Lille's Grammar of Sex: The Meaning of Grammar to a Twelfth-Century Intellectual* (Cambridge, MA: Medieval Academy of America, 1985).

131. Carol A. Newsom, *The Book of Job: A Contest of Moral Imaginations* (Oxford and New York: Oxford University Press, 2003).

132. Edwin M. Good, *In Turns of Tempest: A Reading of Job* (Stanford, CA: Stanford University Press, 1990), 331–337.

133. Gregory, *Moralia*, ed. J. P. Migne, *Patrologiae cursus completus, sive bibliotheca universalis . . . omnium sanctorum patrum*, Series Latine. 221 vols. (Paris, 1844–1864), 76: 429B.

134. "Wise (*sapiens*), so called from taste (*sapore*), because as the sense of taste is able to discern the taste of food, so the wise person is able to distinguish things and their causes, because he understands each thing, and makes distinctions with his sense of the truth." *Etymologies*, 10, S. 240, 228.

135. Rhodes, *Poetry Does Theology*, 183–185.

TWO Of Frogs, Giants, and the Court

1. Illidio Bussani, *Il romanzo cavalleresco in Luigi Pulci* (Turin: Fratelli Bocca Editori, 1933), in particular, ch. 2, "Il mondo del ventre." According to Bussani, Pulci's extensive use of food imagery makes him "un poeta della realtà" (a poet of reality).

2. In his *L'indole e il riso di Luigi Pulci* (Rocca San Casciano: Licinio Cappelli, 1907) Attilio Momigliano states that laughter in the *Morgante* is not of the bitter type of the sonetti (29). Rather, it is "l'espressione più vasta e più forte del gaio spirito del quattrocento" (the broadest and strongest expression of the Quat-

trocento's gay spirit). For Momigliano in the *Morgante* "il riso del medioevo, sarcastico o materiale, cede il luogo alla fine canzonatura e specialmente al riso, che esprime la nuova gioia di vivere" (the medieval laughter, sarcastic and material, is replaced by mockery and especially laughter that expresses the new joie de vivre) (105). The critic also states that "il Pulci ... coglie il lato comico ed umoristico delle cose ... talora per modo da rendere ridicolo quello, che per il più degli uomini è serio" (Pulci ... seizes on the funny side of things ... often to ridicule what most men consider serious) (118).

3. Marco Santagata and Stefano Carrai, *La lirica di corte nell'Italia del Quattrocento* (Milan: Franco Angeli, 1993), 11–39.

4. For a comprehensive discussion on giants and their appetite, see Walter Stephens, *Giants in Those Days* (Lincoln and London: University of Nebraska Press, 1989).

5. On this, see Giuseppe Mazzotta, *Cosmopoiesis: The Renaissance Experiment* (Toronto: University of Toronto Press, 2001), particularly ch. 1: "Poliziano's *Orfeo,* the World as a Fable"; Cesare Vasoli, "La cultura laurenziana," *Lorenzo il Magnifico e il suo mondo: Convegno internazionale di studi: Firenze 9–13 giugno, 1992,* ed. Gian Carlo Garfagnini (Florence: L. S. Olschki, 1994), 153–175.

6. For an enlightening perspective on the enchanted palace in the *Morgante,* see Alessandro Polcri, *Luigi Pulci e la chimera: Studi sull'allegoria nel Morgante* (Florence: Società Editrice Fiorentina, 2010), 155–175.

7. Luigi Pulci, *Morgante,* ed. Franca Ageno (Milan and Naples: Riccardo Ricciardi Editore, 1955), 2.19. All citations are from this edition.

8. English translations are from *Morgante, the Epic Adventures of Orlando and his Giant Friend Morgante,* trans. Joseph Tusiani, intro. and notes Edoardo Lèbano (Bloomington and Indianapolis: Indiana University Press, 1998).

9. Albert Russell Ascoli, *Ariosto's Bitter Harmony: Crisis and Evasion in the Italian Renaissance* (Princeton: Princeton University Press, 1987), especially "The Nature of Education," 168–199.

10. Paolo Orvieto, *Pulci medievale: Studio sulla poesia volgare fiorentina del Quattrocento* (Rome: Salerno, 1978).

11. Lorenzo de' Medici, *Tutte le opere,* ed. Paolo Orvieto (Rome: Salerno, 1992), in particular, "Canti carnascialeschi," 7–56.

12. Francesco Guicciardini draws an accurate portrait of Lorenzo in his *History of Florence:* "Lorenzo possessed many outstanding qualities. He also had certain vices ... He had such great authority that one may say that the city was not free in his time, even though it was rich in all those glories and good fortunes which a city may enjoy when free in name but in fact riled as a tyrant by one of its citizens ... He had a brilliant and outstanding mind ... He committed more than one rash action ... He desired glory and success more than any man. One may criticize him for carrying this passion even into things of small importance, so that even in poetry, in games and other pursuits he would not permit any to imitate or compete with him, and was angry with those who did so. Even in greater things his

ambition was excessive . . . he strove to ensure that all the arts and talents should flourish more brilliantly in Florence than in any other city in Italy . . . So in his lifetime all the best and most famous men in Italy taught there and were very highly paid, for no expense or trouble was spared to get hold of them. Thus the study of the humanities flourished in Florence under Messer Agnolo Poliziano, Greek studies under Messer Demetrio [Calcondila] and later under Lascari, philosophy and arts had Marsilio Ficino, Maestro Giorgio Benigno, Count Pico della Mirandola, and other eminent men. He also equally favored poetry in the vernacular, music, architecture, painting, sculpture, and all the arts of the mind and hand . . . And they flourished all the more because he was able, with his universal taste, to appreciate them and favor their authors accordingly, so that everyone competed in their works to please him. Another factor was his infinite liberality, making abundant provision for able men and providing all the necessary instruments for their work. He was by nature very arrogant, so that, besides not allowing others to oppose him, he also wished them to understand him by allusions . . . in his domestic life rather plain and decent than sumptuous—except in the magnificent feasts which he gave in honor of noble foreigners who came to Florence. He was libidinous, amorous, and faithful in his loves . . . Some held that he had a cruel and revengeful nature . . . His worst fault was his mistrust . . . In short, one must conclude that under him the city was not free, although it would be impossible to find a better and more agreeable tyrant." Cecil Greyson, trans., *Guicciardini History of Italy and History of Florence,* ed. John R. Hale (New York: Twayne, 1964), 2–8.

13. R. C. Trexler, *Public Life in Renaissance Florence* (New York: Academic, 1982), 409, 438–439.

14. Brian P. Copenhaver, "Lorenzo, Ficino and the Domesticated Hermes," *Lorenzo Magnifico e il suo mondo: Convegno internazionale di studi, 9–13 giugno 1992,* ed. Gian Carlo Garfagnini (Florence: L. S. Olschki, 1994), 225–257, particularly 255; Riccardo Fubini, *Quattrocento fiorentino: Politica, diplomazia, cultura* (Pisa: Pacini Editore, 1996), in particular, "Ficino e i Medici all'avvento di Lorenzo il Magnifico," 235–282.

15. For a study on Ficino and Pulci's controversy, see Polcri, *Luigi Pulci e la chimera,* especially the chapter "'Contra hypocritas tantum': L'eresia e i dettagli della filologia," 37–66.

16. Bartolomeo Sacchi (Platina), *On the Right Pleasure and Good Health* (*De honesta Voluptate et Valetudine*), ed. and trans. Mary Ella Milham (Tempe, AZ: Medieval and Renaissance Texts and Studies, 1998), 4.

17. Annaclara Cataldi Palau, "La biblioteca pandolfina," *Italia Medievale e umanistica* 31 (1988): 262.

18. Platina, *On the Right Pleasure and Good Health,* 7.

19. Joseph W. Vehling, *Platina and the Rebirth of Man* (Chicago: Walter M. Hill, 1941).

20. Platina, *On the Right Pleasure and Good Health,* bk. 1.

21. See Lotario Dei Segni (Innocent III), *The miseria condicionis humane*, ed. Robert E. Lewis (Athens: University of Georgia Press, 1978).

22. Leonardo Bruni's translation from Greek of Aristotle's *Nicomachean Ethics* in 1417 set in motion the heated discussion about the *summum bonum*. See Franco Gaeta, *Lorenzo Valla: Filologia e storia nell'umanesimo italiano* (Naples: Istituto italiano per gli studi storici in Napoli, 1945).

23. Mario Fois, *Il pensiero cristiano di Lorenzo Valla nel quadro storico-culturale del suo ambiente* (Rome: Libreria editrice dell'Università Gregoriana, 1969). Also, Giovanni Di Napoli, *Lorenzo Valla: Filosofia e religione nell'umanesimo italiano* (Rome: Edizioni di storia e letteratura, 1971).

24. "Virtue is not to be desired for itself, as something severe, harsh, and arduous, nor is it to be desired for the sake of earthly profits." Lorenzo Valla, *On Pleasure (De voluptate)*, trans. A. Kent Hieatt and Maristella De Panizza Lorch (New York: Abaris, 1977), 267.

25. Ibid., 265.

26. Ibid., 267.

27. Here Valla elucidates: "those who wrote in Latin 'wishing to express (as I think) what they understood as a great experiencing of delight,' chose 'pleasure' [*voluptas*] as a translation." Ibid., 267.

28. "What nature created and shaped cannot be anything but holy and praiseworthy . . . and disposed with rationality, beauty, and utility." Ibid., 75.

29. "Nature has offered a multitude of goods to mortals. It is up to us to know how to enjoy them properly." Ibid., 85.

30. "Pleasure itself is love; but because it is God who creates pleasure, he who receives it loves, and what is received is loved. Loving itself is delight, or pleasure, or beatitude, or happiness, or charity, which is the final end or goal for which all other things are." Ibid., 275.

31. "What else does Paul mean when he proclaims with a loud voice 'all that does not proceed from faith is sin'; and elsewhere: 'The just man lives by faith'; and again: 'Without faith man cannot please God'?" Ibid., 263.

32. "Indeed, a kind of probable pleasure is not lacking in this life, and the greatest such comes from the hope of future happiness, when the mind, which is aware of right action, and the spirit, which unceasingly contemplates divine things, consider themselves a kind of candidate for the heavenly, represent to themselves the promised honors, and in a way make them present—the more happily and zestfully, the more candidates and competitors it has seen." Ibid., 269.

33. "This food and drink will be of such sweetness that I might almost say the sense of taste will conquer the other senses." Ibid., 301.

34. The canonical authors of grammar treatises used in the Middle Ages were Servius, Donatus, and Priscian. See Richard W. Hunt, *The History of Grammar in the Middle Ages: Collected Papers* (Amsterdam: J. Benjamins, 1980); Jeffrey F. Huntsman, "Grammar," *The Seven Liberal Arts in the Middle Ages*, ed. David L. Wagner

(Bloomington: Indiana University Press, 1983). See also, *Il pensiero pedagogico dello Umanesimo*, ed. Eugenio Garin (Florence: Giuntine and Sansoni, 1958), in particular "La pedagogia dell'umanesimo," xi–xxviii.

35. Mirko Tavani, *Latino, grammatica, volgare: Storia di una questione umanistica* (Padua: Antenore, 1984), 152. It is worth noting that Alberti holds a view similar to Valla's for he states: "Italy was repeatedly occupied and dominated by various nations, Gauls, Goths, Vandals, Lombards, and other brutish barbarians . . . Moved by necessity or by their own desire, the people began to learn one or the other of these foreign tongues . . . Similarly, the foreigners became accustomed to our own language, though, I believe, with many barbarisms and much corruption. Because of this mixture, our language, which had once been most elegant and perfect, became debased and uncouth." *The Albertis of Florence: Leon Battista Alberti's Della Famiglia*, trans., intro., and notes Guido Guarini (Lewisburg: Bucknell University Press, 1974), 160.

36. Antonio La Penna, "La tradizione classica nella cultura italiana," *Storia d'Italia* (Turin: Einaudi, 1973), vol. 2, 1353. See also L. Cesarini Martinelli, "Note sulla polemica Poggio-Valla e sulla fortuna delle *Elegantiae*," *Interpres* 3 (1980): 63, n. 66.

37. "Neque enim armis aut cruore aut bellis dominatum adeptus est, sed beneficiis, amore, concordia." Laurentius Valla, "De lingua latinae elegantia," *Opera omnia*, pref. Eugenio Garin (Turin: Bottega d'Erasmo, 1962), 3.

38. Mariangela Regoliosi, *Nel cantiere del Valla: Elaborazione e montaggio delle Elegantie* (Rome: Bulzoni, 1993), 63–70.

39. Valla, "De lingua latinae elegantia," 4.

40. See Tavoni, *Latino, grammatica, volgare*, 116–169, and in particular, 123–125.

41. Poggio Bracciolini was one of his most outspoken critics. See Martinelli, "Note sulla polemica Poggio," 29–79; Riccardo Fubini, *Umanesimo e secolarizzazione da Petrarca a Valla* (Rome: Bulzoni, 1990); David Marsh, "Grammar, Method, and Polemic in Lorenzo Valla's *Elegantiae*," *Rinascimento* 19 (1979): 91–116.

42. Salvatore Camporeale, *Lorenzo Valla: Umanesimo e teologia* (Florence: Istituto nazionale di studi sul Rinascimento, 1972), 190.

43. Platina, *On the Right Pleasure and Good Health*, 243.

44. Pliny the Elder, *Natural History, with an English Translation in Ten Volumes*, trans. H. Rackham, MA (Cambridge, MA: Harvard University Press; London: William Heinemann, 1940), vol. 3, bk. 10, 22.

45. Saint Augustine, *The City of God*, 21.4.

46. See Claudio Benporat, *Cucina Italiana del Quattrocento* (Florence: L. S. Olschki, 1996), 62.

47. Marsilio Ficino, *Three Books on Life (De vita libri tres)*, ed. and trans. C. Kaske and J. R. Clark (Binghamton, NY: Medieval and Renaissance Texts and Studies, 1989).

48. As he writes to his friends Giovanni Battista Buoninsegni and Giorgio Antonio Vespucci, both members of the Platonic Academy, "Walking recently in the manner of the Peripatetics, we talked much together about caring for the health of those who apply themselves assiduously to the study of letters. I have summed this up briefly in a work which I have decided to dedicate especially to you both." *The Letters of Marsilio Ficino*, trans. members of the Language Department of the School of Economic Science, London, vol. 8 (London: Shepeard-Walwyn, 2009), 48–49.

49. Paul O. Kristeller, *Philosophy of Marsilio Ficino* (New York: Columbia University Press, 1943); Eugenio Garin, *L'umanesimo italiano* (Bari: Laterza, 1965), 110.

50. Ficino, *Three Books on Life* (*De vita libri tres*). The work's general title specifies it is dedicated "On Caring of Those Who Devote Themselves to Literary Studies," 107. This idea is reiterated throughout the treatise; see, for instance, bk. 3, ch. 24, where he states: "I am addressing people dedicated to learning," 379.

51. For Ficino's interest in astrology, see Michael J. B. Allen, "Summoning Plotinus: Ficino, Smoke and the Strangled Chickens," *Reconsidering the Renaissance*, ed. M. A. Di Cesare (Binghamton, NY: Medieval and Renaissance Texts and Studies, 1992), 63–88. Also, Eugenio Garin, *L'età nuova: Ricerche di storia della cultura dal XII al XVI secolo* (Naples: Liguori, 1969), 421–427, and idem, *Lo zodiaco della vita: La polemica sull'astrologia dal Trecento al Cinquecento* (Rome: Bulzoni, 1976), ch. 2.

52. It should be noted that in a departure from the Platonists, Ficino differentiates between the astral benefits of medicine and figures: "the things we said cause celestial power in images can have their efficacy rather in medicine than in figures." *Three Books on Life*, bk. 3, ch. 19, 343.

53. To this day Ficino's most accurate biography remains Raymond Marcel's *Marsile Ficin* (Paris: Société d'édition "Les Belles Lettres," 1958).

54. In a letter to Cosimo de' Medici Ficino states that "all men want to live well and to do so they require riches, wealth, beauty, strength, nobility of birth, honors, power, prudence, as well as justice, fortitude and temperance, and above all else, wisdom which comprehends the whole essence of happiness . . . Wisdom makes sure that we rightly use riches and things which are called good. For this reason knowledge is the cause of good and successful action, in the possession, use and working of every gift." *Letters of Marsilio Ficino*, 32–34.

55. J. B. Wadsworth, "Lorenzo de' Medici and Marsilio Ficino: An Experiment in Platonic Friendship," *The Romanic Review* 46 (1955): 90–100.

56. Ficino, *Three Books on Life*, 1.10.20.

57. Ibid., 2.6.45.

58. Ibid., 2.6.53.

59. To my knowledge this is the only meal described as such in the *Morgante*.

60. Alison Brown, "Lorenzo and Public Opinion in Florence: The Problem of Opposition," *Lorenzo il Magnifico e il suo mondo: Convegno internazionale*

di studi, Firenze, 9–13 giugno, 1992, ed. Gian Carlo Garfagnini (Florence: L. S. Olschki, 1994), 61–85.

61. See Claude Grignon, "Commensality and Social Morphology: An Essay of Typology," *Food, Drink and Identity*, ed. Peter Scholliers (Oxford and New York: Berg, 2001).

62. Salvatore Battaglia, *Grande dizionario della lingua italiana* (Turin: UTET, 1961).

63. Barbara Di Pascale, *Banchetti Estensi: La spettacolarità del cibo alla corte di Ferrara nel Rinascimento* (Imola: La mandragora, 1995).

64. Marsilio Ficino, *Commentary on Plato's Symposium on Love*, trans. Sears Jayne (Dallas, TX: Spring, 1985), bk. 2, ch. 8: "Certainly dominion and lover differ thus. The ruler possesses others through himself; the lover recovers himself through another, and the further each of the two lovers is from himself, the nearer he is to the other, and dead in himself, revives in the other." In more explicit terms, in book 2, chapter 9, Ficino states: "Beauty of the body is nothing other than the splendor itself in the ornament of colors and lines. Beauty of the soul also is a splendor in the harmony of doctrine and customs. Not the ears, not smell, not taste, not touch, but the eye perceives that light of the body. If the eye alone recognizes, it alone enjoys. Therefore the eye alone enjoys the beauty of the body. But since love is nothing else except the desire of enjoying beauty, and this is perceived by the eyes alone, the lover of the body is content with sight alone. Thus the desire to touch is not a part of love, nor is it a passion of the lover, but rather a kind of lust and perturbation of a man who is servile."

65. In a letter to Lorenzo Matteo Franco writes, "Gigi (Pulci) è animella delle vostre palle. Havete tolto a mostrare la magnificentia et humanita vostre in tenere a ghalla questo dispecto della generatione humana" (Gigi [Pulci] is a flee of your balls [a direct allusion to the Medici coat-of-arms that also acquires a more obscene meaning]. You have chosen to show your humanity and magnificence in keeping afloat this spite of humanity). Marcel, *Marsile Ficin*, 426. In a letter to Lorenzo Pulci writes, "Racomandomi a te, et spero m'aiuterai; et lungo tempo ho desiderato tu possa ... Aiutami poichè puoi ... perchè senza il tuo aiuto, Lorenzo, a parlare virilmente, sono ancora in più noia non credi" (I entrust myself to you, and I hope you will help me; I have hoped this for a long time ... Help me, because you can ... because to tell you the truth, Lorenzo, without your help I find myself in more trouble than you can imagine). Domenico De Robertis, *Morgante e lettere* (Florence: Sansoni, 1984), 976.

66. Giovanni Getto, in his *Studio sul Morgante* (Florence: L. S. Olschki, 1977), looks briefly at this episode in the chapter "L'avventura dei sentimenti," 102.

67. Albert Rabil Jr., "The Significance of Civic Humanism in the Interpretation of Italian Renaissance," *Renaissance Humanism: Foundations, Forms, and Legacy*, 3 vols., ed. Albert Rabil Jr. (Philadelphia: University of Pennsylvania Press, 1988), 141–174.

68. Jean-Pierre Garrido, "Le theme de la 'grande bouffe' dans le *Morgant* de Luigi Pulci," *La table et ses dessous*, ed. A. Charles Fiorato and A. Fontes Baratto (Paris: Presses de la Sorbonne Nouvelle, 1999), 73–91.

69. Mikhail Bakhtin, *Rabelais and His World*, trans. H. Iswolsky (Cambridge and London: MIT, 1968), 58.

70. Stephens, *Giants in Those Days*, 9–57; Richard Berrong, *Rabelais and Bakhtin: Popular Culture in Gargantua and Pantagruel* (Lincoln and London: University of Nebraska Press, 1986).

71. Bakhtin, *Rabelais and His World*, ch. 4, "Banquet Imagery."

72. "For every body consists entirely of parts that are fixed and individual; if these are removed, enlarged, reduced, or transferred somewhere inappropriate, the very composition will be spoiled that gives the body its seemly appearance." Leon Battista Alberti, *On the Art of Building in Ten Books*, trans. Joseph Rykwert, Neil Leach, and Robert Tavernor (Cambridge, MA, and London: MIT, 1990), bk. 9, ch. 5.

73. Giovanni Pico della Mirandola, *On the Dignity of Man*.

74. Chiara Frenquellucci, "La gastronomia nell'epica cavalleresca: Il *Morgante* di Pulci," *Romance Language Annual* (1996): 172–178.

75. Hans Baron, *The Crisis of the Early Renaissance* (Princeton: Princeton University Press, 1955); Garin, *L'umanesimo italiano*.

76. Mazzotta, *Cosmopoesis*.

77. Ficino, *Theologia Platonica*, 14.1: "The entire striving in our soul is to become God. Such striving is no less natural to men than the effort to fly is to birds. For it is always in men everywhere. Likewise it is not a contingent quality of some men but follows the nature itself of the species." See also Charles Trinkaus, *In Our Image and Likeness: Humanity and Divinity in Italian Humanist Thought*, 2 vols. (Notre Dame, IN: University of Notre Dame Press, 1995), especially "The Human Condition in Humanist Thought: Man's Dignity and His Misery," 171–343.

78. There is an echo here of Alberti's belief in expanding a thematic field beyond what is included and known "since the *istoria* is the greatest work of the painter, in which there ought to be copiousness and elegance in all things, we should take care to know how to paint not only a man but also horses, dogs and all other animals and things worthy of being seen." *On Painting*, trans. John R. Spencer (New Haven and London: Yale University Press, 1966), 95.

79. On this, see Stefano Carrai, *Le muse dei Pulci: Studi su Luca e Luigi Pulci* (Naples: Guida editori, 1985), 95–112.

80. Mary Kuntz, "'The Prodikean Choice of Herakles': Reshaping of Myth," *The Classical Journal* 89 (1993): 163–181.

81. Pollio Vitruvius, *Ten Books on Architecture*, trans. and ed. Ingrid D. Rowland, comm. and illus. Thomas Noble Howe (Cambridge and New York: Cambridge University Press, 1999), xiii, xiv.

82. Ingrid D. Rowland, "From Vitruvian Scholarship to Vitruvian Practice," *Memoirs of the American Academy in Rome* 50 (2005): 15–40.

83. Deborah Howard, "Apartments in Renaissance Italy," *Artibus et Historiae* 43 (2001): 127–135.

84. Vitruvius, *Ten Books on Architecture*, 29.

85. Ibid., 27.

86. The extent of Vitruvius's pseudo-scientific theories comes to full view in ch. 6. Here, in describing the northern populations he states that they "have sluggish minds" because of "the air's thickness." By contrast, southern populations "have acute minds and infinite cleverness of invention . . . ," yet, "when they are called to give a show of strength they give way, because the vigor of their minds has been sucked away by the sun." In contrast to these, "Roman people partake in equal measure of the qualities of both north and south." This fact, according to Vitruvius, sets Roman people apart from all the others. Ibid., 77.

87. Ibid., 29.

88. Matthew 16:18.

89. According to De Robertis, "Pulci parla come i suoi personaggi . . . è uno di loro; e racconta come racconterebbero loro, il suo occhio, la sua partecipazione, il suo modo di inquadrare e commentare quei fatti, è quello di Rinaldo e Margutte" (Pulci speaks like his characters . . . he is one of them; and narrates in the same fashion they would, his perspective, his participation, and his way to frame and comment on those events is Rinaldo's and Margutte's). *Storia del Morgante*, 465.

90. See Mazzotta, *Cosmopoiesis*, 8.

91. "Only the contemplative (men) reach it (sufficiency), for the contemplative life is close to the good itself, which is God" (312); "So, if pleasure is present to the external and corporeal senses, it will be present to the body alone; it will not pass over into the undiluted soul. For the soul enjoys pleasure through inner comprehension, which is called opinion, and through memory and reason and the intellect" (318). Marsilio Ficino, *The Philebus Commentary*, ed. and trans. Michael J. B. Allen (Tempe, AZ: Arizona Center for Medieval and Renaissance Studies, 2000).

92. Which is also akin to Ficino's belief that "the soul is being in itself and outside of itself at the same time." Jorg Lauster, "Ficino as a Christian Thinker," *Marsilio Ficino: His Theology, His Philosophy, His Legacy*, ed. Michael J. B. Allen and Valery Reed (Leiden: Brill, 2002), 63. In cognition the soul draws the divine into itself, through love it extends itself to the infinity of God. *Theologia Platonica*, 14.10

93. See Bruce G. McNair, "Cristoforo Landino and Coluccio Salutati on the Best Life," *Renaissance Quarterly* 47 (1994): 747–769.

94. Valla, *On Pleasure*, 59.

95. Ficino, in his *Theologia Platonica*, 12.6, speaks of the "power of the numbers that is in the soul." And continues: "Yet the judging numbers do temper our individual actions. For whatever it is that prevents and checks us from walking with uneven strides, or beating time to uneven intervals, or chewing with uneven bites of our teeth . . . Whatever it is in any concern that checks us from un-

balanced movements when we do anything using the body's limbs, and silently commands us to observe a certain symmetry, this is in fact some judging thing. This is what gives men much more than the beasts a sense of, an appreciation for, beauty and charm."

96. Ficino explains: "the senses which are absolutely necessary and are diffused through the whole body, namely touch and taste. For the latter are necessary for self-preservation and the production of offspring." *Philebus Commentary*, 320. "From these things it can be apparent to anyone that of those six powers of the soul, three pertain to the body and matter (touch, taste, and smell) whereas the other three (reason, sight, and hearing) pertain to the spirit." Marsilio Ficino, *Commentary on Plato's Symposium on Love*, trans, intro., and notes Sears Jayne (Dallas, TX: Spring, 1985), 85–86.

97. Ficino, *Theologia Platonica*, 14.229.

98. See Orvieto, *Pulci medievale*, particularly ch. 5, "Ancora a proposito di Margutte," 171–212.

99. Bakhtin, *Rabelais and His World*, ch. 4, "Banquet Imagery."

100. "The grotesque image reflects a phenomenon in transformation, an as yet unfinished metamorphosis, of death and birth, growth and becoming." Ibid., 24.

101. Geoffrey G. Harpham, *On the Grotesque: Strategies of Contradictions in Art and in Literature* (Princeton: Princeton University Press, 1982), 6–7. "Grotesque embodies confusion of type, that arises from the clash between the virtuous limitations of forms and a rebellious content that refuses to be constrained."

102. André Chastel, "'Idée' Artistique et problèmes de l'atelier," *Art et humanisme à Florence au temps de Laurent le Magnifique: Études sur la Renaissance et l'humanisme platonicien* (Paris: Presses Universitaires de France, 1959), 335.

103. See Stephens, *Giants in Those Days*.

104. The most renowned recipe collection of this period is the *Ricettario di Maestro Martino*, compiled, as the title suggests, by a Martino de Rubeis (de' Rossi) prior to 1465. He was the cook for the cardinal of Aquileia first, and later, in Rome, for Ludovico Trevisani. There he met Bartolomeo Sacchi (Platina), who had arrived in Rome in 1462, and, like him, became a member of the Accademia Pomponiana. See Benporat, *Cucina italiana del Quattrocento*.

105. Augustine, *The City of God*, ch. 11, 605.

106. Lorenzo Valla, *Dialogue on Free Will, The Renaissance Philosophy of Man*, ed. Ernst Cassirer, Paul Oskar Kristeller et al., trans. C. E. Trinkaus Jr. (Chicago: University of Chicago Press, 1969), esp. 175 ff.

107. "La pernise è carne temperata, molto cordiale e declina al secco come ditto. È carne da zentili e richi homini, imperò se fa preciosa" (Partridge meat is temperate, very mild, and, as mentioned, produces dryness. It is a meat fit for courtly and wealthy men, thus appreciated for its qualities). Michele Savonarola, *Libreto de tutte le cosse che se magnano un'opera di dietetica del sec. XV*, ed. Jane Nystedt (Stockholm: Amquist & Wiksell International, 1988), 115.

108. "La pernice è fraudolento animale, invola e cova l'altrui ovi, ma dapò rimane inganata, ché come quelli animali sono nasciuti e odono la voce dela madre la quale i generò, lassa quelli a che lli ha covato e cussì de robba mal aquistata non fa capitalle" (The partridge is a deceitful bird because it steals and broods the eggs of other birds; but afterwards it is itself deceived. After the little chicks have hatched they recognize their mother's voice and abandon the partridge that brooded them. Thus, what is acquired through theft does not produce wealth). *Libreto de tutte le cosse che se magnano*, 116.

109. "Partridge meat . . . increases strength of the brain, stimulates fertility, and excites flagging passion." Platina, *On the Right Pleasure and Good Health*, 5.14.255–256.

110. Ficino, *Three Books on Life*, 2.17.219.

111. Alberti, in his *On the Art of Building in Ten Books*, speaks of variety as "always a most pleasing spice." Bk. 1, 9, 13–15.

112. "The 'Uncanny,'" *The Standard Edition of the Complete Psychological Works of Sigmund Freud*, ed. James Strachey (London: Hogarth Press, 1955), vol. 17, 240.

113. See Nadia Khouri, "The Grotesque: Archeology of an Anti-Code," *Zagadnienia Rodzajow Literackich* 23, no. 2 (1980): 5–24.

114. Leon Battista Alberti, *Momus*, trans. Sarah Knight, ed. Virginia Brown (Cambridge, MA: Harvard University Press, I Tatti Renaissance Library, 2003), bk. 2, 127.

THREE Banquets of Power

1. Aristotle, *Politics*, bk. 1, 8, 1256a, 19–39.

2. For a brief but valuable article on Boiardo's political and poetic career at the Este court, see Giuseppe Trenti, "L'Orlando dimenticato: Il Boiardo tra corte, feudo e uffici ducali," *L'quila Bianca: Studi di storia estense per Luciano Chiappini*, ed. Antonio Samaritani and Ranieri Varese (Ferrara: Corbo, 2000), 437–455.

3. Emilio Faccioli, ed., *L'arte della cucina italiana* (Turin: Einaudi, 1987).

4. Elvira Garbero Zorzi speaks of the banquet as spectacle because, as she points out, it was organized and directed like a theatrical performance. She notes that the *soprintendente della festa*, like a modern movie director, oversaw the efficient planning of all the parts of the event. In this role, he was not only responsible for coordinating the work of all the individuals necessary to serve an entire meal, but also for overseeing the organization of the performances presented during the *intermezzi*. The *soprintendente* also played a crucial role in designing the elements of *sorpresa* and *meraviglia* that made every banquet a unique occasion to celebrate the host's magnificence. See "La festa cerimoniale del Rinascimento: L'ingresso trionfale e il banchetto d'onore," *Scene e figure del teatro italiano*,

ed. Elvira Garbero Zorzi and Sergio Romagnoli (Bologna: Società Editrice Il Mulino, 1985), 76.

5. The wedding celebrations continued in Ferrara with the arrival of Eleonora on July 4, 1473. See Jadranka Bentini, "Per la ricostruzione del banchetto del Principe," *A tavola con il principe: Materiali per una mostra su alimentazione e cultura nella Ferrara degli Estensi*, ed. Jadranka Bentini, Alessandra Chiappini, Giovanni Battista Panatta, and Anna Maria Visser Travagli (Ferrara: Gabriele Corbo, 1988), 269–307.

6. Ludwig Pastor has a comprehensive description of the event in his *The History of the Popes, from the Close of the Middle Ages*, ed. F. I. Antrobus (London: Routledge and Kegan Paul, 1949), vol. 4, 241–244.

7. An excellent study on the Orsini family and its shifting alliances and enmities with different popes has been authored by Christine Shaw, *The Political Role of the Orsini Family from Sixtus IV to Clement VII: Barons and Factions in the Papal States* (Rome: Istituto Storico Italiano per il Medio Evo, 2007).

8. According to Giles of Viterbo, corruption, venality, and nepotism reached unprecedented levels during the pontificate of Sixtus IV. This fact, in Giles's account, accelerated the downward spiral in the history of papal dissoluteness. See John W. O'Malley, "Egidio da Viterbo and Renaissance Rome," *Egidio da Viterbo, O.S.A. e il suo tempo: Atti del V Convegno dell'Istituto Storico Agostiniano, Roma—Viterbo, 20–23 ottobre 1982* (Rome: Ed. "Analecta Augustiniana," 1983), 111.

9. Bartolomeo Sacchi (Platina), *On the Right Pleasure and Good Health (De honesta Voluptate et Valetudine)*, ed. and trans. Mary Ella Milham (Tempe, AZ: Medieval and Renaissance Texts and Studies, 1998), 236–237.

10. "Alla corte di Ferrara," Antonia Tissoni Benvenuti states, "qualsiasi citazione dell'Ercole mitologico è sempre un sottinteso omaggio al Signore con quel nome" (At the court of Ferrara every reference to the mythological Hercules is always an implied homage to the lord bearing that name). *L'innamoramento de Orlando*, ed. A. Tissoni Benvenuti and C. Montagnani (Milan and Naples: Ricciardi, 1999), 1494. While the critic's description focuses on the situation in Ferrara, it is quite clear that in Rome Riario used the same strategy to curry favor with Ercole I.

11. In 1475, within the first few years of Ercole's rule, Pier Andrea de' Bassi's work on *Laboris Herculis* was printed and widely circulated in Ferrara. According to A. Tissoni Benvenuti, Ercole's personal interest in this work was "forse per una politica dinastica che rafforzando l'immagine paterna, era volta a far dimenticare i fratellastri Leonello e Borso; ma sicuramente anche per motivi onomastici" (perhaps, based on dynastic politics that, by reinforcing the paternal image was intended to erase from memory the figures of the step-brothers Leonello and Borso; surely, it also underscored the link between the mythical hero and his namesake). "L'antico a corte: Da Guarino a Boiardo," *Alla corte degli Estensi: Filosofia, arte e cultura a Ferrara nei secoli XV e XVI*, ed. M. Bertozzi (Ferrara: Università degli Studi, 1994), 394.

12. According to Joseph Manca, Cosmè Tura's drawing of *Hercules and the Nemean Lion* "is one of the earliest representations of this subject in the Renaissance." The critic adds that "most likely it was made for Duke Ercole I," and suggests that the subject of Hercules fighting the lion could relate "to the war between Ferrara and Venice." Through this detail the art historian dates the drawing to 1482–1484 or later. More than just establishing the accurate date of the work, the drawing provides evidence that in his Ferrara Ercole d'Este was celebrated through the mythical hero's iconography. See *Cosmè Tura: The Life and Art of a Painter in Estense Ferrara* (Oxford: Clarendon, 2000), 154–155.

13. This element has been dismissed, or considered irrelevant, by critics who have claimed that meals in general are unimportant to the Renaissance hero's quests. See A. Franceschetti, *"Dall'Innamorato al Furioso," Passare il tempo: La letteratura del gioco e dell'intrattenimento dal XII al XVI secolo. Atti del convegno di Pienza, 10–14 settembre, 1991* (Rome: Salerno Editrice, 1993), 194.

14. Matteo Maria Boiardo, *Orlando innamorato*, 2 vols., ed. Riccardo Bruscagli (Turin: Einaudi, 1995), vol. 1, 15. All citations are from this edition. All English translations are from *Orlando Innamorato*, trans. and intro. Charles S. Ross (Oxford and New York: Oxford University Press, 1995).

15. Cheeses and breads, along with fruit, meat, and fish, are among the foodstuffs that require a natural process of decomposition in their preparations. Wine, along with fruit-based drinks, are elements that require fermentation, which in itself is a process of a natural (chemical) breakdown.

16. See Garbero Zorzi, "La festa cerimoniale del Rinascimento," 73; for table arrangement in general and the use of *baldachino*, see Terence Scully, *The Art of Cookery in the Middle Ages* (Woodbridge: Boydell, 1995), 169.

17. On commensal hierarchy and painting renditions, see Elisa Acanfora, "La tavola," *Rituale, cerimoniale, etichetta*, ed. Sergio Bertelli and Giuliano Crifò (Milan: Bompiani, 1985), especially 58–66.

18. For the representation of dogs sitting at the feet of the banquet table, see *The Duke of Berry sitting at a table* in the illuminated manuscript *The Very Rich Hours of the Duke of Berry* (ca. 1410), and Sandro Botticelli and Bartolomeo di Giovanni's *Nastagio degli Onesti, terzo episodio* (1483). For banquet scenes from the Middle Ages through the Baroque, see also Acanfora, *Rituale, cerimoniale, etichetta*.

19. The practice of tossing leftovers to dogs moving around or lying on the ground at the feet of dinner tables is analyzed by Cristiano Grottanelli, "Cibo, istinti, divieti," *Rituale, cerimoniale, etichetta*, ed. Sergio Bertelli and Giuliano Crifò (Milan: Bompiani, 1985), 43–47.

20. For Niccolò III's pilgrimage to the Holy Land, see G. Nori, "La corte itinerante: Il pellegrinaggio di Niccolò III in Terrasanta," *La corte e lo spazio: Ferrara estense*, ed. G. Papagno and A. Quondam (Rome: Bulzoni, 1982), 233–246.

21. On the portrayal of Turks in the Renaissance, see T. Hampton, "'Turkish Dogs': Rabelais, Erasmus and the Rhetoric of Alterity," *Representations* 41 (1993):

58–82. The Turkish presence in Ferrara is also discussed by Giovanni Ricci, *Ossessione turca* (Bologna: Il Mulino, 2002).

22. See Bartholomaeus Anglicus, *On the Properties of Things* (*De proprietatibus rerum*), trans. John Trevisa, ed. M. C. Seymour et al. (Oxford: Clarendon, 1975–1988), bk. 18.

23. "The ass (*asinus*) and the 'small ass' (*asellus*, dim. of *asinus*) are so called from 'sitting' (*sedere*), as if the word were *asedus*. The ass took this name, which is better suited to horses, because before people captured horses, they began by domesticating (*praesidere*, lit. "sit on") the ass. Indeed, it is a slow animal and balks for no reason." Isidore of Seville, *Etymologies*, 12.1.38.

24. "So the Lord has compassion on those who fear him . . . He remembers that we are dust . . . Man's days are like those of grass . . . The wind sweeps over him and he is gone, and his place knows him no more." Psalm 103:13–16.

25. Michele Savonarola, *Libretto de tutte le cosse che se magnano un'opera di dietetica del sec. XV*, ed. Maria Aurelia Mastronardi (Bari: Palomar, 1996).

26. Louis Marin, *Food for Thought*, trans. Mette Hjort (Baltimore: Johns Hopkins University Press, 1989), 125.

27. Ibid., 122. Here Marin focuses on the function of "transignificance" that food acquires.

28. On this see Giovanni Boccaccio, *Decameron*, ed. Vittore Branca (Florence: LeMonnier, 1965), 1149, n. 2.

29. Interestingly, centuries later, Fusoritto da Narni describes women catching fish as part of a banquet's spectacle in his treatise. Used as an element of *sorpresa*, the fishing he describes is made possible by lifting the dining tables under which a *peschiera* had been set up. From it, the ladies could catch fish "con i loro retini apposta preparati." V. Cervio, *Il Trinciante, ampliato et a perfettione ridotto dal Cavalier Reale Fusoritto da Narni* (Rome: nella stampa del Gubbio, 1593), 86.

30. Tissoni Benvenuti defines Boiardo a poet "istituzionalmente 'di corte', non letterato di professione." "L'antico a corte: da Guarino a Boiardo," 398.

31. Coluccio Salutati states, "Let us be cautious about our actions and our desires and how we apply the indomitable choice of the will to those things which are done through us or press upon us or others from the outside . . . We are certain never to lack grace in acting, if our care will be to temper the will by the rules of right reason." Quoted in Charles Trinkaus, "The Will Triumphant: Coluccio Salutati," *In Our Image and Likeness: Humanity and Divinity in Italian Humanist Thought* (Notre Dame, IN: University of Notre Dame Press, 1995), vol. 1, 97.

32. Dante, *Inferno*, 1.3.

33. Petrarch, Salutati, Valla, quoted in Albert Russell Ascoli, *Ariosto's Bitter Harmony: Crisis and Evasion in the Italian Renaissance* (Princeton: Princeton University Press, 1987), 76.

34. Giuseppe Mazzotta, *The Worlds of Petrarch* (Durham: Duke University Press, 1993), especially the chapter "The Canzoniere and the Language of the Self."

35. Richard M. Tristano, "Matteo Maria Boiardo and Fifteenth-Century Ferrarese Courtly Culture," *Phaeton's Children*, ed. Dennis Looney and Deanna Shemeck (Tempe, AZ: Arizona Center for Medieval and Renaissance Studies, 2005), 129–168.

36. For another perspective on the Este's notion of grandiose magnificence, see Joseph Manca, "The Presentation of a Renaissance Lord: Portraiture of Ercole I d'Este, Duke of Ferrara (1471–1505)," *Zeitschrift für Kunstgeschichte* 52 (1989): 522–538.

37. In describing Ercole's need of money, Ugo Caleffini writes that the duke sold two-year offices to the highest bidders. This strategy ensured him a "renewable" source of revenues: "In questo tempo el duca de Ferrara universalmente tuti li suoi offici, et grandi et piccoli, et de forteze et del Comune, vendeva a chi più ge ne dava, pigliando prima li denari, et vendendo per dui anni et non per più; et però veneva suxo gente incohnite ad avere offitii" (During this time the Duke of Ferrara used to sell great and small positions, pertaining to both fortresses and the *Comune*, to the highest bidders. He would take the money and sell the offices for two-year periods. In this manner, people without any title or well-established family background ended up in positions of authority). Caleffini also portrays Ercole as a leader unconcerned with city's affairs ("se impazava de cosa cosa alcuna"), while deeply engrossed in personal enjoyments. An example he offers is that of Ercole moving through the city during the carnival season, wearing carnival masks to amuse himself "andava in maschara ogni zorno ed davase piacere" (he went around the city every day wearing a mask and enjoying himself). *Diario di Ugo Caleffini (1471–1494)*, 2 vols., ed. Giuseppe Pardi (Ferrara: Premiata Tipografia Sociale, 1938), vol. 2, 206–207.

38. For the use of spices in the Renaissance, see Paul Friedman, "Spices and Late-Medieval European Ideas of Scarcity and Value," *Speculum* 80 (2005): 1209–1227; Stefan Halikowski Smith, "Demystifying a Change in Taste: Spices, Space, and Social Hierarchy in Europe, 1380–1750," *International History Review* 29 (2007): 237–257; Bridget Ann Henisch, *Fast and Feast: Food in Medieval Society* (University Park and London: Pennsylvania State University Press, 1976); and Wolfgang Schivelbusch, trans. David Jacobson, *Tastes of Paradise: A Social History of Spices, Stimulants, and Intoxicants* (New York: Pantheon, 1992), 3–14.

39. On the diffusion of the idea of magnificence throughout Italy, see A. D. Fraser Jenkins, "Cosimo de' Medici's Patronage of Architecture and the Theory of Magnificence," *Journal of the Warburg and Courtauld Institutes* 33 (1970): 162–170; for the rebuilding of Naples, see George Hersey, *Alfonso II and the Artistic Renewal of Naples, 1485–1495* (New Haven: Yale University Press, 1969).

40. Aristotle, *Nicomachean Ethics*, bk. 4, 2, 1122b–1123a.

41. Long periods of droughts or of floods regularly ruined the cultivation of grains, fruit, and vegetables. These periods of extreme climate, more than just resulting in widespread famine, had devastating effects on the economy of the city

and more especially on the lives of the lower-class city- and country-dwellers. Throughout his *Diario Ferrarese* Caleffini regularly speaks of the food scarcity that marked Ercole's reign. For example: "In questo tempo molto pochi dinari erano per la tera, et chi havea uno ducato d'oro gli parea havere assai. Et li cittadini et contadini de Ferrara stavano malissimi (sic) per le caristie, et pochissime facende se facea a Ferrara et in le altrui tere" (At this time there was not much money available; anyone with a gold ducato would feel as though he possessed a lot of money. Famines created terrible conditions for both farmers and Ferrara's citizens. As a result, very little was accomplished in Ferrara and in other places). *Diario di Ugo Caleffini (1471–1494),* vol. 1, 90.

42. On Ercole's war with Venice, see L. Chiappini, *Gli Estensi: Mille anni di storia* (Ferrara: Corbo, 2001), 176–188.

43. "10 maggio (C.) Il duca, conoscendo che certi provvedimenti suggeriti a lui dal soprannominato (Giacomo Trotti, 'cavalero ribaldo, traditore, inimico del sangue di poveri'), gli avevano inimicato il popolo, restituì al Comune la Masseria, rinunciò alla tassa del boccatico per tutti i contadini e condonò le condanne per danni dati e malefizi (grida, che fu ripetuta il giorno dopo); e pose in luogo del Trotti, come giudice dei XII Savi, Bonifacio Bevilacqua, 'perchè sciapeva lui essere grato al populo'" (May 10. Realizing that certain requirements he had suggested to the above mentioned (Giacomo Trotti, a rogue, betrayer, and enemy of poor people) had alienated his people, the duke gave back the Masseria to the Comune, eliminated the food tax, and pardoned convictions (proclamation that was repeated the next day); and he replaced Trotti with Bonifacio Bevilacqua as judge of the XII Savi "because he knew that this man was well liked by the people"). In a note that accompanies this entry, the editor states: "La politica fiscale seguita fin allora per provvedere agli sperperi di Ercole I aveva inasprito il popolo; ma tutta la colpa ne fu addossata al caduto giudice dei XII Savi e il duca si rifece una verginità di fronte ai Ferraresi" (the fiscal policies intended to provide for Ercole I's extravagances had exasperated the people; but all the blame was put on the judge of the XII Savi and the duke regained his innocence in the eyes of the Ferraresi). *Diario di Ugo Caleffini (1471–1494),* vol. 1, 283.

44. See Maria Serena Mazzi, "La fame e la paura della fame," *A tavola con il principe: Materiali per una mostra su alimentazione e cultura nella Ferrara degli Estensi,* ed. Jadranka Bentini, Alessandra Chiappini, Giovanni Battista Panatta, and Anna Maria Visser Travagli (Ferrara: Gabriele Corbo, 1988), 153–169.

45. Francesco Petrarca, *Canzoniere,* ed. Gianfranco Contini (Turin: Giulio Einaudi, 1964), 264.

46. "Virtue and glory," asserts Vergerio, "are the goals for the noble." "The Character and Studies Befitting a Free-Born Youth," *Humanist Educational Treatises,* ed. and trans. Craig W. Kallendorf (Cambridge, MA, and London: Harvard University Press, I Tatti Renaissance Library, 2002), 29.

47. Chrétien de Troyes offers various examples of courtly hospitality where ladies help knights shedding their armor; see, for example, *The Knight of the Cart (Lancelot)*, trans. and intro. William W. Kibler (New York: Penguin, 1991), 220 and 233.

48. Trevor Dean discusses the Estes' attitude toward the power they wielded in *Terra e potere a Ferrara nel tardo medioevo: Il dominio estense: 1350–1450* (Modena: deputazione di storia patria per le antiche province modenesi, 1990).

49. Trevor Dean, "Ferrarese Chroniclers and the Este State," *Phaeton's Children: The Este Court and its Culture in Early Modern Ferrara*, ed. Dennis Looney and Deanna Shemeck (Tempe: Arizona Center for Medieval and Renaissance Studies, 2005), 174.

50. Eugenio Garin, *Educazione umanistica in Italia: Testi scelti e illustrati* (Bari: Laterza, 1949); idem, *Educazione in Europa 1400–1600: Problemi e programmi* (Rome and Bari: Laterza, 1976).

51. Raffaele Donnarumma, "Poetiche romanzesche nel I libro del poema," *Il Boiardo e il mondo estense nel Quattrocento: Atti del convegno internazionale di studi Scandiano-Modena-Reggio Emilia-Ferrara 13–17 settembre 1994*, ed. G. Anceschi and T. Matarrese (Padua: Antenore, 1997), 777–806.

52. Marco Dorigatti, "La favola e la corte: Intrecci narrativi e genealogie estensi dal Boiardo all'Ariosto," *Gli dei a Corte: Letteratura e immagini nella Ferrara estense* (Florence: L. S. Olschki, 2009), 31–54.

53. Riccardo Bruscagli, "Ferrara: Arts and Ideologies in a Renaissance State," *Phaeton's Children: The Este Court and its Culture in Early Modern Ferrara*, ed. Dennis Looney and Deanna Shemeck (Tempe: Arizona Center for Medieval and Renaissance Studies, 2005), 35.

54. Homer, *The Iliad*, trans. Richmond Lattimore (Chicago and London: University of Chicago Press, 1951), 442–445.

55. Antonio Franceschetti, *L'Orlando innamorato e le sue componenti tematiche e strutturali* (Florence: L. S. Olsckhi, 1975), 145. Here Franceschetti speaks of "ragioni esterne" that prevent the hero from consuming his love for Angelica. Donnarumma, on the contrary, states: "non liquiderei l'episodio come una buffonesca manifestazione della buffonaggine di Orlando ... Ma (Orlando) è affetto da un'inconcludente patologia lirica" (I would not dismiss the episode as an example of Orlando's buffoonery ... But [Orlando] is affected by an ineffective lyrical pathology). As model Franceschetti offers Petrarch's and Boiardo's personal lives. "Poetiche Romanzesche," 795.

56. Jo Ann Cavallo, in her *Boiardo's Orlando Innamorato: An Ethics of Desire* (Rutherford, Madison, and Teaneck: Fairleigh Dickinson University Press, 1993), 13, states that "Boiardo's narrator is an ironist ... Even when Boiardo is at his most lyrical, his comments can harbor an ironic smile." Also, in the introduction she speaks of the allegorical structure that governs the poem. To this end, she affirms that "the elements of Boiardo's narrative often function on another level of mean-

ing that aims to further our understanding of human nature from a moral standpoint" (5).

57. Franceschetti, *L'Orlando inamorato,* 13; and Robert Durling *The Figure of the Poet in Renaissance Epic* (Cambridge, MA: Harvard University Press, 1965), 105.

58. Antonia Tissoni Benvenuti in her article "Di alcuni nuovi studi sull' 'Inamoramento de Orlando,'" *Rivista di letteratura italiana* 9 (1991): 289, discusses Boiardo's ways of drawing his readers into the tale he narrates.

59. Michele Savonarola gives a biased account of the sequence of events that took place at the time of Leonello's death. He asserts that the Consiglio dei Savi was gathered at Villa Belriguardo where Lionello died. They, according to Savonarola, after debating the specific qualities that the marquis's successor must embody, opted for Borso and not the legitimate heirs: "incomenzuorono in consiglio a cridare ad alta voce: —Borso marchese! Viva Borso nostro principo!" (During the meeting they began to shout—Borso marchese. Long live our prince Borso!). *Del Felice Progresso di Borso d'Este*, ed. Maria Aurelia Mastronardi (Bari: Palomar, 1996), especially 100–161.

60. See Giuseppe Pardi, "Borso d'Este duca di Ferrara, Modena e Reggio (1450–1471)," *Studi storici* 15 (1906): 3–58, 133–203, 377–415, and 16 (1907): 113–168, cited in Micaela Torboli, *Il duca Borso d'Este e la politica delle immagini nella Ferrara del Quattrocento* (Ferrara: Edizioni Cartografica, 2007).

61. Luciano Chiappini, *Gli Estensi: Mille anni di storia* (Ferrara: Corbo, 2001), 138.

62. "Questa famiglia ha una vera singolarità" (This family has a real uniqueness), wrote Enea Silvio Piccolomini (Pius II), without hiding the sharp irony in his words. "A memoria dei nostri padri nessun figlio legittimo è mai divenuto principe, tanto furono più fortunati i figli delle concubine che non quelli delle mogli: cosa questa contraria non solo alle leggi cristiane ma a quelle di tutte le nazioni" (For as long as we can remember no legitimate son has ever become a prince; indeed, the lovers' sons were luckier than the wives': this fact is not only contrary to Christian laws but also to those of every nation). See E. S. Piccolomini, *I Commentarii*, ed. Luigi Totaro (Milan: Adelphi, 2004), 403. And in fact, Borso was son, grandchild, great-grandchild, and great-great-grandchild of a bastard. See Torboli, *Il duca Borso d'Este e la politica delle immagini nella Ferrara del Quattrocento,* 9.

63. Chiappini, *Gli Estensi*, ch. 6.

64. For Borso's triumphal entrance into Ferrara, see Elvira Garbero and Susanna Cantore, "Le entrate trionfali," *Teatro a Reggio Emilia*, ed. Sergio Romagnoli and Elvira Garbero, 2 vols. (Florence: Sansoni, 1980), vol. 1, 3–28.

65. To this end, see Matteo Provaso, *Il popolo ama il duca? Rivolta e consenso nella Ferrara Estense* (Rome: Vielle, 2011), 57–77. See also Charles M. Rosenberg, *The Este Monuments and Urban Development in Renaissance Ferrara* (New York: Cambridge University Press, 1997), in particular, 83–109.

66. Savonarola, *Del Felice Progresso di Borso d'Este*, 118–138.

67. "Sulle sue labbra molte lusinghe e insieme molte menzogne. Teneva ad apparire magnifico e liberale, più che ad esserlo" (together with many flattering words numerous lies came out of his mouth. He was more interested in appearing as a magnificent and liberal man than actually being one), Piccolomini comments wryly with regard to Borso. *Commentarii*, 405.

68. Yet again Piccolomini offers an unvarnished picture of Borso's propensity for satisfying personal desires rather than attending to the affairs of his state. Called to Mantua by him (Pius II), Borso chose not to go. After a series of unconvincing excuses, Borso opted to go hunting rather than keeping his promise to the pope. Thus, Piccolomini reasons: "non pochi principi . . . assecondano ogni loro desiderio; lasciano andare in rovina lo Stato piuttosto che accettare di rinunciare a un pur piccola parte dei loro piaceri" (not few are the princes . . . that gratify their every desire; they let their State go to ruin rather than renouncing the smallest one of their pleasures). Ibid., 513. Referring specifically to Borso, he goes on to say, "A sentir lui la sua sapienza era grande; per gli altri, ne avea ben poca. E fu piuttosto la fortuna che non la sua prudenza a governare lo Stato: Ferrara divenne prospera per i continiui conflitti dei vicini, non per l'accortezza dei principi" (To hear him, his wisdom was great; but according to others, he possessed little of it. The way he governed his State owed more to fortune than to prudence: Ferrara prospered because of the continuous conflicts its neighbors were involved in rather than the shrewdness of its princes). Ibid., 515.

69. According to Charles M. Rosenberg this is evidenced by the fact that Borso simply substituted his name for Leonello's on the silver coins issued during the first two years of his reign. See "Ferrarese Coinage and the Ideology of Power from Obizzo III to Borso d'Este," *L'quila Bianca: Studi di storia estense per Luciano Chiappini*, ed. Antonio Samaritani and Ranieri Varese (Ferrara: Corbo, 2000), 110–141.

70. Quentin Skinner, *The Foundations of Modern Political Thought* (Cambridge and New York: Cambridge University Press, 1978), 56–57. Also quoted in Rosenberg, *Este Monuments and Urban Development in Renaissance Ferrara*, especially ch. 6.

71. The idea that Borso did not marry for political reasons, to ensure that the marquisate would return to Niccolò III's legitimate heirs, remains unconvincing in spite of Torboli's claim in *Il duca Borso d'Este e la politica delle immagini nella Ferrara del quattrocento*, 24–29.

72. On this subject Chiappini remains vague. According to him, a document attesting to a daughter, and another possibly to a son of Borso, are irrefutable. As for Borso's possible "deviazioni sessuali," Chiappini simply asserts that "non hanno riscontro *per lo meno esplicito—a quanto pare*—in documento alcuno," (there are no explicit proofs—as far as one can tell—in any document) (italics mine). *Gli Estensi*, 158.

73. On the war that was fought between 1482 and 1484, see Ugo Caleffini, *Croniche: 1471–1494* (Ferrara: "Monumenti" della Deputazione provinciale ferrarese di storia patria, 2006), 373–632; B. Zambotti, *Diario ferrarese dell'anno 1476 sino al 1504*, ed. G. Pardi (Bologna: Zanichelli, 1928–1937), 24, 7:2, 101 ff.; Chiappini, *Gli Estensi*, 179–187.

74. "There is a tendency to underestimate Boiardo's abilities as a historian," notes Tristano in "Matteo Maria Boiardo and Fifteenth-Century Ferrarese Courtly Culture," 142. And yet, it is quite evident that throughout his works Boiardo is an acute observer, and recorder, albeit in both poetic and literary forms, of the events shaping the time in which he lives.

75. For the wars Sixtus (and the Church) fought, see D. S. Chambers, *Popes, Cardinals and War: The Military Church in Renaissance and Early Modern Europe* (London and New York: I. B. Tauris, 2006), in particular, 79–89.

76. Werner Gundersheimer, *Ferrara estense: Lo stile del potere*, trans. Vittorio Vendelli (Ferrara: Panini, 1988), in particular, ch. 6, "Hercules Dux Ferrariae."

77. Claudio Benporat, *Cucina italiana del Quattrocento* (Florence: L. S. Olschki, 1996); idem, *Feste e banchetti: Convivialità italiana fra Tre e Quattrocento* (Florence: L. S. Olschki, 2001).

78. There, Sancho yearns for a meal of *olla potrida*. "Y denme de comer" ("And give me food to eat"), he tells the appointed dietician, "o si no, tómense su gobierno, que oficio que no da de comer a su dueño no vale dos habas" ("otherwise you can keep this governor position, for a position that does not provide food is not worth having"). Miguel de Cervantes, *Don Quijote de la Mancha*, ed. Martín de Riquer (Barcelona: Editorial Juventud, 1975), 873.

79. See Cavallo, *Boiardo's Orlando Innamorato*, particularly the chapter "Angelica," 27–35.

80. Sigmund Freud, *Three Contributions to the Theory of Sex* (New York: Dutton, 1962), 1.

81. In tracing the ascent of this family through its acquisitions of land, Dean shows that the Estes established their power by amassing extensive land possessions. See *Terre e potere a Ferrara nel tardo medioevo*, in particular, "Il patrimonio estense," 33–84. The way in which Ercole literally reshaped Ferrara's urban space by expanding the city walls through the "Herculean Addition" after the war with Venice exemplifies his political ambitions as well as his determination to preserve it.

82. Werner Gundersheimer, *Ferrara: The Style of Renaissance Despotism* (Princeton: Princeton University Press, 1973). Also, Dean, *Terre e potere a Ferrara nel tardo medioevo*.

83. Piccolomini, *I Commentarii*, 654.

84. For example, in describing the rebellion of the prince of Taranto and other lords against King Ferdinand, Piccolomini uses again a sharp tone in describing the Estes: "Fra la sorpresa di tutti si rivelò traditore, fra gli altri, anche Ercole della stirpe Estense, figlio del marchese Niccolò, il quale aveva condiviso con

Ferdinando non solo la caccia ma anche i più riposti segreti. Costui aprì al nemico le porte di Lucera dei Saraceni, ove si trovava a passare l'inverno con un grosso squadrone di cavalleria; e ciò avvenne non senza infamia per suo fratello Borso, del quale Ercole disse più tardi di avere eseguito gli ordini" (to everyone's surprise, Ercole d'Este, son of the Marquis Niccolò, revealed himself to be a traitor. This occurred in spite of the fact that he had shared with Ferdinand the most hidden secrets and joined him in hunting expeditions. This Ercole opened the doors of Lucera dei Saraceni, where he was spending the winter with a large troop of cavalry, to the enemy; this fact brought dishonor to his brother Borso. Afterward Ercole admitted that he had followed Borso's orders). Ibid., 645. After Ferdinand received papal assistance, Borso is yet again described as "apertamente non tanto nemico quanto traditore di Ferdinando, benchè presumesse di operare copertamente" (openly not as much as an enemy, rather as a traitor of Ferdinand, even though Borso assumed that his actions were secret). Ibid., 647.

85. Michele Savonarola, *Libreto de tutte le cosse che se magnano un'opera di dietetica del sec. XV*, ed. Jane Nystedt (Stockholm: Amquist and Wiksell International, 1988), 88.

86. Ficino, *Three Books on Life*, 2.5.177.

87. *Libreto de tutte le cosse che se magnano*, 161.

88. Barbara Di Pascale, *Banchetti estensi: La spettacolarità del cibo alla corte di Ferrara nel Rinascimento* (Imola: La mandragora, 1995).

89. See, for example, *Cosmè Tura e Francesco del Cossa: L'arte a Ferrara nell'età di Borso d'Este*, ed. M. Natale (Ferrara: Ferrara Arte, 2007); Salvatore Settis, *Artisti e committenti fra Quattro e Cinquecento* (Turin: Einaudi, 2010); Thomas Tuohy, *Herculean Ferrara: Ercole d'Este 1471–1505, and the Invention of a Ducal Capital* (Cambridge and New York: Cambridge University Press, 1996).

90. *Libreto de tutte le cosse che se magnano*, 162.

91. Leon Battista Alberti, *On Painting*, trans. John R. Spencer (New Haven and London: Yale University Press, 1966), 63.

92. Ficino, *Three Books on Life*, 1.7.125.

93. Dante, *Inferno*, 5.136.

94. "Et fede, sì come dice un savio, è lla speranza della cosa promessa; e dice la legge che fede è quella che promette l'uno e l'altro attende. Ma Tulio medesimo dice in un altro libro *delli offici* che fede è fondamento di giustizia, veritade in parlare e fermezza delle promesse; e questa èe (sic) quella virtude ch'è appellata lealtade" (As a wise man says, faith is hope in that which is promised; and the law states that faith is what one promises and another delivers. Tulio himself says in a book of the *De officiis* that faith is the foundation of justice, truth in speaking, and firmness in promises; and this is that virtue which is called loyalty). *La Rettorica di Brunetto Latini*, ed. Francesco Maggini (Florence: Stab. Tip. Galletti e Cocci, 1915), 7.22–27.19.

95. Aldo Scaglione, *Knights at Court: Courtliness, Chivalry, and Courtesy from Ottonian Germany to the Italian Renaissance* (Berkeley: University of California Press, 1991), 158.

FOUR Meals, Transformations, and the Belly of History

1. Ludovico Ariosto, *Orlando Furioso*, intro. and notes Nicola Zingarelli (Milan: Hoepli, 1954). All citations are from this edition. The English translations are from *Ludovico Ariosto: Orlando Furioso*, trans. Guido Waldman (Oxford and New York: Oxford University Press, 1998). For a study on the various editions of the *Furioso*, see Alberto Casadei, "The History of the *Furioso*," *Ariosto Today: Contemporary Perspectives*, ed. Donald Beecher, Massimo Ciavolella, and Roberto Fedi (Toronto: Toronto University Press, 2003), 55–70; Marco Dorigatti, "Il manoscritto dell'*Orlando Furioso (1505–1515)*," *L'uno e l'altro Ariosto in corte e nelle delizie*, ed. Gianni Ventura (Florence: L. S. Olschki, 2011), 1–44.

2. For Ariosto's biography, see Michele Catalano, *Vita di Ludovico Ariosto*, 2 vols. (Geneva: L. S. Olschki, 1930–1931); Giulio Ferroni, *Ariosto* (Rome: Salerno Editrice, 2008); and Walter Binni, *Metodo e poesia di Ludovico Ariosto e altri studi ariosteschi*, ed. Rosanna Alhaique Pettinelli (Scandicci and Florence: La Nuova Italia, 1996).

3. On Ariosto's critical tone, see Cesare Segre, *Esperienze ariostesche* (Pisa: Nischi-Listri, 1966).

4. On the transient nature of food, see Deane W. Curtin, "Recipes for Values," *Cooking, Eating, Thinking*, ed. D. W. Curtin and Lisa M. Heldke (Bloomington and Indianapolis: Indiana University Press, 1992), 126.

5. For a study on courts and courtiers, see *Princes, Patronage, and the Nobility: The Court at the Beginning of the Modern Age 1450–1650*, ed. Ronald Asch and Adolf Birke (New York: Oxford University Press, 1991).

6. Anthony Grafton and Lisa Jardine, *From Humanism to the Humanities: Education and the Liberal Arts in Fifteenth- and Sixteenth-Century Europe* (London: Duckworth, 1986).

7. Michael Dietler, "Theorizing the Feast," *Feasts: Archaeological and Ethnographic Perspectives on Food, Politics, and Power*, ed. M. Dietler and B. Hayden (Washington, DC, and London: Smithsonian Institution Press, 2001), 66.

8. See David Quint, "The Figure of Atlante: Ariosto and Boiardo's Poems," *Modern Language Notes* 94 (1979): 77–91.

9. In the *Republic*, trans. A. D. Lindsay, MA (London: J. M. Dent and Sons; New York: E. P. Dutton, 1947) Plato speaks of food and drinking as a false pleasure (9.585). In the *Phaedo* the senses are vilified because they give a false perception of reality: "the view of things by means of the eyes is full of deception, as also is that through the ears and the other senses, persuading an abandonment of these so far as it is not absolutely necessary to use them ... The soul of the true philosopher, therefore, ... abstains as much as possible from pleasures and desires, grief and fears." *Five Dialogues of Plato Bearing on Poetic Inspiration*, trans. A. D. Lindsay, MA (London and Toronto: J. M. Dent and Sons; New York: E. P. Dutton, 1927), 83. "Those who have given themselves up to gluttony, wantonness, and drinking, and

having put no restraint on themselves, (they) will probably be clothed in the form of asses and brutes of that kind." Ibid., 82.

10. Pier Paolo Vergerio in his "Character and Studies Befitting a Free-Born Youth," *Humanist Educational Treatises,* trans. and ed. Craig W. Kallendorf (Cambridge, MA, and London: Harvard University Press, I Tatti Renaissance Library, 2002), 85–87, states that "it is not unseemly to relax the mind with singing or playing the lute." And he differentiates between "singing praises of mighty men . . . not love songs." With regard to dancing he explains: "dancing to music and group dances with women might seem to be pleasures unworthy of a man. Yet there might be a certain profit in them, since they exercise the body and bring dexterity to the limbs, if they did not make young men lustful and vain, corrupting good behavior." Ibid., 87. As he goes on to talk about playing games, Vergerio again differentiates among different types of games and the players' objectives. In his view, a game board is acceptable, and not corrupting because "it offers a semblance of fighting and hostile contest." As for the game of dice "those who hunt pleasure (in this game) are slow-witted, as they cannot find any more honorable pleasure. Pleasure is most suitable taken in games that require some or even great skill, and as little chance as possible." Ibid.

11. On the subject of music during this period, see Lewis Lockwood, *Music in Renaissance Ferrara, 1400–1505* (Cambridge, MA: Harvard University Press, 1984).

12. In Baldassarre Castiglione's *Cortegiano,* ed. Ettore Bonora (Milan: Mursia, 1972), 2.11, dressing in different manners (*travestirsi*) at court discloses one's freedom and *licenzia:* "lo esser travestito porta seco una certa libertà e licenzia" (masquerading carries with it a certain freedom and license). English translation is from *The Book of the Courtier,* trans. Charles S. Singleton (Garden City, NY: Doubleday, 1959).

13. For a fascinating study of games at court and their development, see Achille Olivieri, "Giuco, gerarchie e immaginario tra Quattro e Cinquecento," *Rituale, cerimoniale, etichetta,* ed. Sergio Bertelli and Giuliano Crifò (Milan: Bompiani, 1985), 163–180.

14. The existence and advancement of Castiglione's courtier is based on deception and simulation: "(un) bon discipulo . . . sempre ha da metter ogni diligenzia per assimigliarsi al maestro e . . . transformarsi in lui . . . usar in ogni cosa una certa sprezzatura, che nasconda l'arte e dimostri ciò che si fa e dice venir fatto senza fatica e quasi senza pensarvi" (a good pupil must . . . transform himself into his master . . . to practice in all things a certain *sprezzatura,* so as to conceal all art and make whatever is said or done appear to be without effort and almost without any thought about it). *Cortegiano,* 1,26. It is evident, then, that the court exemplifies political and social falsehood, deception, and slyness.

15. Deanna Shemeck, *Ladies Errant: Wayward Women and Social Order in Early Modern Italy* (Durham and London: Duke University Press, 1988).

16. Giorgio Masi, "'The Nightingale in a Cage': Ariosto and the Este Court," *Ariosto Today: Contemporary Perspectives*, ed. Donald Beecher, Massimo Ciavolella, and Roberto Fedi (Toronto, Buffalo, and London: University of Toronto Press, 2003), 71–92.

17. It may be superfluous here to recall Socrates's words in Plato's *Phaedo*: "As long as we are encumbered with the body, we can never fully attain to what we desire; and this, we say, is truth. For the body subjects us to innumerable hindrances on account of its necessary support, and moreover if any diseases befall us, they impede us in our search after that which is; and it fills us with longings, desires, fears of all kinds of fancies, and a multitude of absurdities, so that, as it is said in real truth, by reason of the body it is never possible for us to make any advances in wisdom" (134–135).

18. Throughout the *Cortegiano* the prince, and each highly regarded courtier, must play a role by pretending effortlessness, aloofness, and grace in every activity he undertakes. Castiglione's paramount notion of *sprezzatura* is precisely the charade of "acting as if." From this comes the definition of the court's theatricality. See *La corte e il "Cortegiano: unmodello europeo,"* ed. Adriano Prosperi (Rome: Bulzoni, 1980).

19. Claudio Benporat, in his *Cucina italiana del Quattrocento* (Florence: L. S. Olschki, 1996), lists "Il ricettario di Maestro Martino" as one of the most important recipe collections of this period. Originally, Martino de Rubeis da Como (Martino de' Rossi) was a cook for the Sforza's court. Later, he worked for the patriarch of Aquileia. His *ricettario*—as discussed above—was incorporated into Bartolomeo Sacchi's (Platina) *De honesta voluptate et valitudine*. Other important recipe collection manuals circulating during this period were Michele Savonarola's *Libreto de tutte le cosse che se magnano; un'opera di dietetica del secolo XV* and Cristoforo Messisbugo's *Libro nuovo nel quale s'insegna far d'ogni sorta di vivanda secondo la diversità dei tempi, cose di carne e di pesce*. This treatise was first published in 1549, a year after Messisbugo's death. For an excursus on Renaissance food's manuals and treatises, see Alessandra Chiappini, "Libri e cose che se manzano," *A tavola con il principe: Materiali per una mostra su alimentazione e cultura nella Ferrara degli Estensi*, ed. Jadranka Bentini, Alessandra Chiappini, Giovanni Battista Panatta, and Anna Maria Visser Travagli (Ferrara: Gabriele Corbo, 1988), 217–268; Giovanni Battista Panatta in collaboration with Edgardo Canducci, "La mensa del principe," *A tavola con il principe: Materiali per una mostra su alimentazione e cultura nella Ferrara degli Estensi*, ed. Jadranka Bentini, Alessandra Chiappini, Giovanni Battista Panatta, and Anna Maria Visser Travagli (Ferrara: Gabriele Corbo, 1988), 69–99.

20. Ludovico Ariosto, "Erbolato," *Tutte le opere di Ludovico Ariosto*, 3 vols., ed. C. Segre (Milan: Mondadori, 1984). For the English translation, see Dennis Looney, *"My Muse Will Have a Story to Paint": Selected Prose of Ludovico Ariosto* (Toronto, Buffalo, and London: University of Toronto Press, 2010).

21. Looney, "*My Muse Will Have a Story to Paint,*" 285.
22. On this work, see Dennis Looney, "Ariosto and the Classics in Ferrara," *Ariosto Today: Contemporary Perspectives*, ed. Donald Beecher, Massimo Ciavolella, and Roberto Fedi (Toronto, Buffalo, and London: University of Toronto Press, 2010), 20–31; also, idem, "*My Muse Will Have a Story to Paint.*"
23. To this end Albert R. Ascoli is correct in affirming that in the *Furioso* "culturally negative or subversive outcomes are, on the whole, left implicit . . . Attacks on patrons, or on figures of unassailable prestige . . . can only be deduced by an active interpretation of ostentatious formal features." "Ariosto and the 'Fier Pastor': Form and History in *Orlando Furioso*," *Renaissance Quarterly* 54, no. 2 (2001): 510.
24. As indicated above, in *On the Right Pleasure and Good Health*, Platina specifies that "Non tutti i cibi sono adatti a ogni uomo ma secondo la diversita' dei principi alimentari, dei desideri dell'uomo secondo gli umori, dei gusti di ciascuno così dovranno variare i cibi" (Not all foods are suitable for every man; on the contrary, they must vary according to the different alimentary principles they possess, as well as, man's desires, humors, and taste).
25. Ken Albala, *Eating Right in the Renaissance* (Berkeley and Los Angeles: University of California Press, 2002); *Food and Drink in History: Selections from the Annales, économie, societies, civilization*, ed. Robert Forster and Orest Ranum, trans. Elborg Forster and Patricia M. Ranum (Baltimore: Johns Hopkins University Press, 1979).
26. On the discourse of ethics/etiquette, see Giorgio Patrizi, "Etica/etichetta," *Etiquette*, ed. Alain Montandon (Clermont-Ferrand, France: Association des publications de la Faculté des letters et sciences humaines de Clermont-Ferrand, 1989), 78–99.
27. In the introduction to his *Libreto* dedicated to Borso d'Este, Savonarola specifies that "Imperò vedendo mi tua Signoria a cussì desiderare, caro illustre mio Signore, de tale cosse cussì spesse fiate nelli toi amichevoli convivij da me dimandate, le quale hanno cum sue virtude tua sanitade conservar, che un libreto a te scrivesse, di loro mettendo li documenti e di quelli la correctione. E domandandoti cossa cussì e a mi debita per tuo cussì più sano vivere e tua longa vita menare, disposto me ho a tale tuo desiderio cum ogni mia força diligentia satisfare" (Aware of your lordship's desire that I write a little book about the things we often discussed in the course of your friendly dinner parties, things whose qualities aim at preserving your health, I gathered the information you wished for. So I diligently set myself to fulfill your desire by documenting the attributes of food that will enable you to live a healthy and long life). Michele Savonarola, *Libreto de tutte le cosse che se magnano; un'opera di dietetica del secolo XV*, ed. Jane Nystedt (Stockholm: Almquist and Wiksell International, 1988), 57.
28. As indicated above, in *On the Right Pleasure and Good Health*, Platina specifies that appropriate food must be consumed according to its alimentary value, man's desires, taste, and humors. See note 24.

29. Eduardo Saccone, "Wood, Garden, 'locus amoenus' in Ariosto's *Orlando Furioso*," *Modern Language Notes* 112, no. 1 (1997): 1–20; Ita MacCarthy, "Alcina's Island: From Imitation to Innovation in the *Orlando Furioso*," *Italica* 81, no. 3 (2004): 325–350.

30. Castiglione, *Cortegiano*, 1.26.

31. On desire in the *Furioso*, see Eugenio Donato, "'Per selve e boscherecci labirinti': Desire and Narrative Structure in Ariosto's *Orlando Furioso*," *Literary Theory/Renaissance Texts*, ed. Patricia Parker and David Quint (Baltimore: Johns Hopkins University Press, 1986), 33–62.

32. Aenea Silvius Piccolomini, "The Education of Boys," *Humanist Educational Treatises*, trans. and ed. Craig W. Kallendorf (Cambridge, MA, and London: Harvard University Press, I Tatti Renaissance Library, 2002), 139.

33. Ibid., 143–145. Piccolomini also admonishes boys against playing games that are "lewd and indecent." Ibid., 143.

34. On the importance of magnificence at the Este court, see *Art and Life at the Court of Ercole I d'Este: The "De triumphis religionis" of Giovanni Sabadino degli Arienti*, ed. Werner L. Gundersheimer (Genève: Librairie Droz, 1972), 50–79.

35. Ovid, *Metamorphoses*, trans. A. D. Melville, intro. and notes E. J. Kenney (Oxford and New York: Oxford University Press, 1986), bk. 9, 62–90.

36. "Tasting involves registering the sensation as pleasant or unpleasant. Therefore this sense provides a suitable analogue for judgments of the quality of experience by means of immediate, subjective approval," states Carolyn Korsmeyer in *Making Sense of Taste: Food and Philosophy* (Ithaca and London: Cornell University Press, 1999), 41.

37. "While her attendants were making ready the viands and the wine, for the wassail, she arrayed Alcides in her own garb. She gave him gauzy tunics in Gaetulian purple dipped; she gave him the dainty girdle, which but now had girt her waist. For his belly the girdle was too small; he undid the clasps of the tunics to thrust out his big hands. The bracelets he had broken, not made to fit those arms; his big feet split the little shoes. She herself took the heavy club, the lion skin, and the lesser weapons stored in their quiver." Ovid, *Fasti*, trans. James G. Frazer (London: William Heinemann, 1959), 2, vv. 317–326. Also, Deianira addressing Hercules' submission to Omphale: "Meander as it twists upon its track, / its weary waters always turning back, / Saw, astonished, necklaces bedeck / Hercules' sturdy, sky-supporting neck. / Shamelessly you braceleted your arms, / Embellishing with gems your brawny charms— / To think that those arms had strength to slay / Nemea's scourge, whose hide you wear today! / You even wound a turban round your hair— / A poplar garland would look better there! / Nor, like a harlot, did you think it wrong / to dress up in a Lydian sarong— / . . . They say that you sat spinning too, afraid / Of being scolded, trembling like a maid / . . . It's said, poor wretch, that at your lady's feet you / Cowered terrified that she would beat you." Ovid, *Heroides*, trans. Daryl Hine (New Haven and London: Yale University Press, 1991), 30–31.

38. *Diario di Ugo Caleffini (1471–1494)*, 2 vols., ed. Giuseppe Pardi (Ferrara: Premiata Tipografia Sociale, 1938), 206–207.

39. Interestingly, Castor Durante in *Il Tesoro della sanità* (Rome, 1586); 3rd ed. (Venice: Domenico Imberti, 1643) speaks of gluttons who "search in vain for more delectable morsels, overstimulating their appetites, and finally eating themselves to death." Quoted in Albala, *Eating Right in the Renaissance*, 106.

40. Giovanni Pico della Mirandola, "On the Dignity of Man," trans. Elizabeth Livermore Forbes, *The Renaissance Philosophy of Man*, ed. Ernst Cassirer, Paul Oskar Kristeller, and John Herman Randall Jr. (Chicago and London: University of Chicago Press, 1948), 215–254.

41. Giovanni Pico della Mirandola, *Heptaplus o La settemplice interpretazione dei sei giorni della Genesi*, trans. Eugenio Garin, intro. Alberto Cesare Ambesi (Turin: Edizioni Arktos, 1996), 81–82.

42. "L'uomo infatti era stato fatto per natura in modo che la ragione dominasse i sensi e che dalla legge di questa fosse frenato ogni impulso d'ira e ogni appetito sessuale" (Man was created by nature in such a way that reason would dominate the senses and laws of nature would restrain his every impulse of anger and sexual appetite). Mirandola, *Heptaplus o La settemplice interpretazione dei sei giorni della Genesi*, 83.

43. According to Looney, Ariosto's *Erbolato* "parodies the work of Pico and other neo-platonists." "*My Muse Will Have a Story to Paint*," 24.

44. See Benporat, *Cucina italiana del Quattrocento*, in particular, "banchetti e conviti," 59–70.

45. Cristoforo Messisbugo, *Libro nuovo nel quale s'insegna far d'ogni sorta di vivanda secondo la diversità dei tempi, cose di carne e di pesce* (Venice: al segno di San Girolamo, 1556). Dedicated to Ippolito D'Este, cardinal of Ferrara, the book not only offers significant information about the uses and customs of banquets at the court but also provides priceless descriptions of the confetti molded out of sugar and brought to the banquet tables between courses at regular intervals. For the banquet offered by Ercole to his father and the archbishop of Milan on January 23, 1529, Messisbugo writes that "Furono portate a tavola figure grandi di zucchero 25 le quali significavano le forze di Ercole quando vinse il leone, la cui grandezza era piu' di due palmi e mezzo per ciascheduna, dorate e dipinte con le carnagioni che parevano vive. Et stettero a tavola fino a che si levò il primo mantile" (25 big sugar-figures were brought to the tables. They represented Hercules' strength when he overwhelmed the lion. Each figure measured more than two spans [22.5 inches], was gilded and painted in colors that made the skin seem real. These figures were left on the tables until the end of the first course) (15). For the same dinner Messisbugo records two more sets of twenty-five figures, each representing Ercole's strength (18, 25).

46. For the social meaning of sugar in history, see Sidney W. Mintz, *Sweetness and Power: The Place of Sugar in Modern History* (New York: Viking, 1985).

47. On "The Courtly Universe" and "Court Spectacle," see Sergio Bertelli, Franco Cardini, and Elvira Garbero Zorzi, *The Courts of the Italian Renaissance* (New York: Facts on File, 1986).

48. Bernardino Zambotti in the *Diario ferrarese dell'anno 1476 sino al 1504*, ed. Giuseppe Pardi (Bologna: Zanichelli, 1934–1937) describes Ferrara as a city in which hunger and famine are an integral part of daily life.

49. In his *Corona florida medicinae* Antonius Gazius [Antonio di Gazzo], O5v (Venice: Ioannes et Gregorius de Gregoriis, 1491), mentions the people deceived when they traveled to Venice to buy confections for weddings only to discover back in Padua that they were hollow, without a soft sugar center. Cited in Albala, *Eating Right in the Renaissance*, 212, n. 92.

50. Castiglione in the *Cortegiano* 4.7 speaks of princes who "are ill-balanced within and are heedlessly placed on uneven bases (and) fall to their ruin by reason of their own weight, and pass from one error to a great many: for their ignorance, together with the false belief that they cannot make a mistake and that the power they have comes from their own wisdom."

51. "Princes of today are so corrupted by evil costumes and by ignorance and a false esteem of themselves." Ibid., 4.9.

52. Niccolò Machiavelli, *The Art of War*, trans., ed., and comm. C. Lynch (Chicago: University of Chicago Press, 2003), 90.

53. "Softness or anything that makes men delicate or unwarlike." Ibid., 163.

54. W. L. Gundersheimer, in *Ferrara estense: Lo stile del potere,* trans. Vittorio Vendelli (Ferrara: Panini, 1988), 87, draws a lucid picture of Ercole's aloofness and detachment not only from the people but also in the administration of Ferrara. Also, the duke's imposition of new taxes, even at times when famine and plague regularly afflicted the citizens of his duchy, gives a fuller picture of his self-serving character.

55. Machiavelli, *Art of War*, 163.

56. Giovanni Maria Zerbinati, *Croniche di Ferrara: Quali comenzano del anno 1500 sino al 1527*, ed., intro., and notes Maria Giuseppina Muzzarelli (Ferrara: Deputazione provincial ferrarese di storia patria, 1989).

57. Catalano, *Vita di Ludovico Ariosto*; Adriana Flamigni and Rossella Mangaroni, *Ariosto* (Milan: Camunia, 1989); Giuseppe Toffanin, *La vita e le opere di Ludovico Ariosto* (Naples: Libreria scientifica editrice, 1959). For specific autobiographic information, Ariosto's correspondence is a precious source. See, for instance, Looney, *"My Muse Will Have a Story to Paint"*; and Gianni Scalia, *Lettere dalla Garfagnana di Ludovico Ariosto* (Bologna: Cappelli, 1977).

58. Giorgio Padoan, *"L'Orlando Furioso* e la crisi del Rinascimento," *Lettere italiane* 27 (1975): 286–307.

59. Various letters addressed to the cardinal or his secretaries attest to the poor treatment he reserved for the poet. For this see, for example, Letter 10 in Looney's *"My Muse Will Have a Story to Paint,"* 36–37.

60. Thomas M. Greene describes Ariosto's "complicated position" as a "bourgeois who never entirely lost a certain bourgeois outlook, despite his long service for the d'Este family." "Ariosto and the Earlier Italian Renaissance," *The Descent from Heaven: A Study in Epic Continuity* (New Haven and London: Yale University Press, 1963), 104–143, and particularly 129.

61. "Chi brama onor di sprone o di cappello, / serva re, duca, cardinale o papa; / io no, che poco curo questo e quello" (3.40–42) ("Let the man who hungers for the honors of the / spurs or of the hat serve a king, a / duke, a cardinal, a pope. I will not. Such trifles do not / interest me"); "So ben che del parer de' più mi tolgo / che'l stare in corte stimano grandezza; / ch'io per contrario a servitù rivolgo" (3.28–30) ("Well do I know that I reject the opinion of the / world, which esteems it an honor to live at the court, / for I on the contrary consider it servitude"). *The Satires of Ludovico Ariosto: A Renaissance Autobiography*, trans. Peter DeSa Wiggins (Athens: Ohio University Press, 1976).

62. Zambotti in the *Diario ferrarese* offers many examples of this. Also Luciano Chiappini, in particular, "La fine della signoria estense a Ferrara," *Gli Estensi: Mille anni di storia* (Ferrara: Corbo, 2001), 429–433; Guido Guerzoni, *Le corti estensi e la devoluzione di Ferrara del 1598* (Modena: Archivo Storico, Assessorato alla cultura e beni culturali, 2000).

63. Luciano Chiappini, *Gli Estensi: Mille anni di storia* (Ferrara: Corbo, 2001). Also, Jane F. Bestor, "Kinship and Marriage in the Politics of an Italian Ruling House: The Este of Ferrara in the Reign of Ercole I 1471–1505" (PhD diss. University of Chicago, 1992); Antonio Piromalli, *Cultura a Ferrara al tempo di Ludovico Ariosto* (Florence: La Nuova Italia, 1953).

64. See M. Cattini and M. Romani, "Le corti parallele: Per una tipologia delle corti padane dal XIII al XVI secolo," *La corte e lo spazio: Ferrara estense*, ed. G. Papagno and A. Quondam (Rome: Bulzoni, 1982), 47–82. "Il principe, divenuto il primo dei cortigiani, preferisce la finzione e l'artificio alla realtà e perde sempre più di vista i problemi del governo e le normali cure quotidiane che questo comporta" (The prince, turned first among courtiers, prefers fiction and artifice to reality. Thus he loses sight of the problems the government faces and of the daily care they require) (77).

65. Gundersheimer, *Ferrara estense*. Also, Zerbinati, *Croniche di Ferrara; Lettere dalla Garfagnana di Ludovico Ariosto*, ed. Gianna Scalia (Bologna: Cappelli, 1977).

66. Guerzoni, *Le corti estensi e la devoluzione di Ferrara del 1598*.

67. 1516, 1521, and 1532 are the dates of the three editions. See Catalano, *Vita di Ludovico Ariosto*.

68. Barbara Di Pascale, *Banchetti Estensi: La spettacolarità del cibo alla corte di Ferrara nel Rinascimento* (Bologna: La mandragora, 1995).

69. According to Savonarola, *confettare* means to prepare, to season, and to pickle and, in general, to preserve. *Confetto*, on the contrary, is a sweetened aliment. *Libretto de tutte le cose che se magnano*, 214.

70. On this, see Giuseppe Mazzotta's "The Road to Freedom," *The Humanities Review* 6, no. 2 (2008): 187–201, in particular, 193.

71. Augustine of Hippo, *The City of God*, 11.

72. Lorenzo Valla, *Dialogue on Free Will* in *The Renaissance Philosophy of Man*, ed. Ernst Cassirer, Paul Oskar Kristeller, et al., trans. C. E. Trinkaus Jr. (Chicago: University of Chicago Press, 1979), vol. 1, 175 ff.

73. Giovanni Boccaccio, *Famous Women*, ed. and trans. Virginia Brown (Cambridge, MA, and London: Harvard University Press, 2001).

74. "Semiramis always wore a turban and kept her arms and legs covered so that nothing could reveal the deception and hinder her course of action." Boccaccio, *Famous Women*, 19.

75. "Her accomplishments," writes Boccaccio, "would be extraordinary and praiseworthy and deserving of perpetual memory." Ibid., 21.

76. Ibid., 367.

77. Plutarch, *The Lives of the Noble Grecians and Romans*, trans. J. Dryden (New York: Modern Library, 1932), 1125, states "all he did was done without perfect consideration, as by a man who had no power of control over his faculties, who, under the effect of some drug or some magic, was still looking back elsewhere,"

78. Boccaccio, *Famous Women*, 367.

79. Marin, *Food for Thought*, 137.

80. Ibid., 136.

81. Ovid, *Metamorphoses*, 6.1–141.

82. "In casa mia mi sa meglio una rapa / ch'io cuoca, e cotta s'un stecco me inforco, / e mondo, e spargo poi di acetto e sapa, / che all'altrui mensa tordo sterna o porco / selvaggio; e così sotto una vil coltre, / come di seta o d'oro, ben mi corco" (In my house a turnip tastes better to me that I / cook myself and, when it is done, fork on a stick / and peel and season with vinegar and must, than at / someone else's table thrush, partridge, or wild boar; / and I go to bed at home beneath a humble covering, / as if it were made of silk or of gold brocade) (3.43–48); "Degli uomini son varii li appetiti: / a chi piace la cherchia, a chi la spada, a chi la patria, a chi li strani liti. / Chi vuole andare a torno, a torno vada: . . . a me piace abitar la mia contrada" (Men's appetites are various. The tonsure / pleases one man, while the sword befits another. Some / love their homeland, while others delight in foreign / shores. Let him wander who desires to wander. / . . . / I am content to live in my native land) (3.52–56).

83. " Se ne l'onor si trova o ne la immensa / ricchezza il contentarsi, i'loderei / non aver, se non qui, la voglia intensa; / ma se vediamo i papi e i re, che dei stimiamo in terra, star sempre in travaglio, che sia contento in lor dir non potrei" (If contentment were to be found in prestige or in / immense riches, I would praise a disposition directed / nowhere save toward them; but when we see popes / and kings, whom we consider gods on earth, remain / forever in travail, how can I say

that contentment / resides in honors and wealth?) (3.232–238); and then "Convenevole è ancor che s'abbia cura / de l'onor suo; ma tal che non divenga / ambizione e passi ogni misura" (It is also right that a man pay attention to his honor, / but not so diligently that honor becomes ambition / and passes all measures) (3.256–258).

84. "il vero onore è ch'uom da ben te tenga / ciascuno, e che tu sia . . . / Che cavalliero o conte o reverendo / il populo te chiami, io non te onoro, / se meglio in te che'l titol non comprendo" (The true honor is that everyone / consider you a good man and that you be a good / man . . . / The populace may call you Knight or Count or Reverend, / but I do not honor you unless I perceive / something more in you than your title) (3.259–264).

85. Even though their payments were a source of continuous despair and the reason for the poet's unhappy years at the Garfagnana, "Dimandar mi potreste chi m'ha spinto / dai dolci studi e compagnia sì cara / in questo rincrescevol labirinto. Tu dei saper che la mia voglia avara / unqua non fu, ch'io solea star contento / di quel stipendio che trae a Farrara; / ma non sai forse come uscì poi lento, / succendendo la guerra, e come volse / il Duca che restasse in tutto spento. / Fin che quella guerra durò non me ne dolse; / mi dolse di vedere che poi la mano / chiusa restò, ch'ogni timor si sciolse" (You may wonder what it was that thrust me from / my sweet studies, and the company so dear to me, / into this noisome labyrinth. You must know that it / could never have been my greed, since I used to be / well contented with the stipend I drew in Ferrara. / But perhaps you do not know how tardily he issued / forth after awhile with the coming of the war, and / how the Duke willed then that it should stop entirely. / While the war lasted I did not complain. But later / it grieved me to see the hand still closed after every / fear was vanquished) (4.169–180).

86. William J. Kennedy, "Ariosto's Ironic Allegory," *Modern Language Notes* 88, no. 1 (1973): 44–67.

87. Leon Battista Alberti, in his treatise *On Painting*, speaks of painting as the art that "contains a divine force which not only makes absent men present, as friendship is said to do, but moreover makes the dead seem almost alive," *On Painting*, trans. John R. Spencer (New Haven and London: Yale University Press, 1966), 63.

88. As he speaks of the pleasures derived by the senses, Lorenzo Valla's Epicurean lists drinking wine as one of two elements (the other one being speech) that makes man superior to all other animals. "Men are superior to all other animals on two counts: we can express what we feel, and we can drink wine, sending out the one and ushering in the other." *On Pleasure*, bk. 1, 24, 105.

89. Eugenio Garin, *Educazione in Europa, 1400–1600* (Rome and Bari: Laterza, 1976), 94.

90. Ruggiero's journey back from the world of errors and misguided beliefs bears the mark of the reversed image of Dante's Pilgrim descending into the

world of damnation. Ruggiero's persevering "al suo dritto cammin" (his straight way) (10.40), thus becomes the specular inversion of the Pilgrim's "la diritta via era smarrita." (the straight way was lost). Dante, *Inferno,* 1.3.

FIVE Courtesans and Figs, Art and Nature in Aretino's *Ragionamento*

1. Paul Larivaille, *Pietro Aretino* (Rome: Salerno Editrice, 1997); idem, *Pietro Aretino fra Rinascimento e Manierismo* (Rome: Bulzoni, 1980); Edward Hutton, *Pietro Aretino Scourge of Princes* (London: Constable, 1922); Bertrand Levergeois, *L'Arétin ou l'insolence du Plaisir* (Paris: Fayard, 1999).

2. Fabio Massimo Bertolo, *Aretino e la stampa, strategie di autopromozione a Venezia nel Cinquecento* (Rome: Salerno Editrice, 2003); G. Baldassarri, "L'invenzione dell'epistolario," *Convegno internazionale su Pietro Aretino nel cinquecentenario della nascita: Atti del convegno di Roma-Viterbo-Arezzo-Toronto-Los Angeles 28 settembre–29 ottobre 1992* (Rome: Salerno Editrice, 1995), 157–178. See also Raymond B. Waddington, "Aretino e la cultura della stampa," *Il satiro di Aretino: Sessualità, satira e proiezione di sé nell'arte e nella letteratura del XVI secolo,* trans. Cristiano Spila (Rome: Salerno, 2009), 79–119.

3. Some examples from his letters suffice to give an idea of Aretino's approach. In 1534 to Antonio Da Leva he writes, "i Re hanno abbondanza de i tesori, e carestia de la verità" (kings have an abundance of treasures and scarcity of truth). Pietro Aretino, *Lettere,* 6 vols., ed. Paolo Procaccioli (Rome: Salerno, 1997), 1.41.7–8. All citations from the *Lettere* are from this edition. In 1537, to Frate Vitruvio de i Rossi: "Se i principi che ci comandano, dessero di sprone a le lor promesse, onde corressono, come corrano le vostre, che bel vivere e che bella età saria la nostra" (If the princes that rule us were to keep their promises as you keep yours, what enjoyable living conditions we would have and what a beautiful age ours would be). Ibid., 1.182.1–3. In 1537 to Lionardo Bartolini: "il nascere nobili, il vivere onorato, e il morire glorioso è una concordanza che si vede in pochi" (to be born noble, live honorably, and die gloriously is found only in a few people). Ibid., 1.334.9–10. To Franchini in 1546: "Certo che sua eccellenza in l'arte de la liberalità è singulare, ma quella con il sí poco esserctarla la imbastardisce, sí ch'è peggio che avarizia; e non burlo" (Surely his Excellency is truly unique in practicing the art of liberality. But because he practices this art so rarely he bastardizes it, so that his liberality becomes worse than avarice; and I am not kidding). Ibid., 4.74. To the duke of Urbino in 1554: "Le speranze invero sono Parasite e meretrici de i desiderii, e le promesse ruffiane e bastarde de gli effetti. Tal che le cose promesse e sperate si negoziano non pure per vie de le cortegiane e de le menzogne, ma con il mezzo de le mule e de le Pollastriere" (In truth hopes are desires' parasites and whores; promises are effects' panders and bastards. So that things that are promised and hoped for are not only negotiated through courtesans and lies but worse yet through

animal-like behaviors and procurers). Ibid., 6, 336-1-4. And to M. ETC. (sic) in 1603, "Se io avessi creduto, o fratello, che lo inreverendissimamente Reverendo si dilettasse più de le grasse pernici e dei buoni vini, che dei valenti uomini e de i belli ingegni, le laude che io gli ho dato . . . si convertivano ne i vituperi che mi apparecchio a scrivergli . . . In tanto sua signoria, per essere ministra del piacer de la gola, dee portare di molto odio al suo ventre, poi che non è grande come la sua ingordigia . . . Or tracanni e inghiotta fin che ci crepi e scoppi" (Had I known, brother, that the most unworthy of reverence Reverend would rather enjoy fat partridges and good wines than men of valor and keen intellect the praises I have bestowed on him . . . would turn into the vituperations I am about to hurl at him. . . . Meanwhile, his lordship must hate his belly because, as minister of his pleasure and gluttony, it is not as large as his greed . . . Now let him guzzle and gulp down until he bursts and pops off). Ibid., 5.386.1–5 and 12–20.

4. Larivaille, *Pietro Aretino*; Mario Pozzi, "Note sulla cultura artistica e sulla poetica di Pietro Aretino," *Giornale storica della letteratura Italiana* 145 (1968): 293–313.

5. Larivaille, *Pietro Aretino*, 20.

6. Benvenuto Cellini throughout his *Vita*, ed. Ettore Camesasca (Milan: Biblioteca Universale Rizzoli, 1985) gives lively accounts of artists' lives in Rome during Clement VII's and Leo X's papacies. Of particular interest, however, is book 1. Here, in chs. 19 and 30 prominent historical and artistic figures associated with Aretino appear. See also Larivaille, *Pietro Aretino*, ch. 2.

7. Elizabeth L. Eisenstein, *Printing Press as an Agent of Change: Communications and Cultural Transformation in Early Modern Europe* (Cambridge and New York: Cambridge University Press, 1979); idem, *Printing Revolution in Early Modern Europe* (Cambridge and New York: Cambridge University Press, 2005).

8. On the prestige and status that curial officials benefited from, see Charles L. Stinger, *The Renaissance in Rome* (Bloomington: Indiana University Press, 1985), in particular, "Church Administration and Spiritual Power," 123–140.

9. It is interesting to note that Erasmus of Rotterdam penned his *Praise of Folly* on his return from Rome. The work was published in 1511. In it, Folly is a goddess and her nymphs and companions include Flattery, Inebriation, Ignorance, Madness, Pleasure, Intemperance, Laziness, Wantonness, Self-love, Oblivion, and Dead-sleep. Not surprisingly, these are the same traits that Aretino highlights in the Roman courtiers his Nanna describes.

10. "Ecco il flagello / De principi, il divin Pietro Aretino" (here is the scourge of princes, the divine Pietro Aretino). L. Ariosto, *Orlando furioso*, 46.14; see also Giovangirolamo De' Rossi: "Amò ancora Pietro Aretino perché dei preti, signori e príncipi d'ogni sorte, in voce ed in scritti, era acerbissimo persecutore di modo che lo chiamava per soprannome il flagello dei Signori" (He [Giovanni delle Bande Nere] also loved Pietro Aretino because in words and writings the latter was a sharp critic of priests, lords, and princes of every kind. For this reason, he was

called the scourge of Princes). *La vita di Giovanni de' Medici detto delle Bande Nere*, ed. Vanni Bramante (Rome: Salerno Editrice, 1996), 104.

11. "La sua memoria è infame; un uomo ben educato non pronunzierebbe il suo nome innanzi a una donna" (his memory lives in infamy; a gentleman would never mention his name in the presence of a lady), affirms Francesco de Sanctis, *Storia della letteratura italiana*, ed. N. Gallo, intro. N. Sapegno (Turin: Einaudi, 1966), 624. Also, P. Larivaille, "Pietro Aretino tra infrazione e censura," *Convegno internazionale su Pietro Aretino nel cinquecentenario della nascita: Atti del convegno Roma-Viterbo-Arezzo (28 settembre–1 ottobre 1992), Toronto (23–24 ottobre 1992), Los Angeles (27–29 ottobre 1992)* (Rome: Salerno, 1995), 3–21.

12. Marga Cottino-Jones, in "I *Ragionamenti* e la ricerca di un nuovo codice," n. 1, offers a thorough bibliography of Aretino's dialogue. *Convegno internazionale su Pietro Aretino nel cinquecentenario della nascita: Atti del convegno Roma-Viterbo-Arezzo (28 settembre–1 ottobre 1992), Toronto (23–24 ottobre 1992), Los Angeles (27–29 ottobre 1992)* (Rome: Salerno, 1995).

13. For Paolo Procaccioli Aretino's writings dating back to the Roman years are, above all, examples of *antibembismo*. "Pietro Aretino sirena di antipetrarchismo: Flussi e riflussi di una poetica della militanza," *Autorità, modelli e antimodelli nella cultura artistica e letteraria tra Riforma e Controriforma: Atti del Seminario internazionale di studi, Urbino-Sassocorvaro, 9–11 novembre 2006*, ed. Antonio Corsaro, Harald Hendrix, and Paolo Procaccioli (Rome: Vecchiarelli Editore, 2007), 108. For Nino Borsellino the *Ragionamenti* are specifically set against the courtly systems of Bembo's *Asolani* and Castiglione's *Cortegiano*. According to the critic, against these works, Aretino's *Ragionamento* is the "mirror of a hidden truth." See *L'età italiana: Cultura e letteratura del pieno Rinascimento* (Rome: Vecchiarelli Editore, 2008), 218.

14. "Questo libro tanto vituperato quanto mal noto" (this book is as vituperated as poorly known). Alessandro Luzio, *Pietro Aretino nei primi suoi anni a Venezia e la corte dei Gonzaga* (Turin: Ermanno Loescher, 1888), 112.

15. Enrico Malato, "Per un bilancio in itinere," *In utrumque paratus. Aretino e Arezzo, Aretino a Arezzo: In margine al ritratto di Sebastiano del Piombo. Atti del Colloquio internazionale per il 450o anniversario della morte di Pietro Aretino, Arezzo 21 Ottobre 2006*, ed. Paolo Procaccioli (Rome: Salerno Editrice, 2006), 17–25; idem, "Gli studi su Pietro Aretino negli ultimi cinquant'anni," *Pietro Aretino nel cinquecentenario della nascita: Atti del convegno di Roma-Viterbo-Arezzo (28 settembre–1 ottobre 1992), Toronto* (Rome: Salerno Editrice, 1995), 1127–1150.

16. According to Nino Borsellino, the *Ragionamento* evidences "la volontà di contraffazione nei confronti dei dialoghi platonizzanti di ispirazione cortigiana e accademica, ambientati in dimore e giardini signorili" (the will to mimic and poke fun at the Platonizing dialogues of courtly and academic inspiration set in elegant homes and gardens). In his view, this feature "imprime all'opera una sua netta originalità strutturale rispetto alla corrente produzione libellistica sulla

vita e i costumi delle prostitute" (gives the work its distinct structural originality with respect to the prevalent publications on the lives and customs of prostitutes). *Gli anticlassicisti del Cinquecento* (Rome and Bari: Laterza, 1973), 30.

17. "A Pietro importava di piú ritrovare quanto prima un posto importante nell'*entourage* del 'patrone lasciato cardinale' e adesso diventato papa, e per salire nella sua stima e conseguentemente nella gerarchia cortigiana" (Pietro was mostly concerned with finding an important position within the inner circle of his former patron whom he had left a cardinal and now had become pope and with rising in the latter's esteem and in the courtly hierarchy). Paul Larivaille, "Pietro Aretino nella Roma di Clemente VII," *In utrumque paratus: Aretino e Arezzo, Aretino a Arezzo: In margine al ritratto di Sebastiano del Piombo,* ed. Paolo Procaccioli (Rome: Salerno, 2008), 123.

18. The Sack of Rome is treated at length in Ludwig Pastor, *The History of the Popes, from the Close of the Middle Ages,* 40 vols. (London: Routledge and Kegan Paul, 1949), vol. 9, 272–467; see also Luigi Guicciardini, *The Sack of Rome,* trans. James H. McGregor (New York: Italica, 1993); Judith Hook, *The Sack of Rome, 1527* (London: Macmillan, 1972); E. R. Chamberlin, *The Sack of Rome* (London: Batsford, 1979); Maria Ludovica Lenzi, *Il sacco di Roma del 1527* (Florence: Nuova Italia, 1978). For the cultural impact, see André Chastel, *The Sack of Rome, 1527,* trans. Beth Archer (Princeton: Princeton University Press, 1983); Giuseppe Galasso, "La crisi italiana e il sistema politico europeo nella prima metà del secolo XVI," *Dalla "libertà d'Italia"alle preponderanze straniere* (Naples: Editoriale Scientifica, 1997), 15–59.

19. Giulio Ferroni, "Pietro Aretino e le corti," *Pietro Aretino nel cinquecentenario della nascita* (Rome: Salerno Editrice, 1995), 23–48.

20. "il vero è mio Idolo" (the truth is my Idol), writes Aretino. *Lettere,* 6.169.36. His distance from conventions, as Procaccioli points out, also underscores the divergence between past and present, and between individual and tradition. "Pietro Aretino sirena di antipetrarchismo. Flussi e riflussi di una poetica della militanza," 113.

21. According to Massimo Ciavolella, Aretino's erotic language and subjects are a strategy the writer adopts to uncover the true aspects of his society. See "La produzione erotica di Pietro Aretino," *Convegno internazionale su Pietro Aretino nel cinquecentenario della nascita,* 49–66.

22. On this topic, see Ruth Kelso, *Doctrine for the Lady of the Renaissance* (Urbana: University of Illinois Press, 1956); Joan Kelly, *Women, History and Theory* (Chicago: University of Chicago Press, 1984); Ian Maclean, *The Renaissance Notion of Women* (Cambridge and New York: Cambridge University Press, 1990); Sarah F. Matthews-Grieco, *Erotic Cultures of Renaissance Italy* (Farnham, Surrey, and Burlington, VT: Ashgate, 2010).

23. Borsellino defines the *Ragionamenti* as *unicum* because no other example of "pornographic literature" from the same period or even an earlier one

exists that measures up to it. Borsellino also emphasizes the coherence that Aretino establishes between the courtesans' language and their social background. This, according to the critic, gives full historical-literary rights to the *Ragionamenti*. See *L'età italiana*, 209–222.

24. This association was first emphasized by Sperone Speroni in his *Dialoghi:* "Lo Aretino non ritragge le cose men ben in parole, che Titiano in colori: & ho veduto de suoi sonetti fatti da lui, d'alcuni ritratti di Titiano: & non è facile il giudicare, se li sonetti son nati dalli ritratti, ò li ritratti da loro; certo ambidue insieme, cioè, il sonetto, & il ritratto, sono cosa perfetta: questo dà voce al ritratto, quello all'incontro, di carne, & d'ossa veste il sonetto. E credo che l'esser dipinto da Titiano, et lodato dall'Aretino, sia una nuova regeneratione de gli uomini" (Aretino does not depict objects through words more poorly than Titian does through colors. I read some sonnets he authored and some portraits Titian painted and it is not simple to figure out whether the sonnets were born from the portraits or the portraits from the sonnets: for the first lend voice to the portrait while simultaneously the portrait dresses the sonnets with bones and flesh. And I believe that to be painted by Titian and praised by Aretino represents a new regeneration of man). (*Vinegia: In casa de' figliuli di Aldo,* 1543), 25.

25. Rodolfo Pallucchini, *Tiziano* (Florence: Sansoni, 1969); idem, *Profilo di Tiziano* (Florence: Martello-Giunti), 1977; idem, ed., *Tiziano e il manierismo europeo* (Florence: L. S. Olschki, 1978).

26. Clark Hulse, *The Rule of Art: Literature and Painting in the Renaissance* (Chicago: University of Chicago Press, 1990), 83–114.

27. See, for instance, Carlo Dionisotti, *Umanisti e il volgare fra Quattro e Cinquecento* (Florence: LeMonnier, 1968); Piero Floriani, *Bembo e Castiglione: Studi sul classicismo del Cinquecento* (Rome: Bulzoni, 1976); Robert W. Hanning and David Rosand, eds., *Castiglione: The Ideal and the Real in Renaissance Culture* (New Haven and London: Yale University Press, 1983).

28. See Nuccio Ordine, "Le 'Sei giornate,'" *Convegno internazionale su Pietro Aretino nel cinquecentenario della nascita: Atti del convegno Roma-Viterbo-Arezzo (28 settembre–1 ottobre 1992), Toronto (23–24 ottobre 1992), Los Angeles (27–29 ottobre 1992)* (Rome: Salerno, 1995), 673–716.

29. With regard to language, he writes: "Sterpate da le composizioni vostre i ternali del Petrarca . . . non tenete in casa vostra i suoi 'unquanqui,' i suoi 'soventi,' e il suo 'ancide,' stitiche superstizioni de la lingua nostra; nel replicare l'istorie e i nomi scritti da lui, allontanativigli più che potete, perché son cose troppo trite" (Eliminate from your writings Petrarch's three syllabic words . . . Do not keep his "unquanqui," his "soventi," and his "ancide," for they are unnatural in our language; distance yourselves from repeating the stories and the names he wrote because they are overused and unoriginal). *Lettere,* 1.177.29–34. Also, to Capitano Franciotto: "la lingua de i gran maestri piena sempre di promesse magnifiche, è simile a qual si voglia cipresso eminente, che se ben va con le cime sublimi insuso,

niuno frutto produce, sí che belle ma vane sono le parole di tali; sí come alta ma sterile è la sorte di arbori cosí fatti" (the language of great teachers is always full of magnificent promises; like any perfect cypress, its sublime top reaches upward, yet it does not produce any fruit; so the words of those individuals are beautiful but empty, just like this tall but fruitless tree). Ibid., 4.322.2–6.

30. Christopher Cairns, *Pietro Aretino and the Republic of Venice: Research on Aretino and His Circle in Venice, 1527–1556* (Florence: L. S. Olschki, 1985), ch. 5; Fabio Massimo Bertolo in his *Pietro Aretino e la stampa: Strategie di autopromozione a Venezia nel Cinquecento* (Rome: Salerno Editrice, 2003) argues that Aretino dedicated volume 5 of his *Lettere* and two volumes of letters he received to members of the Del Monte family to ingratiate himself with Pope Julius III. Bertolo describes this strategy as the "procedere ad una manovra di avvicinamento al pontefice, dedicando al fratello *Lettere* V e al nipote i due volumi di *Lettere scritte a Pietro Aretino* (Marcolini 1551–1552), il tutto in prospettiva di una chiamata a Roma e della tanto sospirata porpora cardinalizia" (a maneuver intended to get closer to the pope by dedicating the *Lettere* V to his brother and the two volumes *Lettere scritte a Pietro Aretino* (Marcolini 1551–1552) to his nephew. All of this in the hope that he [Aretino] would be called to Rome and there receive the much hoped for cardinal's hat) (37).

31. Pietro Aretino, *Sei Giornate: Ragionamento della Nanna e della Antonia (1534), Dialogo nel quale la Nanna insegna a la Pippa (1536)*, ed. Giovanni Aquilecchia (Bari: Laterza and Figli, 1969), 8. All Italian references are from this edition. The English translations are from *Dialogues*, trans. Raymond Rosenthal, pref. Alberto Moravia, intro. Margaret E. Rosenthal (Toronto, Buffalo, and London: University of Toronto Press, 2005).

32. According to Raymond B. Waddington, the bestial love nuns typify and divine love that prostitutes exemplify in Aretino's *Ragionamento* represent the exact inversion of Bembo's bestial, human, and divine love in the *Asolani*. "Aretino e la cultura della stampa," *Il satiro di Aretino: Sessualità, satira e proiezione di sé nell'arte e nella letteratura del XVI secolo*, trans. Cristiano Spila (Rome: Salerno, 2009), 62.

33. With regard to Aretino's boldness in outdoing old artistic models, see ibid.,14.

34. Throughout the letters Aretino's partiality toward fine foods emerges. For example, "Il sagrestano m'ha dato i boleti che avete mandati costí da Trevigi, de i quali he goduto . . . E perché i tartufi, le ostrighe e i frutti, non son cibi, ma alettamenti dell'appetito, che sforzano a mangiare fino a i satolli, non vorrei che il piacer che ho preso mangiandogli vi facesse credere che io mi dilettassi nel vizio de la gola . . . Ceratmente il mio animo, se'l modo ci fusse, si pasceria de le grandezze reali, ma la mia bocca, che potria pur trarsi qualche voglia nel gusto, si nudrisce di vivande villane" (The sexton gave me the mushrooms you sent from Treviso. I enjoyed them . . . Since truffles, oysters, and fruit are not food, but ap-

petite's temptations that induce one to gorge, I would not want you to think, because of the pleasure I felt eating them, that I am a glutton. Surely, if there were a way, my soul would feed on royal delicacies, but my mouth, which could well wish to satisfy my taste's cravings, is only nourished by rustic dishes), he writes to Frate Vitruvio De Rossi, *Lettere*, 1.182.3–14.

35. To invite Nicolò Franciotto to dine with him Aretino writes, "Hollo per favore ancora che degnate venirci caso che in voi si senta voglia di mangiare e di bere. Perché berete e mangiarete da principi" (I will consider it a favor if you will deign come if you feel like eating and drinking. Because you will drink and eat like a prince). *Lettere*, 4.615.2–4.

36. Roberto Ridolfi, *The Life of Francesco Guicciardini*, trans. Cecil Grayson (New York: Knopf, 1968), 174–175.

37. Larivaille, *Pietro Aretino*, 180.

38. Marc Bloch, "Sel et produits de remplecement," *Pour une histoire de l'alimentation*, ed. Jean-Jacques Hémardinquer (Paris: Librairie Armand Colin, 1970), 295–296.

39. For example, the war of Venice against Ferrara was fought to gain the territory of Comacchio known for the production of salt, a commodity that generated tax revenues.

40. See, for example, Leon Battista Alberti, *Dinner Pieces*, trans. David Marsh (Binghamton, NY: Medieval and Renaissance Texts and Studies, 1987), in particular, bk. 1, 21–29 and bk. 3, 54–57.

41. For a study of the gardens in the Renaissance, see Terry Comito, *The Idea of the Garden in the Renaissance* (New Brunswick, NJ: Rutgers University Press, 1978).

42. See Ernst Curtius, *European Literature and the Latin Middle Ages*, trans. Willard R. Trask (New York: Pantheon, 1953), 183–202.

43. Terry Comito, "Renaissance Gardens and Paradise," *Journal of the History of Ideas* 32 (1971): 483–506.

44. On *otium* and *negotium*, see Marc Fumaroli, "*Otium, convivium, sermo*," *Rhetorica, a Journal of the History of Rhetoric* 11 (1993): 439–446; Bruce G. McNair, "Cristoforo Landino and Coluccio Salutati on the Best Life," *Renaissance Quarterly* 47 (1994): 747–769; Giuseppe Mazzotta, *The Worlds of Petrarch* (Durham: Duke University Press, 1993), especially "Humanism and Scholastic Spirituality," 147–166.

45. Paul Oskar Kristeller, *The Philosophy of Marsilio Ficino*, trans. Virginia Conant (Gloucester, MA: P. Smith, 1964), 296.

46. For flowers that embellish Renaissance gardens, see Ruth W. Kennedy, *The Renaissance Painter's Garden* (New York: Oxford University Press, 1948).

47. See, for instance, Giorgio Barberi Squarotti, "Il giardino ambiguo," *Regards sur la Renaissance italienne, Mélanges de literature offert à Paul Larivaille* (Nanterres: Université Paris X, 1998), 27–32.

48. Bartolomeo Scappi documented in detail the sumptuous menu for a dinner he prepared in a Trastevere garden and offered in April 1536 by Cardinal Campeggio for the Holy Roman Emperor Charles V. Although chronologically this dinner occurred after the *Ragionamento*'s publication, it still gives an idea of the gastronomic refinements the Roman curia preferred even within the garden context. See Terence Scully, trans., *The Opera of Bartolomeo Scappi (1570): L'arte et prudenza d'un maestro Cuoco (The Art and Craft of a Master cook)* (Toronto, Buffalo, and London: University of Toronto Press, 2008), 397–401.

49. John Dixon Hunt, *Garden and Grove: The Italian Renaissance Garden in the English Imagination: 1600–1750* (Princeton: Princeton University Press, 1986).

50. The garden is a topic that Alberti discusses as an ornament to private buildings in book 9 of his *The Art of Building*.

51. Ibid. Alberti specifies the makeup of the ideal garden: "there should be gardens full of delightful plants, and a garden portico, where you can enjoy both sun and shade. There should also be truly festive space . . . Walks should be lined full of evergreen plants; in a sheltered place plant a hedge of box . . . myrtle, laurel and ivy prefer a shade. Nor should cypresses cloaked in ivy be lacking. In addition, circles, semicircles and other geometric shapes . . . can be modeled out of laurel, citrus, and juniper when their branches are bent back and intertwined . . . Let the garden be green with rare herbs and those that physicians value . . . For hedges, use rose entwined with hazel and pomegranate" (300).

52. See Betty Radice, trans., *The Letters of the Younger Pliny* (New York: Penguin, 1963), 33.

53. For a discussion on the humanists' fondness for villas, gardens, and vineyards in Rome, see Stinger, *Renaissance in Rome*, in particular, 75–76.

54. Georgina Masson, "Pietro Aretino and the Small Roman Renaissance Garden," *The Garden History Society* 8 (1980): 67–68.

55. "You must understand that none of those famous men had any virtue as long as faith, hope, and charity were lacking; if one of these was absent, they could possess no other virtue at all." *A Defense of Life: Lorenzo Valla's Theory of Pleasure*, ed. and trans. Maristella De Panizza Lorch (Munich: W. Fink, 1985), bk. 3, 263.

56. Marsilio Ficino, *Platonic Theology*, trans. Michael J. B. Allen, ed. James Hankins and William Bowen (Cambridge, MA, and London: Harvard University Press, I Tatti Renaissance Library, 2004), 14.1.

57. Ibid., 14.2.

58. Ibid.

59. For an excellent study on the development of the Protestant Reformation, see Anthony Levi, *Renaissance and Reformation: The Intellectual Genesis* (New Haven and London: Yale University Press, 2002).

60. Plutarch, *The Lives of the Noble Grecians and Romans*, trans. John Dryden (New York: Modern Library, 1932), 24–46.

61. Ibid., 26.

62. Augustine, *The City of God*, bk. 3.

63. "The whole city is chargeable with it (crime) because it did not see to its punishment, and thus committed, not both fratricide, but parricide, which is worse. For both brothers were founders of that city, of which the one was by villainy prevented from being a ruler." Ibid.

64. "But unscrupulous ambition has nothing to work upon, save in a nation corrupted by avarice and luxury. Moreover, a people becomes avaricious and luxurious by prosperity." Ibid., bk. 1.

65. To Giovanni Gaddi in 1528 Aretino wrote: "Ma dove se udí mai più che uno, apena vestitosi l'abito di Prelato, cominci a dare e non a torre? Io stupisco più di ciò, che di M. Giulio de i Medici, diventato superbo Pontefice di umile Cavaliere" (Has it ever been heard that as soon as one becomes prelate he begins to give instead of taking? I am more surprised at this than at M. Giulio de' Medici turning into a superb Pope from humble knight). *Lettere*, 1.12.

66. In a letter written to Ersilia da Monte in 1562 Aretino explained: "Ben che ciascuna mia disgrazia insolente deriva da l'odio che porta a i miei vangeli la Corte, le cui obstinate perfidie ebbi per ascendente in le fasce; testimonio, come Leone, Clemente, le diaboliche santità de i quali, in cambio di asciugarmi il sudore de la servitú con le pronte mani del premio, le intinsero con presta crudeltà nel mio sangue, non per altro che per essere io senza inganno; . . . perchè l'adulazione non mi gusta; perchè la crapula fuggo; perchè procedo alla libera" (Every one of my troubles stem from the hatred the Court feels toward my truths. Its obstinate perfidy was my destiny from the time I was a baby; proof of this are Leo and Clement, whose satanic Holiness instead of drying the sweat caused by my slavery with the ready hands of reward, dipped them with quick cruelty in my blood, because I was not deceitful . . . because I hate flattery; because I avoid overeating; because I behave as a free man). Ibid., 6.169.29–36.

67. Barbara Harvey, "Monastic Diet, XIIIth–XVIth Centuries: Problems and Perspectives," *Alimentazione e nutrizione secc. XIII–XVIII, Atti della "Ventottesima Settimana di Studi" 22–27aprile 1996*, ed. Simonetta Cavaciocchi (Florence: Le Monnier, 1997), 611.

68. Again, Scappi's *Opera* offers the best examples of curial gastronomy because, as Scully notes, he knew and worked for various cardinals and several popes, among whom were Leo X, Hadrian VI, Clement VII, Paul III, Julius III, up to and including Gregory XIII. See *Opera of Bartolomeo Scappi*, 7–26.

69. Maristella De Panizza Lorch, *A Defense of Life: Lorenzo Valla's Theory of Pleasure: Lorenzo Valla's Theory of Pleasure* (Munich: W. Fink, 1985), 305.

70. For Valla, pleasure is "a powerful form of joy"; hence "pleasure must be desired for itself by those who wish to experience joy, both in this life and in the life to come." Ibid., 267.

71. Ibid.

72. Ibid., 275.

73. This is the same as saying that another man before Pyramus climbed the wall that divided the lovers.

74. Gerald Christianson, Thomas M. Izbicki, and Christopher M. Bellitto, eds., *The Church, the Councils and Reform: The Legacy of the Fifteenth Century* (Washington, DC: Catholic University of America Press, 2008).

75. For a background on Clement VII's papacy, see David S. Chambers, *Popes, Cardinals and War: The Military Church in Renaissance and Early Modern Europe* (London and New York: I. B. Tauris, 2006), 144–152.

76. For Clement VII's wars and especially political maneuverings, see Maurizio Gattoni, *Clemente VII e la geo-politica dello stato pontificio (1523–1534)* (Vatican City: Archivio Segreto Vaticano, 2002).

77. Guicciardini, *Sack of Rome*, 64.

78. Prince T. Zimmermann, *Paolo Giovio the Historian and the Crisis of Sixteenth Century Italy* (Princeton: Princeton University Press, 1995); Marcello Alberini, *Il sacco di Roma*, intro. Paola Farenga (Rome: Roma nel Rinascimento, 1997); Marjorie Reeves, *Prophetic Rome in the High Renaissance Period* (Oxford: Clarendon; New York: Oxford University Press, 1992); André Chastel, *The Crisis of the Renaissance*, trans. Peter Price (Geneva: Skira, 1968); Hans Joachim Hillerbrand, *The Division of Christendom: Christianity in the Sixteenth Century* (Louisville: Westminster John Knox, 2007).

79. See Levi, *Renaissance and Reformation*, especially "Protestantism: The Defeat of Erasmus," 285–305.

80. Massimo Firpo, *Il problema della tolleranza religiosa nell'età moderna dalla riforma protestante a Locke* (Turin: Loescher, 1978); Per Brooks, ed., *Seven-Headed Luther: Essays in Commemoration of a Quincentenary, 1483–1983* (Oxford: Clarendon, 1983); Mark Edwards Jr., *Luther's Last Battles: Politics and Polemics, 1531–46* (Ithaca and London: Cornell University Press, 1983), especially chs. 5 and 8.

81. Hermann Barge, *Andreas Bodenstein von Karlstadt*, 2 vols. (Leipzig: Friedrich Brandstetter, 1905); Charles Garside, *Zwingli and the Arts* (New Haven and London: Yale University Press, 1966), 28–33.

82. See Bryan D. Mangrum and Giuseppe Scavizzi, trans. and eds., *A Reformation Debate: Karlstadt, Emser, and Eck on Sacred Images: Three Treatises in Translation* (Ottawa: Dovehouse Editions; Toronto: Centre for Reformation and Renaissance Studies, Victoria University, 1991).

83. Ficino, *De vita libri tres*, 2.6.

84. Ibid., 2.9.

85. Ibid., 3.11.117.

86. "primum quidem monstrum est Venereus coitus" (indeed physical intercourse is the first monster). Ibid., 1.7.

87. Giorgio Vasari, *The Lives of the Most Excellent Painters, Sculptors, and Architects*, trans. Gaston du C. de Vere, ed. Philip Jacks (New York: Modern Library, 2006).

88. Mark W. Roskill, ed., *Dolce's Aretino and Venetian Art Theory of the Cinquecento* (Toronto and Buffalo: University of Toronto Press and Renaissance Society of America, 2000), 116.

89. "non vi niego che Michel'Agnolo a nostri dì non sia un raro miracolo dell'arte e della Natura ... e massimamente d'intorno alla parte del disegno, nella quale senza dubbio è profondissimo. Percioche egli è stato il primo, che in questo secolo ha dimostro ai Pittori i bei dintorni, gli scorti, il rilievo le moventie, e tutto quello, che si ricerca in fare un nudo a perfettione: cosa, che non si era veduta inanzi a lui" (I do not deny to you that Michelangelo represents, in our day, a rare miracle of art and nature ... this applies most of all to the field of draftsmanship, in which he is, without a doubt, most profound. For he has been the first artist of this century to provide painters with examples of beautiful outlines, foreshortenings, projection, movement, and indeed all that one can ask for in the execution of a nude to perfection). Ibid., 86.

90. "pittura e' la poesia: Pittura la historia, pittura qualunque componimento de' dotti" (poetry is painting, history is painting, and that any kind of a composition by a man of culture is painting). *Dolce's Aretino and Venetian Art Theory of the Cinquecento*, 100.

91. Ibid., 90.

92. Ibid., 88.

93. "per dire la verità: in servigio dellaquale (sic) ho spesso indirizzata contra i Prencipi, come sapete, la spade della mia virtù, poco curandomi che la verita' partorisca odio" (to tell the truth, in the service of which, as you well know, I have often unsheathed against princes the sword of my intellect, with little heed to the fact that truthfulness begets hate). Ibid., 98.

94. He states: "Giovarebbe anco questo ragionamento peraventura non poco agli studiosi di lettere per la conformità, che al pittore con lo Scrittore" (This discourse of mine may also conceivably offer some assistance to those who study literature, owing to the conformity between painter and writer). Ibid., 98.

95. Ibid., 98.

96. "ma la natura, non ci durando una fatica al mondo il partorisce bello e puro ... La natura istessa de la cui simplicità son secretario, mi detta ció che io compongo; e la patria mi scioglie i nodi de la lingua, quando si raggroppa ne la superstizione de chiacchiere forestieri ... sicchè intendete a essere scultor di sensi, e non miniator di parole" (but nature, without effort gives birth to the pure and beautiful ... Nature itself, of whose simplicity I am secretary, dictates what I write; my homeland unties my tongue's knots when it gets stuck in foreign utterings ... so, learn how to be sculptor of senses and not embellishers of words). Aretino, *Lettere*, 1.155.229–32.

97. To this end, see Henri Bergson, *Laughter: An Essay on the Meaning of the Comic*, trans. Cloudesly Brereton and Fred Rothwell (London: Macmillan, 1911).

98. For instance: "Ah, this is a corrupt world," she exclaims as Nanna describes the abbess being seduced by a Jew (45). "And I thought that the whoring

of nuns could not be bettered, and I was mistaken," she retorts after hearing of the sexual encounter between the hermit and the doctor's pious wife (60) in the section dedicated to the life of married women. "Are there no good nuns, wives, widows, and whores?" she ponders out loud, while Nanna continues her stories (72). Also, reflecting on the accomplishments a whore must pretend to have achieved in order to beguile a man she states: "everything in this world goes hand in hand with deception" (119).

    99. *Alberti e la cultura del Quattrocento: Atti del convegno internazionale del Comitato nazionale VI centenario della nascita di Leon Battista Alberti, Firenze 16–17–18 Dicembre 2004*, ed. Roberto Cardini and Mariangela Rigoliosi (Florence: Polistampa, 2007); Leon Battista Alberti, *Intercenales*, ed. Franco Bachelli and Luca D'Ascia (Bologna: Pendragon, 2003); idem, *Intercenale inedite*, ed. Eugenio Garin (Florence: G. C. Sansoni, 1965); idem, *Libri della famiglia*, ed. Ruggiero Romano and Alberto Tenenti (Turin: Einaudi, 1969).

    100. "D'infima stirpe a tanta altezza venne / Pietro Aretin" are the words used in his epitaph. Giovanni Aquilecchia, "In obitu divini Petri Aretini nel codice Add. 12054 della British Library," *Regards sur la Renaissance italienne, Mélanges de literature offert à Paul Larivaille* (Nanterres: Université Paris X, 1998), 46.

Conclusion

    1. Roland Barthes, *Elements of Semiology*, trans. Annette Lavers and Colin Smith (New York: Hill and Wang, 1967), 27–28.
    2. Roland Barthes, "Toward a Psychology of Contemporary Food Consumption," *Food and Culture: A Reader*, ed. Carole Counihan and Penny Van Esterik (New York and London: Routledge, 1997), 30.
    3. Ibid., 34.
    4. Claude Lévi-Strauss, "The Culinary Triangle," *Food and Culture: A Reader*, ed. Carole Counihan and Penny Van Esterik (New York and London: Routledge, 1997), 43.

BIBLIOGRAPHY

Abulafia, David. "The Italian South." *The New Cambridge Medieval History*. Ed. Michael Jones. Vol. 6. Cambridge and New York: Cambridge University Press, 2008. 488–514.
Acanfora, Elisa. "La tavola." *Rituale, cerimoniale, etichetta*. Ed. Sergio Bertelli and Giuliano Crifò. Milan: Bompiani, 1985.
Albala, Ken. *Eating Right in the Renaissance*. Berkeley and Los Angeles: University of California Press, 2002.
Alberini, Marcello. *Il sacco di Roma*. Intro. Paola Farenga. Rome: Roma nel Rinascimento, 1997.
Alberti, Leon Battista. *On the Art of Building in Ten Books*. Trans. Joseph Rykwert, Neil Leach, and Robert Tavernor. Cambridge, MA, and London: MIT, 1990.
———. *Dinner Pieces*. Trans. David Marsh. Binghamton, NY: Medieval and Renaissance Texts and Studies, 1987.
———. *Intercenales*. Ed. Franco Bachelli and Luca D'Ascia. Bologna: Pendragon, 2003.
———. *Intercenali inedite*. Ed. Eugenio Garin. Florence: G. C. Sansoni, 1965.
———. *Libri della famiglia*. Ed. Ruggiero Romano and Alberto Tenenti. Turin: Einaudi, 1969.
———. *The Alberti of Florence: Leon B. Alberti's Della famiglia*. Trans., intro., and notes Guido A. Guarino. Lewisburg: Bucknell University Press, 1971.
———. *Momus*. Trans. Sarah Knight. Ed. Virginia Brown. Cambridge, MA: Harvard University Press, I Tatti Renaissance Library, 2003.
———. *On Painting*. Trans. John R. Spencer. New Haven and London: Yale University Press, 1966.
Alighieri, Dante. *La commedia secondo l'antica vulgata*. Ed. Giorgio Petrocchi. Turin: Einaudi, 1975.
———. *Il convivio*. Trans. R. Lansing. New York: Garland, 1990.
———. *Inferno*. Trans. and comm. Charles S. Singleton. Princeton: Princeton University Press, 1975.
———. *Vita nuova*. Trans. Mark Musa. Bloomington and London: Indiana University Press, 1973.

Allen, Michael J. B. "Summoning Plotinus: Ficino, Smoke, and the Strangled Chickens." *Reconsidering the Renaissance.* Ed. M. A. Di Cesare. Binghamton, NY: Medieval and Renaissance Texts and Studies, 1992. 63–88.

Althoff, Gerd. "Obbligatorio mangiare: Pranzi, banchetti e feste nella vita sociale del Medioevo." *Storia dell'alimentazione.* Ed. Jean-Louis Flandrin and Massimo Montanari. Rome: Laterza, 1997. 234–242.

Ambrose, Saint. *Hexameron, Paradise, and Cain and Abel.* Trans. John J. Savage. Washington, DC: Catholic University of America Press, 1961.

Aquilecchia, Giovanni. "In obitu divini Petri Aretini nel codice Add. 12054 della British Library." *Regards sur la Renaissance italienne, Mélanges de literature offert à Paul Larivaille.* Nanterres: Université Paris X, 1998. 45–52.

Aquinas, Thomas, Saint. *On Love and Charity: Readings from the Commentary on the Sentences of Peter Lombard.* Trans. Peter A. Kwasniewski, Thomas Bolin, OSB, and Joseph Bolin. Washington, DC: Catholic University of America Press, 2008.

———. *On Evil (De Malo).* Trans. Jean Oesterle. Notre Dame, IN: University of Notre Dame Press, 1995.

———. *Summa Theologica, First Complete American Edition in Three Volumes.* Ed. and trans. Fathers of the English Dominican Province. New York, Boston, Cincinnati, Chicago, and San Francisco: Benziger Brothers, 1947.

Aretino, Pietro. *Lettere.* 6 vols. Ed. Paolo Procaccioli. Rome: Salerno Editrice, 1997.

———. *Dialogues.* Trans. Raymond Rosenthal. Pref. Alberto Moravia. Intro. Margaret E. Rosenthal. Toronto, Buffalo, and London: University of Toronto Press, 2005.

———. *Sei Giornate: Ragionamento della Nanna e della Antonia (1534), Dialogo nel quale la Nanna insegna a la Pippa (1536).* Ed. Giovanni Aquilecchia. Bari: Laterza and Figli, 1969.

Arienti, Giovanni Sabadino degli. *Art and Life at the Court of Ercole I d'Este: The "De triumphis religionis" of Giovanni Sabadino degli Arienti.* Ed. Werner L. Gundersheimer. Geneva: Librairie Droz, 1972.

Ariosto, Ludovico. "Erbolato." *Tutte le opere di Ludovico Ariosto.* 3 vols. Ed. Cesare Segre. Milan: Mondadori, 1984.

———. *Lettere dalla Garfagnana.* Ed. Gianni Scalia. Bologna: Nuova Universale Cappella, 1977.

———. *Orlando Furioso.* Intro. and notes Nicola Zingarelli. Milan: Hoepli, 1954.

———. *Orlando Furioso.* Trans. Guido Waldman. Oxford and New York: Oxford University Press, 1998.

———. *The Satires of Ludovico Ariosto: A Renaissance Autobiography.* Trans. Peter DeSa Wiggins. Athens: Ohio University Press, 1976.

Aristotle. *The Complete Works of Aristotle.* 2 vols. Ed. Jonathan Barnes. Princeton: Princeton University Press, 1984.

Asch, Ronald, and Adolf Birke, eds. *Princes, Patronage, and the Nobility: The Court at the Beginning of the Modern Age 1450–1650.* New York: Oxford University Press, 1991.
Ascoli, Albert Russell. *Ariosto's Bitter Harmony: Crisis and Evasion in the Italian Renaissance.* Princeton: Princeton University Press, 1987.
———. "Ariosto and the 'Fier Pastor': Form and History in *Orlando Furioso*." *Renaissance Quarterly* 54, no. 2 (2001): 487–522.
———. *Dante and the Making of a Modern Author.* New York: Cambridge University Press, 2008. 130–174.
———, and Victoria Kahn, eds. *Machiavelli and the Discourse of Literature.* Ithaca and London: Cornell University Press, 1993. 17–51.
———. "'*Neminem ante nos*': Historicity and Authority in the *De vulgari eloquentia*." *Annali d'italianstica* 8 (1990): 186–231.
———."Pyrrhus' Rules: Playing with Power from Boccaccio to Machiavelli." *Modern Language Notes* 114 (1999): 14–57.
Astbury, Raymond. "Petronius, P. Oxy. 3010, and Menippean Satire." *Classical Philology* 72 (1977): 22–31.
Astell, Ann W. *Eating Beauty: The Eucharist and the Spiritual Arts of the Middle Ages.* Ithaca and London: Cornell University Press, 2006.
Athanasius, of Alexandria, Saint. *The Life of Anthony.* Trans. T. Vivian and N. Athanassakis. Kalamazoo, MI: Cistercian Publications, 2003.
Augustine, of Hippo, Saint. *The City of God.* 2 vols. Trans. and ed. Marcus Dods, DD. New York: Hafner, 1948.
———. *The Confessions.* Trans. Rex Warner. New York: Signet, 1963.
———. *The Literal Meaning of Genesis*, *On Genesis.* Trans. Edmund Hill, OP. Ed. John E. Rotelle. Hyde Park, NY: New City, 2002.
Autrand, Françoise. "France under Charles V and Charles VI." *The New Cambridge Medieval History.* Ed. Michael Jones. Vol. 6. Cambridge and New York: Cambridge University Press, 2008.
Bakhtin, Mikhail. *Rabelais and His World.* Trans. H. Iswolsky. Cambridge and London: MIT, 1968.
Baldassarri, G. "L'invenzione dell'epistolario." *Convegno internazionale su Pietro Aretino nel cinquecentenario della nascita: Atti del convegno di Roma-Viterbo-Arezzo-Toronto-Los Angeles 28 settembre–29 ottobre 1992.* Rome: Salerno Editrice, 1995. 157–178.
Barberi Squarotti, Giorgio. *Le donne al potere e altre interpretazioni: Boccaccio e Ariosto.* San Cesario di Lecce: Manni, 2011.
———. "Il giardino ambiguo." *Regards sur la Renaissance italienne, Mélanges de literature offert à Paul Larivaille.* Nanterres: Université Paris X, 1998. 27–32.
———. *L'onore in corte: Dal Castiglione al Tasso.* Milan: F. Angeli, 1986.
Barge, Hermann. *Andreas Bodenstein von Karlstadt.* 2 vols. Leipzig: Friedrich Brandstetter, 1905.

Baron, Hans. *The Crisis of the Early Renaissance*. Princeton: Princeton University Press, 1955.

———. *Humanistic and Political Literature in Florence and Venice at the Beginning of the Quattrocento: Studies in Criticism and Chronology*. Cambridge, MA: Harvard University Press, 1955.

———. *In Search of Florentine Civic Humanism: Essays on the Transition from Medieval to Modern Thought*. Princeton: Princeton University Press, 1988.

Barthes, Roland. *Elements of Semiology*. Trans. Annette Lavers and Colin Smith. New York: Hill and Wang, 1967.

———. "Toward a Psychology of Contemporary Food Consumption." *Food and Culture: A Reader*. Ed. Carole Counihan and Penny Van Esterik. New York and London: Routledge, 1997.

Bartholomaeus Anglicus. *On the Properties of Things (De proprietatibus rerum)*. Trans. John Trevisa. Ed. M. C. Seymour et al. Oxford: Clarendon, 1975–1988.

Battaglia, Salvatore. *Grande dizionario della lingua italiana*. Turin: UTET, 1961.

Battles, Dominique. *The Medieval Tradition of Thebes: History and Narrative in the OF Roman de Thèbes, Boccaccio, Chaucer, and Lydgate*. New York and London: Routledge, 2004.

Bec, Christian, Stefano Carrai, and Ivano Paccagnella, eds. *Scarpe grosse: Contadini in letteratura*. Turin: Tirrenia Stampatori, 1999.

Beniscelli, Alberto, and Francesco Furlan, eds. *Leon Battista Alberti (1404–72) tra scienze e lettere: Atti del Convegno organizzato in collaborazione con la Société Internationale Leon Battista Alberti (Parigi) e l'Istituto Italiano per gli Studi Filosofici (Napoli) Genova, 19–20 novembre 2004*. Genoa: Accademia Ligure di Scienze e Lettere, 2005.

Benporat, Claudio. *Cucina italiana del Quattrocento*. Florence: L. S. Olschki, 1996.

———. *Cucina e convivialità nel Cinquecento*. Florence: L. S. Olschki, 2007.

———. *Feste e banchetti: Convivialità italiana fra Tre e Quattrocento*. Florence: L. S. Olschki, 2001.

Bentini, Jadranka, Alessandra Chiappini, Giovanni Battista Panatta, and Anna Maria Visser Travagli, eds. *A tavola con il principe: Materiali per una mostra su alimentazione e cultura nella Ferrara degli Estensi*. Ferrara: Gabriele Corbo, 1988.

Bentley, Jerry H. *Politics and Culture in Renaissance Naples*. Princeton: Princeton University Press, 1987.

Bergson, Henri. *Laughter: An Essay on the Meaning of the Comic*. Trans. Cloudesly Brereton and Fred Rothwell. London: Macmillan, 1911.

Bernard, of Clairvaux, Saint. *A Rule of Good Life, 1633*. Trans. Antonie Batt. Menston and Yorkshire: Scholar Press, 1971.

———. "Meditationes piissime ad humane conditionis cognitionem." *Opera*. Lyons: Societas Biblipolarum, 1679.

Berrong, Richard. *Rabelais and Bakhtin: Popular Culture in Gargantua and Pantagruel*. Lincoln and London: University of Nebraska Press, 1986.

Bertelli, Sergio, Franco Cardini, and Elvira Garbero Zorzi, eds. *The Courts of the Italian Renaissance*. New York: Facts on File, 1986.
Bertolo, Fabio Massimo. *Pietro Aretino e la stampa, strategie di autopromozione a Venezia nel Cinquecento*. Rome: Salerno Editrice, 2003.
Bestor, Jane F. "Kinship and Marriage in the Politics of an Italian Ruling House: The Este of Ferrara in the Reign of Ercole I 1471–1505." PhD diss. University of Chicago, 1992.
Binni, Walter. *Metodo e poesia di Ludovico Ariosto e altri studi ariosteschi*. Ed. Rosanna Alhaique Pettinelli. Scandicci and Florence: La Nuova Italia, 1996.
Blamires, Alcuin. *The Case for Women in Medieval Culture*. Oxford: Clarendon, 1997.
———. "Paradox in the Medieval Gender Doctrine of Head and Body." *Medieval Theology and the Natural Body*. Ed. Peter Biller and A. J. Minnis. York: York Medieval Texts, 1997. 3–29.
Bloch, Howard R. *Medieval Misogyny and the Invention of Western Romantic Love*. Chicago and London: University of Chicago Press, 1991.
Bloch, Marc. "Sel et produits de remplecement." *Pour une histoire de l'alimentation*. Ed. Jean-Jacques Hémardinquer. Paris: Librairie Armand Colin, 1970. 295–296.
Boccaccio, Giovanni. *Decameron*. Ed. Vittore Branca. Florence: LeMonnier, 1965.
———. *The Decameron*. Trans. Mark Musa and Peter Bondanella. New York: Penguin, 2002.
———. *Famous Women*. Ed. and trans. Virginia Brown. Cambridge, MA, and London: Harvard University Press, 2001.
Bodel, J. P. "The Freedmen in the Satyricon of Petronius." Ph.D. diss. University of Michigan, 1984.
Boiardo, Matteo Maria. *Orlando inamorato*. 2 vols. Ed. Riccardo Bruscagli. Turin: Einaudi, 1995.
———. *Orlando Innamorato*. Trans. and intro. Charles S. Ross. Oxford and New York: Oxford University Press, 1995.
Bonardi, Giovanna. "Manger à Rome: La mensa pontificale à la fin du Moyen Âge entre cérémoniale et alimentation." *Banquets et manières de table au Moyen Âge*. Aix-en-Provence: CUER MA, 1996. 37–51.
Bonaventure, Saint. "Major Life of St. Francis." *St. Francis of Assisi, Writings and Early Biographies: English Omnibus of the Sources for the Life of St. Francis*. Ed. Marion A. Habig. Chicago: Franciscan Herald, 1983.
Bongrani, Paolo. "Appunti sulle '*Prose della volgar lingua*': In margine a una recente edizione." *Giornale storico della letteratura italiana* 159, no. 506 (1982): 271–290.
Borsellino, Nino. *L'età italiana: Cultura e letteratura del pieno Rinascimento*. Rome: Vecchiarelli Editore, 2008.
———. *Gli anticlassicisti del Cinquecento*. Rome and Bari: Laterza, 1973.

Bradley, Denis J. M. *Aquinas on the Twofold Human Good.* Washington, DC: Catholic University of America Press, 1997.
Bramante, Vanni, ed. *Giovangirolamo De' Rossi: Vita di Giovanni de' Medici detto delle Bande Nere.* Rome: Salerno, 1996.
Branca, Vittore. *Boccaccio e dintorni.* Florence: L. S. Olschki, 1983.
———. *Boccaccio Medievale.* Florence: Sansoni, 1970.
———. *Giovanni Boccacio: Profilo biografico.* Florence: Sansoni, 1977.
Bratton, Susan P. *Christianity, Wilderness, and Wildlife: The Original Desert Solitaire.* Scranton: University of Scranton Press; London and Toronto: Associated University Press, 1993.
Brezzi, Paolo. *La civiltà del medievo europeo.* 4 vols. Rome: Eurodes, 1978.
Brooks, Per, ed. *Seven-Headed Luther: Essays in Commemoration of a Quincentenary, 1483–1983.* Oxford: Clarendon, 1983.
Brown, Alison. "Lorenzo and Public Opinion in Florence: The Problem of Opposition." *Lorenzo il Magnifico e il suo mondo: Convegno internazionale di studi, Firenze, 9–13 giugno 1992.* Ed. Gian Carlo Garfagnini. Florence: L. S. Olschki, 1994. 61–85.
Brown, Peter. *The Body and Society: Men, Women and Sexual Renunciation in Early Christianity.* New York: Columbia University Press, 1988.
Brundage, James A. "Carnal Delight: Canonistic Theories of Sexuality." *Proceedings of the Fifth International Congress of Medieval Canon Law, Salamanca, 21–25 September 1976.* Ed. Stephan Kuttner and Kenneth Pennington. Vatican City: Biblioteca Apostolica Vaticana, 1980. 361–385.
Bruscagli, Riccardo. "Ferrara: Arts and Ideologies in a Renaissance State." *Phaeton's Children: The Este Court and its Culture in Early Modern Ferrara.* Ed. Dennis Looney and Deanna Shemeck. Tempe: Arizona Center for Medieval and Renaissance Studies, 2005.
Bruschi, Arnaldo. "Sull'Alberti architetto." *Leon Battista Alberti: Architettura e cultura. Atti del Convegno internazionale, Mantova 16–19 novembre 1994.* Florence: L. S. Olschki, 1999. 15–26.
Burns, E. Jane. *Bodytalk.* Philadelphia: University of Pennsylvania Press, 1993.
Bussani, Illidio. *Il romanzo cavalleresco in Luigi Pulci.* Turin: Fratelli Bocca Editori, 1933.
Cairns, Christopher. *Pietro Aretino and the Republic of Venice: Research on Aretino and His Circle in Venice, 1527–1556.* Florence: L. S. Olschki, 1985.
Caleffini, Ugo. *Croniche: 1471–1494.* Ferrara: "Monumenti" della Deputazione provinciale ferrarese di storia patria, 2006. 373–632.
———. *Diario di Ugo Caleffini (1471–1494).* 2 vols. Ed. Giuseppe Pardi. Ferrara: Premiata Tipografia Sociale, 1938.
Camporeale, Salvatore. *Lorenzo Valla: Umanesimo e teologia.* Florence: Istituto nazionale di studi sul Rinascimento, 1972.
Camporesi, Piero. *The Anatomy of the Senses.* Trans. Allan Cameron. Cambridge: Polity, 1994.

―――. *Bread of Dreams: Food and Fantasy in Early Medieval Europe*. Trans. David Gentilcore. Cambridge: Polity in association with Basil Blackwell, 1969.

―――. *Carne impassibile: Salvezza e salute tra medioevo e controriforma*. Milan: Saggiatore, 1991.

―――. *Land of Hunger*. Trans. Tania Croft-Murray with the assistance of Claire Foley. Cambridge: Polity; Cambridge, MA: Blackwell, 1996.

―――. *Pane selvaggio*. Bologna: Il Mulino, 1980.

Cappellanus, Andreas. *The Art of Courtly Love*. Trans. John Jay Parry. New York: Columbia University Press, 1960.

Cardini, Roberto, and Mariangela Rigoliosi, eds. *Alberti e la cultura del Quattrocento: Atti del convegno internazionale del Comitato nazionale VI centenario della nascita di Leon Battista Alberti, Firenze 16–17–18 Dicembre 2004*. Florence: Polistampa, 2007.

Carrai, Stefano. *Le muse dei Pulci: Studi su Luca e Luigi Pulci*. Naples: Guida editori, 1985.

Carré, Yannick. *Le baiser sour la bouche au Moyen Age: Rites, symbols, mentalités à travers les texts et les images, XIe–XVe siècles*. Paris: Editions Le Léopard d'Or, 1992.

Casadei, Alberto. "The History of the *Furioso*." *Ariosto Today: Contemporary Perspectives*. Ed. Donald Beecher, Massimo Ciavolella, and Roberto Fedi. Toronto: University of Toronto Press, 2003. 55–70.

Cassiano, Giovanni. *Conferenze ai monaci I–X*. Trans. and ed. Lorenzo Dattrino. Rome: Città Nuova Editrice, 2000.

Castiglione, Baldassarre. *Cortegiano*. Ed. Ettore Bonora. Milan: Mursia, 1972.

―――. *The Book of the Courtier*. Trans. Charles S. Singleton. Garden City, NY: Doubleday, 1959.

Catalano, Michele. *Vita di Ludovico Ariosto*. 2 vols. Geneva: L. S. Olschki, 1930–1931.

Cataldi Palau, Annaclara. "La biblioteca pandolfina." *Italia Medievale e umanistica* 31 (1988): 262.

Catone, il Censore. *L'agricoltura (De re agraria)*. Trans. Luca Canali and Emanuele Lelli. Milan: Mondadori, 2000.

Cattini, M., and M. Romani. "Le corti parallele: Per una tipologia delle corti padane dal XIII al XVI secolo." *La corte e lo spazio: Ferrara estense*. 3 vols. Ed. G. Papagno and A. Quondam. Rome: Bulzoni, 1982. 47–82.

Cavallo, Jo Ann. *Boiardo's Orlando Innamorato: An Ethics of Desire*. Rutherford, Madison, and Teaneck: Fairleigh Dickinson University Press, 1993.

Cellini, Benvenuto. *Vita*. Ed. Ettore Camesasca. Milan: Biblioteca Universale Rizzoli, 1985.

Cervantes, Miguel de. *Don Quijote de la Mancha*. Ed. Martín de Riquer. Barcelona: Editorial Juventud, 1975.

Cervio, Vincenzo. *Il Trinciante, ampliato et a perfettione ridotto dal Cavalier Reale Fusoritto da Narni*. Rome: nella stampa del Gubbio, 1593.

Cesarini Martinelli, L. "Note sulla polemica Poggio-Valla e sulla fortuna delle *Elegantiae*." *Interpres* 3 (1980): 29–79.

Chamberlin, E. R. *The Sack of Rome*. London: Batsford, 1979.
Chambers, David S. *Popes, Cardinals and War: The Military Church in Renaissance and Early Modern Europe*. London and New York: I. B. Tauris, 2006.
Chastel, André. *Art et humanisme à Florence au temps de Laurent le Magnifique: Études sur la Renaissance et l'humanisme platonicien*. Paris: Presses Universitaires de France, 1959.
———. *The Crisis of the Renaissance*. Trans. Peter Price. Geneva: Skira, 1968.
———. *The Sack of Rome, 1527*. Trans. Beth Archer. Princeton: Princeton University Press, 1983.
Chiappini, Alessandra, "Libri e cose che se manzano." *A tavola con il principe: Materiali per una mostra su alimentazione e cultura nella Ferrara degli Estensi*. Ed. Jadranka Bentini, Alessandra Chiappini, Giovanni Battista Panatta, and Anna Maria Visser Travagli. Ferrara: Gabriele Corbo, 1988. 217–268.
Chiappini, Luciano. *Corte estense alla metà del Cinquecento: I compendi di Cristoforo Messisbugo*. Ferrara: Belriguardo, 1984.
———. *Gli Estensi: Mille anni di storia*. Ferrara: Corbo, 2001.
Christianson, Gerald, Thomas M. Izbicki, and Christopher M. Bellitti, eds. *The Church, the Councils and Reform: The Legacy of the Fifteenth Century*. Washington, DC: Catholic University of America Press, 2008.
Ciavolella, Massimo. "La produzione erotica di Pietro Aretino." *Convegno internazionale su Pietro Aretino nel cinquecentenario della nascita: Atti del convegno Roma-Viterbo-Arezzo (28 settembre–1 ottobre 1992), Toronto (23–24 ottobre 1992), Los Angeles (27–29 ottobre 1992)*. Rome: Salerno, 1995.
Cicero, Marco Tullio. *On Duties (De officiis)*. Trans. Harry G. Edinger. Indianapolis and New York: Bobbs-Merrill, 1974.
Clement, of Alexandria, Saint. *Stomateis*. Trans. John Ferguson. Washington, DC: Catholic University of America Press.
Comito, Terry. *The Idea of the Garden in the Renaissance*. New Brunswick, NJ: Rutgers University Press, 1978.
———. "Renaissance Gardens and Paradise." *Journal of the History of Ideas* 32 (1971): 483–506.
Copenhaver, Brian P. "Lorenzo, Ficino and the Domesticated Hermes." *Lorenzo Magnifico e il suo mondo: Convegno internazionale di studi, Firenze, 9–13 giugno 1992*. Ed. Gian Carlo Garfagnini. Florence: L. S. Olschki, 1994. 225–257.
Corsaro, Antonio, Harald Hendrix, and Paolo Procaccioli, eds. *Autorità, modelli e antimodelli nella cultura artistica e letteraria tra Riforma e Controriforma: Atti del Seminario internazionale di studi, Urbino-Sassocorvaro, 9–11 novembre 2006*. Rome: Vecchiarelli, 2007.
Cottino-Jones, Marga. "I *Ragionamenti* e la ricerca di un nuovo codice." *Convegno internazionale su Pietro Aretino nel cinquecentenario della nascita: Atti del convegno Roma-Viterbo-Arezzo (28 settembre–1 ottobre 1992), Toronto (23–24 ottobre 1992), Los Angeles (27–29 ottobre 1992)*. Rome: Salerno, 1995. 933–958.

Culbertson, Diana. *The Poetics of Revelation: Recognition and the Narrative Tradition.* Studies in American Biblical Hermeneutics 4. Macon, GA: Mercer University Press, 1989.
Curtin, Deane W. "Recipes for Values." *Cooking, Eating, Thinking.* Ed. D.W. Curtin and Lisa M. Heldke. Bloomington and Indianapolis: Indiana University Press, 1992.
Curtius, Ernst. *European Literature and the Latin Middle Ages.* Trans. Willard R. Trask. New York: Pantheon, 1953.
Cuthbert, Dom Butler. *The Lausiac History of Palladius: A Critical Discussion Together with Notes on Early Egyptian Monachism.* London: Cambridge University Press, 1898.
Dean, Trevor. "Ferrarese Chroniclers and the Este State." *Phaeton's Children: The Este Court and its Culture in Early Modern Ferrara.* Ed. Dennis Looney and Deanna Shemeck. Tempe: Arizona Center for Medieval and Renaissance Studies, 2005. 169–187.
———. *Land and Power in Late Medieval Ferrara: The Rule of the Este, 1350–1450.* Cambridge and New York: Cambridge University Press, 1988.
———. *Terra e potere a Ferrara nel tardo medioevo: Il dominio estense: 1350–1450.* Trans. Giuseppe Trenti. Modena: deputazione di storia patria per le antiche province modenesi, 1990.
Dei Segni, Lotario (Innocent III). *The miseria condicionis humane.* Ed. Robert E. Lewis. Athens: University of Georgia Press, 1978.
De Robertis, Domenico. *Morgante e lettere.* Florence: Sansoni, 1984.
———. *Storia del Morgante.* Florence: Le Monnier, 1958.
De' Rossi, Giovangirolamo. *La vita di Giovanni de' Medici detto delle Bande Nere.* Ed. Vanni Bramante. Rome: Salerno Editrice, 1995.
de Sanctis, Francesco. *Storia della letteratura italiana.* Ed. N. Gallo. Intro. N. Sapegno. Turin: Einaudi, 1966.
Desiderius, Erasmus. *The Praise of Folly.* Trans. and intro. Clarence H. Miller. Afterword William H. Gass. New Haven and London: Yale University Press, 2003.
Dietler, Michael. "Theorizing the Feast." *Feasts: Archaeological and Ethnographic Perspectives on Food, Politics, and Power.* Ed. M. Dietler and B. Hayden. Washington, DC, and London: Smithsonian Institution Press, 2001.
Di Napoli, Giovanni. *Lorenzo Valla: Filosofia e religione nell'umanesimo italiano.* Rome: Edizioni di storia e letteratura, 1971.
Dionisotti, Carlo. *Machiavellerie: Storie e fortuna di Machiavelli.* Turin: Einaudi, 1980.
———. *Pietro Bembo: Prose e Rime.* Turin: UTET, 1966.
———. *Umanisti e il volgare fra Quattro e Cinquecento.* Florence: LeMonnier, 1968.
Di Pascale, Barbara. *Banchetti Estensi: La spettacolarità del cibo alla corte di Ferrara nel Rinascimento.* Imola: La mandragora, 1995.

Donati, Francesca Pucci. "Dietetica e cucina nel *Regimen Sanitatis* di Maino de' Maineri." *Food and History* 4 (2006): 107–131.
Donato, Eugenio. "'Per selve e boscherecci labirinti': Desire and Narrative Structure in Ariosto's *Orlando Furioso*." *Literary Theory/Renaissance Texts*. Ed. Patricia Parker and David Quint. Baltimore: Johns Hopkins University Press, 1986. 33–62.
Donnarumma, Raffaele. "Poetiche romanzesche nel I libro del poema." *Il Boiardo e il mondo estense nel Quattrocento: Atti del convegno internazionale di studi Scandiano-Modena-Reggio Emilia-Ferrara 13–17 settembre 1994*. Ed. G. Anceschi and T. Matarrese. Padua: Antenore, 1997. 777–806.
Dorigatti, Marco. "La favola e la corte: Intrecci narrativi e genealogie estensi dal Boiardo all'Ariosto." *Gli dei a Corte: Letteratura e immagini nella Ferrara estense*. Florence: L. S. Olschki, 2009. 31–54.
———. "Il manoscritto dell'*Orlando Furioso (1505–1515)*. L'uno e l'altro Ariosto in Corte e nelle Delizie*. Ed. Gianni Venturi. Florence: L. S. Olschki, 2011. 1–44.
Durante, Castor. *Il Tesoro della sanità*. Venice: appresso Andrea Muschio, 1586.
Durling, Robert. *The Figure of the Poet in Renaissance Epic*. Cambridge, MA: Harvard University Press, 1965.
Eck, Caroline van. "The Structure of 'De re aedificatoria' Reconsidered." *Journal of the Society of Architectural Historians* 57, no. 3 (1998): 280–297.
Edwards, Mark, Jr. *Luther's Last Battles: Politics and Polemics, 1531–46*. Ithaca and London: Cornell University Press, 1983.
Eisenstein, Elizabeth L. *Printing Press as an Agent of Change: Communications and Cultural Transformation in Early Modern Europe*. Cambridge and New York: Cambridge University Press, 1979.
———. *Printing Revolution in Early Modern Europe*. Cambridge and New York: Cambridge University Press, 2005.
Faccioli, Emilio, ed. *L'arte della cucina italiana*. Turin: Einaudi, 1987.
Ferroni, Giulio. "Pietro Aretino e le corti." *Pietro Aretino nel cinquecentenario della nascita*. Rome: Salerno Editrice, 1995. 23–48.
———. *Ariosto*. Rome: Salerno Editrice, 2008.
———. *Le voci dell'istrione: Pietro Aretino e la dissoluzione del teatro*. Naples: Liguori, 1999.
Ficino, Marsilio. *Commentary on Plato's Symposium on Love*. Trans. Sears Jayne. Dallas, TX: Spring, 1985.
———. *The Letters of Marsilio Ficino*. 8 vols. Trans. members of the Language Department of the School of Economic Science, London. Pref. Paul O. Kristeller. London: Shepeard-Walwyn, 2009.
———. *The Philebus Commentary*. Ed. and trans. Michael J. B. Allen. Tempe: Arizona Center for Medieval and Renaissance Studies, 2000.
———. *Platonic Theology*. 5 vols. Trans. Michael J. B. Allen. Ed. James Hankins and William Bowen. Cambridge, MA, and London: Harvard University Press, 2005.

———. *Three Books on Life* (*De vita libri tres*). Ed. and trans. C. Kaske and J. R. Clark. Binghamton, NY: Medieval and Renaissance Texts and Studies, 1989.
Fiorato, Adelin Charles, and Anna Fontes Baratto, eds. *La table et ses dessous: Culture, alimentation et convivialité en Italie (XIV–XVI siècles)*. Paris: Presses de la Sorbonne Nouvelle, 1999.
Firpo, Massimo. *Il problema della tolleranza religiosa nell'età moderna dalla riforma protestante a Locke*. Turin: Loescher, 1978.
Flamigni, Adriana, and Rossella Mangaroni. *Ariosto*. Milan: Camunia, 1989.
Flandrin, Jean-Louis. *Chronique de Platine: Pour une gastronomie historique*. Paris: O. Jacob, 1992.
———, and Massimo Montanari. *Food: A Culinary History from Antiquity to Present*. Ed. Albert Sonnenfeld. Trans. Clarissa Botsford et al. New York: Columbia University Press, 1999.
———. *Ordre des mets*. Paris: Odile Jacob, 2002.
———, and Jane Cobbi, eds. *Tables d'hier, tables d'ailleurs: Histoire et ethnologie du repas*. Paris: Odile Jacob, 1999.
Floriani, Piero. *Bembo e Castiglione: Studi sul classicismo del Cinquecento*. Rome: Bulzoni, 1976.
Fois, Mario. *Il pensiero cristiano di Lorenzo Valla nel quadro storico-culturale del suo ambiente*. Rome: Libreria editrice dell'Università Gregoriana, 1969.
Forster, Robert, and Orest Ranum, eds. *Food and Drink in History: Selections from the Annales, économie, sociétes, civilization*. Trans. Elborg Forster and Patricia M. Ranum. Baltimore: Johns Hopkins University Press, 1979.
Franceschetti, Antonio. "*Dall'Innamorato al Furioso.*" *Passare il tempo: La letteratura del gioco e dell'intrattenimento dal XII al XVI secolo. Atti del convegno di Pienza, 10–14 settembre, 1991*. 2 vols. Rome: Salerno Editrice, 1993.
———. *L'Orlando innamorato e le sue componenti tematiche e strutturali*. Florence: Olschki, 1975.
Fraser Jenkins, A. D. "Cosimo de' Medici's Patronage of Architecture and the Theory of Magnificence." *Journal of the Warburg and Courtauld Institutes* 33 (1970): 162–170.
Frenquellucci, Chiara. "La gastronomia nell'epica cavalleresca: Il *Morgante* di Pulci." *Romance Language Annual* (1996): 172–178.
Freud, Sigmund. *Three Contributions to the Theory of Sex*. New York: Dutton, 1962.
Friedman, Paul. "Spices and Late-Medieval European Ideas of Scarcity and Value." *Speculum* 80 (2005): 1209–1227.
Fubini, Riccardo. *Quattrocento fiorentino: Politica, diplomazia, cultura*. Pisa: Pacini Editore, 1996.
———. *Umanesimo e secolarizzazione da Petrarca a Valla*. Rome: Bulzoni, 1990.
Fumaroli, Marc. "Otium, convivium, sermo." *Rhetorica, a Journal of the History of Rhetoric* 11 (1993): 439–446.
Gaeta, Franco. *Lorenzo Valla: Filologia e storia nell'umanesimo italiano*. Naples: Istituto italiano per gli studi storici in Napoli, 1945.

Galasso, Giuseppe. "La crisi italiana e il sistema politico europeo nella prima metà del secolo XVI." *Dalla "libertà d'Italia"alle preponderanze straniere.* Naples: Editoriale Scientifica, 1997,

Garbero, Elvira Zorzi. "La festa cerimoniale del Rinascimento: L'ingresso trionfale e il banchetto d'onore." *Scene e figure del teatro italiano.* Ed. Elvira Garbero Zorzi and Sergio Romagnoli. Bologna: Società editrice Il Mulino, 1985.

———, and Susanna Cantore. "Le entrate trionfali." *Teatro a Reggio Emilia.* 2 vols. Ed. Sergio Romagnoli and Elvira Garbero. Florence: Sansoni, 1980. 3–28.

Garin, Eugenio. *La cultura filosofica del Rinascimento italiano.* Florence: Sansoni, 1961.

———. *Educazione in Europa 1400–1600: Problemi e programmi.* Rome and Bari: Laterza, 1976.

———. *Educazione umanistica in Italia: Testi scelti e illustrati.* Bari: Laterza, 1949.

———. *L'età nuova: Ricerche di storia della cultura dal XII al XVI secolo.* Naples: Liguori, 1969.

———. "Guarino Veronese e la cultura a Ferrara." *Ritratti di umanisti.* Florence: Sansoni, 1967. 69–106.

———. *Medioevo e Rinascimento.* Bari: Laterza, 1961.

———. *L'umanesimo italiano.* Bari: Laterza, 1965.

———. *L'umanesimo italiano: Filosofia e vita civile nel Rinascimento.* Bari: Laterza, 1952.

———. *Lo zodiaco della vita: La polemica sull'astrologia dal Trecento al Cinquecento.* Rome: Bulzoni, 1976.

Garnsey, Peter. *Food and Society in Classical Antiquity.* Cambridge: Cambridge University Press, 1999.

Garrido, Jean-Pierre. "Le theme de la 'grande bouffe' dans le *Morgant* de Luigi Pulci." *La table et ses dessous.* Ed. A. Charles Fiorato and A. Fontes Baratto. Paris: Presses de la Sorbonne Nouvelle, 1999. 73–91.

Garside, Charles. *Zwingli and the Arts.* New Haven and London: Yale University Press, 1966.

Gattoni, Maurizio. *Clemente VII e la geo-politica dello stato pontificio (1523–1534).* Vatican City: Archivio Segreto Vaticano, 2002.

Getto, Giovanni. *Studio sul Morgante.* Florence: L. S. Olschki, 1977.

———. *Vita di forma e forme di vita nel Decameron.* Turin: Petrini, 1986.

Girolamo, San. "Epistola di S. Girolamo ad Eustochio." *Scelta di curiosità letterarie inedite o rare dal secolo XIII al XVII.* Ed. I. G. Isola. Bologna: Presso Gaetano Romagnoli, 1869.

———. *Vite degli eremiti Paolo, Ilarione, e Malco.* Trans. and ed. Bazyli Degórski. Rome: Città Nuova Editrice, 1996.

Good, Edwin M. *In Turns of Tempest: A Reading of Job.* Stanford, CA: Stanford University Press, 1990.

Grafton, Anthony. "Petronius and Neo-Latin Satire: The Reception of the *Cena Trimalchionis.*" *Journal of the Warburg and Courtauld Institutes* 53 (1990): 237–249.

———, and Lisa Jardine. *From Humanism to the Humanities: Education and the Liberal Arts in Fifteenth- and Sixteenth-Century Europe*. London: Duckworth, 1986.
Grayson, Cecil. *Studi su Leon Battista Alberti*. Ed. Paola Claut. Florence: L. S. Olschki, 1998.
Green, Louis. "Florence and the Republican Tradition." *The New Cambridge Medieval History*. Ed. Michael Jones. Vol. 6. Cambridge and New York: Cambridge University, 2000. 469–487.
Green, Roger Lancelyn, trans. *Two Satyr Plays: Euripides' Cyclops and Sophocles' Ichneutai*. Harmondsworth, Middlesex, and Baltimore: Penguin, 1957.
Greene, Thomas M. *The Descent from Heaven: A Study in Epic Continuity*. New Haven and London: Yale University Press, 1963.
Gregory the Great, Saint. *Moralia*. Ed. J. P. Migne. *Patrologiae cursus completus, sive bibliotheca universalis . . . omnium sanctorum patrum*, Series Latine. 221 vols. Paris, 1844–1864. 27, 31, 76.
Greyson, Cecil, trans. *Guicciardini History of Italy and History of Florence*. Ed. John R. Hale. New York: Twayne, 1964.
Grieco, Allen. "Les plantes, les régimes végétariens et la mé à la fin du Moyen Age et au début de la Reniassance italienne." *Le Monde vegetal (XIIe–XVIIe siècles): Savoirs et usages sociaux*. Saint-Denis: Presses Universitaires de Vincennes, 1993.
———. "Alimentazione e classi sociali nel tardo Medioevo e nel Rinascimento in Italia." *Storia dell'alimentazione*. Ed. Jean-Louis Flandrin and Massimo Montanari. Rome: Laterza, 1997. 370–380.
Griffith, Mark. "Slaves of Dionysos: Satyrs, Audience, and the Ends of the *Oresteia*." *Classical Antiquity* 21 (2002): 195–258.
Grignon, Claude. "Commensality and Social Morphology: An Essay of Typology." *Food, Drink and Identity: Cooking, Eating and Drinking in Europe since the Middle Ages*. Ed. Peter Scholliers. Oxford and New York: Berg, 2001.
Grottanelli, Cristiano. "Cibo, istinti, divieti." *Rituale, cerimoniale, etichetta*. Ed. Sergio Bertelli and Giuliano Crifò. Milan: Bompiani, 1985. 43–47.
Guerzoni, Guido. *Le corti estensi e la devoluzione di Ferrara del 1598*. Modena: Archivio Storico, Assessorato alla cultura e beni culturali, 2000.
Guicciardini, Francesco. *Maxims and Reflections*. Trans. Mario Domandi. Philadelphia: University of Pennsylvania Press, 1965.
———. *Ricordi*. Intro. and comm. Emilio Pasquini. Milan: Garzanti, 1975.
———. *The History of Italy*. Trans. and ed. Sidney Alexander. New York: Macmillan, 1969.
———. *Storia d'Italia*. 4 vols. Ed. Costantino Panigada. Bari: Laterza, 1929.
Guicciardini, Luigi. *The Sack of Rome*. Trans. James H. McGregor. New York: Italica, 1993.
Gundersheimer, Werner. *Ferrara: The Style of Renaissance Despotism*. Princeton: Princeton University Press, 1973.
———. *Ferrara estense: Lo stile del potere*. Trans. Vittorio Vendelli. Ferrara: Panini, 1988.

Günther, Hubertus. "Alberti, gli umanisti contemporanei e Vitruvio." *Leon Battista Alberti: Architettura e cultura. Atti del Convegno internazionale, Mantova 16–19 novembre 1994*. Florence: L. S. Olschki, 1999. 33–44.

Halikowski Smith, Stefan. "Demystifying a Change in Taste: Spices, Space, and Social Hierarchy in Europe, 1380–1750." *International History Review* 29 (2007): 237–257.

Hampton, T. "'Turkish Dogs': Rabelais, Erasmus and the Rhetoric of Alterity." *Representations* 41 (1993): 58–82.

Hankins, James. *Humanism and Platonism in the Italian Renaissance*. 2 vols. Rome: Edizioni di Storia e Letteratura, 2003.

Hanning, Robert W., and David Rosand, eds. *Castiglione: The Ideal and the Real in Renaissance Culture*. New Haven and London: Yale University Press, 1983.

Harpham, Geoffrey G. *On the Grotesque: Strategies of Contradictions in Art and in Literature*. Princeton: Princeton University Press, 1982.

Harrison, Robert P. *The Body of Beatrice*. Baltimore: Johns Hopkins University Press, 1988.

Harvey, Barbara. "Monastic Diet, XIIIth–XVIth Centuries: Problems and Perspectives." *Alimentazione e nutrizione secc. XIII–XVIII, Atti della "Ventottesima Settimana di Studi" 22–27 aprile 1996*. Ed. Simonetta Cavaciocchi. Florence: Le Monnier, 1997.

Hedreen, Guy. "'I Let Go of My Force Just Touching Her Hair': Male Sexuality in Athenian Vase-Paintings of Silens and Iambic Poetry." *Classical Antiquity* 25 (2006): 277–325.

Henisch, Bridget Ann. *Fast and Feast: Food in Medieval Society*. University Park and London: Pennsylvania State University Press, 1976.

Herlihy, David. "Life Expectancies for Women." *The Role of Women in the Middle Ages*. Ed. Rosmarie Thee Morewedge. Albany: State University of New York Press, 1975.

———. "Medieval Children." *Women, Family and Society in Medieval Europe*. Ed. and intro. A. Molho. Providence, RI: Berghahn, 1995. 215–243.

———. *Women in Medieval Society*. The Annual B. K. Smith Lecture in History, 1971.

Hersey, George. *Alfonso II and the Artistic Renewal of Naples, 1485–1495*. New Haven: Yale University Press, 1969.

Hillerbrand, Hans Joachim. *The Division of Christendom: Christianity in the Sixteenth Century*. Louisville: Westminster John Knox, 2007.

Hollander, Robert. "Boccaccio's Dante." *Italica* 63 (1986): 278–289.

———. *Boccaccio's Dante and the Shaping Force of Satire*. Ann Arbor: University of Michigan Press, 1997.

———. *Boccaccio's Two Venuses*. New York: Columbia University Press, 1977.

———. "The *Decameron* Proem." *The Decameron First Day in Perspective*. Toronto, Buffalo, and London: University of Toronto Press, 2004. 14–15.

Homer. *The Iliad.* Trans. Richmond Lattimore. Chicago and London: University of Chicago Press, 1951.
Hook, Judith. *The Sack of Rome, 1527.* London: Macmillan, 1972.
Horsfall, Nicholas. "The Use of Literacy and the *Cena Trimalchionis*: I." *Greece & Rome* 36 (1989): 74–89.
Howard, Deborah. "Apartments in Renaissance Italy." *Artibus et Historiae* 43 (2001): 127–135.
Hugh of St. Victor. *Didascalicon of Hugh of St. Victor.* Trans. and ed. Jerome Taylor. New York: Columbia University Press, 1961.
Hulse, Clark. *The Rule of Art: Literature and Painting in the Renaissance.* Chicago: University of Chicago Press, 1990.
Hunt, John Dixon. *Garden and Grove: The Italian Renaissance Garden in the English Imagination: 1600–1750.* Princeton: Princeton University Press, 1986.
Hunt, Richard W. *The History of Grammar in the Middle Ages: Collected Papers.* Amsterdam: J. Benjamins, 1980.
Huntsman, Jeffrey F. "Grammar." *The Seven Liberal Arts in the Middle Ages.* Ed. David L. Wagner. Bloomington: Indiana University Press, 1983.
Hutton, Edward. *Pietro Aretino, the Scourge of Princes.* London: Constable, 1922.
Isidore, of Seville, Saint. *The Etymologies of Isidore of Seville.* Trans. Stephen A. Barney, W. J. Lewis, J. A. Beach, and Oliver Berghof. Cambridge and New York: Cambridge University Press, 2006.
Jeanneret, Michel. *A Feast of Words: Banquets and Table Talk in the Renaissance.* Trans. Jeremy Whiteley and Emma Hughes. Chicago: University of Chicago Press, 1991.
John Cassian. *The Conferences.* Trans. Boniface Ramsey, OP. New York and Mahwah, NJ: Paulist, 1997.
Joliffe, J. W. "Satire: Satira: Σάτupος. A Study in Confusion." *Bibliothèque d'Humanisme et Renaissance* 18 (1956): 84–95.
Jones, Michael. "The Last Capetians and Early Valois Kings, 1314–1364." *The New Cambridge Medieval History.* Ed. Michael Jones. Vol. 6. Cambridge and New York: Cambridge University Press, 2000. 388–421.
Kelly, Joan. *Women, History and Theory.* Chicago: University of Chicago Press, 1984.
Kelso, Ruth. *Doctrine for the Lady of the Renaissance.* Urbana: University of Illinois Press, 1956.
Kennedy, Ruth W. *The Renaissance Painter's Garden.* New York: Oxford University Press, 1948.
Kennedy, William J. "Ariosto's Ironic Allegory." *Modern Language Notes* 88. no. 1 (1973): 44–67.
Khouri, Nadia. "The Grotesque: Archeology of an Anti-Code." *Zagadnienia Rodzajow Literackich* 23, no. 2 (1980): 5–24.
Kilgour, Maggie. *From Communion to Cannibalism: An Anatomy of Metaphors of Incorporation.* Princeton: Princeton University Press, 1990.

Kircher, Timothy. "The Modality of Moral Communication in the *Decameron*'s First Day, in Contrast to the *Mirror of the Exemplum*." *Renaissance Quarterly* 54, no. 1 (2001): 1035–1073.
Kirkham, Victoria. "An Allegorically Tempered *Decameron*." *Italica* 62 (1985): 7.
———. *The Signs of Reason in Boccaccio's Decameron*. Florence: L. S. Olschki, 1993.
Korsmeyer, Carolyn. *Making Sense of Taste: Food and Philosophy*. Ithaca and London: Cornell University Press, 1999.
Kristeller, Paul O. *The Philosophy of Marsilio Ficino*, trans. Virginia Conant. Gloucester, MA: P. Smith, 1964.
———. *Renaissance Concept of Man and Other Essays*. New York: Harper and Row, 1972.
———. *Renaissance Philosophy and the Medieval Tradition*. Latrobe, PA: Archabbey, 1966.
———. *Renaissance Thought and the Arts*. Princeton: Princeton University Press, 1999.
Kuntz, Mary. "'The Prodikean Choice of Herakles': A Reshaping of Myth." *The Classical Journal* 89, no. 2 (Dec. 1993–Jan. 1994): 163–181.
Lacarrière, Jacques. *Men Possessed by God: The Story of the Desert Monks of Ancient Christendom*. Garden City, NY: Doubleday, 1964.
Lambert, Carole, ed. *Du manuscrit à la table: Essais sur la cuisine au Moyen Âge et repertoire des manuscrits médiévaux contenant des recettes culinaires*. Montreal: Les Presses de l'université de Montréal; Paris: Champion-Slatkine, 1992.
La Penna, Antonio. "La tradizione classica nella cultura italiana." *Storia d'Italia*. 2 vols. Turin: Einaudi, 1973.
Larivaille, Paul. *Lettere di, a, su, Pietro Aretino nel fondo Bongi dell'archivio di stato di Lucca*. Nanterre: Université Paris X-Nanterre, Centre de recheches de langue et litérature italienne, 1980.
———. *Pietro Aretino*. Rome: Salerno Editrice, 1997.
———. "Pietro Aretino nella Roma di Clemente VII." *In utrumque paratus: Aretino e Arezzo, Aretino a Arezzo. Colloquio internazionale per il 450o anniversario della morte di Pietro Aretino*. Ed. Paolo Procaccioli. Rome: Salerno, 2008. 113–132.
———. "Pietro Aretino tra infrazione e censura." *Convegno internazionale su Pietro Aretino nel cinquecentenario della nascita: Atti del convegno Roma-Viterbo-Arezzo (28 settembre–1 ottobre 1992), Toronto (23–24 ottobre 1992), Los Angeles (27–29 ottobre 1992)*. Rome: Salerno, 1995.
———. *Pietro Aretino fra Rinascimento e Manierismo*. Rome: Bulzoni, 1980.
———. *Sur la poétique, l'art et les artistes: Michel-Ange et Titien/l'Aretin*. Paris: Belles lettres, 2003.
Laurioux, Bruno. *Gastronomie, humanisme et société à Rome au milieu du XVe siècle: Autur du De honesta voluptate de Platina*. Florence: SISMEL, Edizioni del Galluzzo, 2006.

———. *Histoire culinaire du moyen âge*. Paris: Champion, 2005.
———. *Livres de cuisine médiévaux*. Turnhout and Belgium: Brepols, 1997.
———. *Manger au moyen âge: Pratiques et discours alimentaires en Europe au XIVe et XVe siècle*. Paris: Hachette, 2002.
———, and Laurence Moulinier-Brogi, eds. *Scrivere il medioevo; lo spazio, la santità, il cibo: Un libro dedicato ad Odile Redon*. Rome: Viella, 2001.
Lauster, Jorg. "Ficino as a Christian Thinker." *Marsilio Ficino: His Theology, His Philosophy, His Legacy*. Ed. Michael J. B. Allen and Valery Reed. Leiden: Brill, 2002.
Law, John. "The Italian North." *The New Cambridge Medieval History*. Vol. 6. Ed. Michael Jones. Cambridge and New York: Cambridge University Press, 2000. 442–468.
Le Goff, Jacques. "'Head or Heart': The Political Use of Body Metaphors in the 'Middle Ages.'" *Fragments for a History of the Human Body*. Ed. Michael Feher. New York: Zone, 1986.
———. *Marchands et banquieres du Moyen Age*. Paris: Presses Universitaires de France, 1956.
Lenzi, Maria Ludovica. *Donne e madonne: L'educazione femminile nel primo Rinascimento italiano*. Turin: Loescher, 1982.
———. *Il sacco di Roma del 1527*. Florence: Nuova Italia, 1978.
Levenstein, Jessica. "Out of Bounds: Passion and the Plague in Boccaccio's *Decameron*." *Italica* 73, no. 3 (1996): 313–330.
Levergeois, Bertrand. *L'Arétin ou l'insolence du Plaisir*. Paris: Fayard, 1999.
Levi, Anthony. *Renaissance and Reformation: The Intellectual Genesis*. New Haven and London: Yale University Press, 2002.
Lévi-Strauss, Claude. "The Culinary Triangle." *Food and Culture: A Reader*. Ed. Carole Counihan and Penny Van Esterik. New York and London: Routledge, 1997. 43.
———. *From Honey to Ashes*. Trans. J. and D. Weightman. New York: Harper and Row, 1966.
———. *Origins of Table Manners*. Trans. John and Doreen Weightman. New York: Harper and Row, 1978.
———. *The Raw and the Cooked*. Trans. J. and D. Weightman. Chicago: University of Chicago Press, 1969.
Limentani, Alberto. "Boccaccio traduttore di Stazio." *La rassegna* 8 (1960): 231–242.
Lockwood, Lewis. *Music in Renaissance Ferrara, 1400–1505*. Cambridge, MA: Harvard University Press, 1984.
Looney, Dennis. "Ariosto and the Classics in Ferrara." *Ariosto Today: Contemporary Perspectives*. Ed. Donald Beecher, Massimo Ciavolella, and Roberto Fedi. Toronto, Buffalo, and London: University of Toronto Press, 2003. 20–31.
———. *"My Muse Will Have a Story to Paint": Selected Prose of Ludovico Ariosto*. Toronto, Buffalo, and London: University of Toronto Press, 2010.

———, and Deanna Shemek, eds. *Phaethon's Children: The Este Court and its Culture in Early Modern Ferrara*. Tempe: Arizona Center for Medieval and Renaissance Studies, 2005.

Lorch, Maristella De Panizza. *A Defense of Life: Lorenzo Valla's Theory of Pleasure*. Munich: W. Fink, 1985.

Lugnani, Emanuella Scarano. *Guicciardini e la crisi del Rinascimento*. Rome and Bari: Laterza, 1973.

Luzio, Alessandro. *Pietro Aretino nei primi suoi anni a Venezia e la corte dei Gonzaga*. Turin: Ermanno Loescher, 1888.

MacCarthy, Ita. "Alcina's Island: From Imitation to Innovation in the *Orlando Furioso*." *Italica* 81, no. 3 (2004): 325–350.

Maclean, Ian. *The Renaissance Notion of Women*. Cambridge and New York: Cambridge University Press, 1990.

McNair, Bruce G. "Cristoforo Landino and Coluccio Salutati on the Best Life." *Renaissance Quarterly* 47 (1994): 747–769.

Machiavelli, Niccolò. *The Art of War*. Trans., ed., and comm. C. Lynch. Chicago: University of Chicago Press, 2003.

———. *Discorso o dialogo intorno alla nostra lingua*. Ed., intro., notes, and app. Bortolo Tommaso Sozzi. Turin: Piccola Biblioteca Einaudi, 1976.

———. *The Prince*. Trans. George Bull. Intro Anthony Grafton. New York: Penguin, 1999.

Maggini, Francesco, ed. *La Rettorica di Brunetto Latini*. Florence: Stab. Tip. Galletti e Cocci, 1915.

Malacarne, Giancarlo. *Sulla mensa del principe*. Modena: Il Bulino, 2000.

Malato, Enrico. "Per un bilancio in itinere." *In utrumque paratus. Aretino e Arezzo, Aretino a Arezzo: In margine al ritratto di Sebastiano del Piombo. Atti del Colloquio internazionale per il 450o anniversario della morte di Pietro Aretino, Arezzo 21 Ottobre 2006*. Ed. Paolo Procaccioli. Rome: Salerno Editrice, 2006. 17–25.

———. "Gli studi su Pietro Aretino negli ultimi cinquant'anni." *Pietro Aretino nel cinquecentenario della nascita: Atti del convegno di Roma-Viterbo-Arezzo (28 settembre–1 ottobre 1992), Toronto (23–24 ottobre 1992), Los Angeles (27–29 ottobre 1992)*. 2 vols. Rome: Salerno Editrice, 1995. 1127–1150.

Manca, Joseph. *Cosmè Tura: The Life and Art of a Painter in Estense Ferrara*. Oxford: Clarendon, 2000.

———. "The Presentation of a Renaissance Lord: Portraiture of Ercole I d'Este, Duke of Ferrara (1471–1505)." *Zeitschrift für Kunstgeschichte* 52 (1989): 522–538.

Mangrum, Bryan D., and Giuseppe Scavizzi, trans. and eds. *A Reformation Debate: Karlstadt, Emser, and Eck on Sacred Images: Three Treatises in Translation*. Ottawa: Dovehouse Editions; Toronto: Centre for Reformation and Renaissance Studies, Victoria University, 1991.

Marcel, Raymond. *Marsile Ficin*. Paris: Société d'édition "Les Belles Lettres," 1958.

Marchesi, Ilaria. "Traces of a Freed Language: Horace, Petronius, and the Rhetoric of Fable." *Classical Antiquity* 24 (2005): 307–330.
Marcus, Millicent J. *An Allegory of Form: Literary Self-Consciousness in the Decameron*. Saratoga, CA: ANMA Libri, 1979.
Marin, Louis. *Food for Thought*. Trans. Mette Hjort. Baltimore: Johns Hopkins University Press, 1989.
Marsh, David. "Grammar, Method, and Polemic in Lorenzo Valla's *Elegantiae*." *Rinascimento* 19 (1979): 91–116.
Martelli, Mario. "La lingua poetica di Leon Battista Alberti." *Leon Battista Alberti: Architettura e cultura. Atti del Convegno internazionale, Mantova 16–19 novembre 1994*. Florence: L. S. Olschki, 1999. 79–105.
Masi, Giorgio. "'The Nightingale in a Cage': Ariosto and the Este Court." *Ariosto Today: Contemporary Perspectives*. Ed. Donald Beecher, Massimo Ciavolella, and Roberto Fedi. Toronto, Buffalo, and London: University of Toronto Press, 2003. 71–92.
Masson, Georgina. "Pietro Aretino and the Small Roman Renaissance Garden." *The Garden History Society* 8 (1980): 67–68.
Matthews-Grieco, Sarah F. *Erotic Cultures of Renaissance Italy*. Farnham, Surrey, and Burlington, VT: Ashgate, 2010.
Maxwell-Stuart, P. G. *Satan: A Biography*. Stroud and Gloucestershire: Amberley, 2008.
Mazzi, Maria Serena. "LA fame e la paura della fame." *A tavola con il principe: Materiali per una mostra su alimentazione e cultura nella Ferrara degli Estensi*. Ed. Jadranka Bentini, Alessandra Chiappini, Giovanni Battista Panatta, and Anna Maria Visser Travagli. Ferrara: Gabriele Corbo, 1988. 153–169.
Mazzoni, Cristina. "Sweet Traditions and the Martyrdom of Saint Agatha." *The Women in God's Kitchen: Cooking, Eating, and Spiritual Writing*. New York and London: Continuum, 2005. 74–86.
Mazzotta, Giuseppe. *Cosmopoesis: The Renaissance Experiment*. Toronto: University of Toronto Press, 2001.
———. *Dante Poet of the Desert: History and Allegory in the Divine Comedy*. Princeton: Princeton University Press, 1979.
———. *Dante's Vision and the Circle of Knowledge*. Princeton: Princeton University Press, 1993.
———. "The Road to Freedom." *The Humanities Review* 6, no. 2 (2008): 187–201.
———. *The World at Play in Boccaccio's Decameron*. Princeton: Princeton University Press, 1986.
———. *The Worlds of Petrarch*. Durham: Duke University Press, 1993.
Medici, Lorenzo de'. *Tutte le opere*. Ed. Paolo Orvieto. Rome: Salerno, 1992.
Medine, Peter E. "Isaac Casaubon's Prologomena to the 'Satires' of Persius: An Introduction, Text, and Translation." *English Literary Renaissance* 6 (1976): 271–298.

Messisbugo, Cristoforo. *Libro nuovo nel quale s'insegna far d'ogni sorta di vivanda secondo la diversità dei tempi, cose di carne e di pesce.* Venice: al segno di San Girolamo, 1556.
Migliorini, Bruno. *Storia della lingua italiana.* Florence: Sansoni Editore, 1983.
Migne, J. P. *Patrologiae cursus completus, sive bibliotheca universalis . . . omnium sanctorum partum.* 221 vols. Paris: Garnier-Frères, 1958.
Miles, Margaret R. *Carnal Knowing: Female Nakedness and Religious Meaning in the Christian West.* Boston: Beacon, 1989.
Minnis, Alastair. "*De impedimento sexus:* Women's Bodies and Medieval Impediments to Female Ordination." *Medieval Theology and the Natural Body.* Ed. Peter Biller and A. J. Minnis. York: York Medieval Texts, 1997. 109–139.
Mintz, Sidney W. *Sweetness and Power: The Place of Sugar in Modern History.* New York: Viking, 1985.
———. *Tasting Food, Tasting Freedom.* Boston: Beacon, 1996.
Momigliano, Attilio. *L'indole e il riso di Luigi Pulci.* Rocca San Casciano: Licinio Cappelli, 1907.
———. *Saggio sull' "Orlando Furioso."* Bari: Laterza, 1959.
Montanari, Massimo. *Alimentazione e cultura nel medioevo.* Rome: Laterza, 1989.
———. *La fame e l'abbondanza: Storia dell'alimentazione in Europa.* Rome and Bari: Laterza, 1993.
———. *Il cibo come cultura.* Rome: GLF editori Laterza, 2006.
———. *Les frontiers alimentaires.* Ed. Jean-Robert Pitte. Paris: CNRS, 2009.
———. "Contadini, guerrieri, sacerdoti: Immagine della società e stili di alimentazione." *Storia dell'alimentazione.* Ed. Jean-Louis Flandrin and Massimo Montanari. Rome: Laterza, 1997. 229–232.
———. "Strutture di produzione e sistemi alimentari nell'alto Medioevo." *Storia dell'alimentazione.* Ed. Jean-Louis Flandrin and Massimo Montanari. Rome: Laterza, 1997. 226–228.
———. "Verso un nuovo equilibrio alimentare." *Storia dell'alimentazione.* Ed. Jean-Louis Flandrin and Massimo Montanari. Rome: Laterza, 1997.
———, Giorgio Mantovani, and Silvio Fronzoni, eds. *Fra tutti i gusti il più soave: Per una storia dello zucchero e del miele in Italia.* Bologna: CLUEB, 2002.
Morrison, Karl F. *"I Am You": The Hermeneutics of Empathy in Western Literature, Theology and Art.* Princeton: Princeton University Press, 1988.
Nash, Roderick. *Wilderness and the American Mind.* 3rd ed. New Haven: Yale University Press, 1982.
Natale, Mauro. *Cosmè Tura e Francesco del Cossa: L'arte a Ferrara nell'età di Borso d'Este.* Ferrara: Ferrara Arte, 2007.
Newsom, Carol A. *The Book of Job: A Contest of Moral Imaginations.* Oxford and New York: Oxford University Press, 2003.
Nigro, Salvatore S. *Pulci e la cultura medicea.* Bari: Laterza, 1972.
Noakes, Susan. "The *Heptameron* Prologue." *Studi sul Boccaccio* 20 (1991–1992): 267–275.

Nori, G. "La corte itinerante: Il pellegrinaggio di Niccolò III in Terrasanta." *La corte e lo spazio: Ferrara estense.* 3 vols Ed. Giuseppe Papagno and Amedeo Quondam. Rome: Bulzoni, 1982. 233–246.

Olivieri, Achille. "Giuoco, gerarchie e immaginario tra Quattro e Cinquecento." *Rituale, cerimoniale, etichetta.* Ed. Sergio Bertelli and Giuliano Crifò. Milan: Bompiani, 1985. 163–180.

O'Malley, John W. "Egidio da Viterbo and Renaissance Rome." *Egidio da Viterbo, O.S.A. e il suo tempo: Atti del V Convegno dell'Istituto Storico Agostiniano, Roma—Viterbo, 20–23 ottobre 1982.* Rome: Ed. "Analecta Augustiniana," 1983.

Ordine, Nuccio. "Le 'Sei giornate.'" *Pietro Aretino nel cinquecentenario della nascita: Atti del convegno di Roma-Viterbo-Arezzo (28 settembre–1 ottobre 1992), Toronto (23–24 ottobre 1992), Los Angeles (27–29 ottobre 1992).* 2 vols. Rome: Salerno Editrice, 1995. 673–716.

Orvieto, Paolo. *Pulci medievale: Studio sulla poesia volgare fiorentina del Quattrocento.* Rome: Salerno, 1978.

Ovid. *Fasti.* Trans. James G. Frazer. London: William Heinemann, 1959.

———. *Heroides.* Trans. Daryl Hine. New Haven and London: Yale University Press, 1991.

———. *Metamorphoses.* Trans. A. D. Melville. Intro. and notes E. J. Kenney. Oxford and New York: Oxford University Press, 1986.

Paccagnella, Ivano. "Plurilinguismo letterario: Lingue, dialetti, linguaggi." *Letteratura italiana: II, Produzione e consumo.* Turin: Einaudi, 1983. 103–167.

Padoan, Giorgio. *Boccaccio, le muse, il Parnaso, e l'Arno.* Florence: L. S. Olschki, 1978.

———. "*L'Orlando Furioso* e la crisi del Rinascimento." *Lettere italiane* 27 (1975): 286–307.

Pagels, Elaine. *Adam, Eve, and the Serpent.* New York: Random House, 1988.

Palladius. *The Lausiac History of Palladius.* Trans. W. K. Lowther Clarke. New York: Macmillan, 1918.

Pallucchini, Rodolfo. *Profilo di Tiziano.* Florence: Martello-Giunti, 1977.

———. *Tiziano.* Florence: Sansoni, 1969.

———, ed. *Tiziano e il manierismo europeo.* Florence: L. S. Olsckhi, 1978.

Panatta, Giovanni Battista, and Edgardo Canducci. "La mensa del principe." *A tavola con il principe: Materiali per una mostra su alimentazione e cultura nella Ferrara degli Estensi.* Ed. Jadranka Bentini, Alessandra Chiappini, Giovanni Battista Panatta, and Anna Maria Visser Travagli. Ferrara: Gabriele Corbo, 1988. Pardi, Giuseppe. "Borso d'Este duca di Ferrara, Modena e Reggio (1450–1471)." *Studi storici* 15 (1906): 3–58, 133–203, 377–415; 16 (1907): 113–168.

Pastor, Ludwig. *The History of the Popes, from the Close of the Middle Ages.* 40 vols. London: Routledge and Kegan Paul, 1949.

Patrizi, Giorgio. "Etica/etichetta." *Etiquette.* Ed. Alain Montandon. Clermont-Ferrand, France: Association des publications de la Faculté des letters et sciences humaines de Clermont-Ferrand, 1989. 78–99.

Payne, Alina A. *The Architectural Treatise in the Italian Renaissance: Architectural Invention, Ornament, and Literary Culture*. New York: Cambridge University Press, 1999.

Petrarca, Francesco. *Canzoniere*. Ed. Gianfranco Contini. Turin: Einaudi, 1964.

Petronius Arbiter. *Cena Trimalchionis*. Trans. and ed. Michael, J. Ryan. London and Felling-on-Tine: Walter Scott, 1905.

Piccolomini, Aenea Silvius (Pius II). *I Commentarii*. 2 vols. Ed. Luigi Totaro. Milan: Adelphi, 2004.

———. "The Education of Boys." *Humanist Educational Treatises*. Trans. and ed. Craig W. Kallendorf. Cambridge, MA, and London: Harvard University Press, I Tatti Renaissance Library, 2002.

Pico, Giovanni della Mirandola. "On the Dignity of Man." *The Renaissance Philosophy of Man*. Trans. Elizabeth Livermore Forbes. Ed. Ernst Cassirer, Paul Oskar Kristeller, and John Herman Randall Jr. Chicago and London: University of Chicago Press, 1948. 215–254.

———. *Heptaplus o La settemplice interpretazione dei sei giorni della Genesi*. Trans. Eugenio Garin. Intro. Alberto Cesare Ambesi. Turin: Edizioni Arktos, 1996.

Piromalli, Antonio. *Cultura a Ferrara al tempo di Ludovico Ariosto*. Florence: La Nuova Italia, 1953.

Plato. *Phaedo. Five Dialogues of Plato Bearing on Poetic Inspiration*. Trans. A. D. Lindsay, MA. London and Toronto: J. M. Dent and Sons; New York: E. P. Dutton, 1927.

———. *The Republic*. Trans. A. D. Lindsay, MA. London: J. M. Dent and Sons; New York: E. P. Dutton, 1945.

Pliny, the Elder. *Natural History, with an English Translation in Ten Volumes*. Trans. H. Rackham, MA. Cambridge, MA: Harvard University Press; London: William Heinemann, 1938–1963.

Pliny, the Younger. *The Letters of the Younger Pliny*. Trans. and intro. Betty Radice. New York: Penguin, 1963.

Plutarch. *The Lives of the Noble Grecians and Romans*. Trans. John Dryden. New York: Modern Library, 1932.

Polcri, Alessandro. *Luigi Pulci e la chimera: Studi sull'allegoria nel Morgante*. Florence: Società Editrice Fiorentina, 2010.

Pollitt, Jerome J. *The Ancient View of Greek Art: Criticism, History and Terminology*. New Haven and London: Yale University Press, 1974.

Pollock, Frederick, and William Maitland. *A History of English Law before the Time of Edward I*. 2 vols. Cambridge: Cambridge University Press, 1898.

Pozzi, Mario. *Lingua, cultura, società: Saggi sulla letteratura italiana del Cinquecento*. Alexandria: Dell'Orso, 1989.

———. "Note sulla cultura artistica e sulla poetica di Pietro Aretino." *Giornale storica della letteratura Italiana* 145 (1968): 293–313.

Procaccioli, Paolo. "Pietro Aretino sirena di antipetrarchismo: Flussi e riflussi di una poetica della militanza." *Autorità, modelli e antimodelli nella cultura artistica e letteraria tra Riforma e Controriforma: Atti del Seminario internazionale di studi, Urbino-Sassocorvaro, 9–11 novembre 2006.* Ed. Antonio Corsaro, Harald Hendrix, and Paolo Procaccioli. Rome: Vecchiarelli, 2007.

———. *Studi sul Rinascimento italiano in memoria di Giovanni Aquilecchia.* Rome: Vecchiarelli, 2005.

Procaccioli, Paolo, and Angelo Romano, eds. *Cinquecento capriccioso e irregolare: Eresie letterarie nell'Italia del classicismo: Seminario di letteratura italiana, Viterbo, 6 Febbraio 1998.* Rome: Vecchiarelli, 1999.

Prosperi, Adriano, ed. *La corte e il "Cortegiano: Un modello europeo."* Rome: Bulzoni, 1980.

Provaso, Matteo. *Il popolo ama il duca? Rivolta e consenso nella Ferrara Estense.* Rome: Vielle, 2011.

Pulci, Luigi. *Morgante.* Ed. Franca Ageno. Milan and Naples: Riccardo Ricciardi Editore, 1955.

Quint, David. "The Figure of Atlante: Ariosto and Boiardo's Poems." *Modern Language Notes* 941 (1979): 77–91.

Rabil, Albert, Jr. "The Significance of Civic Humanism in the Interpretation of Italian Renaissance." *Renaissance Humanism: Foundations, Forms, and Legacy.* 3 vols. Ed. Albert Rabil Jr. Philadelphia: University of Pennsylvania Press, 1988. 141–174.

Rad, Gerhard von. *Genesis: A Commentary.* Philadelphia: Westminster, 1973.

Rawson, Beryl. "Banquets in Ancient Rome: Participation, Presentation and Perception." *Dining on Turtles: Food Feats and Drinking in History.* Ed. Diane Kirby and Tanja Luckins. New York: Palgrave Macmillan, 2007.

Redon, Odile, Line Sallmann, and Sylvie Steinberg, eds. *Désir et le gout: Une autre histoire (XIIIe–XVIIIe siècles): Actes du colloque international à la mémoire de Jean-Louis Flandrin, Saint-Denis, septembre 2003.* Saint-Denis: Presses universitaires de Vincennes, 2005.

Reeves, Marjorie. *Prophetic Rome in the High Renaissance Period.* Oxford: Clarendon; New York: Oxford University Press, 1992.

Regoliosi, Mariangela. *Nel cantiere del Valla: Elaborazione e montaggio delle Elegantie.* Rome: Bulzoni, 1993.

Rhodes, James F. *Poetry Does Theology: Chaucer, Grosseteste, and the Pearl-Poet.* Notre Dame, IN: University of Notre Dame Press, 2001.

Ricci, Giovanni. *Ossessione turca.* Bologna: Il Mulino, 2002.

Ridolfi, Roberto. *The Life of Francesco Guicciardini.* Trans. Cecil Grayson. New York: Knopf, 1968.

Riera-Melis, Antoni. "Società feudale e alimentazione (secoli XII–XIII). *Storia dell'alimentazione.* Ed. Jean-Louis Flandrin and Massimo Montanari. Rome and Bari: Laterza, 1997. 307–324.

Roberts, Alexander, and James Donaldson, eds. *The Ante-Nicene Fathers, Translations of the Fathers down to A.D. 325.* 10 vols. Grand Rapids, MI: Eerdmans, 1982.

Rosenberg, Charles M. *The Este Monuments and Urban Development in Renaissance Ferrara.* New York: Cambridge University Press, 1997.

———. "Ferrarese Coinage and the Ideology of Power from Obizzo III to Borso d'Este." *L'quila Bianca: Studi di storia estense per Luciano Chiappini.* Ed. Antonio Samaritani and Ranieri Varese. Ferrara: Corbo, 2000. 110–141.

Roskill, Mark W., ed. *Dolce's Aretino and Venetian Art Theory of the Cinquecento.* Toronto and Buffalo: University of Toronto Press and Renaissance Society of America, 2000.

Rowland, Ingrid D. "From Vitruvian Scholarship to Vitruvian Practice." *Memoirs of the American Academy in Rome* 50 (2005): 15–40.

Rubin, Miri. *Mother of God: A History of the Virgin Mary.* New Haven: Yale University Press, 2009.

Russell, Anthony Presti. "Epic Agon and the Strategy of Reform in Folengo and Rabelais." *Comparative Literature Studies* 34 (1997): 119–148.

Sacchi, Bartolomeo (Platina). *On the Right Pleasure and Good Health (De honesta Voluptate et Valetudine).* Ed. and trans. Mary Ella Milham. Tempe, AZ: Medieval and Renaissance Texts and Studies, 1998.

Saccone, Eduardo. "Wood, Garden, 'locus amoenus' in Ariosto's *Orlando Furioso*." *Modern Language Notes* 112, no. 1 (1997): 1–20.

Samat, Maguelonne Toussaint. *Histoire naturelle & morale de la nourriture.* Paris: Bordas, 1987.

Sanday, Peggy Reeves. *Divine Hunger: Cannibalism as a Cultural System.* Cambridge: Cambridge University Press, 1986.

Sanguineti, Laura White. *La scena conviavile nel "Decameron" e la sua funzione nel mondo del Boccaccio.* Florence: L. S. Olschki, 1983.

Santagata, Marco, and Stefano Carrai. *La lirica di corte nell'Italia del Quattrocento.* Milan: Franco Angeli, 1993.

Santoro, Mario. "L'*Erbolato* o la mercificazione della cultura." *Ariosto e il Rinascimento.* Naples: Liguori, 1989. 365–378.

Savonarola, Michele. *Del Felice Progresso di Borso d'Este.* Ed. Maria Aurelia Mastronardi. Bari: Palomar, 1996.

———. *Libreto de tutte le cosse che se magnano un'opera di dietetica del sec. XV.* Ed. Jane Nystedt. Stockholm: Amquist and Wiksell International, 1988.

Scaglione, Aldo. *Knights at Court: Courtliness, Chivalry, and Courtesy from Ottonian Germany to the Italian Renaissance.* Berkeley: University of California Press, 1991.

———. *Love and Nature in the Middle Ages.* Berkeley and Los Angeles: University of California Press, 1963.

Scalia, Gianni, ed. *Lettere dalla Garfagnana di Ludovico Ariosto.* Bologna: Cappelli, 1977.

Schivelbusch, Wolfgang. *Tastes of Paradise: A Social History of Spices, Stimulants, and Intoxicants.* Trans. David Jacobson. New York: Pantheon, 1992.

Scully, Terence. *The Art of Cookery in the Middle Ages.* Rochester: Boydell, 2005.

———, trans. *The Opera of Bartolomeo Scappi (1570): L'arte et prudenza d'un maestro Cuoco (The Art and Craft of a Master Cook).* Toronto, Buffalo, and London: University of Toronto Press, 2008.

———. "Tempering Medieval Food." *Food in the Middle Ages.* Ed. Melitta Weiss Adamson. New York and London: Garland, 1995. 3–21.

Segre, Cesare. *Esperienze ariostesche.* Pisa: Nischi-Listri, 1966.

———, ed. *Ludovico Ariosto, lingua, cultura, tradizione: Atti del Congresso organizzato dai comuni di Reggio Emilia e Ferrara, 12–16 ottobre 1974.* Milan: Feltrinelli, 1976.

Settis, Salvatore. *Artisti e committenti fra Quattro e Cinquecento.* Turin: Einaudi, 2010.

Shahar, Shulamith. *The Fourth Estate: A History of Women in the Middle Ages.* Trans. Chaya Galai. New York: Routledge, 2003.

Shaw, Christine. *The Political Role of the Orsini Family from Sixtus IV to Clement VII: Barons and Factions in the Papal States.* Rome: Istituto Storico Italiano per il Medio Evo, 2007.

Shemeck, Deanna. *Ladies Errant: Wayward Women and Social Order in Early Modern Italy.* Durham and London: Duke University Press, 1988.

Siraisi, Nancy. *Medicine and the Italian Universities, 1250–1600.* Leiden: Brill, 2001.

Skinner, Quentin. *The Foundations of Modern Political Thought.* Cambridge and New York: Cambridge University Press, 1978.

Smarr, Janet Levarie. *Boccaccio and Fiammetta: The Narrator as Lover.* Urbana and Chicago: University of Illinois Press, 1986.

———. "Boccaccio and Renaissance Women." *Studi sul Boccaccio* (1991–1992): 279–297.

———. "Other Races and Other Places in the *Decameron.*" *Studi sul Boccaccio* (1999): 113–136.

Sozzi, Bartolo Tommaso. *Aspetti e momenti della questione linguistica.* Padua: Liviana, 1955.

Speroni, Sperone. *Dialoghi di M. Sperone Speroni, nuovamente stampati & con molta diligenza riveduti & corretti.* Vinegia: In casa de' figliuoli di Aldo, 1543.

Stephens, Walter. *Giants in Those Days.* Lincoln and London: University of Nebraska Press, 1989.

Stinger, Charles L. *The Renaissance in Rome.* Bloomington: Indiana University Press, 1985.

Strachey, James, trans. *The Standard Edition of the Complete Psychological Works of Sigmund Freud.* London: Hogarth, 1955.

Tavani, Mirko. *Latino, grammatica, volgare: Storia di una questione umanistica.* Padua: Antenore, 1984.

Tetel, Marcel. "Rabelais and Folengo." *Comparative Literature* 15, no. 4 (1963): 357–364.
Tissoni, Antonia Benvenuti. "Di alcuni nuovi studi sull' 'Inamoramento de Orlando.'" *Rivista di letteratura italiana* 9 (1991): 289.

———. "L'antico a corte: Da Guarino a Boiardo." *Alla corte degli Estensi. Filosofia, arte e cultura a Ferrara nei secoli XV e XVI*. Ed. M. Bertozz. Ferrara: Universita' degli studi, 1994. 389–404.

———, and C. Montagnani, eds. *L'innamoramento de Orlando*. Milan and Naples: Ricciardi, 1999.

———. "Il mito di Ercole. Aspetti della ricezione dell'antico alla corte Estense nel primo Quattrocento." *Omaggio a Gianfranco Folena*. Padua: Programma, 1993. 773–792.

Toffanin, Giuseppe. *La vita e le opere di Ludovico Ariosto*. Naples: Libreria scientifica editrice, 1959.
Torboli, Micaela. *Il duca Borso d'Este e la politica delle immagini nella Ferrara del Quattrocento*. Ferrara: Edizioni Cartografica, 2007.
Trachtenberg, Marvin. "An Observation on Alberti's Choice of Antique Models: The Anxious Shadow of a Brunelleschian Anti-Canon." *Leon Battista Alberti: Architettura e cultura. Atti del Convegno internazionale, Mantova 16–19 novembre 1994*. Florence: L. S. Olschki, 1999. 71–77.
Trenti, Giuseppe. "L'Orlando dimenticato: Il Boiardo tra corte, feudo e uffici ducali." *L'quila Bianca: Studi di storia estense per Luciano Chiapppini*. Ed. Antonio Samaritani and Ranieri Varese. Ferrara: Corbo, 2000. 437–455.
Trexler, R. C. *Public Life in Renaissance Florence*. New York: Academic, 1982.
Trinkaus, Charles. *In Our Image and Likeness: Humanity and Divinity in Italian Humanist Thought*. 2 vols. Notre Dame, IN: University of Notre Dame Press, 1995.
Trissino, Giovan Giorgio. *Scritti linguistici*. Ed. Alberto Castelvecchi. Rome: Salerno Editrice, 1986.
Tristano, Richard M. "Matteo Maria Boiardo and Fifteenth-Century Ferrarese Courtly Culture." *Phaeton's Children*. Ed. Dennis Looney and Deanna Shemeck. Tempe: Arizona Center for Medieval and Renaissance Studies, 2005. 129–168.
Trovato, Paolo. *Storia della lingua italiana: Il primo Cinquecento*. Bologna: Il Mulino, 1994.
Troyes, Chrétien de. *The Knight of the Cart (Lancelot)*. Trans. and intro. William W. Kibler. New York: Penguin, 1991.
Tuohy, Thomas. *Herculean Ferrara: Ercole d'Este 1471–1505, and the Invention of a Ducal Capital*. Cambridge and New York: Cambridge University Press, 1996.
Tusiani, Joseph, trans. *Morgante, the Epic Adventures of Orlando and his Giant Friend Morgante*. Intro. and notes Edoardo Lèbano. Bloomington and Indianapolis: Indiana University Press, 1998.

Valla, Lorenzo. *Dialogue on Free Will* in *The Renaissance Philosophy of Man*. Ed. Ernst Cassirer, Paul Oskar Kristeller, et al. Trans. C. E. Trinkaus Jr. Chicago: University of Chicago Press, 1969.
———. "De lingua latinae elegantia." *Opera omnia*. Pref. Eugenio Garin. Turin: Bottega d'Erasmo, 1962.
———. *On Pleasure (De voluptate)*. Trans. A. Kent Hieatt and Maristella De Panizza Lorch. New York: Abaris, 1977.
Vance, Eugene. *Mervelous Signals: Poetics and Sign Theory in the Middle Ages*. Lincoln: University of Nebraska Press, 1986.
Vasari, Giorgio. *The Lives of the Most Excellent Painters, Sculptors, and Architects*. Trans. Gaston du C. de Vere. Ed. Philip Jacks. New York: Modern Library, 2006.
Vasoli, Cesare. "La cultura laurenziana." *Lorenzo il Magnifico e il suo mondo: Convegno internazionale di studi: Firenze 9–13 giugno, 1992*. Ed. Gian Carlo Garfagnini. Florence: L. S. Olschki, 1994. 153–175.
———. *Ficino, Savonarola, Machiavelli: Studi di storia della cultura*. Turin: N. Aragno, 2006.
———. *Filosofia e religione nella cultura del Rinascimento*. Naples: Guida, 1988.
Vehling, Joseph W. *Platina and the Rebirth of Man*. Chicago: Walter M. Hill, 1941.
Velli, Giuseppe. "Cultura e imitazione nel primo Boccaccio." *Annali della Scuola Normale Superiore di Pisa* 2, no. 37 (1968): 65–93.
Vergerio, Pier Paolo. "The Character and Studies Befitting a Free-Born Youth." *Humanist Educational Treatises*. Trans. and ed. Craig W. Kallendorf. Cambridge, MA, and London: Harvard University Press, I Tatti Renaissance Library, 2002.
Viladesau, Richard. *Theological Aesthetics: God in Imagination, Beauty, and Art*. New York and Oxford: Oxford University Press, 1999.
Vitale, Maurizio. *La questione della lingua*. Enhanced ed. Palermo: Palumbo, 1978.
———. *La veneranda favella*. Naples: Morano, 1988.
Vitruvius, Pollio. *Ten Books on Architecture*. Trans. and comm. Ingrid D. Rowland. Comm. and illus. Thomas Noble Howe. Cambridge and New York: Cambridge University Press, 1999.
Waddington, Raymond B. "Aretino e la cultura della stampa." *Il satiro di Aretino: Sessualità, satira e proiezione di sé nell'arte e nella letteratura del XVI secolo*. Trans. Cristiano Spila. Rome: Salerno, 2009. 79–119.
Wadsworth, J. B. "Lorenzo de' Medici and Marsilio Ficino: An Experiment in Platonic Friendship." *The Romanic Review* 46 (1955): 90–100.
Walker Bynum, Caroline. *Holy Feast and Holy Fast: The Religious Significance of Food to Medieval Women*. Berkeley, Los Angeles, and London: University of California Press, 1987.
Warner, Marina. *Alone of All her Sex: The Myth and the Cult of the Virgin Mary*. New York: Knopf, 1976.

Webb, Heather. *The Medieval Heart.* New Haven and London: Yale University Press, 2010.
Wetherbee, Winthrop. "Dante and the *Thebaid* of Statius." *Lectura Dantis Newberryana.* Ed. Paolo Cherchi and Antonio Mastrobuoni. Evanston, IL: Northwestern University Press, 1988. 73–92.
———. "History and Romance in Boccaccio's *Teseida.*" *Studi sul Boccaccio* 20 (1991–1992): 173–184.
Wood, Roy C. *The Sociology of the Meal.* Edinburgh: Edinburgh University Press, 1995.
Woodward, William Harrison. *Vittorino da Feltre and Other Humanist Educators.* Foreword Eugene F. Rice Jr. Toronto, Buffalo, and London: University of Toronto Press, 1996.
Zambotti, Bernardino. *Diario ferrarese dell'anno 1476 sino al 1504.* Ed. Giuseppe Pardi. Bologna: Zanichelli, 1928–1937.
Zatti, Sergio. *The Quest for Epic.* Ed. Dennis Looney. Trans. Sally Hill with Dennis Looney. Intro. Albert Russell Ascoli. Toronto: University of Toronto Press, 2006.
Zerbinati, Giovanni Maria. *Croniche di Ferrara: Quali comenzano del anno 1500 sino al 1527.* Ed., intro., and notes Giuseppina Muzzarelli. Ferrara: Deputazione provinciale ferrarese di storia patria, 1989.
Zimmermann, Price T. *Paolo Giovio the Historian and the Crisis of Sixteenth Century Italy.* Princeton: Princeton University Press, 1995.
Ziolkowski, Jan. *Alan of Lille's Grammar of Sex: The Meaning of Grammar to a Twelfth-Century Intellectual.* Cambridge, MA: Medieval Academy of America, 1985.

INDEX

Acciaiuoli, Piero and Donato, 97
Achelous, 229–33, 257
Achilles, 188
Adam and Eve
   Aretino's *Ragionamento* and, 293, 302–3
   Ariosto's *Orlando Furioso* and, 250–51
   Boccaccio's *Decameron* and, 47, 50, 51, 53–55, 59, 69, 72, 78, 87
   in Dante's *Paradiso*, 332n32
   exegesis of Genesis 1, 34–38, 328n4, 329nn7–9, 330nn11–15
   Pulci's *Morgante* and, 142
akolasia and *akrasia*, 77, 298–99, 306, 339n124
Alan of Lille, 340n130
Alberti, Leon Battista, 2–4, 31
   Aretino's *Ragionamento* and, 288, 314, 378n51
   Ariosto's *Orlando Furioso* and, 257
   Boccaccio's *Decameron* and, 322n9
   Boiardo's *Orlando Innamorato* and, 203
   De pictura, 203, 347n78, 370n87
   De re aedificatoria, 2–4, 288, 321n7, 322n10, 347n72, 350n111, 378n51
   Grammatichetta, 4
   Libri della famiglia, 322n17, 344n35, 382n99

Momus, 151
   Pulci's *Morgante* and, 132, 148, 151, 344n35, 347n78, 350n111
   Valla and, 344n35
Alcuin, 328n4
Alfonso I of Naples, 182
Ambrose of Milan, Saint, 78
Amulius and Numitor, 295
Andreas Cappellanus, *Art of Courtly Love,* 53, 335n66
Andromache, 188–89
anthropological approach to food, 8–9, 317, 319, 325n41
appetite
   for food (*see* food as metaphor in Italian literature)
   for sex (*see* sexual desire and sexual pleasure)
Aquinas. *See* Thomas Aquinas
Arachne, 252–55
architecture, 2–4, 131–33
Aretino, Pietro. *See also Ragionamento*
   career and writings, 266–68
   in Dolce's *Dialogo della Pittura,* 310–12
   Lettere, 266, 371n3, 374n20, 375n29, 376n30, 376n34, 377n35, 379nn65–66, 381n96
   obituary, 382n100
   Platina and, 108
Argyropoulos, John, 97

411

Ariosto, Ludovico. See also *Orlando Furioso*
  Erbolato, 223
  as Este courtier, 216, 228, 241–42, 254–55, 368n60, 370n85
  Satires, 255, 368n61
Aristotle
  Aretino's *Ragionamento* and, 290, 298, 299, 306
  Boccaccio's *Decameron* and, 37, 77, 97, 329n6, 339n124
  on bodily pleasures, 7, 8
  Boiardo's *Orlando Innamorato* and, 153, 182
  Nicomachean Ethics, 325n37, 325n39, 329n6, 339n124, 343n22
  Politics, 153
  Pulci's *Morgante* and, 149
  Rhetoric, 325n37
  Thomas Aquinas and, 7, 8, 325n37, 325n39
Art of Courtly Love (Andreas Cappellanus), 53, 335n66
Art of War (Machiavelli), 239–41, 243, 367n53
Arthurian romances, 175, 188, 190, 356n47
Ascoli, Albert Russell, 332n36, 364n23
Astell, Ann W., 6, 28
astronomy and food, 26–30
Augustine of Hippo
  on Adam and Eve, 35–36, 329nn7–8, 330n15
  Aretino's *Ragionamento* and, 295–96
  Ariosto's *Orlando Furioso* and, 246
  Boccaccio's *Decameron* and, 35–36, 49–50, 55, 64
  City of God, 112, 143, 295–96, 330n11, 333n52, 336n77, 379nn63–64
  Confessions, 28–29
  Literal Meaning of Genesis, The, 329n7
  Pulci's *Morgante* and, 112, 142–43, 146
  on Rome, 295–96

Bakhtin, Mikhail, 127–28, 138, 349n100
Baldus (Folengo, 1517 and later editions), 5, 324n28
Barthes, Roland, 317–18, 319
Bartolini, Lionardo, 371n3
Bassi, Pier Andrea de', 351n11
bear meat, 156–57, 227
Bembo, Pietro, 4, 5, 267–70, 272, 273, 314, 373n13, 376n32
Benporat, Claudio, 363n19
Bernard of Clairvaux, 331n26, 336n83
Bertolo, Fabio Massimo, 376n30
Bevilacqua, Bonifacio, 355n43
birds' meat
  chicken meat, 53–56, 308–9
  Ficino on, 115–16, 308–9
  partridge, 144
  peacocks, 111–13, 115–16
  Platina on, 110–13, 115–16
  starlings, 113
black bile or melancholia, management of, 113–14
Bloch, R. Howard, 333n41
boar meat, 11–13
Boccaccio, Giovanni. See also *Decameron*
  Aretino's *Orlando Furioso* and, 245, 246–50
  Dante and, 333n45, 337n99
  Famous Women, 246–50, 369nn74–75
  Machiavelli on, 5
  Tissano on, 4

Boiardo, Matteo Maria. See also *Orlando Innamorato*
    as Este courtier, 154, 156, 178, 188, 353n30
    observational powers of, 359n74
Bonaventure, 337nn96–97
Borselino, Nino, 373n13, 373n16, 374n23
Bracciolini, Poggio, 344n41
Bratton, Susan P., 338n111, 339nn116–17
Brown, Peter, 72
Bruni, Leonardo, 343n22
Bruschi, Arnaldo, 321n8
Buoninsegni, Giovanni Battista, 345n48
Bussani, Illidio, 89, 340n1

Caleffini, Ugo, 235, 354n37, 354n41
Campeggio, Cardinal, 378n48
cannibalism, 6, 328n68
Carolingian romances, 188, 190
Il castellano (Trissino, 1529), 4
Castiglione, Baldessar. See *Libro del Cortegiano*
Cato, 61, 101
Cattini, M., 368n64
Cavallo, Jo Ann, 356n56
Cellini, Benvenuto, 372n6
Cena Trimalchionis (Petronius Arbiter), 9–16, 219, 326n42, 326nn46–48
Ceres, 233, 234, 235
Cervantes, Miguel de, 195, 359n78
Character and Studies Befitting a Free-Born Youth (Vergerio), 227, 362n10
Charlemagne. See under *Orlando Innamorato*
Charles V (Holy Roman Emperor), 269, 305, 378n48

Chiappini, Luciano, 358n72
chicken meat, 53–56, 308–9
Chigi, Agostino, 266
Chrétien de Troyes, 356n47
Cicero (Tully or Tulio), 13–14, 146, 359n84
City of God (Augustine of Hippo), 112, 143, 295–96, 330n11, 333n52, 336n77, 379nn63–64
Clement VII (pope; formerly Giulio de' Medici), 298, 305–6, 307, 372n6, 379nn65–66, 379n68
Clement of Alexandria, 329n9
Cleopatra, banquets of, 244–50
Colleoni, Bartolomeo, 307
Colonna, Fabrizio, 239
Commedia (Dante), 36. See also *Inferno; Paradiso; Purgatorio*
Commentarii (Piccolomini/Pius II), 199, 357n62, 358nn67–68, 359n84
Commentary on Plato's Symposium on Love (Ficino), 346n64, 349n96
Confessions (Augustine of Hippo), 28–29
confetti
    Ariosto's *Orlando Furioso* and, 216, 217, 237–39, 243–44, 249, 251–52, 257, 259, 261, 368n69
    Boiardo's *Orlando Innamorato* and, 200–203, 206
    confettare versus *confetto*, 368n69
    Gazius on counterfeit Venetian confections, 367n49
    Pulci's *Morgante* and, 122–23, 125, 126
Convivio (Dante), 55, 120
Cortegiano (Castiglione). See *Libro del Cortegiano*
courtly love, 40, 49, 51, 53, 175, 204
cum panis as etymology of company, 26

Dante. See also *Inferno*
  on Adam's fall, 36
  Boccaccio and, 333n45, 337n99
  Commedia, 36
  Convivio, 55, 120
  on cosmology and food, 27–31
  De vulgari eloquentia, 4
  on gluttony, 29, 36, 318
  Paradiso, 330n16, 332n32
  Purgatorio, 263, 318
  Trissino on, 4
  Vita nuova, 27–29
dates in Alibech story, *Decameron*, 77–79
De architectura (*On architecture*; Vitruvius), 2–4, 131–33, 348n86
De falso et vero bono (Valla), 299–300, 306
De honesta voluptate et valetudine (*On Right Pleasure and Good Health*; Platina), 2, 25
  Aretino and Platina, 108
  Ariosto's *Orlando Furioso* and, 200, 363n19, 364n24, 364n28
  on birds' meat, 110–13, 115–16
  Boiardo's *Orlando Innamorato* and, 156, 350n109
  on gluttony, 99, 100
  on power and powerlessness, 98–100, 104, 108–9, 111, 112
  Pulci's *Morgante* and, 97–101, 104–5, 108–16, 144
  Roman curia, critique of, 21, 98–100, 108, 111, 116
De Malo (*On Evil*; Thomas Aquinas), 330n15, 330n17, 340n125
De officiis (Cicero), 14, 360n94
De pictura (*On Painting*; Alberti), 203, 347n78, 370n87
De re aedificatoria (*On the Art of Building in Ten Books*; Alberti), 2–4, 288, 321n7, 322n10, 347n72, 350n111, 378n51

De Robertis, Domenico, 348n89
De vita libri tres (*The Three Books on Life*; Ficino), 21–22, 113–14, 147, 345n48, 345n50, 345n52, 380n86
De voluptate (*On Pleasure*; Valla), 101–4, 135, 146, 290, 343n24, 343nn27–33, 370n88, 378n55, 379n70
De vulgari eloquentia (Dante), 4
Decameron (Boccaccio), 18–20, 33–88, 318–20
  Adam and Eve and, 47, 50, 51, 53–55, 59, 69, 72, 78, 87
  Alibech story, 60–88, 319
  —Dante's Ulysses and, 63, 65–71
  —dates in, 77–79
  —desert asceticism and, 71–74
  —Dioneo as narrator of, 60–61, 338n105
  —on food scarcity/simplicity and carnal desire, 62, 63, 76–79, 80, 84–88
  —marchioness's story compared, 64, 86, 88
  —"putting the devil back in hell" (Job 37:5–8), 62, 80–86
  —return of Alibech to native town, 62, 87
  —Rustico's carnal desires, 61–62, 76, 79–88
  —service of Christian God, Alibech's desire for, 61–65, 67–71, 76, 82–88
  —Statius's *Thebiad* and, 74–76
  Aretino's *Ragionamento* and, 270–71, 277, 289
  Boiardo's *Orlando Innamorato* and, 168, 174–77, 188
  exegesis of Genesis 1 and, 34–38
  Fiametta
  —Dioneo compared, 60–61
  —as narrator of marchioness of Monferrato's story, 60

—story of old King Charles in Messer Neri's garden, 174–77
marchioness of Monferrato's banquet for king of France, 48–60, 318, 319
—Alibech story compared, 64, 86, 88
—Ariosto's *Orlando Furioso* and, 245
—Barthes on language and food, 317, 318
—Charlemagne in first canto of Boiardo's *Innamorato* compared, 168
—chicken-dominated meal, 53–56, 88
—explanation provided by marchioness, 57–59
—Fiametta as narrator of, 60
—king's inability to interpret meaning of banquet, 55–57, 91–92
—Pampinea compared, 51–52, 58, 59
Pampinea's decision to take refuge in countryside, 42–48
—marchioness's tale and, 51–52, 58, 59
—Santa Maria Novella as setting for, 42, 43, 44–45, 47, 59
—sexual transgression, fear of, 332n32
power and powerlessness in, 33–34, 51–53, 58, 82–83, 153
Pulci's *Morgante* and, 89, 100
reason and appetite in, 36–37, 40–43, 46, 61, 65
theology/religion and food (*see under* theology/religion and food)
three codes of behavior adopted in face of plague, 38–41
Del Felice Progresso di Borso d'Este (Savonarola), 357n59

Del Monte family, 376n30
della Rovere, Giuliano, 154, 156, 178
desert asceticism and Alibech story in *Decameron*, 71–74
desserts. See *confetti*
Dialoghi (Speroni), 375n24
Dialogo della Pittura (Dolce, 1557), 310–12, 381nn89–90, 381nn93–94
Dialogue on Free Will (Valla), 143, 246, 301
Dionysus and Dionysian rites, 15–16
Discorso o dialogo intorno alla nostra lingua (Machiavelli), 4–5, 207, 323n22, 323n24, 324n25
Disputation (Karlstadt), 307
dogs, at banquets, 163
Dolce, Ludovico, *Dialogo della Pittura* (1557), 310–12, 381nn89–90, 381nn93–94
Dominicans, 59
Don Quijote de la Mancha (Cervantes), 195, 359n78
Donatus, 343n34
Durante, Castor, 366n39

Education of Boys, The (Piccolomini/Pius II), 227, 365n33
Elegantia lingue latine (Valla), 105–8, 344n37
Eleonora D'Aragona, 1473 banquet to honor, 154–56, 169, 178, 196, 216–17, 279
Epicureans and Epicureanism, 101–4, 135, 290, 300, 370n88
Epistola de le lettere aggiunte ne la lingua italiana (Trissino, 1524), 4
"Epistola di S. Girolamo and Eustochio," 328n4
Erasmus of Rotterdam, 372n9
Erbolato (Ariosto), 223
Erysichthon, 233, 234–35, 238, 246, 257, 269–70

Este, Alberto d', 191, 223
Este, Alfonso d', 242
Este, Borso d', 191–92, 199, 200, 351n11, 357n62, 358nn67–69, 358nn71–72, 359n84
Este, Ercole I d'
  aloofness and detachment of, 367n54
  in Ariosto's *Erbolato*, 223
  banquet in honor of Eleonora D'Aragona (1473) and, 154, 155, 156, 216
  Boiardo's *Orlando Innamorato* and, 181, 182, 184, 188, 191, 195, 351nn10–11, 352n12, 354n37, 355nn42–43
  expansion of Ferrara city walls by, 359n81
  Ferdinand, King, revolt against, 359n84
  Hercules figures constructed for banquets of, 237–40, 249, 366n45
  Machiavelli on, 239–40
  Messisbugo on, 366n45
  sale of offices by, 235
Este, Ippolito d', 237, 241, 366n45
Este, Leonello d', 191, 351n11, 357n59, 358n69
Este, Niccolò III d', 191, 358n71, 359n84
Este, Rinaldo d', 223
Este, Sigismondo d', 191, 223
Este family and court. See also under *Orlando Furioso*; *Orlando Innamorato*
  Aretino's *Ragionamento* and, 268
  land acquisitions and ascent of, 359n81
  Piccolomini on, 199, 357n62, 358nn67–68, 359n84
Etymologies (Isidore of Seville), 6, 51, 86, 164, 285, 324n32, 334n58, 340n134

Eucharistic symbolism in Aretino's *Ragionamento*, 281–83
Eve. See Adam and Eve

Fabius Pictor, 294
Fabrini, Giovan Francesco, 310
famine/hunger
  desert asceticism and Alibech story in *Decameron*, 71–74
  in Ovid's tale of Erysichthon, *Metamorphoses*, 234–35, 238, 246
Famous Women (Boccaccio), 246–50, 369nn74–75
Fasti (Ovid), 365n37
Ferrara. See also entries at Este
  expansion of city walls by "Herculean Addition," 359n81
  war with Venice, 194–95, 377n39
Ficino, Marsilio
  Aretino's *Ragionamento* and, 273, 286–87, 290–92, 308–9
  on bird meat, 115–16, 308–9
  Commentary on Plato's Symposium on Love, 346n64, 349n96
  on *confetti*, 200–201, 202, 206
  conversion to orthodox Christianity, 150
  De vita libri tres, 21–22, 113–14, 147, 345n48, 345n50, 345n52, 380n86
  on gluttony, 135
  on human nature and *summum bonum*, 290–92
  letters of, 345n48, 345n54
  on melancholy or black bile, 114
  as Neo-Platonist, 273
  Philebus Commentary, The, 348n91, 349n96
  Platonic Academy at Careggi, 286–87
  on Platonic love, 301
  Pulci's *Morgante* and (see under *Morgante*)

Theologia Platonica, 114, 135, 347n77, 348n95
fig tree in *Ragionamento* (Aretino), 292–97
fishing, 176–77, 353n29
Florentine (Platonic) Academy, 90, 124, 129, 286–87, 345n48
Folengo, Teofilo, 5, 324n28
food as metaphor in Italian literature, 1–31, 317–20
  aesthetics and ethics of food, 7–8
  anthropological approach to, 8–9
  architecture, language, and food, 2–6
  in Aretino's *Ragionamento,* 25–26, 265–315, 318–20 (see also *Ragionamento*)
  in Ariosto's *Orlando Furioso,* 24–25, 215–63, 318–20 (see also *Orlando Furioso*)
  astronomy and food, 26–30
  in Boccaccio's *Decameron,* 18–20, 33–88, 318–20 (see also *Decameron*)
  in Boiardo's *Orlando Innamorato,* 20–22, 153–213, 318–20 (see also *Orlando Innamorato*)
  in classical literature, 9–16
  as link between literature, philosophy, art, history, and theology, 26–31
  moral/ethical issues, 6–7, 17–18
  multi-layered functions of, 16–17
  power and food (*see* power and powerlessness)
  in Pulci's *Morgante,* 20–22, 89–151, 318, 320 (see also *Morgante*)
  sexuality and food (*see* sexual desire and sexual pleasure)
  as sign of its times, 1–2
  theology/religion and food, 6–7 (*see also* theology/religion and food)

Franceschetti, Antonio, 356n55
Francesco de Sanctis, 373n11
Franciotto, Capitano, 375n29
Franciotto, Nicolò, 377n35
Francis of Assisi, 62, 337n96
Franciscans, 62, 101, 337n97
Franco, Matteo, 94–95, 346n65
free will/freedom, 142–43, 145–47, 149, 235–36, 246
frogs and frog meat, 96–97, 104–5, 117
fruit, 200–202

Gaddi, Giovanni, 379n65
Galen, 98, 113, 132, 165, 200–201
gambling, 136
Gano di Maganza, 188
gardens in Renaissance culture, 286–92, 378n51
Gargantua and Pantagruel (Rabelais), 127–28, 137
gastronomy, etymology of, 30
Gazius, Antonius (Antonio di Gazzo), 367n49
gender issues. *See also* Adam and Eve
  Aretino's *Ragionamento* on women's options, 274–77, 283, 314
  Boccaccio's *Decameron* and role of women in medieval and Renaissance world, 42–48
  exegesis of Genesis 1, 36, 330n12
  feminization and Ariosto's *Orlando Furioso,* 225–27, 248
  in Ovid's *Metamorphoses,* 231–32
  stereotypes of Genesis 3, 142
Genesis
  exegesis of chapter 1, 34–38, 328n4, 329nn7–9, 330nn11–15
  gender stereotypes in Chapter 3, 142
  Pico della Mirandola's exegesis of, 236

418 Index

Ghiberti, Lorenzo, 132
giants
   in Boiardo's *Orlando Innamorato*, 171
   in Pulci's *Morgante* (see *Morgante*)
Giles of Viterbo, 351n8
Giovio, Paolo, 132
gluttony
   Aretino's *Ragionamento* and, 304, 308, 372n3, 376n34
   Ariosto's *Orlando Furioso* and, 235, 361n9, 366n39
   boars and pigs, associated with, 13
   Boccaccio's *Decameron* and, 36, 77, 85, 328n4, 330n15, 330n17, 334n58, 335n65, 340n125
   Boiardo's *Orlando Innamorato* and, 165–66, 171, 204–5
   Dante on, 29, 36, 318
   Ficino on, 135
   lewdness and, 335n65
   Platina on, 99, 100
   Plato on, 361n9
   pride and, 36
   Pulci's *Morgante* and, 22, 99, 100, 120, 134, 135, 136, 150
   Thomas Aquinas on, 36, 77, 340n125
Gonzaga, Ludovico, 97, 98
Gonzaga family, 268
Grafton, Anthony, 326n47, 327n59
Grammatichetta (Alberti), 4
Greene, Thomas M., 368n60
Gregory I the Great (pope), *Moralia*, 335n65, 340n133
Gregory XIII (pope), 379n68
Guarino da Verona, 22, 187
Guicciardini, Francesco, 1–2, 3, 5, 31, 182, 220, 279, 319–20, 341n12
Gundersheimer, W. L., 367n54

Hadrian VI (pope), 379n68
Harphem, Geoffrey G., 138, 349n101
Hector, 188–89
Heptaplus (Pico della Mirandola), 366n43
Hercules, 130–31, 156, 229–32, 237–40, 277, 351nn10–11, 366n45
Hercules and the Nemean Lion (Tura drawing), 352n12
Herlihy, David, 332n39, 333n44
Heroides (Ovid), 365n37
Hollander, Robert, 333n45, 337n98
Homer, 9, 188–89
Hugh of St. Victor, 336n79
humors, medical theory of, 98, 113–14, 132, 165, 200–201
hunger. See famine/hunger

Iliad (Homer), 188–89
Inferno (Dante), 29–30
   Ariosto's *Orlando Furioso* and, 221, 262, 370n90
   Boccaccio's *Decameron* and, 46, 63, 65–71, 338n103
   Boiardo's *Orlando Innamorato* and, 179–80, 209–10
   on gluttony, 318
   Paolo and Francesca story in, 209–10
   Ulysses in, 63, 65–71, 338n103
Isidore of Seville, *Etymologies*, 6, 51, 86, 164, 285, 324n32, 334n58, 340n134

Jardine, Lisa, 327n59
John Cassian, 328n4
Julius III (pope), 376n30, 379n68

Karlstadt, Andreas, 307, 313
Kilgour, Maggie, 328n68
Kirkham, Victoria, 332n33, 337n89, 337n91
knowledge and sex, 35–36, 329n9
Korsmeyer, Carolyn, 365n36

Laboris Herculis (Bassi), 351n11
Lactantius, 330n13
language
   architecture and, 3–4
   Barthes on food and, 317, 318
   Bembo's *Prose della volgar lingua* (1525), 267
   names and naming, 108–9
   Pulci's *Morgante* and, 105–8
   questione della lingua, 4–5
   Valla's *Elegantie lingue latine*, 105–8, 344n37
Larivaille, Paul, 374n17
Lattini, Brunetto, 211, 360n94
Lauster, Jorg, 348n92
Leo X (pope), 297–98, 372n6, 379n66, 379n68
Lettere (Aretino), 266, 371n3, 374n20, 375n29, 376n30, 376n34, 377n35, 379nn65–66, 381n96
Leva, Antonio Da, 371n3
Levenstein, Jessica, 332n32
Lévi-Strauss, Claude, 8–9, 26, 77, 317, 319, 325n41
Libreto de tutte le cosse che se magnano (Michele Savonarola)
   Ariosto's *Orlando Furioso* and, 196, 200–202, 363n19, 364nn27–28, 368n69
   Boiardo's *Innamorato* and, 169, 349n107, 350n108
   on *confettare* versus *confetto*, 368n69
Libri della famiglia (Alberti), 322n17, 344n35, 382n99
Libro del Cortegiano (*The Book of the Courtier;* Castiglione, 1528)
   Aretino's *Ragionamento* and, 267–70, 272, 273, 311, 373n13
   Ariosto's *Orlando Furioso* and, 362n12, 362n14, 363n18, 367nn50–51
   on *questione della lingua*, 4

Libro di cucina (Rossi), 98
Libro nuovo nel quale s'insegna far d'ogni sorta di vivanda secondo la diversità dei tempi, cose di carne e di pesce (Messisbuga, 1549), 363n19, 366n45
linguistics. *See* language
Literal Meaning of Genesis, The (Augustine of Hippo), 329n7
Lives of the Noble Grecians and Romans, The (Plutarch), 294–95, 369n77
Logos, 55, 58, 336n76
Luther, Martin, 307
Luzio, Alessandro, 373n14

Machiavelli, Niccolò, 4–5, 207, 239–41, 243, 323n22, 323n24, 324n25, 367n53
Manca, Joseph, 352n12
Marcus, Millicent J., 333n47
Marin, Louis, 17, 170, 173, 212
Mark's Gospel, fig tree in, 293–94
Mars, 61
Mary (mother of Jesus), Pampineo in *Decameron* compared to, 44–45
Mary Magdalene, 281
Mazzotta, Giuseppe, 338n103
meat. *See also* birds' meat
   bear meat, 156–57, 227
   boar meat, 11–13
   frogs and frog meat, 96–97, 104–5, 117
   lasciviousness and meat-eating, 334n58
   salted meats in Aretino's *Ragionamento*, 284
Medici, Cosimo de', 97, 115, 286, 345n54
Medici, Giulio de' (later Pope Clement VII), 298, 305–6, 307, 372n6, 379nn65–66, 379n68

Medici, Lorenzo de', and Pulci's *Morgante*, 20, 90
    Antea and Rinaldo story (canto 16), 120, 124
    Florinetta story (canto 19), 146, 148, 151
    giants Morgante and Margutte, meeting of (canto 18), 129, 132, 136–37
    Guicciardini's word portrait of Lorenzo, 341n12
    letters to, 346n65
    palace in the desert episode (canto 2), 94–95, 97, 109, 115, 117
Medici family and court, 155, 156, 182, 199, 268. See also under *Morgante*
melancholia or black bile, management of, 113–14
Menippus, 326n42
Messisbugo, Cristoforo, 237, 249, 363n19, 366n45
Metamorphoses (Ovid), 229, 232, 252, 256
Michelangelo, 310, 381n89
migliaccio, 125–26
Miles, Margaret R., 334n60
Momigliano, Attilio, 340n2
Momus (Alberti), 151
Montanari, Massimo, 335n61
Monte, Ersilia da, 379n66
Moralia (Gregory the Great), 335n65, 340n133
Morgante (Pulci), 20–22, 89–151, 318, 320
    Antea and Rinaldo episode (canto 16), dueling and banquets in, 117–27, 143–44
    Aretino's *Ragionamento* and, 291, 292
    Boccaccio's *Decameron* and, 89, 100
    confetti, 122–23, 125, 126
    courtly gastronomy and banqueting culture, 110, 122–23, 144
    Ficino and, 21–22, 309
    —Antea and Rinaldo episode, 120, 123–24, 127
    —Florinetta story, 144, 146–47, 149–51
    —giants Morgante and Margutte, meeting of, 129, 134–37
    —Orlando in desert palace episode, 90, 94–95, 113–16
    Florinetta story (canto 19), 138–51
    —Antea compared, 143–44
    —biblical resonances in, 141–43
    —compliant eating in, 143–45
    —on freedom/free will, 142–43, 145–47, 149
    —gustatory behavior after freeing, 148–49
    —Medici court, food as means of critiquing, 138, 140, 141, 144–48
    —Morgante's selfishness and gluttony, 149–51
    —snakes and vipers consumed by Florinetta in captivity, 139–42, 147
    frogs and frog meat, 96–97, 104–5, 117
    giants Morgante and Margutte, meeting of (canto 18), 127–38
    language and politics, 105–8
    Medici, Lorenzo de' (*see* Medici, Lorenzo de', and Pulci's *Morgante*)
    Medici court, food as means of critiquing, 90
    —in Antea and Rinaldo story, 127
    —in Florinetta story, 138, 140, 141, 144–48
    —giants Morgante and Margutte, meeting of, 128–29, 133–37
    —in Orlando in desert palace episode, 93–96, 109, 114–17

Orlando in desert palace (canto 2), 90–97, 104–5, 109–10, 113, 116–17, 241, 257–58
Platina's *De honesta voluptate et valetudine* and, 97–101, 104–5, 108–16, 144
power and powerlessness in, 153
—Actea and Rinaldo, 119, 121–22, 124, 125
—Florinetta story, 138–42, 146, 148, 149–50
—Morgante and Margutte, 128, 129, 134, 136–38, 138–42
—Orlando in desert palace, 93, 94–95, 96, 110, 116–17
Stoic/Epicurean debate between virtue and pleasure, 101–4
theology/religion and food (*see under* theology/religion and food)
Morrison, Karl E., 328n67

Nafissa, Saint, 301
names and naming, 108–9
Narcissus, 120–21
Narni, Fusoritto da, 353n29
Nash, Roderick, 338n110
"natural" and "truth" in literature and painting. *See* "truth" and "natural" in literature and painting
Natural History (Pliny the Elder), 326n50
negotium and *otium*, 286
Neo-Platonism, 272–73
Nicomachean Ethics (Aristotle), 325n37, 325n39, 329n6, 339n124, 343n22
Nilus, 334n58
Noakes, Susan, 332n40, 336n80
Numitor and Amulius, 295

On Love and Charity (Thomas Aquinas), 339nn120–21
Oration on the Dignity of Man (Pico della Mirandola), 235
Orlando Furioso (Ariosto), 24–25, 215–63, 318–20
Aretino's *Ragionamento* and, 263, 292, 372n10
Astolfo imprisoned in myrtle (canto 6), 233–34
banquet of Alcina for Ruggiero (canto 7), 243–46, 250–52
Boccaccio and, 245, 246–50
Boiardo's *Orlando Innamorato* and, 215, 237
captivity of Ruggiero in Atlante's castle (canto 4), 218–24
confetti, 216, 217, 237–39, 243–44, 249, 251–52, 257, 259, 261, 368n69
escape of Ruggiero from Alcina (canto 10), 259–63
Este family and court and
—Atlante's imprisonment of Ruggiero, 221, 223
—*confetti* constructed for Ercole I d'Este, 237–40, 249
—escape of Ruggiero from Alcina, 261
—Ruggiero in Alcina's paradise, 228, 235, 237–43, 249, 254–55, 257
feminization in, 225–27, 248
Logistilla's realm, 263
magicians' powers to control Ruggiero's decisions in, 236–43
Melissa's interventions, 227–28, 250, 258–59
Ovid's stories and, 229–35, 236, 243, 251, 252–55, 256–57, 263
Pico della Mirandola and, 235–36, 268, 314, 366n43

422 Index

Orlando Furioso (*cont.*)
   power and powerlessness in, 215, 235, 237–38, 246
   Pulci's *Morgante* and, 241, 257–58
   reality and illusion/reason and folly in, 215, 237–38, 249–50, 257, 262, 263
   Ruggiero in Alcina's paradise (canto 6), 224–29, 233–34
   Ruggiero's education, self-knowledge, and achievements, food as instrument for gauging, 215–17
   Semiramis and Cleopatra, banquets of, 244–50
   sexual desire and sexual pleasure in, 216, 225, 246, 248–49, 250–51, 255–58
   transformation and food in, 215–16, 263
   —Alcina in Ruggiero's bedroom (canto 7), 255–58
   —banquet of Alcina for Ruggiero and, 246–47, 249, 250, 252, 254, 257
   —captivity of Ruggiero in Atlante's castle, 219–20, 222, 224
   —Ruggiero in Alcina's paradise, 225, 229–30, 232, 235, 236, 237, 242
Orlando in desert palace, *Morgante* (Pulci, canto 2), 90–97, 104–5, 109–10, 113, 116–17, 241, 257–58
Orlando Innamorato (Boiardo), 22–24, 153–213, 318–20
   Angelica's lust for Rainaldo, 186, 193, 197, 205, 207, 208
   Aretino's *Ragionamento* and, 279–80
   Ariosto's *Orlando Furioso* and, 215, 237
   arrival of Angelica at banquet, 170–78

Boccaccio's *Decameron* and, 168, 174–77, 188
Charlemagne's desire for Angelica, 172–78
Charlemagne's tournament banquet, 157–70
   —appearance versus substance at, 159, 168–69
   —Aretino's *Ragionamento* and, 279
   —Balugante at, 161–62, 165, 168
   —behavior of Charlemagne toward Saracens, 167–68, 187
   —dinner prepared by Angelica for Orlando compared, 197
   —Este court and, 154–56, 169
   —invitation of Saracens to, 157–59
   —non-specification of dishes at, 169–70
   —Pentecost, celebration of, 157, 158, 161, 168, 169, 170, 184
   —Rainaldo insulted by Saracens at, 159–67
   —seating positions at, 162–64
confetti, 200–203, 206
Este family and court
   —Angelica's arrival at banquet and, 178
   —banquet to honor Eleonora D'Aragona (1473), 154–56, 169, 178, 196
   —Charlemagne's tournament banquet and, 154–56, 169
   —meal offered by Angelica to Orlando and, 198–99
   —Orlando's passion for Angelica and, 154–56, 169, 178, 181–82, 184, 187, 188, 191–92, 194–95
Orlando's passion for Angelica, 179–212
   —ambivalence regarding, 179–83
   —anger of Orlando at Rainaldo, 203–5

—arrival of Orlando at fortress of Albracà, 183–86
—bathing and massage, 186–90
—defeat of Marfisa, Angelica's demand for, 198–200
—Este court and, 181–82, 184, 187, 188, 191–92, 194–95
—impotence of Orlando, 189–94, 209
—kiss of Angelica, 185–86
—meal offered by Angelica to Orlando, 195–203
—removal of armor, 184–85
—sleeping Orlando observed and wakened by Angelica, 207–12
—visits of Angelica to Orlando on battlefield, 205–8
power and powerlessness in, 153, 213
—Charlemagne's tournament banquet, 158–59, 163–64, 169, 232
—Orlando's passion for Angelica and, 181–82, 186, 192–95, 197, 198, 204–5, 207–8
refusal of Rainaldo to accept Angelica's advances, 212–13
Ruggiero's lineage in, 188
sexual desire and sexual pleasure in (*see under* sexual desire and sexual pleasure)
sociopolitical role of food in Renaissance and, 153–56, 350n4
theology/religion and food (*see under* theology/religion and food)
Orsini family, 155, 156
otium and *negotium*, 286
Ovid
Ariosto's *Orlando Furioso* and, 229–35, 236, 243, 251, 252–55, 256–57, 263

Fasti, 365n37
Heroides, 365n37
Metamorphoses, 229, 232, 252, 256
Pyramis and Thysbe invoked in Aretino's *Ragionamento*, 299, 304–8

Pandolfini, Pandolfo, 97
Paolo and Francesca story in Dante's *Inferno*, 209–10
papal court. *See* Roman curia
Paradiso (Dante), 330n16, 332n32
partridge meat, 144
Paul II (pope), 109
Paul III (pope), 379n68
Pazzi conspiracy, 178
peacock meat, 111–13, 115–16
Pentecost, celebration of, in *Orlando Innamorato* (Boiardo), 157, 158, 161, 168, 169, 170, 184
Petit, Pierre, 326n47
Petrarch, 4, 5, 132, 149, 181, 183, 188, 356n55, 375n29
Petronius Arbiter, *Cena Trimalchionis*, 9–16, 219, 326n42, 326nn46–48
Phaedo (Plato), 361n9, 363n17
Philebus Commentary, The (Ficino), 348n91, 349n96
philology. *See* language
Physiologus tradition, 111
Piccolomini, Enea Silvio (later Pope Pius II)
Commentarii, 199, 357n62, 358nn67–68, 359n84
Education of Boys, The, 227, 365n33
Pico della Mirandola, Giovanni, 235–36, 268, 314, 366n43
Pius II (pope). *See* Piccolomini, Enea Silvio
Platina (Bartolomeo Sacchi). *See De honesta voluptate et valetudine*

Plato
   Arentino's *Ragionamento* and, 286–87, 301, 373n16
   Boccaccio's *Decameron* and, 33, 51
   Commentary on Plato's Symposium on Love (Ficino), 346n64, 349n96
   on gluttony, 361n9
   Neo-Platonism, 272–73
   Phaedo, 361n9, 363n17
   Pulci's *Morgante* and, 90, 114, 120, 129, 135, 150, 345n48, 345n52
   Republic, 33, 325n38, 328n2, 361n9
   Symposium, 120
   Theologia Platonica (*Platonic Theology*; Ficino), 114, 135, 347n77, 348n95
Platonic (Florentine) Academy, 90, 124, 129, 286–87, 345n48
Platonic love, 301
pleasure and virtue, Stoic/Epicurean debate between, 101–4
Pliny the Elder, 111, 115, 326n50
Plutarch's *Lives*, 294–95, 369n77
Politics (Aristotle), 153
power and powerlessness. See also under *Morgante*; *Orlando Innamorato*
   in Aretino's *Ragionamento*, 265, 275–77, 312
   in Ariosto's *Orlando Furioso*, 215, 235, 237–38, 246
   in Boccaccio's *Decameron*, 33–34, 51–53, 58, 82–83, 153
   names and naming, 108–9
   Platina on, 98–100, 104, 108–9, 111, 112
   Platina's *De honesta voluptate et valetudine* on, 98–100, 104, 108–9, 111, 112
   sociopolitical role of food in Renaissance and, 153–56
   in Valla's *Elegantia lingue latine*, 106–8

Praise of Folly (Erasmus), 372n9
pride and gluttony, 36
Priscian, 343n34
Procaccioli, Paolo, 373n13, 374n20
promises, 210–12
Prose della volgar lingua (Bembo, 1525), 4, 267
Protestant Reformation and Aretino's *Ragionamento*, 306–8
Pulci, Luigi. See *Morgante*
Purgatorio (Dante), 263, 318
Pyramis and Thysbe, 299, 304–8

questione della lingua, 4–5

Rabelais, François, 127–28, 137
Ragionamento (Aretino), 25–26, 265–315, 318–20
   Ariosto's *Orlando Furioso* and, 263, 292, 372n10
   authenticity, efforts to retain, 310–13
   Boccaccio's *Decameron* and, 270–71, 277, 289
   Boiardo's *Orlando Innamorato* and, 279–80
   Dolce's *Dialogo della Pittura* and, 310–12
   Ficino and, 273, 286–87, 290–92, 308–9
   on human nature, 268–71, 290–91, 313–15
   humanist dialogues, as response to, 268, 270, 272–73
   Nana and Antonia dialogue
   —convent banquet, Nana's description of, 298, 308–9
   —Eucharistic symbolism in, 281–83
   —under fig tree, 292–97
   —nun, Nana's description of life as, 297–309, 312–13, 381n98
   —Pippa's future in, 273–78, 283–84, 296–97, 314
   —salted meats in, 284

—table salt in, 285–86
—three-day withdrawal with simple foodstuffs, 278–83
—vineyard location of, 286–92
power and powerlessness in, 265, 275–77, 312
Protestant Reformation and, 306–8
Pulci's *Morgante* and, 291, 292
Pyramis and Thysbe invoked in, 299, 304–8
Roman curia, critique of, 25–26, 266–71
—fig tree, Nana and Antonia's dialogue under, 292, 293, 294
—in Nana and Antonia's discussion of Pippa's future, 273–74, 277–78, 284
—in Nana and Antonia's foodstuffs, 282, 283, 285
—nun, Nana's description of life as, 297–98, 306–8, 312
—vineyard, Nana and Antonia's dialogue in, 287
Rome in, 269, 295–97, 305–8
sexual desire and sexual pleasure in (*see under* sexual desire and sexual pleasure)
theology/religion and food (*see under* theology/religion and food)
Raphael, 132, 310
religion and food. *See* theology/religion and food
Republic (Plato), 33, 325n38, 328n2
Rettorica (Lattini), 211, 360n94
Rhetoric (Aristotle), 325n37
Rhodes, James F., 86
Riario, Pietro, 154–56, 159, 169, 178, 196, 213, 216, 279, 351n10
Ricettario di Maestro Martino (Martino de' Rossi), 349n104, 363n19
Ricordi (*Maxims and Reflections;* Guicciardini), 1–2, 321n2

Roman curia
  Aretino's *Ragionamento* and (see under *Ragionamento*)
  Platina's critique of, 21, 98–100, 108, 111, 116
Romani, M., 368n64
Rome, in Aretino's *Ragionamento*, 269, 295–97, 305–8
Romulus and Remus, 294–96
Rossi, Frate Vitruvio De, 376n34
Rossi, Giovangirolamo De', 372n10
Rossi, Martino de' (Martino de Rubeis da Como), 98, 349n104, 363n19
Roverella, Cardinal, 99–100
Ruminalis, 294
Rykwert, Joseph, 3

Sacchi, Bartolomeo (Platina). See *De honesta voluptate et valetudine*
Sack of Rome, 269, 305–6
Saint Benedict's Rule, 298
Salutati, Coluccio, 353n31
Saluzzo, Ricciarda di, 191
Saracens
  at Charlemagne's tournament banquet *Orlando Innamorato* (see under *Orlando Innamorato*)
  in *Morgante* (Pulci), 95
satire and food, 15–16, 326n42
Satires (Ariosto), 255, 368n61
Saturae Menippeae (Varro), 326n42
satyr plays, Greek, 15–16
Satyricon (Petronius Arbiter), 326n42
Savonarola, Michele. See also *Libreto de tutte le cosse che se magnano Del Felice Progresso di Borso d'Este,* 357n59
Scappi, Bartolomeo, 378n48, 379n68
Scully, Terence, 335n68
seating positions at banquets, 162–64
Semiramis, banquets of, 244–47, 369n74
Seneca, 326n42

Servius, 343n34
sexual desire and sexual pleasure
  in Aretino's *Ragionamento*
  —convent banquet, Nana's description of, 308
  —courtesans' voices in dialogues, 268, 272–73
  —explicitness of, 267, 271, 272
  —fig tree under which Nana and Antonia sit, 292–94
  —nun, Nana's description of life as, 301–5, 312, 381n98
  —Romulus and Remus, wolf/prostitute as nurse of, 295
  —self-defloweration of Nana, 306
  Ariosto's *Orlando Furioso* and, 216, 225, 246, 248–49, 250–51, 255–58
  Boccaccio's *Decameron,* Alibech and marchioness of Monferrato stories in (see under *Decameron*)
  in Boiardo's *Orlando Innamorato*
  —Angelica's lust for Rainaldo, 186, 193, 197, 205, 207, 208
  —arrival of Angelica at banquet, 170–78
  —Charlemagne's desire for Angelica, 172–78
  —Orlando's passion for Angelica (see under *Orlando Innamorato*)
  —prostitute metaphor in opening banquet, 165–67
  —refusal of Rainaldo to accept Angelica's advances, 212–13
  gluttony and lewdness, relationship between, 99–100, 335n65
  knowledge and sex, 35–36, 329n9
  in Pulci's *Morgante,* 119–27, 131, 135, 136
Sforza family and court, 182, 199, 363n19
Silenus, 15

silkworms devouring mulberry leaves, 299
Sixtus IV (pope), 154, 155, 194–95, 351n8
Smarr, Levarie, 333n48
spectacles, banquets as, 350n4
Speroni, Sperone, 375n24
starlings, 113
Statius, 74–76
Stoics and Stoicism, 101–3, 290, 300
Storia della letteratura italiana (Francesco de Sanctis), 373n11
sugar. See *confetti*
Summa Theologica (Thomas Aquinas), 36–37, 325n37, 325n39, 330n18, 331n20
summum bonum, 101, 290–91, 343n22
sweets. See *confetti*
Symposium (Plato), 120

Tertullian, 328n4
Il Tesoro della sanità (Durante, 1586), 366n39
Thebiad (Statius), 74–76
Theologia Platonica (*Platonic Theology;* Ficino), 114, 135, 347n77, 348n95
theology/religion and food. See also Adam and Eve; Genesis
  in Aretino's *Ragionamento*
  —Adam and Eve, 293, 302–3
  —Baptism and salt in, 285
  —Eucharistic symbolism in Nana and Antonia's dialogue, 281–83
  —fig tree, 292–94
  —nun, Nana's description of life as, 297–308
  —Protestant Reformation, 306–8
  —Roman curia, critique of (see under *Ragionamento*)

in Boccaccio's *Decameron*
— Alibech story (see under *Decameron*)
— Messer Neri's daughters, 176–77
— Santa Maria Novella as setting for introduction of, 42, 43, 44–45, 47, 59
in Boiardo's *Orlando Innamorato*
— behavior of Charlemagne toward Saracens, 167–68, 187
— passion of Orlando for Angelica, 185–86
— Pentecost, celebration of, 157, 158, 161, 168, 169, 170, 184
— Rainaldo insulted by Saracens at banquet, 159–67
in Dante's *Vita nuova*, 27–29
exegesis of Genesis 1, 34–38
Mark's Gospel, fig tree in, 293–94
Mary (mother of Jesus), Pampineo in *Decameron* compared to, 44–45
in Pulci's *Morgante*
— in Antea and Rinaldo story, 127
— Florinetta story, biblical resonances in, 141–43
— giants Morgante and Margutte, 133–38, 150
Roman curia
— Aretino's *Ragionamento* and (see under *Ragionamento*)
— Platina's critique of, 21, 98–100, 108, 111, 116
scripture, food and eating metaphors in, 6–7
Trinitarian symbolism, 292–93
Word/*Logos* become flesh, 55, 58
Thomas Aquinas
on Adam's fall and bodily pleasure, 36–37, 325n37, 330n15, 330nn17–18, 331n20
on aesthetics and ethics of food, 7–8

Aristotle and, 7, 8, 325n37, 325n39
on beatitude, 339n120
Boccaccio's *Decameron* and, 36–37, 38, 40–42, 57, 59, 65, 76, 77
De Malo, 330n15, 330n17, 340n125
on etymology of gastronomy, 30
on gluttony, 36, 77, 340n125
On Love and Charity, 339nn120–21
on speculative intellect, 339n121
Summa Theologica, 36–37, 325n37, 325n39, 330n18, 331n20
Tissoni Benvenuti, Antonia, 351nn10–11, 353n30
Titian, 272, 310, 375n24
Tornabuoni, Lucrezia, 97
transformation and food in Ariosto's *Orlando Furioso*. See under *Orlando Furioso*
Trevisani, Ludovico, 349n104
Trimalchio. See *Cena Trimalchionis*
Trinitarian symbolism, 292–93
Trissino, Giovan Giorgio, 4–5, 323n22
Tristano, Richard M., 359n74
Trotto, Giacomo, 355n43
"truth" and "natural" in literature and painting, 310–12
Tully or Tulio (Cicero), 13–14, 146, 359n84
Tura, Cosmè, 352n12

Valla, Lorenzo
Alberti and, 344n35
De falso et vero bono, 299–300, 306
De voluptate (On Pleasure), 101–4, 135, 146, 290, 343n24, 343nn27–33, 370n88, 378n55, 379n70
Dialogue on Free Will, 143, 246, 301
Elegantia lingue latine, 105–8, 344n37
Varro, 326n42

Vasari, Giorgio, 310
Venice and Ferrara, war between, 194–95, 377n39
Venus, 60
Vergerio, Pier Paolo, 227, 355n46, 362n10
Vespucci, Giorgio Antonio, 345n48
vineyards in Renaissance culture, 286–92
virtue and pleasure, Stoic/Epicurean debate between, 101–4

La vita di Giovanni de' Medici detto delle Bande Nere (Giovangirolamo De' Rossi), 372n10
Vita nuova (Dante), 27–29
Vitruvius, Pollio, 2–4, 131–33, 322n14, 348n86

women. *See* gender issues

Zorzi, Elvira Garbero, 350n4

PINA PALMA is professor of Italian at Southern Connecticut State University.